P9-BBU-861

Labor
RELATIONS

DEVELOPMENT,

STRUCTURE,

PROCESS

JOHN A. FOSSUM

Industrial Relations Center
University of Minnesota

SEVENTH EDITION

Boston   Burr Ridge, IL   Dubuque, IA
Madison, WI   New York   San Francisco   St. Louis
Bangkok   Bogotá   Caracas   Lisbon   London
Madrid   Mexico City   Milan   New Delhi   Seoul
Singapore   Sydney   Taipei   Toronto

Irwin/McGraw-Hill

*A Division of The **McGraw-Hill** Companies*

LABOR RELATIONS: DEVELOPMENT, STRUCTURE, PROCESS

Copyright © 1999 by The McGraw-Hill Companies, Inc. All rights reserved. Previous editions ©1979, 1982, 1985, 1989, 1992, and 1995 by Richard D. Irwin, a Times Mirror Higher Education Group, Inc. company. Printed in the United States of America. Except as permitted under the United States Copyright Act of 1976, no part of this publication may be reproduced or distributed in any form or by any means, or stored in a database or retrieval system, without the prior written permission of the publisher.

This book is printed on acid-free paper.

1 2 3 4 5 6 7 8 9 0 DOC/DOC 9 3 2 1 0 9 8

ISBN 0-256-23887-1

Vice president and editorial director: *Michael W. Junior*
Publisher: *Craig S. Beytien*
Senior sponsoring editor: *John E. Biernat*
Editorial assistant: *Erin Riley*
Marketing manager: *Ellen Cleary*
Project manager: *Kimberly Schau*
Manager, new book production: *Melonie Salvati*
Designer: *Jennifer McQueen Hollingsworth*
Supplement coordinator: *Nancy Martin*
Compositor: *GAC/Shepard Poorman*
Typeface: *10/12 Times Roman*
Printer: *R. R. Donnelley & Sons Company*

Library of Congress Cataloging-in-Publication Data

Fossum, John A.
    Labor relations : development, structure, process / John A. Fossum. — 7th ed.
      p.   cm.
    Includes index.
    ISBN 0-256-23887-1
    1. Industrial relations—United States.   2. Collective bargaining—United States.   3. Trade-unions—United States.   I. Title.
HD8072.5.F67   1999
331′.0973—dc21   98-23634

http://www.mhhe.com

To all my parents
Peter, Almeda, Herb, and Jane
To
Alta for vigilance and support
To
Andy, Jean and Steve, and KC for reality, success, and equanimity
And to
Solidarność (the free Polish trade union movement)
*for its central role in overcoming totalitarian rule in eastern Europe and validating the
essential role of democratic trade unions in creating and maintaining a free society*

ABOUT THE AUTHOR

John Fossum is a Professor of Human Resources and Industrial Relations in the Industrial Relations Center, University of Minnesota. He has been a faculty member at the University of Wyoming and the University of Michigan. Professor Fossum holds his M.A. from the University of Minnesota and his Ph.D. from Michigan State University. At Minnesota, he has been Director of the Industrial Relations Center—a teaching, research, and service unit; and Director of Graduate Studies in Human Resources and Industrial Relations, which includes more than 200 masters and 15 doctoral students. He has also held visiting faculty appointments at UCLA, Cornell, Lyon (France), and the Warsaw School of Economics (Poland). He is active in the Academy of Management and the Industrial Relations Research Association, and his research and writing cover a broad area of employment issues.

PREFACE

The seventh edition of *Labor Relations: Development, Structure, Process* is being published twenty years after the introduction of the first edition. The 20 years that have elapsed since the original edition have seen a major and continuing transition in employment. During the period, the economic globalization has grown rapidly, U.S. manufacturing employment continued to decrease as a proportion of total employment, unionization of the work force (in percentage terms) fell by half, the way in which goods and services are produced has been changed dramatically, and the role of government regulation of private sector business has declined markedly. As noted in the preface to the sixth edition, financial performance is an increasingly important driving force in the structure of organizations and employment.

At the same time that unionization has declined in the private sector, it has gained in the public sector as concerns about job security have increased. Research on the effects of unions and unionization on employers and individuals has continued to grow in volume and sophistication. The findings of current reach studies are incorporated into the subject matter of this text and their documentation serves to introduce students to more intensive research into areas of particular interest.

As with the previous editions, the seventh is an evolutionary product. Major changes include: a new chapter on union avoidance and management campaigns during organizing drives (incorporating material from the previous edition's chapter on employee relations in nonunion organizations), a simplified modern job structure for the mock negotiation exercise, expanded material on union-management cooperation, a summary of state labor relations laws applying to public sector employees, and a substantial expansion of the chapter on international and comparative labor relations. All chapters incorporate the results of recent research studies.

I hope that you will see this book as presenting a prespective that reflects and balances the viewpoints of both labor and management; includes economic, institutional, and behavioral perspectives. In developing my approach to this book, I am indebted to many institutions and individuals—my graduate school professors at the University of Minnesota and Michigan State University; my academic colleagues at the University of Wyoming, University of Michigan, UCLA, and now the Industrial Relations Center at the University of Minnesota; and the many academics and practitioners from whom I have received ideas in academic meetings, human resource manager contacts and consulting, and international union representative contacts and consulting.

In an age of mergers and acquisitions, it's important to trace the family tree of a surviving project. There are many people who have contributed to this book's existence and continued success. The first edition was brought forth as a result of the substantial risk-taking of Jim Sitlington and Cliff Francis of Business Publications, Inc. (BPI), a highly successful start-up subsidiary of Richard D. Irwin, Inc. By the fourth edition, BPI was reabsorbed into Irwin, which, in turn, had been sold to Dow Jones. The fifth and sixth editions were published by Irwin under the ownership of the Times Mirror Corporation. Between the sixth and the seventh, Irwin was sold by Times Mirror to McGraw-Hill. Thus, over the 20 year period the book has been in print, it has been published by three different houses under four different owners. What has remained constant is the high quality of the publishing professionals who have worked closely with me on the production and marketing of this project.

By the fifth edition, Irwin had been sold to Times Mirror. The thorough reviews and helpful comments of Hoyt Wheeler of the University of South Carolina (and my first faculty industrial relations colleague as we began our careers at the University of Wyoming) and I. B. Helburn of the University of Texas significantly assisted me in preparing the first edition. The second was aided by suggestions and comments from Jim Chelius of Rutgers University, Sahab Dayal of Central Michigan University, and George Munchus of the University of Alabama at Birmingham. The third was aided by the reviews of George Bohlander of Arizona State University, Richard Miller of the University of Wisconsin, Edmond Seifried of Lafayette College, and Bobby Vaught of Southwest Missouri State University. The fourth benefited from comments and suggestions from Edward Reinier of the University of Southern Colorado and Jack E. Steen of Florida State University. The fifth was helped by A. L. "Bart" Bartlett of Pennsylvania State University, Robert Seeley of Wilkes University, R. H. Votaw of Amber University, and Frank Balanis of San Francisco State University. Ed Suntrup of the University of Illinois at Chicago and Bill Cooke of Wayne State University provided particularly helpful comments on specific portions of the text. The sixth edition was assisted by comments of Alison E. Barber of Michigan State University, Robert A. Bolda of The University of Michigan–Dearborn, Michael R. Buckley of University of Oklahoma, Constance R. Campbell of Georgia Southern University, Paula Phillips Carson of University of Southwestern Louisiana, Paul F. Clark of Penn State University, Harry P. Cohany of Towson State University, Millicent Collier of Chicago State University, Peter Feuille of University of Illinois–Champaign, Robert J. Forbes of Oakland University, Gilbert J. Gall of Penn State University, Denise Tanguay Hoyer of Eastern Michigan University, Foard Jones of University of Central Florida, Gundars E. Kaupins of Boise State University, William R. Livingston of Baker College Flint, Michael P. Long of Oakland University, Kathleen J. Powers of Willamette University, Gary C. Raffaele of University of Texas at San Antonio,

Jerald F. Robinson of Virginia Tech, Stephen Rubenfeld of University of Minnesota–Duluth, Donna C. Summers of University of Dayton, Henry Testa of Herkimer County Community College, Herman A. Theeke of Central Michigan University, Hoyt N. Wheeler of University of South Carolina, and Harold C. White of Arizona State University. The seventh benefited from feedback from Ed Suntrup of University of Illinois–Chicago, Gary Raffaele of University of Texas–San Antonio, Paul Clark of Pennsylvania State University, Mark Widenor of University of Oregon, Donna Blancero of Arizona State University, and Jack Kondrasuk of University of Portland. Tom Pearce of Moorhead State University wrote the teacher's manual (as he did for the sixth edition), applying an additional perspective to the package. Both Kurt Strand and John Biernat have contributed strong editorial assistance on recent editions. Kim Schau coordinated the details of production.

Reference materials are particularly important in preparing a text, and reference librarians are thus helpful in pointing out new information and locating it. I have been assisted by several in preparing this text. For the first two editions, JoAnn Sokkar, Mabel Webb, and Phyllis Hutchings of the Industrial Relations Reference Room at the University of Michigan provided this assistance. Editions three through seven were aided by Georgianna Herman, Mariann Nelson, and Jennifer Clement of the Industrial Relations Center Reference Room at the University of Minnesota. Research assistants for this edition were Chris McGraw (undergraduate degree from Ohio State) and Brye Paetznick (undergraduate degree from Minnesota).

Finally, I owe a permanent debt to all of the parents of my family who provided me with the examples and support to undertake an academic career; to my wife, Alta, who has made the personal sacrifices of moving several times, has subordinated her interests during times when I was writing, and has offered the wisest counsel; and to my children Andy and Jean who have grown up and succeeded despite their father's failings.

John A. Fossum

TABLE OF CONTENTS

3

LABOR LAW AND FEDERAL AGENCIES 58

4

UNION STRUCTURE AND GOVERNMENT 84

8

THE ENVIRONMENT FOR BARGAINING 214

9

WAGE AND BENEFIT ISSUES IN BARGAINING 250

12
IMPASSES AND THEIR RESOLUTION   384

13
UNION-MANAGEMENT COOPERATION   416

14
CONTRACT ADMINISTRATION   456

15
GRIEVANCE ARBITRATION   484

16
PUBLIC-SECTOR LABOR RELATIONS   518

17
A SURVEY OF LABOR RELATIONS IN MARKET ECONOMIES   554

1

INTRODUCTION

Labor relations is the set of processes **unions** and **employers** develop and use to achieve their goals while accommodating the needs of the other side. The term "labor relations" connotes conflict resolution processes. Because of the differences in their goals, conflict between unions and employers is real and, to some extent, always underlies the relationship between the parties. The parties also have some goals in common. The labor relations process tries to accommodate each of the parties' separate goals while enhancing the likelihood of realizing common goals.

The practice of labor relations is governed by laws and regulations that specify and limit its scope and implementation. These rules are ultimately the product of the culture and experiences of the society to which they apply.

Around the world, most countries permit and encourage the collectivization of capital through incorporation. Incorporation creates a legal entity that can act as if it were a person. Individual investors in a corporation have limited liability—they cannot lose more than their original investments. Fractional ownership (shares) in the corporation can be bought or sold without requiring its liquidation. This ability to combine large pools of money with limited liability offers the potential for investors to realize lower risk returns than they could expect in a partnership or sole proprietorship. Publicly held corporations create the opportunity for making capital highly liquid through the sale of shares in the stock market.

Large corporations generally have many owners or shareholders, most of whom do not materially participate in the corporation's day-to-day business. Operational decisions are made by managers hired by the shareholders through their elected Board of Directors.

Shareholders who are dissatisfied with corporate performance can either sell their shares or combine with others to vote to oust the current managers. Shareholders are primarily concerned with the financial performance of the corporation, particularly as reflected in the price of the corporation's stock. Higher profitability, returns on invested capital, and growth rates typically lead to higher share prices. Minimizing costs of inputs relative to the price of outputs is an important goal for managers in seeking to improve profitability. Labor costs are one of the inputs to be minimized.

Enterprises employ workers to produce the goods and services that will be sold to ultimately yield a profit. Employers would like complete freedom to alter the terms and conditions of employment in their workplaces, as necessary, to maximize returns on investments.

While labor is somewhat mobile, with workers able to move between employers as opportunities occur, it is less mobile than financial capital. Workers have investments in houses, occupations, family ties and friendships in a local community, and other intangibles. They would like to reduce the risks associated with employment—particularly the risk that their employers will radically change the terms and conditions of employment.

Unionization is one method employees can use to counter employers' powers to unilaterally change employment conditions. It is, to a large extent, the corollary of incorporation. Members elect officers and may hire agents to bargain an employment contract with the owners' managers. Unionization introduces democracy into the employment relationship. Employees determine first whether a majority desires to be represented; second, who to elect as leaders or hire as agents; third, what workplace issues are most important to them; and fourth, whether to accept a proposed contract or to collectively withhold their labor.

Historically, unions developed to enhance the power of workers to resist employers' unilateral imposition of terms and conditions of employment. Unions emphasize the need to create and maintain solidarity among members of the working class. In general, they favor relative equality in pay across employees and greater worker control of the work environment. Unions also stress the importance of continual improvements in living standards for their members, best attainable through increases in their pay.

Higher pay and other improvements in employment, other things equal, lead to lower returns to capital. Thus, the goals of capitalists and unionists inevitably collide. Unionists believe workers should have more control over the operation of and returns from the workplace while capitalists believe owners should have complete control of the processes and outcomes in facilities they own.

In democracies, laws and regulations are ultimately a reflection of the will of the electorate as expressed in the leaders it elects. If employment conflict is at a level above what the electorate will tolerate, or if the direction of results from this conflict is manifestly different than desired, the electorate ultimately changes the environment through its actions at the ballot box. Thus, the limits within which unions and employers craft their particular relationship is defined by public policy. The degree of conflict that exists depends on how able the parties are to accommodate the goals of their opposite numbers while achieving their own. This text focuses on the bases for the underlying conflicts, the tactics the parties use to gain power to achieve their goals, and how the process works in an ongoing relationship.

An important point to consider in studying labor relations is that employers can exist without unions, but unions cannot exist without employers. Thus, where public policy permits, it's to be expected that some or many employers will try to avoid unionization, to eliminate them if they exist in their workplaces, and to minimize their effectiveness if they do. Unions, on the other hand, rarely try to eliminate a unionized employer in which they represent workers. If a unionized employer is eliminated, the jobs the union represents are also simultaneously eliminated, weakening its long-run power.

It is also important to remember that the shareholders of a corporation ultimately control decisions about its direction; in what to invest; and whether to continue operations, sell, or liquidate, depending on which best meets their interests. Managers are employed to determine how best to put into operation and implement these decisions, but unless they are also shareholders, they have no independent ability to determine the distribution of profits.

Unionization enhances the bargaining power of employees. In collectivizing, the union rather than the individual employee becomes, in a sense, the supplier of labor because the contract establishes the rates for which all labor will be paid.

THE PARTIES INVOLVED

The limits within which labor relations practices are crafted are established by public policy. Within these limits, unions and employers are free to devise and implement their own relationships, usually in the form of contracts and how they are interpreted. Unions are simultaneously economic and political organizations. They have economic ends they want to secure for their members, while at the same time they seek to create and maintain power to influence the direction of laws and regulations, to provide a vehicle for advancing their leaders' purposes, and to survive and grow. Conflicts may also exist between union levels as national union goals may not completely agree with goals at the local level.

Employers have corporate goals and objectives with regard to unions and coping with unionization and **collective bargaining. Line managers** in operations have production and sales goals that must be achieved. Achievement is facilitated or inhibited by how successfully labor relations (or **employee relations** in a nonunion environment) are conducted. In larger organizations, **human resource managers** or **industrial relations managers** and staff advise the organization on how to structure labor relations, negotiate contracts with union representatives, and interpret agreements that have been made.

The actions of all these parties in creating and maintaining labor relations will be examined throughout this book. A recognition of the reality of conflict and the need to make continuing accommodations to it is essential to understanding labor relations.

CONTEMPORARY LABOR RELATIONS

Labor relations and employment have changed markedly since the early 1980s. The proportion of unionized employment has declined substantially due to declining employment in heavily unionized industries and the increasing success of employers in resisting union-organizing campaigns. Many commentators marked the 1981 air traffic controllers' strike and their subsequent discharge by President Reagan as a major event in the decline in union power. Falling membership is particularly marked in the United States, but unionization in other Western countries also declined as employment increasingly moved from goods to service production and from manual to mental labor.[1] Increasing global competition, freer trade, and an emphasis on improved corporate financial performance, continue to strongly influence labor relations.

Union-management relations has simultaneously grown more adversarial and more cooperative since the early 1980s. Employers resist unionization more

---

[1] L. Troy, "Is the U.S. Unique in the Decline of Private Sector Unionism?" *Journal of Labor Research* 11 (1990), pp. 111–43.

vigorously and react strongly to potential and actual strikes by threatening to or hiring replacement workers. At the same time, especially in industries faced with increasing global competition, management and labor have worked together to cut costs, improve profitability, and save jobs.

Although union representation of workers in the United States has declined from 35 percent to between 10 and 15 percent over the past 40 years, unions still exert substantial influence on employment practices through "spillovers." A **spillover** is an employment practice in union firms that tends to be duplicated by nonunion companies as these firms try to avoid unionization by copying what unions have won for their members.

WHAT UNIONS DO

Unions evoke controversy. Many people have strong opinions about their tactics and effects. Unionization creates monopoly power by fixing wages through contracts. It also provides employees a voice in how the employment relationship is implemented in their workplaces. Thus, unions benefit their members **(monopoly power),** at a possible cost to the public, and benefit the public by creating mechanisms requiring employers to respond to employee grievances **(voice power).**[2] Union monopoly power costs about 1 percent of gross domestic product (GDP). Administration costs in obtaining and exercising monopoly power are about .2 percent of GDP. Returns to members' investments, in the form of higher wages and benefits than their nonunion counterparts, are about 12 times larger annually than the cost of union dues.[3]

There are large differences in the degree to which industries and occupations are unionized. Some of the differences relate to the mix of occupations by industries and some to their ages and employment practices. Unionization is more prevalent where jobs require employer-specific knowledge and where internal workplace governance more strongly influences employee outcomes.[4]

Over the past two decades the proportion of employees who are represented by unions has decreased. As Table 1–1 shows, this decrease is largely related to the growth of the labor force and a small decline in union membership. During the 1983–94 period, employment grew by almost 20 million while union membership declined by 1 million. The drop was entirely concentrated in the private sector which declined by 2.3 million while membership increased by 1.3 million in the public sector.

---

[2] R. B. Freeman and J. L. Medoff, *What Do Unions Do?* (New York: Basic Books, 1984).

[3] C. M. Stevens, "The Social Cost of Rent Seeking by Labor Unions in the United States," *Industrial Relations* 34 (1995), pp. 190–202.

[4] G. Hundley, "Things Unions Do, Job Attributes, and Union Membership," *Industrial Relations* 28 (1989), pp. 335–55.

Chapter 1

TABLE 1–1

Changes in Employment and Union Membership, 1983–1994

Sector	Employment		% Unionized	
	1983	1994	1983	1994
U.S. total	88,290	107,988	20.1	15.5
Private sector	72,656	89,649	16.5	10.8
Public sector	15,634	18,339	36.7	38.7
Industry				
Agriculture	1,446	1,491	3.4	2.2
Mining	872	654	20.6	15.6
Construction	4,609	5,409	28.0	20.5
Durable goods manufacturing	7,930	8,014	25.9	17.0
Nondurable goods manufacturing	11,294	11,366	29.2	19.1
Transportation	3,627	5,106	49.9	37.8
Communications and public utilities	1,435	1,517	45.2	28.1
Utilities and sanitary services	1,474	1,521	39.0	32.1
Wholesale trade	3,657	4,002	9.3	6.5
Retail trade	14,510	18,407	8.6	6.2
Finance, insurance, and real estate	5,709	7,132	3.4	3.0
Private households	1,223	948	0.3	0.9
Business and repair	3,672	6,605	6.5	4.1
Personal services	1,897	2,562	9.4	6.8
Entertainment and recreation	1,010	1,805	13.0	10.0
Hospitals	4,358	4,988	17.6	14.5
Medical	2,986	4,895	9.7	8.2
Educational	7,837	9,584	34.7	35.8
Social services	1,315	2,518	10.9	8.7
Other professional	2,561	3,463	4.6	3.7
Forestry and fisheries	118	132	10.6	12.1
Public administration	4,751	5,870	30.0	33.4

SOURCE: Condensed from B. T. Hirsch and D. A. Macpherson, *Union Membership and Earnings Data Book 1994: Compilations from the Current Population Survey* (Washington, DC: Bureau of National Affairs, 1995).

WHY WORKERS UNIONIZE

Employees become union members through one of three processes. First, nonunion employees may organize a union to bargain collectively for them. Second, employees in a unit covered by a collective bargaining agreement may decide to join the union. Third, newly hired employees may be required by the collective bargaining agreement where they work to join the union as a condition of continued employment.

Catalyst for Organization

The monopoly and voice power of unions are attractive to workers, but job content, experience, age, and gender also relate to a willingness to form or join a union.[5] Specific events often trigger organizing activity in a given workplace. Employee dissatisfaction within their workplaces is significantly related to both union activity and actual voting for union **representation** when elections are held.[6]

Employees are more likely to vote for unions as dissatisfaction increases. Also, employees in units that have *any* organizing activity are more dissatisfied than in those units where it does not occur. Individuals are influenced to vote for unions more by dissatisfaction with employment conditions than by job task characteristics. Dissatisfaction with **job security,** economics, and supervisory practices were most predictive of a prounion vote across a set of studied elections.[7] The presence and level of organizing activity in units of a large multilocation company were predicted by poor supervision, co-worker friction, amount of work required, lack of advancement, bad feelings about the company, physical surroundings, and the kind of work done.[8]

Dissatisfaction alone does not automatically mean a union **organizing campaign** will result or an election will be won by the union. Two conditions have to exist to predict organizing attempts and a union win. First, employees have to be dissatisfied and believe they are individually unable to influence a change in the conditions causing their dissatisfaction. Second, a majority of employees have to believe collective bargaining would improve conditions more than changing jobs, and its benefits outweigh the costs.[9]

The creation of unions and the tenacious struggle to secure collective bargaining are examined in Chapter 2. Chapter 6 studies union organizing campaigns. Chapters 9 and 10 consider the specific demands unions and managements make in collective bargaining. All of these issues help explain why workers attempt to unionize. This introduction is concerned with a general explanation of why workers join unions and what they expect unions will accomplish collectively that they are unable to achieve individually.

---

[5] J. Fiorito, D. G. Gallagher, and C. R. Greer, "Determinants of Unionism: A Review of the Literature," in K. Rowland and G. Ferris, eds., *Research in Personnel and Human Resource Management,* vol. 4 (Greenwich, CT: JAI Press, 1986), pp. 269–306.

[6] J. G. Getman, S. B. Goldberg, and J. B. Herman, *Union Representation Elections: Law and Reality* (New York: Russell Sage Foundation 1976); W. C. Hamner and F. J. Smith, "Work Attitudes as Predictors of Unionization Activity," *Journal of Applied Psychology* 63 (1978), pp. 415–21; and C. A. Schreisheim, "Job Satisfaction, Attitudes toward Unions, and Voting in a Union Representation Election," *Journal of Applied Psychology* 63 (1978), pp. 548–52.

[7] J. M. Brett, "Why Employees Want Unions," *Organizational Dynamics* 8, no. 4 (1980), pp. 47–59.

[8] Hamner and Smith, "Work Attitudes," pp. 415–21.

[9] Brett, "Why Employees Want Unions," pp. 48–49.

Individuals and Union Organizing

Several factors influence the organizing process. Dissatisfaction is consistently associated with interests in unionizing. Dissatisfaction is also associated with employee turnover.[10] Since both unionization and turnover are predicted by dissatisfaction, organizing involves other influences as well, with employees believing that their individual outcomes are best leveraged by collective action to improve the outcomes of all employees in the unit.

An integrative model of unionization suggests that a gap between expectations and achievements leads employees to find ways to eliminate it. They may first try nonadversarial methods within the workplace to accomplish change. If they are frustrated, or if part of the gap is due to a perceived threatening environment created by the employer, they may prepare to act against the employer. Decisions leading to readiness are made by assessing conditions that facilitate and inhibit action (see Chapter 6). Workers are expected to rationally calculate whether they expect outcomes to be better or worse if unionization occurs and also to be influenced by their political and/or ideological beliefs. The level of support for unionization emerges from the interplay of these variables.[11] Figure 1–1 displays this relationship. Figure 1–1 contains a "rational calculation" box. The next section examines how this calculation is made and displays the process in Figures 1–2 and 1–3.

In an organizing campaign, people must decide whether unionization is in their interest. To make this decision, people assess what the likely outcomes of unionization will be, whether each outcome is positive or negative, and the likelihood that working for or voting for a union will lead to positive or negative outcomes. An individual might first examine the present job situation and assess the possibility of receiving positive or negative outcomes as a result of holding that job. Where a job has some negative outcomes, individuals may weigh such actions as convincing supervisors or management to behave differently, doing nothing, or organizing to change the situation. A person's experience with the efficacy of a particular action determines whether that action will be pursued or abandoned. Figure 1–2 outlines a model following this approach.[12]

Figure 1–3 depicts a hypothetical belief system for two employees where organizing is being considered. Each employee evaluates likely outcomes from organizing. In the example, the same set of outcomes and valuations is specified

---

[10] J. M. Carsten and P. E. Spector, "Unemployment, Job Satisfaction, and Employee Turnover: A Meta-Analytic Test of the Muchinsky Model," *Journal of Applied Psychology* 72 (1987), pp. 374–81.

[11] H. N. Wheeler and J. A. McClendon, "The Individual Decision to Unionize," in G. Strauss, D. G. Gallagher, and J. Fiorito, eds., *The State of the Unions* (Madison, WI: Industrial Relations Research Association, 1991), pp. 47–84.

[12] This is a variant on the expectancy model of motivation. For further information, see V. H. Vroom, *Work and Motivation* (New York: John Wiley & Sons, 1964); and E. E. Lawler, III, *Motivation in Work Organizations* (Monterey, CA: Brooks/Cole Publishing, 1973).

FIGURE 1–1

An Integrative Model of Factors Related to the Decision to Support Unionization

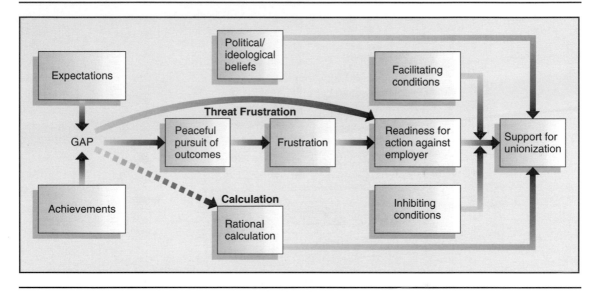

SOURCE: H. N. Wheeler and J. A. McClendon, "The Individual Decision to Unionize," in G. Strauss, D. G. Gallagher, and J. Fiorito, eds., *The State of the Unions* (Madison, WI: Industrial Relations Research Association, 1991), p. 60.

FIGURE 1–2

Rational Calculations

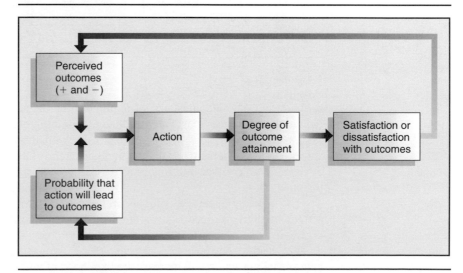

FIGURE 1–3

Beliefs about Organizing

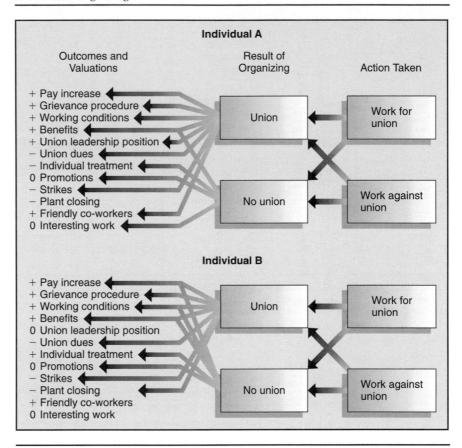

for both, but the outcomes are not required to be the same, especially if major individual differences exist between them. Examining outcomes and their valuations reveals differences between the two individuals. Individual A positively values a union leadership position, while B apparently attaches no positive or negative value to it. Other differences also exist, such as preferences for individual treatment.

The next explanatory component links outcomes with the result of an action—in this case, success or failure in organizing. For individual A, success in organizing is associated with six positive and two negative outcomes. Failure to organize leads to one positive, one negative, and two neutral items. If individual A believes taking action will increase the likelihood of unionization, efforts to do so would be expected because the greater net balance of positive outcomes results from a union. Individual B, on the other hand, expects four positives and three negatives from a union and four positives and one neutral from no union. Individual B would be predicted to oppose the union.

Some consequences could follow directly from actions taken rather than their results. For example, if individual A thinks neither working for nor against the union will affect the organizing campaign outcome, then no effort would be expected. Why? It's easier. But, effort would be predicted from individual A if A thinks it's necessary for organization and believes his or her effort will contribute to winning the election.

Some might argue that this model makes it difficult to predict what people in a group will do. This is the case if group members have diverse backgrounds or widely differing beliefs as to what actions will lead to results or what outcomes will follow from results. However, a number of things probably reduce this diversity.

Employees often see avenues other than union membership to attain valued outcomes from employment. For example, if promotions based on individual merit and interesting work are highly valued but seen as unattainable on jobs likely to be unionized, then many employees desiring them would probably leave. Achievable, positive, past job outcomes become increasingly important to employees. Thus, unionizing attempts may begin because management withholds rewards or changes the system so rewards differ from what people in the jobs have learned to value.

The degree to which unionization is seen as leading to attaining positive and avoiding negative outcomes may also be changed through campaigning, thereby creating more homogeneous attitudes and behaviors. Both labor and management attempt to direct employees toward a stronger belief that unionization will have positive and negative consequences, respectively.

Examining the perceptions and choices individuals make about unions should make it clear that, before unionization is possible, employees must hold a common belief that a union will benefit them. This means a large heterogeneous unit would probably be difficult to organize, whereas a smaller, more stable work group should be easier. Even considering differences among individuals, however, people likely take into account not only their own probable gains and losses, but also their family and other workers important to them.[13] It also means differences among members of a bargaining unit after unionization may be substantial and must be considered by the union in its representational activities.[14]

BELIEFS ABOUT UNIONS

Each of us has beliefs about the appropriate role of unions in society. These beliefs result from our upbringing and experiences, involvement with union members,

---

[13] See D. Knoke, *Organizing for Collective Action* (New York: Walter de Gruyter, 1990).

[14] L. A. Newton and L. M. Shore, "A Model of Union Membership: Instrumentality, Commitment, and Opposition, *Academy of Management Review* 17 (1992), pp. 275–98.

work in union or nonunion employers, and gains or costs we perceive to be associated with organized labor.

A 1988 Gallup Poll survey found 61 percent of respondents approved of labor unions while 25 percent disapproved (the rest were neutral or expressed no opinion). Respondents ascribed a positive role to unions in general, and particularly toward enhancing employment outcomes for all through political efforts influencing legislation. Both those who approve and disapprove of unions believe employees need protection from employers, and close to half of those who disapprove still believe that without unions, laws and benefits employees have gotten would be weakened or repealed and that laws enabling employees to organize should be strengthened. Table 1–2 summarizes many of the poll's findings.[15]

Willingness to Vote for Union Representation

When people are asked whether they would vote for a union to represent them, about one-third respond yes. Prounion sentiments are influenced by the perceived power of the labor movement and its instrumentality for worker gains, and also by specific beliefs employees have about the effects of unions on their personal intrinsic and extrinsic outcomes and introducing more fairness into the workplace.[16] In addition, perceptions that unions are working to better the lot of all working people positively influence an interest in voting for representation.[17] The decline in union membership may relate to changing perceptions about unions. Between 1977 and 1984, beliefs about unions' ability to improve employment conditions fell, while job satisfaction increased for employees in nonunion employers and declined for those in unionized employers.[18] Even those dissatisfied with their jobs are now less likely to be interested in voting for a union than in the past.[19]

[15] For an expanded discussion of this report, see R. B. Freeman and J. Rogers, "Who Speaks for Us? Employee Representation in a Nonunion Labor Market," in B. E. Kaufman and M. M. Kleiner, eds., *Employee Representation: Alternatives and Future Directions* (Madison, WI: Industrial Relations Research Association, 1993), pp. 13–80.

[16] S. P. Deshpande and J. Fiorito, "Specific and General Beliefs in Union Voting Models," *Academy of Management Journal* 32 (1989), pp. 883–97.

[17] J. Fiorito, "Unionism and Altruism," *Labor Studies Journal* 17, no. 3 (1992), pp. 19–34.

[18] H. S. Farber, "Trends in Worker Demand for Union Representation," *American Economic Review,* 79, no. 2 (1989), pp. 161–65.

[19] H. S. Farber and A. B. Krueger, "Union Membership in the United States: The Decline Continues," in B. E. Kaufman and M. M. Kleiner, eds., *Employee Representation: Alternatives and Future Directions* (Madison, WI: Industrial Relations Research Association, 1993), pp. 105–34.

TABLE 1–2

Gallup Survey of Attitudes Toward Representation

	Total Sample	Approve of Labor Unions	Disapprove of Labor Unions
Total sample (percent answering positively)	100	61	25
Labor unions are good for the nation as a whole.	69	87	31
Unions can solve workers' problems on the job even when all other approaches have failed.	55	67	32
Without union efforts, most laws which benefit workers would be seriously weakened or repealed.	68	80	49
Corporations sometimes harass or fire employees who support unions.	69	71	67
Employees should have an organization to discuss and resolve concerns with their employer.	90	94	82
Existing American laws should be strengthened to prevent corporations from denying workers rights to organize.	66	76	47
It's not fair for employers to resist employees' union-organizing efforts.	78	86	62
Workers' rights and abilities to organize unions have faced a strong challenge from corporations in the past few years.	73	81	68
Percent who agree that:			
Labor unions have become too weak to protect their members.	52	56	48
Most unions are not concerned about the welfare of the company with which they are bargaining.	46	38	70
A union establishment is much more likely to go out of business than a nonunion establishment is.	35	33	45
Unions are responsible for much of the decline in U.S. industry.	43	37	80
The presence of a union increases tension between employees and employers.	61	55	78
Most people who form unions are looking for a way to be less productive without suffering any consequences.	31	29	52
Most strikes by union employees are justified.	45	62	27
If employees attempted to form a union in my workplace, serious conflict among employees would be inevitable.	44	46	63

SOURCE: Synopsis of the Gallup Study of Knowledge and Public Opinion Concerning the Labor Movement, as tabled in R. B. Freeman and J. Rogers, "Who Speaks for Us? Employee Representation in a Nonunion Labor Market," in *Employee Representation: Alternatives and Future Directions,* ed. B. E. Kaufman and M. M. Kleiner (Madison, WI: Industrial Relations Research Association, 1993), p. 30.

The Local Community

The attitudes of the local community affect union power. Unions influence the political makeup in the community. The depth of support for the union among its members and citizens who may not be union members influences the union's ability to gain important collective bargaining outcomes. Community influence is most likely when an outcome of a dispute unfavorable to labor strongly threatens the community.[20] Union action may also influence public policy decisions on potentially favorable tax abatements for employers.[21]

Union Member Beliefs

Union members place the highest priorities on their union's handling of grievances, getting feedback from their unions, additional fringe benefits, having a say in the union, better wages, and job security. The preferences of union members for bargaining outcomes will be covered in much greater detail in Chapters 9 and 10. Generally, union members are satisfied with the performance of their unions, particularly on economic issues. Their 73 percent satisfaction rate is about the same as the historic job satisfaction rate in the United States.[22]

Among a sample of public-sector union members who could choose to join or not join the union that represented them, satisfaction with the union's performance was related to beliefs in the goals of the union movement and endorsement of the union's preferred positions on promotions and job security. Less favorable attitudes were found among those who joined for social reasons or who felt pressured to join.[23]

COLLECTIVE BEHAVIOR

Groups form because of mutual interests or similarities among their members. They also form in response to perceived danger or threat. Supervisors who manage "by fear" may face a collective response among group members. "Wagon-circling" is a pervasive phenomenon when a group perceives danger. Assisting or affiliating behavior requires that the danger be applicable to a majority of individuals in an area before group activities occur, however.[24]

When individuals are dissatisfied with their present employment, one might ask why they don't simply leave. Employees may believe they have invested parts

---

[20] J. A. Craft, "The Community as a Source of Union Power," *Journal of Labor Research* 11 (1990), pp. 145–60.

[21] B. Nissen, "Successful Labor-Community Coalition Building," in C. Craypo and B. Nissen, eds., *Grand Designs: The Impact of Corporate Strategies on Workers, Unions, and Communities* (Ithaca, NY: ILR Press, 1993), pp. 209–23.

[22] T. J. Chacko and C. R. Greer, "Perceptions of Union Power, Service, and Confidence in Labor Leaders: A Study of Member and Nonmember Differences," *Journal of Labor Research* 3 (1983), pp. 211–21.

[23] M. E. Gordon and L. N. Long, "Demographic and Attitudinal Correlates of Union Joining," *Industrial Relations* 21 (1981), pp. 306–11.

[24] See, for example, S. Schachter, *The Psychology of Affiliation: Experimental Studies of the Sources of Gregariousness* (Stanford, CA: Stanford University Press, 1959).

of their lives with their employers or alternative employment will be hard to find. One theory suggests that people can dissent in two ways—either by leaving an organization (exit option) or by trying to change conditions within it (voice option).[25] Forming a union enables use of a collective voice in influencing change at work.

Group Cohesiveness

A group is labeled cohesive when low variance in behavior is observed among group members. Studies show the productivity of some work groups remains relatively constant over time and varies little among members. This indicates group members are adhering to a collectively adopted output norm.

What are the underlying reasons for cohesiveness? First, members of the group are likely to hold the same basic values, reflecting for example, a class consciousness, and to agree on the methods used for their attainment. Second, age, seniority, and other background characteristics are probably quite similar. Third, the group has probably informally chosen a group leader. This member often has values closest to the overall values of the group. Finally, cohesiveness may be a function of external threat.

Class Consciousness

Class consciousness has often been suggested as a reason why unions form. Employees and employers often come from different classes, with mobility between classes perceived as unlikely and the income distribution seen as highly unequal and inequitable. Unionization is viewed as a means for equalizing power in dealing with employers. Americans are highly individualistic, however, and American unions have generally followed pragmatic, business-related agendas, downplaying class consciousness.[26] As will be noted later, however, specific differences between managerial and employee privileges and outcomes are frequently used to raise class consciousness during organizing campaigns.

External Threat

If external threat increases cohesiveness, how does it do so, and is the relationship linear or at least monotonic? Expectancy theory can answer the first part of this question. If someone perceives that negative outcomes will occur for one who must act alone but not for one acting within a group, then acting as a group is perceived to have positive consequences. If a united front is perceived to be strong,

---

[25] A. O. Hirschman, *Exit, Voice, and Loyalty* (Cambridge: Harvard University Press, 1970).

[26] M. J. Piore, "The Future of Unions," in G. Strauss, D. G. Gallagher, and J Fiorito, eds., *The State of the Unions* (Madison, WI: Industrial Relations Research Association, 1991), pp. 387–410.

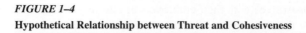

FIGURE 1–4

Hypothetical Relationship between Threat and Cohesiveness

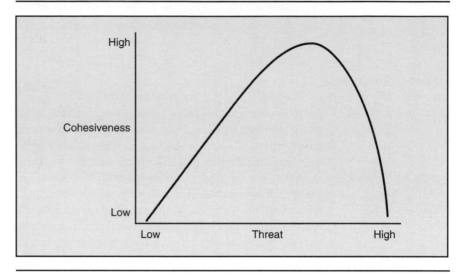

then cohesiveness will be high. If an employer is unwilling to grant a wage increase to a single employee and dares the employee to quit, the same employer might not be willing to risk denying a collectively demanded raise if the alternative is a strike.

How far would group members be expected to go in individually sacrificing for the good of the group? When the costs of membership outweigh the benefits perceived from remaining a group member, cohesiveness will break down. As Figure 1–4 shows, the hypothetical relationship between threat and cohesiveness is an inverted *U*.

Unions cannot ensure similar backgrounds among their members because management makes hiring decisions and unions are obligated to admit all employees who want to join. To maintain cohesiveness, unions must continually convince employees they will receive greater employment benefits through continued unionization, often casting management as a threat to those benefits. To maintain cohesiveness through perceived threat, an adversarial relationship follows. Thus, management actions against individuals or the group may benefit the union because management action can then be rebuffed, modified, or rescinded through group action.

UNIONS, THEIR MEMBERS, AND DECISION MAKING

To understand the activities of unions, it's necessary to recognize that officers are elected and contracts require ratification by the members. Bargaining units are not organized until a majority of employees desire representation; officers are elected or defeated by majorities of **local union** members; and contracts are ratified by a majority of bargaining unit members. Ultimately, the policies of large national unions are influenced strongly by the actions of majorities of local union members.

For specific union decisions requiring votes, it's helpful to understand the **median voter** concept.[27] To obtain a majority in any two-issue decision, the chosen alternative must be favored by the person who occupies the middle political position on that issue because a majority requires 50 percent plus one. Thus, to predict the outcome of an election or ratification, an analyst must understand the preferences of the middle person on a continuum of attitudes toward an issue. The median voter concept will be discussed at several points in this book when examining union decision making.

LABOR UNIONS IN THE 1990s

The 1980s was a decade of accelerating decline for organized labor as economic changes, coupled with employer and governmental initiatives, surprised unions and eroded membership. The 1990s left unions facing crucial structural and functional problems likely to affect their future viability. Some suggest the U.S. legislative climate, along with declining membership, has retarded organizing, representation, and bargaining outcomes relative to the past and compared to Canada.[28] Another position traces the decline to aggressive employer actions to fight organizing campaigns, build new plants where they will not be initially unionized and where antipathy toward unions probably exists, and violate or ignore labor laws aimed at protecting collective bargaining.[29] An alternative position is that larger numbers of employees were unionized in the past than wanted to be represented, partly because of coercive organizing tactics in which union members refused to deal with nonunion employees. Legislation outlawing this behavior coincides with the beginning of the decline in unionization.[30] Still another position argues that satisfaction of nonunion employees has increased to become substantially equivalent to unionized workers, particularly along economic dimensions, eliminating the motivation to organize.[31] Table 1–3 shows these changes. Finally, it's argued that the employment relationship in union and

---

[27] M. D. White, "The Intra-Unit Wage Structure and Unions: A Median Voter Model," *Industrial and Labor Relations Review* 35 (1982), pp. 565–77.

[28] G. N. Chaison and J. B. Rose, "New Directions and Divergent Paths: The North American Labor Movements in Troubled Times," *Labor Law Journal* 41 (1990), pp. 591–95.

[29] R. B. Freeman, "Contraction and Expansion of Unionism in the Private and Public Sector," *Journal of Economic Perspectives* 2, no. 2 (1988), 63–88; P. C. Weiler, "Governing the Workplace: Employee Representation in the Eyes of the Law," in B. E. Kaufman and M. M. Kleiner, eds., *Employee Representation: Alternatives and Future Directions* (Madison, WI: Industrial Relations Research Association, 1993), pp. 81–104.

[30] M. W. Reder, "The Rise and Fall of Unions: The Public Sector and the Private," *Journal of Economic Perspectives* 2, no. 2 (1988), pp. 89–110.

[31] Farber and Krueger, "Union Membership Decline."

TABLE 1–3
Job Satisfaction by Union Status, 1977–1992

	Nonunion Workers			*Union Workers*		
Percentage satisfied with:	1977	1984	1992	1977	1984	1992
Overall	87	89	90	88	85	90
Pay	59	75	76	75	77	87
Job security	73	85	88	76	78	77

SOURCE: Adapted from H. S. Farber and A. B. Krueger, "Union Membership in the United States: The Decline Continues," in *Employee Representation: Alternatives and Future Directions,* ed. B. E. Kaufman and M. M. Kleiner (Madison, WI: Industrial Relations Research Association, 1993), p. 120.

nonunion firms is substantially different. Nonunion employees may be treated more consistently in promotions and pay increases, have more involvement in managing production, be subject to fewer rules, and have a more leisurely work pace.[32]

A historical perspective suggests that the relatively small proportion of the workforce belonging to unions is strongly related to the economic history of the United States. While U.S. unions have waxed and waned at various points during the past two centuries, several conditions may have prevented their empowerment. First, employers fiercely protected, and unions ceded to them the capitalistic, market-driven system the United States has embraced. Thus, prices, and ultimately wages, are controlled by the market rather than by collective bargaining or administrative order. Second, with the exception of the skilled trades, employers have always controlled the content of jobs. Even skilled trades have been increasingly defined by employers through attempts to blur their boundaries. Third, employers have historically been involved with the U.S. educational system, especially the high schools, colleges, and universities that have the closest relationship to developing skills of future employees. Ironically, given organized labor's strong advocacy of free public education, this has occurred within both private and public school systems. Fourth, business has been strongly involved with government, in advocating legislation, in providing executives for public policy positions, and in using the courts to litigate labor problems. Fifth, and probably most telling, the large middle class in the United States has had strong interests in efficiency and productivity. If the middle class perceives income distribution as fair, then support for collective bargaining will not be strong.[33]

The fifth point—the effect of the middle class—appears to be the most important (recognizing that it's also related to the others). The future vitality of the labor movement in its ability to exercise monopoly power depends on a class consciousness developing or a perception by the middle class that the income

---

[32] J. Evansohn, "The Effects of Mechanisms of Management Control on Unionization," *Industrial Relations* 28 (1989), pp. 91–103.

[33] For a provocative expansion of these issues, see D. Montgomery, *The Fall of the House of Labor* (New York: Cambridge University Press, 1987).

distribution is unfair. If the middle class decreases in size, relative to the upper and lower classes, then the lower class could exert more power through unions because efficiency claims would not be as strong. If the income distribution is perceived as unfair, the middle class, as median voters, may seek collective bargaining as a method for restoring an appropriate balance. Recent econometric studies find that income inequality has increased as union coverage declined. A comparison of the United States and Canada shows that inequality is substantially lower in Canada, which has a larger proportion of unionized employees.[34] These issues lead to challenges and opportunities for the labor movement in the 21st century.

Perhaps, however, the greatest challenge facing private-sector unions is the continually increasing globalization of production. As will be noted in more detail in Chapter 8, competition from foreign labor reduces union bargaining power and can lead to the loss of jobs. One study found that for any industry in which more than 10 percent of goods were produced in and imported from low-wage countries, these low wages decreased U.S. wage rates for production employees in those industries.[35] While major employers have increasingly exercised global options, unions around the world have maintained jurisdictions largely within their own countries. In fact, within North America, unionization has become more country-specific during a period in which employment and plant location alternatives have increased.

In understanding the threats facing unions in maintaining or increasing membership, it is important to understand that in many cases economics are international while politics are local. When an employer decides to outsource or move production abroad, the decision frequently sets up internal competition among employees to retain jobs. Often, unionized workers from two different locals of the same national union will offer competitive concessions in order to have their plant be the one that remains open. This may increase job security for the winners, but it erodes union bargaining power on a companywide basis. Companies may also seek tax concessions from governments representing a particular country or geographical region in deciding where to locate.

Bargaining power is higher for unions that represent workers who must deliver services directly to the consumer. For example, in most cases; domestic air travel cannot be provided by French or Indian carriers, and baggage handlers are always domestic workers. These unions are less vulnerable to international competition, but may be vulnerable to nonunion entries in their industries. We would expect these unions to have greater survival opportunities in the future. The same would hold for local construction. Once a site has been selected, there is no geographic competition unless the employer imports workers from other locations.

---

[34] J. DiNardo and T. Lemieux, "Diverging Male Wage Inequality in the United States and Canada, 1981–1988: Do Institutions Explain the Difference?" *Industrial and Labor Relations Review* 50 (1997), pp. 629–51.

[35] R. B. Freeman, "Are Your Wages Set in Beijing?" *Journal of Economic Perspectives* 9, No. 1, (1995), pp. 15–32.

What Should Unions Do?

The challenge to unions involves membership. Traditionally, membership depended on employment in a workplace governed by a collective bargaining agreement. If employment was lost, membership often terminated. Only in the building trades, the maritime unions, and some entertainment unions did membership survive after employment with a particular employer ended. Membership survived because the union was the primary source of employees through union **hiring halls** and other training and development activities. If future employees have increasingly temporary ties to an employer, more unions may take on the same features as the building trades. They could offer continuity in benefits and training programs to improve occupational skills and to enable members to excel in comparison to nonmembers. If industrial unions don't offer these services and act only as a collective bargaining agent, they will find it increasingly difficult to attract members in a transient employment environment.

With the increased mobility of capital experienced during the last 15 years, one source of potential union power and solidarity could be the development of community-based movements.[36] These could reinforce the resolve of employees in employers with difficult labor relations problems, reduce the ability to hire replacement workers for strikers, and galvanize a united local policy on employment.

SUMMARY AND PREVIEW

This study of labor relations will examine the historical development of the labor movement, the structure of union organizations and federal agencies involved in labor relations, and the processes of collective bargaining, including the identification of bargaining issues, negotiations, and contract administration.

The evidence indicates that dissatisfaction leads to interest in organizing. For the most part, the general public sees unions and their leaders as beneficial to the public interest but also likely to increase tensions in the workplace. A significant minority of unorganized employees say they would vote for union representation if an election were held in their work unit.

Cohesiveness appears to be a necessary property for successful organization. Similarities among group members and external threats have a positive influence on cohesiveness. The adversary role that unions take is likely to enhance the cohesiveness of their memberships.

---

[36] Nissen, "Successful Labor-Community Coalition Building," and Piore, "The Future of Unions."

Plan of the Book

The title, *Labor Relations: Development, Structure, Process,* was not chosen haphazardly. The first part of the title indicates a focus on the employment relationship in unionized settings. The words following the colon establish the topical flow of the book.

Development

The present state of the labor movement and collective bargaining results from a variety of economic and social situations in which strategic choices were made by labor leaders and managers. In examining the development of the labor movement, the conditions related to the initial formation of unions must be understood. Public opinion influenced the response of public officials toward the subsequent formation of unions and their operation.

Other areas of interest concern the reactions of employers to unions. Where did unionization begin? In what industrial sectors have unions been most prevalent? How have the parties adapted to each other over the long run? What are the present stances of employers toward unions, and where are the greatest changes occurring?

Chapters 2 and 3 address development issues, tracing the historical evolution and present public policy environment in which American labor operates. Although union activity has occurred throughout the nation's history, effective labor organizations are about 115 years old. These chapters indicate that labor law and its enforcement have played an important role in the conduct of labor relations. The development chapters trace societal and economic changes and detail the statutes that have contributed to the development and particular shape of collective bargaining in the United States—in particular, legislation passed in the 1930s to protect employees in forming unions and engaging in collective bargaining contributed to union growth. The current interpretation of statutes may be hastening the decline.

Structure

The examination of union structure focuses on the office and institutions that make up the labor movement or have major impacts on it. In this regard, the last part of Chapter 3 details the federal institutions involved in regulating collective bargaining. Chapter 4 lays out the structure of the various organizational levels of the labor movement and identifies the location of its power centers. Chapter 4 also discusses the organizational structure of several national unions, the roles played by union officers, and the causes and consequences of the recent increase in union mergers. Chapter 5 examines the attitudes and activities of union members and the political activities of unions. The various structures within which negotiations between labor and management take place are detailed in Chapter 8.

Process

The greatest emphasis in this text is on process. This section concerns methods used to organize employees into unions, identifies issues of importance in bargaining, explains the organization and processes involved in negotiations, and details how labor and management deal with differences that occur during bargaining and after a contract has been signed. These areas are covered in Chapters 6 through 16.

Special Chapters

The last two chapters of the book involve special issues that cut across the areas of development, structure, and process. Chapter 16 covers collective bargaining in the public sector and issues unique to it. Chapter 17 examines some of the differences between unions and labor relations in the United States and other industrialized nations.

Preview

In this text, each chapter begins by introducing the subject and highlighting some major issues that should be explored to gain an understanding of the development, structure, or process of labor-management relations.

Most chapters end with discussion questions. These either relate to relatively broad issues raised in the chapter or ask that a position be formulated for labor or management on one of these issues. Many chapters also conclude with case material. Most of these cases relate to a simulated organization, General Materials & Fabrication Corporation (GMFC), a heavy-equipment manufacturer. The first case involving GMFC follows Chapter 6. Later, a mock negotiation exercise, contract administration cases, and cases discussing arbitration issues arising from the contract are presented. These cases should help you gain a greater appreciation of the process involved in the collective bargaining relationship.

Point of View

Most readers of this book are or have been employed, but most have probably not been union members, and most do not expect to be union members. But readers have likely formed attitudes toward labor unions and collective bargaining through information provided by the news media. Media attention is usually focused on unusual events. In labor relations, this usually means a major negotiation, strike, lockout, or an unlawful practice charge. The media shouldn't be faulted for this—excitement draws viewers and sell newspapers, but it does not reflect day-to-day labor relations in the United States. Overt disagreement, occurring in strikes, lockouts, and unlawful practices, is relatively infrequent.

This text includes information to increase your ability to understand labor relations as it is practiced in the United States. This understanding must be based on the evolution and development of the labor movement to its present form, the subject matter and jurisdiction of labor law, and the practices of the two major parties in the process: management and labor.

The subject should be interesting. In teaching courses in organizational behavior, human resource management, and labor relations, I have found most students are more intrinsically interested in labor relations than in the other two, perhaps because we are likely to have strong attitudes about what we think are the proper roles each party should take in the process and notions about which side should be blamed for the problems surrounding labor relations. I do not expect your basic posture toward labor relations to change as a result of either this book or the course you are in, but I expect you to gain a far greater understanding of why the parties act as they do.

KEY TERMS

Labor relations *2*	Monopoly power *5*
Union *2*	Voice power *5*
Employer *2*	Representation *7*
Collective bargaining *4*	Job security *7*
Line manager *4*	Organizing campaign *7*
Employee relations *4*	Local union *17*
Human resource manager *4*	Median voter *17*
Industrial relations manager *4*	Hiring halls *20*
Spillover *5*	

THE EVOLUTION OF

AMERICAN LABOR

*T*he history of labor relations in the United States is as old as the nation itself. Understanding the present operation and goals of the American labor movement requires an examination of the events, personalities, and philosophies that shaped it. Major milestones include the early development of local **craft unions,** the formation of national unions, the creation of the **American Federation of Labor** (AFL), employer resistance and industrial violence, legislation enabling representation and severely restricting injunctions against union activities, the creation of the **Congress of Industrial Organizations** (CIO), further labor legislation, and the merger of the AFL and CIO.

Immigration and the changing economic environment have been major forces influencing the course of development and success rate of organized labor. Through most of its history, the American labor movement has been predominantly results oriented rather than ideologically oriented. Surviving labor organizations have adapted to change and been responsive to member needs.

As you study this chapter, consider the following questions:

1. How have laws, public policy, and public opinion changed over time? Consider the influences of legislators, judges, and the news media.
2. What ultimate form did the American labor movement develop?
3. What types of events contributed to and detracted from union growth? Do these still operate in the same manner?
4. How have the personalities of the major actors within the labor movement contributed to union growth?
5. Why have American unions generally accepted the capitalist system?

UNION PHILOSOPHIES AND TYPES IN THE UNITED STATES

Since the origin of the union movement, certain ideas have fueled its direction and development. Their intensity has varied across times and between labor organizations, but they underlie the actions of all. The ideas can be summarized as follows: Society has a productive class that ultimately creates the tangible products or services people demand. Labor is thus the ultimate creator of wealth and is entitled to its returns. Society generally includes a monied aristocracy, in which society's wealth is excessively, unequally distributed. Without major efforts to avoid it, education is unequal and undemocratically provided. Class distinctions exist, and the goals of workers and employers differ. Thus, trade unions are necessary to protect workers' rights.[1]

In most democracies, unions have attempted to forward a **corporatist** agenda in which the employment relationship would be jointly governed by unions, employers, and the government.[2] Unions and their members have been involved in political activity designed to establish certain minimum requirements for the terms and conditions of employment and to require consultation and bargaining with management where employees desire them. Laws and regulations reinforce this approach. Employers, particularly in the United States, have strongly opposed a corporatist approach because it restricts the boundaries of permissible employment decisions. As Chapter 17 will note, corporatist approaches are generally in place in much of the European Union, but have eroded in the United States since the 1960s.

Unions can be classified according to their goals. Four categories include: uplift, revolutionary, business, and predatory unions. **Uplift unionism,** concerned with social issues, is aimed at the general betterment of educational and monetary outcomes and labor-management systems for workers. **Revolutionary unionism** is primarily oriented toward changing the fabric of society, overthrowing the capitalistic system, and replacing it with worker ownership of industry. **Business unionism** relates to the representation of employees' immediate employment interests, primarily the regulation of wages, hours, and terms and conditions of employment. This philosophy was typified by Adolph Strasser, one of the AFL's founders, in 1883, when he testified in Congress, "We have no ultimate ends. We are going on from day to day. We are fighting only for immediate objects—objects that can be realized in a few years." **Predatory unionism** occurs when the union's prime goal is to enhance itself at the expense of the workers it represents.[3]

No U.S. union exists in an absolutely pure form; most duplicate the characteristics of business unionism—concern with immediate goals, accepting the system as it is, and working for union goals within that system. Pragmatism has

---

[1] M. F. Neufeld, "Persistence of Ideas in the American Labor Movement: The Heritage of the 1830s," *Industrial and Labor Relations Review* 35 (1982), pp. 207–20.

[2] See N. Lichtenstein, *The Most Dangerous Man in Detroit: A History of Walter Reuther and the UAW* (Charlottesville: University of Virginia Press, 1995), for examples of this philosophy.

[3] R. F. Hoxie, *Trade Unionism in the United States* (New York: Appleton-Century-Crofts, 1921).

contributed to the durability of the labor movement; but as primarily an employee agent rather than a public policy advocate, it has depended to an extent on the tolerance and fortune of employers for its continued existence.

EARLY UNIONS AND THE CONSPIRACY DOCTRINE

The genesis of the American labor movement parallels the birth of the nation. In 1778, New York **journeyman** printers won a wage increase through collective action.[4] However, unions did not grow at the same pace as the nation during most of the following 200 years. Substantial impediments included adverse legal decisions, the predominantly rural nature of 19th-century America, and substantial numbers of relatively unskilled immigrants competing for jobs at relatively low wages.

Philadelphia Cordwainers

The Federal Society of Journeyman Cordwainers (shoemakers) was organized in Philadelphia in 1794.[5] It formed as a result of changes in the way shoes were marketed. Until about 1790, journeymen almost exclusively manufactured "bespoke" (i.e., custom) work. Master shoemakers took orders and supplied material for the journeymen, who produced a pair of shoes or boots for an agreed-upon wage. This arrangement required that the customer be willing to wait to receive the shoes. Because this was inconvenient and expensive, the masters developed three other market classes: "shop," "order," and "market" work. Shop work was for the master's stock, order work was for wholesalers, and market work was to sell in the public market. Each was priced lower than its predecessor, and masters differentiated wage rates depending on the market being supplied. The journeymen cordwainers responded by attempting to fix wages for shoemaking at the rate for bespoke work.

The cordwainers' refusal to work at rates that varied depending on the market for their output was seen by the employers as a criminal act. The court found the collective actions of the cordwainers in pursuit of their personal interests contravened the public's interests and was, hence, a criminal conspiracy. Each member of the union was fined $8 (see Exhibit 2–1).[6] This decision established the **conspiracy doctrine,** under which a union could be punished if either its means or ends were deemed illegal by the courts.

---

[4] U.S. Department of Labor, Bureau of Labor Statistics, *A Brief History of the American Labor Movement,* Bulletin 1000, rev. (Washington, DC: U.S. Government Printing Office, 1970), p. 99.

[5] For a thorough analysis of this group, see J. R. Commons, *Labor and Administration* (New York: Macmillan, 1973), pp. 210–64.

[6] J. S. Williams, *Labor Relations and the Law,* 3rd ed. (Boston: Little, Brown, 1965), p. 18.

EXHIBIT 2–1

Charge to the Jury in the Philadelphia Cordwainers Case

"What is the case before us? . . . A combination of workmen to raise their wages may be considered in a twofold point of view: one is to benefit themselves . . . the other is to injure those who do not join their society. The rule of law condemns both . . . [T]he rule in this case is pregnant with sound sense and all the authorities are clear on the subject. Hawkins, the greatest authority on criminal law, has laid it down, that a combination to maintain one another, carrying a particular object, whether true or false, is criminal . . ."

SOURCE: Condensed from 3 Commons and Gilmore 228–33, which was partially reprinted in J. S. Williams, *Labor Relations and the Law,* 3rd ed. (Boston: Little, Brown, 1965), p. 20.

Commonwealth v. *Hunt*

The conspiracy doctrine was softened substantially in 1842 when the Massachusetts Supreme Court overturned the conviction of Boston Journeymen Bootmakers' Society members for refusing to work in shops where nonmembers worked below the negotiated rate.[7] The court held the society's action was primarily to persuade nonmembers to join rather than to secure criminal ends. The court refused to enjoin organizing activities; however, it did not say that injunctions against other collective activities would be stopped (see Exhibit 2–2).[8]

Pre–Civil War Unions

During the first half of the 19th century, unions were faced with a number of problems, including employers who did not see them as legitimate organizations, courts that enjoined and punished collective activity, and competition from a growing supply of immigrant labor. But even in the face of these impediments, collective activity still occurred. Most was among skilled artisans, such as the cordwainers, but even unskilled textile workers in Massachusetts became involved.

Newly organized workingmen's parties contributed to the election of President Andrew Jackson.[9] Following Jackson, Martin Van Buren issued an executive order decreasing the workday for federal employees to 10 hours. Unions in major U.S. cities successfully used strikes to secure wage increases. Union membership swelled in the early 1830s, but poor economic conditions soon tipped the scales in favor of employers, and union activity waned where membership threatened one's continued employment.

---

[7] 4 Metcalf 111 (1842).

[8] Williams, *Labor Relations and the Law,* p. 22.

[9] See F. R. Dulles, *Labor in America,* 3rd ed. (New York: Crowell, 1966), pp. 35–52.

EXHIBIT 2–2

Interpretation of the Conspiracy Doctrine under *Commonwealth* v. *Hunt*

"The manifest intention of the association is to induce all those engaged in the same occupation to become members of it. Such a purpose is not unlawful. It would give them a power which might be exerted for useful and honorable purposes, or for dangerous and pernicious ones. If the latter were the real and actual object and susceptible of proof, it should have been specially charged . . . In this state of things, we cannot perceive that it is criminal for men to agree to exercise their acknowledged rights in such a manner as best to subserve their own interests."

SOURCE: 4 Metcalf 129, as contained in J. S. Williams, *Labor Relations and the Law,* 3rd ed. (Boston: Little, Brown, 1965), p. 22.

THE BIRTH OF NATIONAL UNIONS

Beginning in the 1850s, a few national trade unions were formed. These early unions have all either disappeared or been merged into surviving unions. Until the end of the Civil War, unions represented certain trades or industries. This pattern ultimately prevailed in the United States. After the Civil War, however, the first major movements were organized on a national basis, without craft or industry distinctions. The early national labor movements were involved heavily in many major public policy issues. Immigration policy posed a problem for unions because, while many members were immigrants, they feared the effects immigration would have on their wage levels. Many civic organizations opposed free immigration and advocated literacy tests. Trade unions gravitated toward these positions at the end of the 1800s, partly in a bid to attain mainstream legitimacy as social institutions.[10]

The National Labor Union

The **National Labor Union** (NLU) was founded in Baltimore in 1866. Its goals were largely political and reformist rather than economic or immediate. Its leader, William Sylvis, had been instrumental in organizing the National Molders' Union in 1859. NLU goals included introduction of the eight-hour workday, establishment of consumer and producer cooperatives, reform of currency and banking laws, limitations on immigration, and establishment of a federal department of labor.

The NLU was open not only to skilled trades workers but also to other interested and sympathetic individuals. Suffragists, particularly prominent at its

---

[10] C. Collomp, "Unions, Civics, and National Identity: Organized Labor's Reaction to Immigration, 1881–1897," *Labor History* 29 (1988), pp. 450–74.

national meetings, attempted to get the NLU to endorse their efforts to gain voting rights for women.

Sylvis was the backbone of the NLU. His death in 1869 and its subsequent alliance with the Greenback party in 1872 doomed the NLU. A lack of leadership and inattention to worker problems contributed to its demise.[11] However, the first attempts to coordinate labor organizations nationally had begun—and would ultimately be successful.

The Knights of Labor

The **Knights of Labor** began in Philadelphia in 1869. Its goals and membership, while different from those ultimately embodied in the U.S. labor movement, more closely approximated the final pattern than the NLU. It was part labor organization and part fraternal lodge. Workers were organized on a city-by-city basis across crafts. When a city assembly (the Knights' local unit) had a group of members from a particular craft large enough to be self-sustaining, it was spun off. A basic position of the Knights of Labor held that all workers had common interests that blurred craft distinctions.

Philosophically, the Knights of Labor was more willing to recognize the short-term legitimacy of capitalism than the NLU. The leaders of the Knights—first Uriah Stephens, then Terence Powderly—were essentially idealists who favored **arbitration** over strikes. Employers used these prestated positions to their advantage. But in confrontations, the rank and file were more militant than their leaders and used strikes effectively.

The Knights of Labor grew slowly, taking three years to gain enough members to establish a second assembly in Philadelphia. By 1875, district assemblies had headquarters in Reading and Pittsburgh, Pennsylvania, as well. Because it was a secret society, the Knights of Labor was in conflict with the Roman Catholic Church. Clergy believed Knights members were required to take secret oaths that might commit them to beliefs inconsistent with Roman Catholic dogma. Ultimately, negotiations between Terence Powderly and James Cardinal Gibbons led to a ruling that Roman Catholics could belong to the Knights.[12]

As had often occurred previously in the 19th century, the country entered a depression in the early 1880s. These periods had taken their toll on labor unions in the past, but this time the Knights' strength grew. In several railroad strikes, the Knights successfully organized workers and won their demands—a sharp contrast to the crushing defeat railroad strikers suffered in 1877. In 1885, when financier Jay Gould attempted to break the union by laying off its members, the union struck the Wabash Railroad and refused to handle its rolling stock on other lines,

---

[11] Dulles, *Labor in America,* pp. 100–113.

[12] P. Taft, *Organized Labor in American History* (New York: Harper & Row, 1964), pp. 84–89.

forcing Gould to cease discriminating against Knights members. The nationally publicized negotiations gave added impetus to organization. By the middle of 1886, membership in the Knights of Labor reached 700,000.[13]

There was irony in the Knights' success against Jay Gould.[14] Many new members joined hoping to gain the same concessions Gould had given. But the leaders' position was oriented toward the long run rather than toward satisfying day-to-day grievances. They did not espouse a collective bargaining approach leading to an ultimate goal on a piecemeal basis. They firmly opposed using strikes as weapons to pressure employers. The leaders' long-run perspective and their belief in "rational" processes for achieving ultimate objectives is typified by these quotes from Powderly and Knights of Labor publications: "You must submit to injustice at the hands of the employer in patience for a while longer," and, "Do not strike, but study not only your own condition but that of your employer. Find out how much you are justly entitled to, and the tribunal of arbitration will settle the rest."[15]

The long-run objectives were inconsistent with the immediate results sought by new members. The differences between the ascetic Powderly (see Exhibit 2–3) and the interests of the burgeoning rank and file hastened the Knights decline. Besides the leadership-membership cleavages, an antagonistic press increasingly linked the Knights with anarchy and radical action. Public pressure, internal power vested in individuals with reformist sentiments, and an inability to get employers to arbitrate, all contributed to a decline in the Knights' membership to 75,000 by 1893. But the withering of the Knights of Labor did not bring an end to national organizations. At the height of the Knights' success, the first enduring national federation was formed.

The American Federation of Labor

The American Federation of Labor (AFL) was created in a meeting of national unions in Columbus, Ohio, in 1886.[16] It was born out of the frustration craft unionists felt about the mixing of skilled and unskilled workers in Knights of Labor assemblies and its increasingly reformist orientation. The Knights also tended toward centralization of authority, diminishing the autonomous power of individual craft unions.

Twenty-five national labor groups representing 150,000 members initially formed the federation. The national unions maintained autonomy and control over their trades while ceding authority to the AFL to settle disputes among them.[17] The

---

[13] Dulles, *Labor in America,* pp. 139–41.
[14] N. W. Chamberlain and D. E. Cullen, *The Labor Sector,* 2nd ed. (New York: McGraw-Hill, 1971), pp. 97–98.
[15] Ibid., p. 98.
[16] Dulles, *Labor in America,* p. 161.
[17] Ibid.

EXHIBIT 2–3

The Ascetic Terence Powderly on Labor Picnics

"I will talk at no picnics. When I speak on the labor question, I want the individual attention of my hearers, and I want that attention for at least two hours, and in that two hours I can only epitomize. At a picnic where the girls as well as the boys swill beer I cannot talk at all . . . If it comes to my ears that I am advertised to speak at picnics . . . I will prefer charges against the offenders for holding the executive head of the Order up to ridicule . . ."

SOURCE: F. R. Dulles, *Labor in America: A History,* 3rd ed. (New York: Crowell, 1966), p. 136.

AFL was formed by unions of skilled employees. During most of its history, it maintained a skilled-worker, or craft, orientation and an antipathy toward organizing the unskilled. The AFL concentrated on winning tangible gains by entering into collective agreements with employers. It aimed at rationalizing the workplace through labor contracts.

The early direction of the AFL was influenced by the philosophies of its first president, Samuel Gompers. As a member of the New York Cigarmakers local, he had seen radical action punished by civil authorities and experienced the Knights of Labor's advocacy of unskilled demands. As a labor leader, these experiences led Gompers to pay close attention to the workers he represented, not necessarily the interests of all laborers. Experience also led him to take a pragmatic approach, seeking gains through bargaining rather than legislation. His long incumbency—from 1886 to 1924 except for one year—is in large part responsible for the "business" orientation of U.S. unions.

Gompers and other early leaders, such as Adolph Strasser, cemented the base on which the American trade union movement stands. Their approach accepted the system as it existed and worked within it. They were primarily concerned with improving the lot of the members they represented. This approach is basically retained in the present agency role taken by unions in representation.

Taking this pragmatic, business-oriented viewpoint limited the AFL in sponsoring social reforms. It advocated legislation only when it could not bargain successfully for its objectives. The absence of an underlying ideology is best typified in Gompers's answer to a question asking what labor's goals were: "More, more, more."

Another aspect of the pragmatic genius of the AFL's founders was their structural design for the federation. The structure preserves the autonomy of its member international unions and makes their locals subsidiary to them. This approach serves two purposes: first, the leaders' focus is toward the job problems unique to the trade they represent; second, discipline is maintained over the locals' activities. Thus a more united and rational front is presented when initiating actions or responding to management.

LABOR UNREST

Bitter labor struggles marked the decades between 1870 and 1910. The period was characterized by frequent financial panics resulting in depressions, continuing adamancy by owners who refused to recognize or negotiate with unions, and intervention by government on the side of employers. Some unrest was localized and grew out of radical political action or the nationalistic solidarity of immigrant groups, but much was general to an area or industry.

In the 1870s, coal miners in Pennsylvania struck when operators unilaterally cut wages below an agreed minimum. As the strike dragged on, some miners returned, but a few diehards formed a secret organization (which became known as the Molly Maguires) to continue resisting the owners. This group sabotaged mines, threatened owners and supervisors, and conducted terrorist activities until it was infiltrated by James McParlan, a Pinkerton detective hired by the owners. As a result of his testimony, 10 of the Molly Maguires were hanged, and another 14 were jailed, ending the mine warfare.[18]

In the summer of 1877, railroads cut wages while paying high dividends to their stockholders. In the East, rail employees struck and in some instances seized railway property. In Pittsburgh, federal troops were called in to retake the property, but not before 25 people had been killed. Widespread rioting broke out. Railroad property was burned, and local business establishments were looted.[19]

In 1886, violence broke out between strikers and strikebreakers at the Chicago McCormick Harvester plant. Police intervened, and four people were killed. A rally was held in Haymarket Square to protest the use of police. As the peaceful meeting was dispersing, police arrived, ordering everyone to leave. Just then a bomb exploded among the police, killing one. Before the carnage was over, seven more police and four workers were killed, and more than 100 were injured. The riot was blamed on anarchists. Eight were arrested and charged with murder. Seven were ordered hanged and the eighth imprisoned. All were pardoned six years later. Those still alive were released.[20]

Two major strikes in the 1890s helped split the labor movement while raising doubts about the power of unskilled workers to win their demands. These were the 1892 Homestead strike in the Carnegie Steel Company and the 1894 Pullman Company strike.

After Homestead workers refused to accept a company-ordered wage cut, they were locked out by Henry Frick, Carnegie's general manager. The workers correctly assumed Frick would use strikebreakers to reopen the works. To accomplish this, 300 armed Pinkerton detectives were barged up the Monongahela River behind the plant. As they neared the works, the entrenched workers opened fire,

---

[18] Ibid., pp. 117–18.
[19] Ibid., pp. 119–20.
[20] Ibid., pp. 123–25.

used a small cannon to try to sink the barges, and poured burning oil onto the river. After a daylong battle, the Pinkertons surrendered.

The workers' victory was short lived. The governor ordered the militia to take over the plant, which Frick reopened with strikebreakers. The union was crushed so badly that no serious attempt was made to organize the steel mills until the 1930s.[21]

The Pullman Company produced railroad cars. Pullman workers were required to rent company-owned houses. In 1893, the company laid off half its employees, and cut wages of the rest up to 40 percent. However, rents were not reduced, and shareholders continued to receive dividends.

Pullman employees attempted to get the company to adjust their economic grievances, but it refused and fired several of their leaders. The Pullman locals of the American Railway Union (ARU) reacted by striking. The company refused the union's offer to arbitrate the differences. As a result, ARU leader Eugene Debs ordered members not to handle Pullman rolling stock. Railroad employees throughout the country stopped trains and uncoupled cars manufactured by Pullman. The railroads retaliated by discharging employees found cutting out Pullman cars. But whole train crews quit and abandoned their trains if one was fired.

One management strategy led to the end of the strike. When trains were assembled, Pullman cars were connected to U.S. mail cars. If the Pullman cars were later uncoupled and the mail car was also cut out, this interfered with the mail, a federal offense. The federal government intervened, supplying federal troops and permanently enjoining interference with mail delivery and the movement of goods in interstate commerce. Debs was sent to jail for conspiracy to obstruct the mails, and the strike was broken.[22]

The failure of these industrial actions convinced one faction of the labor movement that to achieve worker goals, socialism needed to replace capitalism.[23] Revolutionary unions were spawned in the West in mining and timbering and in textiles in the East.

The IWW and the Western Federation of Miners

The inability of the Knights of Labor to win important settlements and the antipathy of the AFL to industrial organization led to more radical approaches. Just as Eugene Debs's jail term convinced him that revolutionary unionism and the abolition of capitalism were necessary, so too, did the results of numerous mine strikes and wars convince "Big Bill" Haywood that miner solidarity and resistance were the answers to employer intransigence.

Haywood played an active role in organizing the Western Federation of Miners (WFM), which had withdrawn from the AFL in 1897. After the

---

[21] Ibid., pp. 166–69.

[22] Ibid., pp. 171–79.

[23] See J. R. Constantine, "Eugene V. Debs: An American Paradox," *Monthly Labor Review* 114, no. 8 (1991), pp. 30–33.

EXHIBIT 2-4

Preamble to the IWW Constitution

The working class and the employing class have nothing in common. There can be no peace so long as hunger and want are found among millions of working people and the few who make up the employing class have all the good things of life.

Between these two classes a struggle must go on until the workers of the world organize as a class, take possession of the earth and the machinery of production, and abolish the wage system.

We find that the centering of management of the industries into fewer and fewer hands makes the trade unions unable to cope with the ever-growing power of the employing class. The trade unions foster a state of affairs which allows one set of workers to be pitted against another set of workers in the same industry, thereby helping defeat one another in wage wars. Moreover, the trade unions aid the employing class to mislead the workers into the belief that the working class have interests in common with their employers.

These conditions can be changed and the interest of the working class upheld only by an organization formed in such a way that all its members in any one industry, or in all industries if necessary, cease work whenever a strike or lockout is on in any department thereof, thus making an injury to one an injury to all.

Instead of the conservative motto, "A fair day's wage for a fair day's work," we must inscribe on our banner the revolutionary watchword, "Abolition of the wage system."

It is the historic mission of the working class to do away with capitalism. The army of production must be organized, not only for the everyday struggle with capitalists, but also to carry on production when capitalism shall have been overthrown. By organizing industrially we are forming the structure of the new society within the shell of the old.

---

long-smoldering Cripple Creek, Colorado, strike was crushed in 1904, the WFM realized it needed national support. Thus, in 1905, Haywood, Debs, and other leading socialists banded their unions together to form the **Industrial Workers of the World** (IWW) (see Exhibit 2–4).[24]

Immediately embroiled in internal political struggle, the IWW was decimated by the WFM's withdrawal in 1906, while Haywood stayed with the IWW. Its rhetoric was radical, but its demands were not. When involved in collective action, the IWW's usual demands related to wages and hours rather than usurpation of management functions.[25] And although strike violence occasionally broke out, these incidents were often sparked by management action similar to that facing the 19th-century industrial labor movement. It is important to note, however, that the purpose of the IWW was not to achieve better wages and working conditions—but to abolish the wage system. This may be why it encountered such resistance from employers and why it had little success in building permanent organizations.

---

[24] Dulles, *Labor in America,* pp. 208–11.

[25] J. G. Rayback, *A History of American Labor* (New York: Free Press, 1966), p. 248.

The most successful IWW strike occurred in 1912 in Lawrence, Massachu-setts, after textile workers suffered a wage cut. Although mostly unorganized, 20,000 workers walked out, and IWW organizers took over the strike's direction. After two months, during which several violent incidents occurred (perpetrated by all sides), worker demands were met, and the mills reopened.[26]

Despite this victory, the IWW lost a subsequent textile strike in 1913 in Paterson, New Jersey. This outcome, coupled with the advent of World War I, dur-ing which the IWW stated that its members would fight for neither side since only the capitalists would benefit, led to the IWW's demise. Haywood and other lead-ers were tried and convicted of sedition for allegedly obstructing the war effort. The IWW was effectively finished.[27]

The Boycott Cases

The strike was not the only weapon labor used against employers. While local employees struck, national unions urged union members and the public to **boycott** struck or "unfair" products. Two major national boycotts to support strikes, the *Danbury Hatters* and *Bucks Stove* cases, led to sharp legal reverses for labor organizations.

In *Danbury Hatters,* the employer retaliated by charging the union with con-spiring to restrain trade, a violation of the **Sherman Antitrust Act.** Under Sher-man Act provisions, if restraint is found, actual damages can be punitively trebled. The union lost, and it appeared that employees would have to pay damages, but the AFL and the United Hatters' national organization "passed the hat" and paid the fines.[28] In *Bucks Stove,* a federal district court enjoined the boycott and held Samuel Gompers in contempt of court. The conspiracy doctrine specter reappeared in the application of court injunctions halting union actions. Strikes, union organizing, and other union activities were increasingly interpreted by federal courts as restraints on interstate commerce and, hence, enjoinable and punishable.[29]

Injunctions, such as those issued in the railroad strikes, had a substantial effect on union activities. Their use not only ended the strikes at which they were aimed, but also reduced the willingness of workers in other situations to strike, particu-larly if they were called in sympathy for other strikes or involved issues of work-place control.[30]

---

[26] Dulles, *Labor in America,* pp. 215–19.

[27] Ibid., pp. 219–22.

[28] Ibid., p. 197.

[29] Rayback, *A History of American Labor,* pp. 224–26.

[30] H. J. McCammon, " 'Government by Injunction': The U.S. Judiciary and Strike Action in the Late 19th and Early 20th Centuries," *Work and Occupations* 20 (1993), 174–204. See also, W. E. Forbath, *Law and the Shaping of the American Labor Movement* (Cambridge: Harvard University Press, 1991).

Early Legislation

Early collective actions on an industrial scale by unions were usually met by a two-pronged attack: adamant resistance by employers and court injunctions. To balance the power between the parties and to substitute statutory for court-made common law, Congress passed the Erdman Act in 1898, prohibiting discrimination against railroad employees based on union membership. However, it was held unconstitutional in 1908 as an abridgment of personal liberty and the rights of property.[31]

Union leaders felt the Supreme Court's application of the Sherman Act to the boycott cases hamstrung collective activity. With the election of President Woodrow Wilson and a Democratic Congress, labor expected relief to be forthcoming. In 1914, the Clayton Act was passed, hailed by Samuel Gompers as the "industrial Magna Carta upon which the working people will rear their structure of individual freedom."[32]

The removal of labor from the jurisdiction of the Sherman Act and limitations on the use of federal injunctions, contributed to Gompers's euphoria. However, enthusiasm was short lived because its ambiguous wording led to judicial interpretations that disappointed labor.[33] The Supreme Court held that, even though unions could not be construed as rendering trade unions illegal per se, their actions might still be construed as restraining trade.[34] It also held that strikes terminated the normal employer-employee relationship, thereby removing the protection against injunctions for lawful employee activities.[35] Thus, the Clayton Act lost whatever teeth labor had believed it had gained.

TRADE UNION SUCCESS AND APATHY

World War I

Although World War I spelled the end of the IWW, AFL unions made solid gains. During 1917, numerous strikes, often fomented by the IWW, protested static wages as inflation grew. To reduce strikes, the National War Labor Board was established in 1918. It included five representatives each from labor and management, with two cochairs to represent the public's interest. Labor's right to organize and bargain collectively was recognized. By the end of the war, average

---

[31] *Adair* v. *United States,* 208 U.S. 161 (1908).

[32] S. Gompers, "The Charter of Industrial Freedom," *American Federationist* 31, no. 11 (1914), pp. 971–72.

[33] S. I. Kutler, "Labor, the Clayton Act, and the Supreme Court," *Labor History* 3 (1962), pp. 19–38.

[34] *Duplex Printing* v. *Deering,* 254 U.S. 445 (1921).

[35] D. L. Jones, "The Enigma of the Clayton Act," *Industrial and Labor Relations Review* 10 (1957), pp. 201–21.

earnings of even semiskilled union members exceeded $1,000 annually, and the AFL had added more than a million members, thus exceeding 4 million in 1919.[36]

The American Plan

A variety of factors eroded labor's growth after World War I. The 1920s was a decade of relative prosperity. A decline in immigration reduced competition for jobs among unskilled workers. With the prosecution of several leaders of the IWW for sedition, management identified labor as politically extremist. Although the IWW did not represent a large portion of the labor movement, it became a symbol of its danger in the public's eye. At the same time, the Bolsheviks gained power in Russia, and Americans were warned that this pattern could be duplicated in the United States if trade unions became too strong.

Against this backdrop, the **American Plan** was implemented. Employers subtly associated the union movement with foreign subversives and questioned whether it was appropriate for workers to be represented by union officials who were not employed at their plant. Employers championed the **open shop,** ostensibly to preserve the freedom of employees to refrain from joining unions. But the freedom to join was discouraged through the use of **yellow-dog contracts,** which applicants and employees were required to sign, indicating they understood union membership was grounds for discharge. As the decade wore on, yellow-dog contracts were seen increasingly as instruments of coercion, severely restricting the private rights and potential economic power of employees.[37]

Communities organized open-shop committees to protect citizens from outside labor organizers. Reinforcing the idea of local control–local concern, many employers improved wages and working conditions in unorganized plants. Where employees began to organize, employers encouraged establishment of a company union, autonomous from a national union but not necessarily the employer (see Exhibit 2–5).[38]

The End of an Era

The 1920s was a decade of transition for the United States. The country shifted from an agricultural to an industrial society. Mass production and the assembly line reduced skill requirements, creating an industrial rather than a craft orientation. Immigration quotas reduced the influx of impoverished potential employees. While the AFL took a stand-pat approach to industrial organization, some of its newer leaders began to see the importance of organizing unskilled workers.

---

[36] Dulles, *Labor in America,* pp. 226–28.

[37] D. Ernst, "The Yellow-Dog and Liberal Reform, 1917–1932," *Labor History* 30 (1989), pp. 251–74.

[38] See Chamberlain and Cullen, *Labor Sector,* 109–10; and Taft, *Organized Labor,* chap. 27.

EXHIBIT 2–5

Charles M. Schwab, Chairman of the Board of Bethlehem Steel, in a Speech to a Chamber of Commerce Audience, 1918

"I believe that labor should organize in individual plants or amongst themselves for the better negotiation of labor and the protection of their own rights; but the organization and control of labor in individual plants and manufactories, to my mind, ought to be made representative of the people in those plants who know the conditions; that they ought not to be controlled by somebody from Kamchatka who knows nothing about what their conditions are."

SOURCE: C. M. Schwab, "Capital and Labor: A Reconstruction Policy," *Annals of the American Academy of Political and Social Science,* January, 1919, p. 158.

The 1920s marked the end of the Gompers era, which spanned almost 50 years. His parting words to the AFL are capsuled in Exhibit 2–6.[39] On its surface, the AFL appeared to be in decline, conserving a shrinking base. In terms of internal politics, it might be seen as a festering mass of irreconcilable factions. But the economic turmoil of the Depression, combined with changes in the direction of the labor movement, signaled a sea change in U.S. public policy and labor-management relations.

EXHIBIT 2–6

Samuel Gompers's Farewell Words to the AFL

"I want to live for one thing alone—to leave a better labor movement in America and in the world than I found it when I entered, as a boy . . ."

SOURCE: *AFL Proceedings,* 1924, p. 281.

INDUSTRIAL UNIONS

Until the 1930s, attempts to organize **industrial unions** were generally unsuccessful. A number of factors contributed to this lack of success, including the continuing supply of unskilled workers provided by immigration, the AFL's relative disinterest in industrial unions, and the tendency of industrially oriented unions to adopt revolutionary goals. By the mid-1930s, a new set of circumstances created an atmosphere more favorable for industrial organizing. The Depression and legislative initiatives in labor-management relations helped. Established union leaders with a business-union orientation took up the industrial organizing crusade. Elected officials became more tolerant of, or actively favored, union activity.

---

[39] I. Yellowitz, "Samuel Gompers: A Half-Century in Labor's Front Rank," *Monthly Labor Review* 112, no. 7 (1989), pp. 27–33.

The Industrial Union Leadership

The leadership for industrial organizing efforts came from within the AFL. John L. Lewis and other officials of the United Mine Workers (UMW), an AFL union, spearheaded the drive over the objections of the craft unions. Lewis realized the UMW faced membership erosion in a declining industry. He decided in the early 1930s the time had come to push for industrial organizing, but was not prepared for the adamant opposition he met within the AFL. In an acrimonious debate at its 1935 convention, Lewis and "Big Bill" Hutcheson, president of the Carpenters' Union, actually came to blows (see Exhibit 2–7). The convention voted against embarking on industrial organizing. Afterwards, Lewis and Philip Murray of the UMW, and leaders of the Amalgamated Clothing Workers, International Ladies' Garment Workers, Typographical Union, Textile Workers, cap and millinery department of the United Hatters, Oil Field, Gas Well, and Refining Workers, and Mine, Mill, and Smelter Workers met to form the **Committee for Industrial Organization** (CIO).[40]

EXHIBIT 2–7

Lewis and Hutcheson at the 1935 AFL Convention

The industrial union report was defeated, but the question kept recurring. Delegates from rubber, radio, mine, and mill kept urging a new policy. Their way was blocked, though, not least by the towering figure of Big Bill Hutcheson, powerful head of the Carpenters' Union. Hutcheson and Lewis had always held similar views and frequently worked together. Like Lewis, Hutcheson was a big man, 6 feet tall and 220 pounds. When a delegate raised the question of industrial unions in the rubber plants, Hutcheson raised a point of order. The question had already been settled, he contended. Lewis objected; the delegate should be heard on a problem facing his own union. "This thing of raising points of order," he added, "is rather small potatoes."

"I was raised on small potatoes," Hutcheson replied.

As Lewis returned to his seat, he paused to tell Hutcheson that the opposition was pretty small stuff. "We could have made you small," was the reply. "We could have kept you off the executive council, you crazy bastard."

Lewis swung a wild haymaker. It caught Hutcheson on the jaw; the two men grappled, crashed against a table, and fell awkwardly to the floor. President Green wildly hammered his gavel as delegates tried to separate the two heavyweights.

SOURCE: D. F. Selvin, *The Thundering Voice of John L. Lewis* (New York: Lathrop, Lee, & Shepard, 1969), pp. 103–4.

Organizing the Industrial Workforce

Major efforts were begun to organize workers in the steel, textile, rubber, and auto industries. Philip Murray headed the Steel Workers Organizing Committee

---

[40] Rayback, *History of American Labor,* pp. 348–50.

EXHIBIT 2–8

Telegram from Sit-Down Strikers to Governor Murphy

"Governor, we have decided to stay in the plant. We have no illusions about the sacrifices which the decision will entail. We fully expect that if a violent effort is made to oust us many of us will be killed and we take this means of making it known to our wives, to our children, to the people of the state of Michigan and of the country that if this result follows from the attempt to eject us you are the one who must be held responsible for our deaths."

SOURCE: S. Fine, *Sit-Down: The General Motors Strike of 1936–1937* (Ann Arbor: University of Michigan Press, 1969), p. 278.

(SWOC), establishing 150 locals totaling over 100,000 members by the end of 1936. In early 1937, secret efforts of John L. Lewis and Myron Taylor, head of U.S. Steel, resulted in the SWOC's recognition as the bargaining agent for U.S. Steel employees. The steelworkers won an 8-hour day, 40-hour week, and a wage increase. Other steel firms were not so readily organized. During an organizing parade at Republic Steel on Memorial Day, 1937, violence broke out, and 10 strikers were killed by Chicago police.[41]

The autoworkers were next. Despite relatively high wages pioneered by Henry Ford, jobs were tedious and fatiguing, and owners had established private police forces to keep workers in line.[42] In 1936, the United Automobile Workers (UAW) sought recognition from General Motors. GM refused, but worker sentiments were so strong that "quickie" strikes resulted.[43]

In late 1936, workers at GM's Fisher body plants in Flint, Michigan, took over the plants and refused to leave. GM viewed this **sit-down strike** as criminal trespass, but the workers asserted that job rights were superior to property rights. Injunctions to oust the workers were ignored (see Exhibit 2–8). Attempts to persuade Michigan Governor Frank Murphy to mobilize the militia to enforce the injunction failed. Realizing the workers could hold out, GM capitulated in February 1937, agreeing to recognize the UAW and promising not to discriminate against union members.[44]

This tactic was used to organize Chrysler workers as well as the glass, rubber, and textile industries. Industrial unionization had been achieved. By 1938, the CIO membership of 3.7 million exceeded membership in the older AFL by 300,000.[45]

---

[41] Dulles, *Labor in America,* pp. 299–302.

[42] M. J. Gannon, "Entrepreneurship and Labor Relations at the Ford Motor Company," *Marquette Business Review,* Summer 1972, pp. 63–75.

[43] Rayback, *History of American Labor,* p. 353.

[44] S. Fine, *Sit-Down: The General Motors Strike of 1936–1937* (Ann Arbor: University of Michigan Press, 1969).

[45] Rayback, *History of American Labor,* pp. 354–55.

LEGISLATION

In the 1930s, public policy toward unions shifted radically. Before the Railway Labor Act in 1926, no laws facilitated organizing or bargaining. Courts routinely enjoined unions from striking, organizing, picketing, or other activities, even if peacefully conducted. State laws limiting injunctive powers of state courts were struck down.[46]

Norris-LaGuardia Act (1932)

By the time the **Norris-LaGuardia Act** was passed in 1932, Congress had recognized the legitimacy of collective bargaining. Until Norris-LaGuardia, acceptance of a collective bargaining relationship had to devolve from a voluntary employer action.[47]

The act severely restricted the power of federal courts to issue injunctions against union activities. The act also forbade federal courts from enforcing the yellow-dog contract, which required employees or job applicants to agree, as a condition of employment, not to join a labor union. Courts had previously upheld their legality.[48]

While the Norris-LaGuardia Act protected numerous previously enjoinable activities, it was a neutral policy—it did not open any right to demand employer recognition. Other than the removal of the yellow-dog contract, explicit federal ground rules for employer conduct in labor-management relations still did not exist. This would change after the inauguration of President Franklin D. Roosevelt.

National Industrial Recovery Act (1933)

The National Industrial Recovery Act (NIRA), adopted in 1933, encouraged employers to band together to set prices and production quotas through industrial codes. To complete an industrial code, however, employers were required to enable employees to bargain through representatives of their own choosing, free from employer interference. However, the Supreme Court ruled the NIRA unconstitutional in 1935.[49]

Wagner Act (National Labor Relations Act, 1935)

As the NIRA safeguards for unions were lost, the **Wagner Act** resecured organizing rights and specified employer illegal activities. Section 7, the heart of the act, specifies the rights of employees to engage in union activities:

---

[46] *Truax* v. *Corrigan,* 257 U.S. 312 (1921).

[47] B. Taylor and F. Witney, *Labor Relations Law,* 2nd ed. (Englewood Cliffs, NJ: Prentice Hall, 1975), pp. 144–46.

[48] *Hitchman Coal Co.* v. *Mitchell,* 245 U.S. 229 (1917).

[49] *Schechter Poultry Corp.* v. *United States,* 295 U.S. 495 (1935).

> Employees shall have the right to self-organization, to form, join, or assist labor organizations, to bargain collectively through representatives of their own choosing, and to engage in concerted activities, for the purpose of collective bargaining or other mutual aid or protection.

Section 8 broadly forbade interference with employees' rights to be represented, to bargain, to have their labor organizations free from employer dominance, to be protected from employment discrimination for union activity, and to be free from retaliation for accusing the employer of an unlawful (unfair) labor practice.

To investigate violations of Section 8 and to determine whether employees desired representation, the Wagner Act established the **National Labor Relations Board** (NLRB), whose major duties were to determine which, if any, union was the employees' choice to represent them and to hear and rule on alleged unfair labor practices.

The Wagner Act also established the concept of **exclusive representation** in the agency relationship between the union and the employees. Where a majority of employees chose a union, that union would represent all employees in the unit in bargaining over issues of wages, hours, and terms and conditions of employment.

The Wagner Act did not apply to all employers and employees. Specifically exempted were those who worked for federal, state, and local governments; and those subject to the Railway Labor Act. Supervisors and managers, agricultural workers, domestic employees, and family workers were also excluded from coverage.

Passage of the Wagner Act did not immediately presage a shift in U.S. labor relations. With NIRA recently having been declared void by the Supreme Court and with Section 7 of the Wagner Act closely duplicating the NIRA section, some employers expected the courts to rule against Congress on a constitutional challenge.

EMPLOYER INTRANSIGENCE

Unions saw the Wagner Act as creating a mechanism for employees to use to gain representation. Organizing was a crucial activity with almost half of the strikes between 1935 and 1937 not over bargaining issues but over obtaining recognition.

Many employers doubted the constitutionality of the Wagner Act. Firms engaged a variety of strategies in opposition to union-organizing activities. Some fostered company unions. Other tactics included exploiting differences between the AFL and CIO.[50] Company unions received managerial support, but gradually some became relatively independent and effective as companies were scrutinized

---

[50] D. Nelson, "Managers and Nonunion Workers in the Rubber Industry: Union Avoidance Strategies in the 1930s," *Industrial and Labor Relations Review* 43 (1989), pp. 41–52.

to determine whether the unions were illegally dominated by management.[51] Employers also used the so-called **Mohawk Valley formula,** linking unions with agitators and communists. Proponents of this strategy organized back-to-work drives during strikes, got local police to break up strikes, and aligned local interests against the focus of union activities.[52]

Congress investigated company attempts to thwart or rebuff union activities and found they spent almost $10 million for spying, strikebreaking, and munitions between 1933 and 1937. To prepare for potential strikes, Youngstown Sheet and Tube amassed 8 machine guns, 369 rifles, 190 shotguns, 450 revolvers, 109 gas guns, 3,000 rounds of gas, and almost 10,000 rounds of shotgun shells and bullets. Republic Steel allegedly possessed the largest private arsenal in the United States.[53] The Ford Motor Company established an internal police force that numbered between 3,500 and 5,000 (about 1 for every 25 workers), enforced plant rules, spied on union activity, and fomented beatings of union organizers.[54]

Constitutionality of the Wagner Act

Both sides had reasons to believe their positions to be legitimate. Management had seen a long line of Supreme Court decisions adverse to labor, not the least of these the striking down of the NIRA, which was partially similar to the Wagner Act. Labor had seen sympathy for its position grow throughout the country. With President Roosevelt consolidating his position through the overwhelming electoral endorsement of the New Deal in 1936, labor believed the court would find it difficult to invalidate the law.[55]

Opposition to the Wagner Act by employers was probably related to ideological, legal, and economic factors. Employers' creation and use of the American Plan, Mohawk Valley formula, and other devices reflected their ideological opposition to industrial unionization. Employers believed unionization would raise their labor costs. A study of the economic effects of the Wagner Act indicates the market value of companies unionized after passage of the Wagner Act decreased relative to that of nonunion firms. Thus, the reduced ability to avoid unionization following passage of the act had an economic cost for employers.[56]

The Wagner Act was ruled constitutional by the Supreme Court on April 12, 1937.[57] Earlier, the NLRB determined that Jones & Laughlin Steel had violated

---

[51] S. M. Jacoby, "Reckoning with Company Unions: The Case of Thompson Products, 1934–1964," *Industrial and Labor Relations Review* 43 (1989), pp. 19–40.

[52] Dulles, *Labor in America,* p. 278.

[53] Ibid., pp. 277–78.

[54] See Lichtenstein, *The Most Dangerous Man in Detroit,* and S. Norwood, "Ford's Brass Knuckles: Harry Bennett, The Cult of Muscularity, and Anti-Labor Terror—1920–1945," *Labor History* 37 (1996), pp. 365–91.

[55] Taylor and Witney, *Labor Relations Law,* pp. 161–64.

[56] C. A. Olson and B. E. Becker, "The Effects of the NLRA on Stockholder Wealth in the 1930s," *Industrial and Labor Relations Review* 44 (1990), pp. 116–29.

[57] *NLRB* v. *Jones & Laughlin Steel Corp.,* 301 U.S. 1 (1937).

the act by discriminating against union members. It ordered 10 employees reinstated with back pay and told the firm to cease unfair labor practices. The appeals court had held the NLRB's action was beyond the range of federal power.

In a five-four decision, the Court sided with the board, holding that Congress may regulate employer activities under the Constitution's commerce clause. It reaffirmed employee rights to organize and recognized Congress's authority to restrict employer activities likely to disrupt unionization. The Court ruled that manufacturing, even if conducted locally, was a process involving interstate commerce. Further, it was reasonable for Congress to set rules and procedures governing employees' rights to organize. Finally, the Court found the board's conduct at the hearing and its orders were regular, within the act's meaning, and protected. With the Wagner Act upheld, an era of rapid industrial unionization was opened.

LABOR POWER

The CIO's momentum increased for the rest of the 1930s. Both federations raided each other's members, with employers caught in the midst. These **jurisdictional disputes** created public hostility and led to some state laws outlawing certain union activities.[58]

Although labor had been instrumental in getting its friends elected to public office in the 1930s, its ranks split in 1940 when John L. Lewis announced his support for Wendell Wilkie, the Republican candidate for president. The split originated in 1937 when Lewis had expected the Democratic administration to repay labor for its campaign assistance by providing help during the GM sit-down strike. During the strike, Lewis said:

> For six months the economic royalists represented by General Motors contributed their money and used their energy to drive [Roosevelt's] administration out of power. The administration asked labor for help, and labor gave it. The same economic royalists now have their fangs in labor. The workers of this country expect the administration to help the workers in every legal way and to support the workers in General Motors plants.[59]

President Roosevelt did nothing except urge meetings between the UAW and the company. During the strike, some of Lewis's other pronouncements were equally dramatic (see Exhibit 2–9).

The period before World War II was a time of great political ferment. Many questioned the capitalist system's ability to overcome and avoid depressions. Radical political agendas were created, with government regulation or operation of the economy proposed. However, most of the influential new industrial union

---

[58] A jurisdictional dispute occurs when two or more unions claim to (1) simultaneously represent or attempt to bargain for the same employee group or (2) simultaneously assert that their members are entitled by contract to perform a certain class of work.

[59] Rayback, *History of American Labor,* p. 368.

EXHIBIT 2–9

The Rhetoric of John L. Lewis

[The mid-1930s were] a time of virtual class warfare. The National Guard was called out more than a dozen times a year; strikes were broken not only by goons and ginks and company finks, in the words of the old labor song, but by tear gas and machine guns. And when a particularly disdainful Chrysler president asked for Lewis's comment in the midst of a negotiation inspired by a spontaneous sit-down at Chrysler, the six-foot-two Lewis stood up and said, "I am 99 percent of a mind to come around the table right now and wipe that damn sneer off your face." Lee Pressman, of the new CIO, later observed, "Lewis's voice at that moment was in every sense the voice of millions of unorganized workers who were being exploited by gigantic corporations. He was expressing at that instant their resentment, hostility, and their passionate desire to strike back."

. . . When F.D.R. lumped labor with management, declaring his famous "plague on both your houses" . . . Lewis intoned: "Labor, like Israel, has many sorrows. Its women weep for their fallen, and they lament for the future of the children of the race. It ill behooves one who has supped at labor's table and who has been sheltered in labor's house to curse with equal fervor and fine impartiality both labor and its adversaries when they become locked in deadly embrace."

The "sup" to which he had made reference was a $500,000 UMW contribution to F.D.R.'s 1936 campaign. Lewis was unabashed about demanding his money's worth. "Everybody says I want my pound of flesh, that I gave Roosevelt $500,000 for his 1936 campaign, and I want quid pro quo. The UMW and the CIO have paid cash on the barrel for every piece of legislation gotten . . . Is anyone fool enough to believe for one instant that we gave this money to Roosevelt because we are spellbound by his voice?"

. . . Although Lewis was rarely photographed smiling ("That scowl is worth a million dollars," he once confided to a friend), one can see the demon gleam in his eye as he scratched out his answer (to Roosevelt's plea for a wartime no-strike pledge). "If you want to use the power of the state to restrain me, as an agent of labor, then, sir, I submit that you should use the same power to restrain my adversary in this issue, who is an agent of capital. My adversary is a rich man named Morgan, who lives in New York." Signed, in letters which ran two and a half inches tall, "Yours humbly."

SOURCE: V. Navasky, "John L. Lewis, Union General," *Esquire,* December 1983, pp. 264–66.

---

leaders gave priority to trade union matters.[60] As the 1930s wore on, it became apparent that an increasingly large number of industrial union staff positions were held by communists. They did not join in President Roosevelt's support for the Allies after Germany and Russia signed a nonaggression pact in 1939.

The year 1941 was one of crisis for labor-management relations. The ambivalent stand of some industrial union leaders toward the war allowed employers to brand them nonpatriotic. When Philip Murray became CIO president in 1940 the

---

[60] K. Boyle, "Building the Vanguard: Walter Reuther and Radical Politics in 1936," *Labor History* 30 (1989), pp. 433–48.

stand shifted, but the label was not entirely removed. Employers refused to recognize unions, although organizing at Ford and Little Steel was finally successful. For the first time, labor's goal of "more, more, more now" was becoming intolerable to the general public. More than 4,300 strikes broke out in 1941, involving more than 8 percent of the workforce. This widespread industrial disruption would probably have been moderated by congressional action had not the attack on Pearl Harbor involved the United States in World War II.[61]

World War II

At the outbreak of World War II, AFL, CIO, and management representatives pledged to produce together to meet the war effort. Labor pledged not to strike if a board were established to handle unresolved grievances. Management did not entirely concede, and, as a result, President Roosevelt established the National War Labor Board (NWLB). As the war got under way, prices rose rapidly. Labor's demands for wage increases grew. The NWLB tried to maintain a policy whereby wage increases would equal changes in the cost of living. Labor objected to the check on collective bargaining and NWLB policy on wages, but it was not changed.[62]

Although no-strike pledges had been given, in 1945, 4,750 strikes involved 3,470,000 workers, and 38 million worker-days were lost. This exceeded the prewar high of 28.4 million days in 1937. Major sporadic strikes in the coal industry, led by John L. Lewis, were particularly evident to the public. At one point, the coal mines were seized and run by Secretary of the Interior Harold Ickes (see Exhibit 2–10).[63]

The strike activity led Congress to pass the War Labor Disputes Act over President Roosevelt's veto. This act authorized the seizure of plants involved in labor disputes, made strikes and lockouts in defense industries a criminal offense, required 30 days' notice to the NWLB of a pending dispute, and required the NLRB to monitor strike votes.[64]

Accommodation and innovation in bargaining was also evident during World War II. Even overtly communist unions supported no-strike agreements since this aided the Soviet-American alliance in Europe.[65] In only 46 of 17,650 dispute cases before the NWLB did parties fail to reach or accept agreements. The war experience also led to a widespread acceptance of fringe benefits in lieu of wage increases. Holidays, vacations, sick leaves, and shift differentials were approved by the NWLB as part of labor contracts. Labor shortages led to policies

---

[61] Rayback, *History of American Labor,* pp. 370–73.

[62] P. Taft, *Organized Labor in American History* (New York: Harper & Row, 1964), pp. 546–52.

[63] Ibid., pp. 553–56.

[64] Ibid., p. 557.

[65] M. Torigian, "National Unity on the Waterfront: Communist Politics and the ILWU During the Second World War," *Labor History* 30 (1989), pp. 409–32.

EXHIBIT 2–10

Comments by President Roosevelt on Coal Strikes during 1943

On June 23, the president issued a statement in which he said that "the action of the leaders of the United Mine Workers coal miners has been intolerable—and has rightly stirred up the anger and disapproval of the overwhelming mass of the American people."

He declared that the mines would be operated by the government under the terms of the board's directive order of June 18.

He stated that "the government had taken steps to set up the machinery for inducting into the armed services all miners subject to the Selective Service Act who absented themselves, without just cause, from work in the mines under government operation." Since the "Selective Service Act does not authorize induction of men above 45 years into the armed services, I intend to request the Congress to raise the age limit for non-combat service to 65 years. I shall make that request of the Congress so that if at any time in the future there should be a threat of interruption of work in plants, mines, or establishments owned by the government, or taken possession of by the government, the machinery will be available for prompt action."

SOURCE: A. Suffern, "The National War Labor Board and Coal," in *The Termination Report of the National War Labor Board,* vol. 1: *Industrial Disputes and Wage Stabilization in Wartime* (Washington, DC: U.S. Government Printing Office, 1948), p. 1009.

advocating equal employment opportunities for minorities and equal pay for men and women in the same jobs.[66]

Reconversion

As the war ended, consumers anticipated the return of durable goods. Labor looked forward to wage increases to offset cost-of-living increases that had occurred during the war. The inevitable clash of labor and management led to the greatest single-year period of labor conflict in U.S. history. Between August 1945 and August 1946, 4,630 strikes involved 4.9 million workers and the loss of 119.8 million worker-days (or 1.62 percent of total days available). Major strikes affected the coal, rail, auto, and steel industries. These were settled with wage increases averaging about 18.5 cents per hour; and some, especially in steel, resulted in price increases as well.[67]

CHANGING THE BALANCE

The end of the war, the strikes, and the election of a more conservative Congress led to legislation to balance the power between unions and managements. The strikes of 1941, the coal problems during World War II, and the 1946 strikes

---

[66] Taft, *Organized Labor,* pp. 559–62.
[67] Ibid., pp. 563–78.

stimulated legislation to expand and clarify rules applied to the practice of U.S. labor relations.

The Wagner Act had addressed only employers' unfair labor practices. The labor movement's critics argued that unions also could coerce individual employees and refuse to bargain collectively. The Wagner Act was amended and added to with the enactment of the Labor Management Relations Act of 1947, better known as **Taft-Hartley.**

Taft-Hartley Act

Employee rights were expanded to include the right to refrain from union activities beyond membership or paying dues. Congress went further by enabling states to enact so-called **"right-to-work" laws** prohibiting union membership as a condition of continued employment.[68] Organized labor refers to them as "right-to-wreck" laws, enabling free riders to receive union gains applicable to an entire bargaining unit without contributing money or effort to the cause. Proponents see the laws as essential to freedom of association and protective of the right to join or not join organizations.

Union unfair labor practices were defined, recognizing the agency role the union plays for all bargaining unit members. Unions were required to bargain in good faith with employers and forbidden to strike to gain recognition or to put pressure on uninvolved second parties to get at a primary employer.

The **Federal Mediation and Conciliation Service** (FMCS) was established to aid settlement of unresolved contractual disputes. Assistance could be requested by the parties or offered directly. Provision was made for intervention in strikes likely to create a national emergency. If the president determined a labor dispute imperiled the nation, a board of inquiry could be convened to determine the issues and positions of the parties. Provisions were included for an 80-day "cooling-off" period during which strikes were prohibited and NLRB elections on final contract proposals would be conducted.

Union officials were forbidden to accept money from employers, and employers could not offer them inducements. Secondary boycotts to force an employer to cease doing business with others (i.e., a struck or nonunion firm) were made illegal. Corporations and labor unions were forbidden to make political contributions. Finally, federal employees were forbidden to strike.

The overall thrust of the legislation balanced the relative power of the contenders and provided mechanisms to reduce the likelihood of a recurrence of labor strife of the magnitude seen in 1946. Because the bill represented a retreat from the initiatives labor had previously enjoyed, it was not greeted with enthusiasm in that quarter. But the bill satisfied business, Congress, and the public. It passed by wide margins in both houses, was vetoed by President Truman, and repassed over

---

[68] States passing these laws include Alabama, Arizona, Arkansas, Florida, Georgia, Iowa, Kansas, Louisiana, Mississippi, Nebraska, Nevada, North Carolina, North Dakota, South Carolina, South Dakota, Tennessee, Texas, Utah, Virginia, and Wyoming.

his veto. The passage of Taft-Hartley and other legislation brought an end to free-wheeling administratively initiated change. Rule-making became subject to court review. Instead of the government promoting unionization as a counterbalance to big business, it assumed more of a referee role.[69]

The New Production Paradigm

The decade and a half of labor-management turmoil embedded in the Great Depression and World War II led to a pervasive and fundamental shift in productivity regimes in the United States. Prior to this period, employers institutionalized the **"drive system"** in which supervisors (foremen) intensively directed and monitored the workforce and had ultimate power in hiring, firing, and pay decisions. Foremen relied on fear and orders to meet production quotas. Collective bargaining reduced the power of supervisors and raised wages. Increased effort came from the ability to hire employees with higher ability and the funding of wage improvements through productivity increases. An era of **capital-labor accords** was begun.[70]

RETRENCHMENT AND MERGER

Organized labor realized two things after Taft-Hartley. First, it would have to exert more influence in legislative activity and adopt a more publicly advocative stance on labor issues. Second, the strength of management and labor had been changed by the act. The time had come to direct labor's energies toward unity. The old guard who sundered the AFL was disappearing. William Green and Philip Murray both died in 1952. Their deaths resulted in the election of a new president of the AFL, George Meany, and of the CIO, Walter Reuther. John L. Lewis's UMW was unaffiliated, thus greatly reducing the historic friction.[71]

The 1950s began a nearly 20 year period in which most large unionized employers accepted unions as legitimate representatives. Longer-term contracts were negotiated. Wage and productivity increases were closely related. Living standards and profits increased during the period. Conditions that led to the formation of the CIO—animosity from craft unionists and adamant opposition to unionization from large employers—had been mostly overcome. CIO unionists had equalized their power with the AFL, and unification became possible.[72]

---

[69] R. O'Brien, "Taking the Conservative State Seriously: Statebuilding and Restrictive Labor Practices in Postwar America," *Labor Studies Journal* 21, no. 4 (1997), pp. 33–63.

[70] D. M. Gordon, "From the Drive System to the Capital-Labor Accord: Econometric Tests for the Transition between Productivity Regimes," *Industrial Relations* 36 (1997), pp. 125–59.

[71] Dulles, *Labor in America,* pp. 360–72.

[72] For more information on the CIO, see R. H. Zieger, "The CIO: A Bibliographical Update and Archival Guide," *Labor History* 31 (1990), pp. 413–40.

Merger

The first step toward rapprochement was the ratification of a no-raid agreement in 1954. A Joint Unity Committee was established to study the feasibility of a merger. On February 9, 1955, a merger formed the combined AFL–CIO with George Meany as its president.[73]

Meany reendorsed Gompers's concept of "more" as it applied to a person's standard and quality of living. He reaffirmed labor's commitment to collective bargaining. He was unwilling to involve labor in management but demanded that management's stewardship be high.[74] He reiterated the business unionism approach of the U.S. union movement, while recognizing that advances for its members may lead to advances for society.

The merged AFL–CIO did not become more powerful than the two federations had been in the past. In fact, union membership as a proportion of the labor force reached its peak in 1956 at about one-third. By 1964, this proportion had fallen to 30 percent, and a decline of 700,000 members had been recorded. Parts of the decline were due to less aggressive organizing, perhaps partly related to a reduction in competition for members, to better nonunion employee relations, and to the reduced relative proportion of blue-collar manufacturing workers in the labor force.

Whatever the reasons, the 1956–65 decade was one of malaise and retreat for the labor movement.[75] Unions also gained some unwanted notoriety as congressional investigators uncovered gross malfeasance by some major national union officers.

Corruption

For two and one-half years, beginning in 1957, the American public watched televised hearings in which a parade of labor officials invoked the Fifth Amendment to avoid self-incrimination. The Teamsters Union drew the lion's share of the spotlight as witnesses disclosed that its president, Dave Beck, had converted union funds to his own use, borrowed money from employers, and received kickbacks from labor "consultants." James R. Hoffa was accused of breaking Teamster strikes and covertly running his own trucking operation. "Sweetheart" contracts with substandard benefits and guaranteeing labor peace were uncovered in New York area Teamster locals operated by racketeers.

Other unions, including the Bakery and Confectionery Workers, Operating Engineers, Carpenters, and United Textile Workers, were also involved.

---

[73] Dulles, *Labor in America,* pp. 372–74.

[74] G. Meany, "What Labor Means by 'More,'" *Fortune* 26, no. 3 (1955), pp. 92–93.

[75] Dulles, *Labor in America,* pp. 377–81.

Management contributed to the corruption by providing payoffs for sweetheart contracts that prevented other unions from organizing while paying substandard rates.[76]

The publicity associated with the hearings cast a pall over the entire labor movement. By inference, all labor was corrupt. The AFL–CIO investigated internally and considered charges against the Allied Industrial Workers, Bakers, Distillers, Laundry Workers, Textile Workers, and Teamsters. The Textile Workers, Distillers, and Allied Industrial Workers agreed to mandated changes. The Bakers, Laundry Workers, and Teamsters refused and were expelled from the AFL–CIO in 1957.[77] Meanwhile, the congressional investigations led to legislation to reduce the likelihood of corrupt practices and to amend the Taft-Hartley Act.

Landrum-Griffin Act

The **Landrum-Griffin Act** of 1959 established rights of individual union members to freedom of speech, equal voting rights, control of dues increases, and copies of labor agreements under which they worked. Unions were required to file periodic reports of official and financial activities and financial holdings of union officers and employees, and employers were required to report financial transactions with unions. Internal union political activities involving election of officers and placing subordinate bodies under trusteeship were regulated. Recently convicted felons were barred from holding office. Extortionate picketing was prohibited.

PUBLIC SECTOR UNION GROWTH

As private-sector organizing activity sank into the doldrums of the late 1950s and early 1960s, public employees became increasingly interested in unionization. The Taft-Hartley Act had forbidden strikes in the federal service. Most state statutes forbade strikes by public employees, generally made strikers ineligible for any gains won by striking, and included summary discharge as a penalty. Concomitantly, most federal and state statutes had no mechanism for recognizing bargaining representatives.

Federal Executive Orders

In 1962, President Kennedy issued **Executive Order 10988,** a breakthrough for federal employee unions. This order enabled a majority union to bargain collectively with a government agency. Negotiations were restricted to terms and

---

[76] Taft, *Organized Labor,* pp. 698–704.
[77] Ibid., p. 704.

conditions of employment, not wages. Unions could not represent employees if they advocated strikes or the right to strike. Executive Order 11491 established procedures for determining appropriate bargaining units, required Landrum-Griffin-type reporting by unions, granted arbitration as a final settlement procedure for grievances, specified unfair labor practices and created procedures for redressing them, and created a Federal Impasse Panel to render binding decisions when negotiations reach a deadlock. This provision ameliorated the statutory no-strike provisions facing federal government employees. Executive Order 11616 allowed professionals in an agency to decide whether to join a bargaining unit, allowed individuals to pursue unfair labor practice charges through grievance channels or through the assistant secretary of labor for labor-management relations, required a grievance procedure in exclusively represented units (while narrowing the range of issues allowed arbitration), and allowed some negotiating on government time.[78]

Civil Service Reform Act

Title VII of the Civil Service Reform Act of 1976 regulates labor-management relations in the federal service. The act codifies the provisions written into the executive orders. It also establishes the **Federal Labor Relations Authority,** which acts as the federal service equivalent of the NLRB. Requirements and mechanisms for alleviating bargaining impasses and unresolved grievances under the contract are also spelled out.[79]

PASSING THE TORCH

The American Federation of Labor marked its 100th anniversary in 1982. In that century, with the exception of a one-year period, the AFL and its successor, the AFL–CIO, had only four presidents: Samuel Gompers, William Green, George Meany, and Lane Kirkland. George Meany retired from the presidency in 1979 at the age of 85 and died in 1980. Meany's service to the labor movement was great, but his passing, like the earlier passings of Green and Murray, created opportunities for rapprochement and change. After Lane Kirkland took office, the United Auto Workers and the Teamsters both reaffiliated with the AFL–CIO. John Sweeney's ascension to the presidency in 1994 is the first election of an insurgent candidate, and may signal increased labor militancy in the future. Exhibit 2–11 furnishes excerpts from George Meany's farewell address, delivered just two months before his death.

---

[78] Ibid., pp. 550–55.
[79] H. B. Frazier III, "Labor-Management Relations in the Federal Government," *Labor Law Journal* 30 (1979), pp. 131–38.

EXHIBIT 2–11

Excerpts from George Meany's Farewell Address, November 1979

Today is the last time I will have the honor of opening a convention of the AFL–CIO. By coincidence it is also an historic anniversary for the American trade union movement.

Ninety-eight years ago on this day—in Pittsburgh, Pennsylvania—107 trade unionists established the first, continuing national trade union center. The AFL–CIO is its direct descendant.

On November 15, 1881, the Federation of Organized Trades and Labor Unions was born for one simple reason—the unions of that day knew—as we know—that in unity there is strength.

Of course, there were many trade unions, assemblies and councils in many cities, even national and international labor unions in 1881. They had already made many important gains. But the founders of this great movement knew that much more could be accomplished through a combination of all those organizations.

So they organized and adopted a charter to "promote the general welfare of the industrial classes and secure that justice which isolated and separated trade and labor unions can never fully command."

Each succeeding generation of trade unions has given that charter life and breath. It has been a torch handed down from generation to generation—sometimes flickering, but never dimmed. It is now our responsibility—individually and collectively—to preserve that charter, to give it life and meaning in our time, and to pass it, intact and shining, to those who follow us; to carry that torch high, with pride, with honor.

Despite what some of my friends in the media may believe, I did not attend that convention in 1881. But I have read the proceedings and I believe Gompers, Foster, Leffingwell and all the courageous founders of our movement would look with favor upon the stewardship of their successors . . .

I am confident that the labor movement is about to embark on another period of significant growth and expansion. The growth in unionization among public workers is continuing at a strong pace—and there are significant organizing breakthroughs by unions in the service trades. White-collar and professional workers are seeking organization. Farm workers are proving their strength against the most oppressive tactics used by any employers anywhere in the nation . . .

Today the American trade union movement is vital, dynamic, growing. It is strong and unified.

But it needs to continue to grow, to consolidate its strength. And, I predict with certainty, it will.

SUMMARY

The following major points should be apparent in examining the early U.S. labor movement:

1. Labor organizations have been an integral part of the nation's growth at all stages.
2. Before the end of the 1920s, labor was faced with a hostile national environment.
3. Most of labor's activities could be—and were—enjoined by the courts when they were effective.
4. Most successful labor leaders were concerned about labor's role in representing their members' immediate concerns and refrained from advocating ideological positions.

In summary, labor encountered several hurdles in its early organization: the conspiracy doctrine, initial uplift union movements, the link with radicals, and injunctions aimed at union activities. Personalities who shaped the early American labor movement included Terence Powderly and Uriah Stephens, Samuel Gompers and Adolph Strasser, Eugene Debs and "Big Bill" Haywood.

The 1920s was a decade of retrenchment. Beneath the surface was a growing interest in industrial union organization, particularly by John L. Lewis, president of the United Mine Workers. Interest in labor legislation was growing. Then the Depression began. The 1930s saw most present labor legislation being shaped and many present-day industrial unions formed. It was a decade of turbulence, formation, and definition and an adolescence necessary for America's labor-management relations to endure to reach adulthood and relative maturity.

The 1930s provided the environment necessary for successful industrial unions. Both the Norris–LaGuardia and Wagner acts were passed, eliminating injunctions against most union activities and establishing collective bargaining as the preferred mode for resolving employment disputes.

The CIO was formed by dissident AFL leaders. It began by organizing efforts in primary industries, such as auto, steel, and rubber. Employers strongly resisted, but sit-down strikes and changes in public policy toward unions strengthened the CIO's efforts. By 1937, membership in the CIO was moving toward 4 million and had surpassed the AFL.

Industrial strife increased until the outbreak of World War II. The National War Labor Board was established to cope with employment problems during the wartime mobilization and to resolve disputes. Arbitration of grievances was introduced and later incorporated into collective bargaining agreements.

After the war, strikes reached unprecedented levels. In 1947, Congress passed the Taft-Hartley Act over President Truman's veto. The act provided for national emergency dispute procedures, established the Federal Mediation and Conciliation Service, and designated several union unfair labor practices. In 1959, the Landrum-Griffin Act limited the possibility of corruption in union-management relations.

The AFL and the CIO merged in 1955; but, shortly after, the union movement reached its maximum growth as a share of the labor force. With the exception of the public sector, union membership has recently been declining. Later chapters identify the causes of these changes and their consequences for the labor movement.

DISCUSSION QUESTIONS

1. Trace the evolution of the legal status of American unions. What activities were restricted by laws and courts? Did constraints increase or decline with time?
2. What were the major contributing causes to the failure of uplift unionism?
3. What were the advantages and disadvantages of taking a "business union" approach as opposed to advocating a labor political party?
4. Who were the leading personalities in labor relations? Which ones contributed to the definition of labor relations in the United States?
5. Who were the most effective union leaders during the 1930s and 1940s? What are your criteria for effectiveness? Would these same leaders be effective now?

KEY TERMS

Craft union   *25*

American Federation of Labor   *25*

Congress of Industrial
  Organizations   *25*

Corporatist   *26*

Uplift unionism   *26*

Revolutionary unionism   *26*

Business unionism   *26*

Predatory unionism   *26*

Journeyman   *27*

Conspiracy doctrine   *27*

National Labor Union   *29*

Knights of Labor   *30*

Arbitration   *30*

Industrial Workers of the World   *35*

Boycotts   *36*

Sherman Antitrust Act   *36*

American Plan   *38*

Open shop   *38*

Yellow-dog contracts   *38*

Industrial unions   *39*

Committee for Industrial
  Organization   *40*

Sit-down strike   *40*

Norris–LaGuardia Act   *42*

Wagner Act   *42*

National Labor Relations Board   *43*

Exclusive representation   *43*

Mohawk Valley formula   *44*

Jurisdictional dispute   *45*

3

LABOR LAW AND

FEDERAL AGENCIES

This chapter covers federal law and federal agencies charged with regulating collective bargaining. Relevant laws include the Railway Labor Act, Norris-LaGuardia Act, Wagner Act (as amended by Taft-Hartley and later legislation), Landrum-Griffin Act, and Civil Service Reform Act. The chapter gives an overview of the statutes, major government agencies, and their organizational structures. This chapter also examines briefly some of the effects of how laws are enforced by federal government agencies, and how employees react to protections granted by some employment laws.

In studying this chapter, keep the following questions in mind:

1. What specific types of activities are regulated?
2. In what areas have regulations been extended or retracted?
3. What employee groups are excluded or exempted from various regulations?
4. How do administrative agencies interact with employers and unions in implementing laws and regulations?

OVERVIEW

Statutory labor law is the result of the interaction of the positions of a variety of interest groups in society. When a pluralistic coalition of interest groups results, the climate necessary for passage is created.[1] New laws or the amendment of existing laws require the bonding of interest groups around issues or an agenda. As will be noted later in this chapter, organized labor in the United States has seldom expended much effort toward developing its own political party, but has been actively involved politically in supporting an overall agenda friendly to labor and liberal social positions.

Current laws governing organizing and collective bargaining date back to 1926, when the Railway Labor Act was enacted. Since then, five other significant pieces of legislation have followed: Norris-LaGuardia (1932), Wagner (1935), Taft-Hartley (1947), Landrum-Griffin (1959), and the Civil Service Reform Act, Title VII (1978). Each was enacted to clarify and/or constrain the roles of management and labor. Table 3–1 lists each piece of major legislation and the areas of labor relations to which it applies.

RAILWAY LABOR ACT (1926)

The **Railway Labor Act** (RLA) applies to rail and air carriers and their nonmanagerial employees. The act has five general purposes:

1. Avoiding service interruptions.
2. Eliminating any restrictions on joining a union.
3. Guaranteeing the freedom of employees in any matter of self-organization.
4. Providing for prompt dispute settlement.
5. Enabling prompt grievance settlement.

In railroads, engineers, maintenance of way employees, conductors, ticket agents, shop workers, and others are covered, regardless of whether they are personally involved in moving passengers or freight. Similarly, in airlines, pilots, cabin attendants, mechanics, reservations agents, baggage handlers, and others are covered. In 1996, the Federal Aviation Authorization Act extended jurisdiction to include air express companies, including their ground employees. This extension brings Federal Express (FedEx) within RLA jurisdiction, but leaves United Parcel Service (UPS) outside because FedEx is considered primarily an air express company while UPS is seen as primarily a ground carrier.

---

[1] For an extended and insightful treatment of the interaction between labor organizations and the state, see R. J. Adams, "The Role of the State in Industrial Relations," in D. Lewin, O. S. Mitchell, and P. D. Sherer, eds., *Research Frontiers in Industrial Relations and Human Resources* (Madison, WI: Industrial Relations Research Association, 1992), pp. 489–523. See also W. Forbath, *Law and the Shaping of the American Labor Movement* (Cambridge: Harvard University Press, 1991).

TABLE 3–1
Federal Labor Laws

Law	Coverage	Major Provisions	Federal Agencies
Railway Labor Act	Private-sector nonmanagerial rail and airline employees and employers.	Employees may choose bargaining representatives for collective bargaining, no yellow-dog contracts, dispute settlement procedures include mediation, arbitration, and emergency boards.	National Mediation Board, National Railroad Adjustment Board
Norris-LaGuardia Act	All private-sector employers and labor organizations.	Outlaws injunctions for nonviolent labor union activities. Makes yellow-dog contracts unenforceable.	
Labor Management Relations Act (originally passed as Wagner Act, amended by Taft-Hartley and Landrum-Griffin Acts).	Private sector nonmanagerial and nonagricultural employees not covered by Railway Labor Act; postal workers.	Employees may choose bargaining representatives for collective bargaining; both labor and management must bargain in good faith; unfair labor practices include discrimination for union activities, secondary boycotts, and refusal to bargain; national emergency dispute procedures established.	National Labor Relations Board, Federal Mediation and Conciliation Service.
Landrum-Griffin Act	All private-sector employers and labor organizations.	Specification and guarantee of individual rights of union members. Prohibits certain management and union conduct. Requires union financial disclosures.	U.S. Department of Labor.
Civil Service Reform Act, Title VII	All nonuniformed, nonmanagerial federal service employees and agencies.	Employees may choose representatives for collective bargaining; bargaining rights established for noneconomic and nonstaffing issues. Requires arbitration of unresolved grievances.	Federal Labor Relations Authority.

The RLA enables employees to choose, by majority vote, an organization to exclusively represent them for collective bargaining purposes. Under the RLA, employees within a given craft (or occupation) are entitled to be represented separately within their employers, and initial **representation elections** would be held within a single defined occupational group. Unions or associations seeking to represent employees must be free of employer domination or assistance.

Majority representatives become the exclusive bargaining agent for the employees within the bargaining unit and are entitled to negotiate with the carrier over wages, terms, and conditions of employment. Negotiated contracts must contain a grievance procedure consistent with the requirements of the RLA.

As will be contrasted below, contract negotiations under the RLA are substantially different than those under virtually all other private- and public-sector laws. Under the RLA, the provisions of a contract remain in place, even after its stated expiration date, until a new agreement is reached. Before a contract can be altered, one of the parties has to give the other written notice 30 days before the intended changes would go into effect. At this point, the parties start to prepare for and commence the bargaining process. They may also request assistance from the **National Mediation Board** (NMB) in attempting to reach an agreement. The board may also offer its services without the request of the parties. No unilaterally imposed changes or strikes can occur (if settlement is not reached) unless an impasse has been declared by the NMB, and then only if the parties reject arbitration of their differences. Finally, if the president believes a work stoppage would substantially disrupt interstate commerce, an Emergency Board can be convened to investigate the dispute and render a report. No changes or strikes can take place until at least 30 days after the completion of an emergency board's report. Thus, relatively long periods often elapse between the beginning of negotiations and the conclusion of a new agreement. Exhibit 3–1 covers President Clinton's appointment of a board in the American Airlines–Allied Pilots Association contract dispute in early 1997.

Two federal agencies are created by the RLA: the **National Railroad Adjustment Board** (NRAB) and the NMB. The NRAB is supposed to consist of an equal number of union and management members and is empowered to settle grievances of both parties. If the board deadlocks on a grievance, it obtains a referee to hear the case and make an award. Awards are binding, and prevailing parties may sue in federal district courts to enforce the awards. In reality, most disputes are handled by Public Law Boards and Special Boards of Adjustment, which involve ad hoc arbitrators or rotating boards of neutrals who hear and rule on deadlocked disputes.

The NMB is composed of three members appointed by the president. It handles representation elections, mediates bargaining disputes on request, urges parties to arbitrate when mediation is unsuccessful, interprets mediated contract agreements, and appoints arbitrators if disputing parties cannot agree upon one.

Compared with later acts, dispute handling under the Railway Labor Act is highly detailed. Subsequent laws generally leave this up to the parties. The RLA also required employees to be organized by craft (or occupational area), forcing employers to bargain with several unions, often with conflicting goals. Over time, bargaining by craft has changed somewhat as mergers have formed new unions such as the United Transportation Union (UTU) and the Transportation Communications International Union (TCIU). The TCIU constitutes a merger among employees in blue- and white-collar railroad and airline occupations.

EXHIBIT 3–1

Clinton Blocks Strike: He'll Appoint Team to Study Disagreement

President Clinton stepped in late Friday [February 14, 1997] to head off a pilots' walk-out at American Airlines, putting the largest airline strike in history on hold for up to 60 days.

Mr. Clinton's announcement came even as Allied Pilots Association president Jim Sovich and other union officials announced that they were going on strike.

Mr. Clinton said he would appoint a Presidential Emergency Board to review the dispute between the union and management. The board has up to 30 days to make a recommendation, and a subsequent 30-day cooling-off period would have to pass before pilots could walk off.

. . . The walkout would have forced more than 200,000 passengers a day to seek transportation on other carriers or be stranded. American chairman Robert L. Crandall had estimated that a strike would cost the airline $50 million a day; a U.S. Department of Transportation study put the daily loss to the U.S. economy at more than $100 million.

The carrier's 9,000 pilots had prepared to walk off their jobs at 11:01 P.M. Dallas time Friday in a dispute over pay raises, stock options, pay rates for junior pilots and whether they would get to fly small jets.

SOURCE: T. Maxon and M. Zimmerman, "Clinton Blocks Strike," *Dallas Morning News,* February 15, 1997.

There have been differences in the way the law has been implemented in the rail and airline industries. Arbitration of intracontract disputes in the airline industry is generally conducted like that in industries covered by the NLRA. In addition, contrary to the technical wording of the law, some railway supervisors, such as yardmasters, are represented by unions.

NORRIS–LAGUARDIA ACT (1932)

The Norris-LaGuardia Act was the first law to protect the rights of unions and workers to engage in union activity. The act forbids federal courts to issue **injunctions** (orders prohibiting certain activities) against a variety of specifically described union activities and outlaws yellow-dog contracts (in which employees agree that continued employment depends on abstention from union membership or activities). These contracts had been upheld previously by the Supreme Court.[2] Since enactment, federal courts have construed Norris-LaGuardia provisions strictly.

The act recognizes that freedom to associate for collective bargaining purposes is the corollary of the collectivization of capital through incorporation. Injunctions and yellow-dog contracts interfere with freedom of association.

---

[2] *Hitchman Coal & Coke Co.* v. *Mitchell,* 245 U.S. 229 (1917).

Besides the absolute prohibition of yellow-dog contracts, injunctions against specific activities are prohibited regardless of whether the act is done by an individual, a group, or a union. The following cannot be enjoined:

1. Stopping or refusing to work.
2. Union membership.
3. Paying or withholding strike benefits, unemployment benefits, and the like to people participating in labor disputes.
4. Aid or assistance for persons suing or being sued.
5. Publicizing a labor dispute in a nonviolent, nonfraudulent manner.
6. Assembly to organize.
7. Notifying anyone that any of these acts are to be performed.
8. Agreeing to engage or not engage in any of these acts.
9. Advising others to do any of these acts.

The Norris-LaGuardia Act also finally and completely laid to rest the 18th-century conspiracy doctrine. Section 5 prohibits injunctions against any of the above activities if pursued in a nonviolent manner. The effects of the *Danbury Hatters* decision (which required union members to pay boycott damages) were substantially diminished by Section 6.[3] That section mandates that an individual or labor organization may not be held accountable for unlawful acts of its leadership unless those acts were directed or ratified by the membership.

Section 7 ensures that the act may not be used as a cover for violent and destructive actions. An injunction may be issued if:

1. Substantial or irreparable injury to property will occur.
2. Greater injury will be inflicted on the party requesting the injunction than the injunction would cause on the adversary.
3. No adequate legal remedy exists.
4. Authorities are either unable or unwilling to give protection.

Before an action can be enjoined, the union must have the opportunity for rebuttal. If immediate restraint is sought and there is insufficient time for an adversary hearing, the employer must deposit a bond to compensate the union for possible damages done to it by the injunction. Injunctions cover only those persons or associations actually causing problems.

Section 8 further restricts injunction-granting powers by requiring the requester to try to settle the dispute before asking for an injunction. Section 9 states that the injunction cannot be issued against all union activities in the case, only those leading to the injury. For example, mass picketing might be enjoined if

---

[3] *Loewe* v. *Lawlor,* 208 U.S. 274 (1908).

it is violent, but the strike, payments of strike benefits, and so on could not be enjoined.

While the Norris-LaGuardia Act did not require an employer to recognize a union or bargain with it, it did provide labor some leverage in organizing and bargaining. Labor could, henceforth, bring pressure on the employer through strikes, boycotts, and the like without worrying about federal court injunctions.

WAGNER AND TAFT–HARTLEY ACTS (AS AMENDED)

The Wagner and Taft-Hartley Acts were enacted 12 years apart, with Taft-Hartley amending and extending the Wagner Act. In 1959, the Landrum-Griffin Act added amendments. The latest major amendments, in 1974, extended jurisdiction to private nonprofit health care organizations and modified some provisions for these organizations only. These acts established a statutory preference for using collective bargaining to resolve differences in the employment relationship and for roughly balancing the power of management and labor. The Wagner Act, passed during a period of relative weakness for organized labor, spoke only to employer practices. As the pendulum swung in the other direction, Taft-Hartley added union practices to the proscribed list. Finally, Landrum-Griffin aimed to fine-tune the law to match day-to-day realities.

The heart of the act, Section 7, embodies public policy toward the individual worker and collective bargaining. It reads:

> Employees shall have the right to self-organization, to form, join, or assist labor organizations, to bargain collectively through representatives of their own choosing, and to engage in other concerted activities for the purpose of collective bargaining or other mutual aid or protection, and shall also have the right to refrain from any or all of such activities except to the extent that such right may be affected by an agreement requiring membership in a labor organization as a condition of employment as authorized in Section 8(a)(3).

Definitions

The most important definitions are related to the terms employer, employee, supervisor, and professional employee.

Employer
An **employer** is an organization or a manager or supervisor acting on its behalf. However, certain types of organizations are specifically excluded from the act's jurisdiction. These are federal, state, and local governments or any organizations wholly owned by these agencies (except the U.S. Postal Service); persons subject to the Railway Labor Act; and union representatives when acting as bargaining

agents. Where a person works on a contract basis for a temporary agency or in other unusual situations, specialized definitional rules apply.[4]

Employee
An **employee** need not be an employee of an organization in which a labor dispute occurs. For example, if firm A is struck and employees of firm B refuse to cross picket lines, even though no dispute exists with B, the workers at firm B are considered employees under the act. An individual also remains an employee if on strike for a contract or if on strike or fired because of an employer's unfair labor practice. Employees remain within this definition, even if employers do not consider them such, until they are rehired at or above a level equivalent to their previous jobs. Domestic workers, agricultural workers, independent contractors,[5] individuals employed by a spouse or parent,[6] or persons covered by the Railway Labor Act are excluded.

Supervisor
A **supervisor** is an employee with independent authority to make personnel decisions and to administer a labor agreement. Examples of personnel decisions include hiring, firing, adjusting grievances, making work assignments, and deciding pay increases. A supervisor may belong to a union (although this is unlikely outside the construction or maritime industries), but groups of supervisors may not organize and bargain collectively.

Professional Employee
A **professional employee** is one whose work is intellectual in character, requiring independent judgment or discretion; whose performance cannot readily be measured in a standardized fashion; and whose skills are learned through prolonged, specialized instruction.[7] Professional employees may organize, but may not be included in a nonprofessional unit without a majority vote of the professionals.

National Labor Relations Board

The National Labor Relations Board (NLRB) consists of five members appointed by the president and confirmed by the Senate. Members serve five-year terms and may be reappointed. One member, designated by the president, chairs the board. The NLRB is responsible for conducting representation elections and resolving or determining unfair labor practice charges.

[4] R. A. Posthuma and J. B. Dworkin, "The Joint Employer, the NLRB, and Changing Rights of Contingent Workers," *Labor Law Journal* 48 (1997), pp. 19–28.

[5] *P.Q. Beef Processors, Inc.,* 231 NLRB 179 (1977).

[6] *Viele & Sons, Inc.,* 227 NLRB 284 (1977).

[7] See N. A. Beadles II and C. Scott, "Professionals under the Labor Management Relations Act: Lessons from the Health Care Industry," *Journal of Collective Negotiations in the Public Sector* 24 (1995), pp. 285–300.

The board may delegate its duties to a subgroup of three or more members. It can also delegate authority to determine representation and election questions to its regional directors. The board has a general counsel responsible for investigating charges and issuing complaints. More details on the board's organization, function, and performance will be covered later in this chapter.

Unfair Labor Practices

The amended labor acts specify a variety of employer tactics presumed to interfere with employees' freedom of choice in being represented by their chosen advocates. They also specify union tactics that might coerce employees of a nonunion organization to join a union or would interfere with a nonunion employer's ability to operate. The specified **unfair labor practices** (ULPs) are contained in Section 8; part (a) applies to employers, part (b) to unions.

Employer Unfair Labor Practices

An employer may not interfere with an employee engaging in any activity protected by Section 7. The employer may not assist or dominate a labor organization. If two unions are vying to organize a group of workers, an employer may neither recognize one to avoid dealing with the other nor express a preference for one over the other. The employer may not create a company-sponsored union and bargain with it. Employers may not create employee groups within the organization and ask them to participate in setting wages, hours, and terms and conditions of employment.

An employer may not discriminate in hiring, assignment, or other terms of employment on the basis of union membership. However, employers and unions may negotiate contract clauses requiring union membership as a condition of continued employment (a **union shop** agreement). But if such a clause is negotiated, the employer cannot discriminate against nonmembership if the union discriminatorily refuses to admit an employee to membership.

Employees may not be penalized or discriminated against for charging an employer with unfair labor practices.

Finally, employers may not refuse to bargain with a union over issues of pay, hours, or other terms and conditions of employment.

Union Unfair Labor Practices

Unions may not coerce employees in the exercise of Section 7 rights, but this does not limit union internal rule making, discipline, fines, and so forth. Unions cannot demand or require an employer to take action against an employee for any reason except failure to pay union dues.

Unions are also forbidden to engage in—or encourage individuals to engage in—strikes or refusals to handle some type of product or work if the object is to accomplish any of the following ends:

1. Forcing an employer or self-employed person to join an employer or labor organization or to cease handling nonunion products (except in certain cases, detailed later).
2. Forcing an employer to bargain with an uncertified labor organization; that is, one whose majority status has not been established.
3. Forcing an employer to cease bargaining with a certified representative.
4. Forcing an employer to assign work to employees in a particular labor organization unless ordered to do so or previously bargained to do so.
5. Requiring excessive initiation fees to become a union member.
6. Forcing an employer to pay for services not rendered.
7. Picketing an employer to force recognition of the picketing union if:
    a. The picketing group has not been certified as the employees' representative;
    b. Either no union election has taken place within the past 12 months or the picketing union requests a representation election within 30 days after picketing begins; but
    c. Nothing can prohibit a union's picketing to advise the public that an employer's employees are not unionized, provided the picketing does not interfere with pickups and deliveries.

Protected Concerted Activity
Where no evidence of threat, reprisal, or promise of benefit exists, the parties involved in collective bargaining activities are free to express views in any form.

Duty to Bargain
Unions and employers have a mutual duty to bargain in good faith about wages, hours, and terms and conditions of employment. Each must meet with the other when requested to negotiate an agreement, reduce it to writing, and interpret its meaning if disagreements arise. Neither is required to concede any issue to demonstrate good faith. Notifying the Federal Mediation and Conciliation Service (FMCS) is required as a condition to modify a contract. Specific and more stringent requirements are laid out for health care organizations.

Prohibited Contract Clauses
Except in the construction and apparel industries, employees and unions cannot negotiate contracts providing that particular products of certain employers will not be used. This is the so-called **hot cargo** issue. For example, a trucking union could not negotiate a contract prohibiting hauling goods manufactured by a nonunion employer. But a construction union could refuse to install nonunion goods if a contract clause had been negotiated.

Construction Employment
Contractors can make collective bargaining agreements with construction unions, even without a demonstration of majority status. The agreements may require

union membership within seven days of employment and give the union an opportunity to refer members for existing job openings. These exceptions recognize the short-run nature of many construction jobs. Labor agreements may also provide for apprenticeship training requirements and may give preference in job openings to workers with greater past experience.

Health Care Picketing

A union anticipating a strike or picketing at a health care facility must notify the Federal Mediation and Conciliation Service (FMCS) 10 days in advance.

Representation Elections

The act provides that when a majority of employees in a particular unit desires representation, all employees (regardless of union membership) will be represented by the union regarding wages, hours, and terms and conditions of employment. Individuals can present and have their own grievances adjusted if the resolution is consistent with the contract.

The NLRB determines what group of employees would constitute an appropriate unit for a representation election and subsequent bargaining. Its discretion is limited, however. First, it cannot include professional and nonprofessional employees in the same unit unless a majority of the professionals agree. Second, it cannot deny separate representation to a craft solely on the basis that it was part of a larger unit determined appropriate by the board. Third, it cannot include plant guards and other types of employees in the same unit. Also, supervisors are not employees as defined by the act; so, for example, a unit of production supervisors would be an inappropriate group for representation.

In cases of questionable union majority status, the board is authorized to hold elections (subject to certain constraints, detailed in Chapter 6). The board may also conduct elections to determine whether an existing union maintains a continuing majority status.

Unfair Labor Practices Charges and NLRB Procedures

If the board finds that an unfair labor practice (ULP) occurred, it can issue cease-and-desist orders, require back pay to make wronged persons whole, and petition a court of appeals to enforce its orders. Board activities with regard to ULPs are detailed later in this chapter.

"Right-to-Work" Laws

Section 14(b), one of the most controversial in the act, permits states to pass right-to-work laws. In states with these laws, employees represented by unions cannot be compelled to join a union or pay dues as a condition of continued employment. Union and **agency shop** clauses are unenforceable in these states.

Religious Objections to Union Membership in Health Care Organizations

Health care organization employees whose religious beliefs preclude membership in a union may donate a sum equal to union dues to a nonreligious charity in lieu of the dues.

Federal Mediation and Conciliation Service

The act indicates that maintaining stable labor relations is in the public interest. If conflicts between the parties interfere with stability, the government should be able and willing to offer assistance. Thus, the FMCS was created to offer mediation services whenever disputes threaten to interrupt commerce or where it involves a health care organization. The FMCS is directed to emphasize services in contract negotiations, not grievance settlements.

National Emergency Disputes

If, in the opinion of the president, a labor dispute imperils the nation, a board of inquiry may be appointed to investigate the issues surrounding the dispute. After the board submits its report, the attorney general may be directed to ask a district court to enjoin a strike or lockout. If the court agrees that the dispute threatens national security, an injunction may be issued. If an injunction is ordered, the board is reconvened and monitors the settlement process. If an agreement is not reached after 60 days, the board reports the positions of labor and management and includes management's last offer. Over the next 15 days, the NLRB holds an election among the employees to determine whether a majority favors accepting management's last offer. Five more days are taken to certify the results. At this time (or earlier, if a settlement was reached), the injunction will be discharged. If a settlement was not reached, the president forwards the report of the board, the election results, and the president's recommendations to Congress for action. While used occasionally in the past, national emergency dispute procedures have not been used for over 20 years.

Suits, Political Action, and Financial Relationships

Unions may sue on behalf of their members and can be sued and found liable for damages against organizational assets, but not those of members. Financial dealings between an employer and the representative of its employees are forbidden. Union agents are forbidden from demanding payment for performing contractual duties. Certain regulations relating to the establishment of trust funds are also included.

Unions and corporations are forbidden to make political contributions in any elections involving the choice of federal officeholders.

Summary

The important aspects of Taft-Hartley relate to the establishment, function, and powers of the NLRB, the delineation of employer and union unfair labor practices, the promulgation of rules governing representation and certification, the creation and functions of the FMCS, and the national emergency injunction procedures. These aim at balancing the power of labor and management and stabilizing industrial relations.

LANDRUM-GRIFFIN ACT (1959)

The Landrum-Griffin Act, formally the Labor-Management Reporting and Disclosure Act of 1959, resulted from congressional hearings into corrupt practices in labor-management relations. It regulates internal activities of employers and unions covered by both Taft-Hartley and the Railway Labor Act.

Bill of Rights for Union Members

Unions are required to provide equal rights and privileges to members in nominating, voting, participating in referenda, meetings, and so on. Each member has a right to be heard and to oppose the policies of the leadership insofar as this does not interfere with the union's legal obligations. Dues, initiation fees, and assessments cannot be increased without a majority vote to approve the increase. Members' rights to sue their unions are guaranteed as long as they have exhausted internal union procedures and are not aided by an employer or an employer association. Members of unions cannot be expelled unless due process consistent with this section is followed. Copies of the labor agreement between the employer and the union must be provided to every member.

Reports Required of Unions and Employers

All unions are required to file constitutions and bylaws with the secretary of labor. Unions must file annual reports detailing assets and liabilities, receipts, salaries and allowances of officers, loans made to officers or businesses, and other expenditures as prescribed by the secretary of labor. The report must also be made available to the membership. Employees covered by union contracts have little access to information on union expenditures to influence political outcomes, litigation, and the like before it is filed with the department of labor.[8]

Every officer and employee (except clerical and custodial employees) must submit annual reports to the secretary of labor detailing any family income or

---

[8] M. F. Masters, R. S. Atkin, and G. W. Florkowski, "An Analysis of Union Reporting Requirements under Title II of the Landrum-Griffin Act," *Labor Law Journal* 40 (1989), pp. 713–22.

transaction in stocks, securities, or other payments (except wages) made by a firm where the union represents employees; income or other payments from a business with substantial dealings with these firms; or any payments made by a labor consultant to such a firm.

Employers must report payments made to union officials (even if only to reimburse expenses); report payments to employees to convince other employees to exercise or not exercise their rights to organize and bargain collectively; and report payments to obtain information about unions or individuals involved in disputes with the employer. Employers must also report agreements with or payments to a labor relations consultant hired to oppose union organizing campaigns.

Trusteeships

A union may act against a subsidiary for breaching the union's constitution or bylaws. To reduce the possibility of stifling dissent, a **trusteeship** can be imposed only to restore democratic procedures, correct corruption or financial malfeasance, or assure performance of collective bargaining agreements or other legitimate union functions. If a trusteeship is imposed, the union must file a report with the secretary of labor detailing the reasons for the takeover. It must also disclose the subsidiary's financial situation. A union exercising a trustee relationship cannot move assets from the subsidiary or appoint delegates to conventions from it (unless they were elected by secret ballot of the membership). For example, the United Food and Commercial Workers (UFCW) placed its local P-9, which represents employees of Hormel's Austin, Minnesota, plant, under trusteeship for refusing to end a strike. Exhibit 3–2 contains some background information on the controversy surrounding the trusteeship.

OTHER FEDERAL LAWS AND REGULATIONS

Byrnes Act (1936)

The Byrnes Act of 1936 makes it illegal to recruit and/or transport individuals across state lines for the purpose of interfering forcefully or threateningly with peaceful picketing or the right of self-organization.

Copeland Anti-Kickback Act (1934)

This law prohibits anyone from requiring or coercing employees on a public works construction project (or a project financed by loans or grants from the federal government) to kick back part of their compensation as a condition of continued employment.

EXHIBIT 3–2

P-9 Trusteeship Gets Judge's Approval; Local Leadership Out

A federal judge ruled Monday [June 3, 1986] that the United Food and Commercial Workers (UFCW) union can take control of striking Local P-9 of Austin, Minn.

The ruling clears the way for the international union to negotiate a labor contract with Geo. A. Hormel & Co., according to the international and Hormel.

It also enforces the suspensions of P-9 officers. They contended in their fight with the international that they were elected by the membership and could not be replaced as the sole bargainers for the striking meatpackers.

Joe Hansen, an international vice president, district director of the UFCW and the international's trustee, said late yesterday that Hormel has agreed to meet later this week to resume contract negotiations in the nearly 10-month-old labor dispute.

"The trustee is the bargaining agent for Local P-9," said Hansen. "Jim Guyette (P-9's president) and all of the officers of P-9 have been suspended and all business of the local will be conducted with me or with the (two) deputy trustees."

U.S. District Judge Edward Devitt [said], "Since Local P-9 did not comply with the international's directive to cease its strike against Hormel (in March) or to cease its roving picket line activities, the international acted within its authority in appointing the trustee to manage P-9's affairs."

SOURCE: N. St. Anthony, "P-9 Trusteeship Gets Judge's Approval; Local Leadership Out," *Minneapolis Star Tribune*, June 3, 1986, pp. 1A, 9A.

Racketeer Influenced and Corrupt Organizations (RICO) Act (1970)

RICO was passed by Congress in 1970 to increase penalties for corruption through the forfeiture of interests gained illegally. Penalties are assessed at triple the amount of the corrupt gain. State laws have also been enacted to attempt to reduce or eliminate corruption. Evidence in the New Jersey casino industry suggests the laws work well in policing employers, but unions are more difficult to control because local unions may represent employees in both casinos and other service organizations. Thus, representation by corrupt union officers is possible through a majority being represented in corrupt relationships.[9] An economic analysis of corruption in the New York City construction industry suggests that the coordination necessary in construction coupled with the potential monopoly power of unions to supply skilled labor could lead to organized crime involvement in monitoring or facilitating activities. The effect of possible corruption on wages of union construction workers appears not to be significant—somewhat surprising

---

[9] B. A. Lee and J. Chelius, "Government Regulation of Union-Management Corruption: The Casino Industry Experience in New Jersey," *Industrial and Labor Relations Review* 42 (1989), pp. 536–48.

given the relatively high unionization of construction workers relative to those in the rest of the United States.[10]

EFFECTS OF IMPLEMENTATION OF LAWS

An intriguing analysis of labor law and labor history suggests courts have consistently interpreted new statutory law to reinforce market-oriented practices. For example, the Supreme Court, while finding the Wagner Act constitutional, reiterated management's exclusive right to make certain decisions unless it voluntarily agreed to bargain about them. Further, it is argued that courts have generally been permissive toward employer-sponsored participation plans, not finding them to be dominated labor organizations.[11] Laws, as interpreted, appear to be based on a pluralist assumption that management, labor, and government operate together, with the government facilitating market activities through the operation of labor-management conflict resolution mechanisms.[12]

Employers are more likely to engage in actions that are later found to be unfair labor practices when the differences between union and nonunion wages are greater. The NLRB has difficulty coping with these problems because complaints cannot be processed quickly without increased staff, which must be appropriated by Congress, and the board can levy no penalties above the requirement that workers be made whole for the effects of violations.[13]

FEDERAL DEPARTMENTS AND AGENCIES

All three branches of government—legislative, executive, and judicial—are involved in labor relations. Congress writes and amends the law; the executive agencies implement and regulate within the law; and the judiciary examines the actions of the other two in light of the Constitution, the statutes, and common law. This section examines the departments and agencies concerned with labor relations functions.

---

[10] C. Ichniowski and A. Preston, "The Persistence of Organized Crime in New York City Construction: An Economic Perspective," *Industrial and Labor Relations Review* 42 (1989), pp. 549–65.

[11] G. Grenier and R. L. Hogler, "Labor Law and Managerial Ideology: Employee Participation as a Social Control System," *Work and Occupations* 18 (1991), pp. 313–33.

[12] R. L. Hogler, "Critical Labor Law, Working-Class History, and the New Industrial Relations." *Industrial Relations Law Journal* 10 (1988), pp. 116–43; and R. L. Hogler, "Labor History and Critical Labor Law: An Interdisciplinary Approach to Workers' Control," *Labor History* 30 (1989), pp. 185–92. For a comprehensive review and commentary on labor law and regulation, see B. E. Kaufman, ed., *Government Regulation of the Employment Relationship* (Madison, WI: Industrial Relations Research Association, 1997).

[13] R. J. Flanagan, "Compliance and Enforcement Decisions under the National Labor Relations Act," *Journal of Labor Economics* 7 (1989), pp. 257–80.

Department of Labor

The Department of Labor, created in 1913, has a broad charter.

> The U.S. Department of Labor is charged with preparing the American workforce for new and better jobs, and ensuring the adequacy of America's workplaces. It is responsible for the administration and enforcement of over 180 federal statutes. These legislative mandates and the regulations produced to implement them cover a wide variety of workplace activities for nearly 10 million employers and well over 100 million workers, including protecting workers' wages, health and safety, employment and pension rights; promoting equal employment opportunity; administering job training, unemployment insurance and workers' compensation programs; strengthening free collective bargaining and collecting, analyzing and publishing labor and economic statistics.[14]

The organization of the Department of Labor is shown in Figure 3–1.

Employment Standards Administration
The Employment Standards Administration (ESA) contains several agencies responsible for collecting information, promulgating regulations, and enforcing laws and regulations. There are four offices within the ESA: Labor-Management Standards, Federal Contract Compliance Programs, Wage and Hour Division, and the Workers' Compensation Programs.

Labor-Management Standards.   The Office of Labor-Management Standards is responsible for administering and enforcing provisions of the Landrum-Griffin Act and Civil Service Reform Act.

Federal Contract Compliance Programs.   The Office of Federal Contract Compliance Programs administers laws and regulations banning employment discrimination based on race, sex, color, religion, national origin, disability, and veterans' status for employers with federal contracts. It also administers affirmative action provisions of Executive Order 11246 and the Vietnam Era Veterans' Readjustment Act (1974).

Wage and Hour Division.   The Wage and Hour Division enforces various wage and hour laws requiring minimum wage and overtime premium payments for covered workers. It also enforces several other laws such as the Family and Medical Leave Act (1993).

Workers' Compensation Programs.   The Office of Worker Compensation Programs administers worker compensation programs for federal employees and maritime and coal-mining worker compensation laws.

---

[14] U.S. Department of Labor, www.dol.gov, March 29, 1997.

FIGURE 3–1

Department of Labor Organizational Chart

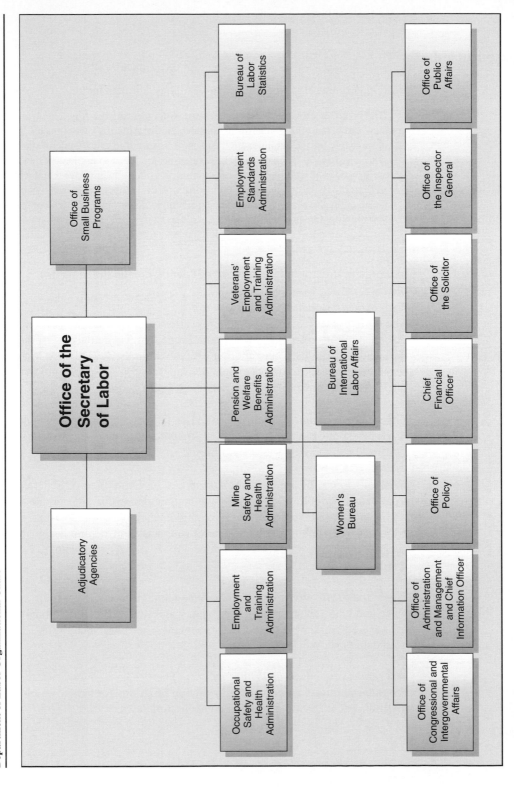

SOURCE: U.S. Department of Labor, www.dol.gov/dol/public/aboutdol/org/orgchart.htm, September 2, 1998.

Occupational Safety and Health Administration

OSHA is responsible for the interpretation and enforcement of the Occupational Safety and Health Act of 1970. It investigates violations and assesses penalties through hearings held by Department of Labor administrative law judges. Workers who are better educated or unionized appear to be more knowledgeable about hazards, and workers who are better protected in the exercise of their rights are more likely to refuse unsafe work.[15]

Employment and Training Administration

The Bureau of Apprenticeship and Training in the ETA assists employers and unions in establishing high-quality skilled trades training programs with consistent standards.

Bureau of Labor Statistics

The BLS collects, maintains, and publishes data that interested persons use to assess the current state of the economy—nationally, regionally, or locally. It publishes the consumer price index, conducts area wage surveys, and provides unemployment data.

Bureau of International Labor Affairs

The Bureau of International Labor Affairs represents the United States on multilateral trade bodies such as the General Agreement on Tariffs and Trade (GATT), the International Labor Organization (ILO), and the Organization for Economic Cooperation and Development (OECD). It also manages the labor attaché program in U.S. embassies abroad and monitors conformance with internationally recognized worker rights.

Women's Bureau

The Women's Bureau focuses on the priorities of working women. Its objectives include alerting women about their rights in the workplace, proposing legislation that benefits working women, researching work aspects of concern to women, and reporting its findings to the president and Congress.

Federal Mediation and Conciliation Service

The Federal Mediation and Conciliation Service (FMCS) was established by the Taft-Hartley Act to help parties resolve labor disputes. In contract negotiation, it may mediate either through invitation or on its own motion. **Mediators** assist the parties in bargaining but have no power to impose settlements or regulate bargaining activity.

The FMCS offers preventive mediation and alternative dispute resolution programs, including expertise to resolve problems involving federal agencies as

---

[15] V. Walters and M. Denton, "Workers' Knowledge of Their Legal Rights and Resistance to Hazardous Work," *Relations Industrielles* 45 (1990), pp. 531–45.

mandated by the Alternative Dispute Resolution and Negotiated Rulemaking Acts of 1990. It aids local labor-management cooperation programs through grants and technical assistance enabled by the Labor-Management Cooperation Act of 1978. To foster peaceful conflict resolution of employment issues internationally, the FMCS has provided mediator training in developing economies around the world.[16]

It also maintains lists of arbitrators from which parties may choose to settle disputes within the contract. In listing or delisting an arbitrator, the FMCS applies established qualification rules.

National Mediation Board

A 1934 amendment to the Railway Labor Act established the National Mediation Board (NMB). It mediates contract disputes between carriers and their unions and certifies representatives of employees for bargaining. It refers grievances to the National Railroad Adjustment Board (NRAB). The NMB may appoint a referee to assist in making NRAB awards when the panel is deadlocked.

The NMB is also responsible for notifying the president if an unsettled, mediated dispute threatens to cripple transport in some section of the country. The president may then appoint an emergency board to study the situation and make recommendations.

National Labor Relations Board

The NLRB was established by the Wagner Act. It determines whether employees desire union representation and whether unions or companies have committed unfair labor practices as defined by federal law. The NLRB has jurisdiction over most for-profit employers; private, profit and nonprofit hospitals; and the U.S. Postal Service. Figure 3–2 shows the structure of the board.

The NLRB does not initiate action but only responds to complaints from the involved parties.[17] The board receives about 45,000 cases per year through its 33 regional offices. About 80 percent are unfair labor practice (C) cases and about 20 percent representation election (R) cases. When a C case is filed, the regional office investigates. If the charge appears not to be meritorious (about two-thirds of all C cases), the charging party is asked to withdraw it, or charges are dismissed. These decisions can be appealed to the general counsel, but less than 4 percent are reversed. If the case has merit, the regional director works with the parties to try to fashion a remedy and settle the case. This succeeds in over 90 percent of cases. Failing that, the case is heard within one to three months by an **administrative**

---

[16] J. C. Wells, "FMCS: Past, Present, and Future," *Proceedings of the Industrial Relations Research Association* 48 (1996), pp. 396–406.

[17] For complete details, see K. C. McGuinness, *How to Take a Case before the National Labor Relations Board,* 4th ed. (Washington, DC: Bureau of National Affairs, 1976).

FIGURE 3–2
National Labor Relations Board

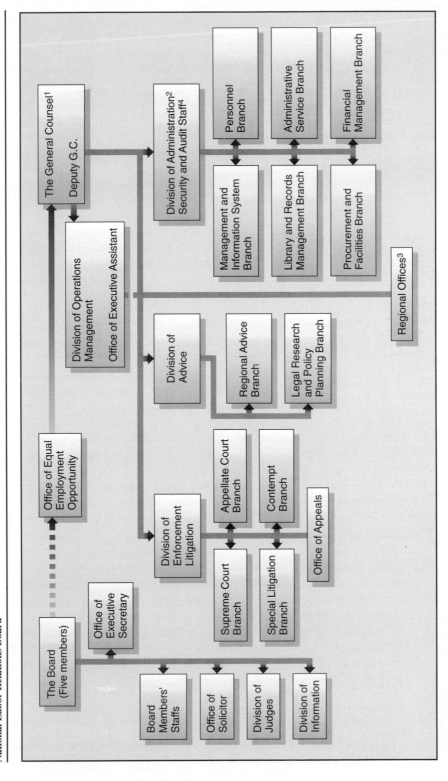

[1] The authority and responsibility of the general counsel in certain administrative matters is derived by delegation from the board.

[2] Division of Administration is also responsible to the board for administrative support services required in the performance of board functions.

[3] Includes exercise by regional director of board authority under Section 9 of the act, in representation cases, by delegation from the board.

[4] The auditor is authorized to bring findings directly to the board or general counsel as appropriate.

SOURCE: "NLRB Organizations and Functions," Rules and Regulations and Statements of Procedure (Washington, DC: U.S. Government Printing Office, 1987), p. 281.

law judge. After the judge issues a ruling, exceptions can be filed, and the case is assigned to a board member. The board must then study the case, and a three-member panel issues a ruling.[18]

If a party does not comply with an NLRB decision, the board may petition a U.S. court of appeals for enforcement. Board orders must be publicized to employees and/or union members. The board may issue cease-and-desist orders, bargaining orders, and decisions making employees whole for illegal personnel actions, such as termination for union activity.

Very few initial unfair labor practice charges are ever heard by administrative law judges and passed on to the NLRB for its review. Cases that are not settled before board review are of two general types: (1) those involving a complex or unsettled issue for which there is no clear precedent, and (2) those that one party (usually management) expects to have decided against itself, but believes that delay in a final determination is to its advantage.

As noted earlier, the five members of the NLRB are appointed for fixed terms by the president (with the consent of the Senate). Board members are individuals with expertise in labor-management relations, almost invariably attorneys, and usually members of the president's political party. To be confirmed, nominees must be knowledgable about the law and appear fair, regardless of their political orientation. Thus, board members may be Democrats appointed by a Democratic President (Dem-Dem), Republicans appointed by a Democratic President (Rep-Dem), Democrats appointed by a Republican President (Dem-Rep) or Republicans appointed by a Republican President (Rep-Rep). Democrats may be presumed to favor labor more often when precedents are not clear, while Republicans may be expected to favor management. Board members may also be expected to pay attention to the position of the president who appointed them, and to some extent to the makeup of the Congress.

A careful study of board decisions found that in complex cases, relative to Dem-Dem members, Rep-Rep and Rep-Dem members were more likely to decide for management, while labor was favored more often during periods when Congress appeared to favor labor's political agenda, when unemployment was high, and when there were large changes in unemployment. In simpler cases, decisions favoring employers were more likely from Dem-Rep members, during high unemployment, and where the regional officer and administrative law judge ruled for the employer. Negative factors were influential when the regional officer and administrative law judge ruled for the union and where the case occurred in a southern right-to-work state. Dem-Dems decided against the employer in almost all cases.[19] This is contrary to the conventional wisdom that Rep-Rep members are the most doctrinaire in their decisions and the most likely to disregard precedent.

---

[18] D. L. Dotson, "Processing Cases at the NLRB," *Labor Law Journal* 35 (1984), pp. 3–9; updated data from www.nlrb.gov, March 29, 1997.

[19] W. N. Cooke, A. K. Mishra, G. M. Spreitzer, and M. Tschirhart, "The Determinants of NLRB Decision-Making Revisited," *Industrial and Labor Relations Review* 48 (1995), pp. 237–57.

The general counsel's political orientation may also strongly influence outcomes because that office decides which cases should be referred to the board members for decisions. A comparison of unfair labor processing in Ontario (Canada) and the United States found that in Ontario, charges were more likely to be heard and heard promptly. There was also a lower frequency of filings and less intervention by courts in reviewing administrative decisions. Unlike the United States, the parties in Ontario pay the cost of processing an unfair labor practice charge.[20]

Regional staff decisions also affect how charges are handled. One study of regional staff decisions during the Reagan years—a period in which a substantial body of NLRB precedents were reversed—indicated that regional directors dismissed many fewer cases and sent more on to Washington. Evidence also indicated that unions withdrew many more charges, probably fearing adverse decisions and establishments of new precedents by the board once it hears a case.[21]

NLRB decisions may alter the bargaining power between labor and management if a previously used practice is prohibited. Filing rates are influenced by the level of economic activity, and they increase for both unions and managements when it appears that board composition will lead to more favorable decisions for management. Employers may increase their filings because they believe pro-management decisions may deter union tactics.[22]

LABOR LAW REFORM: A CONTINUING CONTROVERSY

Much controversy surrounds recent NLRB decisions, with union leaders suggesting they might be better off without labor legislation.[23] Shortly after President Clinton's first inauguration, a commission was established to study the employment relationship and make recommendations for labor law reform. Among its recommendations were several to facilitate union organizing and to financially penalize employers who were using stalling tactics. With the election of a Republican majority in Congress in 1994, which interpreted its victory as one in favor of reducing rather than increasing regulation, the recommendations could be diagnosed as "dead on arrival."[24]

---

[20] P. G. Bruce, "The Processing of Unfair Labor Practice Cases in the United States and Ontario," *Relations Industrielles* 45 (1990), pp. 481–509.

[21] D. E. Schmidt, "Partisanship in the NLRB and Decision Making in Regional Offices," *Labor Law Journal* 42 (1991), pp. 484–90.

[22] M. Roomkin, "A Quantitative Study of Unfair Labor Practice Cases," *Industrial and Labor Relations Review* 34 (1981), pp. 245–56.

[23] See, for example, *NLRB at 50: Labor Board at the Crossroads* (Washington: Bureau of National Affairs, 1985). For a comprehensive and cogent look at the status of modern labor law with suggestions for change, see W. B. Gould IV, *Agenda for Reform: The Future of Employment Relationships and the Law* (Cambridge: MIT Press, 1993).

[24] Commission on the Future of Worker Management Relations, *Final Report and Recommendations* (Washington, DC: U.S. Government Printing Office).

The controversy continues with calls for more latitude for employers to establish employee work teams and communications programs without violating Section 8(a)(2) of the labor acts. The so-called "Team Act" was passed by Congress in 1996, but vetoed by President Clinton. Some argue that the internationalization of trade has made increased regulation of employment a liability, and that responsiveness by employers is required to survive in a new economic era the labor acts never contemplated.[25] Others argue that relatively minor changes need to be made to the labor acts to enhance competition and worker outcomes.[26]

TRADE TREATIES

Trade treaties often include provisions for minimum labor standards. These are usually included to protect jobs in high wage countries. Developing countries seldom can afford to duplicate conditions experienced in first-world countries. Prohibitions on child labor and forced (prison) labor may be somewhat easier to enforce.[27] Area trade treaties, such as the North American Free Trade Agreement (NAFTA), offer opportunities for international cooperation by unions. To this point, however, evidence suggests they have had a greater effect on nurturing national identities rather than international development.[28]

S U M M A R Y

U.S. labor law consists primarily of the Railway Labor, Norris-LaGuardia, Wagner, Taft-Hartley, and Landrum-Griffin acts. These enable collective bargaining, regulate labor and management activities, and limit intervention by the federal courts in lawful union activities.

The legislative branch of government enacts the laws, the executive branch carries them out, and the court system tests their validity and rules on conduct within their purview.

As a cabinet department, the Department of Labor is primarily responsible for implementing human resource programs and monitoring activities. It has little direct influence on collective bargaining.

Rule-making, interpretive, and assistance agencies have major influences on employers through either direct intervention or regulation. The Federal Mediation

---

[25] M. L. Wachter, "Labor Law Reform: One Step Forward and Two Steps Back," *Industrial Relations* 34 (1995), pp. 382–401. See also L. Galloway and R. Vedder, "Labor Laws: Then and Now," *Journal of Labor Research* 17 (1996), pp. 253–76.

[26] R. N. Block, "Labor Law, Economics, and Industrial Democracy: A Reconciliation," *Industrial Relations* 34 (1995), pp. 402–16.

[27] C. L. Erickson and D. J. B. Mitchell, "Labor Standards in International Trade Agreements: The Current Debate," *Labor Law Journal* 47 (1996), pp. 763–75.

[28] J. Cowie, "National Struggles in a Transnational Economy: A Critical Analysis of U.S. Labor's Campaign Against NAFTA," *Labor Studies Journal* 21, no. 4 (1997), pp. 3–32.

and Conciliation Service and National Labor Relations Board have the greatest impact on collective bargaining.

DISCUSSION QUESTIONS

1. In the absence of federal labor laws, what do you think the scope and nature of labor relations would be in the United States?

2. Should workers now under the Railway Labor Act be brought within the jurisdiction of the LMRA?

3. Are current laws strong enough to preserve individual rights in collective bargaining?

4. To what extent should the federal government have power to intervene in collective bargaining activities?

5. Should such administrative agencies as the NLRB be allowed to render administrative law decisions that can be enforced by the courts, or should an agency be required to go directly to court?

6. Are current labor laws capable of dealing with labor-management problems, or should they be abolished? If abolished, what should their replacements (if any) address?

KEY TERMS

Railway Labor Act   *60*

Representation elections   *61*

National Mediation Board   *62*

National Railroad Adjustment
  Board   *62*

Injunctions   *63*

Employer   *65*

Employee   *66*

Supervisor   *66*

Professional employee   *66*

Unfair labor practice   *67*

Union shop   *67*

Hot cargo   *68*

Agency shop   *69*

Trusteeship   *72*

Mediators   *77*

Administrative law judge   *78*

4

UNION STRUCTURE

AND GOVERNMENT

*E*mployers and labor unions are governed differently. Employees are hired to perform tasks to accomplish employer-defined objectives. Most have little voice in choosing the objectives. These are determined by high-level managers who are monitored by owners or boards of directors elected by shareholders or, in the case of public agencies, by their elected or appointed boards. Managers are responsible to their constituencies: a corporation's shareholders, a city's voters, a union's members. Union goals reflect member interests. Union leaders must generally be responsive to member desires to remain in office.

This chapter examines the organizational components, functions, and governance of unions and how these relate to and involve the membership. Union political activities are also explored. This chapter addresses the following major questions:

1. What are the major organizational levels within the labor movement?
2. What roles do the local union, the international, and the AFL–CIO play?
3. How do international union organizational structures and internal politics differ?
4. To what extent are unions autocratically or democratically governed?
5. How have international unions responded to the continuing decline in membership?

The U.S. labor structure consists of three major components: the local union, the national union, and the labor federation. These are described in the following sections.

The Local Union

The local union represents employees in day-to-day dealings with the employer. Local union jurisdictions are defined along four major dimensions: (1) the type of work performed or the industry in which it is accomplished (craft and industrial jurisdictions), (2) a specified geographic area, (3) the type of activity involved (organizing, bargaining, and so on), and (4) the level of union government applying the jurisdiction.[1] A local's constituency varies within these parameters. Many local unions operate in a specific municipality, represent workers in a single industry or trade, and frequently bargain with a single employer.

Examples of local unions include a relatively small unit (less than 100) of close-knit employees who work for a single employer, a large unit of mixed occupations with a preponderance of members in semi- or unskilled jobs who work for a single employer in one or more plants located in a single city, a skilled trade unit whose members work for many employers and whose employment changes frequently, or a unit whose members work for many different employers in different types of jobs. Units in these examples might typify a professional local, a manufacturing company local, a building trades local, and a general local.[2]

Local unions are most often chartered by and affiliated with a national union (e.g., a local union representing auto parts industry workers affiliated with the United Auto Workers). Occasionally, local unions will affiliate directly with the AFL–CIO or remain independent. Independent locals form where employees of a particular employer (often within a single plant) organize without external assistance. Some independent unions predate the Wagner Act and are adaptations of company unions originally created with employer assistance, often to avoid representation by a local established by a national union.

A local union's jurisdiction affects its size, constitution, officers, and organizational structure. A president, vice president, recording secretary, financial secretary, treasurer, sergeant at arms, and trustees are usually elected. Unless the local is large, these posts are part time and usually unpaid. Locals with over 1,000 members are likely to have full-time paid officers. Only about one-third of top-level officers got their position through defeating an incumbent. More often they are elected following a retirement or are appointed. Most presidents are able to successfully endorse a successor. About half of all local presidents return to bargaining unit jobs after they leave office.[3]

Locals dealing with several employers often hire a **business agent.** Business agents ensure that contracts are being followed and refer members to available employment. They are most necessary where local members work on a project

---

[1] J. Barbash, *American Unions: Structure, Government, and Politics* (New York: Random House, 1967).

[2] G. Strauss, "Union Democracy," in G. Strauss, D. G. Gallagher, and J. Fiorito, eds., *The State of the Unions* (Madison, WI: Industrial Relations Research Association, 1991), pp. 201–36.

[3] M. J. Goldberg, "Top Officers of Local Unions," *Labor Studies Journal* 19, no. 4 (1995), pp. 3–23.

basis and move between employers as work is finished on one project and becomes available on another.[4]

Two major committees operate within most locals: the **executive committee** (made up of the local's officers) and the grievance or **negotiation committee.** The executive committee establishes local policy; the negotiation committee reviews member grievances and negotiates with management over grievances and contract changes. Other committees deal with organizing and membership, welfare, recreation, and political action.

At the work-unit level, **stewards** are elected or appointed. Stewards ensure that first-line supervisors comply with the contract. Stewards act as spokespersons in presenting grievances. They collect dues and solicit participation in union activities. Many collective bargaining contracts recognize the vulnerability of the steward's advocative position by according it **superseniority.** As long as one remains a steward, he or she is, by definition, the most senior member of the unit. Stewards are often inexperienced in representing employees before assuming their positions. Union training helps them accomplish their responsibilities—particularly understanding the goals of the union movement, understanding the contract, and communicating with members.[5] Stewards are activists. Most are involved in other organizations off the job. Stewards average about 12 years of job experience and about 5.5 years of steward experience. About half are appointed, and only about 25 percent are opposed in elections.[6] Exhibit 4–1 provides an example of how one local sees the responsibilities of the steward.

Higher-level local union officers in larger units are generally granted leaves of absence by their employers. As local officers, they are responsible to their national unions and the local's members, as well as remaining attached to their employer.

Local Union Democracy

Local union governance resembles municipal politics. Union elections usually generate only moderate interest. Incumbents are usually reelected unless the rank and file believes a critical issue has been mishandled. A local typically holds regular business meetings, open to all members. Two aspects of local union government and politics bear examination: (1) the type of business conducted by unions in their meetings, and (2) the degree to which the local union is democratically operated. Local business meetings are fairly mundane unless contract negotiations are approaching. They deal mostly with reporting disbursements, communications, and pending grievances.

---

[4] L. R. Sayles and G. Strauss, *The Local Union*, rev. ed. (New York: Harcourt Brace Jovanovich, 1967), pp. 2–5.

[5] B. Broadbent, "Identifying the Education Needs of Union Stewards," *Labor Studies Journal* 14 (1989), pp. 28–45.

[6] P. A. Roby, "Becoming Shop Stewards: Perspectives on Gender and Race in Ten Trade Unions," *Labor Studies Journal* 20, no. 3 (1995), pp. 65–82.

EXHIBIT 4–1

The Role of the Steward

East Chicago, Ind.—Alan Moseley, still sweating from his workday in the steel mill, lumbers into the office of United Steelworkers Local 1010 and slams his briefcase down in frustration.

Mr. Moseley is a union "griever," or shop steward, as he would be called in some unions, handling union members' complaints against his employer, Inland Steel Industries Inc. His frustration at the time results from a year of sometimes rancorous talks with Inland over whether eight new jobs in its plant should go to union or salaried workers.

Yanking the complaint from his bulging briefcase, he grouses that a tentative agreement is meeting resistance from his own members. "It's total unrest out there," Mr. Moseley says, gesturing toward Inland's sprawling mill down the street. "It's a daily battle over jobs."

. . . Mr. Moseley's recent struggle over the eight new jobs at Inland reflects the deep tension. As his negotiations with the company dragged on, workers grew angry at the delay. Last summer, they circulated a cartoon depicting Mr. Moseley as a fat hog with a hoof in the company's till. Enraged, Mr. Moseley telephoned dozens of members but failed to find out who distributed the cartoon.

"You've got to have a leather hide in this business, but that hurt me," the 41-year-old Mr. Moseley says.

After more than a year of effort, Mr. Moseley in February finally worked out a compromise with the company: Inland promised to let union members take four of the eight jobs in a new automated steel-testing laboratory.

. . . But despite all the frustrations and despite a high defeat rate among grievers who seek reelection, Mr. Moseley has continued to run every three years. Shunning the hard-hat decals many candidates pass out, Mr. Moseley laboriously handwrites a letter to each member, asking for his vote.

He continues at this often-thankless job, he says, "because of the injustices out there." He recalls handing out food last Christmas to a long line of laid-off workers: "It made me want to hold on to the jobs I have." Besides, he adds, "I enjoy defending people. If I had my life to do over, I'd probably be a lawyer."

SOURCE: Excerpted from Alex Kotlowitz, "Grievous Work: Job of Shop Steward Has New Frustrations in Era of Payroll Cuts," *The Wall Street Journal* 68, no. 118 (1987), pp. 1, 20.

Only a minority of members generally attend meetings. Smaller locals and those with higher-skilled members have higher attendance. Typical rates might vary between 1 and 33 percent.[7] Meeting agendas also affect attendance. Meetings to ratify contracts, discuss contract demands, and elect officers usually have the highest attendance rates.

Low attendance raises questions about the breadth of support and democracy of unions. Local member involvement seems low given that their collective bargaining interests are centered there. Local union democracy is manifested in the

---

[7] Sayles and Strauss, *Local Union*, p. 97.

way factions combine into coalitions around certain issues. It is also demonstrated by contested and occasionally close elections for major offices. Local union democracy is highest in newer, small locals. Elections tend to be closer in larger units with more specialized jurisdictions, where management is not viewed as hostile and the election does not involve an incumbent.[8]

Unions are relatively democratic. Pressures by members to handle grievances and improve conditions require responses by union officers. But if management is intransigent, the pressure to maintain a united front may lead to suppression of dissent.[9]

Functional Democracy

Are local unions run democratically? If democracy requires two or more relatively permanent factions, the answer is generally no. But if democracy demands only that leaders respond to individuals and groups, the answer is generally yes. Local constitutions require elections of officers and limited terms. Further, the Landrum-Griffin Act requires local elections at least once every three years. Finally, under exclusive representation requirements, the union must apply the terms of the contract equally to all bargaining unit employees.

Democratic operation requires individual commitment to union activity. While most members believe their union works to their benefit, many were not involved in its founding and may view the union simply as their agent in employment matters. In return for dues, many members expect the union to relieve them of the effort and details involved in regulating the employment relationship. What members may want is representation in return for their dues, not participation and involvement in the union.

In unionized employment, one is simultaneously an employee and a union member. In the **functional democracy** of employment, the parties are the employer and the union.[10] Union members are entitled to due process under at least two sets of rules: the local's constitution and the labor contract. Each is administered by separate sets of officials: the local by the executive board and the contract(s) by the negotiation committee(s). An internal check-and-balance system helps ensure the contract is consistent with union standards and administered fairly for all bargaining unit members.[11]

Figure 4–1 pictures the idea of **dual governance.** Assume a local includes three **bargaining units** in an open-shop industry. Three separate contracts are administered by three negotiation committees. All bargaining unit union members

---

[8] J. C. Anderson, "A Comparative Analysis of Local Union Democracy," *Industrial Relations* 17 (1978), pp. 278–95.

[9] Sayles and Strauss, *Local Union*, pp. 135–47.

[10] N. W. Chamberlain and D. E. Cullen, *The Labor Sector*, rev. ed. (New York: McGraw-Hill, 1971), pp. 194–96.

[11] A. H. Cook, "Dual Governance in Unions: A Tool for Analysis," *Industrial and Labor Relations Review* 15 (1962), pp. 323–49.

FIGURE 4–1
Dual Governance in Unions

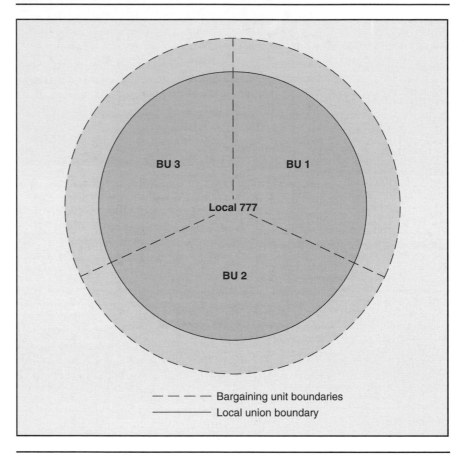

vote for the officers of the local. Each bargaining unit's employees vote on the contract. The shaded area represents workers who are both union and bargaining unit members, while those outside the local circle are bargaining unit members only.

Local unions are probably less democratic electorally than governmental units. This may not be a problem because union members are interested generally in similar types of outcomes, view the union as their agent, and evaluate it on the outcomes produced rather than the ideological stand of a faction.[12] Members do not generally feel a need to be "protected" from their union; on the contrary, it is management they worry about. If members are concerned about a lack of democracy, they can oust the leadership, turn down contracts, or vote to decertify the

---

[12] Sayles and Strauss, *Local Union*, p. 141.

local. Legal safeguards are sufficient to require responsiveness, if not democracy, and that appears to be enough for most members.

The local union is not an autonomous, freestanding organization. It most often owes its existence to—and almost certainly must comply with—the directives of a parent international, unless it is directly affiliated with the AFL–CIO or an independent.

Independent Local Unions

Independent local unions represent only employees of a single employer and are not affiliated with an international or the AFL–CIO. Most were formed in the 1920s and 1930s through initiatives under the American Plan or with employer assistance prior to the Wagner Act. TRW employees have had a long history of independent union representation. Wages of employees represented by independent unions are about the same as members belonging to affiliated locals.[13] Independent locals may be more effective in representing local interests, but have less bargaining power than affiliated locals who can act in concert with others during contract negotiations in multifacility operations.

INTERNATIONAL UNIONS

International unions originally established jurisdictions over workers in specific crafts, industries, or other job territories. Many have members in Canada as well as in the United States. As noted in Chapter 2, the (inter)national union is the unit in which authority is vested within the union movement. Most local unions are chartered by a parent national, and many local activities are constrained or must be approved by the national body.

There are more than 135 national unions, of which 78 are affiliated with the AFL–CIO. Affiliated nationals account for about 80 percent of the total U.S. union membership of about 16.3 million.[14] The latest figures find 36 unions claim more than 100,000 members each. Over half of all union members belong to the seven largest national unions. Table 4–1 lists national unions claiming 100,000 or more members in 1996. The median number of locals affiliated with a national union is about 350.

Most national unions are full-time operations. Officers are full-time unionists. Departments are established and staffed with appointed and hired specialists. Most elect officers at their conventions, legally required to meet at least every five years. Delegates to the convention are chosen by each local and sent on a per capita basis or are national union officials and **field representatives.** The union

---

[13] S. M. Jacoby and A. Verma, "Enterprise Unions in the United States," *Industrial Relations* 31 (1992), pp. 137–58.

[14] C. D. Gifford, *Directory of U.S. Labor Organizations, 1997 Edition* (Washington, DC: Bureau of National Affairs, 1997).

TABLE 4–1

National Unions with More than 100,000 Members

National Education Association[u]	2,200,000
Teamsters	1,440,000
Food and Commercial Workers	1,400,000
State, County, and Municipal Employees	1,300,000
Service Employees	1,112,000
Teachers	907,000
Auto Workers	790,000
Laborers	750,000
Brotherhood of Electrical Workers	679,000
Machinists	675,000
Communications Workers	600,000
Carpenters	500,000
Steelworkers	403,000
Operating Engineers	365,000
Letter Carriers	311,000
Plumbers	300,000
Postal Workers	300,000
Needletrades	285,000
Paperworkers	252,000
Fraternal Order of Police[u]	250,000
Hotel and Restaurant Employees	241,000
Fire Fighters	225,000
Nurses[u]	205,000
Government Employees	200,000
Transportation (UTU)	159,000
Treasury Employees[u]	155,000
Federal Employees[u]	150,000
Electronic, Electrical	135,000
Painters	125,000
Bakery, Confectionery, and Tobacco Workers	122,000
Musicians	120,000
Transportation Communications	120,000
Health and Human Service Employees	117,000
California State Employees[u]	112,000
Sheet Metal Workers	106,000
Iron Workers	105,000

[u] unaffiliated with the AFL–CIO.

SOURCE: Developed from data included in C. D. Gifford, *Directory of U.S. Labor Organizations, 1997 Edition* (Washington: Bureau of National Affairs, 1997).

convention is similar to a political convention. If the national leadership can appoint many delegates, its chances of staying in office are greatly enhanced.

National Union Goals

As noted in Chapter 1, groups of workers unionize when they believe a union would improve their employment outcomes. Chapter 2 noted that unionists have traditionally believed that income inequality is excessive in the United States.[15] Chapter 3 examined the legal environment for labor relations and recognized that U.S. labor law limits the union movement in representing employees. The exclusive agency relationship created in collective bargaining stimulates a competitive environment for employee relations services that influences how both unions and managements operate.

National unions have two major goals: organizing an increasing number and share of the labor force and providing representation services to enhance the well-being of their members. These goals are obviously interrelated. Organizing success depends to an extent on the success the union has had in representing employees in a manner visible to potential new members. Successful representation depends on organizing a group of employees through which bargaining power can be exerted on the employer.

National unions formed for economic reasons. As transportation facilities developed, U.S. industry became more national, resulting in a decline in local bargaining power. National unions exert greater pressure on employers and assist locals during difficult periods when they might not survive on their own. Support and control are thus lodged in the nationals.

National unions have their own goals. But what common elements help predict what each might do? Unions are generally composed of members who expect services and permanent employees who supply them. Members evaluate whether they want continued representation by comparing contract outcomes and services received from their union with those available from alternative sources (other unions or nonunion human resource departments). Leaders desire growth to enhance their power and stability, and strong unionization within an industry to promote bargaining power. Elected leaders and appointed full-time unionists need membership approval to retain their posts.[16] Thus, leaders might be expected to promote organizing, while the rank and file would probably prefer services for present members first. Unions in highly organized industries spend a smaller proportion of their resources on organizing than do those in jurisdictions with lower union penetration.[17]

---

[15] M. F. Neufeld, "The Persistence of Ideas in the American Labor Movement: The Heritage of the 1830s," *Industrial and Labor Relations Review* 36 (1982), pp. 207–20.

[16] R. N. Block, "Union Organizing and the Allocation of Union Resources," *Industrial and Labor Relations Review* 34 (1980), pp. 101–13.

[17] Ibid.

The economic environment in which organized labor participates has changed markedly over the past 20 years. Sometimes it is more difficult for national unions than locals to recognize the magnitude of change and the needs to respond and adapt to it. Nationals often have less knowledge about actual workplace experiences than locals, are buffered from pressures to change given their overall financial stability, and have difficulty in implementing organizationwide change because of their decentralized and political nature.[18]

National Union Strategies and Planning

Some commentators today believe organized labor is critically ill. Advocates argue that organized labor is essential to the survival and vitality of democracy, that labor needs to turn its attention more broadly, moving away from a firm-level economic bargaining orientation, toward a broad member service approach, more intensely involved in economic decision-making with employers at the industry level.[19]

National unions vary in their interest and capabilities to adapt and innovate. A study of national unions found that planning for change was positively related to the use of environmental scanning techniques, effective structuring of management and administrative activities, and larger size—and negatively related to democratic structures.[20]

Some national unions are developing plans and strategies for the future.[21] Figure 4–2 displays a union strategic planning model. Nationals that paid more attention to planning devoted larger proportions of their resources to organizing in their traditional and new jurisdictions, participated in **corporate campaigns,** and formed **political action committees.**[22] Education, budgeting, and political action are the most frequent topics of long-range planning. Plan implementation is influenced by the use of consultants, support from the union's president, and involvement in representing employees in the service or utility industries.[23] Levels at which planning occurs, the type of planning, and variables associated with planning are depicted in Figure 4–3.

The union movement is also looking at alternative forms of representation that do not involve exclusive agency. More people will join associations than will vote for union representation. Associations have often been precursors of unions, particularly among professional and public-sector employees.[24] Also, many

---

[18] T. Fitzpatrick and W. Waldstein, "Challenges to Strategic Planning in International Unions," *Proceedings of the Industrial Relations Research Association* 46 (1994), pp. 73–84.

[19] J. Rogers, "A Strategy for Labor," *Industrial Relations* 34 (1995), pp. 367–81.

[20] J. T. Delaney, P. Jarley, and J. Fiorito, "Planning for Change: Determinants of Innovation in U.S. National Unions," *Industrial and Labor Relations Review* 49 (1996), pp. 597–614.

[21] C. L. Schenck and G. W. Bohlander, "The Planning Practices of Labor Organizations: A National Study," *Labor Studies Journal* 15, no. 4 (1990), pp. 69–84.

[22] K. Stratton and R. B. Brown, "Strategic Planning in U.S. Labor Unions," *Proceedings of the Industrial Relations Research Association* 41 (1988), pp. 523–31.

[23] Y. Reshef and K. Stratton-Devine, "Long-Range Planning in North American Unions: Preliminary Findings," *Relations Industrielles* 48 (1993), 250–65.

[24] C. Ichniowski and J. S. Zax, "Today's Associations, Tomorrow's Unions," *Industrial and Labor Relations Review* 43 (1990), pp. 191–208.

FIGURE 4-2

A Union Strategic Planning Model

Phase 1	Phase 2	Phase 3	Phase 4	Phase 5	Phase 6

Define the union's purpose and establish a strategic mission	Scan the external environment:
	• Demographics
	• Economics
	• Political
	• Legislative
	• Technology
	• Foreign competition
	• Industry trends
	• Federal and state taxing and spending policies
	• Other union activities
		Identify the labor organization's strengths and weaknesses
		• Staff
		• Financial
		• Organizing
		• Procedures
		• Specific expertise or knowledge
			Develop objectives, goals, and performance targets
			1. Short run
			  • Collective bargaining
			  • Political/legislative
			  • Organizing
			2. Long run
			  • Mergers
			  • Political/legislative
			  • Collective bargaining
			  • Organizing
				Formulate a strategy to achieve target objectives and performance	Evaluate performance and redo strategic planning as needed

Redefine as needed	Revise on a consistent time frame	Reassess on a consistent basis	Reformulate as needed	Replan as needed	Recycle to phases 1, 2, 3, 4, or 5 as needed

SOURCE: C. L. Schenck and G. W. Bohlander, "The Planning Practices of Labor Organizations: A National Study," *Labor Studies Journal* 15, no. 4 (1990), p. 82.

FIGURE 4–3

A Union Planning Framework

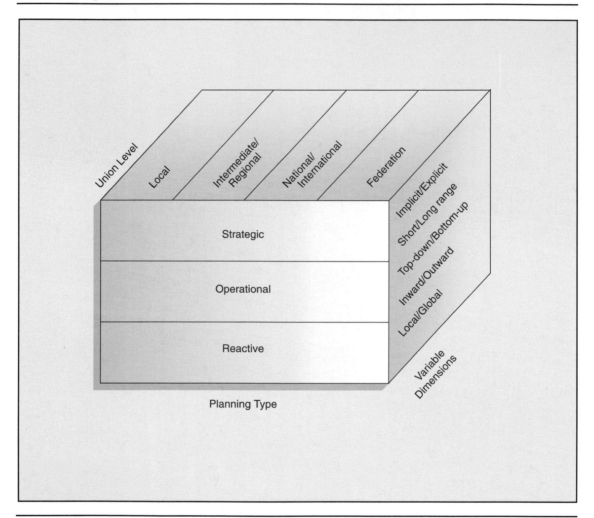

SOURCE: K. Stratton-Devine and Y. Reshef, "Union Planning: A Framework and Research Agenda," *Relations Industrielles* (1996), p. 512.

employees now work part time or for small employers who do not have personnel or other employee relations functions. The union could act as a vehicle for counseling about workplace problems; providing information on job opportunities elsewhere; purchasing group medical, dental, and other insurance benefits; and other activities. In return, **associate members,** or nonrepresented members would pay a service fee or dues to the union.[25] Attitudes toward consumer benefits affect

[25] T. A. Kochan, H. C. Katz, and R. B. McKersie, *The Transformation of American Industrial Relations* (New York: Basic Books, 1986), pp. 221–23.

EXHIBIT 4–2

New Methods of Advancing the Interests of Workers

First, unions must develop and put into effect multiple models for representing workers tailored to the needs and concerns of different groups. For example, in some bargaining units, workers may not desire to establish a comprehensive set of hard and fast terms and conditions of employment, but may nonetheless desire a representative to negotiate minimum guarantees that will serve as a floor for individual bargaining, to provide advocacy for individuals, or to seek redress for particular difficulties as they arise. In other units, a bargaining approach based on solving problems through arbitration or mediation rather than through ultimate recourse to economic weapons may be most effective.

Second, . . . unions must continually seek out and address new issues of concern to workers. For example, the issue of pay inequity has become a proper concern of women workers; collective action provides the surest way of redressing such inequities. There is a strong concern among workers about health and safety issues and a high degree of impatience with the inadequacy of government programs in this area. Again, collective action through labor unions can develop constructive steps to meet these concerns . . .

Approximately . . . 27 million workers . . . are former union members; most . . . left their union only because they left their unionized jobs. There are hundreds of thousands more nonunion workers who voted for a union in an unsuccessful organizing campaign . . . These individuals might well be willing to affiliate with a union with which they have had contact or with which they have had some logical relationship provided that the costs were not prohibitive; this would be especially true to the extent unions offered services or benefits outside of the collective bargaining context . . . New categories of membership could be created by individual unions or on a federationwide basis to accommodate individuals who are not part of organized bargaining units, and affiliates should consider dropping any existing barriers to an individual's retaining his membership after leaving an organized unit.

SOURCE: *The Changing Situation of Workers and Their Unions,* Report of the AFL–CIO Evolution of Work Committee, February 1985, pp. 18–19.

---

interest in joining an association but not a union. Strong pro-union attitudes predict a willingness to join both.[26] Exhibit 4–2 is an excerpt from an AFL–CIO statement on the need for changing representation patterns.

National Union Jurisdictions

National unions have traditionally operated as either craft or industrial unions. Craft unions formed the AFL, and industrial unions formed the CIO. Craft and industrial jurisdictional boundaries blurred as AFL and CIO unions competed for members before their merger and as craft and industrial employment patterns changed.

---

[26] P. Jarley and J. Fiorito, "Associate Membership: Unionism or Consumerism?" *Industrial and Labor Relations Review* 43 (1990), pp. 209–24.

National unions often concentrate on certain jurisdictions, and many define their jurisdictions in their constitutions. For example, the jurisdiction of the Carpenters' Union is asserted as follows:

> The trade autonomy of the United Brotherhood of Carpenters and Joiners of America consists of the milling, fashioning, joining, assembling, erection, fastening or dismantling of all materials of wood, plastic, metal, fiber, cork and composition, and all other substitute materials. The handling, cleaning, erecting, installing and dismantling of machinery, equipment and all materials used by members of the United Brotherhood.
>
> Our claim of jurisdiction, therefore, extends over the following divisions and subdivisions of the trade: Carpenters and Joiners, Millwrights, Pile Drivers, Bridge, Dock, Wharf Carpenters, Divers, Underpinners, Timbermen and Core Drillers, Shipwrights, Boat Builders, Ship Carpenters, Joiners and Caulkers; Cabinet Makers, Bench Hands, Stair Builders, Millmen; Wood and Resilient Floor Layers, and Finishers; Carpet Layers; Shinglers, Siders; Insulators; Acoustic and Dry Wall Applicators; Shorers and House Movers; Loggers, Lumber, and Sawmill Workers; Furniture Workers; Reed and Rattan Workers; Shingle Weavers; Casket and Coffin Makers; Box Makers, Railroad Carpenters and Car Builders, regardless of material used; and all those engaged in the operation of woodworking or other machinery required in the fashioning, milling or manufacturing of products used in the trade, or engaged as helpers to any of the above divisions or subdivisions, and the handling, erecting and installing material on any of the above divisions or subdivisions; burning, welding, rigging and the use of any instrument or tool for layout work, incidental to the trade. When the term "carpenter(s)" or "carpenter(s) and joiner(s)" are used, it shall mean all the divisions and subdivisions of the trade.[27]

The largest U.S. nationals tend to have broad jurisdictions. The Teamsters originally organized transportation and warehouse employees outside the railroads. Now, more than half of all Teamster members work in occupations and industries with no primary relationship to transportation. The National Education Association represents both public and private schoolteachers at primary, secondary, and postsecondary educational institutions. The United Auto Workers has expanded its organizing to nonteaching employees in colleges and universities. The American Federation of State, County, and Municipal Employees organizes in many occupations across a broad spectrum of nonfederal public and private nonprofit employers. The International Brotherhood of Electrical Workers began as a craft union but has successfully organized in electrical equipment manufacturing. Where employment in traditional jurisdictions declines, union leaders push for expanding jurisdictions.

National Structure

National unions depend on members to survive—primarily through their locals acting as exclusive bargaining agents for groups of employees. Their ability to

---

[27] *Constitution and Laws of the United Brotherhood of Carpenters and Joiners of America,* as amended (Washington, DC: United Brotherhood of Carpenters and Joiners, 1975), pp. 6–7.

obtain and maintain membership depends on environmental characteristics such as the employer's resistance to unionization, employment patterns, laws and regulations, and the political environment. Employment patterns result from the ultimate demand for goods and services and the quality of the labor supply. Unions have virtually no control over the former, and only limited control over the latter unless they provide employee training, as in the building trades.[28]

In turn, these environmental factors influence the goals of the union movement. Some of these can be realized internally (workplace goals) through collective bargaining, while others require public policy changes (external goals). The goals and services important to union members influence the strategies chosen and the organizational structures created to deliver them. Among the strategies, collective bargaining, legislative enactment, mutual insurance (unilateral regulation), and confrontation (strikes, etc.) are blended to react to employer initiatives and to advance union agendas.[29] Figure 4–4 displays a model of the determinants of union organizational structures.

The organizational structure of national unions is influenced by the interaction of two factors: the types of services members demand and the bargaining structure that has evolved with the organizations in which the union represents employees. As the bargaining structure changes, union organization changes with it. To demonstrate these relationships and the differences between national unions, profiles of the United Auto Workers, the International Association of Machinists, the International Union of Operating Engineers, the International Brotherhood of Teamsters, and the American Federation of State, County, and Municipal Employees will be presented.

The United Auto Workers

The UAW has traditionally organized workers in industries that fabricate and assemble autos and trucks, airplanes, construction and agricultural equipment, and associated parts suppliers. Final assemblers are highly concentrated (i.e., relatively few manufacturers account for most of the production). Around 1980, virtually all U.S.-made automobiles were assembled by four manufacturers: American Motors, Chrysler, Ford, and General Motors. Since then, BMW, Honda, Mazda, Mercedes, Mitsubishi, Nissan, and Toyota have opened U.S. assembly plants, and Chrysler has acquired American Motors (and recently merged with Daimler-Benz). To best serve members in a consistent manner across these major manufacturers, the UAW established **national departments.** Because U.S.-based domestic automaker production facilities were virtually 100 percent unionized, national departments concentrated on representation rather than organizing activities. Figure 4–5 shows the UAW's organization at the national level.

---

[28] J. Fiorito, C. L. Gramm, and W. E. Hendricks, "Union Structural Choices," in G. Strauss, D. G. Gallagher, and J. Fiorito, eds., *The State of the Unions* (Madison, WI: Industrial Relations Research Association, 1991), pp. 103–38.

[29] Ibid.

FIGURE 4–4

A Model of the Key Determinants of Union Organizational Structure

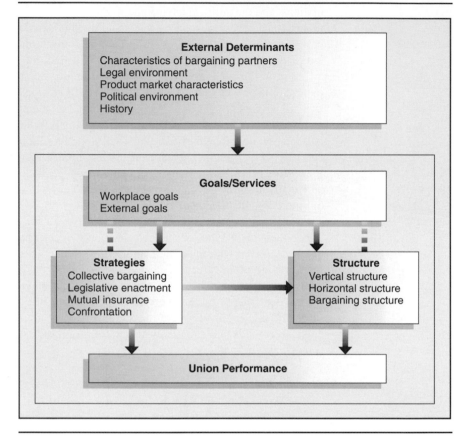

SOURCE: J. Fiorito, C. L. Gramm, and W. E. Hendricks, "Union Structural Choices," in G. Strauss, D. G. Gallagher, and J. Fiorito, eds., *The State of the Unions* (Madison, WI: Industrial Relations Research Association, 1991), p. 106.

National departments are the line portion of the organization. This is where national-local interfaces occur. Each national department has a council consisting of delegates from that department's locals. In turn, the councils form subcommittees based on common interests of the members, such as seniority and work rules. Subcommittees designate members to take part in the national negotiation council from that department.

Staff departments provide information for the national departments and also assist locals through the UAW's international representatives. Besides having a "product-line" approach in its national departments, the UAW is also broken into geographical regions based on the concentration of UAW members in a given area. Regional staffs conduct organizing drives and assist remote local unions or those not closely affiliated with national departments in negotiation,

FIGURE 4–5

Organizational Structure of the UAW

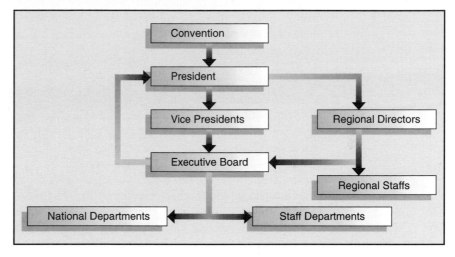

National Departments

General Motors
Ford
Chrysler
Aerospace
Agricultural Implements
Competitive Shops
Heavy Trucks
Transnationals and Joint Ventures
Skilled Trades and Technical, Office, and
    Professionals

Staff Departments

Accounting
Arbitration
Auditing
Circulation
Community Action Program
Civil Rights
Community Services
Retired Workers
Purchase and Supply
Conservation and Resource Development
Consumer Affairs
Education
Health and Safety
Information Systems
Legal
Organizing
Public Relations and Publications
Recreation and Leisure-Time Activities
Research
Research Library
Social Security
Strike Insurance
Time Study and Engineering
Veterans' Issues
Washington Office
Governmental and International Affairs
Legislative
Women's Issues

SOURCE: Abstracted from *You and Your Membership in the UAW*, publication 383 (Detroit: United Auto Workers, 1978), and updated from www.uaw.org, February 14, 1998.

administration, and grievance handling. Regional staffs may also have experts in such areas as health and safety or industrial engineering.

The centralized organizational makeup of the UAW is largely a function of employer concentration and the level at which economic bargaining occurs. However, as automakers close older, less efficient plants, local economic concessions may be traded for job security, necessitating more concern by the UAW for local bargaining issues.

The International Association of Machinists

The International Association of Machinists and Aerospace Workers was founded in a railroad locomotive pit in Atlanta in 1888 and affiliated with the AFL in 1895. Over time it expanded its jurisdiction by establishing metal trades and railway employees departments, admitting auto mechanics, organizing some occupations in the airline industry, and creating an electronics department. Many workers in the aerospace industry are represented by the Machinists.

The international union consists of several conferences and departments (related to industries in which the Machinists represent or are attempting to organize workers). There are also several staff departments that provide service to the national, locals, and members. Figure 4–6 depicts the union's current departmental structure. The union's membership peaked in 1968 at more than 1,000,000 members; about 700,000 currently belong.

The International Union of Operating Engineers

The International Union of Operating Engineers represents primarily heavy equipment operators, mechanics, and surveyors in the construction industry and stationary engineers operating equipment in building and industrial complexes. It also represents a broad group of health care workers and public employees. There are about 200 locals, most of which cover a relatively large geographical territory, particularly in construction. It has about 400,000 members and is the 12th largest union in the AFL–CIO.[30] Many of the union's services are provided at the local level, particularly through joint union-employer apprenticeship programs.

The International Brotherhood of Teamsters

The Teamsters union is the closest to a general union of any in the United States. After its expulsion from the AFL–CIO in 1960, it broadened its jurisdiction from trucking and warehousing to cover all workers. The mergers of several smaller nationals, such as the Brewery Workers, into the Teamsters made it the dominant union within several industries. The Teamsters reaffiliated with the AFL–CIO in 1987.

Given the early background of the Teamsters and the local or regional nature of much of the trucking industry, its organization is somewhat decentralized, particularly with regard to representation and organizing. The executive board of the Teamsters consists of the general president, the general secretary-treasurer, and

---

[30] www.iuoe.org, February 14, 1998.

FIGURE 4–6
Departmental Structure of the Machinists

Organizing	Safety and Health/Crest Apprenticeship/Scholarship
Government Affairs	Communications
International Affairs	Political and Legislative Action
Human Rights	Transportation
Placid Harbor (Training Facility)	Strategic Resources
Women's Department	Community Services/Retirees
Aerospace	High Performance Work Organizations

SOURCE: http://www.iamaw.org/departments/departments.htm, February 15, 1998.

several vice presidents. Some of the vice presidents are also international directors of Teamster area conferences. Twelve trade divisions address the bargaining issues associated with the industries in which Teamster members are employed: airline; automotive, petroleum, and allied trades; building material and construction; convention and exposition centers; freight; food processing; laundry; warehouse; newspaper drivers; parcel and small package; trade show and movie making; and public employees. Four trade conferences (Bakery, Communications, Brewery and Soft Drink Workers, and Dairy) coordinate activities in these industries.

The Teamsters' Union has about 50 local joint councils. These semiautonomous bodies administer activities among affiliated locals. Each local is required to belong to a joint council and must get council permission to sign a contract or to strike. Each joint council is indirectly controlled by the executive branch. Thus, much of the grass-roots organizing and representation activity is initiated or controlled at the joint council level.

The Teamsters have had a long history of difficulty with the federal government. General presidents in the 1950s and 1960s such as Dave Beck and James R. Hoffa were forced to resign for a variety of federal offenses involving the use of their positions of leadership for personal advantage. In the 1980s, the federal government imposed an external trustee following the conviction of Roy Lee Williams, then general president, for gang-related activities. Ron Carey, an insurgent leader, was elected general president following lifting of federal control. However, in late 1997, he was ruled ineligible to succeed himself owing to money laundering activities surrounding his election campaign. In late 1998 James R. Hoffa's son, James P. Hoffa, a Carey opponent, was elected Teamster president.

The American Federation of State, County, and Municipal Employees

AFSCME is an industrial-type union asserting jurisdiction over nonelected public employees outside the federal government and employees in private, nonprofit public-service organizations. The union is led by its president and secretary-treasurer who are elected at its biennial convention. They are joined by 31 international vice presidents who are elected from 24 legislative districts (some entitled to more than one vice president). At the next level are 63 regional councils responsible for coordinating bargaining and political activities among locals in their regions.[31]

AFSCME's structure reflects the fact that its members are employed in a variety of governmental jurisdictions and bargain under many different laws. Unlike most industrial unions, locals in AFSCME do not require the national's approval of their contract settlements or the decision to strike. All locals are expected to affiliate with one of the regional AFSCME councils, which are operated within jurisdictions relating to the bargaining laws associated with the occupations represented.

Services provided by the national union include research, legislative, legal, organizational, educational, public relations, and other activities.[32] AFSCME's federal nature results from the fact its affiliated locals bargain with public employers operating under a myriad of collective bargaining laws that may apply differently to various occupations within the same jurisdiction.

AFSCME expends between 10 percent and one-third of its total budget on lobbying and other political activities.[33] Issues related to job security are particularly important to the union. Since most of its membership is employed in the public sector, the ability to influence legislators and county and municipal elected officials is particularly important to its survival and growth.

National-Local Union Relationship

National unions charter locals, provide services, and usually require locals to obtain permission to ratify contracts or strike, reducing the possibility of competition between locals and increasing the discipline of locals when necessary to pressure a large national employer.

Service to locals, especially from industrial unions, is provided by international representatives, who are usually recruited and appointed by national union officers from local officer positions or activists interested in a union career. National unions may hire staff from other unions,[34] creating career mobility opportunities for staff experts. Large differences exist between unions in the intensity of services they provide through professional staff members. Comparative figures indicate a relatively high level of staff per union member in the Steelworkers (1 to 677) while the ratio is quite low in the Teamsters (1 to 9,013).[35] The ratio of staff to members has increased recently. As a result, administrative efficiency is reduced, but greater staff intensity may allow the national to

---

[31] M. F. Masters, "AFSCME as a Political Union," *Journal of Labor Research* 19 (1998), pp. 313–49.

[32] http://www.afscme.org/afscme/about/structur.htm, February 14, 1998.

[33] Masters, "AFSCME as a Political Union," pp. 313–49.

[34] P. F. Clark and L. S. Gray, "The Management of Human Resources in National Unions," *Proceedings of the Industrial Relations Research Association* 44 (1992), pp. 414–23.

[35] P. F. Clark, "Organizing the Organizers: Professional Staff Unionism in the American Labor Movement," *Industrial and Labor Relations Review* 42 (1989), pp. 584–99.

better serve member interests. However, increases in staff may also tend to perpetuate oligarchical practices.[36]

Newly elected national union officers may discharge permanent staff employees as long as it doesn't interfere with their roles as union members,[37] but elected union officers are protected by the Landrum-Griffin Act's Title I free speech provision and cannot be removed for expressing dissenting opinions.[38]

International representatives, unlike many local union officers, are full-time union employees. Their major responsibilities are to organize nonunion employers in industries or occupations in which the national union has an interest, to provide assistance to employees interested in organizing, and to assist in representing union members, particularly in negotiating contracts and processing grievances. International representatives are typically assigned to regional staffs and may be responsible for a number of locals. International representatives implement consistent policies across employers and provide expertise and presence where locals are relatively small, where local officers lack sophistication, and where the area is thinly organized.

Union clerical and professional employees frequently organize to bargain collectively with the leaders of the unions for which they work. Organized staff units are most common in larger industrial unions. Some unions have strongly opposed the organization of their staff members, while others have welcomed organizing attempts. Few unions have written human resource policies.[39] Staff unions generally bargain for the same types of employment issues that unions in general seek, but they seldom strike in support of their demands.[40]

Union administration has become more sophisticated as employers have increasingly opposed unionization and concession bargaining has increased. Unions rely on consultants more than in the past, and internal management is operated on a more businesslike basis.[41]

National Union Politics

National unions are ultimately governed by their conventions, which establish broad policies, may amend their constitutions, and frequently elect officers. The degree of member participation in national union activities depends on the method used to choose convention delegates and elect union officers. Although national

---

[36] P. F. Clark, "Professional Staff in American Unions: Changes, Trends, Implications," *Journal of Labor Research* 13 (1992), 381–92.

[37] *Finnegan* v. *Leu*, No. 80-2150, U.S. Supreme Court, 1982.

[38] *Sheet Metal Workers' International Association* v. *Lynn*, No. 86–1940, U.S. Supreme Court, 1989.

[39] Clark and Gray, "Management of Human Resources."

[40] Clark, "Organizing the Organizers."

[41] For more details on union administration, see P. F. Clark and L. S. Gray, "Union Administration," in G. Strauss, D. G. Gallagher, and J. Fiorito, eds., *The State of the Unions*, Madison (WI: Industrial Relations Research Association, 1991), pp. 175–200; and J. T. Dunlop, *The Management of Labor Unions* (Lexington, MA: Lexington, 1990).

unions are required by law to hold conventions and elect officers at least every five years, they differ greatly in the extent to which member involvement is sought and democratic ideals are applied to their operation.

National union democracy can be measured by the degree of control members have in the major decision-making areas unions face: contract negotiations, contract administration, service to members, union administration, and political and community activities. Members' control in each area could range from complete autocracy to consultation, veto power, or full decisional control and participation.[42] Desire for democracy may be inferred through the level of union member participation in decisions open to them and their satisfaction levels in relation to opportunities for, or actual participation in, union decision-making activities.

Most national unions do not have two-party systems, but a union's constitution affects the degree to which dissent may lead to a change in the union's direction. Unions electing officers on an at-large basis among all the eligible voters (either as delegates or through a general referendum) are much less likely to be responsive to factional viewpoints than unions that elect executive board members on a geographic basis.[43] In the Mineworkers and the Steelworkers (both of which have changed national general presidents because of internal dissent), regionally elected executive boards have served as springboards to national campaigns. If officers are elected by convention and if the delegates to the international convention include not only those selected at a local level but also officials appointed by the incumbent, then the chance of ousting the incumbent is virtually nonexistent.[44]

Leaders of national unions generally come from union backgrounds. Their family economic conditions are generally modest, and while most have some post–high school education, few are college graduates. Most joined unions because their employers had agreed to a union shop. They began their union careers early, usually as local union officers. Many had mentors, and most are very satisfied with their chosen careers.[45]

National Unions and Public Policy

Representation aims at enhancing union members' employment outcomes through collective bargaining. Unions also serve member needs by attempting to influence public policy. Some attempts are aimed at membership interests in particular industries, while others focus on improving outcomes for all members or an identifiable subgroup across industries.

---

[42] A. Hochner, K. Koziara, and S. Schmidt, "Thinking about Democracy and Participation in Unions," *Proceedings of the Industrial Relations Research Association* 32 (1979), pp. 16–17.

[43] S. Gamm, "The Election Base of National Union Executive Boards," *Industrial and Labor Relations Review* 32 (1979), pp. 295–311.

[44] A. L. Fox II and J. C. Sikorski, *Teamster Democracy and Financial Responsibility* (Washington, DC: Professional Drivers Council for Safety and Health, 1976).

[45] P. L. Quaglieri, "The New People of Power: The Backgrounds and Careers of Top Labor Leaders," *Journal of Labor Research* 9 (1988), pp. 271–84.

Examples of public policy initiatives that cut across industries include support of occupational safety and health legislation, opposition to lower minimum wages for younger workers, and the elimination of pay inequality between men and women. Special interest groups within the labor movement advocate specific positions. For example, the Committee of Labor Union Women (CLUW) was a strong proponent of equal pay and civil rights legislation enabling women workers to be paid similarly to men in equal jobs.[46] While wage equality would lead to gains primarily for women, it's also squarely within the equalitarian approach of trade unionism. Other social issues that have strong appeal to subgroups within the labor movement, such as abortion, can lead to cleavages and loss of support from traditional allies if pursued and to internal strife if not aired.[47]

As competition changes within industries, unions may advocate legislation to restrict the employment-cutting options of employers. For example, deregulation of the airline and trucking industries has created incentives for employer efficiency by reducing barriers to entry for new employers. Because these new employers have neither senior employees nor labor unions, competition between union and nonunion employees is injected. Where domestic markets have opened to foreign competition (e.g., autos and steel), lower wage costs among foreign competitors reduce the demand for domestic unionized employees. Thus, unions advocate protective legislation in the form of tariffs, domestic content laws, or reregulation. Exhibit 4–3 is an example of Teamster Union opposition to granting the president fast-track authority in further trade treaty negotiations.

Different unions advocate different issues. Mature unions representing skilled workers urge more legislation to protect unions as organizations, while emerging unions and those representing employees in service industries urge more attention to income redistribution.[48] The internal politics of union political action and an assessment of the level of success of union political activity will be explored in the next chapter.

THE AFL–CIO

When national unions attempt to speak as one voice on public policy, they use the AFL–CIO. The AFL–CIO is a federation of national unions banded together to provide some overall direction to the labor movement and technical assistance to individual nationals. It also has a number of directly affiliated independent local unions. To maintain membership in the AFL–CIO, a national union must comply with the federation's Ethical Practices Code, avoid dominance by nondemocratic

---

[46] C. Kates, "Working Class Feminism and Feminist Unions: Title VII, The UAW and NOW," *Labor Studies Journal* 14, no. 2 (1989), pp. 28–45.

[47] S. B. Garland, "How the Abortion Issue Is Shaking the House of Labor," *Business Week*, August 6, 1990, p. 39.

[48] D. B. Cornfield, "Union Decline and the Political Demands of Organized Labor," *Work and Occupations*, 16 (1989), 292–322.

EXHIBIT 4–3

Teamster Union Opposition to Fast Track Authority

Big Victory for Teamster Members!

We've Stopped NAFTA Fast Track . . .

Big corporations' move to expand the job-destroying NAFTA trade deal is dead for this year.

President Clinton and Republican leader Newt Gingrich have announced that they don't have the votes in Congress to pass their "Fast Track" proposal for NAFTA expansion.

Clinton and Gingrich both admitted that phone calls, letters, rallies, and other grass-roots action by Teamster members and other working families made the difference.

. . . But We're Not Done Yet

Big corporations could try to bring up NAFTA fast track again in Congress early in 1998.

In addition, they are pressuring Clinton to put in place the part of NAFTA that would allow U.S. companies to use unsafe trucks from Mexico on every highway in America.

U.S. trucking companies want to exploit drivers from Mexico—who are paid as little as $7 a day—to haul freight now handled by U.S. drivers.

Clinton has delayed that part of NAFTA for the past two years. But the American Trucking Association and politicians like Texas Gov. George W. Bush and California Gov. Pete Wilson are pressuring Clinton to lift the delay.

Call your member of Congress at 1-888-723-5246.

Tell them you're concerned about good jobs and safety on the highway and ask them to urge President Clinton to keep the NAFTA trucking delay in place.

SOURCE: http://www.teamster.org/nafta_vic.html, February 15, 1998.

ideologies, and agree to submit interunion disputes for mediation and adjudication by the AFL–CIO.[49]

---

[49] *Directory of National Unions and Employee Associations 1982–1983* (Washington, DC: Bureau of National Affairs, 1982), pp. 7–10.

The AFL–CIO simultaneously coordinates national union interests and directs state and city central body activities. Figure 4–7 shows its general organization structure. The biennial national convention consists of delegates apportioned to the convention on the basis of national union size and are elected or appointed according to their national's policy. Other delegates are sent by directly affiliated locals, state and city central bodies, and national industrial and trade departments. The convention amends the constitution, elects officers, and expresses official positions. The general board consists of the executive council, presidents of each affiliated national, and a representative from each constitutional department.

The ongoing business of the AFL–CIO is handled by the top executives, their staffs, and the constitutional departments. One set of constitutional departments— the nine trade and industrial departments—relates to jurisdictional interests of the national members: building trades, food trades, industrial union, maritime trades, metal trades, professional employees, public employees, transportation, and union label. The staff portion of the organization consists of the standing committees and their equivalent departments. These include: accounting, building management, civil and human rights, community services, economic research, education, facilities management, field services, general counsel, information services, international affairs, legislation, occupational safety and health, organizing, personnel, political action, public affairs, support services, and working women.[50] Political activity and lobbying are major activities of the AFL–CIO. Many issues before Congress have potential direct and indirect effects on the labor movement.

STATE AND LOCAL CENTRAL BODIES

In addition to its departments, the AFL–CIO has a direct relationship with almost 800 state and local **central bodies.** These bodies reflect the composition of the parent AFL–CIO and the particular industrial mix of their geographical areas. The state and local centrals are directly responsible to the AFL–CIO, not to the internationals.

State and local central bodies are primarily involved in politics and lobbying. Their positions in national election must be consistent with those of the AFL–CIO.[51] Central bodies endorse state and local candidates, and testify and lobby on local and state legislative proposals. The AFL–CIO consists predominantly of affiliated internationals, while state and local central bodies involve local unions. Figure 4–8 shows the relationship of state and local central bodies to the AFL–CIO.

---

[50] C. D. Gifford, *Directory of U.S. Labor Organizations* (Washington, DC: Bureau of National Affairs, 1997), p. 11.

[51] *Rules Governing AFL–CIO State Central Bodies,* Publication No. 12 (Washington, DC: AFL–CIO, 1973), p. 21.

FIGURE 4–7

Structural Organization of the American Federation of Labor and Congress of Industrial Organizations

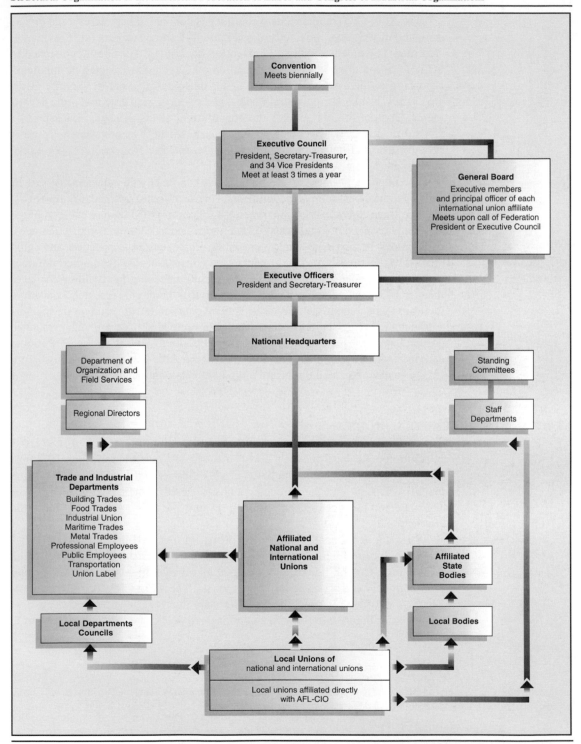

SOURCE: C. D. Gifford, *Directory of U.S. Labor Organizations* (Washington, DC: Bureau of National Affairs, 1997), p. 2.

FIGURE 4–8

The Relationship of the AFL–CIO to State and Local Central Bodies

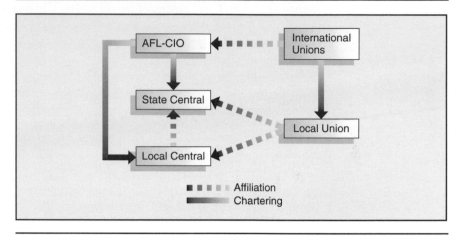

SOURCE: Adapted from J. G. Kilpatrick and M. C. Stanley, *Handbook on Central Labor Bodies: Functions and Activities,* West Virginia University Bulletin, series 64, no. 4–6 (October 1963), p. 5.

Overview of the Union Hierarchy

Power in the labor movement clearly resides in the nationals, with locals and the federation deriving their authority from the nationals. Local unions are structured to handle the day-to-day activities of the membership. Much of their effort involves policing the contract and handling grievances.

A national union could be compared with the corporate staff division of a large company, where policies are developed, actions are audited to ensure conformity to policy, and advice is given to generalists in plants (or locals) on specific issues. Although the convention ultimately governs the national, many national presidents have broad powers to take interim actions and to influence the delegate composition of future conventions.

The AFL–CIO is similar to a trade association, a chamber of commerce, or a national association of manufacturers. It coordinates activities among the nationals and amplifies their voices. The federation's prime functions are information, integration, and advocacy. Its greatest areas of autonomy relate to legislative and political processes.

NATIONAL UNION MERGERS

The recent past has witnessed a large number of corporate mergers and acquisitions. Organizational change in the labor movement has mirrored these activities, although hostile takeovers are not possible in the labor movement. Union mergers appear to take two forms: absorption, in which a small or rapidly declining union becomes a part of a larger national[52] (e.g., the 450-member Window Glass Cutters League's 1975 merger into the 80,000-member Glass Bottle Blowers); and amalgamation, in which two unions of roughly equal size merge to form a new union (e.g., the 1979 merger of the 500,000-member Amalgamated Meat Cutters and Butcher Workers with the 700,000-member Retail Clerks to form the United Food and Commercial Workers).[53]

Mergers take three forms: (1) symbiotic, in which two unions represent workers whose outputs are interdependent; (2) commensalistic, in which two unions have competed for the organization of the same employees; and (3) scale, wherein a large union seeks to increase its efficiency or power. Symbiotic mergers prevail when unions are expanding membership, and commensalistic mergers are more common during contraction. Recessions are associated with greater merger activity.[54]

Mergers are complicated by duplicate national union officers and services unless staffs are consolidated. Symbiotic mergers are probably the easiest because the needs of the merged membership may have little overlap. Commensalistic mergers require agreements on the role of present union officers and the fate of local unions following the merger. Mergers are eased when few integration issues exist, such as where craft identities are preserved, the regional penetration of one union is great, important historical traditions are preserved, leadership duplication problems are accommodated, and merged structures are based on strong individual union identities.[55] Union leaders perceive several benefits from merger, including increased power of the merged unions, greater strategic capability, greater possibilities for growth, staff job security, and greater achievement possibilities for the leaders.[56]

Three of the larger national unions affiliated with the AFL–CIO are already in the process of merging to create the largest affiliated union in the United States. The UAW, Machinists, and Steelworkers plan to merge before the year 2000 to create an organization of about 1,800,000 members. The merger aims to increase union bargaining power in mature, high-wage industries. Table 4–2 shows union mergers that occurred between 1993 and 1997.

A study examining demographic characteristics and attitudes of a local union's members who were voting on merging an independent union into a national found that votes for the merger were predicted by the perceived effectiveness of the merger, support for the merger by influential co-workers, and the importance of the recommendation for the merger by the independent union's

---

[52] C. J. Janus, "Union Mergers in the 1970s: A Look at the Reasons and Results," *Monthly Labor Review* 102, no. 10 (1978), pp. 13–23.

[53] G. N. Chaison, "Union Growth and Union Mergers," *Industrial Relations* 20 (1981), pp. 98–108.

[54] J. Freeman and J. Brittain, "Union Merger Process and the Industrial Environment," *Industrial Relations* 16 (1977), pp. 173–85.

[55] G. N. Chaison, "Union Mergers and the Integration of Union Governing Structures," *Journal of Labor Research* 3 (1982), pp. 139–51.

[56] K. Stratton-Devine, "Union Merger Benefits: An Empirical Analysis," *Journal of Labor Research* 13 (1992), pp. 133–43.

TABLE 4–2
Union Mergers between 1993–97

1993

United Food and Commercial Workers (AFL–CIO)
International Union of Life Insurance Agents (Ind.)

United Food and Commercial Workers (AFL–CIO)
Retail, Wholesale and Department Store Union (AFL–CIO)

United Paperworkers International Union (AFL–CIO)
Allied Industrial Workers of America (AFL–CIO)

Communications Workers of America (AFL–CIO)
Union of Professional and Technical Employees (Ind.)

United Electrical Workers (Ind.)
Iowa United Professionals (Ind.)

United Electrical Workers (Ind.)
National Industrial Workers Union (Ind.)

Service Employees International Union (AFL–CIO)
United Service Workers of America (Ind.)

1994

International Brotherhood of Boilermakers (AFL–CIO)
Stove, Furnace, and Allied Appliance Workers (AFL–CIO)

Service Employees International Union (AFL–CIO)
International Brotherhood of Firemen and Oilers (AFL–CIO)

International Brotherhood of Electrical Workers (AFL–CIO)
United Association of Office, Sales and Technical Employees (Ind.)

1995

Amalgamated Clothing and Textile Workers Union (AFL–CIO)
International Ladies' Garment Workers Union (AFL–CIO)
(formed Union of Needletrades, Industrial and Textile Employees, AFL–CIO)

United Food and Commercial Workers (AFL–CIO)
Distillery, Wine and Allied Workers (AFL–CIO)

Communications Workers of America (AFL–CIO)
Newspaper Guild (AFL–CIO)

United Steelworkers of America (AFL–CIO)
United Rubber, Cork, Linoleum and Plastic Workers (AFL–CIO)

United Food and Commercial Workers (AFL–CIO)
United Textile Workers of America (AFL–CIO)

1996

United Food and Commercial Workers (AFL–CIO)
International Chemical Workers Union (Ind.)

1997

United Auto Workers (AFL–CIO)
Mechanics Educational Society (AFL–CIO)

International Association of Machinists (AFL–CIO)
International Woodworkers of America (AFL–CIO)

Note: Italicized union is the survivor.
SOURCE: L. Williamson, "Union Mergers, 1985–94 Update," *Monthly Labor Review* 118, no. 2, pp. 18–25.

leadership. Negative votes were predicted by beliefs that dues would increase, strikes would increase, and the perceived importance of the employer's campaign against the merger.[57]

UNION FINANCES

Union finances are generally related to two different functions. The first involves the day-to-day operations of the union, and the second is associated with the fiduciary obligation of officers in some unions to the collection, trusteeship, and disbursement of pension and welfare benefits to members. The latter is usually found in craft unions or unions in which employers are too small or marginal to administer their own pension programs.

Organization Receipts and Disbursements

Three major sources of revenue are available to unions: dues from members; fees, fines, and assessments from members; and investment income. Dues and fees are collected at the local level. The nationals and the AFL–CIO levy a per capita tax on the locals. The current AFL–CIO per capita tax is 45 cents monthly; many nationals require locals to remit about 50 percent of dues for their operations.[58] Dues vary widely among unions; some require a flat fee while others scale fees to earning levels. The parent national usually sets minimum and maximum levels, and the local can adjust within those limits. Occasionally, an assessment is added to replenish or maintain strike funds.

The most recent study available indicates about 85 percent of local unions require an initiation fee. Most new members pay $40 or less to become members. Dues vary among locals, but a common rule of thumb is to set them equal to two hours' wages per month.[59]

As of 1995, total assets of national unions, intermediate bodies, and local unions totaled roughly $10.1 billion, with about 43 percent held by nationals, 10 percent with intermediate bodies, and 47 percent by locals. Revenues for 1995 totaled about $12.7 billion (less than $1,000 per member from all income sources). About 40 percent was attributed to nationals, 13 percent to intermediate bodies, and 48 to locals. The seven largest national unions in terms of asset base account for 43 percent of all assets held by unions. Unions have large differences in the degree to which assets are held at the national or local level. In general, unions representing manufacturing workers are likely to hold a larger share of assets at the national level. Since 1979, operating income for 28 major unions has

---

[57] J. A. McClendon, J. Kriesky, and A. Eaton, "Member Support for Union Mergers: An Analysis of an Affiliation Referendum," *Journal of Labor Research* 16 (1995), pp. 9–24.

[58] *This Is the AFL–CIO,* Publication No. 20 (Washington, DC: AFL–CIO, 1980), p. 5.

[59] C. W. Hickman, "Labor Organizations' Fees and Dues," *Monthly Labor Review* 100, no. 5 (1977), pp. 19–24.

declined by about 23 percent while net worth has increased by about 6 percent and 23 percent per member. Increasing net worth reflects cost cutting during a period of adversity. Increasing net worth per member increases the ability of the union to provide negotiating services or strike benefits as they are needed in the future.[60]

A union's ability to service the workers it represents depends, to a certain extent, on the dues members pay. As noted earlier in the discussion of functional democracy, all employees who are represented are not necessarily members. In federal government employment, union shop clauses cannot be negotiated and unions cannot strike. Presently, **free riding** (representation by a union without joining or paying dues) by nonmember federal employees approaches almost two-thirds of the total number of employees represented by the American Federation of Government Employees and other federal-sector unions. This has led to low solvency and the need to borrow money to cover operating expenses during certain periods. It also has probably reduced the effectiveness of the unions in bargaining and contract administration.[61]

Financial Malfeasance

The Landrum-Griffin Act and state criminal codes specify a variety of illegal financial transactions for labor unions. In 1998, Teamsters General President Ron Carey was barred from ever holding union office again as a result of money laundering that funneled funds to his re-election campaign in 1997. In general, national unions have been free of financial transgressions by their officers. And, given the large number of local and intermediate bodies that exist, relatively few instances of embezzlement have taken place in these organizations. During a two-year period between 1993 and 1995, 104 persons were convicted under the federal statute prohibiting embezzlement from unions. In general, losses tended to be under $25,000, the victimized unions were small in both membership and financial resources, and the perpetrators were usually part-time officers, male, and acted alone.[62]

Pension Administration

Pension plans are frequently administered by craft and other unions where the size of employers is small or employment is transient. Craft union dues are greater than those in industrial unions, with a portion set aside for benefits. Other unions require employers to make a per capita payment, as in the National Master Freight

---

[60] M. F. Masters and R. S. Atkin, "The Finances of Major U.S. Unions," *Industrial Relations* 36 (1997), pp. 489–506.

[61] M. F. Masters and R. S. Atkin, "Financial and Bargaining Implications of Free Riding in the Federal Sector," *Journal of Collective Negotiations in the Public Sector* 22 (1993), pp. 327–40.

[62] A. L. Bowker, "Trust Violators in the Labor Movement: A Study of Union Embezzlements," *Journal of Labor Research* 19 (1998), pp. 571–79.

Agreement with the Teamsters (1998), which called for $1.45 per employee per hour in health, pension, and welfare payments.

Administering pension programs has become an increasingly important issue for both union administrators and members. The Employee Retirement Income Security Act of 1974 requires pension administrators to safeguard and invest prudently all contributions made toward retirement. Certain investment practices, such as risky or low-interest loans, are illegal. Investments in one's own organization are also largely precluded. Given equivalent expected returns, however, unions may channel financing toward projects that will enhance employment of their members. For example, building trades unions may provide financing for housing projects and other activities that will require increased employment of building trades workers.

SUMMARY

Organized labor has essentially a three-tiered structure (local, national, and AFL–CIO), with power concentrated at the second level. At the local level, the most typical structure is the single employer bargaining unit. Multiemployer units are perhaps most common in the construction industry. National unions are of two major types: craft, representing workers in a specific occupation, and industrial, representing occupations in a specific industry. The AFL–CIO is the only major U.S. labor federation, with over three-quarters of the nation's union and association members affiliated with it since the Teamsters rejoined.

Although the local union is the workers' direct representative, members' interests in internal affairs are generally low. They appear to view the union as their employment agent and allow a cadre of activists to control its internal politics.

National union structures, particularly the industrials, adapt to both the breadth of their constituencies and the concentration within their industries. For example, the UAW has a General Motors Department.

Whether unions operate democratically depends on the definition of the term. Most do not have two-party systems, and many equate dissent with attempts to undermine union goals. On the other hand, local officers are directly elected, and international officials are chosen in a manner similar to a presidential nominating convention. Unions introduce democracy into the work setting by requiring a bargaining contract. Within unions, the checks and balances initiated through its constitution and contracts increase democracy and safeguards for members.

DISCUSSION QUESTIONS

1. If you were recommending an organizational structure for a national union, what factors would you advise that it consider (industrial concentration, occupations it represents, and so on)?

2. Should unions enroll associate members or continue only to act as bargaining agents?
3. How could a union local increase the involvement of its membership?
4. Defend or attack the usual method of electing an international president (through local delegates and international staff members at the convention).

KEY TERMS

Business agent   *86*
Executive committee   *87*
Negotiation committee   *87*
Stewards   *87*
Superseniority   *87*
Functional democracy   *89*
Dual governance   *89*
Bargaining units   *89*

International unions   *91*
Field representatives   *91*
Corporate campaigns   *94*
Political action committees   *94*
Associate members   *96*
National departments   *99*
Central bodies   *109*
Free riding   *115*

5

UNIONS: MEMBER AND LEADER ATTITUDES, BEHAVIORS, AND POLITICAL ACTIVITIES

*C*hapter 4 examined the structure of the labor movement, detailing its components, offices, and activities. Individuals employed in unionized establishments work in a unique environment. In nonunion organizations, employers retain the right to make all legal decisions regarding the direction of the workplace. With unionization, wages, hours, and terms and conditions of employment are determined on a bilateral basis, and ongoing workplace governance is shared by the employer and union.

Once unionized, individuals are simultaneously employees and union members. Employers continue to have explicit expectations about employee effort and performance within their jobs. Employees take responsibility for operating their union and bargaining with the employer. Levels of commitment and participation of union members may vary substantially depending on the local employment environment and the governance structure of the union. This chapter examines the behavior of individuals in their role as union members, their participation and commitment, the role of national unions in influencing the external environment through political action, and the future for unions. As you study this chapter, consider the following questions:

1. What factors influence the willingness of union members to participate in local union activities?
2. Can one be simultaneously committed to both employer and union goals?
3. What effect does national union political action have on outcomes important to organized labor?
4. What factors influence the participation of women and minorities in local and national unions?

THE INDIVIDUAL AND THE LOCAL UNION

Most people who are union members joined after being hired by a unionized employer. As will be described in more detail in Chapter 10, unions usually negotiate union security clauses into collective bargaining agreements that require represented employees to join the union or pay an **agency fee** for representation services. In states with right-to-work laws, federal employment, and most state and local public employment, employees may not be required to join unions if represented, and most often are not required to pay agency fees.

In some occupations, union membership strongly facilitates employment. Where employment is transient (as in the construction and maritime industries) and when the union takes a leading role in occupational skill training (as in the building trades), entrée to employment opportunities is most often through the union. Thus, membership in these unions does not usually follow from taking employment with a particular employer but is a prerequisite for being referred to many opportunities.

Joining and Socialization

Employers usually orient new employees to their workplaces. Most often a cohort of new employees starts work at the beginning of a pay period. They usually attend a group meeting at which they receive information about the company, policies and procedures, enroll in benefit programs, and the like. Then they move off to their work areas, meet their supervisors, are assigned work stations, meet their fellow employees, and begin on-the-job training. Sometimes there may be a formal training period before they begin the job. New employees are often hired in a probationary capacity—making the transition to so-called permanent employment after a training and adaptation period. While new employees in a unionized bargaining unit are represented by the union from the outset, labor contracts usually reserve the company's right to terminate a probationary employee for any reason without recourse to the grievance procedure.

Most collective bargaining agreements exempt probationary employees from union representation or payment of union agency fees. If there is a **union shop** agreement in the contract, new employees will be required to join immediately after the probationary period. At this point, they must pay an initiation fee and begin to pay monthly dues.

Generally, the steward enrolls new members in a work unit. The steward explains to employees the union's role in representation activities and how the collective bargaining agreement benefits them. The steward makes employees aware of union activities and tries to involve new members in them. Since the union's ability to represent employees requires it to be able to demonstrate majority support, it's important for it to be able to spell out gains it has previously negotiated to present and potential members. Aspects of the contract related to protection from unilateral discipline and rationalizing job opportunities through seniority clauses reflect the operationalization of union values.[1] The steward's role in socializing new members to the union appears to be much more important than formal programs. Socialization positively influences attitudes toward the union and later commitment to the union's programs and activities.[2]

Where there is no union shop clause or agency fee required, employees need not join the union to receive contractual benefits. This is **free-riding.** Employees who are socialized into the union (or develop feelings of union solidarity) avoid free-riding. Employees with lower attachment to their occupations or who have less fear of arbitrary employer actions may be more willing to free-ride. Employees who do not believe the net benefits gained through collective bargaining exceed the costs of dues and other efforts would also be less likely to join. An adversarial relationship between the union and employees will be more likely to create the perceived need for union protection.[3] Unionized employees who perceive that the labor relations climate in their workplaces is adversarial are likely to decrease their commitment to both the employer and the union.[4] Factors found to be associated with higher rates of free-riding (holding other factors constant) include employment in the private sector in a right-to-work state, lower earnings, employment in a white-collar occupation, higher education levels, and being younger, white, or a woman.[5]

Member Participation

Union member participation involves administrative activities, attending meetings, and voting in elections, strike authorizations, and contract ratifications. One set of activities relates to the local union as an organization (e.g., meeting attendance, voting in officer elections, running for office), while the other involves the union's role as bargaining agent (e.g., voting on contract ratifications, picketing). The steward's role combines both sets in enrolling union members and encouraging involvement in its ongoing activities, and in processing grievances and preparing for contract negotiations.

---

[1] P. F. Clark, C. Fullager, D. G. Gallagher, and M. E. Gordon, "Building Union Commitment among New Members: The Role of Formal and Informal Socialization," *Labor Studies Journal* 18, no. 3 (1993), pp. 3–16.

[2] C. J. A. Fullager, D. G. Gallagher, M. E. Gordon, and P. F. Clark, "Impact of Early Socialization on Union Commitment and Participation: A Longitudinal Study," *Journal of Applied Psychology* 80 (1995), pp. 147–57.

[3] S. J. Deery, R. D. Iverson, and P. J. Erwin, "Predicting Organizational and Union Commitment: The Effect of Industrial Relations Climate," *British Journal of Industrial Relations* 32 (1994), pp. 581–98.

[4] J. B. Fuller and K. Hester, "The Effect of Labor Relations Climate on the Union Participation Process," *Journal of Labor Research* 19 (1998), pp. 173–88.

[5] G. N. Chaison and D. G. Dhavale, "The Choice between Union Membership and Free-Rider Status," *Journal of Labor Research*, 13, 355–369, although "true" free-riding, where the value of benefits exceeds the costs appears to be equal in both right-to-work and non-right-to-work states, see R. S. Sobel, "Empirical Evidence on the Union Free-Rider Problem: Do Right-to-Work Laws Matter?" *Journal of Labor Research* 16 (1995), pp. 346–65.

A study of attitudes toward union participation found three correlated dimensions: administrative support, intermittent support during certain types of events, and supportive attitudes toward fellow members.[6] A study of union member participation found that activities can be hierarchically ordered with participation in a higher-level activity indicating involvement in activities below it. Increasing levels of participation would begin with reading union literature and progress through voting on collective bargaining issues, voting in union elections, attending union meetings, serving on committees; and ending in holding union office.[7]

In this study, the level of union participation was directly predicted by willingness to work for the union and leadership of the member's shop steward. In turn, willingness to work for the union was predicted by loyalty and feelings of responsibility to the union. Responsibility was predicted by union loyalty and Marxist work beliefs, while union loyalty was predicted by subjective norms about unions, the perceived instrumentality of the union in gaining important outcomes, first-year socialization into the union, and shop steward leadership. Subjective norms are the individual's beliefs about how important referents, such as friends and family, feel about unions. Participation in union activities, in turn, was associated with lower intrinsic and extrinsic job satisfaction. Marxist work beliefs also independently contributed to lower feelings of satisfaction. Figure 5–1 displays the model and the relationships between components.[8] Later research suggested that low job satisfaction predicts participation only in adversarial labor relations climates.[9] As Chapter 6 will note, some components predicting participation in the union also predict a willingness to vote for the union in representation elections.

It's important to note the negative relationship between union participation and job satisfaction measures as moderated by the labor relations climate. While Chapter 1 noted general equivalence in satisfaction between union and nonunion employees, these results suggest union activists are less satisfied. A poor work climate is usually necessary to trigger organizing activity. Those who are most dissatisfied with their work situation can be expected to put in the most effort to change it. Activism may be reasonable since those who perceive higher union instrumentality see unionization as necessary to gain job outcomes they perceive the employer is unwilling to grant unilaterally.

Participation in Administration
Participation in local union administration is predicted primarily by interest in union business, educational level, seniority, beliefs in the value of unions, and low

---

[6] J. M. Parks, D. G. Gallagher, and C. J. A. Fullager, "Operationalizing the Outcomes of Union Commitment: The Dimensionality of Participation," *Journal of Organizational Behavior* 16 (1995), pp. 533–56.

[7] E. K. Kelloway and J. Barling, "Members' Participation in Local Union Activities: Measurement, Prediction, and Replication," *Journal of Applied Psychology* 78 (1993), pp. 262–79.

[8] Ibid.

[9] Fuller and Hester, "The Effect of Labor Relations Climate . . ."

FIGURE 5–1

Predictors of Union Participation

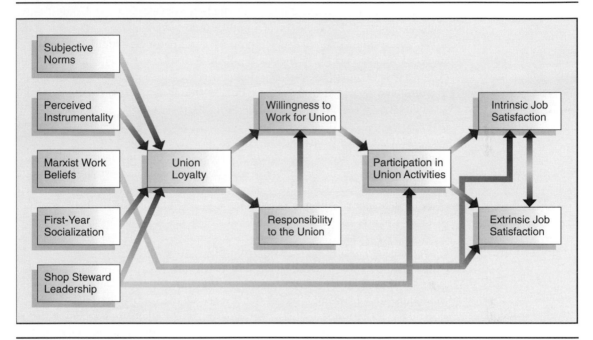

SOURCE: E. K. Kelloway and J. Barling, "Members Participation in Local Union Activities: Measurement, Prediction, and Replication, *Journal of Applied Psychology* 78 (1993), p. 274.

job involvement.[10] One study found that members who attended union meetings were more likely to be committee activists, voters, campaigners, and union newspaper readers. Participation was not greater among members with employment grievances.[11] Race differences do not appear to be associated with participation,[12] and increasing proportions of minorities in a unit do not decrease the members' willingness to use formal and informal means to force changes.[13] Some evidence suggested that women are less likely to participate because of duties at home, underestimation of their abilities, and the belief that men would make better union

[10] S. L. McShane, "The Multidimensionality of Union Participation," *Journal of Occupational Psychology* 59 (1986), pp. 177–87.

[11] J. C. Anderson, "Local Union Participation: A Re-Examination," *Industrial Relations* 18 (1979), pp. 18–31.

[12] M. M. Hoyman and L. Stallworth, "Participation in Local Unions: A Comparison of Black and White Members," *Industrial and Labor Relations Review* 40 (1987), pp. 323–35.

[13] R. Hodson, "Do Racially Mixed Work Forces Undermine Worker Solidarity and Resistance?" *Proceedings of the Industrial Relations Research Association* 46 (1994), pp. 239–46.

officers.[14] However, increases in the proportion of women in union leadership positions increases participation of women in all union activities.[15]

Active members see the union as a vehicle for developing and demonstrating leadership among nonprofessional employees where the job design does not provide decision-making opportunities. Strong participation in union activities may also reflect differences in values and political orientations when compared with managers and employers. Local union leaders are less satisfied with their jobs than nonparticipating members. They also report more stress and higher role ambiguity and conflict given their union roles.[16]

Participation and Satisfaction

Evidence is mixed on the relationship between participation in union activities and satisfaction with the union. In a U.S. sample, participation was higher among members who expressed dissatisfaction with their unions, but it was also higher when members indicated their unions were effective in gaining member goals and were interested in both intrinsic and extrinsic goals of members.[17]

Participation and Other Factors

Participation varies with the environment in which the union operates. The union's willingness to encourage democracy appears greater when it is not faced with a hostile employer. Political processes may be more active in larger unions, but rank-and-file participation declines for many activities. The reduction in participation in larger unions may not be contrary to member desires, since participation and satisfaction do not appear to be linked in good labor relations climates.[18]

As noted in Chapter 4, local union member participation in activities tends to be greater for contract and other employment issues than for union administration. Over time, participation may be decreased by bureaucratization of union activities through the administration of the contract. The contract spells out how most disputes will be handled. Negotiation committees are established within the local to decide how to deal with disputes that aren't immediately resolved. Unless the committees fail to operate to the satisfaction of the rank and file, there is little

---

[14] G. N. Chaison and P. Andiappan, "An Analysis of the Barriers to Women Becoming Local Union Officers," *Journal of Labor Research* 10 (1989), pp. 149–62.

[15] S. Mellor, "Gender Composition and Gender Representation in Local Unions: Relationships between Women's Participation in Local Office and Women's Participation in Local Activities," *Journal of Applied Psychology* 80 (1995), pp. 706–20.

[16] E. K. Kelloway and J. Barling, "Industrial Relations Stress and Union Activism: Costs and Benefits of Participation," *Proceedings of the Industrial Relations Research Association* 46 (1994), pp. 442–51.

[17] T. J. Chacko, "Member Participation in Union Activities: Perceptions of Union Priorities, Performance, and Satisfaction," *Journal of Labor Research* 6 (1985), pp. 363–73. See also D. G. Gallagher and G. Strauss, "Union Membership Attitudes and Participation," in G. Strauss, D. G. Gallagher, and J. Fiorito, eds., *The State of the Unions* (Madison, WI: Industrial Relations Research Association, 1991), pp. 139–74.

[18] McShane, "Multidimensionality of Union Participation."

need for them to be involved. The union is fulfilling its role as the employee's bargaining agent. If significant numbers of present members are replaced by new employees with a different value system, and there is no strong effort to orient them to the union, then increased participation is likely and bureaucratic structures would be deinstitutionalized.[19]

Commitment to the Union

Commitment to the union involves a psychological investment in its goals. Commitment is behaviorally reflected in participation, espousing union goals, and persuading others to join and work toward them. Commitment is reflected not only in the pursuit of specific local goals, but also to overall goals of the union movement.

Where membership is voluntary, commitment to the union is facilitated by early involvement and socialization in union activities and continued participation. Commitment to the union is promoted by new member orientation programs, communications to members, and participation by members.[20] Commitment to the union appears related, in order, to the following factors: loyalty, responsibility to the union, willingness to work for the union, and belief in unionism.[21]

Attitudes reflecting commitment to the union are stronger than expressions of willingness to assist in obtaining union goals. Comparing a sample of U.S. and Canadian white-collar union members, Canadians expressed greater loyalty.[22] Satisfied union members are also more likely to be satisfied with management, although the union is seen as more important among less-satisfied employees.[23]

During the 1980s, many local unions went through major crises with reductions in membership as plants closed or substantial layoffs occurred. Commitment to the union was positively related to the severity of job loss, indicating an increase in cohesion during a crisis. At the same time, satisfaction with both the

[19] V. G. Devinatz, "A Study in the Development of Trade Union Bureaucratization: The Case of UAW Local 6, 1941–1981," *Proceedings of the Industrial Relations Research Association* 44 (1992), pp. 450–57.

[20] S. Kuruvilla, D. G. Gallagher, and K. Wetzel, "The Development of Members' Attitudes toward Their Unions: Sweden and Canada," *Industrial and Labor Relations Review* 46 (1993), pp. 499–514.

[21] R. T. Ladd, M. E. Gordon, L. L. Beauvais, and R. L. Morgan, "Union Commitment: Replication and Extension," *Journal of Applied Psychology* 67 (1982), pp. 640–44. See also L. M. Shore, L. E. Tetrick, R. R. Sinclair, and L. A. Newton, "Validation of a Measure of Perceived Union Support," *Journal of Applied Psychology* 79 (1994), pp. 971–77 who found union attitudes include commitment, support for the union as an institution, and union instrumentality beliefs.

[22] J. W. Thacker, L. E. Tetrick, M. W. Fields, and D. Rempel, "Commitment to the Union: A Comparison of United States and Canadian Workers," *Journal of Organizational Behavior* 12 (1991), pp. 63–72.

[23] M. E. Gordon, J. W. Philpot, R. E. Burt, C. A. Thompson, and W. E. Spiller, "Commitment to the Union: Development of a Measure and an Examination of Its Correlates," *Journal of Applied Psychology* 65 (1980), pp. 479–99.

company and the union was more likely to decline in situations where severe job loss occurred.[24]

Dual Commitment

In unionized employment, one is simultaneously an employee and a union member. To which is allegiance owed, or can one serve two masters simultaneously? If an employee is committed simultaneously to both employer and union goals, **dual commitment** is said to exist.

Commitment to the union and to the employer has been demonstrated to be independent.[25] Figure 5–2 shows the suggested antecedents of dual commitment. Simultaneous (dual) commitment to the employer and the union has been found to be related to both individual differences[26] and a positive labor relations climate.[27] Involvement in union activities is related to higher commitment to both the union and the employer.[28] Commitment is also higher where employees perceive they have greater job influence and an active cooperative labor-management program is operating.[29] Higher commitment to employers among involved local union members should be expected because their local union activities depend on continued local membership, which is most often dependent on continued employment with the represented employer.

Local Union Effectiveness and Member Behavior

Unions are effective if they can attain goals salient to their members. One study of public sector local unions identified five dimensions of union activities assumed to be associated with effectiveness: member participation, preparations for future negotiations, involvement in political and civil activities, a union mentality, and the union's leadership. Holding other factors constant, political involvement was related to the relative percentage of employees organized and the size of wage increases.[30]

---

[24] S. Mellor, "The Relationship between Membership Decline and Union Commitment: A Field Study of Local Unions in Crisis," *Journal of Applied Psychology* 75 (1990), pp. 258–67.

[25] B. Bemmels, "Dual Commitment: Unique Construct or Epiphenomenon?" *Journal of Labor Research* 16 (1995), pp. 401–22.

[26] C. V. Fukami and E. W. Larson, "Commitment to Company and Union: Parallel Models," *Journal of Applied Psychology* 69 (1984), pp. 367–71.

[27] H. L. Angle and J. L. Perry, "Dual Commitment and Labor-Management Climates," *Academy of Management Journal* 29 (1986), pp. 31–50.

[28] C. Fullager and J. Barling, "Predictors and Outcomes of Different Patterns of Organizational and Union Loyalty," *Journal of Occupational Psychology* 64 (1991), pp. 129–44.

[29] P. D. Sherer and M. Morishima, "Roads and Roadblocks to Dual Commitment: Similar and Dissimilar Antecedents of Union and Company Commitment," *Journal of Labor Research* 10 (1989), pp. 311–30.

[30] T. H. Hammer and D. L. Wazeter, "Dimensions of Local Union Effectiveness," *Industrial and Labor Relations Review* 46 (1993), pp. 302–19.

FIGURE 5–2
Antecedents of Dual Commitment

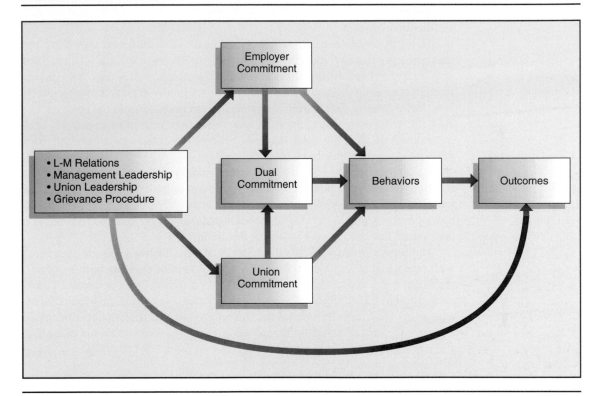

SOURCE: B. Bemmels, "Dual Commitment: Unique Construct or Epiphenomenon?" *Journal of Labor Research* 16, p. 405.

The Individual as a Union Officer

In the local union, the individual might hold an executive office such as president, secretary-treasurer, or the like; be a member of a standing committee such as the negotiating committee; or be a steward in a work unit.

Stewards

In most locals, there are probably more stewards (or committee-persons) than any other type of officer. As noted in Chapter 4, stewards are either appointed or elected. Steward turnover is relatively high. They are directly responsible to their constituents for advocating positions of work group members, and also responsible to the leadership of the union for communicating information and positions to work unit members. If either the work unit members or the leadership is dissatisfied with the steward's performance, the steward is likely to be replaced.

The successful recruiting of minorities and women into steward positions in white male majority locals appears to require one-to-one contact, persuasion, and mentoring.[31] In turn, successful recruiting should lead to more integrated rank-and-file involvement.

Stewards are often seen by work unit employees as a buffer between them and management, thereby reducing the stresses of the workplace.[32] Unresolved stresses are related to dissatisfaction with the union.[33] Stewards gain power through their ability to solve workplace problems jointly with work unit supervisors. Power does not stem from formal rights and perquisites in the contract, but from the steward's ability to obtain results. Private-sector stewards generally have more power than public-sector stewards, generally because supervisors and managers have more latitude to make decisions.[34]

Interests in co-workers and commitment to union goals is related to lower role conflict between their positions as employees and union representatives than for individuals who were stewards for personal reasons.[35] Stewards in the former category probably have fewer worries about internal union politics and its effects on their future leadership opportunities in the union.

The local is interested not only in the steward's ability to adjust grievances with management, but also in his or her ability to communicate with work unit members and enhance their commitment and participation in activities. Grassroots training for stewards influences interaction with and transmission of information to rank-and-file employees.[36] Training on organizational citizenship increases the stewards' support for the union as an organization and for addressing and supporting the needs of co-workers.[37]

Dual Commitment of Stewards

The situation of the steward—as a full-time company employee and also the work unit's employee representative when they have grievances against the employer—is paradoxical. To whom is the steward committed—the union, the employer, or both? A study of about 200 stewards at one employer found that about 80 percent were committed to the union, 36 percent were committed to the employer, and 12 percent were committed to neither. Union commitment was related to perceived

---

[31] P. A. Roby, "Becoming Shop Stewards: Perspectives on Gender and Race in Ten Trade Unions," *Labor Studies Journal* 20, no. 3 (1995), pp. 65–82.

[32] Y. Fried and R. B. Tiegs, "The Main Effect Model versus Buffering Model of Shop Steward Social Support: A Study of Rank-and-File Auto Workers in the U.S.A.," *Journal of Organizational Behavior* 14 (1993), pp. 481–94.

[33] G. S. Lowe and H. C. Northcott, "Stressful Working Conditions and Union Dissatisfaction," *Relations Industrielles* 50 (1995), pp. 420–42.

[34] P. A. Simpson, "A Preliminary Investigation of Determinants of Local Union Steward Power," *Labor Studies Journal* 18, no. 2 (1993), pp. 51–68.

[35] J. E. Martin and R. D. Berthiaume, "Stress and the Union Steward's Role," *Journal of Organizational Behavior* 14 (1993), pp. 433–46.

[36] J. W. Thacker and M. W. Fields, "An Evaluation of Steward Training," *Proceedings of the Industrial Relations Research Association* 44 (1992), pp. 432–39.

[37] D. P. Skarlicki and G. P. Latham, "Increasing Citizenship Behavior Within a Labor Union: A Test of Organizational Justice Theory," *Journal of Applied Psychology* 81 (1996), pp. 161–69.

immobility, belief that the union should use grievances to punish the employer, involvement in union activities and decision making, and employment in larger establishments. Unilateral commitment to the union was predicted by low economic outcomes, perceived involvement in the union, and lack of support from the employer.

Commitment to the employer was predicted by tenure; perceptions of immobility, supervisor support, promotion opportunities, and influence on the employer; and employment in smaller establishments.

Almost 30 percent were committed to the union and the employer simultaneously. Dual commitment was related to stewards' positive perceptions about the employer's supervisors, the promotional opportunities, and the union's influence on the employer; positive beliefs about the union's decision-making process; perceptions of low job opportunities with other employers; and beliefs that the grievance procedure is not a tool to punish supervisors. High dual commitment was predicted by involvement in union decision making, perceived immobility and influence on the employer, being a woman, and being unskilled.[38]

Local Officers

Local officers are elected by the members. In single bargaining unit locals, election issues are often strongly related to collective bargaining issues. Dissatisfaction with recent contract negotiation outcomes is related to election of insurgent candidate slates. Union politics are more complicated when the local negotiates several contracts. One situation might occur where the local has separate contracts for several occupational groups within the same employer. This is more likely to occur under Railway Labor Act jurisdictions because the act requires bargaining units based on occupation. The dominant occupation in the unit is likely to have the greatest effect on the election of officers. However, where a majority is required for election and no single group constitutes a majority, coalitions will develop depending on their perceptions of how local officers are achieving outcomes. Labor relations become more difficult in this environment as officers need to accomplish increasingly better outcomes to remain in power. Exhibit 5–1 details some of the political issues involved in leadership changes in the Machinist union unit that simultaneously represents mechanics, clerks, and baggage handlers at Northwest Airlines.

Another situation might occur with the local union that has contracts with several employers. As in the single employer situation, if the employees of one employer constitute a majority, they are likely to be able to elect officers from their group. On the other hand, if there are a number of bargaining units, to avoid the possibility of shifting coalitions, union officers would probably attempt to negotiate a multiemployer agreement to reduce internal political pressures (among other reasons). (Multiemployer bargaining will be covered in Chapter 8.)

---

[38] J. E. Martin, J. M. Magenau, and M. F. Peterson, "Variables Related to Patterns of Union Stewards' Commitment," *Journal of Labor Research* 7 (1986), pp. 323–36.

EXHIBIT 5–1

Northwest Airlines Machinist Unit Leadership Changes

. . . Predictably, [Tom] Pedersen has become a favorite punching bag for those who believe the [IAM] didn't do enough to keep their paychecks from getting smaller. The average machinist took an 11 percent pay cut in exchange for [Northwest Airlines] stock.

The concessions episode did little to mend political divisions that remain from Pedersen's first presidential bid, when he defeated incumbent Guy Cook in 1991.

. . . He's been branded a weak leader by critics, who fondly recall the strong presence of Cook. Cook returned to his job as a baggage handler after the last election.

. . . Beyond personalities, some question whether the IAM has become too much like a business partner in its approach to Northwest Airlines.

. . . Sentiment is strongest among the mechanics, who are the highest paid of the 23,000 Northwest workers represented by the IAM. The union also represents Northwest sales agents, ground service workers, clerks and cleaners . . .

. . . Northwest played hardball with unions, threatening Chapter 11 bankruptcy if workers didn't sign on for the majority of the $886 million concession tab.

The IAM had to try two times to get a concessions pact OK'd by the rank and file. Pedersen and other union leaders found themselves in the unenviable position of having to convince members that Northwest meant business with its bankruptcy threat.

Pedersen didn't carry the Twin Cities local when he beat Cook by less than 400 votes in 1991. His support is considered strong at Alaska Airlines, and among non-mechanics at the nearly 50 locals outside the Twin Cities.

He continues to tussle with rivals here, and he faces fifth-degree assault charges related to an incident in the union offices last summer . . . [in which he is accused of] twice shov[ing] a [union] member into a wall during an argument in union offices.

[Pedersen subsequently lost the election.]

SOURCE: D. Iverson, "The Post-Concessions Election," *St. Paul Pioneer Press,* March 21, 1994, pp. 1B–2B.

Differences also exist between occupational categories. Members with lower skills often form a majority. If they dominate the leadership and the negotiating committee, then the interests of skilled employees may not be addressed thoroughly. This creates internal pressure and may lead to tensions in the administration of the bargaining agreement (see **fractional bargaining** in Chapter 14). Education and expertise are valuable in enabling more effective accomplishment of leadership roles.[39] Thus, skilled employees may be overrepresented among the leadership relative to their numbers in the local if they pay attention to the bargaining interests of the majority.

Women and Minorities
In addition to potential differences among employees in different bargaining units, identifiable subgroups within a local may also have interests in officer positions

---

[39] See G. Strauss, "Union Democracy," in G. Strauss, D. G. Gallagher, and J. Fiorito, eds., *The State of the Unions* (Madison, WI: Industrial Relations Research Association, 1991), pp. 201–36.

and influence election results. It was noted that African-Americans participate at equivalent rates in local activities.[40] Chapter 6 will note minority group members are more interested in and likely to vote for representation. However, if they are a minority in a local union, they may be underrepresented in officer positions if elections are on an at-large basis.

A study of Massachusetts local unions found women to be represented in officer positions at about the same rate as their proportion in the overall membership, but they were underrepresented as presidents or members of negotiation committees.[41] To the extent the negotiation committee influences the types of grievances pursued and decides the issues of greatest importance in contract negotiations, concerns of women may not receive a degree of attention commensurate with their numbers in the local.[42]

Officer Commitment to the Labor Movement

Commitment is an important issue for higher-level local union officers. While generally granted leaves of absence from work in larger units, they still remain attached to their employers and also bear responsibility to their national unions as well as their local memberships. Local officers are committed strongly to the labor movement, but are less positive about the fairness of national union elections than they are about local elections. They are willing to advocate issues favored by their national union, but they are more closely wedded to the traditional goals of the labor movement than to new approaches.[43]

NATIONAL UNIONS AND THEIR ENVIRONMENT

National unions are particularly interested in the environment for organizing, including the laws and regulations governing permissible activities of unions and employers, employment law applying generally to workplaces and the administration and enforcement of those laws, and the state of the economy and the effect it has on the organizing and bargaining power of unions. One of the major vehicles for influencing all of these areas is political action, including lobbying, financial support for candidates, and assistance in election campaigns.

Employment Law and Administration

Since the founding of the American Federation of Labor, the union movement in the United States has consistently taken a business-oriented approach. As noted in

---

[40] Hoyman and Stallworth, "Participation in Local Unions."

[41] D. Melcher, J. L. Eichstedt, S. Eriksen, and D. Clawson, "Women's Participation in Local Union Leadership: The Massachusetts Experience," *Industrial and Labor Relations Review* 45 (1992), pp. 267–80.

[42] See also A. H. Cook, "Women and Minorities," in G. Strauss, D. G. Gallagher, and J. Fiorito, eds., *The State of the Unions* (Madison, WI: Industrial Relations Research Association, 1991), pp. 237–58.

[43] M. F. Masters, R. S. Atkin, and G. Schoenfeld, "A Survey of USWA Local Officers' Commitment-Support Attitudes," *Labor Studies Journal* 15, no. 3 (1990), pp. 51–80.

Chapter 1, its primary objectives have been to enhance the economic outcomes of its members and to create and maintain a mechanism for redressing grievances in the workplace.

The historic bargain between labor and management and the resulting laws and regulations have basically created a system in which unions have agreed to allow employers to make innovations in production while working to enhance economic outcomes of represented employees.[44] From a regulatory perspective, this means unions have been interested in creating an environment that facilitates the collectivization of labor to accomplish workplace goals. It has not intruded on the property rights of owners and managers (and would be vigorously opposed by management if it did so).

Representation and Bargaining Rules

Unions support legislation and regulations facilitating representation and bargaining. Clearly, the Norris-LaGuardia and Wagner acts helped to accomplish this. Establishment of the National Labor Relations Board (NLRB) created an agency for interpreting labor law and provided a forum for disputes where unions saw employers as unfairly interfering with employee rights to organize and bargain.

National unions feel frustrated by inconsistency in the NLRB's interpretation of labor law and delays involved in the election process and hearing unfair labor practice charges. In addition, employer threats to hire strikebreakers when impasses are reached in contract negotiations (see Chapter 12), are viewed by unions as interfering with worker rights to engage in protected concerted activity. Legislation was introduced but not enacted to prohibit the use of strike replacements. Most Canadian provinces prohibit employment of strike replacements. Exhibit 5–2 portrays the union movement's frustration with the enforcement of collective bargaining legislation.

Regulating Employer Decisions in the Workplace

Employers make hiring decisions without union intervention except when the union supplies workers, as in the building trades. Unions have traditionally favored civil rights legislation, requiring employers to make employment decisions without regard to race, gender, age, and national origin. At the same time, tensions may occur within national unions as the composition of the workforce changes. The leadership of national unions and the AFL–CIO tends to reflect the majority of members within each of the unions, but not the proportion of members in various subgroups. For example, except in women-dominated unions, there are no women national union presidents; except in unions dominated by racial minorities, there are no minority presidents. Exhibit 5–3 is an indication of problems underrepresented groups feel they encounter.

---

[44] D. Brody, "Labor's Crisis in Historical Perspective," in G. Strauss, D. G. Gallagher, and J. Fiorito, eds., *The State of the Unions* (Madison, WI: Industrial Relations Research Association, 1991), pp. 277–312.

EXHIBIT 5–2

Union Frustration with Labor Law Enforcement

The last time labor law reform was a serious possibility, Jimmy Carter was President . . . In 1978, labor law reform legislation died by the slimmest of margins. The very notion of reform was laughable during the 80's, a period during which most unionists came to regard not losing too much ground as a victory.

. . . A month ago, at a demonstration at the headquarters of the [NLRB] in Washington, two dozen people, including Jesse Jackson and several labor leaders and activists, were arrested. Two weeks ago, 10,000 members of some 30 unions held simultaneous demonstrations in 10 cities across the country, according to the demonstrations' organizers.

The unions contend that 1 worker in 10 is fired for organizing and that it takes two years for the board to rule on illegal firings. The NLRB pegs the number at closer to 1 in 60. It acknowledges that a complaint can take years or more to adjudicate fully but that most are taken care of early in the process . . . "Cases can get complicated and elaborate," said David Parker, an NLRB spokesman. "It's not like Judge Wapner. You don't have a commercial break and then the judge renders a decision."

Unions argue that companies manipulate the NLRB process. Even when workers get their jobs back, unions say, potential members are frightened off. "Nobody knows what workers go through in campaigns," said Peter Goldberger, assistant director of organizing at the Amalgamated Clothing and Textile Workers Union, one of the unions sponsoring the recent demonstration. "Corporations break the law and the Government's response is totally inadequate."

SOURCE: B. P. Noble, "Unions Call Out Their Troops," *New York Times,* June 6, 1993, section 3, p. 25.

Unions have also strongly favored legislation regulating health and safety conditions, worker compensation for injuries incurred in the line of work, and unemployment insurance to compensate employees when they are involuntarily laid off. Extension of these laws to all employers somewhat removes their cost from competition between employers. While differences exist in costs between industries, reduction of costs within employers for worker compensation and unemployment insurance would result primarily from reductions in injuries and layoffs.

The Economy

As noted in Chapter 2, the state of the economy has historically influenced union outcomes. With the exception of the Great Depression, unions have traditionally had difficulty during economic downturns. Organizing has depended on the ability of unions to demonstrate to potential members that it would be to their economic advantage to organize. As Chapter 9 will note, substantial evidence exists that unionization affects wages positively, but the radical restructuring that has occurred in the contemporary economy has reduced beliefs about its long-run ability to enhance job security.

EXHIBIT 5–3

Problems of Underrepresentation in the Union Leadership

Although the ranks of women in the nation's trade unions have more than doubled in recent decades, organized labor's national leadership ranks remain largely the political preserve of white males.

A new study by the International Labor Organization, an arm of the United Nations, shows that while women now account for 37 percent of all trade union members in the United States, only two of the 95 unions in the AFL–CIO have women presidents, and that the number of women in top national leadership positions has increased very little in the last decade.

. . . At the local and regional levels, women are taking more of a leadership role, according to the study. But even here, it said, the numbers are deceiving because the leadership jobs women are filling "are not at the center of union activities, such as bargaining and grievances."

"Unions are reflecting the problems of women in the workplace," said the study's author, Susan C. Eaton, who examined the role of women in trade unions in both the United States and Canada . . . "I see this as a big lost opportunity for the unions," she said.

. . . 14.8 percent of all working women in the United States are union members, while 21.3 percent of the men belong to unions. In the past decade, however, overall trade union membership has been a relatively static 20 million.

As a result, Eaton said, U.S. unions need to begin paying attention to the voices of the growing numbers of women in their ranks, if for no other reason than to guarantee the survival of the trade union movement.

"Unions have to take on some of these nontraditional issues to make themselves more attractive to women," Eaton said.

SOURCE: F. Swoboda, "Women Aspiring to Union Leadership Roles Find Limits There Too," *Washington Post*, February 14, 1993, section M, p. 2.

To secure economic gains, either employee productivity must increase faster than wages and competitive labor costs, or employers must be able to pass labor cost increases on to consumers. With the advent of global competition, the latter is becoming increasingly difficult. Industries in which the largest wage premiums exist relative to productivity are potentially the most vulnerable. In addition, if workers in other locations (or countries) can immediately be made more productive by investing in more modern equipment that costs less than the future costs of expected union wages, then rational employers will do so as long as free trade is available.

NAFTA and Organized Labor

Canada, Mexico, and the United States ratified the North American Free Trade Agreement (NAFTA) in 1993, substantially reducing tariffs on imports between these nations. The basic notion driving the treaty is that the populace in each country will see an increase in its welfare as a result of lower prices for goods and services. In turn, the country of origin of these goods and services will see its

EXHIBIT 5–4

Labor's Position on NAFTA

Leaders of American labor unions, who are [in San Francisco] to set goals for the next two years, say that nothing—not health care, not the long erosion of blue-collar wages, not even the Reagan and Bush Presidencies—has stirred worker passions as has the proposed North American Free Trade Agreement.

The prospect of deregulated trade with Mexico so angers some unions that they are vowing to take the unusual step of making the vote of a member of Congress on the agreement a single-issue test of loyalty to labor. The unions say they will use their money and skills to drive from office those who support the agreement.

"We see this as a life-and-death issue," said Jay Mazur, president of the Ladies Garment Workers' Union. "We won't support people who vote for NAFTA."

William H. Bywater, president of the electrical workers and organized labor's most outspoken foe of the agreement, said "We're going to go out and defeat every congressman who votes for NAFTA."

Leaders of the big teamsters and machinists unions are saying much the same. George J. Kourpias, president of the machinists union, said he had not yet issued ultimatums against lawmakers who vote for NAFTA. "But," he added, "I can tell you, we will get no requests from our members back home to support them. They're steamed up about this." George Poulin, a machinists vice president in the Northeast who is also here, said: "Knock them off. That's our position."

SOURCE: P. T. Kilborn, "Unions Gird for War over Trade Pact," *New York Times,* October 4, 1993, p. A14.

output receive the highest approval through consumer purchases. To the extent that cost is a consideration in consumer decisions, competition between producers in different countries will put pressure on labor costs and wages.

NAFTA was negotiated by representatives of the three nations during the Bush administration and placed on a "fast-track" process before President Bush left office. Both President Salinas of Mexico and Prime Minister Mulroney of Canada, who earlier had secured passage of a joint U.S.-Canadian pact, were strong supporters of NAFTA.

Organized labor strongly opposed NAFTA and campaigned against President Bush, although Clinton also supported NAFTA during the 1992 campaign and was to do so after his inauguration. The congressional vote in late summer 1993 was very close, with labor indicating that votes on the treaty would be considered "a litmus test" for continued labor endorsement and support. The political risks were great since Prime Minister Mulroney had resigned and the Conservative party was overwhelmingly defeated in Canadian elections, but NAFTA had been ratified. Labor's position is reflected in Exhibit 5–4.

Labor's opposition to NAFTA was grounded in its objections to a perceived lack of environmental and employment safeguards in Mexico. Concerns were raised that a country's competitive advantage could be gained through lower costs

EXHIBIT 5–5

UAW Leaders Call on GM to Treat Mexican Workers Fairly

In the wake of a strike in June by Mexican autoworkers at four General Motors Delco plants in Reynosa, Tamaulipas, Mexico, in which it was reported that plant guards mistreated workers and reporters, and workers were fired or pressured to resign, UAW leaders have strongly urged GM to behave more responsibly towards its Mexican workforce.

In a letter sent on Wednesday to GM Chairman Jack Smith, UAW President Stephen P. Yokich and Vice President Richard Shoemaker stated, "The treatment of GM workers in Reynosa, and in all GM facilities in Mexico, is an important issue for us and for all UAW-GM workers."

The four Reynosa plants are part of a large and growing GM presence in Mexico which totals about 70,000 workers. According to reports from the Coalition for Justice in the Maquiladoras, the strike occurred at four Delco plants on June 11 and 12 over the inadequacy of a profit sharing payment to the workers which amounted to about $30.

"The situation in Reynosa reflects the situation throughout much of Mexico: economic hardship and reduced buying power for Mexican workers contribute to lower labor costs and higher profits for multinational corporations operating there," Yokich and Shoemaker continued.

The UAW leaders pointed out that, "As a major Mexican employer, GM benefits substantially from the policies that have produced this result. The announced revised profit sharing payment of 350 pesos (about $44) and the 250 pesos food coupon bonus (worth about $32) do not come close to making up for the advantage GM derives from the low level of wages in Reynosa."

"The UAW believes that GM must behave responsibly toward its Mexican workers and compensate them fairly," Yokich and Shoemaker stated, concluding, "We will speak out strongly and support Mexican workers whenever GM fails to meet this test."

SOURCE: http://www.uaw.org/publications/releases/1997/mexico_ys.html

---

resulting from a reduced need to attend to worker welfare and implementation of pollution controls. Fears regarding the abilities of workers to unionize and to gain voice power in the workplace were also expressed (see Exhibit 5–5).

A more fundamental concern had to do with the large gaps between U.S. and Canadian wages on the one hand and Mexican wages on the other. In 1990, using the United States as a base, Mexican hourly manufacturing compensation costs were only 12.5 percent of U.S. wages, while Canadian wages were 7.5 percent above.[45] In labor-intensive industries, labor saw the substantial wage premium earned by U.S. and Canadian workers as likely to lead to the wholesale movement of jobs to Mexico. Thus, NAFTA put wages back into competition in industrial

---

[45] U.S. Department of Labor, Bureau of Labor Statistics, *International Comparisons of Hourly Compensation Costs for Production Workers in Manufacturing,* Report 803 (Washington, DC: U.S. Government Printing Office, 1991).

sectors where substantial success had been achieved in reducing differentials between employers.[46]

Political Action

Political action takes four basic forms: (1) financial support from **political action committees** (PACS) to candidates favoring union positions, (2) volunteer work by union members in campaigns, (3) endorsement of candidates and get-out-the-vote efforts, and (4) lobbying. Labor has been involved increasingly in political activity since the AFL and CIO merged.[47] Although political action has increased, it will be noted later that labor's success in mobilizing voting for endorsed candidates has recently been lower. Given the increase in single-issue politics, labor's position is weakened by a variety of internal factions organized around these issues.[48] However, political action by public-sector unions, particularly at the state and local level, has been effective. Evidence indicates that the degree of political activity of public-sector unions is positively related to public-sector salary levels and the number of public employment jobs.[49]

Financial Support for Candidates

Union Characteristics.   Union political action efforts involve choices about how to best deploy resources. National union political activities increased markedly in the 1980s, particularly among unions representing public employers and those in which executive boards are democratically chosen.[50] One study found medium-sized unions spend more per capita on political action than smaller or larger unions, and spending increases as dues increase. The proportion of women in a national is also related to political activity expenditures, although evidence suggests there is less political activity than members desire.[51] Table 5–1 shows total and per capita PAC expenditures of a variety of national unions over the past several years. In general, contributions are around $1 per member with a small number of notable exceptions. Local union officers contribute substantially more,

---

[46] For positions of proponents and opponents of the treaty, and an appraisal of likely effects, see M. F. Bognanno and K. J. Ready, eds., *The North American Free Trade Agreement: Labor, Industry, and Government Perspectives* (Westport, CT: Praeger, 1993).

[47] For a detailed summary of activities and research on union political action, see J. T. Delaney and M. F. Masters, "Unions and Political Action," in G. Strauss, D. G. Gallagher, and J. Fiorito, eds., *The State of the Unions* (Madison, WI: Industrial Relations Research Association, 1991), pp. 313–46.

[48] J. T. Delaney, "The Future of Unions as Political Organizations," *Journal of Labor Research* 12 (1991), pp. 373–87.

[49] K. M. O'Brien, "Compensation, Employment, and the Political Activity of Public Employee Unions," *Journal of Labor Research* 13 (1992), pp. 189–203.

[50] M. F. Masters and J. T. Delaney, "The Causes of Union Political Involvement," *Journal of Labor Research* 6 (1985), pp. 341–62.

[51] J. T. Delaney, J. Fiorito, and M. F. Masters, "The Effects of Union Organizational and Environmental Characteristics on Union Political Action," *American Journal of Political Science* 32 (1988), pp. 616–42.

TABLE 5–1

Top Union PAC Contributions, 1978–1982

Union	1978	1980	1982	Per Member (1982)
		(in $000s)		
Auto Workers	$1,165	$1,492	$1,699	$ 1.25
AFL–CIO	1,979	997	1,151	—
Marine Engineers	759	1,033	1,150	47.94
Steelworkers	600	601	715	0.58
Transportation Workers	559	582	556	2.93
Machinists	545	861	1,445	1.92
Communications Workers	471	437	643	1.17
National Education Association	450	406	1,273	0.76
Seafarers	414	689	851	10.61
Food and Commercial Workers	398	575	736	0.56
Railway Clerks	319	376	539	3.00
Carpenters	316	567	680	0.87
Ladies Garment Workers	283	480	618	1.92
Teamsters	278	310	403	0.21
AFSCME	273	371	643	0.59
Laborers	252	396	304	0.50
Operating Engineers	235	436	862	2.04
Airline Pilots	222	294	282	4.78
Hotel and Restaurant Employees	184	158	149	0.37
Electrical Workers	157	252	443	0.42
Teachers	146	205	335	0.61

SOURCE: J. T. Delaney and M. F. Masters, "Unions and Political Action," in *The State of the Unions,* ed. G. Strauss, D. G. Gallagher, and J. Fiorito (Madison, WI: Industrial Relations Research Association, 1991), p. 323.

with donations from officers with longer tenure, more education, higher income, greater willingness to support the union, and residence in a state with no right-to-work law predicting the magnitude.[52]

Candidate Characteristics.   Union PAC contributions are not evenly distributed across candidates, even when endorsements are taken into account. One factor that strongly influences the level of support is the committee assignment of congress members. Those who serve on congressional committees with jurisdiction over labor matters receive higher union PAC contributions.[53]

---

[52] M. F. Masters and R. S. Atkin, "Local Union Officers' Donations to a Political Action Committee," *Relations Industrielles* 51 (1996), pp. 40–61.

[53] J. W. Endersby and M. C. Munger, "The Impact of Legislator Attributes on Union PAC Campaign Contributions," *Journal of Labor Research* 13 (1992), pp. 79–97.

PACs were important vehicles for providing financial support to campaigns of candidates friendly to labor. The receipt of PAC contributions by a candidate who subsequently is elected or reelected is related directly to roll-call voting records and indirectly to the number of candidates elected.[54] PACs do not, however, give contributions to all who support their causes. Contributions appear to depend on the willingness of the organization to give, the compatibility of the candidate's ideology with that of the contributing PAC, the probability of the candidate's winning (with more money given when the race is close), and the magnitude of the vote margin an incumbent candidate had in the last election.[55] Contributions also appear related to an incumbent's committee assignment to interests of labor, voting record, and electoral security.[56]

Endorsements and Get-Out-the-Vote Drives

Political endorsements and get-out-the-vote campaigns have some value. Union members are more likely to vote in general elections than nonmembers (or their own family members), and they vote for endorsed candidates about 15 to 20 percent more often than nonmembers. But members do not vote more often in primaries, and about 50 percent split their votes between endorsed and unendorsed candidates.[57] Table 5–2 details voting and political activity of union and nonunion members from 1952 through 1986. The table indicates that union members are significantly more active than nonmembers in both presidential election years and off-year elections, with higher votes in 14 of 16 elections, and more participation in 13 of 16.

The AFL–CIO **Committee on Political Education** (COPE) endorses candidates for congressional elections. COPE does not endorse a candidate in every contest, but since 1980 it has endorsed the majority of all candidates who were elected. A larger proportion of candidates for the House of Representatives was elected than for the Senate.[58]

Union members are more likely than nonmembers to vote for candidates of the Democratic party. Table 5–3 shows that differences are greater for presidential candidates than for members of Congress. Note how they vary depending on the election in question.

---

[54] G. M. Saltzman, "Congressional Voting on Labor Issues: The Role of PACs," *Industrial and Labor Relations Review* 40 (1987), pp. 163–79.

[55] A. Wilhite and J. Theilmann, "Unions, Corporations, and Political Campaign Contributions: The 1982 House Elections," *Journal of Labor Research* 7 (1986), pp. 175–86.

[56] K. B. Grier and M. C. Munger, "The Impact of Legislator Attributes on Interest-Group Campaign Contributions," *Journal of Labor Research* 7 (1986), pp. 349–59.

[57] J. T. Delaney, M. F. Masters, and S. Schwochau, "Unionism and Voter Turnout," *Journal of Labor Research* 9 (1988), pp. 221–36; and J. T. Delaney, M. F. Masters, and S. Schwochau, "Union Membership and Voting for COPE-Endorsed Candidates," *Industrial and Labor Relations Review* 43 (1990), pp. 621–35.

[58] Delaney and Masters, "Unions and Political Action."

TABLE 5–2

Voter Turnout and Electoral Participation by Union Status, 1952–1986

Year	Voter Turnout (%)†*		Participation Index†*	
	Union	Nonunion	Union	Nonunion
1952	76.3	73.0	9	3
1954	—	—	—	—
1956	75.8	71.9	19	9
1958	61.0	56.5	−17	−28
1960	76.9	80.2	23	25
1962	—	—	—	—
1964	82.8	76.1	27	18
1966	62.8	62.2	−9	−12
1968	76.1	75.8	21	17
1970	59.7	59.3	−9	−7
1972	75.3	72.1	17	13
1974	49.6	53.6	−26	−23
1976	77.4	70.0	25	16
1978	56.9	53.9	−8	−14
1980	74.6	70.6	20	12
1982	65.0	59.2	0	−10
1984	78.7	72.3	24	14
1986	55.0	51.9	−13	−18

* Voter turnout is measured as the percentage of respondents in each union-status category who indicated that they had voted in the election.

† The electoral participation index takes voting and five other political activities into account, such as wearing a political button or suggesting how others should vote. The measure is calculated as the percentage of respondents who voted *and* participated in at least one other way minus the percentage who *did not* vote *and did not* participate in any other way. This measure can range between −100 and 100. As the index number increases, electoral participation is greater.

SOURCE: J. T. Delaney and M. F. Masters, "Unions and Political Action," in *The State of the Unions,* ed. G. Strauss, D. G. Gallagher, and J. Fiorito (Madison, WI: Industrial Relations Research Association, 1991), p. 331, as tabled from W. E. Miller and S. A. Traugott, *American National Election Studies Data Sourcebook, 1952–1986* (Cambridge: Harvard University Press (1989), pp. 305, 309.

Lobbying

The AFL–CIO takes political positions on issues of importance to the employment of its members. Business groups such as the Chamber of Commerce also take positions on these issues. Other politically oriented organizations such as the American Conservative Union and the Americans for Democratic Action (ADA) establish comprehensive agendas on a wide range of issues. In general, the AFL–CIO and Chamber of Commerce line up on opposite sides of employment-related issues except for interests in trade reform. Without the advocacy of the AFL–CIO, many issues such as civil rights in employment, worker safety,

TABLE 5–3
Democratic Share of the Vote by Union Status, 1948–1986

	Presidential Vote		Congressional Vote	
Year	Union	Nonunion	Union	Nonunion
1948	80	44	—	
1952	56	36	61	44
1954	—	—	65	49
1956	53	36	62	49
1958	—	—	78	55
1960	64	44	69	51
1962	—	—	—	—
1964	83	62	80	59
1966	—	—	68	53
1968	56	43	58	50
1970	—	—	63	52
1972	46	33	62	53
1974	—	—	71	59
1976	64	47	72	52
1978	—	—	70	54
1980	55	40	65	51
1982	—	—	70	54
1984	57	37	62	53
1986	—	—	64	59

SOURCE: J. T. Delaney and M. F. Masters, "Unions and Political Action," in *The State of the Unions,* ed. G. Strauss, D. G. Gallagher, and J. Fiorito (Madison, WI: Industrial Relations Research Association, 1991), p. 332.

collective bargaining rights, and the like would be unsupported by parties interested in employment.[59]

Effectiveness of Activities

While unions are heavily involved in PAC activities, the attitudes of union members are not monolithic and, in most cases, seem less liberal than the positions taken by their unions' PACs. PACs appear to be more successful in influencing legislation in peripheral areas (e.g., education) than in central areas of interest to labor (e.g., labor law reform).[60] However, a recent study found that PAC contributions are related to votes for COPE-oriented legislation. This study found

---

[59] For a comprehensive examination of these and other political representation issues, see J. Delaney and S. Schwochau, "Employee Representation through the Political Process," in B. E. Kaufman and M. M. Kleiner, eds., *Employee Representation: Alternatives and Future Directions* (Madison, WI: Industrial Relations Research Association, 1993), pp. 265–304.

[60] M. F. Masters and J. T. Delaney, "Union Political Activities: A Review of the Empirical Literature," *Industrial and Labor Relations Review* 40 (1987), pp. 336–53.

other factors positively influencing pro-labor votes, including the percent of the U.S. labor force that is unionized and the ADA rating of the U.S. senator. Negative factors included corporate PAC donations to the incumbent's election opponent, the percent of the populace voting Republican in the most recent presidential election, the proportion of women in the labor force, and being a Republican senator. Over time increasing PAC contributions have more than offset the effect of the loss of union membership in influencing votes on legislation.[61]

Another point to consider, besides labor's ability to deliver its members, is the number of members labor has. Assume an electorate of 100 million potential voters. In the mid-1950s, labor constituted one-third of the labor force while it presently represents no more than 15 percent. Assume two-thirds of voters are members of the labor force. Assume further that three-quarters of union members vote, while only 60 percent of the electorate does so. Assume finally that two-thirds of union members vote Democratic and one-third vote Republican while the remaining voters split 54–46 Republican.

Of the electorate, about 66.7 million are in the labor force. When labor represents a third, about 22.2 million are members. Of these, three-quarters, or 16.7 million vote; with 11.1 million voting Democratic and 5.6 million voting Republican. There are 77.8 million more potential voters, of whom 60 percent, or 46.7 million vote. Of these, 54 percent or 25.2 million vote Republican and 46 percent or 21.5 million vote Democratic. The Democratic majority is 32.6 million to 30.8 million.

With labor dropping to 15 percent of the labor force, it would represent 10 million members. Of these, 7.5 million vote, with 5.0 million voting Democratic and 2.5 million voting Republican. Of the other 90 million potential voters, 60 percent, or 54 million, vote. If 54 percent or 29.2 million vote Republican and 46 percent or 24.8 million vote Democratic, the Republicans win a majority of 31.7 million to 29.8 million.

Thus, union membership levels are critical to the ability of organized labor to gain attention for their agenda from politicians. Even if labor can deliver the same share of the vote as it has in the past, the absolute numbers have fallen substantially.

FUTURE UNIONS

A good deal of pessimism has been expressed about the health of the labor movement. Union membership has been in decline for over 30 years. In addition to changes in industrial concentration and occupational mix, other factors also have influenced the drop-off. Enforcement of laws and regulations supporting

---

[61] W. J. Moore, D. R. Chachere, T. D. Curtis, and D. Gordon, "The Political Influence of Unions and Corporations on COPE Votes in the U.S. Senate, 1979–1988," *Journal of Labor Research* 16 (1995), pp. 203–21.

collective bargaining as the preferred method for handling industrial disputes has become increasingly lax, reducing the ability of unions to organize and employees to secure their rights to bargain.[62] It has also been argued that nonunion employees are now as satisfied with their job outcomes as their unionized counterparts. Thus, the demand for unions has decreased, and membership numbers reflect this phenomenon.[63]

One view of the present situation suggests that the bottom of the decline is near or over. Slower workforce growth, more gradual restructuring, tighter labor markets, and more efficient organizing by unions could stem the decline.[64] But, with increasingly freer trade and global competition, it seems unlikely that tighter labor markets will exist for many occupations, particularly those at lower skill levels.

Union leaders offer a negative assessment of the present state of the movement. Major problems are seen as related to the relatively narrow set of issues included in collective bargaining, the operation of the NLRB, decreasing member solidarity, and leaders who are out of touch with members' most important issues and the problems the labor movement is encountering.[65] For example, a recent survey of Carpenters Union members found that workers believed it was very important to implement technology in their jobs, but they did not perceive their union as being actively involved in technological issues. Older members, members with an interest in technology, and union meeting attendees had particularly strong interests.[66]

At the same time, there are areas of change. Unions are gaining support among unskilled workers for their ability to advocate "voice" issues and bring justice to the governance of the workplace. However, unions are losing support among skilled workers as employers increasingly involve them in decision-making processes.[67]

Chapter 1 noted that unions have been more successful where they have been able to engage the community in which their members live in seeing a

[62] P. C. Weiler, "Governing the Workplace: Employee Representation in the Eyes of the Law," in B. E. Kaufman and M. M. Kleiner, eds., *Employee Representation: Alternatives and Future Directions* (Madison, WI: Industrial Relations Research Association, 1993), pp. 81–104.

[63] H. S. Farber and A. B. Krueger, "Union Membership in the United States: The Decline Continues," in B. E. Kaufman and M. M. Kleiner, eds., *Employee Representation: Alternatives and Future Directions* (Madison, WI: Industrial Relations Research Association, 1993), pp. 105–34.

[64] C. McDonald, "U.S. Union Membership in Future Decades: A Trade Unionist's Perspective," *Industrial Relations* 31 (1992), pp. 13–30.

[65] M. H. Leroy, "State of the Unions: Assessment by Elite American Labor Leaders," *Journal of Labor Research* 13 (1992), pp. 371–79.

[66] W. Malakoff and D.-O. Kim, "Computerized Technology, Jobs and the Union's Role: The Views of Union Members in a Skilled Craft Industry," *Labor Studies Journal* 20, no. 4 (1996), pp. 3–20.

[67] J. D. Reid, Jr., "Future Unions," *Industrial Relations* 31 (1992), pp. 122–36; and T. A. Mahoney and M. R. Watson, "Evolving Modes of Work Force Governance: An Evaluation," in B. E. Kaufman and M. M. Kleiner, eds., *Employee Representation: Alternatives and Future Directions* (Madison, WI: Industrial Relations Research Association, 1993), pp. 135–68.

communality between union and community success. As we will note in Chapter 8, bargaining structures have tilted away from the national level and toward the local level as organizations find it easier to close plants, sell facilities, and move elsewhere. Where everyone's job is at risk, saving them becomes much more critical to the community. It's possible that a return to enterprise unionism with unaffiliated, or directly affiliated, locals may occur.

SUMMARY

Union attention through new member socialization leads to higher participation and commitment. Participation involves activities such as attending meetings; voting in union elections, strike authorizations, and contract ratifications; and being a union officer. Loyalty to the union, Marxist work beliefs, and the perceived leadership of the steward influence participation. Persons who participate at higher rates are less satisfied with intrinsic and extrinsic factors of their jobs.

Commitment to the union is predicted by many of the same factors as participation. Evidence exists that members can be simultaneously committed to their unions and their employers. Studies of stewards have found dual commitment to be high where there was a good working relationship with the employer, and the steward believed that his or her career was strongly linked to a present employer.

Women and minorities participate at the same rate in union activities as men and majority employees, but women are less likely to be found in high leadership positions.

National unions are strongly involved in political activity. While per capita support is relatively modest, legislators who are friendly to labor and on key committees likely to influence labor outcomes receive financial assistance. Since 1980, a majority of candidates elected to Congress have had AFL–CIO COPE endorsement. Union members vote at higher rates in general elections than the public at large. They also are more likely to vote for Democratic candidates.

DISCUSSION QUESTIONS

1. Do the predictors of union participation suggest that union leaders will likely be involved in an adversarial relationship with management?
2. How can the inclusion of women in top leadership positions in local and national unions be increased?
3. How do you reconcile the fact that a majority of those elected to Congress are endorsed by COPE and the failure of Congress to pass any significant labor law reform?
4. Since unions represent all employees in bargaining units they have organized, should they be allowed to endorse particular candidates for office?

KEY TERMS

Agency fee   *120*
Union shop   *120*
Free-riding   *121*
Dual commitment   *126*
Fractional bargaining   *130*

Political action committee (PAC)
  137
Committee on Political Education
  (COPE)   *139*

6

UNION ORGANIZING

CAMPAIGNS

*T*his chapter is the first of a two-chapter set examining union and management approaches to organizing. Chapter 6 will cover union organizing campaigns, the election process, and the role of the National Labor Relations Board (NLRB). Chapter 7 will cover employers' overall strategies with regard to unionization.

Recall from Chapter 2 the long history of employer resistance to organizing in the United States. The Wagner Act in the mid-1930s strongly facilitated and institutionalized collective bargaining as a method to represent worker interests and create governance mechanisms in the workplace for employees who preferred to use this method.

Recall also from the introductory chapters that employer representation in the workplace takes place only if a single union receives the votes of a majority of employees in the unit. The concept of **exclusive representation** establishes a "winner-take-all" outcome in representation elections. This requirement contributes to the creation of the adversarial relationship that exists between employers and unions beginning with the organizing campaign.

Union organizing is highly adversarial and heavily regulated. Most employers actively resist unionization. Union campaigns usually stress unfair treatment by employers and the necessity of employees to organize to gain outcomes that the employer should be able but is unwilling to grant without unionization. Organizing campaigns are intensive on both sides. The National Labor Relations Board (NLRB) or National Mediation Board (NMB) acts as a referee in the process. Where recognition disputes occur, the boards provide a forum for their settlement and rule on the permissibility of the parties' campaign conduct, if questioned. From a regulatory standpoint, this chapter will focus primarily on the NLRB's role since the preponderance of elections are conducted under its auspices. Employers covered by the NMB are mostly very large and already heavily unionized (with some notable exceptions like Southwest Airlines and some short-haul railroads).

Chapter 1 examined some of the reasons workers desire representation. This chapter examines the flow of organizing campaigns, involvement of the NLRB, strategies and tactics used by employers and unions during election campaigns, and recent results in NLRB-monitored representation elections. Chapter 7 focuses in detail on the increasing interest of employers in operating "union free" and the strategies and tactics associated with union avoidance outside the organizing campaigns themselves.

As you study this chapter, consider the following questions:

1. At what points and in what ways is the NLRB involved in representation elections?
2. What effects have employer campaigns had on union organizing success?
3. What common strategies and tactics do employers and unions use during organizing campaigns?
4. How successful are unions in organizing new units?

ORGANIZING AND UNION EFFECTIVENESS

It was noted in Chapter 1 that unions create an opportunity for employees to have a voice in addressing workplace deficiencies and also, through negotiated contracts, to effectively create a monopoly in supplying labor to the employer. This monopoly power generally confers a wage premium for unionized employees.

The ability to gain a wage premium depends to some extent on how much of an industry is organized. This means that unions have a strong interest in organizing workers in industries and labor markets where nonunion competition reduces their monopoly power.

Membership also determines the financial resources available to the union through the collections of dues. There are also economies of scale available through larger memberships. Thus, to some extent effectiveness is related to size. Organizing new units, accreting expanded facilities, and merging with or absorbing other unions, are all mechanisms used to expand membership and enhance union effectiveness. Strategies and tactics that increase the probability of success in organizing should lead to greater chances for effectiveness in bargaining and representation.

HOW ORGANIZING BEGINS

Campaigns to organize unrepresented workers begin at either the local or national level of a union. National union-organizing campaigns target specific employers and send professional organizers to encourage and assist local employees in unionizing. Sometimes organizers apply for jobs in the target firm to gain closer contact with employees. Employers may not legally refuse to hire applicants based on union membership or concurrent employment by a union even if their primary purpose is to attempt to organize the workforce.[1] National union campaigns often occur when a unionized firm opens a new nonunion plant. The union representing employees in the firm's other plants campaign to organize the new plant to maintain common employment practices across the organization. National organizing attempts may also target nonunion firms in predominantly unionized industries. Most organizing attempts begin at the local level when some employees decide they would be better off if they could bargain collectively with the employer.[2]

The campaign pits the union against the employer in terms of which party workers see as best able to develop and implement the employment practices they prefer. Figure 6–1 provides an overview of the sequence and actors involved in the process.

The Framework for Organizing

Union organizing begins with an authorization card campaign and ends with the NLRB's certification of the election results. Figure 6–2 presents a generalized sequence of the organizing events to be described in the following sections. This section will cover activities leading to a recognition request, petitions to the NLRB for elections, and elections in which bargaining unit determination is uncontested. Subsequent sections examine bargaining unit determination, the election campaign, and election certifications.

Authorization Card Campaign

An **authorization card** campaign tries to enroll as many employees as possible in the work unit the union seeks to represent. Organizers contact employees individually to try to convince them to sign cards authorizing the union to act as their agent in negotiating wages, hours, and terms and conditions of employment. Figure 6–3 provides an example of an authorization card.

Recognition Requests

If a majority of employees sign cards, the union can directly request the employer to recognize it as the bargaining agent. A union will not usually make a recognition request unless a substantial majority of employees sign authorization cards; the union prefers a large margin because employers often question the eligibility of some workers to be represented or to vote in the election. Employers faced with

---

[1] *NLRB* v. *Town & Country Electric Inc.*, Sup. Ct. 1995, 150 LRRM 2897. See also M. D. Lucas "Salting and Other Union Tactics: A Unionist's Perspective," *Journal of Labor Research* 18 (1997), pp. 55–64.

[2] For another detailed examination of organizing activities, see J. J. Lawler, "Union Organizing and Representation," in J. A. Fossum, ed., *Employee and Labor Relations*, SHRM-BNA Series, vol. 4 (Washington, DC: Bureau of National Affairs, 1990), pp. 4–134 to 4–179; and J. J. Lawler, *Unionization and Deunionization: Strategy, Tactics, and Outcomes* (Columbia: University of South Carolina Press, 1990).

FIGURE 6–1

Theoretical Model of the Certification Election Process

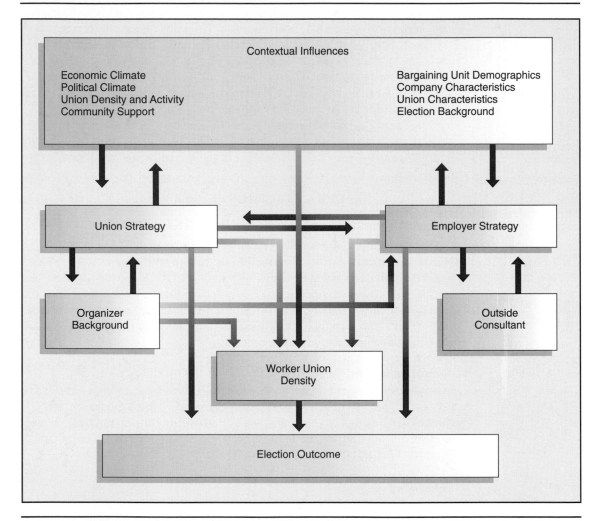

SOURCE: K. Bronfenbrenner, "The Role of Union Strategies in NLRB Certification Elections," *Industrial and Labor Relations Review* 50, p. 197.

a recognition request usually claim that the union's majority status is doubtful. The union may offer to have a neutral third party match the authorization card signatures with a list of employees to establish that a majority actually exists. If a majority has signed and the employer is satisfied with the appropriateness of the proposed bargaining unit, recognition can be granted voluntarily.[3]

_____

[3] See J. W. Budd and P. K. Heinz, "Union Representation Elections and Labor Law Reform: Lessons from the Minneapolis Hilton," *Labor Studies Journal* 20, no. 4 (1996), pp. 3–20 for an example of a situation in which the employer agreed ahead of time to a card check as an appropriate method for determining majority status.

FIGURE 6–2

Sequence of Organizing Events

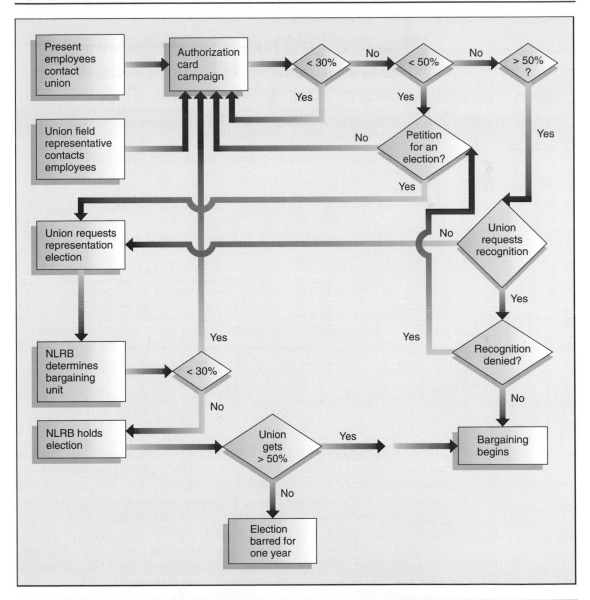

A union may picket an unorganized employer for up to 30 days, demanding that it be recognized as the employees' bargaining agent. If this occurs, the employer can petition the NLRB for an election in the employee unit the union seeks to represent. If the union loses, further **recognitional picketing** would be an unfair labor practice.

FIGURE 6–3
Authorization Card

YES, I WANT THE IAM

I, the undersigned employee of

(Company) _____

authorize the International Association of Machinists and Aerospace Workers (IAM) to act as my collective bargaining agent for wages, hours and working conditions. I agree that this card may be used either to support a demand for recognition or an NLRB election, at the discretion of the union.

Name (print) _____ Date _____

Home Address _____ Phone _____

City _____ State _____ Zip _____

Job Title _____ Dept. _____ Shift _____

Sign Here X _____

Note: This authorization to be SIGNED and DATED in Employee's own handwriting. YOUR RIGHT TO SIGN THIS CARD IS PROTECTED BY FEDERAL LAW.

RECEIVED BY (Initial) _____

Representation Elections

Representation elections are held to determine whether a majority of employees desires union representation, and if so, by which union. Elections in units where employees are not currently represented are called **certification elections.** If employees are currently represented, but at least 30 percent indicate they do not want continued representation, a **decertification election** is held. If a majority votes against representation, the union loses representation rights. So-called **raid elections** occur when at least 30 percent of employees indicate they would prefer a different union to represent them. Elections may not be held if an election result was certified within the previous year. Decertification elections may not be held while a contract is in effect. Figure 6–4 shows that if interest in an election is sufficient, the union (or the employer in the absence of a demand for recognition) can petition the NLRB to hold an election to determine the desires of the employees. This section will trace the basic steps involved.

Election Petitions

The union may petition the NLRB to hold a representation election in the unit it is trying to organize. It includes the signed authorization cards as evidence of

FIGURE 6–4

Avenues to Election Petitions

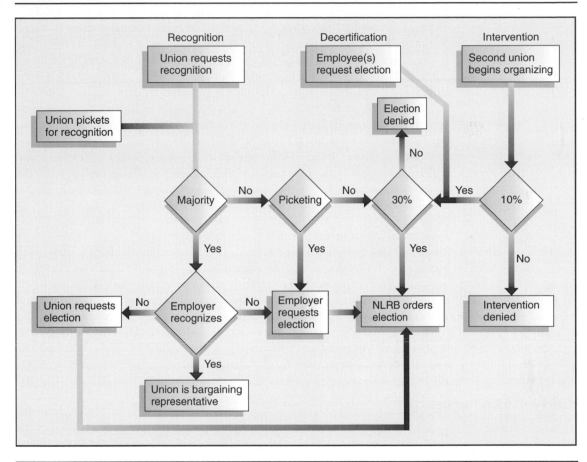

support. The NLRB checks the signed cards against a roster of employees in the work unit. If fewer than 30 percent have signed, the petition is dismissed for lack of sufficient interest. If more than 30 percent sign, the union is legally within its jurisdiction, and if the employer doesn't contest the appropriateness of the proposed bargaining unit, the NLRB schedules an election. The makeup of an **appropriate bargaining unit** is frequently contested by the employer, requiring the NLRB to decide which employees should be included. The criteria the board uses to determine the proposed unit's appropriateness are discussed later in this chapter.

When an appropriate bargaining unit is defined and at least 30 percent of employees in that unit have signed authorization cards, the NLRB will order an election unless the union withdraws its petition. If the union receives a majority of the eligible votes cast in the election, the board certifies it as the employees' bargaining agent and negotiations on a contract can begin. If the union loses, the board certifies the results, and representation elections in that unit are barred for one year. In effect, certification guarantees the union or nonunion status of a bargaining unit for a period of at least one year.[4]

An election petition may be filed by a labor organization, an employer, or an individual. In certain types of elections, however, employers are precluded from filing petitions because early petitions might preempt union campaign efforts. Proof of interest must be shown in a petition or within 48 hours. The union must specify the group of employees it desires to represent. If an employer has had a recognition demand from a union, it can directly petition the board to hold an election. A union or an employee (but not an employer) can file a decertification petition asking removal of the present bargaining agent. Under certain stringent conditions, an employer may petition for an election if it has evidence leading it to doubt the union's continued majority status.[5]

Preelection Board Involvement
There are two types of elections: (1) **consent elections,** in which the parties agree on the scope of the proposed bargaining unit and which employees will be eligible to vote; and (2) **board-directed (or petition) elections,** in which the NLRB **regional director** determines, after hearings, an appropriate bargaining unit and voter eligibility. In a petition election, the employer must provide within seven days a so-called *Excelsior* **list** containing names and addresses of employees in the proposed bargaining unit.[6] After 10 days but within 30 days, the election will normally be held. Figure 6–5 details board procedures before the election.

The Election
The NLRB supervises the secret ballot election. Company and union observers may challenge voter eligibility but not prohibit anyone from voting. Challenges are determined subsequent to the election. After the ballots are counted, the choice receiving a majority of votes cast is declared the winner. If more than two alternatives (e.g., two different unions and no union) are on the ballot and none obtains an absolute majority, a runoff will be held between the two highest choices. After any challenges are resolved, the regional director certifies the results. Figure 6–6 is an example of an NLRB election ballot.

BARGAINING UNIT DETERMINATION

The NLRB considers a variety of factors in bargaining unit determination including (1) legal constraints, (2) the constitutional jurisdiction of the organizing union,

---

[4] *Brooks* v. *NLRB*, 348 U.S. 96 (1954).

[5] C. Scott, K. Hester, and E. Arnold, "Employer-Initiated Elections, 1968–1992," *Journal of Labor Research* 18 (1997), pp. 315–31.

[6] *Excelsior Underwear, Inc.*, 156 NLRB 1236 (1966).

FIGURE 6–5

NLRB Involvement: Petition to Election

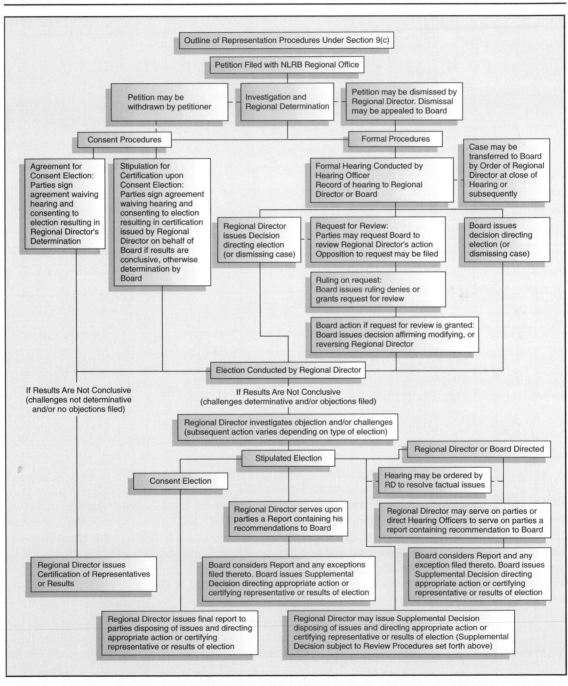

FIGURE 6–6
Specimen NLRB Ballot

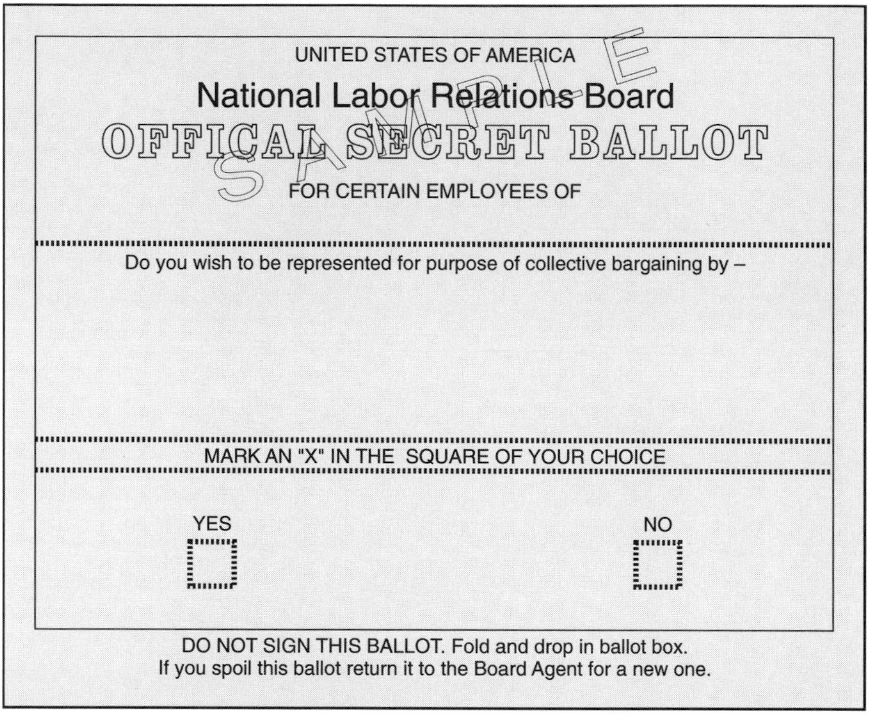

UNITED STATES OF AMERICA
National Labor Relations Board
OFFICAL SECRET BALLOT
FOR CERTAIN EMPLOYEES OF

Do you wish to be represented for purpose of collective bargaining by –

MARK AN "X" IN THE SQUARE OF YOUR CHOICE

YES   NO

DO NOT SIGN THIS BALLOT. Fold and drop in ballot box.
If you spoil this ballot return it to the Board Agent for a new one.

---

(3) the union's likely success in organizing and bargaining, (4) the employer's desires in resisting organizing or promoting stability in the bargaining relationship, and (5) its own philosophy.

Bargaining units can differ depending on whether the focus is on organizing or contract negotiations. For example, several retail stores in a given chain may constitute an appropriate bargaining unit for representation election purposes, while for negotiating purposes, several retail stores owned by different companies may practice **multiemployer bargaining.** The discussion in this chapter is concerned only with representation activities, while bargaining units for negotiations are discussed in Chapter 8.

Legal Constraints

Legal constraints limit the potential scope of a bargaining unit, but within these the contending parties—labor and management—are free to jointly determine an appropriate unit. If they do, a consent election results. If they don't, the NLRB is responsible for determining unit appropriateness.

Section 9(b) of the Taft-Hartley Act constrains unit determination. First, no unit can include both professional and nonprofessional employees without majority approval of the professionals. Second, a separate craft unit within an employer's operation may not be precluded from forming simply because the board had earlier included it in a broader group; however, this subsection has been broadly interpreted by the NLRB in continuing to include craft groups in larger units. Third, no bargaining unit may jointly consist of guards hired by employers to enforce the company's rules and other employees. Fourth, supervisors and managers may not be included in a unit and/or bargain collectively because Section 2 defines their roles as agents of the employer.

The 1974 amendments to Taft-Hartley permitting representation in private, nonprofit health care facilities established special constraints on bargaining. Since then, the board has wrestled with the issue of appropriate bargaining units and has engaged, for the first time, in rule making rather than case-by-case rulings. Units found appropriate by the board include registered nurses, physicians, other professionals, technical employees, skilled maintenance workers, business office clericals, guards, and all other nonprofessional employees. These rules have been challenged and upheld.[7]

While this chapter does not detail organizing in employers covered by the Railway Labor Act, it should be noted that the National Mediation Board handles elections in those units. The major difference between the two jurisdictions is that the Railway Labor Act requires bargaining units to be formed initially on a craft basis.

Jurisdiction of the Organizing Union

Some unions concentrate on organizing certain occupations or industries. Many others organize outside their traditional jurisdictions because of a shrinking employment base. If an AFL–CIO union is organizing where another affiliate already represents employees, the NLRB will notify the AFL–CIO when a petition is filed to allow it to adjudicate the problem internally according to its constitution. Problems are usually resolved because agreeing to let the federation resolve internal disputes is a condition of affiliation. "Raid" elections have declined recently and will continue to recede now that the Teamsters have reaffiliated with the AFL–CIO.[8]

The Union's Desired Unit

A union faces several problems in deciding which bargaining unit configuration it desires. It must balance the optimal configuration of a unit to win an election

---

[7] *American Hospital Association* v. *NLRB*, Sup. Ct., No. 90-97, April 23, 1991.

[8] C. Odewahn and C. Scott, "An Analysis of Multi-Union Elections Involving Incumbent Unions," *Journal of Labor Research* 10 (1989), pp. 197–206.

against its objectives in later contract negotiations. A craft union would likely seek a bargaining unit that includes only workers of relatively similar skills. Industrial unions seek representation of most employees (coverable under the law) within a given plant or company.

A union must be recognized before it can bargain. Thus, it might suggest a unit in which a majority has signed authorization cards or that it believes will be easy to organize. However, organizing a unit that would have little impact on business if the union were to strike would be futile. For example, gaining a majority in a manufacturing plant custodial unit may be relatively easy, but negotiating a favorable contract would be difficult because the employer could readily subcontract the work for little incremental cost during a strike.

The bargaining unit goals of the union, then, are twofold: (1) a "winnable" unit and (2) a unit that will have bargaining power with the employer.

The Employer's Desired Unit

The employer's desired unit is often different from—but not necessarily opposite of—the union's desired unit. It usually prefers a unit the union is unlikely to win. If a craft union is organizing, the employer generally favors a plantwide unit. In some cases, the employer seeks to exclude craft groups from an inclusive unit if most of the organizing strength is among the rank-and-file workforce. Figure 6–7 details a situation in which management might argue for a smaller unit than the organizing union desires. In this case, assume that 60 percent of the production and maintenance employees desire representation, while only 40 percent of skilled trades, 45 percent of shipping and receiving, and 45 percent of clericals do. If the election were held in the union's desired unit and all employees voted, it would win the entire unit by 890 to 760. If management were able to exclude the

FIGURE 6–7
Conflicting Unit Desires

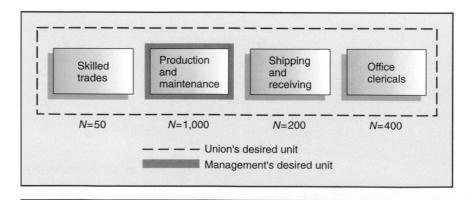

other employee groups, only the production and maintenance employees would be unionized.

The firm also would like the unit configured to minimize the union's bargaining power if it wins. Thus, management might desire functionally independent units, which would allow continued operations if a strike occurred. On the other hand, it also would like to avoid fragmented units, which might require continuous bargaining if different contract expiration dates enable the union to whipsaw the company by threatening a sequence of strikes.

NLRB Policy

NLRB policy determines bargaining unit appropriateness where disputes exist. Although not completely consistent in determining units, it has applied the following criteria.[9]

1. *Community of interests.* The mutuality of interests among employees in bargaining for wages, hours, and working conditions is frequently applied.[10] However, the **community of interests** criterion is difficult to interpret because no benchmark is used to define the degree of similarity necessary between employee groups.

2. *Geographic and physical proximity.* The more separated in distance two or more locations are, the more difficult it is for a single union to represent employees. This factor may be given considerable weight when the employer's policies differ substantially across locations.

3. *Employer's administrative or territorial divisions.* If labor relations or personnel management within a firm were uniform over a given territory (e.g., 46 grocery stores located in five counties of southeastern Michigan and managed as a territorial subdivision of a multistate chain), then this unit rather than a single store or subset may be appropriate.

4. *Functional integration.* This factor relates to the degree to which all potentially includable employees are required to maintain the company's major production processes. For example, in the *Borden Company* decision the NLRB recognized that although 20 different facilities having varying personnel policies were involved in the seemingly independent processes of manufacturing (3) and distributing (17) ice cream, an appropriate unit would contain all 20 plants because of the interrelationships among facilities necessary to market the final product.[11]

---

[9] J. E. Abodeely, R. C. Hammer, and A. L. Sandler, *The NLRB and the Appropriate Bargaining Unit*, rev. ed., Labor Relations and Public Policy Series, report no. 3 (Philadelphia: Industrial Research Unit, Department of Industry, Wharton School of Finance and Commerce, University of Pennsylvania, 1981).

[10] *Continental Baking Co.*, 99 NLRB 777 (1952), and *NLRB* v. *Action Automotive*, (Sup. Ct. 1985, 118 LRRM 2577).

[11] *Borden Co., Hutchinson Ice Cream Div.*, 89 NLRB 227 (1950).

5. *Interchange of employees.* If employees transfer frequently across plants or offices, their community of interest may be similar, leading the board to designate a multiplant unit.

6. *Bargaining history.* In applying this factor, the board may consider the past practices of the union and the employer (if it were a decertification or unit clarification election) or typical industry practices in bargaining.[12] For example, if an employer had a companywide unit that had served the mutual bargaining interests of both the employer and the union, the board would probably leave it undisturbed.

7. *Employee desires.* Early in the board's history, the *Globe Doctrine* was developed.[13] Where a bargaining history involving several units exists, the board may allow employees to vote for or against their inclusion in a more comprehensive unit.

8. *Extent of organization.* After these factors have been analyzed, the board may consider the degree to which organizing has occurred in a proposed unit, although this is not considered the prime factor.[14] The Supreme Court has ruled that the board could consider it because Section 9(c)(5) of the Taft-Hartley Act requires consideration of allowing employees the fullest freedom in exercising their rights.

Many of these factors are interrelated. For example, employee interchange more likely occurs within a defined administrative unit, and, in turn, an interchange should establish a broader community of interests. Thus, the board's determination frequently rests on several factors. Although these factors are generally utilized, there have been exceptions to each.[15]

Craft Severance

The term **craft severance** means that a group of employees with a substantially different community of interests is allowed to establish a separate unit. Craft severance can occur during initial unit determination or when a group of employees votes to leave their bargaining unit. Severance is easier during the initial organizing.

The NLRB will allow craft severance only when the following conditions are present: (1) a high degree of skill or functional differentiation and a tradition of separate representation; (2) a short bargaining history in the present unit and low degree of likely disruption if severance were granted; (3) a distinct separateness in the established unit among members of the proposed unit; (4) a different collective bargaining history in the industry; (5) low integration in production; and (6) a high degree of experience as a representative for that craft of the union desiring

---

[12] *Dallas Morning News*, 285 NLRB No. 106, 126 LRRM 1346 (1987).

[13] *Globe Machine and Stamping Co.*, 3 NLRB 294 (1937); Abodeely et al., *NLRB and the Appropriate Bargaining Unit*, 66–68.

[14] *NLRB* v. *Metropolitan Life Insurance Co.*, 380 U.S. 438 (1965).

[15] Abodeely et al., *NLRB and the Appropriate Bargaining Unit*, pp. 11–86.

severance.[16] Craft severance has been allowed in cases of a recognizable difference in the communities of interest when no prior contrary bargaining history exists.[17]

What Factors Are Used?

Except in health care, no administrative rules apply. The board determines bargaining unit appropriateness on a case-by-case basis. For severance, the overriding factor is bargaining history, buttressed by functional integration in an employer's operation. For representation, community of interest and functional integration are important. The workers' community of interest is affected by the production process, transfer policies, geographical proximity, and administrative decision making.

Judicial precedents are few; NLRB bargaining unit determinations are unappealable because they are not "final orders." If an employer were dissatisfied with the board's determination, it would refuse to bargain after losing an election and have the courts determine the appropriateness of the board's determination.[18] In most cases, the courts leave it undisturbed.

Other Issues in Unit Determination

Organizational structures change over time. What was initially an appropriate unit may no longer be so. Major factors involved in the ongoing definition of a unit include new facilities and acquisitions, reorganization, job reclassification, or sale to another firm.

Accretion

Accretion occurs when a new facility is included in the bargaining unit or when an existing union in an organization gains representation rights for employees previously represented by another union. The NLRB generally applies the same standards to accretion as it does to initial unit determination. However, the board tends to give extra weight to the desires of employees in the unit subject to accretion.[19]

Reorganization and Reclassification

An employer occasionally reclassifies jobs or reorganizes administrative units. These changes might make a previously defined bargaining unit inappropriate,

---

[16] *Mallinckrodt Chemical Works*, 162 NLRB 387 (1966).

[17] *E. I. duPont de Nemours & Co.*, 162 NLRB 413 (1966), and *Anheuser-Busch, Inc.*, 170 NLRB No. 5 (1968).

[18] Abodeely et al., *NLRB and the Appropriate Bargaining Unit*, pp. 28–29.

[19] Compare *Consolidated Edison Co.*, 132 NLRB 1518, 1961, 48 LRRM 1539 (no accretion to an established bargaining unit, but a distinct unit); with *Textile Inc.*, NLRB No. 16-RC-2704, 1960, 46 LRRM 1264 and *Special Machine & Engineering Inc.*, 282 NLRB No. 172, 1987, 124 LRRM 1219, (where accretion occurred); and *Honeywell, Inc., Semiconductor Division*, 140 LRRM 1147 (where no accretion was allowed due to employee desires).

and the parties may redefine the unit by consent. Failing this, the employer would have to refuse to bargain, and the union would have to file an unfair labor practice charge in order for the board to reexamine appropriateness.

Successor Organizations

Generally, a firm acquiring or merging with another assumes contractual bargaining obligations accrued up to the time of the merger.[20] An employer who assumes another firm's operations where the employees simply change employers is obligated to recognize the union but need not honor the predecessor's contract with the union.[21] But a substantial and apparent continuity in operations does not create an obligation if the union lacks majority status, even if the absence of a majority occurs because of layoffs and new hires by the successor.[22] When a firm is restarted by new owners after operations had been discontinued, such as from a liquidation, the bargaining relationship continues if a majority of the new employees are persons who worked for the previous company and were in a represented unit.[23]

THE ORGANIZING CAMPAIGN

During the early part of the campaign, organizing may be done surreptitiously to avoid an employer reaction. Most employers have installed preventive measures to make organizing by nonemployees difficult.

No Distribution or Solicitation Rules

Most employers prohibit solicitations by any organization on company property or on company time. These rules prohibit labor organizers from gaining easy access to employees, because legally they cannot be treated differently from representatives of other organizations. An organizing campaign is much more difficult if workers must be contacted off the job, especially if the organizer does not know where they live.

No-solicitation rules do not apply to employees. Employee organizers can solicit fellow workers on company premises (during nonworking time) unless it's clearly shown that solicitation interferes with production.[24] Nonemployee organizers (e.g., international union field representatives) can, in most instances, be

---

[20] *John Wiley & Sons, Inc.* v. *Livingston,* 376 U.S. 543 (1964).

[21] *NLRB* v. *Burns International Security Services,* 406 U.S. 272 (1972).

[22] *Howard Johnson Co., Inc.* v. *Detroit Local Joint Executive Board, Hotel and Restaurant Employees & Bartenders International Union,* AFL–CIO, 417 U.S. 249 (1974).

[23] *Fall River Dyeing* v. *NLRB,* 107 S. Ct. 2225 (1987); see also, R. F. Mace, "The Supreme Court's Labor Law Successorship Doctrine after *Fall River Dyeing,"* *Labor Law Journal* 39 (1988), pp. 102–9.

[24] *Republic Aviation Corp.* v. *NLRB*; and *NLRB* v. *LeTourneau Co.,* 324 U.S. 793 (1945).

barred from soliciting on company property.[25] Thus, early in-plant support is necessary for a drive to be successful.

In special cases, organizers may solicit on company property where reasonable access to employees is unavailable, as in remote operations such as logging, or where workers live in a company town.[26] But organizers may not take advantage of the quasi-public nature of some of the company's property, such as retail store parking lots or shopping malls, to solicit workers.[27] Employers can reduce opportunities to solicit by requiring employees to leave working areas and plants immediately after their shifts end. Employer property rights generally receive precedence over the rights of employees to organize in determining the legality of campaign activities.[28]

Union Strategy and Tactics

A union organizing campaign has three distinct sequential goals: (1) obtaining a majority of signed authorization cards in the unit it seeks to represent, (2) either voluntary recognition based on a card count or a board-directed election, and (3) the successful negotiation, ratification, and implementation of a first contract.

Obtaining an authorization card majority requires a sufficient number of employees to sign a card and give it to an organizer. To do this, the union organizer needs to be able to contact employees, convince them that unionization is to their benefit, and indicate what strategy the union has to prevent the employer from successfully retaliating against union adherents. While Section 7 forbids employers and unions from interfering with employees' rights to join or not join a union, employers frequently retaliate against activists. Exhibit 6–1 illustrates the point that employers may not deal differently with employees based on their actual or suspected union involvement.

Union organizing needs to gain the support of workers and may also need to proactively blunt management's campaign or potential retaliation. Where the employer is a significant economic entity in the local area, **community action** is an important adjunct. When the employer is not particularly dependent on the local community but is well known to the public or can be linked to other organizations that are, the union may also undertake a **corporate campaign** to inform and pressure the employer to conduct a fair campaign.

---

[25] *NLRB* v. *Babcock & Wilcox Co.*; *NLRB* v. *Seamprufe, Inc.*; and *Ranco, Inc.* v. *NLRB*, 351 U.S. 105 (1956).

[26] *Marsh* v. *Alabama*, 326 U.S. 501 (1946); *Lechmere Inc.* v. *NLRB*, Sup. Ct. 139 LRRM 2225, 1992.

[27] *Central Hardware Co.* v. *NLRB*, 407 U.S. 539 (1972); and *Hudgens* v. *NLRB*, 91 LRRM 2489 (U.S. Supreme Court, 1976).

[28] R. N. Block, B. W. Wolkinson, and J. W. Kuhn, "Some Are More Equal than Others: The Relative Status of Employers, Unions, and Employees in the Law of Union Organizing," *Industrial Relations Law Journal* 10 (1988), pp. 220–40; see also A. Story, "Employer Speech, Union Representation Elections, and the First Amendment," *Berkeley Journal of Employment and Labor Law* 16 (1995), pp. 356–457.

EXHIBIT 6–1

Edward G. Budd Manufacturing Co. *v.* NLRB

United States Court of Appeals, Third Circuit, 1943, 138 F. 2d 86, Biggs, Circuit Judge . . .

The complaint alleges that the petitioner, in September 1933, created and foisted a labor organization known as the Budd Employee Representation Association upon its employees and thereafter contributed financial support to the association and dominated its activities. The amended complaint also alleges that in July 1941 the petitioner discharged an employee, Walter Weigand, because of his activities on behalf of the union . . .

The case of Walter Weigand is extraordinary. If ever a workman deserved summary discharge it was he. He was under the influence of liquor while on duty. He came to work when he chose, and he left the plant and his shift as he pleased. In fact, a foreman on one occasion was agreeably surprised to find Weigand at work and commented upon it. Weigand amiably stated that he was enjoying it. He brought a woman (apparently generally known as the "Duchess") to the rear of the plant yard and introduced some of the employees to her. He took another employee to visit her, and when this man got too drunk to be able to go home, punched his time card for him, and put him on the table in the representatives' meeting room in the plant in order to sleep off his intoxication. Weigand's immediate superiors demanded again and again that he be discharged, but each time higher officials intervened on Weigand's behalf because as was naively stated he was "a representative" (of the association, found to be a dominated union). In return for not working at the job for which he was hired, the petitioner gave him full pay and on five separate occasions raised his wages. One of these raises was general; that is to say, Weigand profited by a general wage increase throughout the plant, but the other four raises were given Weigand at times when other employees in the plant did not receive wage increases.

The petitioner contends that Weigand was discharged because of cumulative grievances against him. But about the time of the discharge it was suspected by some of the representatives that Weigand had joined the complaining CIO union. One of the representatives taxed him with this fact, and Weigand offered to bet a hundred dollars that it could not be proved. On July 22, 1941, Weigand did disclose his union membership to the vice chairman (Rattigan) of the association and to another representative (Mullen) and apparently tried to persuade them to support the union. Weigand asserts that the next day he, with Rattigan and Mullen, were seen talking to CIO organizer Reichwein on a street corner. The following day, according to Weigand's testimony, Mullen came to Weigand at the plant and stated that he, Mullen, had just had an interview with Personnel Director McIlvain and Plant Manager Mahan. According to Weigand, Mullen said to him, "Maybe you didn't get me in a jam." And, "We were seen down there." The following day Weigand was discharged.

As this court [has] stated . . . an employer may discharge an employee for a good reason, a poor reason, or no reason at all so long as the provisions of the National Labor Relations Act are not violated. It is, of course, a violation to discharge an employee because he has engaged in activities on behalf of a union. Conversely an employer may retain an employee for a good reason, a bad reason, or no reason at all, and the reason is not a concern of the board. But it is certainly too great a strain on our credulity to assert, as does the petitioner, that Weigand was discharged for an accumulation of offenses. We think that he was discharged because his work on behalf of the CIO had become known to the plant manager. That ended his sinecure at the Budd plant. The board found that he was discharged because of his activities on behalf of the union. The record shows that the board's finding was based on sufficient evidence . . .

Over the last several years, the AFL–CIO and affiliated national unions have developed new organizing strategies. Traditional campaigns have made heavy use of handbills, letters to employees in the unit, and mass recruiting meetings. These may be supplemented, less often, with community action, corporate campaigns, and negotiating for recognition (chiefly in the building trades).[29] The new strategies are much more focused on one-to-one rank-and-file intensive campaigning.[30] These campaigns use national union representatives trained in organizing to work alongside a developed internal cadre.

Campaigns proceed in establishing individual contacts through home visits, small group meetings, and one-to-one solicitation during nonworking times at work. The campaign stresses themes related to fairness, dignity, and justice, downplaying but not ignoring economic issues.

As the campaign gains momentum, an internal organizing committee is established. Solidarity days are scheduled when signed-up members wear union buttons and/or T-shirts to work to signal their strength. A negotiating committee may also be established to begin defining the specific issues it believes are important to obtain in the first contract. This both personalizes the campaign to the unit and gets workers to realize that winning the campaign is instrumental for realizing desired bargaining outcomes.[31]

Many campaigns still use traditional strategies, with one-third of campaigns using resource coordination and community action. Corporate campaigns are used in about one-quarter of organizing efforts while negotiating with employers for preferential hiring is used least often.[32] Table 6–1 indicates the percentage of a sample of elections in which each of several tactics was used. Leaflets and cartoons may be distributed. Figure 6–8 shows a suggested leaflet used late in the campaign. In terms of raising issues, unions have an advantage over management because they can speculate on changes likely to occur after unionization, while employers may not legally communicate future benefits that would result from an organizing failure.

After an election petition is filed, the union's tactics become more open for three reasons. First, those most in favor of unionization have already signed up, thus each additional union vote requires increasingly concentrated collective

---

[29] R. B. Peterson, T. W. Lee, and B. Finnegan, "Strategies and Tactics in Union Organizing Campaigns," *Industrial Relations* 31 (1992), pp. 370–81.

[30] K. Bronfenbrenner, "The Role of Union Strategies in NLRB Certification Elections," *Industrial and Labor Relations Review* 50 (1997), pp. 195–212.

[31] Ibid. For a detailed plan for organizing see K. Gagala, *Union Organizing and Staying Organized*, (Reston, VA: Reston Publishing, 1983), pp. 95–195.

[32] Peterson et al, "Strategies and Tactics . . . ," pp. 370–81.

TABLE 6–1

Percentage Use of Various Union Organizing Tactics

Tactic	%
Traditional	
Handbilling	77
Mailing letters	100
Holding meetings	100
Signing authorization cards	100
Corporate Campaigns	
Attacking source of finance	30
Action of stockholders	10
Confronting employers on antiunion stands	33
Isolating employer	7
Conducting boycotts	6
Using private intelligence	22
Negotiating	
Neutrality pledge language	7
Accretion agreements	6
Preferential transfers	4
Preferential hiring language	33
Coordinating resources with other unions	35
Working closely with community leaders to facilitate community acceptance of union	33

SOURCE: Adapted from R. B. Peterson, T. W. Lee, and B. Finnegan, "Strategies and Tactics in Union Organizing Campaigns," *Industrial Relations* 31 (1992), p. 375.

pressure. Second, secrecy is no longer necessary because the employer is now publicly aware of the campaign. Third, publicity eliminates the employer's ability to claim ignorance of organizing as a defense if action is taken against employee activists.

Studies indicate grievance handling, job security, and economics are important issues. If the bargaining unit is predominantly female, face-to-face organizing tactics are more successful, and opportunities for advancement and technical training become more salient.[33] Minorities are significantly more likely to favor unionizing.[34] Individual characteristics of organizers also influence organizing outcomes.[35] Women organizers and organizers for the Service Employees (SEIU) focus more on participation in the workplace, women's issues, and union consciousness in their campaigns.[36] Personal contact is associated with election

[33] M. L. Lynn and J. Brister, "Trends in Union Organizing Issues and Tactics," *Industrial Relations* 28 (1989), pp. 104–13.

[34] S. M. Hills and G. DeSouza, "Women's Intentions to Vote for Union Certification across Time," *Labor Studies Journal* 21, no. 4 (1997), pp. 64–80.

[35] T. F. Reed, "Do Union Organizers Matter? Individual Characteristics and Representation Election Outcomes," *Industrial and Labor Relations Review* 43 (1989), pp. 103–19.

[36] M. Crain, "Gender and Union Organizing," *Industrial and Labor Relations Review* 47 (1994), pp. 227–48.

FIGURE 6–8

Specimen Union Communication

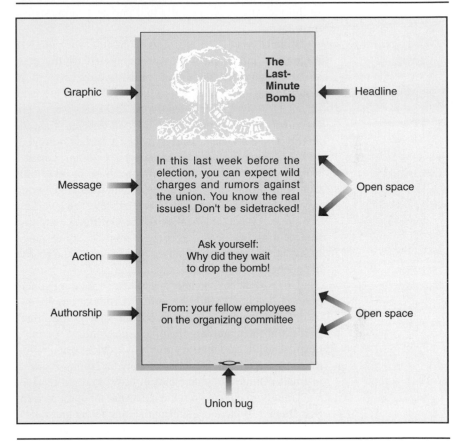

success for unions.[37] Voters are influenced by co-worker and family member attitudes toward unionization but not generally by supervisors or managers. These influences, combined with beliefs about the union's instrumentality for achieving attractive outcomes, predict actual votes very well.[38]

The success of union campaigns within industries is related to firm size, capital intensity, the ratio of labor to total costs, and extremes in profitability. In

[37] D. M. Savino and N. S. Bruning, "Decertification Strategies and Tactics: Management and Union Perspectives," *Labor Law Journal* 43 (1992), pp. 201–10.

[38] B. R. Montgomery, "The Influences of Attitudes and Normative Pressures on Voting Decisions in a Union Certification Election," *Industrial and Labor Relations Review* 42 (1989), pp. 262–79; and J. G. Rosse, T. J. Keaveny, and J. A. Fossum, "Predicting Union Election Outcomes: The Role of Job Attitudes, Union Attitudes, and Coworker Preferences" (Boulder: College of Business Administration, University of Colorado, 1986).

general, large, unprofitable firms are most vulnerable.[39] Unless there are salient employee issues for unionizing, even well-orchestrated drives are likely to fail as did the AFL–CIO's efforts to organize several state Blue Cross–Blue Shield insurers.[40]

An analysis of 261 elections found both the percentage of employees voting for unions and union wins were predicted by the percentage that had signed authorization cards, the use of solidarity days (buttons and T-shirts), establishing a bargaining committee before the election, and focusing on fairness and justice issues. Organizing drives led by the Teamsters were significantly less successful. Organizational size and an election unit different than the petition unit were negatively related. Delay, contrary to most other findings, was positively related to success in one-to-one style campaigns. Unemployment levels and union density were positively related as was unionization of other units in the same company. Company profitability and a preexisting quality-of-work-life program were negatively related. Units in which wages were low, workers were younger, women comprised 60 percent or more of the workforce, and minorities also were represented in higher percentages were more likely to unionize. Finally, organizers based in an international union with at least one to five years of rank-and-file experience ran more successful campaigns.[41]

Unions that have greater success in organizing generally use more innovative methods, specialize in representing particular employee groups, and do not have centralized control.[42] From an overall standpoint, nonaffiliated locals are more successful in organizing than AFL–CIO unions or the Teamsters.[43] In the nonhospital health care industry, unions win more often in for-profit units; when organized by the UFCW, RWDSU, American Nurses Association, or an independent; in smaller units; and where the employees are professionals.[44]

Union organizers do not expect that all campaigns will be successful on the first attempt. If there is a substantial union vote that fails to achieve a majority and if the turnover rate is relatively low, the union can rely on an established cadre to work on a subsequent campaign. In these situations, the union's future campaigns focus on tracking whether management fulfilled postelection promises that it made to address employee problems.[45]

---

[39] C. L. Maranto, "Corporate Characteristics and Union Organizing," *Industrial Relations* 27 (1988), pp. 352–70.

[40] H. R. Northrup, "The AFL–CIO Blue Cross-Blue Shield Campaign: A Study of Organizational Failure," *Industrial and Labor Relations Review* 43 (1990), pp. 525–41.

[41] Bronfenbrenner, "The Role of Union Strategies . . . ," pp. 195–212.

[42] J. Fiorito, P. Jarley, and J. T. Delaney, "National Union Effectiveness in Organizing: Measures and Influences," *Industrial and Labor Relations Review* 48 (1995), pp. 613–35.

[43] M. H. Sandver and K. J. Ready, "Trends in and Determinants of Outcomes in Multi-Union Certification Elections," *Journal of Labor Research* 19 (1998), pp. 165–172; and V. G. Devinatz and D. P. Rich, "Information, Disinformation, and Union Success in Certification and Decertification Elections," *Journal of Labor Research* 17 (1996), pp. 199–210.

[44] C. Scott, A. Seers, and R. Culpepper, "Determinants of Union Election Outcomes in the Nonhospital Health Care Industry," *Journal of Labor Research* 17 (1996), pp. 701–15.

[45] Lawler, *Unionization and Deunionization*, pp. 23–24.

Management Strategy and Tactics

Management strategy and tactics are planned at both corporate offices and the facility at which organizing activities occur. Unless the organization is in the public sector or already heavily unionized, top management almost always resists organizing. It sends out advisors at the first sign of union activity, and may also try to rid itself of presently unionized situations. Many major firms have specific goals for repelling or containing union organizing activities.[46]

Many organizations periodically sample employee attitudes and ask supervisors to keep alert for signs of potential organizing activity. When organizing occurs, consultants may be hired to assist management in conducting an antiunion campaign.[47] Uncovering union activity in a covert manner, restricting solicitations, waging an intense campaign, and opposing a consent election influence election outcomes in management's favor.[48] If an election is sought, management almost always contests the proposed bargaining unit to gain time to mount an intensive campaign in opposition.

Management campaigns emphasize that unions are outsiders less concerned than the employer with employee welfare, that conditions may not improve after unionization, and that employees will be unable to deal individually with employers on employment conditions. Management communicates personally with employees to oppose the union. Figure 6–9 is an example of an employer communication urging employees to vote against the union.

Consultants suggest that employers engage large-scale employee communications efforts, including mass meetings, small-group discussions with management representatives, and individual interviews giving information on present (not anticipated) company human resource programs.[49] Supervisors, a key group in communicating with rank-and-file employees, need extensive briefings on the company's position and on the avoidance of unfair labor practices.[50]

Undecided employees tend to vote for the company rather than the union.[51] Unless an employee makes an effort to gain exposure to the union's position, he or she will have heard much more management information before the vote is taken.

---

[46] A. Freedman, *Managing Labor Relations* (New York: Conference Board, 1979), p. 33; and A. Freedman, *The New Look in Wage Policy and Employee Relations* (New York: Conference Board, 1985), pp. 5–6.

[47] B. E. Kaufman and P. E. Stephan, "The Role of Management Attorneys in Union Organizing Campaigns," *Journal of Labor Research* 16 (1995), pp. 439–55.

[48] K. F. Murrmann and A. A. Porter, "Employer Campaign Tactics and NLRB Election Outcomes: Some Preliminary Evidence," *Proceedings of the Industrial Relations Research Association* 35 (1982), pp. 67–72.

[49] For an overview and incidents involving consultants for both sides, see *Labor Relations Consultants: Issues, Trends, and Controversies* (Washington, DC: Bureau of National Affairs, 1985).

[50] L. Jackson and R. Lewis, *Winning NLRB Elections* (New York: Practising Law Institute, 1972).

[51] J. Getman, S. Goldberg, and J. B. Herman, *Union Representation Elections: Law and Reality* (New York: Russell Sage Foundation, 1976), pp. 100–8.

FIGURE 6–9
Specimen Employer Communication

Home mailing

Wednesday

Dear Fellow Employee:

At our plant gate yesterday, the union distributed a leaflet in which it discussed how it will back up its demands at our company.

In other words, the union is stating that it can fulfill its promise by the use of force. This is absolutely untrue. While the union can make promises and threaten to force us to do things, it is the company that pays your wages and provides you with benefits.

I think you should know some facts about what the union *cannot do* to your company, and some of the things they *can do* to you.

First, let's look at what it *cannot* force your company to do:

1. It cannot force the company to agree to any proposal that the company is unwilling or unable to meet.
2. It cannot increase any wages or benefits unless the company feels it is in its best interest to do so.
3. It cannot guarantee job security or furnish you a day's work or a day's pay.

Now let's work at what it *can* "force" employees to do.

1. It can force the employees to pay dues each and every month where there is a union-shop clause in the contract.
2. It can force members to stand trial and pay fines for violation of any of the provisions of the "book of rules" (constitution).
3. It can force members to pay assessments whenever the union treasury requires more money.

Consider the many advantages and benefits you now enjoy. These have been provided without a union. Consider the many disadvantages of union membership. When you do, I am sure you will vote "no."

Sincerely,

General Manager

SOURCE: L. Jackson and R. Lewis, *Winning the NLRB Elections* (New York: Practising Law Institute, © 1972), p. 134.

A vigorous and successful management campaign uses tactics that gain early warnings of union activity and combine outside consultants, strong inside involvement, and delays.[52] Union win rates decreased when employers gave wage increases (illegal), made promises about future changes (illegal), had frequent captive audience meetings, and mailed several letters to employees during the campaign. However, in the set of elections studied, union tactics were about three times as influential as management tactics.[53]

Some employers, particularly those with low wages and poor working conditions,[54] purposely commit unfair labor practices to blunt organizing drives. The cost to employers of restoring discriminatorily fired union activists with back pay is far outweighed by the potential costs of negotiated wage increases if the union wins. The consequences for unlawful discrimination are slight, usually occurring where unionization is pervasive and among employers who have previously violated the labor acts.[55] Discrimination against employees engaging in union activities decreases union organizing success by an average 17 percent.[56] Employees who perceive that their employers committed unfair labor practices in campaigns are less likely to vote for representation than those who have not, other things being equal.[57] Employers involved in multiple campaigns increase their likelihood of committing unfair labor practices.[58] Unfair labor practice charges by unions have increased substantially since 1970 at the same time that their success in elections and the number of elections conducted have fallen. Table 6–2 is a summary of studies looking at the effects of management activity on election results.[59]

THE ROLE OF THE NLRB

The NLRB's responsibility is to conduct the election and certify the results. If unfair campaign practices are charged, it must decide if they occurred and interfered with employees' Section 7 rights to freely choose. The NLRB's position is

---

[52] Murrmann and Porter, "Employer Campaign Tactics"; J. Lawler, "Labor-Management Consultants in Union Organizing Campaigns: Do They Make a Difference?" *Proceedings of the Industrial Relations Research Association* 34 (1981), pp. 374–80; and J. J. Lawler, "Union Growth and Decline: The Impact of Employer and Union Tactics," *Journal of Occupational Psychology* 59 (1986), pp. 217–30.

[53] Bronfenbrenner, "The Role of Union Strategies . . . ," pp. 195–212.

[54] R. B. Freeman and M. M. Kleiner, "Employer Behavior in the Face of Union Organizing Drives," *Industrial and Labor Relations Review* 43, 1990, pp. 351–365.

[55] M. M. Kleiner, "Unionism and Employer Discrimination: Analysis of 8(a)(3) Violations," *Industrial Relations* 23 (1984), pp. 234–43.

[56] W. N. Cooke, "The Rising Toll of Discrimination against Union Activists," *Industrial Relations* 24 (1985), pp. 421–42.

[57] T. J. Keaveny, J. Rosse, and J. A. Fossum, "Campaign Tactics and Certification Election Outcomes," (Milwaukee, WI: Marquette University, 1989).

[58] Lawler, *Unionization and Deunionization,* pp. 76–77.

[59] R. B. Freeman, "Contraction and Expansion of Unionism in Private and Public Sectors," *Journal of Economic Perspectives* 2, no. 2 (1988), pp. 63–88.

TABLE 6–2

Effects of Management Activity on NLRB Representation Election Results

Study and Sample	Measurement of Management Activity	Does Activity Have Effect?
1. National Industrial Conference Board, 140 union organizing drives of white-collar workers 1966–67	Amount of communication by management	Yes
2. AFL–CIO, 495 NLRB election, 1966–67	Amount of opposition by management	Yes
3. Prosten (1978), analysis of probability of union win in 130,701 elections in 1962–77	Amount of time delay between election and petition	Yes
4. Lawler (1984), 155 NLRB elections, 1974–78	Company hires consultant	Yes
5. Drotning (1967), 41 elections ordered void and rerun by NLRB	Amount of communication by management	Yes
6. Roomkin-Block (1981), 45,155 union representation cases, 1971–77	Delay between petition and election	Yes
7. Seeber and Cooke (1983), proportion of workers voting for union representation by state, 1970–78	Employers object to election district	Yes
8. US General Accounting Office (1982), analysis of 8(a)(3) illegal findings or other discrimination for union involvement in 368 representation elections	Employer committed unfair labor practice	Yes
9. Aspin (1966) study of 71 NLRB elections in which reinstatements were ordered	Employer fired worker for union activity	Yes, unless reinstated before election
10. Getman, Goldberg, and Herman (1976) analysis of 1,293 workers in 31 elections in 1972–73	Campaign tactics employer	Not statistically significant
11. Dickens (1983) study of 966 workers in 31 elections in 1972–73 (using data set in #10)	Legal and illegal campaign tactics by employer	Yes
12. Catler (1978) study of 817 NLRB elections	Unfair labor practices and delay	Yes
13. Kochan, McKersie, and Chalykoff (1986), 225 firms	Employer emphasizes union avoidance strategy	Yes

SOURCE: Richard B. Freeman, "Contraction and Expansion of Unionism in Private and Public Sectors," *Journal of Economic Perspectives* 2, no. 2 (1988), p. 83.

that an election should "provide a laboratory in which an experiment may be conducted, under conditions as nearly ideal as possible, to determine the uninhibited desires of the employees."[60] Employer conduct in interrogating employees, scheduling meetings, and campaigning during the day before the election may be examined. The board may also assess the totality of conduct of the parties in an election.

---

[60] *General Shoe Corp.*, 77 NLRB 127 (1948).

Interrogation

Interrogation would probably be legal if used only to test a claim of majority status[61] but would be unfair if (1) the employer has a history of hostility toward unions, (2) information is likely to be used against a particular individual, (3) the questioner is a high-level manager, (4) the interrogation is performed in an intimidating manner, or (5) the respondents are fearful.[62]

Communications

Employees may be required to attend meetings on company premises during working hours to hear management presentations opposing the union.[63] However, if solicitation is barred during nonworking time (as in a retail establishment), the union may be entitled to equal access.[64]

The NLRB has long considered communication content in both employer and union campaigns. Employers cannot promise employees new benefits if the union loses, but they can point out that if the union is certified, all present levels of wages and benefits will be subject to negotiation. If racial propaganda is used in campaigns and it is extraneous to the situation, the NLRB is likely to order a rerun if objections are filed.[65]

"Truth in campaigning" has been controversial. Since 1977, the NLRB has reversed itself three times on whether campaign distortions are an unfair practice. Before 1977, the board followed the *General Shoe* laboratory condition rule requiring truthfulness.[66] Presently, it no longer considers the truthfulness of campaign claims, reasoning that voters have experienced political campaigns and many have voted before in union representation elections. Thus, they would not easily be swayed by rhetoric or claims. Voters appear to make their decisions relatively early in the campaign; thus, truth or falsity may have little effect during the waning days.[67]

The 24-Hour Rule

Because it would be impossible for a union or an employer to rebut a last-minute campaign statement, the *Peerless Plywood* rule prohibits employers or unions

---

[61] *Blue Flash Express Co.*, 109 NLRB 591 (1954).

[62] *Bourne* v. *NLRB*, 322 F. 2d 47 (1964).

[63] *Livingston Shirt Corp.*, 33 LRRM 1156 (1953).

[64] *May Department Stores Co.*, 136 NLRB 797 (1962).

[65] N. A. Beadles and C. M. Lowery, "Union Elections Involving Racial Propaganda: The *Sewell* and *Bancroft* Standards," *Labor Law Journal* 42 (1991), pp. 418–24.

[66] Beginning with *Hollywood Ceramics Co.*, 140 NLRB 221 (1962), which required truthfulness; adopting *Shopping Kart Food Markets, Inc.*, 229 NLRB 190 (1977), which did not; shifting to *General Knit of California, Inc.*, 239 NLRB 101 (1978), which did; and concluding with *Midland National Life*, 263 NLRB No. 24 (1982), which did not.

[67] J. M. Walker and J. J. Lawler, "Union Campaign Activities and Voter Preferences," *Journal of Labor Research* 7 (1986), pp. 19–40.

from holding a captive-audience presentation within the 24 hours directly preceding the election.[68]

The Effects of Unfair Practices

The vigor of management's campaign influences its likelihood of winning the election. Unfair labor practices during a vigorous campaign influence voters away from the union and may not involve large costs to the employer, even if the employer is penalized. Using the *Union Representation Elections* data, a study simulated the relative effects of various employer practices on the outcomes of elections.[69] In the *Union Representation Elections* study, an NLRB administrative law judge reviewed the campaigns to determine whether an unfair labor practice was committed by either party during the campaign. Actual charges were filed in some of the elections, and the NLRB issued rulings on them. In 31 campaigns that had elections, the board issuing **bargaining orders** (discussed in the next section) in 9, and 13 resulted in other remedies (e.g., election reruns for 12 of the campaigns). Thus, the sample showed both fair and unfair conduct.

Analysis found several campaign practices influenced election outcomes. Among the most important were one legal practice (early meetings with employees) and one unfair practice (threats and actions against union supporters). Table 6–3 shows the effects of individual background, election background, and campaign measures on voting behavior. In the actual campaigns, unions won 36 percent of the elections. Table 6–4 shows the effects of various campaign types on simulated election outcomes. Compared with the average, if the company fails to campaign against the union, the union's probability of winning increases by about 31 percent. In an intense legal campaign, unions lose 14 percent more frequently; an intense campaign using both legal and illegal approaches reduces union victories by about 32 percent to only 4 percent (or 1 in 25 elections). Although employees may not pay much attention to many of the issues raised, they do respond to early employer campaign efforts and illegal tactics. On the other hand, an analysis of Canadian campaigns found employer practices had only a marginal effect on elections.[70]

ELECTION CERTIFICATIONS

After the election, ballots are counted to determine which alternative, if any, received a majority. If no objections or unfair campaign charges are filed, the NLRB certifies the results. If a union wins the election unit, it becomes the exclusive

---

[68] 107 NLRB 427 (1953).

[69] W. T. Dickens, "The Effect of Company Campaigns on Certification Elections: *Law and Reality* Once Again," *Industrial and Labor Relations Review* 36 (1983), pp. 560–75.

[70] T. Thomason, "The Effect of Accelerated Certification Procedures on Union Organizing Success in Ontario," *Industrial and Labor Relations Review* 47 (1994), pp. 207–26.

TABLE 6–3

Estimates of the Reduced-Form Voting Model*

	Specification	
Independent Variable	Specific Violations—Average Percent Impact	NLRB Remedy—Average Percent Impact
Individual background		
1. Tenure < year	.008%	.010%
2. Part-time worker	−.064	.066
3. Age code	.047†	.044
4. Age code squared	−.011	−.010
5. Married	−.047†	−.051†
6. No. of dependents	.008	.008
7. Education code	−.018	.021†
8. White	−.000	−.001
9. Relative a union member	.057‡	.065§
10. Initial disposition	.430§	.427§
11. Not asked to sign card	−.158§	−.159§
12. Potential wage change	.127§	.130§
Election background		
13. UAW	−.213§	−.180§
14. Teamsters	−.150§	−.115§
15. Steelworkers	.173§	.226§
16. Retail clerks	−.320‡	−.316‡
17. Machinists	−.416§	−.339§
18. Percent for union	.006§	.006§
19. Average education	.264§	.354§
20. No. of workers	.003§	.003§
Campaign measure		
21. Illegal speech	−.022	—
22. Illegal actions	−.024	—
23. Threats and actions vs. union supporters	−.155‡	—
24. Early letters	.010‡	.021§
25. Late letters	−.037§	−.035§
26. Early meetings	−.052‡	−.068§
27. Late meetings	−.025	.004§
28. Percent talked to by supervisor	.001	−.001
29. Remedy is bargain	—	−.073
30. Other remedy	—	−.051†

* Dependent variable equals one if the worker voted union and zero if otherwise.
† Significant at the .10 level in a one-tailed test.
‡ Significant at the .05 level in a one-tailed test.
§ Significant at the .01 level in a one-tailed test.
SOURCE: W. T. Dickens, "The Effect of Company Campaigns on Certification Elections: *Law and Reality* Once Again," *Industrial and Labor Relations Review* 36 (1983), p. 568.

TABLE 6–4

Simulated Effects of Campaigns on Election Outcomes, in Percentages of 3,100 Simulated Elections Won by the Union

		Type of Campaign					
Specification	Actual Campaign	All Violations Committed in Every Case	No Violations Committed in Any Case	No Company Campaign in Any Case	Intense Company Campaign in Every Case	Intense Legal Campaign in Every Case	Light Legal Campaign in Every Case
NLRB remedy	36%	25%	44%	66%	5%	9%	58%
Specific violations	36	17	47	67	4	22	63

SOURCE: W. T. Dickens, "The Effect of Company Campaigns on Certification Elections: *Law and Reality* Once Again," *Industrial and Labor Relations Review* 36 (1983), p. 572.

representative of the employees and can begin bargaining with the employer. If it loses and challenges are unsuccessful, then an **election bar** takes effect, barring another election for one year. Even if a winning union lost its majority status within the year, the board wouldn't permit a new election. The Supreme Court and the board reason that certification is equivalent to an elected term in office, even if the official's constituents no longer support him or her.[71] If the union loses the election, the employer cannot legally take action against its supporters. Even though they are not represented by the union, the supporters are legally protected from discrimination.

Setting Aside Elections

If challenges are filed and the board finds the activity interfered with the employees' abilities to make a reasoned choice, the election will be set aside and rerun. If the violations are trivial, the board certifies the results.

Bargaining Orders

In some cases, the board considers the **totality of conduct** by an employer; that is, employer conduct is so coercive it erodes an already demonstrated majority. For example, assume a majority signs authorization cards and attends union-organizing meetings, and the employer interrogates employees, threatens cutbacks and possible plant closings, or will take a strike over bargaining issues rather than concede if the union wins. If the union loses and the board finds employer conduct undermined an actual union majority, it issues a bargaining order, requiring the employer to recognize and negotiate with the union. The remedial approach is imposed because the union would have won but for the employer's illegal conduct.[72]

---

[71] *Brooks* v. *NLRB*, 348 U.S. 96 (1954).

[72] *NLRB* v. *Gissel Packing Co.*, 395 U.S. 575 (1969); for a case in which the NLRB issued a bargaining order where no majority had been demonstrated but where the employer's behavior was seen as preventing its establishment, see G. R. Salem, "Nonmajority Bargaining Orders: A Prospective View in Light of *United Dairy Farmers*," *Labor Law Journal* 32 (1981), pp. 145–157.

The Impact of Board Remedies

Unions do not win rerun elections as frequently as initial elections. This is consistent with the evidence that intensive employer campaigns reduce union win rates. Bargaining orders do not necessarily lead to a contract either. In an examination of a large number of *Gissel*-type cases, only about 39 percent of unions were able to achieve a contract. Success in getting a contract is apparently independent of unit size, extent of organization, or type of employer Section 8 violation.[73]

In addition to election reruns or bargaining orders, the NLRB can issue cease-and-desist orders for unfair labor practices during organizing drives. If individuals have been discriminated against on the basis of union activity (e.g., being discharged), the board will order their reinstatement with back pay and interest to cover differences between wages they would have earned and what they actually earned during discrimination.

Election Outcomes

In 1996, 219,073 persons were eligible to vote in 3,277 NLRB-conducted representation elections. Of these, 2,792 were requested by unions, employees, or employers in initial representation (RC and RM) cases, and 485 were filed by employees seeking decertification (RD cases). Table 6–5 shows the size of bargaining units, number of employees eligible to vote, total elections, and percent won by a union in 1996 initial certifications. Over half were conducted in units of less than 30 employees. Unions won about 47 percent of all certification elections and 31 percent of decertification elections. Unions win rates are higher in white-collar units, and independent unions win more frequently than unions affiliated with the AFL–CIO.

Economic returns from union representation are substantially greater than costs of organizing for employees in most industries. The cost of organizing an additional worker is roughly equal to the annual earnings increase of covered workers.[74] Thus, unions recoup their investment through dues, and employees receive an increasing and continuing wage premium compared to nonunion employees.

Other Types of Representation Changes

Some events that occur during a bargaining relationship might lead an employer to question the continuing majority status of a union. Low membership, little activity in bargaining, lack of interest shown by national union representatives,

---

[73] B. W. Wolkinson, N. B. Hanslowe, and S. Sperka, "The Remedial Efficacy of *Gissel* Bargaining Orders," *Industrial Relations Law Journal* 10 (1989), pp. 509–30.

[74] P. B. Voos, "Union Organizing: Costs and Benefits," *Industrial and Labor Relations Review* 37 (1983), pp. 576–91.

TABLE 6–5

Election Success by Unit Size (RC elections)

Size of Unit	Number Eligible	Total Elections	% Won by Union
<10	3188	553	62.2
10 to 19	7352	521	49.9
20 to 29	7918	326	45.1
30 to 39	8911	260	45.4
40 to 49	7739	175	48.0
50 to 69	14770	253	45.5
70 to 99	18044	214	43.9
100 to 149	23714	197	36.0
150 to 199	17286	101	33.7
200 to 299	19584	80	26.3
300 to 399	11553	34	29.4
400 to 499	12101	27	37.0
500 to 999	25687	40	20.0
1000+	16215	11	36.4
TOTAL	194062	2792	

SOURCE: Adapted from *Sixty-First Annual Report of the National Labor Relations Board* (Washington, D.C.: Government Printing Office, 1998), p. 150.

and significant changes in the workforce all might contribute to this questioning. In cases where there have been strikes, the employer might have replaced the strikers. Even though the unit consists of new employees, the employer cannot presume that replacements oppose the current union. In the absence of an election, other evidence such as union inactivity, violence, and the like may be necessary to support a withdrawal of recognition.[75]

If conditions necessary to decertify existed (certification gained more than one year ago and no contract in force), another union could supplant the current bargaining representative. So-called raid elections require showings of interest similar to initial representation elections. Incumbent unions win raid elections more often in situations with high unemployment, large units, and local union affiliation with a national union.[76]

Contextual Characteristics Influencing Elections

The probability of the union winning a representation election is negatively related to the size of the unit in which the election is held. Union, environmental, and individual characteristics are also associated with election outcomes.

---

[75] E. C. Stephens, B. Vaught, and R. Robinson, "Withdrawal of Union Recognition: Good-Faith Doubt after *Curtin Matheson Scientific*," *Labor Law Journal* 42 (1991), pp. 221–29.

[76] E. Arnold, C. Scott, and J. Rasp, "The Determinants of Incumbent Union Victory in Raid Elections," *Labor Law Journal* 43 (1992), pp. 221–28.

Union Characteristics

Unaffiliated unions win more often than AFL–CIO unions. They may be more in tune with workplace interests.[77] Larger and more democratic unions win more often. Direct benefits to members and relatively lower dues enhance organizing success for white-collar employees but make no difference for blue-collar workers.[78] Teamster win rates are generally lower.

Environmental Characteristics

Economic conditions play a role in union outcomes. High unemployment rates during the previous years and a high degree of unionization in the industry being organized are associated with union victories.[79] Organizing is easier in units where employees are in relatively homogeneous skill groups. If job design changes increase the skill mix, lower organizing success could be expected.[80] State right-to-work laws appear to damage the credibility of organized labor. Organizing attempts decrease about 50 percent in the first five years after their passage and an additional 25 percent over the next five years. Membership is reduced between 5 and 10 percent.[81]

Preferences for unionism among private- and public-sector employees differ. Private-sector preferences are associated with beliefs that the union will be instrumental for workplace changes because the employer will not positively change the workplace, perceptions of the union's image in general, and job dissatisfaction. Public-sector employees are most influenced by the union's image and their view that the employer is unable to positively change the workplace. Public-sector employees respond more positively to job security issues during campaigning than those in the private sector.[82]

In hospitals, previous union activity, the presence of other unions, and the opportunity to organize influence union victories. Nonmedical jobs and nonprofit or religious hospitals are associated with union losses. Size is generally negatively related to organizing across all hospitals, although positively related in larger cities.[83]

[77] V. G. Devinatz and D. P. Rich, "Representation Type and Union Success in Certification Elections," *Journal of Labor Research* 14 (1993), pp. 85–92.

[78] C. L. Maranto and J. Fiorito, "The Effect of Union Characteristics on the Outcome of NLRB Certification Elections," *Industrial and Labor Relations Review* 40 (1987), pp. 225–39.

[79] W. N. Cooke, "Determinants of the Outcomes of Union Certification Elections," *Industrial and Labor Relations Review* 36 (1983), pp. 402–14.

[80] R. S. Demsetz, "Voting Behavior in Union Representation Elections: The Influence of Skill Homogeneity and Skill Group Size," *Industrial and Labor Relations Review* 47 (1993), pp. 99–113.

[81] D. T. Ellwood and G. Fine, "The Impact of Right-to-Work Laws on Union Organizing," *Journal of Political Economy* 95 (1987), pp. 250–73.

[82] J. Fiorito, L. P. Stepina, and D. P. Bozeman, "Explaining the Unionism Gap: Public-Private Sector Difference in Preferences for Unionization," *Journal of Labor Research* 17 (1996), pp. 463–78.

[83] B. E. Becker and R. U. Miller, "Patterns and Determinants of Union Growth in the Hospital Industry," *Journal of Labor Research* 2 (1981), pp. 307–28; and J. T. Delaney, "Union Success in Hospital Representation Elections," *Industrial Relations* 20 (1981), pp. 149–61.

Individual Characteristics

Most models of voting in union representation elections focus on attitudes and characteristics predicting an intent to vote, and the relationship between intent and actual votes.[84] Race and ethnic characteristics have been examined as predictors. In general, only African Americans have a stronger preference for representation.[85] In a South Florida sample, African Americans had more favorable attitudes toward unions than whites, who in turn had more favorable attitudes than Hispanics. Women were more willing to vote for unions than men.[86] Recent immigrants are less likely to be unionized than earlier immigrants, but this appears to be related to declining unionization in general, since rates for recent immigrants are the same as for other new entrants to the labor force.[87] Family values and work beliefs predict attitudes toward unions with people whose families were union members, and who have Marxist and/or humanistic work beliefs indicating a stronger interest in joining a union.[88]

Organizing and Membership Trends

Union membership rates indicate that both the absolute and relative numbers of employees who are union members have fallen for several years. Membership has been falling absolutely since 1979.[89] Whether this trend will continue is open to speculation. There are many more certification than decertification elections. Although unions lose a majority of representation elections, many more employees are gained in new bargaining units each year than are lost through decertification. Countervailing explanations help resolve this apparent paradox. First, much of the change is the result of declining employment in heavily unionized industries.[90] Second, the median size of bargaining units in which elections are held is

---

[84] For a comprehensive summary and analysis of this research, see H. N. Wheeler and J. A. McClendon, "The Individual Decision to Unionize," in G. Strauss, D. G. Gallagher, and J. Fiorito, eds., *The State of the Unions,* (Madison, WI: Industrial Relations Research Association, 1991), pp. 47–84.

[85] G. DeFreitas, "Unionization among Racial and Ethnic Minorities," *Industrial and Labor Relations Review* 46 (1992), pp. 284–301.

[86] R. Silverblatt and R. J. Amann, "Race, Ethnicity, Union Attitudes, and Voting Predilections," *Industrial Relations* 30 (1991), pp. 271–85.

[87] E. Funkhouser, "Do Immigrants Have Lower Unionization Propensities than Natives? *Industrial Relations* 32 (1993), pp. 248–61.

[88] J. Barling, E. K. Kelloway. and E. H. Bremermann, "Preemployment Predictors of Union Attitudes: The Role of Family Socialization and Work Beliefs," *Journal of Applied Psychology* 76 (1991), pp. 725–31.

[89] E. C. Kokkelenberg and D. R. Sockell, "Union Membership in the United States, 1973–1981," *Industrial and Labor Relations Review* 38 (1985), pp. 497–543.

[90] W. T. Dickens and J. S. Leonard, "Accounting for the Decline in Union Membership, 1950–1980," *Industrial and Labor Relations Review* 38 (1985), pp. 323–34. For a more detailed look at the employment changes of unionized and nonunion workers, see L. T. Adams, "Changing Employment Patterns of Organized Workers," *Monthly Labor Review* 108, no. 2 (1985), pp. 25–31.

declining. Third, if unionized firms existing in the same industry as nonunion firms have higher wage costs, they are either more vulnerable to closure or require productivity increases to balance increasing wage costs.[91] The frequent, long-run reaction to increased wages is to substitute capital for labor.[92]

A recent study found that changes in the race and sex distribution of the labor force and employer resistance to unionization have had little effect on membership. Rather, increasing average education levels, changes in the occupational distribution toward professional and service careers, and reductions in economies of scale in organizing as potential units have decreased in size appear to have contributed most to the decline.[93]

SUMMARY

Organizing is an extremely complex issue involving unions, employers, and the National Labor Relations Board. The union's goal is to organize a majority of employees; the employer seeks to avoid unionization. The NLRB's role is to preserve the free choice of employees to be represented or to remain unorganized.

Crucial aspects of organization include the authorization card campaign, bargaining unit determination, the postpetition campaign, and certification. The NLRB's decisions on bargaining units and unfair campaign charges have important bearings on many election outcomes.

The organizing campaign involves communications from the union and employer, attempts by the union to contact every potential voter, and supervisory contact with employees. Employees don't attend to most of the issues raised by either side during the campaign.

Recent results show that most union election victories occur in smaller units where employees may be more homogeneous or closer geographically. Recent behavioral research suggests that prepetition management activity is more influential on election outcomes than postpetition activity and that unfair practices do influence employee voting decisions. At the same time, a well-designed and executed union campaign is more influential on the ultimate outcome.

---

[91] For a thorough presentation of union membership and representation data, see M. A. Curme, B. T. Hirsch, and D. A. Macpherson, "Union Membership and Contract Coverage in the United States, 1983–1988," *Industrial and Labor Relations Review* 44 (1990), pp. 5–33.

[92] For a comprehensive examination of major determinants of union decline in membership, see G. N. Chaison and J. B. Rose, "The Macrodeterminants of Union Growth and Decline," in G. Strauss, D. G. Gallagher, and J. Fiorito, eds., *The State of the Unions* (Madison, WI: Industrial Relations Research Association, 1991), pp. 3–46.

[93] K. A. Bemder, "The Changing Determinants of U.S. Unionism: An Analysis Using Worker-Level Data," *Journal of Labor Research* 18 (1997), pp. 403–23.

DISCUSSION QUESTIONS

1. To what extent should the NLRB get involved in determining bargaining units? Shouldn't the vote be in the unit preferred by the employees?
2. Should union organizers have greater or less access to employees in organizing campaigns than they have now?
3. What do you think explains the relatively poor recent record for unions attempting to organize large bargaining units?
4. Do employers have an unfair tactical advantage in union-organizing situations?

KEY TERMS

Exclusive representation   *147*

Authorization card   *149*

Recognitional picketing   *151*

Representation election   *152*

Certification election   *152*

Decertification election   *152*

Raid election   *152*

Appropriate bargaining unit   *153*

Consent election   *154*

Board-directed (or petition) election   *154*

Regional director   *154*

Excelsior list   *154*

Multiemployer bargaining   *156*

Community of interests   *159*

Craft severance   *160*

Accretion   *161*

Community action   *163*

Corporate campaign   *163*

Bargaining orders   *174*

Election bar   *176*

Totality of conduct   *176*

C A S E
GMFC CUSTOM CONVEYER DIVISION

Last year, General Materials and Fabrication Corporation (GMFC) acquired a manufacturer of custom-built conveyer equipment used in the freight forwarding industry. The nonunion plant, renamed the Custom Conveyer Division (CCD), employs about 120 production employees, 3 supervisors, a general supervisor, a production manager, 2 engineers, 3 office clericals, and a plant manager. The production employees are in five semiskilled job classifications: fabricator, welder, prepper, painter, and assembler.

The fabricators convert raw material, such as steel plates and tubes, into parts using presses, sheers, numerical control cutting equipment, and the like. Welders take the fabricated parts and create frames for conveyer subassemblies. They also weld sheet metal into complex slides and chutes. Preppers clean welding slag, grind welds, degrease welded assemblies, and perform other cleaning functions for painting. Painters spray paint assemblies using a variety of paints and painting equipment, taking special care not to paint areas where additional parts will be attached. Assemblers, working in teams, use the welded subassemblies and purchased parts such as rollers, chains, sprockets, belts, motors, switches, and the like to assemble the equipment and test its operation. They then travel to the installation site to combine the subassemblies and test the completed custom installation.

The plant is located in Cumberland, a small rural town of about 2,500. All of the employees are hired from within a 20-mile radius around the plant. The starting wage for all classifications is $8.00 per hour, with an increase to $8.50 after a 60-day probationary period. Wages increase to a maximum of $10.00 per hour in three 50-cent increases at six-month intervals. About 75 percent of the employees are earning the maximum hourly rate. CCD pays

for comprehensive health insurance for all employees and provides for 80 percent of the cost of dependent coverage. Turnover is very low, averaging about 5 percent per year from all causes. Two other plants in Cumberland hire employees with the same types of skills and pay a starting wage of $7.00 per hour. Most of GMFC's employees have been hired from those plants.

The plant earned over $1.25 million before taxes last year on gross revenues of $9 million. Five other competitors manufacture this type of equipment, but GMFC-CCD has established a reputation for high quality and low cost, and its market share is expanding. Because most of the conveyer systems are used in airports and warehouse operations in large cities, transportation is required for each unit shipped. GMFC paid about $15.5 million for the operation when it was purchased last year.

Union Organizing

The district director of the United Steelworkers in the region in which Cumberland is located wants to increase the number of members in the district. He received a letter today from Dave Neumeier, an employee of GMFC-CCD, who is a former Steelworker member. Dave suggested that CCD was ripe for organizing given the $2 to $5 per hour difference in wages between CCD ($10.00 maximum) and workers in GMFC's main Central City operation. He said some of the preppers were dissatisfied, too, because their work was much more repetitive and dirtier than the other jobs, but the pay was the same.

The district director assigned two of his newest organizers, Rebecca Shea and Rick Anderson, to attempt to organize the plant. Rebecca just graduated from the state university with a bachelor's degree in labor studies. Rick was a welder for a heavy equipment manufacturer. The district director has given them a copy of the GMFC contract currently in force (see the mock negotiating exercise after Chapter 10). Rebecca and Rick have been instructed to try to get jobs at the plant and begin organizing internally. If that's not possible, they are to contact Neumeier and get names and addresses. In either event, they need to formulate a strategy for organizing.

Management

James Holroyd, the plant manager, has just held his weekly supervisors' meeting. A supervisor, Steve Christian, reported that a new employee who just moved to the area, Dave Neumeier, has a Steelworkers local sticker on the inside of his toolbox. While there has been no union activity at CCD, Holroyd was told by GMFC top management to make sure the operation remained nonunion. While work has been steady lately, a layoff is possible in two months if new orders aren't received.

The plant has a generous recreational program for employees with a party every quarter, an out-board runabout, recreational vehicle, and an extensive videocassette library employees can borrow from for free. Turnover is low, and the company has had no problem filling open positions with qualified applicants.

Problem

If you have a union organizer role, develop a strategy for organizing this plant. Consider such things as the authorization card campaign, contacts with employees, campaign literature, comparisons you want employees to make, bargaining unit determination, coping with delays, and potential unfair labor practice charges.

If you have a management role, develop a strategy to maintain a nonunion employment situation. How would you determine whether an organizing threat is likely? Create employee communications, supervisory training programs, and so forth. Consider how you would respond to potentially untruthful campaign literature. How will you deal with Dave Neumeier if he starts to talk up a union to employees?

7

UNION AVOIDANCE:

RATIONALE,

STRATEGIES, AND

PRACTICES

*C*hapter 6 examined union organizing campaigns, covering the events associated with a campaign, union strategies and tactics, management responses, the role of the National Labor Relations Board, and the factors influencing election outcomes. At several points in the chapter, employer responses to unionization attempts make clear that, except in isolated instances, most employers strongly resist organizing drives.

This chapter explores in greater depth the reasons for employer resistance to organizing drives, strategies that a growing number are using to create and maintain a "union-free" employment environment, tactics to prevent union success in organizing, the role of decertifications in deunionizing partially unionized employers, and the effects of organization and job structure changes on the limitation of unionization within employers.

As you study this chapter, consider the following questions:

1. Are employers increasing or decreasing their opposition to unions in the current era? What is the evidence to support your position?
2. What are the economic effects of initial unionization on the employer?
3. What additional activities appear necessary for an employer to avoid unionization?
4. If an employer faces an organizing campaign, what components and processes are included in a typical employer response?
5. What is a decertification election, and how does it differ from other NLRB elections?

HISTORICAL OVERVIEW

The business and labor history of the United States, going back to the Philadelphia Cordwainers, is replete with examples of employer resistance to unionization. The fundamental differences in philosophies, goals, and values of capitalists and trade unionists make this resistance inevitable and accommodation after unionization difficult.

Capitalistic and Trade Union Philosophies

Capitalists (either single entrepreneurs or corporations representing collections of investors) use their resources to create productive processes that will enable them to develop and sell goods and services in the marketplace at prices high enough to yield a return greater than other alternative investments. Employees may be hired to produce the output and are paid wages to do so. These employees are free to leave at any time, and the capitalists would like to have the freedom to terminate them, individual or collectively, as necessary to achieve their business purposes. Capitalists assume the risk that they might not realize a positive yield from their investments and ideas. If they fail, their investments will be diminished or lost. They also expect that if they are successful in the marketplace—that is, their returns are greater than they might realize through riskless investment—they will be able to keep these returns as a reward for taking the risk. If a relatively small proportion is successful, then the returns will become concentrated among a relatively small number of capitalists.

Trade unionists believe that wealth is ultimately created by the workers who produce the products or deliver the services to the consumer. In cases where the firm is successful in the market (i.e., it makes a profit), unions attribute a large measure of the success to the efforts of employees. Their actions are seen as ultimately adding the value to the inputs that make the products and services attractive in the market. From a union perspective, these gains need to be shared with the employees. While employers would like complete freedom to hire, fire, and assign workers to jobs, unions see employees as becoming increasingly invested in their jobs with employers. Unions also believe that job property rights are established over time and that employers should be constrained in the types of decisions they can make about employees as employees accrue seniority and firm-specific skills. Unions also believe that employees should have a role in determining the rules that will be used to decide how these gains will be distributed and how the workplace will be governed. Employees are seen as investing a substantial part of their lives in employment, often with a particular employer. As such, they are entitled to a role in determining how the social system in which they are involved should be operated.

Employer Resistance before World War II

As Chapter 2 noted, employers created and operated a number of strategies and tactics to avoid unionization or reduce its power. From the late 1800s until World War II, large employers often used security forces to police the workforce, forcibly keep out organizers, or ferret out internal union activists or sympathizers. These practices were particularly prevalent in steel and automobile production plants.

Employer resistance was greatest and most successful where workers were essentially unskilled and employers controlled entry into occupations or were the dominant employer in a given location. The organization of the workplace gave a great deal of power to foremen (supervisors) in the direction, control, and discipline of the workforce. The ability of an employee to retain a position depended to a large extent upon pleasing the supervisor. This approach has been labeled the "drive system" and held sway in manufacturing for most of the first third of the 20th century.[1]

During the 1920s and 1930s, employers implemented their own versions of "community action" plans, the American Plan and the Mohawk Valley Formula. Both of these sought to link labor unions with interests outside the community—especially with foreign ideologies. The Mohawk Valley Formula, in particular, mobilized community leaders and police against organizing and strikes. Both stressed the need for workers to be able to refrain from joining unions and to be able to deal directly with their employers rather than through outside agents. Where unionization seemed unavoidable, employers worked with sympathetic employees to help establish so-called **company unions** that would not be affiliated with a larger international union and would be less militant and more familiar and sympathetic to the employer's situation.[2] The passage of the Wagner Act, however made employee organizations established and assisted by employers illegal.

The Corporatist Period

From the late 1940s through the middle to late 1970s, large U.S. employers and unions moved through a period during which unions were essentially conceded a permanent role in a tripartite employment environment involving employers, unions, and the government as reflected in public policy toward employment.

---

[1] D. M. Gordon, "From the Drive System to the Capital-Labor Accord: Econometric Tests for the Transition between Productivity Regimes," *Industrial Relations* 36 (1997), pp. 125–59.

[2] S. M. Jacoby, "Reckoning with Company Unions: The Case of Thompson Products, 1934–1964," *Industrial and Labor Relations Review* 43 (1989), pp. 19–40; and D. Nelson, "Managers and Nonunion Workers in the Rubber Industry: Union Avoidance Strategies in the 1930s," *Industrial and Labor Relations Review* 43 (1989), pp. 41–52.

Laws and regulations favored collective bargaining as the method for dealing with industrial disputes. Productivity rose at a steady rate and wage increases could be financed without substantial inflationary pressure until the late 1960s.

However, the advent of the oil shocks of the 1970s and their effects on inflation along with the beginnings of economic globalization led employers to increase resistance to wage increases and additional unionization. At the same time, productivity gains declined substantially and the economies of Japan and Western Europe were beginning, for the first time, to outstrip major segments of U.S. manufacturing industries. Economic returns to shareholders had gone flat in the early 1970s and the U.S. economy was stagnating in low productivity, inflation, and uncompetitiveness in an increasingly global economy.

"Union-Free" Employment

Employers in newer or more rapidly growing industries such as information technology, financial products and services, retailing, and personal services had never been unionized to any extent or were experiencing many new entrants who were not unionized. Employers in established industries like autos and steel were heavily unionized and faced substantial economic problems. In steel, for example, the creation of so-called minimills could produce low-end commodity products at substantially cheaper prices with much lower investments and lower-wage non-union employees.

To gain increased flexibility in work design and employee assignments and to reduce wage levels, employers embarked on a variety of "union-free" strategies (detailed in this chapter). These strategies were aimed at avoiding unionization in currently nonunion facilities and reducing or eliminating unionization in the rest of their facilities. This approached represented a shift in management strategy from trying to secure the "best bargain" to "union avoidance".[3] This process was aided by a shift in public policy under the Reagan administration away from the corporatist approach and toward greater freedom for labor and management to use whatever legal tactics each wanted to achieve its objectives. Some argue that the scales were tipped to the extent that previously illegal tactics were either reinterpreted to be legal or overlooked as administrative oversight was reduced.[4]

THE ECONOMIC RATIONALE

Chapter 1 noted that unions introduced voice and monopoly power into the workplace. The introduction of monopoly power potentially decreases profitability for the employer. Higher wages have an immediate and sustained effect on shareholder value because higher wages, all else equal, reduce profits.

---

[3] A. Freedman, *Managing Labor Relations* (New York: Conference Board, 1979).

[4] W. B. Gould, IV, *Agenda for Reform: The Future of Employment Relationships and the Law* (Cambridge: MIT Press, 1993), pp. 11–62.

Productivity

As will be noted in Chapter 10, unionization usually leads to changes in policies and practices employers can use to promote, transfer, and lay off employees. Over periods of time, various work rules and production standards are also established. These have the potential for negatively influencing productivity because they may reduce the ability of the employer to include merit as a criterion in making personnel decisions, and flexibility in adapting to change might be reduced by restrictive work rules.

Substantial research has been conducted to measure the effects of unionization on productivity. Industry-level studies have found unionized establishments to be 24 percent more productive on average than nonunion establishments. If the extent of unionization in the industry is considered, the productivity effect increases to 30 percent. Unionization also apparently has an impact on worker quality within the establishment as measured by experience, training, schooling, and the like. Evidence indicates production worker quality in union establishments is 11 percent higher, while nonproduction worker quality is lower by 8 percent.[5]

Within industries, unionization appears to have differential effects. Research on construction industry productivity found that unionized workers on private-sector projects were up to 51 percent more productive than their nonunion counterparts. The differentials decreased markedly in public-sector construction projects where prevailing wage laws often take wages out of competition.[6] In education, student achievement was negatively affected by unionization among public schoolteachers through increased use of administrators and reductions in instruction time, but student achievement was positively influenced through increased preparation time, teacher experience, and smaller student-teacher ratios.[7] In hospitals and nursing homes, productivity was higher among unionized establishments in the private sector, but little difference was noted in the public sector.[8] A study in the auto parts industry found little difference in productivity levels between organized and unorganized establishments, and that failure to account for firms which may have gone out of business may upwardly bias the effects of unions on productivity.[9]

Higher turnover in nonunion organizations (see Chapter 10) is a possible explanation for productivity differentials. If experience is related to skill levels,

---

[5] R. B. Freeman and J. L. Medoff, "The Impact of Collective Bargaining: Illusion or Reality?" in J. Stieber, R. B. McKersie, and D. Q. Mills, eds., *U.S. Industrial Relations, 1950–1980: A Critical Assessment* (Madison, WI: Industrial Relations Research Association, 1981), pp. 47–98.

[6] S. G. Allen, "Further Evidence on Union Efficiency in Construction," *Industrial Relations* 27 (1988), pp. 232–40.

[7] R. W. Eberts, "Union Effects on Teacher Productivity," *Industrial and Labor Relations Review* 37 (1984), pp. 346–58.

[8] S. G. Allen, "The Effect of Unionism on Productivity in Privately and Publicly Owned Hospitals and Nursing Homes," *Journal of Labor Research* 7 (1986), pp. 59–68.

[9] R. S. Kaufman and R. T. Kaufman, "Union Effects on Productivity, Personnel Practices, and Survival in the Automotive Parts Industry," *Journal of Labor Research* 8 (1987), pp. 333–50.

unionized firms will have higher skill levels, leading to greater productivity. Because union contracts reduce the wage dispersion within jobs in firms, employees may believe nonperformance-based pay systems eliminate competition between workers for a wage pool and enable them to willingly share job information and train new employees.

While evidence shows labor productivity in the United States has grown more slowly than in other industrialized countries (e.g., United Kingdom, France, Japan, and Germany), the U.S. employment level in manufacturing was the only one to have increased across countries during the mid-1970s.[10] This would suggest that the cost of labor relative to the cost of capital is lower in the United States than in other industrialized countries and that capital in the United States is substituted for labor at a much lower rate. Where negative productivity rates exist, it is likely that low capacity utilization occurs and relatively large proportions of machinery and plants are unused.

Several conclusions can be drawn from these studies. First, unionization is related to productivity improvements. This is probably due to two factors: In most cases there is an increasing economic advantage for employees to be unionized—therefore they turn over less frequently and their greater experience makes them more productive; and management needs to make work processes more efficient. The work pace in nonunion organizations is more leisurely than in equivalent unionized employers.

Second, in general, productivity increases are not as great as wage increases subsequent to unionization. In addition, employers usually need to adjust to a more capital intensive mix given the relative increase in the cost of labor. Thus, the productivity increase is not solely the result of worker quality and effort.

Profitability

Firms that are unionized are less profitable than nonunion firms and become even less profitable subsequent to unionization.[11] Decreases in profitability may occur as a result of the extension of negotiated wage and benefit increases to nonrepresented employees so that employers can avoid further unionization. While productivity increases have been found in some firms following unionization for represented employees, this may not carry over to nonunion employees who also received increased pay.[12]

---

[10] D. Q. Mills, "Management Performance," in J. Stieber, R. B. McKersie, and D. Q. Mills, eds., *U.S. Industrial Relations, 1950–1980: A Critical Assessment* (Madison, WI: Industrial Relations Research Association, 1981), pp. 99–128.

[11] Freeman and Medoff, *What Do Unions Do?* pp. 181–90.

[12] B. E. Becker and C. A. Olson, "Unions and Firm Profits," *Industrial Relations* 31 (1992), pp. 395–415.

Shareholder Value

Shareholder returns are reduced following unionization. A study tracking organizing success following passage of the Wagner Act in the 1930s found that organized firms had about a 20 percent lower rate of return to shareholders than firms that remained nonunion.[13] Firms involved in organizing drives and whose securities are publicly traded experience a reduction in share prices when an election petition is filed,[14] a reduction of about 4 percent following a successful campaign—and a 1.3 percent loss even if the union lost.[15] The latter probably occurs because firms facing union activity increase wages more than those who don't, win or lose.[16] If unionization leads to lower shareholder returns, other things being equal, top managers, as the agents of shareholders, could be expected to try to reduce unionization in their firms, particularly if a substantial proportion of their compensation is in the form of stock options.[17] On the other hand, lower returns in unionized firms are accompanied by lower risk because security prices are less volatile, perhaps reflecting increased risk sharing by employees through layoff procedures.[18]

Industrial Structure

Evidence suggests productivity differences are greatest in the construction industry, where there are greater opportunities to take advantage of worker skill differences between union and nonunion sectors. In the service industries, unionized worker quality is lower than that of their nonunion counterparts, relatively speaking. The service sector is expanding relative to the size of the manufacturing and construction sectors. To the extent that lower unionized service worker quality translates into lower productivity, greater resistance to unionization should be seen in the service sector. The service sector's relative growth could be a primary contributor to the increased resistance of employers in general to union organizing activities.

---

[13] C. A. Olson and B. E. Becker, "The Effects of the NLRA on Stockholder Wealth in the 1930s," *Industrial and Labor Relations Review* 44 (1986), pp. 116–29.

[14] S. G. Bronars and D. R. Deere, "Union Representation Elections and Firm Profitability," *Industrial Relations* 29 (1990), pp. 15–37.

[15] R. S. Ruback and M. B. Zimmerman, "Unionization and Profitability: Evidence from the Capital Market," *Journal of Political Economy* 92 (1984), pp. 1134–57.

[16] R. B. Freeman and M. M. Kleiner, "Impact of New Unionization on Wages and Working Conditions," *Journal of Labor Economics* 8 (1990), pp. S8–S25.

[17] This and other issues are discussed and analyzed in B. E. Becker and C. A. Olson, "Labor Relations and Firm Performance," in M. M. Kleiner, R. N. Block, M. Roomkin, and S. W. Salsburg, eds., *Human Resources and the Performance of the Firm* (Madison, WI: Industrial Relations Research Association, 1987), pp. 43–86.

[18] B. E. Becker and C. A. Olson, "Unionization and Shareholder Interests," *Industrial and Labor Relations Review* 42 (1989), pp. 246–61.

UNION-FREE APPROACHES

A "union-free" organization is one that is entirely unorganized in its U.S. operations. Many companies fit this label, but among very large companies they are found more often in the financial services industry. Among U.S. firms with manufacturing operations, IBM and Hewlett-Packard are examples of large firms without organized employees.

A study of large nonunion organizations concluded that two types of firms operate without unions. The first type is called doctrinaire. A **doctrinaire organization** explicitly desires to operate without unions and implements personnel policies it believes will lead employees to resist them. Its personnel policies frequently mimic what unions have won in similar organizations through collective bargaining; for example, paying wages equal to or exceeding what unions have negotiated in that industry.[19] The second type is called **philosophy laden.** Such companies have no unions, but the employee relations climate explains the lack of organizing activities. Management engages in human resource practices it believes are right.[20] The policies are evidently congruent with employee desires because union-organizing activities in these firms are practically nonexistent. These two approaches will be examined as the personnel policies of both are explored.

Environmental Factors Associated with Union Avoidance

A variety of environmental factors is associated with union avoidance, some of which employers consider in making locational choices. Union penetration is highest in the Northeast and Midwest and lowest in the South and rural areas. Employers may locate in lightly unionized areas for two reasons. First, employers may believe employees in areas where unions have relatively little membership may be less willing to join unions. Mixed evidence exists on this point, as discussed in Chapters 1 and 6. Second, plants located in areas without unions seldom enable employees to compare economic benefits provided by union and nonunion organizations and, as a result, their employees may not organize for economic reasons. This assumption rests on the belief that employees will choose local plants as a logical comparison, not other plants in the industry. However, the evidence suggests that union organizing around the issues of justice, fairness, and dignity is more successful than that which emphasizes economics.[21]

---

[19] D. G. Taras, "Managerial Intentions and Wage Determination in the Canadian Petroleum Industry," *Industrial Relations* 36 (1997), pp. 178–205.

[20] F. K. Foulkes, *Personnel Policies in Large Nonunion Companies* (Englewood Cliffs, NJ: Prentice Hall, 1980), pp. 45–57.

[21] K. Bronfenbrenner, "The Role of Union Strategies in NLRB Certification Elections," *Industrial and Labor Relations Review* 50 (1997), pp. 195–212.

Employers may associate plant size as a factor to use in avoiding unions. Evidence on union election success covered in Chapter 6 found that plants with fewer than 100 employees were more vulnerable to unionization than larger plants. While very large plants are difficult to organize, employers may also believe that the type of human resource management they would prefer to implement is difficult to inculcate in a large plant. Thus, the trend appears to be toward siting plants in labor market areas capable of supporting medium-sized operations and planning that these plants will not exceed 500 employees unless returns to scale are large. One problem with smaller plants is that they may not be optimally productive given the appropriate capital-labor mix.[22] Plants also should not be smaller than 200 employees because a union can capitalize quickly on an issue in a smaller plant, and the plant population may be relatively homogeneous, enabling quicker and nearly unanimous agreement among employees on whether to be represented.

Differences also exist between and within industries. Industries with a large proportion of white-collar workers (e.g., finance) are less likely to be unionized. But within industries, some firms have not been organized while others are completely unionized. In construction, relatively new organizations remain nonunion through guaranteed employment during usual layoff periods and through the implementation of human resource policies on the organizational level. Newly incorporated, technically oriented industries also have had a relatively low level of unionization, even when they have been located in areas of traditionally high unionization. Some of this is probably due to employment security resulting from rapid growth and abundant alternative employment opportunities, while other aspects of resistance to organization may be related to progressive employee relations policies and practices.

A Philosophy-Laden Approach to Employee Relations

A model has been constructed to explain how a philosophy-laden approach to employee relations results in a variety of outcomes, one of which is the likely absence of a union. The model shows that environmental factors similar to those mentioned above may be involved in the location and demographics of the organization's establishments, the variety of substantive policies implemented, and company characteristics that promote the ability to achieve specific outcomes. These, in turn, lead to a particular climate or culture. The by-products of this culture are a variety of behaviors and attitudes associated with a reluctance to join unions, an avoidance of industrial conflict, and a belief the company is a good place to work. Figure 7–1 depicts the model. This model will be explored in some detail in the following sections.

---

[22] M. Milkman and M. Mitchell, "Union Influence on Plant Size," *Journal of Labor Research* 16 (1995), pp. 319–29.

FIGURE 7–1

Top Management's Stated Beliefs in the Worth of the Individual, Equity, Leadership by Example, and Other Attitudes, Values, Philosophies, and Goals Concerning Employees

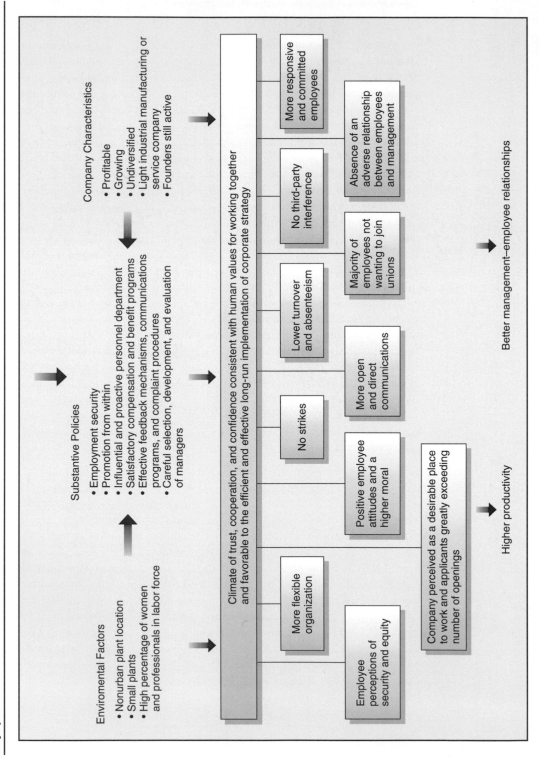

SOURCE: F. K. Foulkes, "Large Nonunion Employers," in *U.S. Industrial Relations, 1950–1980: A Critical Assessment*, ed. J. Steiber, R. B. McKersie, and D. Q. Mills (Madison, WI: Industrial Relations Research Association, 1981), p. 135.

Wage Policies

Large nonunion organizations generally try to lead the market in their pay levels. They try to anticipate what unions will gain at the bargaining table and provide pay increases equal to or exceeding that level, awarding them before unions gain theirs. Nonunion organizations may also implement merit pay policies, using performance measures to differentiate pay increases. Attention is paid to communicating pay and benefit levels and practices to employees.[23] More recently, companies are likely to have implemented skill-based pay programs to support new organizational structures stressing team designs. Additionally, increasing numbers of companies are considering or implementing profit-sharing or gain-sharing programs.

To accomplish these wage goals, an organization must compare favorably with others in its ability to pay.[24] Location in a growing industry with relatively high profits or a position as market leader in the industry should enable an organization to maintain its ability to pay. In turn, a high-paying employer may have an advantage in recruiting and retaining high-quality employees who are motivated to retain their high-paying jobs.[25]

If employee preferences are considered, as a philosophy-laden organization is expected to do, then benefit levels in nonunion organizations should closely lead those in union organizations because there won't be any "stickiness" associated with contractual provisions. Companies might be expected to react quickly to changing needs associated with changing age and gender mixes in their workforces.

Nonwage Policies

Union organizations generally have lower turnover and higher rates of internal promotion and transfer than nonunion organizations. If an organization sought to emulate the conditions employees desire, it would have a rationalized internal labor market with high levels of information on job opportunities available to employees.

Nonunion firms studied generally had formalized job-posting systems, with clearly communicated and unambiguous promotion criteria emphasizing both seniority and skills. Development opportunities were emphasized so that employees could develop the skills necessary to take advantage of openings likely to occur.[26]

Philosophy-laden firms have generally taken a career-oriented approach toward employment. Full-time nonprobationary employees are assumed to be likely to spend their entire careers with the organization. Thus, nonunion firms

---

[23] Foulkes, *Personnel Policies,* pp. 158–63.

[24] Ibid., pp. 165–67.

[25] J. Yellen, "Efficiency Wage Models of Unemployment," *American Economic Review* 74, no. 2 (1984), pp. 200–205.

[26] Foulkes, *Personnel Policies,* pp. 123–45.

frequently require longer probationary periods or hire substantial numbers of part-time employees to provide a buffer for permanent employees during periods of fluctuating product demand.[27] Increasingly, retirement programs are structured to support earlier retirement from full-time employment coupled with part-time or seasonal work with the same employer. Employers are increasingly stressing to employees the importance of continual upgrading of skills and assisting them to develop and potentially market themselves to new employers, if necessary.

Human Resource Expenditures

In unionized organizations, union representation and the negotiated contract take the place of many human resource programs devised by nonunion employers. Management has less need to attend closely to employee desires because this is the union's responsibility, and the contract spells out how employee relations will be handled. Staffing and development needs are handled through on-the-job training, and retention of employees is gained through negotiated seniority clauses and the employees' initial and continuing interest in being represented.

Nonunion organizations have higher human resource expenditures, and more human resource workers are involved in employee relations. The organization must pay more attention to compensation because it usually tries to match or exceed what unions negotiate or to construct a particular package to attract and retain employees. Development activities are emphasized. Supervisory support for problem solving is offered through the human resource department instead of the grievance system.

Employment Security

Union members have the rules for determining their employment security spelled out in the contract. Almost always, increasing competitive status seniority is associated with greater rights to continued employment in a present job or another job for which one is qualified. Recently, these rights have been of lower value where organizations have opted to close entire facilities—but even there, entitlements to transfers and severance pay are often spelled out in contracts, and benefit levels increase with seniority.

Employees in nonunion organizations have their employment rights determined by their employers. Unless otherwise provided, it's legally assumed that an employee is hired at the will of the employer and can be terminated for a good reason, a bad reason, or no reason at all as long as the termination is not for a reason prohibited by employment law. However, courts have increasingly narrowed employers' rights to terminate at will, particularly where employers are judged to have acted in bad faith.[28] Even where employers have contracts with

---

[27] Ibid., pp. 99–122.

[28] E. C. Wesman and D. C. Eischen, "Due Process," in J. A. Fossum, ed., *Employee and Labor Relations,* SHRM-BNA Series, vol. 4 (Washington, DC: Bureau of National Affairs, 1990), pp. 4–117.

employees and where a discharge could lead to a breach of contract suit, employers may be vulnerable to heavier tort damages for bad faith behavior associated with a discharge.[29]

In the reciprocal relationship that develops in employment, employees may come to feel an implied contract exists between them and their employer. With investments in developing skills needed by their present employer and through conscientious application of effort, employees see themselves producing benefits for the employer. In turn, employees may build expectations of long-term employment in return for effort and loyalty.[30]

A variety of methods are used by nonunion employers to enhance employment security for at least some employees. Given increasing needs for flexibility in the workforce, employers are increasingly subcontracting or allocating jobs that require relatively little training about the employer's specific mode of operation to supplemental or complementary workforces of temporary employees. Frequently, these employees are hired on a contract basis for a particular term—usually a year or less. These employees are explicitly told they have no employment security guarantee beyond the period for which they are hired. When faced with a need for major employment reductions, employers have increasingly implemented expanded separation incentives, redeployment to other facilities with or without retraining, training programs for new occupational assignments, expanded personal leaves, and work-sharing programs involving salary and hour cuts to save jobs or provide incentives for those willing to terminate employment.[31]

Employee "Voice" Systems

Lower turnover in unionized situations (detailed in Chapter 10) might be related to an opportunity to voice needs for change through the grievance and negotiation processes. Where these mechanisms are absent, employees who desire change may be able to achieve it only by "voting with their feet."[32]

In unionized organizations, employees are able to exercise their voice on immediate matters through grievance procedures and on long-run matters through participation in negotiation committees. Those having the greatest disagreements with the organization's operations might be expected to have the most motivation to be involved in union activities at the employer level.

In nonunion employers, employees have no contractual entitlement to redress grievances or to have a voice in how the organization should be run. Some nonunion organizations, particularly those with philosophy-laden backgrounds,

---

[29] M. J. Keppler, "Nonunion Grievance Procedures: Union Avoidance Technique or Union Organizing Opportunity," *Labor Law Journal* 41 (1990), pp. 557–62.

[30] Fossum, "Employee Relations," pp. 4–12 to 4–14.

[31] F. K. Foulkes, "Employment Security: Developments in the Nonunion Sector," *Proceedings of the Industrial Relations Research Association* 41 (1988), pp. 411–17.

[32] A. O. Hirschman, *Exit, Voice, and Loyalty* (Cambridge: Harvard University Press, 1970).

EXHIBIT 7–1

The Open-Door Policy

The Open-Door Policy is deeply ingrained in [the company's] history. This policy is a reflection of our belief in respect for the individual. It is also based on the principle that every person has a right to appeal the actions of those who are immediately over him in authority. It provides a procedure for assuring fair and individual treatment for every employee.

Should you have a problem which you believe the company can help solve, discuss it with your immediate manager or your location's personnel manager or, in the field, with the manager of your location. You will find that a frank talk with your manager is usually the easiest and most effective way to deal with the problem.

Second, if the matter is still not resolved, or is of such a nature you prefer not to discuss it with your immediate manager or location personnel manager, you should go to your local general manager, regional manager, president or general manager of your division or subsidiary, whichever is appropriate.

Third, if you feel that you have not received a satisfactory answer, you may cover the matter by mail, or personally, with the Chairman of the Board.

SOURCE: Fred K. Foulkes, *Personnel Policies in Large Nonunion Companies* (Englewood Cliffs, NJ: Prentice Hall, 1980), p. 300.

---

have constructed elaborate systems enabling employees to voice complaints and get action on them.[33]

A model system enables an employee to communicate directly with the firm's chief executive officer, who has a department that directly investigates causes of complaints and reports its findings. The complaining employee's superiors may be a focus of the investigation, but the employee is not identified, and no reprisals may be taken against the group from which the complaint is made. Exhibit 7–1 is a commentary on how one of these systems works.

Several methods have been devised to reduce the possibility of employee cynicism about management's commitment to neutral grievance procedures in nonunion organizations. For example, IBM operates a system that allows employees direct anonymous access to high-level management on complaints. When complaints are received, investigations are required, and the remedial action to be taken, if any, is communicated back to the grievant. Follow-up is monitored by high-level management.

These so-called open-door policies vary substantially in their real access to higher-level managers—in terms of the types of complaints or questions that can be taken up and also the degree to which employees must first contact lower-level supervisors and managers before higher-level managers will see a complaint.[34]

---

[33] For an overview, see R. Bernbeim, *Nonunion Complaint Systems: A Corporate Appraisal* (New York: Conference Board, 1980).

[34] D. M. McCabe, "Corporate Nonunion Grievance Procedures: Open Door Policies—A Procedural Analysis," *Labor Law Journal* 41 (1990), pp. 551–56.

Another innovative approach is creating an employee review board to act as an impartial group to resolve outstanding grievances. Where this is used, a review board of randomly chosen employees or persons at the same relative organizational level as the grievant hears evidence and renders a decision binding on the employer and the grievant.

Employees may have concerns about due process. For due process to operate, a procedure must necessarily include an objective investigator and decision maker who has the power to make a binding decision on both employee and employer.[35] Unless the employee believes the employer's procedures allow a valid appeal, the employee may prefer to take an employment grievance to court as a tort issue (suit to recover for an injury).[36] Nonunion procedures in the public sector are relatively similar to union grievance procedures. Peer review panels are sometimes included. Their effectiveness is related to encouraging employees to use them, training in their operation, assistance by management in processing complaints and obtaining information for grievants, and full and fair hearings together with an explanation of the decision.[37] Table 7–1 summarizes the characteristics found in several comprehensive nonunion employee grievance programs.

Some large nonunion organizations also periodically conduct attitude surveys to obtain an early identification of potentially troublesome areas. These might include certain employee groups or certain employee relations policies such as advancement, pay, or development opportunities. Given that attitudes may be precursors of subsequent behaviors, the diagnosis of potential problem spots allows management to conduct remedial activities to eliminate the potential areas of contention.

Grievance procedures introduce justice systems into the workplace. Several different types of justice can be defined: distributive (methods used to decide the apportionment of outcomes), procedural (methods used to determine how decisions are reached), and interactional (methods used to communicate). Perceptions of organizational justice are influenced by all three, but procedural justice is the strongest, followed by interactional and distributive. Employee input in the process and independence of decision-makers are important components of all three justice types.[38]

In some organizations, supervisors and managers are evaluated by their subordinates as well as by other performance indicators. They are expected to maintain a work environment leading to positive employee attitudes as measured by periodic surveys. When attitude surveys point out a problem, they may be required to devise action plans to eliminate difficulties.

---

[35] D. W. Ewing, *Justice on the Job: Resolving Grievances in the Nonunion Workplace* (Boston: Harvard University Press, 1989).

[36] Keppler, "Nonunion Grievance Procedures."

[37] G. W. Bohlander and K. Behringer, "Public Sector Nonunion Complaint Procedures: Current Research," *Labor Law Journal* 41 (1990), pp. 563–67.

[38] D. Blancero, "Nonunion Grievance Systems: Perceptions of Fairness," *Proceedings of the Industrial Relations Research Association* 44 (1992), pp. 458–64.

TABLE 7–1

Data on Boards in 11 Companies

	Citicorp	Control Data	Donnelly Corporation	Federal Express	General Electric (Columbia, Maryland, plant)
Name of board	Problem Review Board	Review Board	Equity Committee (5 in company)	a. Boards of Review b. Appeals Board	Grievance Review Panel
Years established	1977	1983	Late 1970s	1981	1982
Number of voting members	5	3	ca. 10–25 each	a. Boards of Review: 5 b. Appeals Board: 3	5
Terms	Ad hoc	Ad hoc	2 years	a. Boards of Review: ad hoc b. Appeals Board: ex officio	Ad hoc
Cases per year	ca. 12	ca. 8	3–4	a. Boards of Review: 37 (1986) b. Appeals Board: 209 (1986)	ca. 19
Number of cases per 1,000 employees	0.23	0.25	3	a. Boards of Review: 1 (1986) b. Appeals Board: 5 (1986)	20
Arbitration allowed as final step?	No	No	No	No	No
Reversal rate	n/a	22% (1985)	n/a	a. Boards of Review: 67% (1986) b. Appeals Board: 28% (1986)	n/a
Complaints processed by personnel staff	1982: 293 1984: 374 1986: 700	n/a	n/a	726 (1986) 62% of decisions appealed overturned	n/a

SOURCE: D. W. Ewing, *Justice on the Job: Resolving Grievances in the Nonunion Workplace* (Boston: Harvard University Press, 1989), pp. 80–81.

Grievance procedures are found in about half of nonunion firms. Predictors of having a procedure include higher proportions of managers and professional employees, firm size, the value of human resource management to the firm, having no unionized employees, and not being in high-technology industries. Some grievance procedures include binding arbitration if unresolved. Characteristics associated with third-party resolution include union avoidance strategies, smaller firms, low assets per employee, not being in manufacturing, and a high-tech firm.[39]

[39] J. T. Delaney and P. Feuille, "The Determinants of Nonunion Grievance and Arbitration Procedures," *Proceedings of the Industrial Relations Research Association* 44 (1992), pp. 529–38.

TABLE 7–1
(continued)

Honeywell (DSD-USD)	John Hancock	Northrop	Polaroid	SmithKline Beecham (Pharmaceutical Division)	TWA
Management Appeal Committee	Employee Relations Committee	Management Appeal Committee	Personnel Policy Committee	Grievance Procedure	System Board of Adjustment
1981	1981	1946	1946	ca. 1971	Early 1950s
7	5	3	3	3	3
3 years	Indefinite	Ex officio	Ad hoc	Ad hoc	Ad hoc
ca. 2	15–20	15–20	ca. 20	ca. 8	50–75
0.33	1.5–2.0	0.33	2	1.3	7.1–10.7
No	No	Yes—1 case in 1984, 13 in 1986	Yes	No	No
n/a	n/a	60% (1984)	n/a	n/a	Over 50% in 1985; less than 25% in 1987–88
n/a	ca. 120 (1985)	n/a	ca. 1,000– 2,000	n/a	n/a

Other Innovative Techniques

Some organizations have begun to hold mass meetings between employees and top-management officials to get a sense of possible problems. One approach involves meetings between top managers and groups of lower-level employees to present current problems and gripes. This "deep-sensing" approach may give top managers a better reading on the pulse rate of employee morale, and employees in turn might expect more action on their problems.

Another approach is vertical staff meetings, in which about a dozen employees from various levels are picked at random to meet with the division's president at a monthly meeting. Problems disclosed by the attendees are followed up by the president's report to the participants.[40]

Employer/Employee Committees

Employers have formed various types of management-employee committees. Quality circles are one example. Others involve employees in making recommendations to management about hiring, personnel assignments, hours, terms and conditions of employment, and other similar issues, which are the subject of collective bargaining in unionized employers.

Taft-Hartley forbids dominance of a labor organization by an employer. The *Electromation* decision narrows an employer's ability to broadly ask employees to consider employment issues.[41] Involvement of employees in nonmandatory bargaining issues is unlikely to lead to successful charges of employer dominance.

Communicative activities in some of these committees may be similar to collecting attitude survey data from a sample of the plant population and using these data as a representation of employee attitudes. It also enables both groups to enrich their understanding of what each perceives as problems in the workplace and their causes.

In some situations, employers have also vested some supervisory activities in work groups. For example, General Foods established work groups in one plant in which the group made its own work assignments, created and operated training programs, and made recommendations on staffing decisions.[42] These were found not to be employer-dominated labor organizations.[43]

Developing Practices in Nonunion Employee Relations

An increasing number of companies have explicit union avoidance policies and tailor employee relations practices to support these goals. Several of the areas in which differences exist between companies with an explicit union avoidance policy and those without include providing more information to employees about their work group's productivity, more work group discussion of quality or productivity issues, more encouragement of participative mechanisms such as quality circles and autonomous work teams, work sharing in preference to layoffs, and

---

[40] For additional perspectives on employee voice, see T. A. Mahoney and M. R. Watson, "Evolving Modes of Work Force Governance: An Evaluation," in B. E. Kaufman and M. M. Kleiner, eds., *Employee Representation: Alternatives and Future Directions* (Madison, WI: Industrial Relations Research Association, 1993), pp. 135–68. For an overview of recent research on nonunion grievance procedures, see R. B. Peterson, "The Union and Nonunion Grievance System," in D. Lewin, O. S. Mitchell, and P. D. Sherer, eds., *Research Frontiers in Industrial Relations and Human Resources* (Madison, WI: Industrial Relations Research Association, 1992), pp. 131–62.

[41] *Electromation, Inc.* 309 NLRB No. 163 (1992).

[42] R. E. Walton, "The Diffusion of New Work Structures: Explaining Why Success Didn't Take," *Organizational Dynamics* 3, no. 3 (1975), pp. 2–22.

[43] *General Foods,* 231 NLRB 1232 (1977).

TABLE 7–2

Company Practices among Nonunion Employees

Company Initiative	Number of Companies in which:	
	Managers Are Encouraged to Develop or Sustain	Practice Exists
Information-related		
Employees are given information about competitive or economic conditions of plant or business		431
Employees track their group's quality or productivity performance		264*
Participation-related		
Employee-participation programs (quality circles, quality-of-work-life programs)	364*	
Autonomous work teams	107*	
Employees meet in small work groups to discuss production or quality		340*
Compensation-related		
Profit-sharing, gainsharing, or bonus programs for nonexempt employees	191	
Employees receive productivity or other gainsharing bonuses		121
"Payment for knowledge" compensation systems	107	
All-salaried compensation systems	173	
Miscellaneous		
Formal complaint or grievance system	378*	
Work sharing instead of layoffs	176*	
Flextime or other flexible work schedules	162	

* Statistically significant relationship with a company preference for union avoidance, at .05 or better.

SOURCE: A. Freedman, *The New Look in Wage Policy and Employee Relations* (New York: Conference Board, 1985), p. 17.

the development and operation of formal complaint systems.[44] Table 7–2 shows the number of positive responses toward a variety of employee relations practices among a sample of large employers.

    In addition to differences in communication and participation, a major difference between new nonunion situations and traditional unionized facilities is the organization of the workplace. In an effort to increase flexibility, employers have substantially reduced the number of job classifications in manufacturing facilities. In many situations, employees are organized into teams and each team is responsible not only for production but also for maintenance of its equipment. The team

[44] A. Freedman, *The New Look in Wage Policy and Employee Relations* (New York: Conference Board, 1985), pp. 16–20.

may have only one or two different jobs, which are defined on the basis of skill level rather than the functional specialty of the jobholder.[45]

PREVENTIVE PROGRAMS

Specific preventive programs are aimed at avoiding organizing activities. Employers implement programs designed to influence employees to identify with management and the goals and culture of the organization, control contextual attributes that unions typically argue they can improve, and monitor attitudes and behaviors of employees to gain early evidence of any changes or situations that might encourage attempts to organize.[46] Table 7–3 lists several of the initiatives management implements in each of these areas.

Some of the activities under contextual control and monitoring may be traded off or be used with increased emphasis. For example, intensive employee screening may be implemented to reduce the need for later surveillance and to create a workforce with more company-oriented attitudes.[47] Some activities within contextual control may also be exchanged. For example, high wages and good fringe benefits vary in amounts depending on the location in which the comparison is made. If labor costs are an issue, the firm may decide to locate in a lower-wage area and then pay at rates exceeding the competition. In any case, implementing these activities requires a more intensive employee relations–human resource management effort than it would in a unionized setting. The employer needs to determine that the long-run benefits exceed the costs.

MANAGEMENT ELECTION CAMPAIGN TACTICS

Campaign tactics depend to an extent on the size and sophistication of the employer. Smaller employers or units based in more remote locations often rely on labor relations consultants or attorneys to assist in organizing and implementing the campaign. As Chapter 6 noted, the use of consultants has a negative effect on union success rates. As in preventive processes, employers may implement a variety of influence, contextual control, and monitoring activities to reduce the chances of the organizing union gaining recognition.[48] Table 7–4 lists the activities frequently used by employers. Table 7–5 shows the frequency of a variety of common employer campaign themes that were used in a sample of 201 elections.

---

[45] T. A. Kochan, H. C. Katz, and R. B. McKersie, *The Transformation of American Industrial Relations* (New York: Basic Books, 1986), pp. 81–108.

[46] J. J. Lawler, *Unionization and Deunionization: Strategies, Tactics, and Outcomes* (Columbia: University of South Carolina Press, 1990), pp. 118–28.

[47] Saltzman, G. M., "Job Applicant Screening by a Japanese Transplant: A Union-Avoidance Tactic," *Industrial and Labor Relations Review* 49 (1995), pp. 88–104.

[48] Lawler, *Unionization and Deunionization,* pp. 139–60.

TABLE 7–3

Employer Influence, Contextual Control, and Monitoring Tactics

Objective	Employer Activities
Influence	Orientation programs
	Quality circles (especially blue collar)
	Management-by-objectives (MBO) (especially for white collar and professional employees)
	Information sharing
	Attitude surveys
	Structuring of group interaction
	Empathetic management style
Contextual control	Plant location
	Small plant size
	Outsourcing and use of flexible employment arrangements
	Employee screening
	Supervisor selection and training
	Influential human resource management (HRM) department
	Desirable working conditions
	High wages, good fringe benefits
	Job security
	Career advancement opportunities
	Grievance program
	Restrictions on workplace solicitations by union supporters
Monitoring	Attitude surveys
	Surveillance
	Reports from operatives and management loyalists
	Review of employee complaints
	Review of personnel records

SOURCE: Adapted from J. J. Lawler, *Unionization and Deunionization: Strategies, Tactics, and Outcomes* (Columbia: University of South Carolina Press, 1990), pp. 120–21.

Management often uses a variety of consultants in opposing unionization once an organizing campaign begins. Consultants may include attorneys, campaign advisers, advocates of positive labor relations, security services who will provide investigation resources, trade and industry associations who provide expertise gained from previous campaigns, advocacy groups who oppose unions in general, and educational institutions who might provide union avoidance information.[49]

Several tactics, such as improving wages, hours, and terms and conditions of employment or treating union supporters in a discriminatory manner, are unfair labor practices. Evidence suggests that an aggressive campaign that includes unfair labor practices is associated with management victories.[50] The fact that the costs of having been found to have committed an unfair labor practice are very

---

[49] Lawler, *Unionization and Deunionization*, p. 90.

[50] W. T. Dickens, "The Effect of Company Campaigns on Certification Elections: *Law and Reality* Once Again," *Industrial and Labor Relations Review* 36 (1983), pp. 560–75.

TABLE 7–4

Employer Election Campaign Tactics

Objective	Employer Activity
Influence	Captive audience speeches
	Small group and individual meetings
	Letters, posters, handbills, and other written communications
	Threats and/or inducements
	Films, slide shows
Contextual control	External
	Use of regulatory agency procedures
	Election delays
	Linkages with community institutions (banks, police, newspapers, churches, etc.)
	Intraunit
	Supervisor training
	Discriminatory treatment of union supporters
	Short-term improvement in wages, working conditions
	Establish or support employee antiunion committee
	Refuse workplace access to union organizers
	Restrictions on workplace solicitations by union supporters
	Excelsior list misreporting
	Neutrality agreements
Monitoring	Attitude surveys
	Surveillance
	Interrogation
	Reports from operatives and management loyalists

SOURCE: Adapted from J. J. Lawler, *Unionization and Deunionization: Strategies, Tactics, and Outcomes* (Columbia: University of South Carolina Press, 1990), pp. 141–42.

low relative to the costs of unions winning elections actually reinforces employer choices to commit them.

The greater the differential between union wages in an industry and the employer's wage, the greater management resistance will be. Employer resistance increases more rapidly with differentials than with desires for unionization by the employees.[51] An active union avoidance strategy for new facilities decreases the likelihood of organizing from about 15 percent to 1 percent.[52]

---

[51] R. B. Freeman, "The Effect of the Union Wage Differential on Management Opposition and Union Organizing Success," *American Economic Review* 76 (1986), pp. 92–96.

[52] T. A. Kochan, R. B. McKersie, and J. Chalykoff, "The Effects of Corporate Strategy and Workplace Innovations on Union Representation," *Industrial and Labor Relations Review* 39 (1986), pp. 487–501; see also J. J. Lawler and R. West, "Impact of Union-Avoidance Strategy in Representation Elections," *Industrial Relations* 24 (1985), pp. 406–20.

TABLE 7–5

Relative Frequencies of Common Employer Campaign Themes

Campaign Theme	Frequency (%)
Bargaining Impact Themes	66
Strikes may occur	40
High union dues	33
Potential for fines and assessments by the union	24
Unions cannot guarantee any changes	14
Possible plant closing	14
Bargaining may actually reduce wages, benefits, etc.	5
Antiunion themes	35
Union will interfere with good worker-management relations	7
Union dominated by "outsiders"	13
Union has failed elsewhere	6
Union is corrupt	9
Union is radical or leftist	6
Union will subject workers to rules	6
Unionism is inconsistent with employee and community values	1
Procompany Themes	20
Management is a friend to workers	7
Workers already enjoy high wages and/or good working conditions	9
Give company another chance	8

SOURCE: Adapted from J. J. Lawler, *Unionization and Deunionization: Strategies, Tactics, and Outcomes* (Columbia: University of South Carolina Press, 1990), p. 149.

DECERTIFICATIONS

Once certified, unions face risks in continuing their representation role. A majority may vote to oust the union after the one-year certification period ends if no contract is in effect. Decertification elections tend to be more successful in small units lacking local leadership, with low member involvement in union activities, a changing composition of represented employees, and affiliation with a large national union.[53] Economywide variables associated with decertification elections include inflation, low union density in the industry, frequency of strikes, and small bargaining units.[54]

The ratio of decertification to certification elections has increased from 1 in 20 during the 1950s and 1960s to 1 in 4 in the last several years. While decertifications are strongly related to macroeconomic measures, institutional changes reflected in increasing unfair labor practices, reductions in relative social

---

[53] See J. C. Anderson, G. Busman, and C. A. O'Reilly III, "What Factors Influence the Outcome of Union Decertification Elections?" *Monthly Labor Review* 102, no. 11 (1979), pp. 32–36.

[54] D. A. Ahlburg and J. B. Dworkin, "The Influence of Macroeconomic Variables on the Probability of Union Decertification," *Journal of Labor Research* 5 (1984), pp. 13–28.

spending as unemployment increased, and a Republican administration in office were found to be stronger predictors.[55]

FIRST CONTRACTS

If a union wins a representation election, it still can face formidable barriers in achieving its role as a participant in shaping the employment relationship. Before bargaining can commence, the NLRB has to certify the results of the election. Employers may object to a variety of campaign irregularities and, if the election was close, the eligibility of some of the voters. If objections are raised, some time will inevitably elapse until the board issues a ruling. While the delay is occurring, the company may take a number of employee relations actions that indicate it will take a tough stance toward the union. In addition, it may discriminatorily take action against union activists, thereby committing unfair labor practices, but which may also reduce longer-run interests in remaining unionized. If the union is faced with an intransigent management strategy, it will need to use substantial energy and resources to combat the employer.[56]

For its part, the union needs to shift its tactics from an organizing to a negotiating mode. Organizing is highly adversarial, while negotiating requires the parties, especially the union, to start from the position that joint agreement on a settlement is a primary goal. If a national union has been involved in assisting in organizing, this may be the point at which a different representative—one not involved in organizing—is brought in to assist the new local.[57] Local union members also have no experience in negotiating so they need training and assistance from the national. An unaffiliated local often has difficulty in learning how to negotiate, but this weakness may be offset by greater worker involvement in its organization and operation.

An employer may also undermine the union during the bargaining process. It might refuse to bargain on technical grounds such as the appropriateness of the bargaining unit. This will require NLRB intervention and a bargaining order. It might also bargain in a defiant or evasive manner. Defiance may be marked by making it difficult for the union to get information about the employer's situation, and starting with an offer that includes conditions and wages lower than what is presently implemented.[58]

---

[55] E. A. Nilsson, "The Growth of Union Decertification: A Test of Two Nonnested Theories," *Industrial Relations* 36 (1997), pp. 324–48.

[56] W. N. Cooke, "Failure to Negotiate First Contracts," *Industrial and Labor Relations Review* 38 (1985), pp. 163–78; and W. N. Cooke, "The Rising Toll of Discrimination against Union Certification Elections," *Industial Relations* 24 (1985), pp. 421–41.

[57] T. F. Reed, "Nice Guys Don't Always Finish Last: The Impact of the Union Organizer on the Probability of Securing a First Contract," unpublished paper, Texas A&M University, 1989.

[58] R. W. Hurd, "Union-Free Bargaining Strategies and First Contract Failures," *Proceedings of the Industrial Relations Research Association* 48 (1996), pp. 145–52.

If the employer can forestall reaching an agreement for at least one year after initial certification, employees could (with sufficient interest) petition for a decertification election. It's also possible that the union could fail to enroll a majority of workers as union members and conclude that interest in representation is waning. It might, in unusual circumstances, abandon the negotiations and walk away from the situation.

Evidence suggests that newly organized employers have been taking a harder line in negotiating first contracts, especially since there are few real penalties the NLRB can implement for refusing to bargain. Where management is particularly intransigent, community action and/or corporate campaigns may be the only effective strategy the union can use to buttress its attempts to win an initial contract.

JOB STRUCTURING

Employers and unions may be involved in a continual battle to determine whether jobs fall within the jurisdiction of the bargaining unit or not. At the time that an election is held, the NLRB defines what jobs and what employees are within the bargaining unit. As noted, the law requires professionals to agree affirmatively to be part of a bargaining unit before they can be included. If a set of jobs is changed radically and skill requirements are increased, the employer may argue that they are no longer a part of the bargaining unit as it was defined at election time.

At the same time, if low-skilled jobs are outsourced, the bargaining unit is gradually hollowed out by job design changes, and bargaining power is lost.

SUMMARY

Differences between capitalist and trade union philosophies related to the operation of the workplace cause inevitable conflicts. Employers have long resisted attempts to unionize, with industrial-type unions having little success in organizing workers until passage of the Wagner Act. Following a "corporatist" period of about 30 years following World War II during which management generally conceded a legitimate role for labor, employers took a harder line against organizing and bargaining beginning in the late 1970s. Currently, many employers have a goal of "union-free" employment and implement strategies to avoid new organization and eliminate current unionization in their firms.

Unionization has a variety of economic effects on employers. In general, productivity of unionized workers is higher than nonunion workers in manufacturing and construction, but not in the service sector. Union members earn a substantial pay premium. Where unions have negotiated wage and benefit improvements, employers generally pass these along to unorganized workers as well. Thus, the cost of unionization is not fully related only to unionized workers. Studies of stock price changes associated with unionization and deunionization generally find that share prices fall at a higher than expected rate when unionization or attempts to unionize occur.

Employers implement a variety of practices in an attempt to remain union free. Employers adopting a "philosophy-laden" approach create an employment relationship that fits a particular culture and manner of treating employees. As a result, employees see their situations as being, in most respects, as good as or better than what they would be able to negotiate if they were represented. In other, more traditional approaches, employers may purposely implement a set of employment practices that closely mimic a unionized environment, thereby reducing the likelihood that issues would arise to lead to unionization.

In their avoidance of unionization, nonunion employers focus on plant location decisions, wage and benefit policies, staffing practices, and employee grievance systems, among others. Preventive programs involve attitude surveys, surveillance, employee communications, and supervisor training. If an organizing attempt takes place, intensive communications, hiring consultants, and procedural delays are often implemented. If the union wins recognition, the employer may take an intransigent approach to bargaining an initial contract.

Decertifications are an increasing proportion of NLRB-conducted elections. These must be initiated by employees during a period in which a contract is not in effect.

DISCUSSION QUESTIONS

1. Is the increasing resistance of employers to unionization a new phenomenon or simply a return to the historic relationship that has existed between unions and managements in the United States?

2. Would you expect a stronger antiunion response from an employer in manufacturing or in a service industry?

3. In today's increasingly competitive employment environment, would you expect to find many (or any) employers taking a "philosophy-laden" approach?

4. Should public policy change in some way so that unions who win representation rights have a guarantee that they will be able to negotiate a first contract?

KEY TERMS

Company union   *189*   Philosophy-laden   *194*
Doctrinaire organization   *194*

CASE

GMFC—LOCATING THE NEW RECREATIONAL VEHICLE PLANT

GMFC is planning to expand its U.S. operations by building a new plant that will employ about 500 production workers. This new plant will manufacture motorized recreational equipment, including all-terrain vehicles, personal watercraft, and snowmobiles. The equipment will assemble mechanical components produced in other GMFC operations or purchased from suppliers. The new plant will fabricate fiberglass body parts and complete the final assembly process.

GMFC would like to operate the new plant "union free." It's likely that the United Auto Workers (UAW) and perhaps other internationals will attempt to organize the workforce within a year after startup. You are a member of a planning committee for the new plant. Your primary area of responsibility involves issues related to potential unionization and labor costs. What advice would you provide to the company on plant size, location, staffing, wages and benefits, and other employee relations issues that would help GMFC keep the new plant union free and competitive?

THE ENVIRONMENT

FOR BARGAINING

*O*rganizing campaigns focus on the individual employer and union trying to organize a bargaining unit. While organizing is in progress, both parties concentrate on the issue at hand—whether the employees desire representation. If employees vote to be represented, the employer and the union must bargain within the realities of the environment in which they operate. Environmental aspects that influence bargaining include the degree of competition in the employer's product market, the employer's financial condition, the employer's capital-labor mix, the bargaining issue interests of the union, the effects of unionization on the employer's relationship with the labor market, and any laws and regulations related to the industry in which the employer operates or the fact that it is now unionized.

This chapter begins a four-chapter section on bargaining issues and negotiations. Chapter 8 explores (1) the economic environment in which collective bargaining occurs, (2) the influence of the economic environment and the bargaining structure on bargaining power, and (3) bargaining structures that unions and managements design. Chapter 9 focuses on wage and benefit issues and evidence related to the effects of unions in these areas. Chapter 10 concentrates on nonwage issues and the perceptions of union members of their union's effectiveness. Chapter 11 covers the organizational structures in which employers and unions negotiate, important employer and union bargaining goals, the negotiation process, and the identification and quantification of contract costs.

As you study this chapter, consider the following questions:

1. How does the degree of competition within the product market influence the bargaining behavior of the parties?
2. What effect does unionization have on the wage and employment decisions of employers?

3. What influence do laws and regulations have on collective bargaining?
4. How does globalization of certain markets affect employers and unions?
5. What joint decisions do employers and unions make in their bargaining relationship to attempt to insulate themselves from market conditions?
6. How do economic conditions, product market concentration, and bargaining structure influence bargaining power?

THE PRODUCT AND SERVICE MARKET

Both private- and public-sector organizations create products and services. Some result from responses to consumer demands, while others come from new discoveries and developments that consumers will demand in the future. Consumer demand for certain products or services, the level of competition among suppliers, and the availability of acceptable substitutes all influence how employers relate to the market.

To create products and services, employers combine raw materials, capital, and labor. To produce steel, iron ore, limestone, scrap iron, coke, and other ingredients (raw materials) are combined in a furnace within a steel mill (capital) operated by steelworkers and their supervisors (labor). This combination of production factors is not as obvious where services, such as education, are provided. In a university, students (raw materials) use cafeterias, dormitories, libraries, laboratories, classrooms, computers, and audiovisual equipment (capital), with the assistance of faculty, librarians, clericals, food service and residence workers, and maintenance employees (labor) to obtain a degree.

The economy is a dynamic process in which consumer purchase levels are influenced by their current wealth; the degree of competition among producers; and the prices of raw materials, capital, and labor used to produce their outputs. Changes in product prices influence the amount of a given output consumers purchase. The producer's demand for factors of production is said to be derived from consumers' final demand for the output produced.

How consumers react to price changes determines the elasticity of demand. Demand is inelastic if price changes (up or down) have relatively little effect on the amount of a product or service purchased, while demand is elastic if purchases are highly sensitive to price changes. Figure 8–1 shows examples of relatively elastic (D_E) and inelastic (D_I) demand schedules where Q is the quantity sold and P is the price.

Levels of demand vary over time. Some changes are cyclical (the demand for types of clothing is related to seasons), while others are secular (long-term changes related to shifts in demand or the introduction of substitutes, such as fewer men's and women's hats or increased use of PCs relative to mainframes or contact lenses for eyeglasses). Short-run (or cyclical) demand changes mean employers will change their derived demands for inputs. In most instances, however, capital usage cannot be changed rapidly. For example, when the demand for

FIGURE 8–1

Examples of Elastic and Inelastic Demand

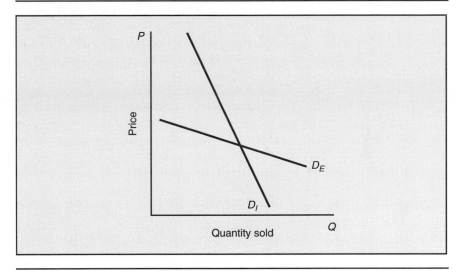

automobiles declined during the late 1970s and early 1980s, auto producers did not immediately respond by selling plants. Instead, they purchased less steel, fiberglass, aluminum, tires, and parts and laid off workers at various levels (production employees first) to accommodate the reduction in overall demand. In the long run, some plants closed, but substantial reductions in raw material and labor purchases occurred first.

If there are several suppliers of relatively similar products and services, the consumer can pick and choose among them based on price. Where a relatively small capital investment is necessary to enter a product market, more competition should result. It's no accident that travel agents outnumber airlines, because the capital outlay required to operate a travel agency is far less than required to provide air travel. The more producers there are, the more elastic is the demand for the products of each because the consumer has a greater ability to choose on the basis of price.

The willingness of consumers to substitute one product for another or the degree to which the demand for one product is influenced by the demand for another is also important to the employer. Consider fast food, for example. As menus expand, consumers have more price-quality-taste decisions to make. If hamburger prices go up and consumers switch to chicken or fish sandwiches, these are substitutes. As a result, beef purchases decrease, resulting in decreased demand for packinghouse workers, cattle, and beef-processing plants. Conversely, fishing and fishery workers, chicken-processing employees, and chicken producers will be positively influenced by the change. There are also complementary relationships between products. If the demand for fish sandwiches goes up, so will the demand for tartar sauce.

If the relative prices of the factors of production change, employers will change the ratios in which they use each. For example, when the price of silver increased substantially in 1980, printers installed devices to recapture silver from photographic plates. Capital was substituted for raw materials. Automakers substitute capital for labor when they install robots on assembly lines. When homeowners install insulation to reduce heating costs, labor (installation) and capital (insulating materials) are substituted for raw materials (gas, oil, or electricity).

Public policy constraints on markets have also been enacted. Some retard the changes that would occur rapidly as the result of major market shifts (e.g., rationing or allocations during fuel shortages), while others prohibit forming or operating monopolies.

PUBLIC POLICY AND INDUSTRIAL ORGANIZATION

Since the passage of the Sherman Antitrust Act in 1890, public policy has limited industrial concentration and collusive activities between producers in a single industry. Excessive industrial concentration is not defined in the statute, by the courts, or by the Federal Trade Commission. On the other hand, price fixing and other collusive activities have been vigorously prosecuted when discovered, and persons or organizations who have been harmed by them have been entitled to recover treble damages.

The growth and maturation of most industries seem to follow a general pattern. During an industry's infancy, production is labor intensive. Characteristics of products are relatively diverse. As consumer preferences are revealed, some producers go out of business because their products do not meet consumer needs. As production methods become standardized, capital and cheaper labor are substituted for skilled craft work, and more efficient producers lower prices, thus driving marginal producers from the industry. Over time, an industry becomes dominated by relatively few firms, and the less dominant either mimic the leader or occupy niches in which the leader chooses not to produce. In the microcomputer industry, various microprocessors and operating systems have been tried, with Intel microprocessors and Microsoft Windows operating systems overwhelming the competition. Software producers must design products to run on Intel-based equipment using Microsoft operating systems in order to have a place in the market. Competitive hardware must follow established standards to be compatible with the software designed to run on the dominant producer's equipment.

In competitive markets, price has a major effect on the quantity each producer sells. Thus, they face very elastic product demand curves. For example, at colleges and universities with several bookstores, prices for textbooks are lower than where there is only one. If the bookstores are within a reasonable distance of campus, student purchase decisions are highly price related. A price-cutting bookstore will increase its market share rapidly. Competition will probably not increase the overall demand for textbooks at a university because students purchase only one copy of each required text. As noted later, the elasticity of demand for a firm's products has a major effect on its demand for labor.

Highly concentrated markets have only one dominant producer or a few major producers. Concentration occurs in most goods-producing industries. Companies with high costs resulting from inefficiency, poor management, or other factors will be forced out of business as competitors drop prices to increase market share. This process will take longer when the product market is growing (which would lead to a more elastic demand for each), but ultimately concentration would be expected. The greater the industrial concentration, the greater the ability of producers to raise prices to consumers without reducing quantities sold.

Regulation and Deregulation

Regulation of certain industries was a tradition in the United States for almost a century. The Interstate Commerce Act was passed in 1887 to regulate interstate rail freight rates. Congress intended to reduce or eliminate price discrimination between small and large shippers and to maintain an incentive for transportation companies to provide service to rural areas. Other industries that have had services and charges regulated include communications, banking, petroleum products and natural gas, electric utilities, interstate trucking, and airlines. But over the past several years, federal regulation in many of these areas has been reduced or eliminated. The initial result has been the elimination of monopolies and the restoration of price competition.

Deregulation enabled new companies to enter these markets and created competition in wages between union and nonunion sectors of the industries. Until now, wages and employment have been most affected by deregulation in trucking, air carriers, and telecommunications. One study found that airline deregulation had relatively little effect on mechanics, but the salaries of pilots fell 22 percent and flight attendants 39 percent from what would have been expected had deregulation not occurred.[1] Mechanics would have alternative employment opportunities in other industries, an advantage not enjoyed by pilots and flight attendants. Following deregulation in the trucking industry, coverage of truckers by the National Master Freight Agreement negotiated by the Teamsters and Trucking Management, Inc., fell by two-thirds. Wages fell by 27 percent and return on equity by 22 percent between 1977 and 1990.[2] The effects of deregulation continue to occur in other industries. Exhibit 8–1 contains information about employment issues in the 1998 local phone company strikes.

---

[1] P.-Y. Cremieux, "The Effects of Deregulation on Employee Earnings: Pilots, Flight Attendants, and Mechanics, 1959–1992," *Industrial and Labor Relations Review* 49 (1995), pp. 223–42.

[2] M. H. Belzer, "Collective Bargaining after Deregulation: Do the Teamsters Still Count?" *Industrial and Labor Relations Review* 48 (1995), pp. 636–55.

EXHIBIT 8–1

CWA and US West Still Dealing with Effects of Deregulation

The Communications Workers of America (CWA), claiming victory Monday at the end of its 15-day strike against U S West, accused the company of fostering bitter negotiations and using union-busting tactics in talks that it characterized as unusually bitter for a Baby Bell.

The strike, which ended late Sunday with the announcement of a tentative agreement, idled 32,000 union phone workers in 13 states.

The CWA seemed the clear winner in the struggle, and Monday claimed to have won several important battles, including limits on what it called excessive overtime work, modifications to a controversial pay-for-performance plan, and the scrapping of a health plan that would have been more costly for and given fewer choices to its members.

[CWA Vice President Sue] Pisha said the agreement is "very much in line" with those the CWA has signed with other telephone companies.

U S West said some aspects of the proposed contract are better than previous CWA contracts. "We believe that the tentative agreement represents a 'best' in the industry in the wage and benefits package," said Mary Hisley, a U S West spokeswoman.

[The contract includes a voluntary pay-for-performance program to be jointly designed by the company and union, overtime capped at 16 hours a week in January 1999 and reducing to 8 hours by January 2001, a reduction from two to one free medical plan per market to be jointly reviewed by the company and union, a wage increase of 10.9 percent over three years, and pension increases of 21 percent over three years.]

SOURCE: Steve Alexander, "Union Criticizes U S West Tactics," *Minneapolis Star Tribune*, September 1, 1998, p. D1–D2.

GLOBAL COMPETITION

Many manufacturers encounter substantial foreign competition. Steel is an example. Because it's essentially a commodity, differences in production and shipping costs cannot be passed on to consumers. Certain fixed costs for plants and equipment, incurred whether operating or not, lead producers to sell steel at a loss for a short time rather than shut down a plant. Where excess capacity exists in the short run, foreign firms may "dump" steel in the U.S. at prices below their costs. Services can also be dumped, Exhibit 8–2 capsulizes complaints of European air carriers who argued that U.S. carriers were "dumping" seats in the North Atlantic market in 1993.

American automakers encountered global competition in the mid-1970s as a result of increased fuel prices. Vehicle efficiency became a more important criterion in consumer purchase decisions. Over time, increased consumer attention to quality began to dominate purchase decisions within various price ranges. Differences in labor costs in various producing countries led to price advantages for producers in some nations. These differences include variations in both wages and labor productivity. Relative costs increase or decrease depending on the exchange rate between the dollar and foreign currencies.

EXHIBIT 8–2

European Community Air Carriers Complain about U.S. Carrier "Dumping"

The European Community [EC] has adopted measures limiting air fare cuts and access by United States [U.S.] carriers, in a move that could fuel a trans-Atlantic trade war, government officials say.

The General Accounting Office . . . reported this week that these measures include a prohibition against non-[EC] airlines' introducing low fares on routes between [EC] countries.

The measures, which took effect on January 1, provided that only [EC] airlines could introduce fares lower than existing ones, or introduce "new products" on routes within the [EC]. They also prevent [EC] nations from establishing bilateral agreements with non-[EC] governments that would provide greater access for non-[EC] airlines.

. . . Some [EC] governments fear that their national airlines would be devoured in a no-holds-barred competition against their American rivals. One sign of mounting tensions across the Atlantic was a blistering attack on American aviation policy on Wednesday by Bernard Attali, the chairman of Air France.

Mr. Attali called on the [EC] to counter what he called American carriers' practice of "price dumping" cheaper fares overseas, according to a report in Thursday's *Journal of Commerce*. Mr. Attali said that as a result of the intense competition in the domestic U.S. market, American carriers were introducing increasingly competitive overseas fares.

SOURCE: M. Tolchin, "Europe's New Airline Rules Displease U.S.," *New York Times,* May 15, 1993, p. 134.

When these types of changes occur, the elasticity of demand for a particular firm's products increases substantially because the industry is no longer concentrated. Wage increases cannot be as easily passed through. Wage concessions initiated in the 1980s were due partly to labor costs (combined with other costs) that would not permit U.S. manufacturers to operate at a profit. After short-run reductions in wages (labor) and parts suppliers' prices (raw materials), some obsolete plants (capital) were shut down to reduce the cost content of new vehicles.

Global competition in basic industries has drastic effects on the wages and employment of unionized workers.[3] Domestic producers are moving some labor-intensive operations to countries with lower labor costs. On the other hand, German automobile manufacturers such as Mercedes-Benz and BMW opened plants in the United States and began buying auto producers in lower-wage European countries such as Great Britain. Changes enabled by NAFTA were opposed by unions because they threatened the availability of high-wage jobs.

---

[3] R. B. Freeman, "Are Your Wages Set in Beijing?" *Journal of Economic Perspectives* 9, No. 3, 1995, pp. 15–32.

EMPLOYER INTERESTS

As noted in Chapter 4, private-sector firms are ultimately governed by their share-holders. Labor is hired to accomplish organizational objectives. Shareholders seek a higher-risk adjusted return than other investments offer, which means a firm's original purpose may no longer be the one by which investors can best realize their objectives. Firms might be expected to leave previous markets and enter new ones as the environment changes the rates of return for various industries. The increase in mergers and acquisitions reflects the mobility of capital. If a firm is not making an acceptable return on its equity, a lower-earning division can be divested, forcing unions to deal with successor owners. Part of an organization can also be spun off as General Motors is doing with parts of its parts-producing operations. Exhibit 8–3 provides information on the reasons behind this action.

To meet investor objectives, management seeks to maximize profits in its present operations and to shift investment from areas with declining returns to those where improvement is anticipated with the greatest amount of flexibility possible.

Labor as a Derived Demand

Labor is necessary to produce and sell products. Total sales depend on aggregate consumer purchases. Thus, the demand for labor is derived with the level of employment influenced by the elasticity of demand for the employer's products. The derived demand for labor is more inelastic: (1) the more essential a given type of labor is in the production of the final products, (2) the more inelastic the demand for the final products, (3) the smaller the fraction of total cost accounted for by the item in question, and (4) the more inelastic the supply of competing production factors.[4] These situations indicate skilled trades in relatively small bargaining units where substitutes are not readily obtainable and where price has little influence over sales would be least likely to cause employers to resist wage increases.

When an employer is a relatively small factor in a labor market and/or when there is substantial unemployment, its supply of labor will likely be very elastic, and hiring more employees will have little effect on the wage rate. But if several employers hire the same type of labor simultaneously and/or unemployment is low, a wage increase will be necessary to obtain a larger supply. Employers are likely to be able to pass on the cost of a wage increase if they are in a noncompetitive product market, because a price increase will not greatly reduce quantities sold if demand is inelastic.

Employers view labor from a short-run perspective. When more employees are needed, they can be hired; when less are needed, they can be laid off. The amount of labor hired would be determined by the price of output, the elasticity of

---

[4] A. Marshall, *Principles of Economics*, 8th ed. (New York: Macmillan, 1920).

EXHIBIT 8–3

GM Plans to Spin Off Delphi Car Parts Unit

In a move that could improve its competitive position but worsen its already tattered labor relations, General Motors said Monday that it will divest its huge Delphi auto parts unit next year.

Though not a household name, Delphi would emerge from the complex stock transaction with 200,000 employees and rank as the nation's 25th-largest company—bigger than Intel, Chase Manhattan, or Lockheed Martin.

Delphi, which posted 1997 sales of $31.4 billion, produces AC sparkplugs, radiators and steering components, among much else. The deal is valued by analysts at more than $10 billion.

Although long expected, the deal's announcement comes only five days after the giant automaker settled a 54-day labor dispute that erupted in part over GM's desire to close down inefficient Delphi operations.

The United Auto Workers union has consistently opposed the Delphi divestiture and late Monday responded sharply to GM's announcement, saying it would do whatever is necessary to protect the jobs of Delphi hourly workers.

GM Chairman John F. Smith Jr. said the Delphi sale represents a historic, strategic shift away from vertical integration, in which GM produces everything from the smallest part to assembling and delivering a vehicle.

. . . Ford Motor and Chrysler produce far fewer of their own parts, as do many of the nation's heavy manufacturers. GM is making its move long after the shift away from vertical integration has become a business trend . . . GM makes more of its components than rivals, who can buy the same parts cheaper at outside, often nonunion, suppliers. GM makes about 65 percent of its own parts, compared with less than 50 percent at Ford and 30 percent at Chrysler. (Ford is also expected to spin off its Visteon parts unit soon.)

The union fears that Delphi's sale will lead to plant closings and possible layoffs. In addition, the partsmaker is likely to push in future years for contract concessions, such as lower wages, once it is separated from GM.

SOURCE: D. W. Nauss, "GM Plans to Spin Off Delphi Car Parts Unit," *Los Angeles Times,* August 4, 1988, p. D–1.

---

demand, and the firm's productivity given its capital equipment. Economic theory suggests additional workers will be added until the wage rate equals the value of the additional product the last hired worker adds. This value (the amount of the product times the price) is called the **marginal revenue product** (MRP). If the demand curve shifted or changed its elasticity, the employer would need more or fewer workers and would like to react accordingly.

In the short run, the marginal product of additional labor declines because the employer is using a fixed amount of capital. For example, a university contains a fixed number of classrooms. At some point, hiring additional faculty would not lead to more classes because there would be no place to teach them. The declining marginal product of labor means labor demand is somewhat inelastic (downward sloping), even though demand for the company's product might be completely

elastic. In concentrated industries, the demand for a firm's product is never completely elastic because each firm is a large proportion of the industry, and each
firm's products have some unique characteristics. Therefore, the labor demand is
less elastic than in the competitive situation because marginal revenue at the point
where market demand intersects the labor supply price would be less than the
price of labor. Figure 8–2 gives examples of employment change comparisons in
competitive and concentrated situations.

Labor-Capital Substitution

Labor and capital are required to produce products and services. Besides being
interested in moving in and out of product and service markets quickly, employers would also like to change the capital-labor mix as the relative costs of the two
change. For example, inventory and checkout processes in a supermarket might
be handled in two ways. In one, the checker would total prices using a conventional tape-printing cash register. Stock clerks would track shelf and backroom
inventory and tell the store manager when to order certain items. In the other
supermarket, the checker would use an optical scanner to read universal product

FIGURE 8–2

Effects of Product Market Concentration on Employment When Demand Changes

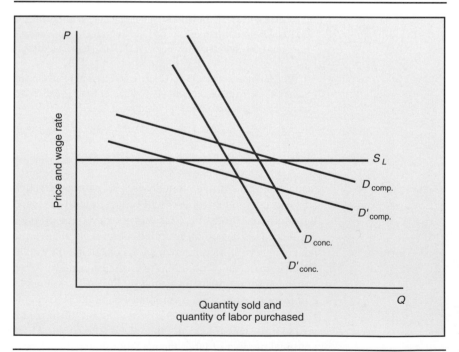

codes, retrieve prices from a computer, print them on the register tape, and simultaneously subtract the purchased item from the stock in the store's inventory. When sufficient purchases are made, the item automatically would be added to a reorder list.

Assume in the first situation that one stock clerk is required to keep track of inventory for every eight checkers. Each employee is paid $35,000 in wages and benefits annually. If a store had 16 checkers, its annual payroll costs would be $630,000. Assume with scanners that the checkers are slightly less productive (scanning takes slightly longer than checking), so another checker is needed. But stock clerks are no longer needed. Assume the cost of the scanners is $2,000 per checker per year. But the scanners' rapid feedback and greater precision in ordering reduces stockouts, excessive inventories, and outdated goods, so the store makes an additional profit of $15,000 per year. Under the new system, payroll costs would be $595,000 (17 checkers and no stock clerks), equipment costs would increase by $34,000 (17 checkout counters), and inventory management-related profits would increase by $15,000. The net savings of the new system would be $16,000 per year. As a result, the store would reduce its staff by one (add one checker and eliminate two stock clerks) while expanding its use of capital.

Employers would like to make adjustments whenever a different combination of factors would improve returns. Changes in the use of capital are generally based on relatively long-run payoffs. To the extent that labor contracts fix wages and restrict layoffs, the use and costs of labor are not changeable in the short run, leaving the employer with what it believes is a suboptimal combination. If negotiations result in increased wages, the employer can be expected to reduce the use of labor and potentially increase the use of capital. Figure 8–3 depicts a graphical example of the type of adjustments an employer would make over a period of time following a wage settlement that increased wages while the price of capital remained constant.

The cost of capital (K) is graphed on the vertical axis and labor (L) on the horizontal axis. Points K and L represent the amounts of each that can be purchased with a budget of a given size. The straight line connecting K and L (KL) is a *budget line* representing all combinations of capital and labor that can be purchased with this budget amount. The arc labeled 100 is an *isoquant* representing all combinations of labor and capital that could be combined to produce 100 units of output. The lowest point on this arc is the most efficient combination of labor and capital necessary to produce this level of output. In Figure 8–3, the arc contacts the budget line at this most efficient point. The corresponding points on the K and L axes are k and l. No other combination of labor and capital that could produce 100 units of output could be purchased with the current budget.

If labor's wage increases, the amount of labor that can be purchased with this budget decreases. The new budget line (KL') lies below the old budget line at all points except K (purchase only capital). No part of the line contacts the 100-unit output isoquant. Thus, the employer's *real income* has declined because it cannot

FIGURE 8–3

Capital-Labor Trade-offs When Wages Increase

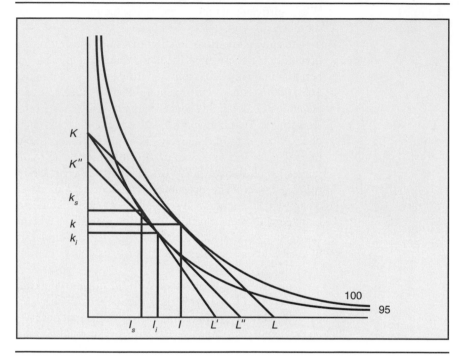

purchase as much as before with the same amount of money. If the employer maintains the same budget, it would have to lower production to a level at which the budget line contacted a lower isoquant, say 95.

The point at which KL' contacts the 95-unit isoquant determines the new most efficient use of each input k_s, l_s. The moves from k to k_s and l to l_s represent a substitution of capital for labor. If the previous labor–capital price–wage relationship continued, then the $K''L''$ budget line would contact the 95-output unit isoquant at a point that k_i, l_i capital and labor would be used. The changes from k to k_i and l to l_i represent the income effect. The changes from k_i to k_s and l_i to l_s represent the substitution effect. Thus, all else being equal, a wage increase will increase the use of capital relative to labor due to the change in relative input prices and decrease the use of one or both due to the drop in real income.

Labor Markets

One of the outcomes of unionization is that the union acquires monopoly power over the labor supply. The union doesn't actually supply the labor, but the contract it negotiates with management fixes its price. Since unions are most attracted to firms that have power to influence prices in the product market or wages in the

FIGURE 8–4

Monopsony Wage and Employment Decisions

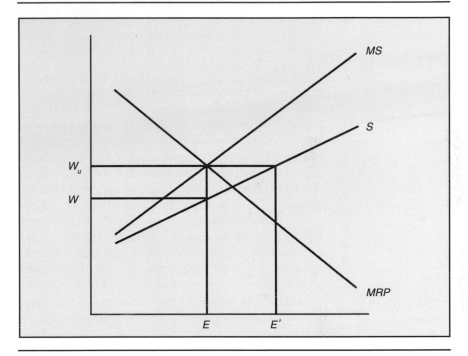

labor market—because these are the employers most able to finance wage increases—what contracting does is to elasticize the labor supply at the contracted rate (assuming a wage premium has been negotiated).

Figure 8–4 demonstrates what happens to an employer who is a monopsonist (single purchaser of labor in a given market) following unionization. In the pre-unionization situation the *marginal revenue product (MRP)* curve reflects the declining productivity of added labor. The *S* curve represents the labor supply curve in the market. Since the firm is a monopsonist, this is its supply curve. The **marginal supply curve** (*MS*) curve represents the additional cost associated with expanding the workforce. For example, if one worker could be hired at $6 but the wage would need to increase to $7 before a second worker would take the job, the cost (marginal supply) of adding the second worker is a $7 + $1 increase for the previously hired worker, or $8. The firm will hire no more workers than necessary to maximize profit (*MS* = *MRP*). This would be equal to *E* measured at its intersection with the *S* curve. *W* would be the wage necessary to hire *E* workers.

The union could negotiate a wage at any level up to the intersection of *MS* and *MRP*, say W_u. Any increase beyond *W* would reduce the employer's profits, but the employer would also now be able to expand employment (if needed) out to *E'* without incurring greater costs than the negotiated wage for each additional worker. Unionization has transferred some level of profits into wages, but has also increased the ability of the employer to respond to increases in demand with an elastic labor supply.

EMPLOYEE INTERESTS

Employee interests are different from those of employers. Employers are interested in accomplishing the organization's objectives, which in the private sector is to maximize long-run profits. Employees want to maximize the long-run return to their investment in skills and the effort they exert in employment. Investors diversify their risks across a portfolio while employees, usually tied to a single occupation, are generally unable to diversify their employment risks. To the extent that employees invest in skills specific to their current employer, their long-run returns depend on job security and the employer's ability and willingness to pay.

A variety of job outcomes are important to employees. Union members believe that grievance handling, fringe benefits, wages, and job security are the most important issues.[5] The relative importance of each probably varies with the economic and employer environment. For example, when layoffs are rising, job security is more important than wage and fringe benefit improvements.

Employees' interests can often be met in their employment, but where they are not and when they do not have other opportunities, forming a union can create bargaining power by monopolizing the internal labor supply.

UNION INTERESTS

Employees unionize to obtain through collective bargaining outcomes they believe are unavailable to them as individuals. Member desires have a major impact on union bargaining goals. It has been suggested that contract demands reflect the preferences of the "median voter" in a unit,[6] requiring the contract to be acceptable to at least a majority to be ratified. Local union officers are often elected by a single bargaining unit. Bargaining success directly influences their ability to be reelected. Where local unions service several bargaining units, local officers might be less concerned about the contents of individual contracts.

Unions demonstrate their effectiveness by negotiating contracts improving employment conditions for their members, attracting new members, and organizing additional units. As an institution, the union desires security as the employees' representative through negotiated union shop agreements.

---

[5] T. A. Kochan, "How American Workers View Labor Unions," *Monthly Labor Review* 102, no. 4 (1979), pp. 23–31.

[6] M. D. White, "The Intra-Unit Wage Structure and Unions: A Median Voter Model," *Industrial and Labor Relations Review* 35 (1982), pp. 565–77.

Two major goals of labor organizations are higher wages and increased membership.[7] Labor is presumed to prefer both, but in its dealings with management, the union often makes trade-offs between them. If wages increase relative to competitors, an employer might find it necessary to reduce employment (membership). To expand employment, wages must rise less rapidly than productivity. However, a national union might be willing to sacrifice some small fraction of employment in a unit to gain higher wages that will increase its organizing leverage in nonunion units with increasingly lower relative wages.

Generally, unions would be predicted to seek wage gains for present members before pursuing expanded employment. Figure 8–5 shows the presumed direction of preferred union trade-offs. The theoretical preference path is not straight because union members may not value employment changes and wages equally. For example, members may favor wage increases over additional membership, preferring stable wages with employment security given risk aversion associated with an inability to diversify employment risks. Employers may actually be the party that prefers expanded employment because they can gain **bargaining power** by threatening layoffs of unit members if negotiated wages were to increase.[8] A study of British trade union leaders found they preferred to maximize pay for present members, but also had a weak interest in expanding employment (which would increase their power as officers).[9] Evidence indicates that unions do not contract for added employment.[10] When facing a cutback, senior members (if they are the median voters) may prefer employment reductions to wage cuts. On the other hand, if a bargaining unit faces the alternative of making a wage concession or the potential closing of a plant, the median voter would be likely to favor concessions where job security guarantees are granted.[11]

LEGAL REQUIREMENTS

Public policy establishes the ground rules for the issues the parties must discuss and the way negotiations will be conducted. Section 8(d) of the Labor-Management Relations Act of 1947 sets forth in one sentence the essence of collective bargaining in the United States.

> For the purposes of this section, to bargain collectively is the performance of the mutual obligation of the employer and representative of the employees to meet at

---

[7] A. M. Cartter, *Theory of Wages and Employment* (Homewood, IL: Richard D. Irwin, 1959), pp. 88–94.

[8] W. J. Wessels, "Contract Curve or Implicit Contract: Which Will a Union Choose?" *Journal of Labor Research* 12 (1991), pp. 73–89.

[9] A. Clark and A. Oswald, "Trade Union Utility Functions: A Survey of Union Leaders' Views," *Industrial Relations* 32 (1993), pp. 391–411.

[10] W. J. Wessels, "Do Unions Contract for Added Employment?" *Industrial and Labor Relations Review* 45 (1991), pp. 181–93.

[11] P. Cappelli, "Concession Bargaining and the National Economy," *Proceedings of the Industrial Relations Research Association* 35 (1982), pp. 362–71.

FIGURE 8–5
Wage-Employment Preference Path

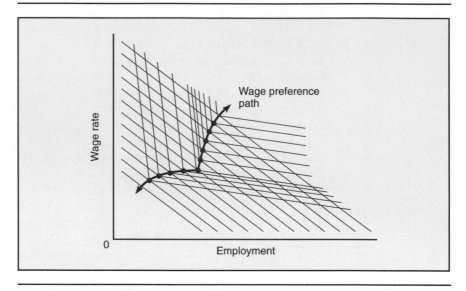

SOURCE: A. M. Cartter, *Theory of Wages and Employment* (Homewood, IL: Richard D. Irwin, 1959), p. 91. Copyright © 1959 by Richard D. Irwin, Inc.

reasonable times and confer in good faith with respect to wages, hours, and terms and conditions of employment, or the negotiation of an agreement, or any question arising thereunder, and the execution of a written contract incorporating any agreement reached if requested by either party, but such obligation does not compel either party to agree to a proposal or require the making of a concession.

This broad definition affects both the process and the issues. For example, for process, what does "good faith" mean? On issues, what do "wages, hours, and other terms and condition of employment" signify? Unions, employers, the NLRB, and the courts have all grappled with these. Novel demands and bargaining tactics have been challenged to determine whether they conform to the statute. Chapters 11, 12, 14, and 15 examine **good faith bargaining** and its impact on process. Chapters 9 and 10 examine the meaning of "wages, hours, and other terms and conditions of employment" issues.

Bargaining issues can be divided into three legal categories: mandatory, permissive, and prohibited. **Mandatory issues** fall within the definition of wages, hours, and other terms and conditions of employment. Wages and hours are straightforward, dealing with economics and work schedules. "Terms and conditions of employment" is a more amorphous concept. A reasonable test of whether an issue is within this area asks if the practice would have a direct and immediate effect on union members' jobs, and is strongly determined by labor cost factors.[12] A plant closing or a reassignment of work between job groups are examples. **Permissive demands** do not require a response because they have no direct impact on management or labor costs. A demand by a union to have a say in the establishment of company product prices would be permissive. **Prohibited issues,** such as demands that employers use only union-produced goods, are statutorily outlawed. Another distinction between mandatory and permissive issues is that neither party may go to **impasse** (refuse to agree on a contract) over a permissive issue. Figure 8–6 describes tests used to distinguish between mandatory and permissive issues.

The labeling of issues as mandatory and permissive seems to affect their appearance in contracts. Permissive issues are not included as frequently in situations where the distinction is imposed. The bargaining power of the union also appears to increase the likelihood of the inclusion of permissive issues in contract clauses in the negotiated agreement.[13]

BARGAINING POWER

Bargaining power does not necessarily reside in the degree to which the employer controls its output market. Bargaining power is better conceptualized as "my cost of disagreeing on your terms relative to my cost of agreeing on your terms."[14] For example, a grocer in a highly competitive market may find that agreeing to a wage demand will eliminate its profit margin. Thus, the grocer would object to a union wage proposal. The employees would likely pressure the union to lower its demands unless strike benefits were equivalent to present wages or unless alternative employment were available. On the other hand, an employer who sells products in a less-than-competitive market may accept a relatively large wage demand because the costs can be largely passed on to consumers.

The elasticity of demand for products and labor has a major effect on bargaining power. Power is enhanced by obtaining a monopoly in the product or service market. For example, a remote community with only one food store would be at the monopoly's mercy. As prices increased, customers might buy less of each commodity, but total revenues would continue to rise with lower volume because the community would need to eat. Sooner or later, news about the amazing profits made by the remote food store would spread, and a new store would be built to get a share of those profits. Competition would ensue, and prices would fall.

[12] J. T. Delaney, D. Sockell, and J. Brockner, "Bargaining Effects of the Mandatory-Permissive Distinction," *Industrial Relations* 27 (1988), pp. 21–36.

[13] J. T. Delaney and D. Sockell, "The Mandatory-Permissive Distinction and Collective Bargaining Outcomes," *Industrial and Labor Relations Review* 42 (1989), pp. 566–83.

[14] N. W. Chamberlain and D. E. Cullen, *The Labor Sector*, 2d ed. (New York: McGraw-Hill, 1971), p. 227.

FIGURE 8–6

How Mandatory (M) or Permissive (P) Status is Determined

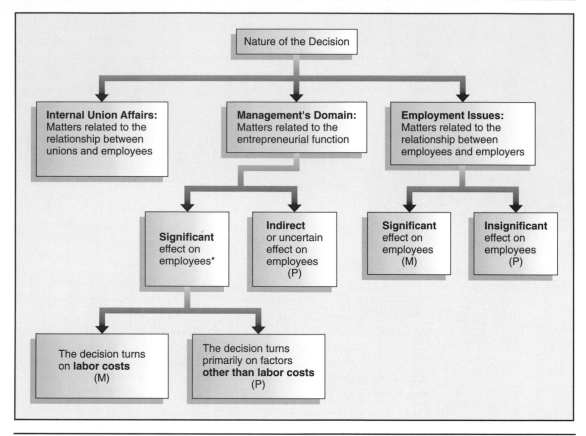

* The duty to engage in effects-bargaining typically attaches to such issues.

SOURCE: J. T. Delaney, D. Sockell, and J. Brockner, "Bargaining Effects of the Mandatory-Permissive Distinction," *Industrial Relations* 27 (1988), p. 24.

Unionization can reduce the elasticity of the supply of labor, and some bargaining relationships can create characteristics of a product market monopoly. When unions are able to organize an employer in a purely competitive industry, negotiating a wage increase (other things being equal) will necessarily lead to a reduction in employment as the employer will be forced to replace labor with capital or to cut back on employment in the short run to remain in the black. Thus, it is to the union's benefit to cooperate in creating a more inelastic demand curve in the employer's product market.

A grocery clerks' union in the remote food store example should be able to gain a large wage increase because the cost can be passed through to the store's customers. But how might the union gain a wage increase in a large city with hundreds of food stores? By bargaining in a unit that includes all stores, each store will pay the same wage increase and will attempt to pass the increase through to consumers simultaneously. No store with the same capital-labor mix would gain a competitive advantage. Less motivation would exist for any single store to resist a wage increase because all stores would encounter the same wage outcomes, leading to relatively little impact on the volume of sales if the market demand curve is relatively inelastic. This rationale, the establishment of multiemployer bargaining units, is discussed later in this chapter.

Ability to Continue Operations (or Take a Strike)

In addition to demand and supply characteristics of the product market in which a firm operates, employer bargaining power is enhanced substantially by its ability to take a strike. Many conditions influence this ability, including timing, perishability of the product, technology, the availability of replacement employees, and competition.

Timing

A strike will have less impact on an employer if it comes during off-peak periods. Facetiously, a strike of Santa Clauses on December 26 wouldn't faze an employer. If timing cannot be controlled, a company can frequently neutralize it by having large inventories or accelerating deliveries to customers prior to a strike.

Perishability of the Product

A food processor would be at a relative disadvantage if a strike occurred just when the fruits or vegetables it was going to pack were ripening. There might be a window during which the produce must be processed or it will spoil. Similarly, striking transportation carriers would permanently lose quasi-perishable goods, such as business travel, because the opportunity to take them will not recur for the customer.

Technology

If the firm is highly capital intensive, it frequently can continue to operate by using supervisors in production roles. For example, oil refiners and telecommunications providers can frequently operate for a considerable time period, if struck, given their high levels of automation.

Availability of Replacements

Strike replacements might come from either of two sources. First, and most possible in capital-intensive firms, supervisors may be able to perform enough of the duties of strikers to maintain operations. Second, the looser the labor market and the lower the skill level of the jobs, the easier it will be for an employer to hire and utilize replacements effectively. In several recent instances, hiring replacements or the threat of hiring them has influenced negotiations.

Multiple Locations and Staggered Contracts

If an employer has several plants producing the same product and different contract expiration dates, production can be shifted to the nonstruck plants and a large fraction of normal output can be continued.

Integrated Facilities

When output from one plant is necessary for production in several others, there is more bargaining power in the supplier plant. This situation frequently occurs in the auto industry at plants producing parts such as electrical equipment or radiators for all vehicles in a manufacturer's line. Problems associated with strikes in supplier facilities have become more critical as manufacturers have moved toward just-in-time parts deliveries.

Lack of Substitutes

The ability of an employer to take a strike increases if no adequate substitutes for the organization's outputs are available. Revenues are not irretrievably lost, only postponed until the firm is in production. Public education is an example of this type of product or service.

Union Bargaining Power

Just as employer bargaining power is enhanced by its ability to take a strike, union bargaining power is increased by its ability to impose costs with a strike. Union wage gains in bargaining are higher where significant barriers to entry exist for new employers, industrial concentration is high, and foreign competition is low. Within the industry, high union coverage by a dominant union also facilitates bargaining power.[15]

Studies of airlines following deregulation demonstrated that union bargaining power—as measured by their ability to resist concessions—is highest among those representing occupations employed in other industries (mechanics, as compared to pilots and cabin attendants), where the wage cut associated with changing employers is smaller (cabin attendants, as compared to pilots), and where the national union exerts strong control over the approval of negotiated contracts (International Association of Machinists).[16]

Union bargaining power is also increased when it exerts a measure of control over the external labor supply or occupational practices. Where rights and benefits are portable between employers and where the occupation establishes performance standards and establishes disciplinary procedures,[17] bargaining power would be higher.

---

[15] L. Mishel, "The Structural Determinants of Union Bargaining Power," *Industrial and Labor Relations Review* 40 (1986), pp. 90–104.

[16] P. Cappelli and T. H. Harris, "Airline Industrial Relations in Transition," *Proceedings of the Industrial Relations Research Association* 37 (1984), pp. 437–46.

[17] D. S. Cobble, "Organizing the Postindustrial Work Force: Lessons from the History of Waitress Unionism," *Industrial and Labor Relations Review* 44 (1991), pp. 419–36.

BARGAINING STRUCTURES

The election unit is not necessarily the unit in which bargaining occurs. The parties may decide a larger negotiating unit would be mutually beneficial. This section explores variations in bargaining unit structures presently used for negotiating contracts.

Bargaining structures for negotiation often aggregate employer units, either collecting numbers of small employers who operate in the same industry in a given region or lumping together various geographically separated plants or units of a single employer. Less often, unions representing employees within a single employer have coordinated bargaining. Bargaining units larger than election size occasionally bargain over wage issues only and leave nonwage issues for local determination. This is the reason why General Motors suffered a debilitating intra-contract strike in a parts stamping plant in Summer 1998.

Aggregations of employer units will be explored first, followed by the union side, including public policy issues influencing the structure of the negotiating relationship.

Multiemployer Bargaining

Many industries comprise large numbers of relatively small employers in any single geographic region. Examples include contract construction, garments, and retail and wholesale trade. Within the industries, the issues leading to unionization will likely be relatively common across employers, and a single union is often the bargaining agent for employees in many employer units.

In the local market, these employers compete for sales. Since all employers in the local industries (e.g., grocers) offer essentially similar goods and services, the demand for each employer's products is highly elastic (price sensitive). Thus, a wage increase would be difficult to pass through to customers. To remain competitive, the employer must cut back on its use of labor and also produce less. Figure 8–7 shows why this result occurs.

From the union's standpoint, besides the political risks associated with job loss, employer differences in their willingness to grant wage increases will lead to a varied pattern of wages throughout the area, and union members in units where wage increases are lower may become dissatisfied with their representation. Employers will also be more motivated to compete on the basis of labor cost differences.

To reduce these problems and to gain the monopolist's advantage in passing wage increases on to consumers, employers and unions frequently form **multiemployer bargaining** units. In a multiemployer unit, a single set of negotiators speaks for all employers, and the negotiated wage applies to all members of the bargaining association. The contract expires at the same time for all, so everyone faces the same economic risk of strikes. Each employer faces a product and service demand curve essentially equivalent to the market demand curve because

FIGURE 8–7

Effect of a Wage Increase for a Single Employer in a Competitive Product Market

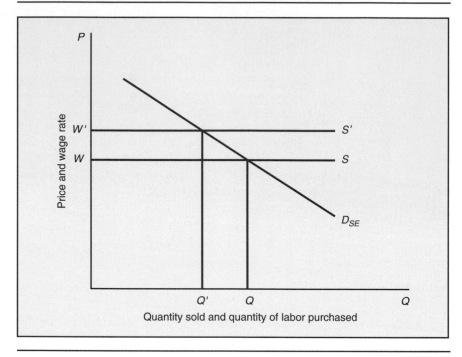

wage-related costs will be passed through by all members simultaneously. Figure 8–8 shows the effects of a wage increase in a multiemployer bargaining unit. If the market demand for the employers' goods and services is quite inelastic, most of the wage increases can be passed through with relatively minimal effects on employment.

The most successful multiemployer bargaining occurs when employers have roughly comparable nonlabor costs, all employers are unionized, and new firms have a relatively high cost of entry. If so, employers in the bargaining unit would probably not be differentially affected by a wage increase, nor would the union have to compete against nonunion labor.

Industrywide Bargaining

While most multiemployer bargaining is done within a relatively small geographic area, it also occurs on an industrywide basis when products or services are essentially commodities. In the trucking industry, major unionized interstate truckers are represented by an employers association that bargains with the Teamsters Union, resulting in the National Master Freight Agreement. However, maintaining an **industrywide bargaining** structure is a perilous proposition. As

FIGURE 8–8

Effect of a Wage Increase in a Multiemployer Bargaining Unit

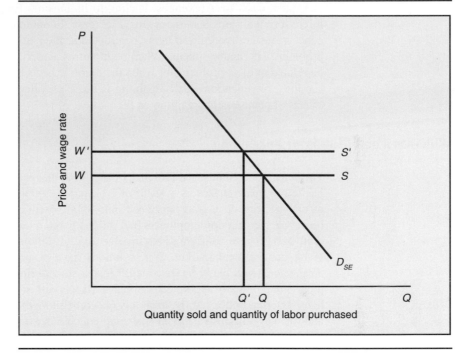

more employers are included, their sizes and abilities to take strikes become dissimilar. In trucking, employers face significant competition from nonunion sources.

Political considerations within the union also affect bargaining structures. As unions become involved in industrywide bargaining, the power and autonomy of local or regional officials decrease. Some commentators have suggested that the Master Freight Agreement is vulnerable to regional factionalism within the Teamsters Union.

National/Local Bargaining

In some firms, bargaining occurs on a companywide basis for wages and benefits and locally for the terms and conditions of employment. In most cases, plant managers and local unions negotiate work rules and other items after a national economic agreement is reached. Work rules may be negotiated simultaneously, but strikes are usually prohibited over local issues until a national economic settlement is concluded. If the local represents employees in a critical plant (e.g., a sole supplier of parts necessary for all final assembly products), the local may have considerable bargaining power.

Plant labor intensity varies given the production technology used; thus, wage increases have varied effects on costs across plants. In one plant, a wage increase may push costs over revenues, leading to its closing. Employees in that local might lose their jobs due to a national increase. Economic settlements involving concessions are more often being negotiated at the plant level, especially when problems vary among plants. When both parties perceive contract difficulties to be related to local problems or when the union expects to get trade-offs for concessions, organizationwide bargaining is more prevalent.[18] Exhibit 8–4 reports effects of plant-level bargaining on the parties.

Wide-Area and Multicraft Bargaining

The construction industry traditionally bargains at the local level. Decentralization has led to many strikes as a result of cross-craft comparisons in bargaining. In most instances, each craft bargained individually with employers. Increasingly, however, construction employers and unions bargain on a wide-area and multicraft basis. These configurations involve all craft unions of a particular set in a given geographical market. Where unions have strong national leaders, this arrangement will likely be successful because it solidifies their positions through the use of politically appointed regional staffs to assist in bargaining. On the other hand, internal politics at the local level become more difficult, because the rank and file may still pressure local leaders to match other settlements instead of concentrating on smoothing the bargaining process.[19]

Pattern Bargaining

In highly concentrated industries, the dominant union chooses a major employer as a bargaining target. Negotiations are concentrated on this target firm, which is struck if agreement is not reached. When agreement is reached, the union moves on to the remaining firms in turn and usually quickly concludes an agreement along the lines of the initial bargain. **Pattern bargaining** has occurred frequently in the auto and rubber industries.[20]

Another form of pattern bargaining involves a large-scale approximation of the multiemployer bargaining model, such as the old Coordinating Committee of Steel Companies (CCSC) consisting of representatives of the major steel producers, led by the chief negotiator at U.S. Steel, and their national and local union counterparts in the Basic Steel Industry Conference of the United Steelworkers

---

[18] Cappelli, "Concession Bargaining."

[19] P. T. Hartmann and W. H. Franke, "The Changing Bargaining Structure in Construction: Wide-Area and Multicraft Bargaining," *Industrial and Labor Relations Review* 34 (1980), pp. 170–84.

[20] For detailed examinations of the history and present bargaining structures in these (and other) industries, see H. C. Katz, "Automobiles," and M. D. Karper, "Tires," in D. B. Lipsky and C. B. Donn, eds., *Collective Bargaining in American Industry* (Lexington, MA: Lexington Books, 1987), pp. 13–54, 79–102.

EXHIBIT 8–4

EXHIBIT 8–4

Plant-Level Talks Rise Quickly in Importance

It is nothing new for work rules to come up in local talks, but the importance of these discussions is rising rapidly. "Almost every plant involved in the basic steel industry has made some form of accommodations in crew size and job combinations that lend to more efficient operations," says Sam Camens, a United Steelworkers official. Moreover, 12 of GM's 22 assembly plants have "competitive" agreements, in most cases because the local unions agreed to reopen local contracts before their September 1987 expiration. The contract changes usually consist of reducing classifications (increasing the variety of jobs that one worker can do) and limiting the times workers can switch jobs . . .

But not only are the companies benefiting from the changes. For industrial workers, job security has become the top issue. While union leaders are struggling to make some headway in that area at the national table, the companies are making it clear that a "competitive" local contract is the best thing a union can do to keep a plant open or to retain work in-house.

GM was scheduled to close its Fairfax, Kansas, plant by the end of this year, but, in 1985, it said it would replace it with a new plant that it might put near the antiquated facility. Two months after the union local signed a letter of intent saying it would consider drastic changes, the company agreed to build the new plant there. Local 31 believes its cooperation was "damn important" to preserving the 4,900 hourly jobs, says Charles Knott, the local's president. "Had we taken a hard line and said we weren't willing to look at anything, chances are we wouldn't have a $1.05 billion plant along the Missouri River."

However, unions are increasingly afraid that the emphasis on local talks is threatening their power. Workers at Mack Truck plants in Hagerstown, Maryland, and Allentown, Pennsylvania, recently approved concessionary local contracts providing various wage cuts and a no-strike clause in return for job guarantees. But the UAW International vetoed the agreements, saying they would "compel accommodations by our members . . . at present and future Mack facilities."

SOURCE: Abridged from J. M. Schlesinger, "Plant-Level Talks Rise Quickly in Importance; Big Issue: Work Rules," *The Wall Street Journal*, March 16, 1987, pp. 1, 13.

(BSIC). The CCSC was dissolved in 1985 when its members—Armco, Bethlehem, Inland, LTV, and U.S. Steel—unanimously agreed to end it.[21]

Some say pattern bargaining broke down during the 1980s because of major variations in plant efficiency levels among employers with several plants and between old and new plants in areas with low unionization. Managers responsible for bargaining increasingly cited firm profitability and labor cost measures as more important than industry wage patterns in their bargaining stances.[22] Unions, on the other hand, want to maintain a pattern to avoid internal political problems

---

[21] J. P. Hoerr, *And the Wolf Finally Came* (Pittsburgh, PA: University of Pittsburgh Press, 1988), pp. 474–76.

[22] A. Freedman, *The New Look in Wage Policy and Employee Relations* (New York: Conference Board, (1985), p. 9.

and serve as a base for launching demands for wage increases.[23] Moving away from a pattern results in more variance in wages across employers. However, evidence suggests that variance decreased between 1977 and 1983.[24] By the late 1980s, the UAW was able to reestablish patterns within industries in which it represented employees, with the exception of aerospace and agricultural equipment.[25] Internal politics within the UAW help to reinforce pattern bargaining. Political factions coalesce around differences in settlements, serving as a strong motivation for union officers to maintain a pattern in order to remain in office.[26]

How can these differences be resolved? First, during the late 1970s, inflation increased rapidly at the same time that labor contracts ran for multiyear periods. Thus, newly negotiated contracts established new patterns at the same time inflation led to large variances. Second, during the 1980s, waves of concessions occurred within fairly short periods, resulting in low wage variance as companies and unions bargained down to lower wage levels. However, large differences existed in other contract provisions such as early retirement, job security, union-management participation, profit sharing, and so forth.[27]

Conglomerates and Multinationals

A conglomerate is a business operating in several distinct industries. For example, a firm may operate a fast-food chain, sell data-processing services, manufacture agricultural chemicals, and produce household appliances. This firm bargains differently than one specializing in a single industry, often bargaining with several unions and having contracts with different expirations. By its nature, a conglomerate has high bargaining power. No part of its business is large relative to others, and its parts do not depend on each other for components or processes. Thus, it could afford to take a long strike at any subsidiary.[28] If a conglomerate is struck, unions gain less than in firms operating in a single industry.[29]

Multinational organizations have great bargaining power because they operate in different countries. Because unions representing U.S. employees do not represent offshore employees, the firm can withstand strikes by shifting production to another country or forgoing small proportions of revenues.

---

[23] Cappelli, "Collective Bargaining," pp. 4-191 to 4-193.

[24] K. J. Ready, "Is Pattern Bargaining Dead?" *Industrial and Labor Relations Review* 43 (1990), pp. 272–79.

[25] C. L. Erickson, "A Re-Interpretation of Pattern Bargaining," *Industrial and Labor Relations Review* 49 (1996), pp. 615–34.

[26] J. W. Budd, "The Internal Union Political Imperative for UAW Pattern Bargaining," *Journal of Labor Research* 16 (1995), pp. 43–55.

[27] Hoerr, *And the Wolf Finally Came.*

[28] C. Craypo, "Collective Bargaining in the Conglomerate, Multinational Firm," *Industrial and Labor Relations Review* 29 (1975), pp. 3–25.

[29] D. C. Rose, "Are Strikes Less Effective in Conglomerate Firms?" *Industrial and Labor Relations Review* 45 (1991), pp. 131–44.

Coordinated and Coalition Bargaining

Coordinated bargaining occurs where two or more national unions represent employees of a single major employer. In coordinated bargaining, unions seek comparable agreements with common expiration dates. Each union agrees that the other can sit in on bargaining and make suggestions to the other union's negotiators. **Coalition bargaining** involves a combination between unions which constitute a bargaining team made up of members from each union that negotiate identical pacts with the company. The largest continuing example of coordinated bargaining involves General Electric and the Electronic Workers and United Electrical Workers. Other unions negotiate similar economic terms following the initial settlement and ratification.[30]

Craft Units within an Employer

In railroads and airlines, the Railway Labor Act requires bargaining units to be organized on a craft basis. This means employers with organized employees will have to bargain with several unions. Not all of the unions have equivalent bargaining power because the employer may continue to operate if particular unions strike (and others are willing to cross their picket lines). Evidence in airline strikes indicates that only pilots and mechanics have the power to inflict substantial economic costs on employers.[31]

Centralization and Decentralization in Bargaining

Increased competition poses problems for both labor and management not only in structuring the bargaining relationship between the parties, but also with their own organizations. For management, the uniqueness of particular plant and work group issues and the shifting of responsibilities for profitability to business units has reduced the involvement of corporate staffs and other industrial relations professionals in bargaining and administering the contract. With the focus moving from a corporate to a business unit perspective, unions have lost leverage on economic issues.[32]

Tension may exist between the national union and its locals. The degree of control nationals exert is reflected in the degree to which locals must allow national participation in negotiations, permissions to strike, and vetoes over negotiated agreements. Control may extend to process and/or content issues in bargaining. As noted above, unions must be able to reduce competition with both

---

[30] For the terms of their 1988 settlement, see G. Ruben, "GE, Coalition Settle Dispute Union Split," *Monthly Labor Review* 11, no. 3 (1988), p. 46.

[31] R. A. DeFusco and S. M. Fuess, Jr., "The Relative Effects of Craft-Level Strikes: The Case of the Airlines," *Journal of Labor Research* 12 (1991), pp. 411–17.

[32] H. C. Katz, "The Decentralization of Collective Bargaining: A Literature Review and Comparative Analysis," *Industrial and Labor Relations Review* 47 (1993), pp. 3–22.

nonunion and union workers to improve conditions. Nonunion competition is reduced through the extension of organizing while union competition is reduced by requiring equivalent pattern agreements. Locals may not have adequate information to negotiate competitive agreements. The national can provide a means for gathering and disseminating information across a wide number of units.[33] Figure 8–9 contains a model suggesting some of the variables likely to be related to the centralization of bargaining processes and bargaining content.

Changes in Industrial Bargaining Structures and Outcomes

A recent set of studies examined changes that had occurred in collective bargaining in several industries that were heavily organized in the past but have undergone major changes over the past two decades.[34]

The paper industry enjoyed a period of increasing demand with no pressure from imports outside North America. Papermaking generally requires highly skilled workers and the industry had become increasingly automated, requiring more sophistication with equipment operations. Workers are largely represented by the United Paperworkers International Union. Even in the face of increasing demand, employers gained concessions on work rules, weekend overtime premiums, and wage restraints. Lump sums were negotiated. Employers used plant location and equipment investment decisions as levers in bargaining. The industry has always had a tradition of local-level economic negotiations, which decreased the union's ability to protect wages during the period.[35]

The steel industry was downsized substantially during the 1980s; several large integrated producers either exited the business or merged with others. Over the decade, capacity was reduced by 25 percent and employment by 50 percent (over 250,000 workers). Real wages fell over the period, but the economic pattern has been reestablished while local industrial relations practices differ. Current contracts attempt to link compensation more closely to firm performance.[36]

Auto unions faced the same level of employment decline as steel (48 percent from 1978 to 1993) as employers increasingly used lean production techniques. Unlike their counterparts in steel, autoworkers experienced an increase in real wages. While employment has been reduced, guarantees of job security and limitations on the lengths of layoffs were negotiated. Automakers have used investment decisions to gain leverage in work rule changes.[37]

---

[33] W. E. Hendricks, C. L. Gramm, and J. Fiorito, "Centralization of Bargaining Decisions in American Unions," *Industrial Relations* 32 (1993), pp. 367–90.

[34] P. B. Voos, ed., *Contemporary Collective Bargaining in the Private Sector* (Madison, WI: Industrial Relations Research Association, 1994).

[35] A. Eaton and J. Kriesky, "Collective Bargaining in the Paper Industry: Developments Since 1979," in Voos, *Contemporary Collective Bargaining in the Private Sector,* pp. 25–62.

[36] J. B. Arthur and S. K. Smith, "The Transformation of Industrial Relations in the American Steel Industry," in Voos, *Contemporary Collective Bargaining in the Private Sector,* pp. 135–180.

[37] H. Katz and J. P. MacDuffie, "Collective Bargaining in the U.S. Auto Assembly Sector," in Voos, *Contemporary Collective Bargaining in the Private Sector,* pp. 181–224.

FIGURE 8–9

A Model of Centralization of Control over Collective Bargaining in National Unions

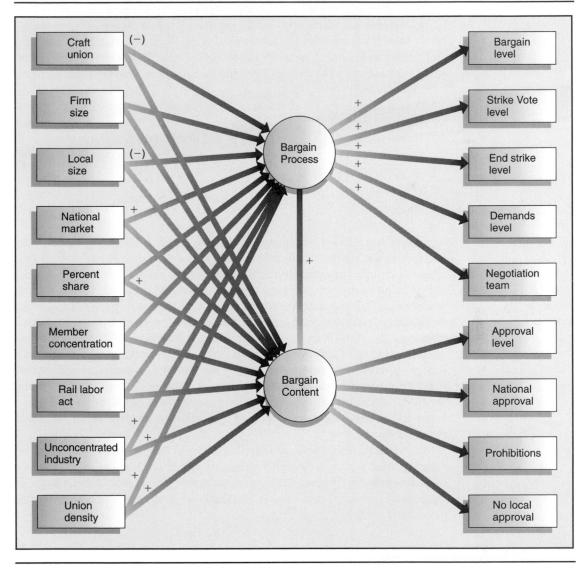

SOURCE: W. E. Hendricks, C. L. Gramm, and J. Fiorito, "Centralization of Bargaining Decisions in American Unions," *Industrial Relations* 32 (1993), p. 375.

Major changes have occurred in auto parts supply. Some parts of the industry have used an employee involvement approach, others have made concessions, and still others focus on cost savings. Earnings have declined and the nonunion sector increasingly leads in practices. There is less of a linkage with the overall

UAW pattern, particularly as the large auto producers are divesting their parts operations.[38]

In telecommunications, overcapacity has been a problem and worker productivity increases have declined. There is substantial nonunion competition, particularly from Northern Telecom. Jobs are being restructured out of the bargaining unit toward management and professional jobs. Union coverage at AT&T shrank by 55 percent from 1984 through 1992 and the ratio of managers to nonmanagers increased 1:4 to 1:3.[39]

Unionization in the construction industry has declined from 50 to 25 percent as employers have increasingly established nonunion subsidiaries (a practice called double-breasting). Union power is also decreased when employers escape previously negotiated prehire agreements. Unions have responded by "salting" union organizers in nonunion contractors to encourage unionization.[40]

Public Policy and Court Decisions

Legislation has affected bargaining structure. As noted, employers covered by the Railway Labor Act are required to bargain on a craft basis. Hence, airline gate agents may be represented by the Brotherhood of Railway and Airline Clerks (BRAC), pilots by the Air Line Pilots Association, and mechanics by the Machinists. Craft bargaining and perishability of air travel (passages to certain destinations at certain times) enhance each union's bargaining power because a strike by a single union might shut an airline down.[41] On the other hand, bargaining under Railway Labor Act provisions is often quite protracted, since no strike is possible until an impasse is declared by the National Mediation Board. At that point, the union may not strike until another 30 days has elapsed. Then, if a strike is called, the union runs the risk that the president will establish an emergency board and prohibit the continuation of the strike for 60 days while the board examines the situation.

In the past, airlines insulated themselves from the perishability problem by securing strike insurance through a mutual aid pact.[42] The legislation deregulating the airline industry eliminated this tactic, but deregulation reduced union bargaining power by allowing new carriers that used nonunion labor to enter the market more easily.

---

[38] J. Cutcher-Gershenfeld and P. P. McHugh, "Collective Bargaining in the North American Auto Supply Industry," in Voos, *Contemporary Collective Bargaining in the Private Sector,* pp. 225–58.

[39] J. Keefe and K. Boroff, (1994) "Telecommunications Labor-Management Relations after Divestiture," in Voos, *Contemporary Collective Bargaining in the Private Sector,* pp. 303–72.

[40] S. G. Allen, "Developments in Collective Bargaining in Construction in the 1980s and 1990s," in Voos, *Contemporary Collective Bargaining in the Private Sector,* pp. 411–46.

[41] W. Hendricks, P. Feuille, and C. Szerszen, "Regulation, Deregulation, and Collective Bargaining in Airlines," *Industrial and Labor Relations Review* 34 (1980), pp. 67–81.

[42] S. H. Unterberger and E. C. Koziara, "The Demise of Airline Strike Insurance," *Industrial and Labor Relations Review* 34 (1980), pp. 82–89.

The NLRB permits coordinated and coalition bargaining,[43] and required General Electric to bargain with a negotiating committee representing several unions as long as each union represented GE employees. Outside representatives could not vote on offers but could observe and comment. Unions have also been permitted to demand common contract expiration dates among employers in a single industry.[44]

At its most elemental level, a bargaining unit is what labor and management say it is. This is a seeming tautology, but Chapter 6 noted that the NLRB ordered consent elections in companies where labor and management did not dispute the makeup of the bargaining unit for representation purposes and no prohibited employees were included. But once past the representation stage, the parties are free to make the bargaining unit more (but not less) inclusive in negotiations, which may lead to novel bargaining structures to accommodate peculiarities of the unions, firms, or industries involved.

The expansion of a bargaining unit results only from the voluntary agreement of the parties. In a case where a union charged a company with refusing to bargain when it would not consider a companywide fringe benefit program, the NLRB held that only the local units are certified and any expanded unit would have to be by mutual agreement.[45]

Where employers and unions have negotiated a multiemployer unit, the NLRB and the courts have generally held that employers cannot unilaterally withdraw from the unit during negotiations without the consent of the union, even if a bargaining impasse has been reached. The Supreme Court did not see impasses as unusual in bargaining or sufficiently destructive of group bargaining to allow the withdrawal of unit members.[46]

Figure 8–10 represents a flowchart that predicts the type of bargaining structures that could evolve in the special situations discussed.

Influence of Bargaining Power and Structure

Bargaining structures can influence bargaining power, and the relative effects for both unions and managements can be altered by the structures they agree to use. The next two chapters examine a variety of bargaining issues. Just as the inelasticity of demand for labor influences the degree to which management can grant wage increases, the inelasticity of demand related to any of the separate demands of labor will influence the outcome of the bargaining relationship. The employer is much more likely to grant in total a demand expected to have relatively little effect on overall costs than one that will broadly affect outcomes. This is one

---

[43] *General Electric Co.*, 173 NLRB 46 (1968).

[44] *AFL-CIO Joint Negotiating Committee for Phelps-Dodge* v. *NLRB*, 3rd Circuit Court of Appeals, No. 19199, 1972, 313.

[45] *Oil, Chemical, and Atomic Workers* v. *NLRB*, 84 LRRM 2581, 2nd Circuit Court of Appeals, 1973.

[46] *Bonanno Linen Service* v. *NLRB*, 109 LRRM 2557, Sup. Ct., 1982.

FIGURE 8–10

Bargaining Patterns

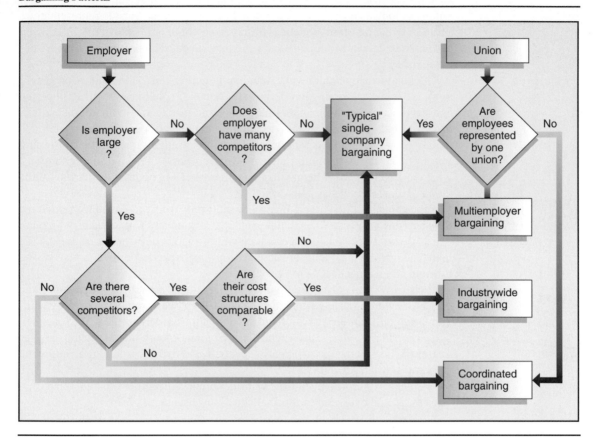

reason pension benefits and health care have grown from small-cost to large-cost items in the labor contract. Figure 8–11 is a helpful diagram of several of the variables that shape bargaining power and its effect on bargaining outcomes.

SUMMARY

Labor, capital, and raw materials combine to produce products or services. Employers generally adjust labor and raw material inputs in the short run and capital in the long run. Labor is a derived demand depending on the level of consumers' demands for the firm's goods and services. The elasticity of this demand influences wages and employment. In the United States, legislation prohibits employers from creating product or service market monopolies; thus, employers compete regarding the costs of their products and attempt to reduce labor costs.

FIGURE 8–11

A Conceptual Framework for the Determinants of Bargaining Outcomes

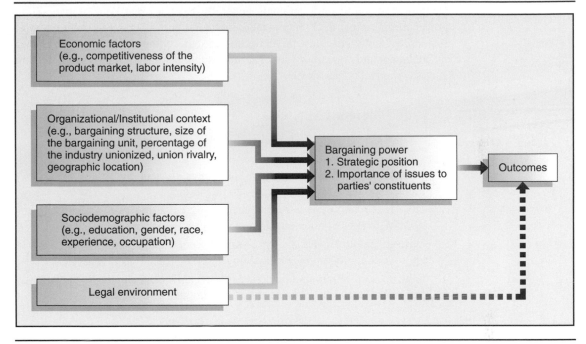

SOURCE: J. T. Delaney and D. Sockell, "The Mandatory-Permissive Distinction and Collective Bargaining Outcomes," *Industrial and Labor Relations Review* 42 (1989), p. 571.

Deregulation and foreign competition have recently increased the elasticity of consumer demand for products and have allowed competition by lower-cost forms of labor: nonunion and foreign. This situation has led to concessions by unionized employees in industries affected by these changes.

Employers generally create strategies allowing them to concentrate in product and service markets with the greatest returns on investment. Where necessary, they want to be able to substitute capital for labor if its efficiency is higher. Employees, concerned about gaining a return on their investment in training and employment, require job security and wages commensurate with their investment.

Bargaining power is determined by assessing whether one's costs of agreeing are greater or less than the costs of disagreeing. Bargaining power relationships are sometimes purposely altered to create more power in the product or service market vis-à-vis consumers. Multiemployer bargaining is an example of this strategy.

Several different bargaining structures exist. The election unit may be expanded as the result of mutual agreements between the employer and the union. Small employers often form multiemployer bargaining units to deal with a single union. Occasionally, nationally based employers form industrywide units to bargain with a national union. Pattern bargaining, in which one company's settlements serve as a basis for negotiating in the rest of the industry, is declining. Conglomerates and multinationals generally have a great deal of bargaining power because of their fragmented business and bargaining relationships. Increased attention to competitiveness has led to decentralization in bargaining for management and concern by national unions that local agreements might lead to whipsawing and concessions.

DISCUSSION QUESTIONS

1. What effect does a lower elasticity of demand have on the wage and employment outcomes for the employer and the union?
2. How is bargaining power influenced by deregulation and foreign competition? Who is most affected by these changes—labor or management?
3. Why are employers less likely to approve coalition bargaining than unions to approve of multiemployer bargaining?
4. Why does the current public policy for bargaining that applies to the Railway Labor Act sector create more bargaining impasses?

KEY TERMS

Marginal revenue product   *223*   Prohibited issues   *231*

Marginal supply curve   *227*   Bargaining structure   *235*

Good faith bargaining   *230*   Multiemployer bargaining   *235*

Mandatory issues   *230*   Industrywide bargaining   *236*

Permissive issues   *231*   Pattern bargaining   *238*

Impasse   *231*   Coordinated bargaining   *241*

Bargaining power   *231*   Coalition bargaining   *241*

CASE

MATERIAL HANDLING EQUIPMENT ASSOCIATION BARGAINING GROUP

GMFC is a charter member of the Material Handling Equipment Association (MHEA). The organization was started in the late 1940s and now includes 30 members producing over 95 percent of all domestic material handling equipment. Presently, these manufacturers produce 70 percent of the material handling equipment sold in the United States. About 80 percent of the association's total production is for the domestic market. Primary foreign markets are in Europe and Latin America, with increasing marketing emphasis in Eastern Europe.

All members are unionized to some extent, with the proportions of production jobs organized ranging from 25 percent to 100 percent. GMFC is 80 percent unionized. Most companies bargain with the Steelworkers, the Auto Workers, or the Machinists. Some variations exist between contracts within employers and across employers in the association. Unions have been particularly interested in negotiating relatively similar contracts across employers and national-level agreements within employers.

Industrial relations executives of the MHEA recently studied the possibility of industrywide bargaining. Coincidentally, since they are proposing to merge, the major unions representing MHEA employees explored potential coalition bargaining arrangements.

Taking either a management or union role, formulate arguments for or against (1) industrywide bargaining with each separate union, (2) industrywide bargaining with coalition bargaining representing employees, (3) bargaining at the local level on all issues with the union that happens to represent the employees.

9

WAGE AND BENEFIT

ISSUES IN

BARGAINING

Wages have always been a major issue in bargaining. Management is concerned with wage and benefit issues because its ability to compete depends to some extent on its labor costs. Firms producing equivalent output with lower labor costs will have higher profits and be better able to operate during downturns.

Both labor and management are concerned about a variety of pay aspects. Each is concerned with the overall level of pay, but both are also concerned about how pay rates and pay increases are determined for different jobs and about the mix of wages and benefits paid to employees.

This chapter examines the components of union wage demands, bargaining on specific aspects of the pay program, the effects unions have on pay levels in both union and nonunion organizations, and the prevalence of wage and benefit issues in contracts.

As you study this chapter, consider the following issues and questions:

1. What are the strongest current arguments unions and/or managements use in the proposal or defense of present or future wages and benefits?
2. What effect do wages and benefits have on the economic performance of the employer and on nonunion employment of the same or other employers?
3. How does the form of wages influence employer and employee outcomes?
4. How does the system for allocating salary increases differ in union and nonunion organizations?
5. How does the usual structuring of union wage and benefit demands alter the structure of wage differentials in an organization over time?

UNION AND EMPLOYER INTERESTS

The union movement has traditionally argued that wealth is ultimately created by labor, in all its forms, and that the distribution of income is excessively unequal. While not denying employers' rights to a return on investment, unions would not necessarily agree that profit maximization is a firm's primary goal. Unionization aims to increase the power of workers to increase their share of the firm's output.

Private sector employers are ultimately interested in maximizing shareholder value. They would also prefer the greatest possible flexibility in structuring their operations, including the mobility of capital. They would like to structure pay programs to minimize labor costs by managing pay programs in such a way as to obtain the most output per dollar.

The next sections will examine the background of union wage demands and the components of pay programs.

COMPONENTS OF WAGE DEMANDS

In framing its wage demands, the union relies on three major criteria: equity within and across employers, the company's ability to pay, and the standard of living. These criteria suggest that the union makes a number of comparisons in formulating wage demands.

Equity

With regard to equity, unions want wages for jobs they represent to exceed—or at least be consistent with—those of equivalent nonunion jobs in the firm. They also expect equivalence in insurance benefits across jobs because personal risks are not related to job or salary level. Unions attend to bargains forged in other industries but, because of global competition and deregulation, upward pattern bargaining has declined. Unions also want uniformity in wage rates for the same jobs in different locations of the same company. For example, an auto assembly worker at Ford's Twin Cities (Minnesota) assembly plant earns the same rate as another on a similar job in Wixom, Michigan, or Atlanta, Georgia. These patterns within a single employer are eroding, however, as plant-level negotiations often lead to concessions in older, less efficient plants to avoid shutdowns and the resulting loss of jobs.

Inequality of income distributions is also a component of the equity demand. An unequal distribution is one in which different workers in different jobs earn different pay. From a union standpoint, excessive inequality would be represented by differences between production workers, professionals, and executives that are larger than members can justify. Inequality suggests that there may be an opportunity to redistribute income from higher- to lower-level jobs. Income inequality has increased substantially since 1980. Some of this can be attributed to occupational changes, but the reduction in union coverage is a major contributor.[1] Union coverage is an important factor because inequality had decreased in the public sector over the same period as union membership grew.[2]

Ability to Pay

While **ability to pay** takes two forms, the primary argument relates to a firm's profitability. When employers' profits are increasing, unions expect to receive pay increases. They avoid accepting reduced pay when profits decline, but may concede when employers have incurred substantial losses and job losses for union members would be the alternative. Some internal union critics have condemned concessions, arguing that past labor leaders would not have accepted them. Exhibit 9–1 recalls the position of Walter Reuther, long-time president of the UAW, as told by Douglas Fraser, the UAW president during initial auto concessions in the early 1980s.

Ability to pay is also related to the proportion of labor costs in a company's total costs. Generally, unions believe that the lower a firm's labor intensity (i.e., the lower the share of costs going to labor), the greater its ability to pay. This assumption is based on the relatively lower elasticity of the derived demand for labor in capital-intensive firms. Table 9–1 illustrates the effects of wage increases on the costs of labor- and capital-intensive firms.

Standard of Living

The **standard of living** component of labor's demands takes on two meanings. One relates to the purchasing power of employees' pay (real wages). If prices increase by 10 percent for the things the average worker buys, but wages rise only 6 percent over the same period, real wages have eroded by 4 percent. Where negotiated, **cost-of-living adjustments** (COLA) are aimed at maintaining parity between wages and prices over time.

Standard-of-living issues also arise with unions' beliefs that the purchasing power of their members needs improvement to enable them to enjoy higher qualities of goods and services; for example, owning a home rather than renting. Some comparison or equity aspects are included here, but the comparison is with society in general, not with a specific work group.

---

[1] J. DiNardo and T. Lemieux, "Diverging Male Wage Inequality in the United States and Canada, 1981–1988: Do Institutions Explain the Difference?" *Industrial and Labor Relations Review* 50 (1997), pp. 629–51; and N. M. Fortin and T. Lemieux, "Institutional Changes and Rising Wage Inequality: Is There a Linkage?" *Journal of Economic Perspectives* 11, no. 2 (1997), pp. 75–96.

[2] M. A. Asher and R. H. DeFina, "The Impact of Changing Union Density on Earnings Inequality: Evidence from the Private and Public Sectors," *Journal of Labor Research* 18 (1997), pp. 425–37.

EXHIBIT 9–1

Douglas Fraser Recalls Walter Reuther's Position on Concessions

Fraser . . . urge[d] a change in union behavior, in speeches to UAW groups. There were always critics present who challenged him, invoking Reuther's name as the final authority.

Fraser told me about one such meeting when I visited him in 1985 . . . "I went into one lion's den last week, a union meeting," Fraser said, "and there was this old Commie there who I knew would raise that precise issue, 'Reuther spinning in his grave.'" Fraser chuckled and rummaged in a desk drawer. He pulled out a mimeographed text of a speech.

So I brought this along and read it:

All industries and all companies within an industry do not enjoy the same economic advantages and profit ratios. We cannot blind ourselves to this fact at the bargaining table. As an employer prospers, we expect a fair share, and if he faces hard times, we expect to cooperate . . . Our basic philosophy toward the employers we meet at the bargaining table is that we have a great deal more in common than we have in conflict, and that instead of waging a struggle to divide up scarcity, we have to find ways of cooperating to create abundance and then intelligently find a way of sharing that abundance.

Fraser showed me the first page of the text. It was an address delivered by Walter P. Reuther in 1964 at the University of Virginia . . .

SOURCE: J. P. Hoerr, *And the Wolf Finally Came* (Pittsburgh, PA: University of Pittsburgh Press, 1988), p. 195.

TABLE 9–1

Cost Comparisons for Labor and Capital-Intensive Firms

	Labor-Intensive Firm	Capital-Intensive Firm
Material cost	$ 500,000	$ 500,000
Capital cost	100,000	400,000
Labor cost	400,000	100,000
Total cost	$1,000,000	$1,000,000
Cost of 10 percent wage increase	40,000	10,000
Net total cost	$1,040,000	$1,010,000

Figure 9–1 presents the wage demand components just discussed. Equity relates to both internal and external comparisons, ability to pay profits and labor intensity, and standard of living to real wages and absolute improvement. Although equity issues were discussed first, none of these pay issues is, a priori, more important than another. Both sides will emphasize issues they believe will enhance their bargaining power.

FIGURE 9–1

Wage Demand Components

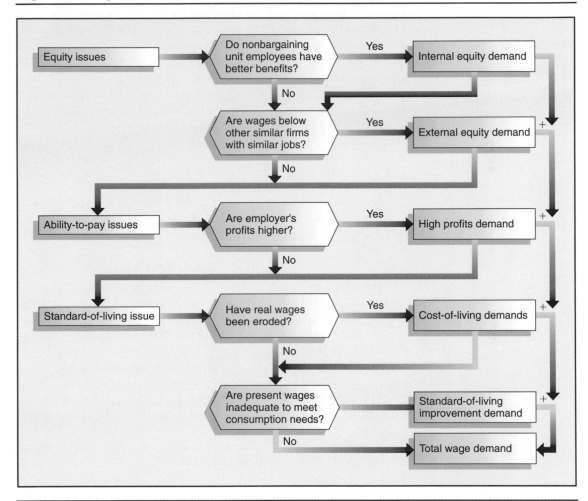

PAY PROGRAMS

Collective bargaining alters the status quo in pay administration by substituting a contract for management's unilaterally determined practices. A useful way to understand pay programs is to divide decisions about them into four major components: pay level, pay structure, pay form, and pay system.[3] **Pay level** refers to

---

[3] H. G. Heneman III and D. P. Schwab, "Work and Rewards Theory," in D. Yoder and H. G. Heneman, Jr., eds., *ASPA Handbook of Personnel and Industrial Relations* (Washington, DC: Bureau of National Affairs, 1979), pp. 6-1–6-2.

how an employer's average pay rates for jobs compare with other employers' rates. **Pay structure** consists of the sets of wage rates the employer applies to different jobs and the ranges of wage rates possible within specific jobs in the organization. **Pay form** is the method by which compensation is received; it includes cash, insurance payments, deferred income, preferential discounts, payments in kind, and recreational and entertainment programs. **Pay system** refers to the methods used to determine how much each individual will earn within a job. The system might be based on piece rates, other productivity or performance indexes, skill level, time worked, seniority with the organization, or other factors. Union and management goals relating to these pay program components are examined in the following sections.

Pay Level

The basic components associated with pay level changes were those shown in Figure 9–1: ability to pay, equity, and standard of living.

Ability to Pay

A variety of considerations influence ability to pay. The general level of business activity influences profits. When the economy is strong and unemployment declines, wage demands increase and the incidence of strikes to support bargaining demands rises. Employers who have relatively capital-intensive production processes or who bargain with several relatively small units do not have the incentive to avoid large wage increases that labor-intensive organizations have. The ability to pay is usually an issue raised by the union, but employers experiencing reduced profits (or losses) or changes in their industries' competitive level argue for pay reductions. Pay level comparisons become more difficult to make as pay form becomes more complex.

Employers are interested in reducing the fixed proportion of pay. Employees may also be interested in making pay flexible if it leads to more job security. Profit sharing has been increasingly negotiated into contracts as a quid pro quo for concessions. For example, auto workers have significant opportunities for profit sharing if their organizations do well. If profits are down or losses occur, a lower level of base pay enables the employer to make a profit at lower levels of output or to cut losses.

In attempting to reduce the rate of growth in employees' base wage levels, firms have offered lump-sum bonuses for agreeing on a contract. For example, assume the union seeks a 4 percent pay increase for employees earning about $25,000 annually. If the employer pays a $1,250 bonus instead, it may be saving money because the base for future increases remains at $25,000 and no additional benefits are paid on the $1,250. If the proportion of wage-tied benefits is greater than 20 percent, the employer saves in the first year.

Equity

Achieving equity across employers in a given industry is important for unions because it has the effect of taking wages out of competition. All employers pay essentially the same, so advantages must be earned through more marketable products or greater productive efficiency.

Some have argued that major national unions respond to the bargaining success of their counterparts. To remain competitive with other unions in organizing and representation, trade union leaders will need to obtain settlements equivalent to or better than others recently wrung from management. Major settlements are presumed to be key-comparison or pattern-setting agreements; however, wage imitation is likely to be decreased by (1) differences between industries in which employers operate, (2) differences in the ability to pay within these industries, and (3) the time between pattern-setting and later settlements.[4] As competition has increased in many industries, management bargainers have increasingly emphasized company productivity trends and profit levels and de-emphasized industry patterns and settlements in other industries.[5] Table 9–2 indicates a relatively wide range in recent settlements across manufacturers whose employees are represented by the United Auto Workers.

Standard of Living

Inflation increases the importance unions place on maintaining a standard of living. The negotiation of COLAs increased rapidly during the 1970s when inflation was high. However, the escalation of wages in response to inflation is usually lower than the measured inflation rates.[6] During the 1980s, firms increasingly made the deferral, modification, or elimination of COLAs a major concession bargaining objective.[7]

Where COLAs exist, pay levels within the contract period are tied to changes in the consumer price index (CPI). Contracts usually provide for quarterly payments based on the difference between the CPI at the time the contract became effective and the index level at the end of the current quarter. As an example, assume that a contact effective January 1, 1999, provided for a base wage of $10 per hour and a COLA of 1 cent for each 0.3 point increase in the CPI. If the CPI increased 6 points by December 31, 1999, then employees would receive a lump-sum payment of 20 cents for each hour worked during the preceding quarter.

A very important COLA consideration is whether increases are incorporated into the base wage. Unions prefer to include them in the base before the current expiration because, if inflation were high, an extremely large increase would be

---

[4] D. J. B. Mitchell, *Unions, Wages, and Inflation* (Washington, DC: Brookings Institution, 1980), p. 50.

[5] A. Freedman, *The New Look in Wage Policy and Employee Relations* (New York: Conference Board, 1985), pp. 7–12.

[6] Mitchell, *Unions, Wages, and Inflation,* pp. 48–50.

[7] Freedman, *New Look in Wage Policy,* pp. 10–12.

TABLE 9–2
Recent UAW Contract Settlements

Ford Motor Company—September 1996, nationwide, 3 years
  $2,000 signing bonus, 3% base increase in 2nd and 3rd years.
  Permanent lower wages for parts workers
  95% workforce size guarantee

Chrysler Corporation—October 1996, nationwide, 3 years
  $2,000 signing bonus, 3% base increase in 2nd and 3rd years
  One-time 2 cent diversion from COLA in December 1996
  Christmas bonus up to $600 each year
  95% workforce size guarantee

Frigidaire, Greenville, WI—October 1996, 2,100 production workers, 3 years
  Introduce team concept in production
  Base increases of 30, 25, and 25 cents in 1st, 2nd, and 3rd years
  10 cent to $1.20 inequity increases for 25% of employees being paid below skill levels
  Pension increase from $20 to $21 per year of credited service
  Medical co-pay begins at $5 per week for single, $10 per week for family if indemnity
    plan chosen, no co-pay for HMO
  Modified mandatory overtime for up to 10 hours per week

Saturn Corporation, Spring Hill, TN, and Troy, MI—December 1996, 3 years
    (self-renewing)
  $2,000 signing bonus, 3% base increase in 2nd and 3rd years
  30 cent skilled trade allowance

American Axle, Detroit, Buffalo, and Tonawanda NY—7,800 production workers, 3 years
  $2,000 signing bonus, 3% base increases in 2nd and 3rd years
  New hires receive 70% of base rate, increasing to full scale in 3 years
  95% workforce size guarantee

Johnson Controls, Plymouth, MI, and Oberlin, OH—500 production workers, 3 years
  Starting wage increased from $9.50 to $10.86, top scale from $10.50 to $12.00 in
    Plymouth, $8.20 to $9.42 and $10.20 to $11.42 in Oberlin
  Starting wage increased from $10.86 to $12.50, top scale from $12.00 to $14.00 in third
    year, $9.42 to $10.35 and $11.42 to $12.35 in Oberlin
  Oberlin workers receive a $1,000 bonus at ratification
  401(k) retirement plans converted to a defined benefit pension plan

---

needed to bring the base up to a real-income standard equivalent to that earned at
the end of the expiring contract.

Pay Structure

Pay structure refers to the pattern of wage rates for jobs within the organization.
Within the bargaining unit, the union negotiates these with management. Pay differentials may be negotiated on a job-by-job basis or result from using a negotiated job evaluation system. Job-by-job negotiations often create difficulties over
time because the original job structure established a hierarchy of jobs separated
by specific pay differences. Bargaining often results in across-the-board pay

increases of equal magnitude for all bargaining unit jobs. While absolute wage differentials are maintained, relative differences shrink, causing wage compression. For example, two jobs with original pay rates of $5 and $10 per hour have a 50 percent differential. Over time, across-the-board increases of $5 per hour shrink the relative differential to 33 percent. Establishing rates for new jobs during the contract and determining rates for jobs where no external comparisons exist also cause problems. Job evaluation methods help employers and unions deal with these problems.

Job Evaluation

Job evaluation determines the relative position of jobs within a pay structure. The procedure has several steps and requires decision-making rules that must be negotiated. In general, job evaluation includes the following steps: (1) the jobs to be evaluated must be specified (usually the jobs covered by the contract); (2) jobs must be analyzed to determine the behaviors required to be performed and/or the traits or skills necessary to perform the job; (3) of the behaviors or traits identified, those that vary across jobs and are agreed to be of value to the employer are grouped into compensable factors; (4) for evaluation purposes, each factor is clearly defined, and different degrees of involvement for each factor are determined; (5) point values are assigned to factors and degrees within a factor; (6) job evaluation manuals used to apply the method are written; (7) all jobs are rated.[8] Table 9–3 is an example of identified factors, point assignments, and degree levels within factors. Figure 9–2 is a specimen of the types of definitions assigned to factors and degrees within a factor.

Job evaluation involves either (1) using a union-management committee to determine compensable factors and the degree to which they're required in bargaining unit jobs or (2) negotiating the points to be applied to evaluations completed by management. Advantages associated with a well-designed and well-administered job evaluation system include reduction of compression in wage differentials if increases are given as a percentage of the total points assigned to the job and the ease with which new jobs can be slotted into an existing pay structure. The primary disadvantage is the requirement for initial agreement between the union and management on the identification, definition, and point assignments associated with compensable factors.

Skill-based Pay

Most pay structures in unionized settings base pay differences on employees' grades and job classifications. **Skill-based pay** (SBP) ties pay to employee skills. An employee is hired at a base rate that may be lower than average starting wages in the area. As the employee learns prescribed skills, pay is increased. Relatively few job classifications exist, and employees can be moved between assignments

---

[8] For more information on job evaluation techniques, see G. T. Milkovich and J. M. Newman, *Compensation,* 5th ed. (Burr Ridge, IL: McGraw-Hill–Irwin, 1996), pp. 125–46.

TABLE 9–3
Points Assigned to Factors and Degrees

	Percent	Degrees and Points						Weight in Percent
		1st Degree	2nd Degree	3rd Degree	4th Degree	5th Degree	6th Degree	
Skill	50%							
1. Education and job knowledge		12 points	24 points	36 points	48 points	60 points	72 points	12%
2. Experience and training		24	48	72	96	120	144	24
3. Initiative and ingenuity		14	28	42	56	70	84	14
Effort	15							
4. Physical demand		10	20	30	40	50	60	10
5. Mental and/or visual demand		5	10	15	20	25	30	5
Responsibility	20							
6. Equipment or tools		6	12	18	24	30	36	6
7. Material or product		7	14	21	28	35	42	7
8. Safety of others		3	6	9	12	15	18	3
9. Work of others		4	8	12	16	20	24	4
Job conditions	15							
10. Working conditions		10	20	30	40	50	60	10
11. Unavoidable hazards		5	10	15	20	25	30	5
Total	100%	100%	100%	100%	100%	100%	100%	100%

SOURCE: H. Zollitsch and A. Langsner, *Wage and Salary Administration*, 2nd ed. (Cincinnati: South-Western Publishing, 1970), p. 186.

FIGURE 9–2

Definition of Factor and Degrees within Factor

1. Knowledge

This factor measures the knowledge or equivalent training required to perform the position duties.

1st Degree

Use of reading and writing, adding and subtracting of whole numbers; following of instructions; use of fixed gauges, direct reading instruments and similar devices; where interpretation is not required.

2nd Degree

Use of addition, subtraction, multiplication and division of numbers including decimals and fractions; simple use of formulas, charts, tables, drawings, specifications, schedules, wiring diagrams; use off adjustable measuring instruments; checking of reports, forms, records and comparable data; where interpretation is required.

3rd Degree

Use of mathematics together with the use of complicated drawings, specifications, charts, tables; various types of precision measuring instruments. Equivalent to 1 to 3 years applied trades training in a particular or specialized occupation.

4th Degree

Use of advanced trades mathematics, together with the use of complicated drawings, specifications, charts, tables, handbook formulas; all varieties of precision measuring instruments. Equivalent to complete accredited apprenticeship in a recognized trade, craft or occupation; or equivalent to a 2-year technical college education.

5th Degree

Use of higher mathematics involved in the application of engineering principles and the performance of related practical operations, together with a comprehensive knowledge of the theories and practices of mechanical, electrical, chemical, civil or like engineering field. Equivalent to complete 4 years of technical college or university education.

SOURCE: G. T. Milkovich and J. M. Newman, *Compensation,* 4th ed. (Homewood, IL: Irwin, 1993), p. 137.

based on the employer's needs. This pay plan combines structural (job or task relationships) and system (pay changes based on individual behavior or skills) aspects. The practice supports team-based production, which sharply blurs job boundaries and, thus, is not found in many unionized plants. Where it exists in unionized settings, it was usually implemented before representation.[9]

[9] T. A. Kochan, H. C. Katz, and R. B. McKersie, *The Transformation of American Industrial Relations* (New York: Basic Books, 1986), p. 158.

Two-Tier Pay Plans

Two-tier pay plans lower wage costs by decreasing the starting rate offered to new employees. Two types of two-tier pay plans exist. The first starts employees at a lower rate and requires a longer period for them than for present employees to reach top rates. The second creates a permanent differential in which newly hired employees are never expected to earn the top rate of present employees. Managements benefit most when turnover is high or the company plans to expand. The rate of change is most rapid when retirement rates are also increasing. Both the employer and the union might expect problems when lower-tier employment levels begin to exceed half of the total. Successful implementation of these plans requires careful employee communications and assurances that job security will be enhanced.[10]

Two-tier pay plans are more prevalent in unionized firms and are usually negotiated without significant management concessions.[11] In the airline industry, two-tier plans were usually installed in the absence of financial distress or market share shifts and frequently negotiated following other union concessions. Airlines justified two-tier plans as aligning their pay rates more closely to comparable jobs in the market for persons with equivalent skill levels.[12] The effects of two-tier pay plans on firm performance is mixed, with slightly positive effects on shareholder value. Given longer-run employee dissatisfaction with these plans and their relatively low returns, it is no surprise that they have not been widely adopted.[13]

Unless many new employees are hired, the union shouldn't incur severe political problems from new members for some time. Management may face problems, in that employees doing equal work will receive unequal pay. Employees in two-tier pay plans can compare their pay among themselves or with employees in other organizations. As pay tends to fall behind what is earned from other higher-paying employers, dissatisfaction results. Dissatisfaction may also occur if employees compare their outcomes given effort unfavorably with others in the organization.[14]

Pay Form

Pay components not received in cash are received as either insurance or deferred compensation. Insurance typically applies to hospital and medical needs, life, disability, and dental benefits. Deferred compensation usually involves pension

---

[10] Ibid., pp. 132, 170.

[11] S. M. Jacoby and D. J. B. Mitchell, "Management Attitudes toward Two-Tier Pay Plans," *Journal of Labor Research* 7 (1986), pp. 221–37.

[12] D. J. Walsh, "Accounting for the Proliferation of Two-Tier Wage Settlements in the U.S. Airline Industry, 1983–1986," *Industrial and Labor Relations Review* 42 (1988), pp. 50–62.

[13] S. L. Thomas and M. M. Kleiner, "The Effect of Two-Tier Collective Bargaining Agreements on Shareholder Equity," *Industrial and Labor Relations Review* 45 (1992), pp. 339–51.

[14] R. T. Lee and J. E. Martin, "Internal and External Referents as Predictors of Pay Satisfaction among Employees of a Two-Tier Wage Setting," *Journal of Occupational Psychology* 64 (1991), pp. 57–66.

benefits. Nonmonetary wage forms have advantages and disadvantages. For the employee, the benefit of the form depends partly on usage. Employees with dependents need life and family health care more than those who do not. On the other hand, the value of many of the benefits is untaxed income. When the company directly purchases medical insurance, the value is not reported as income to the recipient. A wage earner purchasing an equivalent amount may have already been taxed on the money paid for the individual benefit. Some benefits, such as holiday or vacations, are paid in cash at the employee's rate.

Employers are increasingly concerned about the form of pay for all employees because contracts often specify the amounts of insurance coverage rather than employer contributions. Unorganized employees often hope the union receives a large settlement, which might obligate management to do the same for them. In the past, the form of the economic package was generally considered the union's province. An employer willing to give an equivalent of 50 cents per hour in wages (see Figure 9–3) did not care how it was apportioned. As benefits became more complex and as medical, dental, and other health care costs began to escalate more rapidly than the cost of other goods, employer interests in the allocation of pay increased. Table 9–4 details what might happen to costs over the course of a contract. Given employers' desires for certainty or predictability in the contract's effects, their resistance to benefit packages with unknown future costs would be expected; these packages generally specify coverages, not costs. The example in Table 9–4 shows that a health insurance program costing $1,800 per employee decreases in cost per hour as the number of hours worked increases. A $30 per month premium increase would cost between $0.87 and $1.30 per hour depending on the time worked. In this example, if health care premiums increase by $45 instead of $30 per month, the relative difference for overtime is decreased slightly. Health care cost containment has increased in importance for both parties. Managements have sought to negotiate contribution limits rather than to pay for

FIGURE 9–3
Wage Forms

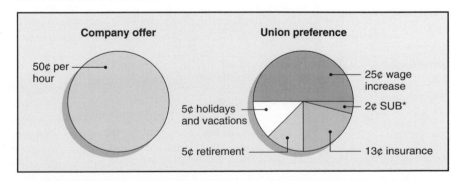

* Supplementary unemployment benefits (SUB).

TABLE 9–4

Cost per Employee for Wage and Fringe Increases

	Present Rate	Total Cost/Year	Cost per Hour	Increase Offered	Anticipated Cost	Cost per Hour	Possible Cost	Cost per Hour
Full-time (2,080 hr./yr.)								
	$10/hour	20,800	10.00	$.40/hr.	21,632	10.40	21,632	10.40
	$150/mo.	1,800	0.87	$30/mo.	2,160	1.04	2,340	1.13
		22,600	10.87		23,792	11.44	23,972	11.53
Part-time (1,664 hr./yr.)								
	$10/hour	16,640	10.00	$.40/hr.	17,306	10.40	17,306	10.40
	$150/mo.	1,800	1.08	$30/mo.	2,160	1.30	2,340	1.41
		18,440	11.08		19,466	11.70	19,646	11.81
Overtime (2,496 hr./yr.)								
	$10/hour	27,040	10.83	$.40/hr.	28,122	11.27	28,122	11.27
	$150/mo.	1,800	0.72	$30/mo.	2,160	0.87	2,340	0.94
		28,840	11.55		30,282	12.13	30,462	12.20

Possible health care cost example assumes premiums go up by $45 instead of $30.

coverage, or at least to require deductibles or co-payments, and/or move plans to managed care providers.

Pensions have also been a problem for unions and managements. Before actuarially based funding was required by the Employee Retirement Income Security Act of 1974 (ERISA), an aging labor force often led to staggering costs for employers providing pensions as a current expense. Contracted increases for already retired employees create an immediate cost to employers because the increases will be unfunded.

The two major types of pension plans are **defined benefit** and **defined contribution** plans. **Defined benefit pension plans** specify rules used to determine future pension benefits; for example, 2 percent of hourly pay at retirement times number of years of service. **Defined contribution pension plans** specify what the employer will set aside for the employee's retirement each year; for example, 3 percent of total pay per hour. Employers face funding risks with defined benefit plans because of variations in investment returns over time. Employees prefer to avoid a defined contribution plan because the investment risk is shifted to them.

As workforces become increasingly diversified demographically, unions and managements will likely negotiate agreements facilitating employment for nontraditional groups. The Communications Workers agreement with AT&T provides for newborn care, family care, tax-free dependent care reimbursement accounts, resources and referrals for professional family care, adoption assistance, flexible hours, and a fund for family care program development.[15]

Because federal wage and hour laws require that employees receive a 50 percent premium for more than 40 hours per week, an employer might reduce costs by hiring new employees when more work is needed. However, if employee-tied benefits such as insurance and paid time off exceed 50 percent of base pay, an employer would prefer overtime unless there were a higher premium in the contract. Benefits now add about 41 percent to salaries.[16] Thus, labor's position favoring benefits restricts new entries and may reduce opportunities for its present members. Even if benefits are below 50 percent, if costs incidental to hiring and benefits exceed the overtime premium, new hiring will be resisted.[17]

Pay System

The pay system refers to methods used to decide pay for each employee. All methods for bargaining unit employees will be specified in the contract. In this section, we identify many of the negotiated arrangements for individual employee pay changes.

Membership
Contracts often provide some forms of compensation simply for membership in the organization. Many employee-tied fringe benefits (e.g., health, life, and disability insurance) are based on membership. They are usually unrelated to the number of hours worked in a given month, as long as the employee was active during a designated period.

Tenure
Several pay system features are related to seniority. **Benefit status seniority** refers to entitlements individuals accrue from continued employment. Many pay systems provide for step pay increases based on length of service within a job or grade level. These increases usually have a cap because a certain range is assigned to a given job.

Participation in pension plans also may be based on service. ERISA requires employees over age 21 to participate in an employer's noncontributory retirement plan. In a noncontributory plan, the employee makes no contributions toward future retirement benefits. However, contributions do not become vested (owned) until the employee has met certain statutorial minimum-service requirements.

---

[15] B. B. Brown and K. Peters-Hamlin, "AT&T's Family-Care Union Agreement: A Harbinger of Change in Corporate America?" *Employment Relations Today* 16 (1989), pp. 205–10.

[16] U.S. Chamber of Commerce, *Employee Benefits, 1997,* Washington: Chamber of Commerce.

[17] J. A. Fossum, "Hire or Schedule Overtime? A Formula for Minimizing Labor Costs," *Compensation Review* 1, no. 2 (1969), pp. 14–22.

Frequently, entitlements to longer vacations are based on length of service. Low-service employees frequently earn only one or two weeks' vacation annually while long-service employees may accrue five or more weeks.

Tenure may entitle employees to use accrued benefits such as retirement. Some contracts allow employees to retire after a defined length of service (e.g., 30 years), rather than at a specific age. Autoworkers pioneered these benefits in the private sector; in the public sector, they are most prevalent in the uniformed services.

Time Worked

Most contracts base pay on the amount of time worked and when it is worked. Wages are calculated on an hourly basis in these cases. In addition, the level of wages frequently depends on the amount of time worked during a given period (overtime) and the time of day during which the work is accomplished (shift differentials).

Productive Efficiency

Slightly more than 31 percent of contracts base wages of some bargaining unit employees on output levels.[18] These incentive plans have a bargained base output level, above which employees receive extra compensation. Depending on the plan, these additions are on a straight-line, increasing, or decreasing basis as production increases.

Negotiating an appropriate base is often difficult, and grievances frequently occur when employees are transferred to jobs where they lack sufficient experience to exceed the standard. Circumstances beyond the employees' control can intrude, reducing chances to achieve high output (e.g., poorly fitting components on an assembly job).

Group incentive plans are often of greater interest to unions because they avoid competition among employees. Implementing the plans frequently requires significant management-union cooperation. These plans are covered in detail in Chapter 13.

Profit Sharing

To make labor costs more flexible, employers have proposed and implemented profit-sharing plans when workers agree to forgo increases in their base wages. The employee's total pay is based on both job level and employer profitability. Profit sharing has been most visible among U.S. auto producers. The size of an employee's bonus depends on his or her proportion of total pay in the unit, the size of the employer's profit, and the agreed formula for determining the size of the pool to share. Exhibit 9–2 contains the UAW–GM formula for profit sharing.

Profit sharing makes compensation more flexible. During economic downturns, pay decreases as profits drop, potentially reducing the need for employers

---

[18] *Collective Bargaining Negotiations and Contracts* (Washington, DC: Bureau of National Affairs, 1984), tab sect. 93.

EXHIBIT 9–2

Profit Sharing in the General Motors–UAW Contract

2.14 **"Profits"** . . . means income earned by U.S. Operations before income taxes and "extraordinary" items . . . Profits are before any profit sharing charges are deducted. Profits also are before incentive program charges for U.S. Operations.

2.18 **"Total Profit Share"** . . . means an obligation of the Corporation for any Plan Year in an amount equal to the sum of:

    (a) 6 percent of the portion of the Profits . . . which exceeds 0.0 percent of Sales and Revenues . . . but does not exceed 1.8 percent . . . ;

    (b) 8 percent of the portion of the Profits . . . which exceeds 1.8 percent of Sales and Revenues . . . but does not exceed 2.3 percent . . . ;

    (c) 10 percent of the portion of the Profits . . . which exceeds 2.3 percent of Sales and Revenues . . . but does not exceed 4.6 percent . . . ;

    (d) 14 percent of the portion of the Profits . . . which exceeds 4.6 percent of Sales and Revenues . . . but does not exceed 6.9 percent . . . ;

    (e) 17 percent of the portion of the Profits . . . which exceeds 6.9 percent of Sales and Revenues.

4.02 **Allocation of Profit Sharing Amount to Participants**

    The portion of the Total Profit Share for the Plan Year allocated to this Plan . . . will be allocated to each Participant entitled to a distribution . . . in the proportion that (a) the Participant's Compensation Hours for the Plan Year bears to (b) the total Compensated Hours for all Participants in the Plan entitled to a distribution for the Plan Year.

---

to lay off employees. Some evidence exists that as unemployment increases, firms with profit sharing are less likely to lay off employees.[19]

Time Not Worked

Employees receive pay when not at work for a variety of reasons. Contracts provide for paid holidays, vacations, sick leave, jury duty, and so forth. Supplementary employment benefits (SUB) are paid during layoffs under some contracts. SUB adds income from a trust fund to required state unemployment insurance benefits. Typically, the addition enables a worker to maintain income close to regular straight-time wages. If layoffs are pervasive and of long duration, total benefit payments may exceed the funds available to pay them, and SUB ends until the funds are restored.

UNION EFFECTS ON PAY

Unionization fixes wages for the unionized employer. High levels of unionization within industries and within industry pattern bargaining decrease competition

---

[19] D. L. Kruse, "Profit-Sharing and Employment Variability: Microeconomic Evidence on the Weitzman Theory," *Industrial and Labor Relations Review* 44 (1991), pp. 437–53.

among employers. This section examines union influences on wages and some specific environmental characteristics involving unions that relate to wage differences.

Union Effects on Pay Levels

There is substantial debate about the effect of unions on pay. If a wage increase is defined as an increase in the share of costs of labor as compared to capital, then economic theory argues that labor's share would not increase in the long run, because employers could increase their return on investment by substituting capital for labor unless labor productivity increased. For example, if arc welders can make 200 welds an hour on a given product and are paid $12 per hour, the labor cost of welds is 6 cents each. If an industrial robot could produce 200 welds an hour and had a useful life of three years (ignoring interest and the depreciation advantages of tax laws) and it cost less than $72,000, the employer would prefer robots over arc welders (assuming a one-shift operation). If robots cost $80,000, the firm would replace welders with robots whenever welders' pay exceeded $13.33 per hour without an increase in their productivity.

An exhaustive analysis of evidence on the role of unions in influencing wages finds consistent, significant positive effects for unions on employees' wages.[20] The effects can be examined at the industrial, occupational, and individual levels. Wage effects are substantially greater for increased unionization within an industry than for increased unionization within an occupation. The size of industrial effects is inversely related to the level of competition in the industry, while occupation effects are most pronounced through increased union representation at the local level.[21] Where a firm has built a degree of asset specificity—that is, methods or processes unique to the organization—unions are able to capture larger than normal increases.[22] Wage premiums do not come without a cost to labor, however. Industries with the highest union wage premium were those in which employment declined the most during the 1970s.[23] A variety of union effects on wages occurs across definable groups. Figure 9–4 shows that employees who have less education, are nonwhite, younger or older, male, short tenure, transport operatives, or laborers are more highly advantaged.[24] Across worker subgroups, becoming unionized, remaining unionized, or becoming employed in unionized

---

[20] R. B. Freeman and J. L. Medoff, *What Do Unions Do?* (New York: Basic Books, 1984), pp. 43–60.

[21] W. J. Moore, R. J. Newman, and J. Cunningham, "The Effect of the Extent of Unionism on Union and Nonunion Wages," *Journal of Labor Research* 6 (1985), pp. 21–44; M. A. Curme and D. A. MacPherson, "Union Wage Differentials and the Effects of Industry and Local Union Density: Evidence from the 1980s," *Journal of Labor Research* 12 (1991), pp. 419–27.

[22] J. K. Cavanaugh, "Asset-Specific Investment and Unionized Labor," *Industrial Relations* 37 (1998), pp. 35–50.

[23] P. D. Linneman, M. L. Wachter, and W. H. Carter, "Evaluating the Evidence on Union Wages and Employment," *Industrial and Labor Relations Review* 44 (1990), pp. 34–53.

[24] Freeman and Medoff, *What Do Unions Do?* p. 49.

FIGURE 9–4

The Union Wage Advantage by Demographic Group, for Blue-Collar Workers, 20–65, 1979

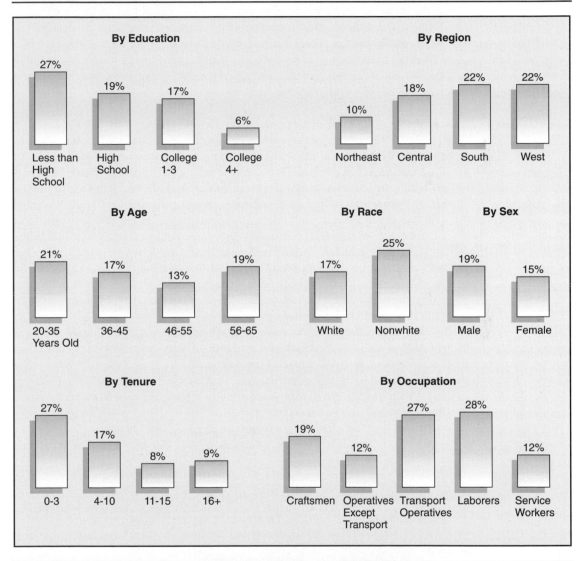

SOURCE: R. B. Freeman and J. L. Medoff, *What Do Unions Do?* (New York: BasicBooks, 1984), p. 49.

organizations is associated with higher wages.[25] Unionization may have occurred because of dissatisfaction with low wages compared to the wages of other employers or other workers in one's community. Thus, unions can also raise

---

[25] Ibid., pp. 46–47.

wages from a below-average position to one of equivalence with others.[26] A study of wage levels in firms facing organizing drives found that in the year subsequent to the drive pay levels were higher than those of a control group facing no union activity. The study also found that firms in which organizing activity occurred had pay levels lower than comparative levels before the drive began. The premium following unionization activity was nowhere near the level found between union and nonunion firms, in general, with initial contract demands focusing more heavily on issues of workplace democracy.[27]

Wage Level Difference Effects over Time

The last 70 years have seen wide swings in the level of union wage premiums. Premiums have ranged from a high of 46 percent in the early 1930s to a low of 2 percent in the late 1940s.[28] Premiums were greater during recessions and narrowed during inflation, perhaps because of the rigidity of rates in long-term contracts.[29] Improved productivity and reduced labor intensity are both associated with larger wage increases. Profits and wage increases are negatively related. This may mean that wage increases have been granted independently of profitability, causing future profits to suffer. Employers were most willing to grant increases in less concentrated industries with improving productivity. Bargaining power in these is reduced because competitive products would be easy substitutes.[30] In the short run, union wages are insensitive to changes in the unemployment rate compared to wages in the nonunion sector.[31]

On the other hand, there is no evidence that union wage premiums declined as a result of wage concessions in negotiations.[32] Real wage concessions did not occur in the early 1980s. Inflation abated faster than nominal wages.[33] Where concessions have been negotiated, they have been more likely in small, high-paying firms with lower union coverage. A history of layoffs and poor stock performance also increased their likelihood.[34]

From 1967 to 1977, union workers received a 24 percent premium, other things being equal. Nonwhites, Southerners, and low-educated persons gained

---

[26] See O. Ashenfelter and G. E. Johnson, "Unionism, Relative Wages, and Labor Quality in U.S. Manufacturing Industries," *International Economic Review,* October 1972, pp. 488–507.

[27] R. B. Freeman and M. M. Kleiner, "The Impact of New Unionization on Wages and Working Conditions," *Journal of Labor Economics* 8 (1990), pp. S8–S25.

[28] G. Johnson, "Changes over Time in the Union/Nonunion Wage Differential in the United States" (Ann Arbor: University of Michigan, 1981), Table 2.

[29] Mitchell, *Unions, Wages, and Inflation,* pp. 80–83.

[30] D. Singh, C. G. Williams, and R. P. Wilder, "Wage Determination in U.S. Manufacturing," 1958–1976: A Collective Bargaining Approach," *Journal of Labor Research* 3 (1982), pp. 223–37.

[31] P. V. Wunnava and A. A. Okunade, "Countercyclical Union Wage Premiums? Evidence for the 1980s," *Journal of Labor Research* 17 (1996), pp. 289–96.

[32] M. E. Haggerty and D. E. Leigh, "The Impact of Union Wage Concessions on Union Premiums," *Industrial Relations* 32 (1993), pp. 111–23.

[33] J. W. Budd, "Union Wage Concessions in the 1980s: Adding Realism to Nominalism," *Proceedings of the Industrial Relations Research Association* 48 (1996), pp. 311–18.

[34] L. A. Bell, "Union Wage Concessions in the 1980s: The Importance of Firm-Specific Factors," *Industrial and Labor Relations Review* 48 (1995), pp. 258–75.

particularly high premiums. Real wages for both the union and the nonunion sector increased in tandem during this period.[35] A large set of studies of the union-nonunion wage gap concluded that the average gap is about 10 percent; narrowing occurs during periods of expansion and widening during periods of high unemployment as a result of the rigidities of contracts.[36]

Structural and Legal Factors

An analysis of employees surveyed in 1977 found that union members' wages were about 18.3 percent over those who were not represented, other things being equal. For both unionized and nonunion workers, however, the inverse relationship between unemployment and wages became more pronounced in the early 1980s.[37] Other factors positively influencing wage levels were plant size (about 5.3 percent per 1,000 employees) and industrial concentration (about 7.4 percent when the largest four firms produce 50 percent rather than 30 percent of the total product of the industry).[38]

Global competition influences union pay premiums. For every 10 percent increase in market share gained by imports in an industry, the differential narrowed about 2 percent. The most heavily unionized industries were most resistant to a narrowing of differentials.[39] Foreign production by U.S. firms appears to have little effect on employment of union members.[40]

In states with right-to-work laws, employees cannot be required to belong to a union as a condition of continued employment. For union members, right-to-work laws or strong campaign activity for such laws are associated with lower wages.[41] Right-to-work laws are also associated with increased inequality in income distributions while unionization decreases inequality.[42]

Deregulation occurred broadly during the 1980s and might have affected wages. However, a study of airline workers found that their wages declined only slightly through 1989.[43]

---

[35] W. J. Moore and J. Raisian, "The Level and Growth of Union/Nonunion Relative Wage Effects, 1967–1977," *Journal of Labor Research* 4 (1983), pp. 65–79.

[36] S. P. Jarrell and T. D. Stanley, "A Meta-Analysis of the Union-Nonunion Wage Gap, *Industrial and Labor Relations Review* 44 (1990), pp. 54–67.

[37] J. W. Budd and Y. Nho, "Testing for a Structural Change in U.S. Wage Determination," *Industrial Relations* 36 (1997), pp. 160–77.

[38] J. E. Kwoka, Jr., "Monopoly, Plant, and Union Effects on Worker Wages," *Industrial and Labor Relations Review* 37 (1983), pp. 251–57.

[39] D. A. MacPherson and J. B. Stewart, "The Effect of International Competition on Union and Nonunion Wages," *Industrial and Labor Relations Review* 43 (1990), pp. 434–46.

[40] T. Karier, "U.S. Foreign Production and Unions," *Industrial Relations* 34 (1995), pp. 107–18.

[41] W. J. Wessels, "Economic Effects of Right-to-Work Laws," *Journal of Labor Research* 2 (1981), pp. 55–75.

[42] M. Nieswiadomy, D. J. Slottje and K. Hayes, "The Impact of Unionization, Right-to-Work Laws, and Female Labor Force Participation on Earnings Inequality across States," *Journal of Labor Research* 12 (1991), pp. 185–95.

[43] N. B. Johnson, "Airline Workers' Earnings and Union Expenditures under Deregulation," *Industrial and Labor Relations Review* 45 (1991), pp. 154–65.

Union Spillovers

Union wage increases lead to nonunion increases, but the reverse is not true. High unemployment dampens the union increase rate, while increasing costs of living raise them. Union-union spillovers are also found, suggesting that pattern bargaining has influenced union settlements. Political and equity issues promote spillovers over and above market forces.[44] Nonunion wage changes do not appear to have any subsequent effect on union wage levels.[45]

Union Effects on Pay Structures

When unionized organizations are compared with nonunion firms in the same industries, variances in wage rates within jobs are more often lower in unionized firms. In a national sample of employees, individuals who moved from nonunion to union employment had lower wage dispersions, while those who made opposite moves had increased dispersions. Compression in wages is increased by across-the-board wage increases. The average decrease in dispersions attributed to unionization is about 22 percent.[46] Figure 9–5 shows differences between hypothetical union and nonunion wage dispersions. The results are consistent with negotiating contracts that focus on the desires of the median voter and put together coalitions best served by settlements that reduce variance in wage increases. They are also consistent with the ideal that unions favor a reduction in the inequality of wages.

Union Effects on Pay Form

Union members prefer larger proportions of their pay to be in the form of fringe benefits. Managements prefer a lower proportion. In terms of costs, unions have the greatest impact on small or low-wage employers; and they most greatly influence the costs of insurance, followed by vacations and holidays, overtime premiums, and pensions. When compared to nonunion situations, unions have the greatest relative influence on pensions—possibly reflecting the returns to seniority included in most contracts—followed by insurance and vacations and holidays. Unions have a negative effect on the use of overtime (but not premium rates), sick leave, and bonuses. Evidence suggests that the union impact is 17 percent greater for fringe benefits than it is for straight-time pay.[47]

---

[44] J. W. Budd, "Institutional and Market Determinants of Wage Spillovers: Evidence from UAW Pattern Bargaining," *Industrial Relations* 36 (1997), pp. 97–116.

[45] S. Vroman, "The Direction of Wage Spillovers in Manufacturing," *Industrial and Labor Relations Review* 36 (1982), pp. 102–12.

[46] R. B. Freeman, "Union Wage Practices and Wage Dispersion within Establishments," *Industrial and Labor Relations Review* 36 (1982), pp. 3–21.

[47] R. B. Freeman, "The Effect of Unionism on Fringe Benefits," *Industrial and Labor Relations Review* 34 (1981), pp. 489–509.

FIGURE 9–5

Hypothetical Union and Nonunion Wage Structures

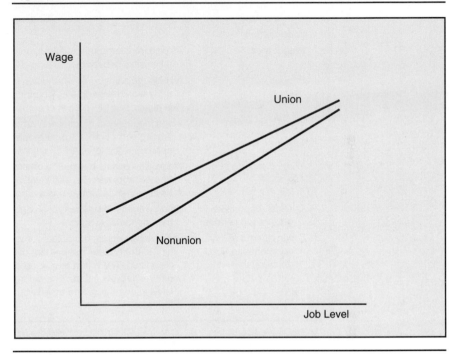

Pension wealth is substantially greater for unionized employees than for comparable nonunion employees. Differences in plans appear greatest for collectively bargained plans having higher initial benefits, earlier retirement opportunities, and larger postretirement increases in benefits.[48]

Union Effects on Pay Systems

Little is known about how unions influence pay systems, and existing data are based at the industry level. Unionized employees are much more likely to have pay increases determined by easily identifiable criteria and by automatic progressions and are less likely to have merit reviews or other forms of individual determinations. Across-the-board increases related to membership are frequent, causing compression in the pay structure.[49] Table 9–5 summarizes the effects of unions on various aspects of pay.

---

[48] S. G. Allen and R. L. Clark, "Unions, Pension Wealth, and Age-Compensation Profiles," *Industrial and Labor Relations Review* 39 (1986), pp. 502–517

[49] Freeman, "Union Wage Practices, pp. 3–21."

TABLE 9–5

Evidence on Union/Nonunion Differences Based on Cross-Sectional Data

Variable	Finding
Compensation	
Wage rates	All else (measurable) the same, union/nonunion hourly wage differential is between 10% and 20%.
Fringes	All else the same, union/nonunion hourly fringe differential is between 20% and 30%. The fringe share of compensation is higher at a given level of compensation.
Wage dispersion	Wage inequality is much lower among union members than among comparable nonmembers and total wage dispersion appears to be lowered by unionism.
Wage structure	Wage differentials between workers who are different in terms of race, age, service, skill level, and education appear to be lower under collective bargaining.
Cyclical responsive-ness of wage rates	Union wages are less responsive to labor market conditions than nonunion wages.
Determinants of compensation differential	Other things equal, the union compensation advantage is higher the greater the percent of a market's workers who are organized. The effect of market concentration on wage differentials is unclear. The differentials appear to be very large in some regulated markets. They appear to decline as firm size increases.

SOURCE: R. B. Freeman and J. L. Medoff, "The Impact of Collective Bargaining: Illusion or Reality?" in *U.S. Industrial Relations, 1950–1980: A Critical Assessment,* ed. J. Stieber, R. B. McKersie, and D. Q. Mills (Madison, WI: Industrial Relations Research Association, 1981), p. 50.

UNION EFFECTS ON ORGANIZATIONAL EFFECTIVENESS

Unionization and the usually resulting seniority rules change employees' orientations toward long-run employment and the benefits accruing with seniority. The effect of unionization on mobility and turnover is explored in the next chapter, but it should be recognized that unionized employees are older and more experienced, other things being equal, than their nonunion counterparts. Estimates indicate human capital per worker (knowledge, skills, and abilities related to the job) is about 6 percent higher in unionized settings.[50]

Productivity

Because the evidence suggests a unionized workforce increases wage costs, in contrast with unorganized firms in the same industries, a unionized firm should be at a competitive disadvantage, other things being equal. But these other things are

---

[50] R. B. Freeman and J. L. Medoff, "The Impact of Collective Bargaining: Illusion or Reality?" in J. Stieber, R. B. McKersie, and D. Q. Mills, eds., *U.S. Industrial Relations, 1950–1980: A Critical Assessment* (Madison, WI: Industrial Relations Research Association, 1981), pp. 47–98.

not all equal. Industry-level studies have found unionized establishments to be 24 percent more productive on average than nonunion establishments. If the extent of unionization in the industry is considered, the productivity effect increases to 30 percent. Unionization also apparently has an impact on worker quality within the establishment as measured by experience, training, schooling, and the like. Evidence indicates production worker quality in union establishments is 11 percent higher, while nonproduction worker quality is lower by 8 percent.[51]

Within industries, unionization appears to have differential effects. Research on construction industry productivity found unionized workers on private-sector projects were up to 51 percent more productive than their nonunion counterparts. The differentials decreased markedly in public-sector construction projects, however.[52] In education student achievement was negatively affected by unionization among public schoolteachers through increased use of administrators and reductions in instruction time, but student achievement is positively influenced through increased preparation time, teacher experience, and smaller student/teacher ratios.[53] In hospitals and nursing homes, productivity was higher among unionized establishments in the private sector, but little difference was noted in the public sector.[54] A study in the auto parts industry found little difference in productivity levels between organized and unorganized establishments, and failure to account for firms that may have gone out of business may upwardly bias the union effects on productivity.[55]

Higher turnover in nonunion organizations is a possible explanation for productivity differentials (examined in Chapter 10). If experience is related to skill levels, unionized firms will have higher skill levels, leading to greater productivity. Because union contracts reduce the wage dispersion within jobs in firms, employees may believe nonperformance-based pay systems eliminate competition between workers for a wage pool and enable them to willingly share job information and train new employees.

Organizational Investment and Growth Decisions

Since unionization generally leads to wage premiums, unless productivity increases as rapidly as labor costs, labor becomes more expensive relative to capital. Production technologies shift somewhat, moving somewhat away from least-cost combinations.[56]

---

[51] Ibid.

[52] S. G. Allen, "Future Evidence on Union Efficiency in Construction," *Industrial Relations* 27 (1988), pp. 232–40.

[53] R. W. Eberts, "Union Effects on Teacher Productivity," *Industrial and Labor Relations Review* 37 (1984), pp. 346–58.

[54] S. G. Allen, "The Effect of Unionism on Productivity in Privately and Publicly Owned Hospitals and Nursing Homes," *Journal of Labor Research* 7 (1986), pp. 59–68.

[55] R. S. Kaufman and R. T. Kaufman, "Union Effects on Productivity, Personnel Practices, and Survival in the Automotive Parts Industry," *Journal of Labor Research* 8 (1987), pp. 333–50.

[56] R. W. Eberts, "Unionization and Cost of Production: Compensation, Productivity, and Factor-Use Effects," *Journal of Labor Economics* 9 (1991), pp. 171–85.

Evidence indicates that unionized firms invest about 20 percent less in physical capital and have lower research and development budgets compared to equivalent nonunion firms.[57] These differences may be related to the belief that returns to investment have been decreased by higher labor costs associated with unionization. Unionization leads to increased capital intensity.[58]

Employment growth rates in unionized plants is also about 3 to 4 percent lower on average than in comparable nonunion plants.[59]

Profitability and Returns to Shareholders

Unionized firms are less profitable than nonunion firms and less profitable subsequent to unionization.[60] The negative effects are related to a reduction in investment growth.[61] Shareholder returns are reduced following unionization. A study tracking organizing success following passage of the Wagner Act in the 1930s found organized firms had about a 20 percent lower rate of return to shareholders than firms remaining nonunion.[62] Firms involved in organizing drives and whose securities are publicly traded experience about a 4 percent reduction in equity value following a successful campaign—and a 1.3 percent loss even if the union lost.[63] The latter probably occurs because firms facing union activity increase wages more than those who don't, win or lose.[64] If unionization leads to lower shareholder returns, other things being equal, as the agents of shareholders, top managers could be expected to try to reduce unionization in their firms.[65] On the other hand, lower returns in unionized firms are accompanied by lower risk because security prices are less volatile, perhaps reflecting increased risk sharing by employees through layoff and recall procedures.[66]

Decreases in profitability may occur as a result of employers extending wage increases to nonrepresented employees to avoid further unionization. While

[57] B. T. Hirsch, "Firm Investment Behavior and Collective Bargaining Strategy," *Industrial Relations* 31 (1992), pp. 95–121.

[58] S. G. Bronars, D. R. Deere, and J. S. Tracy, "The Effects of Unions on Firm Behavior: An Empirical Analysis Using Firm-Level Data," *Industrial Relations* 33 (1994), pp. 426–51.

[59] J. S. Leonard, "Unions and Employment Growth," *Industrial Relations* 31 (1992), pp. 80–94; and R. J. Long, "The Effect of Unionization on Employment Growth of Canadian Companies," *Industrial and Labor Relations Review* 46 (1992), pp. 691–703.

[60] Freeman and Medoff, *What Do Unions Do?* pp. 181–90.

[61] Bronars et al., "Effects of Union on Firm Behavior."

[62] C. A. Olson and B. E. Becker, "The Effects of the NLRA on Stockholder Wealth in the 1930s," *Industrial and Labor Relations Review* 44 (1986), pp. 116–29.

[63] R. S. Ruback and M. B. Zimmerman, "Unionization and Profitability: Evidence from the Capital Market," *Journal of Political Economy* 92 (1984), pp. 1134–57.

[64] Freeman and Kleiner, "Impact of New Unionization."

[65] This and other issues are discussed and analyzed in B. E. Becker and C. A. Olson, "Labor Relations and Firm Performance," in M. M. Kleiner, R. N. Block, M. Roomkin, and S. W. Salsburg, eds., *Human Resources and the Performances of the Firm* (Madison, WI: Industrial Relations Research Association, 1987), pp. 43–86.

[66] B. E. Becker and C. A. Olson, "Unionization and Shareholder Interests," *Industrial and Labor Relations Review* 42 (1989), pp. 246–61.

productivity increases have been found following unionization for represented employees, this may not carry over to nonunion employees who also received increased pay.[67]

Wage concessions in airlines during the 1980s and 1990s were related to share price increases. Concessions in one airline were seen as advantageous from a profitability standpoint since shares in other airlines dropped on the announcement. Prior to deregulation, investors responded positively to increases for flight attendants but negatively to cuts for mechanics. Following deregulation, cuts for flight attendants, clericals, and pilots were positive, reflecting the general unavailability of alternative opportunities for these occupations.[68]

Takeovers of unionized firms result in higher shareholder return (41 percent) compared with takeovers of nonunion employers. Wage concessions following acquisition of nonunion firms have averaged about 8 percent or half of the union premium.[69]

WAGE ISSUES IN CURRENT CONTRACTS

Contracts differ in the degree to which they contain particular types of wage and benefit clauses. Table 9–6 displays major types of wage and benefit clauses and the proportions in which they appear in recent U.S. collective bargaining agreements.

Between 1979 and 1995, the pervasiveness of certain types of contract clauses has changed. Dental insurance has increased, but hospitalization and other forms of medical insurance have decreased. Income maintenance has remained at about the same level, while cost-of-living allowances have declined. Concessionary situations have often been accompanied by improvements in job security clauses.

SUMMARY

Wage demands are a central part of every contract negotiation. In forming their bargaining positions, unions are often concerned with equity among employee groups, the ability of the company to pay an increase, and the change in the standard of living of its members since the last negotiation.

Pay programs, whether negotiated in contracts or formulated by the employer, address issues related to the level of pay in relation to the market, the structure of pay rates for jobs within the organization, the form in which pay is received as wages or benefits, and the system used to determine individual entitlements to

---

[67] B. E. Becker and C. A. Olson, "Unions and Firm Profits," *Industrial Relations* 31 (1992), pp. 395–415.

[68] S. L. Thomas, D. Officer, and N. B. Johnson, "The Capital Market Response to Wage Negotiations in the Airlines," *Industrial Relations* 34 (1995), pp. 203–17.

[69] B. E. Becker, "Union Rents as a Source of Takeover Gains among Target Shareholders," *Industrial and Labor Relations Review* 49 (1995), pp. 3–19.

TABLE 9–6
Basic Wage Clauses in Contracts (1995)

Clause	Percent Containing Clause
Insurance	
Accidental death and dismemberment	75%
Alcohol and drug abuse treatment	58
Comprehensive medical	70
Dental care	82
Doctors' appointments	29
Hospitalization	30
Life	99
Major medical	46
Maternity	42
Medical-related insurance	64
Miscellaneous medical expense	23
Optical care	43
Prescription drugs	47
Sickness and accident	81
Surgical	52
Pensions	
Disability	89
Early retirement	98
Noncontributory plan	93
Some provisions	99
Income maintenance	
Severance pay	40
Some provision	53
Supplementary unemployment benefits	14
Work or pay guarantee	13
Wages	
Cost-of-living adjustments	34
Deferred increases	89
Hiring rates	11
Incentive plans	42
Job classification procedures	60
Lump sum payments	23
Shift differentials	86
Two-tier structure	27
Termination pay	15
Work progression	49
Wage reopeners	8

SOURCE: Compiled from *Collective Bargaining Negotiation and Contracts* (Washington, DC: Bureau of National Affairs, 1995).

varied pay treatments. A variety of concerns are subject to negotiation, with unions stressing equality and ability-to-pay issues and management favoring pay programs that positively influence employee behavior. Managements have also been increasingly interested in lowering base-pay levels and in making a larger proportion of pay flexible and responsive to changes in economic conditions.

Recent evidence suggests that unionization is associated with significantly higher pay levels. Pay structures tend to be somewhat flatter than in nonunion organizations, with a larger proportion of pay given in benefits. Collective bargaining agreements generally contain fewer contingencies surrounding pay increases and have a larger proportion of pay in the form of deferred compensation and insurance.

Evidence suggests organized companies are about 20 percent more productive than unorganized ones. However, they are also about 20 percent less profitable. Productivity differences in favor of unionized organizations appear confined to blue-collar occupations and the private sector. Unionization is also generally associated with lower shareholder returns.

DISCUSSION QUESTIONS

1. What are the costs and benefits for management in allowing the union to decide how the economic package should be divided?
2. What demands would most likely be advocated by union leaders interested in obtaining contract ratification?
3. What information would you use to make predictions about the economic demands and probable settlement for a particular union-management negotiation?
4. What are the economic benefits of union membership to employees, and to what extent can these benefits be increased before employers face problems?
5. What are the trade-offs among increased wages for unions, productivity effects, and profitability effects on organizations?

KEY TERMS

Ability to pay   *253*

Standard of living   *253*

Cost-of-living adjustments   *253*

Pay level   *255*

Pay structure   *256*

Pay form   *256*

Pay system   *256*

Job evaluation   *259*

Skill-based pay   *259*

Two-tier pay plans   *262*

Defined benefit pension plan   *264*

Defined contribution pension plan   *264*

Benefit status seniority   *265*

C A S E
HEALTH CARE COSTS AND EMPLOYMENT LEVELS

During the past year, health care costs per employee provided under the GMFC-Local 384 contract have increased by 11 percent. With the increased penetration of the domestic market by foreign producers and the resulting pressure on prices, GMFC is exploring ways in which health care costs can be contained or reduced. It is concentrating on subcontracting and negotiating an arrangement to hire part-time employees who would not be eligible for health care benefits.

Local 384 would like to avoid benefits reduction, subcontracting, and part-time workers. The first would be a concession in an environment in which reductions have already been conceded. The second and third would lead to a reduction in the membership of the local or a reduction in the proportion of employees who are represented.

Assuming that this issue will be a major one in the upcoming negotiations, prepare either a union or management position on the issue of health care cost containment, recognizing that the employer will be decreasingly able to compete if total compensation costs increase as they have been recently with these types of year-to-year changes in health care costs.

10

NONWAGE ISSUES

IN BARGAINING

Wage and nonwage issues are not completely separable. Both involve economics for the employer. For example, contract provisions relating to hours of work frequently specify when entitlements to overtime premiums begin. This chapter first considers issues primarily associated with hours and terms and conditions of employment and then examines the effects of unions on nonwage outcomes for individuals and organizations.

Nonwage issues are important to both union members and management. For management, the length of the contract and the scope of management rights clauses are important. For union members, job security provisions (particularly those related to promotions and layoffs), grievance procedures, and work schedules are important. As an institution, the union is concerned with securing its representation rights through contractual requirements for employee membership in the union. How promotions and layoffs are handled influence outcomes important to each party.

As you study this chapter, consider the following questions:

1. What impacts do federal regulations and contract provisions have on management decision making as it relates to hours of work?

2. How do discipline and discharge procedures operate, and what procedures are available for redress of improper discipline by management?

3. How do job classification and job design affect the employment relationship?

4. What effect do seniority clauses have on employee behavior?

5. What impact does collective bargaining appear to have on the job satisfaction of represented employees?

NONWAGE PROVISIONS OF CURRENT CONTRACTS

Just as trends and patterns exist for wage issues, certain types of contract clauses appear in a relatively large proportion of collective bargaining agreements. Table 10–1 displays the prevalence of nonwage contract terms in a sample of recent contracts.

Contract clauses relating to issues included in Table 10–1 have become more prevalent during the past several years. For example, recognition of seniority as a criterion for employment decision making and clauses related to entitlement to, restrictions on, and acceptance of overtime have increased. However, union security provisions have not increased recently.

UNION AND MANAGEMENT GOALS FOR NONWAGE ISSUES

Chapter 9 suggested that unions are concerned with equity, ability to pay, and standards of living in formulating wage demands and have simultaneous economic and membership goals. Employers are expected to resist demands interfering with their abilities to be flexible, to be certain of their probable costs, and to respond to changes in their operating environments through the introduction of new production technologies.

Many nonwage issues relate directly to the union's membership goals. To the degree that employer costs increase through overtime rates, hiring more employees is seen as a cost-saving alternative, leading to higher union membership. Contract provisions are negotiated to ration job opportunities during cutbacks or when employers introduce labor-saving equipment. Several issues involve management's decision-making discretion to direct and deploy the workforce in ways most likely to achieve important objectives if business conditions change. To accomplish these ends, contracts frequently contain clauses recognizing the legitimacy of both parties and spelling out the rights and responsibilities of each in their day-to-day relationships.

DESIGN OF WORK

Job design has important cost and flexibility implications for employers and job security consequences for employees. Ironically, job security provisions tied to work design in the past may now exacerbate layoffs, while changes toward more flexible jobs, along with more flexible compensation, may improve job security in the long run and employment levels in the short run. Union-management cooperation in these issues will be discussed in Chapter 13.

Part of work design involves specifying the tasks, duties, and responsibilities assigned to particular jobs. Jobs have been narrowly defined where the production process requires relatively few specific tasks and where necessary training time is short. Jobs may also be narrowly defined where necessary skill sophistication is

TABLE 10–1

Basic Nonwage Clauses in Contracts (1995)

Clause	Percent Containing Clause	Clause	Percent Containing Clause
Contract term		Layoff, rehiring, and work sharing—*Cont.*	
1 year	1%	Notice to employees required—*Cont.*	
2 years	15	3–4 days	16%
3 years	64	5–6 days	14
4 years or more	9	7or more	18
Contract reopeners	9	Bumping permitted	63
Automatic renewal	90	Manufacturing contracts	75
Discipline and discharge		Nonmanufacturing contracts	40
General grounds for discharge	97	Leaves of absence	
Specific grounds for discharge	84	Personal	76
Grievance and arbitration		Union	78
Steps specified	99	Maternity	78
Arbitration as final step	99	Family	35
Hours and overtime		Paternity, child care, or adoption	13
Daily work schedules	87	Funeral	86
Weekly work schedules	71	Civic	82
Overtime premiums	98	Paid sick	31
Daily overtime premiums	92	Unpaid sick	50
Sixth-day premiums	26	Military	72
Seventh-day premiums	29	Management and union rights	
Pyramiding of overtime prohibited	66	Management rights statement	80
Distribution of overtime work	69	Restrictions on management	87
Acceptance of overtime	30	Subcontracting	56
Restrictions on overtime	44	Supervisory work	58
Weekend premiums	67	Technological change restrictions	26
Lunch, rest, and cleanup	62	Plant shutdowns or relocations	25
Waiting time entails	16	In-plant union representation	54
Standby time	4	Union access to plant	54
Travel time	33	Union bulletin boards	71
Voting time	6	Union right to information	56
Holidays		Union activity on company time	35
None specified	2	Union-management cooperation	57
Less than 7	5	Seniority	
7, 7½	5	Probational periods at hire	89
8, 8½	7	Loss of seniority	80
9, 9½	11	Seniority lists	68
10, 10½	21	As factor in promotions	42
11, 11½	21	As factor in transfers	57
12 or more	31	Status of supervisors	28
Eligibility for holiday pay	88	Strikes and lockouts	
Layoff, rehiring, and work sharing		Unconditional pledges (strikes)	63
Seniority as criterion	91	Unconditional pledges (lockouts)	70
Seniority as sole factor	47	Limitation on union liability	43
Notice to employees required	50	Penalties for strikers	47
No minimum	14	Picket line observance	25
1–2 days	16		

TABLE 10–1

(continued)

Clause	Percent Containing Clause	Clause	Percent Containing Clause
Union security		Vacations—*Cont.*	
Union shop	64%	Based on service	89%
Modified union shop	10	Work requirement for eligibility	55
Agency shop	10	Vacation scheduling by management	87
Maintenance of membership	4	Working conditions and safety	
Hiring provisions	23	Occupational safety and health	89
Checkoff	95	Hazardous work acceptance	27
Vacations		Safety and health committees	50
Three weeks or more	88	Safety equipment provided	43
Four weeks or more	86	Guarantees against discrimination	
Five weeks or more	62	Guarantees mentioned	95
Six weeks or more	22	EEO pledges	17

SOURCE: Compiled from *Collective Bargaining Negotiation and Contracts* (Washington, DC: Bureau of National Affairs, 1995).

great, such as in carpentry or electrical work. Typically, manufacturing has had a relatively large number of jobs. These jobs are arranged to allow employees to advance as the result of learning additional skills and/or accumulating seniority. Frequently, more senior workers bid for jobs with better working conditions requiring less physical effort.

Manufacturing employers have been particularly interested in reducing the number of distinct job classifications in both production and maintenance to gain flexibility in staffing and avoid downtime for maintenance operations when a task is outside of a narrow job's jurisdiction. Broader capability requirements in broader job classifications may also require less supervision. Managers believe resistance to change will be higher where unions have negotiated technological change clauses into contracts.[1] Auto industry evidence indicates that a reduction in job classifications is associated with a reduction in supervision required, small improvements in the quality of output, and a small increase in total labor hours required for an equivalent level of output.[2]

In return for increased job security guarantees, employers have negotiated team-oriented production designs where workers have responsibilities for several tasks and an employee can be assigned to what would have been a variety of jobs. The GM–UAW agreement for its Saturn division reduces job classifications substantially. So-called cell-manufacturing techniques require substantially more knowledge and skill in tracking inventories, measuring quality, and determining how production activities will be undertaken. This approach requires higher skill levels, which potentially decrease interest in unionization as the lines between

[1] B. Bemmels and Y. Reshef, "Manufacturing Employees and Technological Change," *Journal of Labor Research* 12 (1991), pp. 231–46.

[2] J. H. Keefe and H. C. Katz, "Job Classifications and Plant Performance in the Auto Industry," *Industrial Relations* 29 (1990), pp. 111–18.

professional and production employees are blurred.[3] Unionized blue-collar employees have a higher likelihood of receiving off-the-job training.[4]

On the other hand, jobs represented by the union are more likely to be deskilled when new technology is introduced if management is successful in designating the jobs to be outside of the bargaining unit. Contractual seniority requirements may entitle jobs to employees who are not the most able to fully operate new equipment. Management is particularly unwilling to include jobs requiring computer programming within the bargaining unit when new technology is installed.[5]

Some work rule changes try to increase efficiency by more fully utilizing equipment (e.g., Teamster drivers previously hauled less than full-load shipments).[6] Others are aimed at increasing employee flexibility through greater skills and management's ability to assign employees to an increased variety of tasks.

Work rules that reserve certain responsibilities to certain jobs reduce efficiency, but may preserve employment levels. One study of the construction industry found that restrictive work rules increase labor costs by about 5 percent. In terms of their bargaining power, building trade unions appear willing to give up about 5 percent in wages to increase staffing levels by 3 percent.[7] Exhibit 10–1 covers some of these issues.

HOURS OF WORK

Hours of work are a mandatory bargaining issue and are regulated by federal and state wage and hour laws. Union campaigns for shorter work hours have been a priority since the early 1800s, with the National Labor Union proposing an eight-hour day after the Civil War. The federal government regulated work hours for civil servants during President Van Buren's administration and imposed overtime penalties for employers beginning in the 1930s.

Federal Wage and Hour Laws

Congress enacted the **Fair Labor Standards Act** (FLSA) in 1937 to regulate wages, hours, and working conditions of private-sector employers involved in interstate commerce. Briefly, the legislation requires employees not performing

---

[3] K. Knauss and M. Matuszak, "Responding to Technological Innovations: Unions and Cell Manufacturing," *Labor Studies Journal* 17, no. 1 (1992), pp. 29–48.

[4] P. Osterman, "Skill, Training, and Work Organization in American Establishments," *Industrial Relations* 34 (1995), pp. 125–46.

[5] M. R. Kelley, "Unionization and Job Design under Programmable Automation," *Industrial Relations* 28 (1989), pp. 174–87.

[6] T. A. Kochan, H. C. Katz, and R. B. McKersie, *The Transformation of American Industrial Relations* (New York: Basic Books, 1986), pp. 117–18.

[7] S. G. Allen, "Union Work Rules and Efficiency in the Building Trades," *Journal of Labor Economics* 4 (1986), pp. 212–42.

EXHIBIT 10–1

Job Targeting in the Construction Industry

Some [building trades] unions have used a controversial tactic known as job targeting. Under this approach, the union gives a contractor a rebate covering part or all of the difference between union and open-shop rates so the contractor can land a particular project that otherwise would have gone to the open shop. This approach has proven popular in some locals because all members pay into the fund, thereby spreading the cost of the concession beyond those working at a particular job site.

SOURCE: S. G. Allen, "Developments in Collective Bargaining in Construction in the 1980s and 1990s," in P. B. Voos (ed.), *Contemporary Collective Bargaining in the Private Sector,* Madison, WI: Industrial Relations Research Association, 1994, p. 438.

---

supervisory roles, outside sales positions, or jobs that require independent discretion using complex knowledge to be paid a 50 percent premium over their regular pay rates for more than 40 hours per week. This premium requirement covers all employees whose work is of a routine nature or requires close supervision and direction. The legislation also establishes a minimum wage level and prohibits persons under certain ages from working in specific occupations or industries.

Congress had previously enacted the **Davis-Bacon Act** (1931) and **Walsh-Healy Government Contracts Act** (1936), which required overtime premiums for employees with similar job duties after 40 hours per week and wages equal to those paid in the local area or industry if they were involved in government contract construction work or produced manufactured goods for the federal government. The laws, passed during the Depression, were intended to stimulate expanded employment and to take wages out of competition for federal government work. Employers would save by hiring more employees rather than having existing employees work overtime.

Collective Bargaining and Work Schedules

Unions have continually favored reducing the workweek and workday. The 40-hour week is typical in most union contracts, but in certain contracts unions have been able to further reduce the workweek. For example, Local 3 of the International Brotherhood of Electrical Workers gained a 25-hour workweek during 1962 negotiations in the construction industry. Few electricians worked only 25 hours a week, but overtime pay commenced after this threshold.[8] Average hours worked per year are less for full-time employees in more heavily unionized sectors of the economy than in nonunion sectors, but full-time schedules are more likely in unionized sectors.[9] Recently, however, overtime in some unionized

---

[8] See R. L. Rowan, "The Influence of Collective Bargaining on Hours," in C. E. Dankert, F. C. Mann, and H. R. Northrup, eds., *Hours of Work* (New York: Harper & Row, 1965), pp. 17–35.

[9] J. S. Earle and J. Pencavel, "Hours of Work and Trade Unionism," *Journal of Labor Economics,* 8 (1990), pp. S150–S174.

EXHIBIT 10–2

CWA Strikes U S WEST to Preserve Job Standards, Quality Service and Health Security for Workers' Families

DENVER—The Communications Workers of America announced a strike at 12:01 a.m. this morning by 35,000 union workers against U S WEST and its subsidiary U S WEST Business Resources Inc.

Strike issues included a package of company concession demands that would jeopardize the health security of workers and their families, take thousands of dollars a year out of workers' pockets, and seriously threaten service quality for telephone customers, CWA said.

"It became clear to us this past week that U S WEST was not serious about a fair and peaceful settlement, but instead wanted a showdown to attempt to force our members to accept terms that would destroy their working conditions and job standards," said CWA Vice President Sue Pisha, head of the union's District 7 headquartered here.

. . . On another key issue, instead of addressing CWA's concern over abusive levels of mandatory overtime hours for the workers, U S WEST actually proposed terms that worsen the problem. "We've been complaining about thousands of workers being forced to regularly work 60 hours or more every week for the past two or three years. The company's demand is unlimited levels of forced overtime the rest of this year, and a supposed limit next year of 65 hours per week," said Vice President Pisha.

"This is a family issue, it's a health and safety issue, it's very much a customer service issue—and it's just unacceptable in the United States of America in 1998," she stated.

To make matters worse, the company also wants to slash premium pay for overtime hours so that workers could be compelled to work 12 or 14 hours a day at "straight time." "The whole idea of premium pay for overtime was to discourage employers from driving workers to exhaustion and stealing time from their families," CWA's Pisha said, adding: "U S WEST seeks to turn the calendar back 60 years to the time Americans struggled to establish the 8-hour day."

In the past five years, U S WEST has slashed union jobs by 12.5 percent while the number of its access lines has grown by 20 percent. To make up the difference, U S WEST is squeezing the extra hours out of too few employees, according to CWA. Extreme downsizing has caused the widely reported service problems in U S WEST territory while enabling the company to milk bigger profits from its telephone operation to finance new businesses, such as its cable venture.

SOURCE: CWA web site. (http://www.cwa-union.org/pressreleases/pressRelease.asp?id=57)

---

sectors, particularly autos and telecommunications, have been the subject of intense negotiations and strikes. Exhibit 10–2 illustrates the Communication Workers of America's position in the 1998 U.S. West strike.

Entitlements to and Restrictions on Overtime

Contracts usually specify rules for assigning overtime. Overtime is often rotated among workers based on seniority, balancing hours in the work group before returning to the senior worker to begin a new cycle. Some contracts allow employees to refuse more than a specified number of overtime hours per week. Employees who have not met this threshold would be subject to discipline for refusing to work scheduled overtime.

Shift Assignments and Differentials

In organizations where continuous-flow operations are most efficient (e.g., chemical manufacturers and refiners) or where product demand levels and plant investment are high enough to justify multishift operations, contracts specify which employees are entitled to work which schedules. Employees may transfer shifts as jobs become available in their specialties and if they are senior to other eligible employees. Rotating shifts may also be used. For example, an entire shift might work from midnight until 8 A.M. for four weeks, then rotate to the 8 A.M. to 4 P.M. shift for four weeks, and then move to the 4 P.M. to midnight shift for four weeks.

Innovative Work Schedules

A variety of innovative work schedules has been designed to meet employee desires and employer requirements. Most have been implemented in nonunion organizations, and most have expanded daily work hours and shortened the number of days in the workweek.[10]

Unions often oppose long workday schedules because they have stressed the impact of fatigue, safety, and long-term health in arguing for shorter days. However, worker satisfaction improves and fatigue does not appear to be a problem even in strenuous occupations.[11] Where employees want to work fewer days and off-job demands in a given day are not great, compressed workweeks may benefit both employers and employees. However, employers should be aware of employee preferences before proposing the issue.[12] The union must also be aware of member preferences. In one case, a union opposing compressed work schedules was threatened with decertification if it did not go along with the schedule change.[13]

---

[10] For a complete summary of these innovations, see J. L. Pierce, J. W. Newstrom, R. B. Dunham, and A. E. Barber, *Alternative Work Schedules* (Boston: Allyn & Bacon, 1989).

[11] H. R. Northrup, "The Twelve-Hour Shift in the North American Mini-Steel Industry," *Journal of Labor Research* 12 (1991), pp. 261–78.

[12] See, for example, M. D. Fottler, "Employee Acceptance of a Four-Day Workweek," *Academy of Management Journal* 20 (1977), pp. 656–68; and S. Ronen and S. B. Primps, "The Compressed Work Week as Organizational Change: Behavioral and Attitudinal Outcomes," *Academy of Management Review* 7 (1981), pp. 61–74.

[13] H. R. Northrup, J. T. Wilson, and K. M. Rose, "The Twelve-Hour Shift in the Petroleum and Chemical Industries," *Industrial and Labor Relations Review* 32 (1979), pp. 312–26.

Paid Time Off

Paid time off includes holidays, vacations, and certain leave periods. These benefits are relatively straightforward, although management may place restrictions on their entitlement or use. For example, employees must normally work the days before and after a holiday to receive holiday pay. Employers may also restrict vacation schedules. If operations are highly integrated and insufficient numbers of employees are available to work in the absence of vacationing workers, management usually sets aside a period for vacations and shuts down. Other organizations may require vacations to be taken during slack periods.

LENGTH OF CONTRACTS

Most contract lengths exceed one year, with three years the most common. Some provide for wage reopeners during the agreement, especially when cost-of-living adjustments (COLAs) are not included. Employers try to avoid one-year contracts because they believe short contracts lead to more strikes and contract administration problems, lower employee morale, and higher and more unpredictable labor costs.[14] Longer-term contracts are more difficult to negotiate, especially when economic environments are changing. Renegotiating long-term contracts was found to be harder when global competition was great; where capacity utilization, selling price of the company's products, and number of vacant positions substantially varied during the contract period; where buyer or seller concentration in the industry was high among larger employers; and during periods of high inflation.[15] Durations have increased independently of many of these factors to provide greater certainty for both labor and management.[16] New agreements often exceed three years.

UNION AND MANAGEMENT RIGHTS

Contracts specify the union's representation rights. Most relate to the number of union stewards or representatives permitted within the bargaining unit, their rights of access to employees in various plant areas, the amount of time off available for union representation activities and who is responsible for compensating this time,

---

[14] S. M. Jacoby and D. J. B. Mitchell, "Employer Preferences for Long-Term Union Contracts," *Journal of Labor Research* 5 (1984), pp. 215–28.

[15] J. M. Cousineau and R. Lacroix, "Imperfect Information and Strikes: An Analysis of Canadian Experience, 1967–82," *Industrial and Labor Relations Review* 39 (1986), pp. 377–87.

[16] K. J. Murphy, "Determinants of Contract Duration in Collective Bargaining Agreements," *Industrial and Labor Relations Review* 45 (1992), pp. 352–65.

office space, access to bulletin boards, and access of nonemployee union officials to the workplace.

Most contracts reserve exclusively to management the right to act in areas not constrained by the agreement. Typical reserved rights include the right to subcontract work that could be performed by the bargaining unit,[17] to assign bargaining unit work to supervisors in emergencies or to train new employees, to introduce technological changes to improve efficiency, and to determine criteria for plant shutdowns or relocations.[18] When management does not reserve these rights, the union is entitled to bargain during the course of the contract if changes involving job security occur. For example, if a plant shutdown would result in layoffs, the absence of a clause leaving this determination to management requires bargaining on the effects of the shutdown if the union requests it.

Outsourcing, or permanently shifting some part of the operation to another employer, is an area of increasing concern to unions because it threatens job security and leads to pressure for concessions, particularly if the new source is a lower-wage nonunion operation. Unions are also concerned with an employer selling or spinning off part of its operations to another company or establishing a new firm. In these instances, the new owner or firm is often more able to reduce wages and/or employment.

Management rights clauses frequently specify rights to direct the workforce, to establish production levels, and to frame appropriate company rules and policies. The establishment of rules and procedures and the direction of the workforce form the basis for clauses relating to discipline and discharge.

DISCIPLINE AND DISCHARGE

Most contracts specify that employees can be discharged or disciplined for just cause. Some reasons are spelled out in the contract, and others relate to violations of rules the employer may promulgate under power retained in a management rights clause.

Specific grounds in discipline and discharge clauses most often cover intoxication, dishonesty or theft, incompetence or failure to meet work standards, insubordination, unauthorized absence, misconduct, failure to obey safety rules,

---

[17] The Supreme Court decision in *Fibreboard Paper Products* v. *NLRB*, 379 U.S. 203 (1964) requires bargaining by management if the union requests when subcontracting is being considered, unless the union has expressly waived its right in this area; however, this rule has been relaxed somewhat by *First National Maintenance* v. *NLRB*, 107 LRRM 2705 (Sup. Ct., 1981), and later by the NLRB when it held that removal of union work to another facility of the company would be permissible if bargaining had reached an impasse (*Milwaukee Spring Div. of Illinois Coil Spring Co.*, 115 LRRM 1065 [1984], enforced by the U.S Court of Appeals, District of Columbia Circuit, 119 LRRM 2801 [1985]), or for a legitimate business reason if there were no antiunion animus (*Otis Elevator Co.*, 115 LRRM 1281 [1984]).

[18] Unless the basic nature of the operation is changed, relocation is a mandatory subject of bargaining. See C. J. Griffin, Jr., and M. A. Jones, "Work Relocations—The Changing Rules Represent a Victory for Organized Labor," *Employee Relations Law Journal* 17 (1991), pp. 389–404.

violations of leave provisions, or general violations of company rules.[19] Committing a violation does not necessarily mean an offender will be automatically discharged but rather will be subject to discipline. However, the organization must be consistent in the way it metes out discipline if it is to successfully defend its disciplinary actions from grievances.

Discipline and discharge clauses may also spell out the due process procedures necessary before discipline can be imposed. Renegotiation of a long-term contract frequently requires that disciplinary action taken before a certain period be removed from an employee's file.

GRIEVANCE AND ARBITRATION

Grievance procedures are a high-priority bargaining issue for unions because they allow employees to object to unilateral management action during the term of the agreement. For example, assume that an employee believes a supervisor unjustly suspended him or her for a work rule violation. Without a grievance procedure, no review of the supervisor's action would be possible. Grievance procedures are also useful to management because the aggrieved employee is expected to use this forum when an alleged violation occurs, rather than to refuse a work assignment or walk off the job.

Grievance procedures usually specify who receives a grievance, the right of employees to representation at various steps in the process, the path a grievance follows if it cannot be resolved by the parties after it has been filed, and the time limits at each step before some action is required. Chapter 14 presents grievance procedures in considerable detail.

Most contracts specify that when parties cannot agree on the disposition of a grievance, a third party will arbitrate the dispute and render a decision binding on both parties. The contract specifies how an arbitrator will be selected, how arbitrators are paid, the powers of the arbitrator, and the length of time an arbitrator has to render a decision. Arbitration of contract interpretation disputes are dealt with in Chapter 15.

High grievance rates are associated with decreased productivity. While low morale might be a hypothesized cause, productivity decreases also occur because employees and supervisors are involved in grievance processing rather than production.[20] Where production rates and methods change, grievance rates might be influenced. For example, in a long-term study of grievances in an aircraft manufacturer, the level of planned production and an increase in the variety of production methods used, which would cause frequent job classifications changes, were

---

[19] For more details, see *Collective Bargaining Negotiation and Contracts* (Washington, DC: Bureau of National Affairs, updated as necessary), tab sect. 40.

[20] C. Ichniowski, "The Effects of Management Practices on Productivity," *Industrial and Labor Relations Review* 40 (1986), pp. 75–89.

both associated with higher grievance rates.[21] Thus, grievance rates may reduce productivity and follow from higher productivity requirements.

STRIKES AND LOCKOUTS

Pledges by unions and managements to avoid strikes and lockouts while the agreement is in force appear in most contracts. Managements frequently demand a no-strike agreement in return for arbitrating unresolved grievances. Unions usually do not give up the right to strike during the contract if management refuses to comply with an arbitration award. Some work stoppages are permitted by contracts, including refusal to cross picket lines of other unions striking the same employer and performing struck work. Some contracts reserve the right to strike over work rule changes during the contract's duration. Exhibit 10–3 recounts issues in the 1998 GM–UAW strike in Flint, Michigan.

Many contracts require that when unauthorized work stoppages, or **wildcat strikes,** occur, the union will disavow the strike and urge employees to return to work. If employees strike in violation of the agreement, many contracts specifically indicate they can be discharged.

UNION SECURITY

Because the union is the exclusive representative of employees in the bargaining unit, it desires that they be required to join and pay dues for the representational services the union renders on their behalf. Different levels of **union security** may be negotiated. Except in states with right-to-work laws, contracts may contain agency or union-shop clauses. The following are definitions of various forms of union security.

1.   **Closed shop** requires employers to hire only union members. Although this requirement is illegal, a contract clause can require the employer to offer the union an opportunity to fill vacant assignments. These arrangements occur most frequently in the construction and maritime industries, where many employers are relatively small and have relatively short-run demands for certain occupations.

2.   **Union shop** requires any bargaining unit employee employed with the firm for a specific time (not less than 30 days, 7 days in construction) to become a union member as a condition of continued employment.

3.   **Modified union shop** requires any bargaining unit employee who was hired after a date specified in the agreement to become a union member within a specific time as a condition of continued employment.

---

[21] M. M. Kleiner, G. Nickelsburg, and A. Pilarski, "Monitoring, Grievances, and Plant Performance," *Industrial Relations* 34 (1995), pp. 169–89.

EXHIBIT 10–3

Disputed Hourly Pay Rule at Heart of G.M. Strike

Until the strike began a month ago, Steven M. White's work day at a General Motors parts factory [in Flint, Michigan] followed a familiar routine. Arriving at 6:30 every morning, he stood at an assembly line welding steel rails in semidarkness, wearing heavy protective clothing in a factory with no air-conditioning and temperatures exceeding 100 degrees on summer days.

Mr. White's job has been to grab a 30-pound, 6-foot-long steel rail from a conveyor belt with his right hand, pull it across to his left hand, lower it into a brace and weld a bumper bracket on the side. He has to do the work partly by feel, he said, because a low ceiling was erected several years ago over his place on the line to ward off a leak in the 45-year-old factory's roof, and no light has been installed under the ceiling.

What makes Mr. White's job controversial, and one of the core issues in a showdown between G.M. and the United Automobile Workers union, is the hours that he keeps. "If everything runs without any breakdowns, we'll get done by 1:30 or 2," including a half-hour lunch break, Mr. White said. For working six and a half or seven hours, Mr. White draws eight hours' pay, at $19 an hour.

G.M. is now fighting to eliminate the practice of allowing Mr. White and others here to collect full pay once they produce a certain number of parts. G.M. has delayed plans to invest $180 million in Mr. White's factory until the union agrees to abolish the practice, known as a "pegged rate." But the U.A.W. has resisted, noting that a local agreement last year with G.M. already calls for the practice to be phased out for any new auto parts production assigned to the factory.

The strike by 3,200 workers at the factory here, combined with a three-week-old strike by nearly 6,000 sympathetic workers at another G.M. auto parts factory in Flint, has crippled production at the world's largest company. G.M. has closed 26 of its 29 assembly plants in North America for lack of parts and has declared an after-tax loss of $1.18 billion through June 30. The strikes have forced G.M. to lay off 161,000 workers temporarily, while outside suppliers have laid off thousands more.

Pegged rates were common in the auto industry in the late 1940's, when foreign auto makers posed little threat to domestic companies and the U.A.W.'s power was at its height. The rates have virtually disappeared since then, as companies have demanded longer hours to become more competitive. Indeed, many longtime industry executives were surprised to learn they still existed.

But they have persisted in a few G.M. parts factories where local U.A.W. units have negotiated separate deals. These are factories that produce parts needed by so many assembly plants for so many car and truck models that G.M. decided to pay the rates rather than risk a strike—until now, that is.

Because those covered by pegged rates have been stopping work early, G.M. had to pay $33 million in unnecessary overtime last year, said Donald Hackworth, group vice president for North American car operations. The overtime contributed heavily to a $50 million loss for the factory, he said, adding, "The insidious work practice here quite frankly is totally noncompetitive and we've got to do something about it."

Outside experts have also found the factory to be inefficient. Harbour & Associates, a manufacturing consulting firm in Troy, Mich., has concluded that labor costs at G.M.'s steel parts factories are higher than any competitors' costs—and that the Flint factory has unusually high costs even by G.M. standards.

continued

But Norwood Jewell, the bargaining committee chairman of the local union here, said that the inefficiency was G.M.'s fault. Unlike the assembly lines in other factories, certain slow-moving equipment here is connected directly to the main production line, instead of making parts separately nearby, he said. This hurts productivity because the entire line must operate at the speed of the slowest equipment, Mr. Jewell said, adding that G.M. had already told him of plans to change the factory's layout.

Poor productivity has "nothing to do with our people, nothing to do with standards or pegged rates," Mr. Jewell said. "It's poor engineering."

SOURCE: K. Bradsher, "Disputed Hourly Pay Rule at Heart of G.M. Strike," *New York Times,* July 7, 1997, p. D-1.

---

4.   Agency shop requires any bargaining unit employee who is not a union member to pay a service fee to the union for its representation activities.

5.   Maintenance of membership requires any bargaining unit employee who becomes a union member to remain one as a condition of continued employment as long as the contract remains in effect.

Contracts also frequently provide for a dues **checkoff** in which employers deduct union dues from members' pay and forward the amount directly to the union. The process benefits all parties. First, it avoids workplace disruptions involved in collection. Second, it insulates employees from union disciplinary action for nonpayment of dues. Third, it ensures a smooth cash flow for the local union's financial operations.

Unions usually bargain for the highest form of union security attainable, but one might argue that a union or agency shop is not necessarily in the individual member's best interest. If union membership were not compulsory, those who joined or remained members would see to it that the union accomplished important ends efficiently. State right-to-work laws enable a preliminary test of whether union membership is influenced by the efficiency of the local union, because individuals can choose whether to join. One study found that the costs of a local's operation were lower in right-to-work states but there were no differences in dues levels, provision of benefits or services, compensation of union officers, or profitability of investments existed.[22] Right-to-work laws increase free-riding (coverage without paying dues) by about 8 percent. Of the increased amount, about 30 percent appear to free ride because membership can't be required, while the other 70 percent wouldn't work in an establishment where union membership was compulsory.[23] Right-to-work laws have a significantly negative effect on union density in the private sector.[24] Some evidence shows that the proportion of union

---

[22] J. T. Bennett and M. H. Johnson, "The Impact of Right-to-Work Laws on the Economic Behavior of Local Unions—A Property Rights Perspective," *Journal of Labor Research* 1 (1980), pp. 1–28.

[23] R. S. Sobel, "Empirical Evidence on the Union Free-Rider Problem: Do Right-to-Work Laws Matter?" *Journal of Labor Research* 16 (1995), pp. 346–65.

[24] J. C. Davis and J. H. Huston, "Right-to-Work Laws and Union Density: New Evidence from Micro Data," *Journal of Labor Research* 16 (1995), pp. 223–34.

members in the bargaining unit influences the union's bargaining power because wage levels increase with higher representation.[25]

WORKING CONDITIONS AND SAFETY

Working conditions and safety clauses are concerned primarily with providing safety equipment, the right to refuse hazardous work, and the creation of management-union safety committees. Many health and safety collective bargaining concerns have been superseded by the Occupational Safety and Health Act (OSHA). Unions may negotiate higher standards than what the act requires.[26] Unions have an additional effect beyond OSHA, however. In the construction industry, unionized worksites are visited by OSHA inspectors more often, maintain a higher level of safety, and have higher penalties for violations.[27] A British study found that safety committees appointed by the union rather than management were more effective in reducing accidents.[28] Exhibit 10–4 details a program introduced in one IBP plant in an agreement with the United Food and Commercial Workers to reduce injuries in the meatpacking industry in response to OSHA findings.

Employers have also taken initiatives in this area with programs aimed at detecting and reducing substance abuse. Many employers have adopted prehire drug screening programs over which unions have no control because applicants have no representation rights. Unions and employers may potentially clash on bargaining over and administration of periodic or random drug tests, with unions arguing that these tests constitute an invasion of privacy and may not be supported by just cause, while employers argue that they are entitled to control the operation of the workplace and need to operate as safely as possible.[29]

SENIORITY AND JOB SECURITY

Seniority issues cut across several of the economic and noneconomic bargaining issues. Seniority may entitle employees to higher pay levels or to overtime, preferences on vacation periods, lengths of vacations, eligibility for promotions and

---

[25] S. Christenson and D. Maki, "The Wage Effect of Compulsory Union Membership," *Industrial and Labor Relations Review* 37 (1983), pp. 230–38.

[26] For an extended overview of occupational safety and health issues, see H. G. Heneman, III, D. P. Schwab, J. A. Fossum, and L. D. Dyer, *Personnel/Human Resource Management*, 4th ed. (Homewood, IL: Richard D. Irwin, 1990), pp. 688–713.

[27] D. Weil, "Building Safety: The Role of Construction Unions in the Enforcement of OSHA," *Journal of Labor Research* 13 (1992), pp. 121–32.

[28] B. Reilly, P. Paci, and P. Holl, "Unions, Safety Committees, and Workplace Injuries," *British Journal of Industrial Relations* 33 (1995), pp. 275–88.

[29] For more details, see E. C. Wesman and D. E. Eischen, "Due Process," in J. A. Fossum, ed., *Employee and Labor Relations*, SHRM-BNA Series, Vol. 4. (Washington, DC: Bureau of National Affairs, 1990), pp. 4-96–4-100.

EXHIBIT 10–4

Meat-Packing Plant Acts to Curb Injuries

Cumulative trauma injuries, which have become of increasing concern in a number of industries, were addressed in a program adopted by IBP Inc. and the United Food and Commercial Workers for the company's flagship meatpacking plant in Dakota City, Nebraska. A company official explained that other IBP plants were initially excluded so that the program could be tried in a controlled environment, not helter-skelter. Some results might be seen in six months or so; other results might take two years.

Cumulative trauma injuries (e.g., carpal tunnel syndrome) usually result from repetitive motions, such as those performed by workers on slaughtering lines.

The agreement calls for:

Training certain workers as "ergonomics monitors" to identify injury-inducing jobs and recommend solutions (disputes, if any, between union and management regarding the solutions will be resolved by a joint committee).

Training new employees in avoiding stressful work methods.
Developing new workstation layouts to ease physical strain on employees.
Initiating a medical program to treat and rehabilitate injured employees.

The three-year agreement came less than two years after the Food and Commercial Workers began a campaign to publicize alleged unsafe working conditions at the plant. Later, the Occupational Safety and Health Administration intensified enforcement activity in the meatpacking industry, culminating in a 1987 proposal to fine IBP $5.7 million for alleged safety and record-keeping violations. In return for the company's adopting the new safety program, OSHA reduced the fine to $975,000.

SOURCE: G. Ruben, "Developments in Industrial Relations," *Monthly Labor Review* 112, no. 4 (1989), p. 41.

---

transfers, and insulation against layoffs. Seniority provisions have been shown to positively influence the pay level of blue-collar workers represented by unions.[30]

A distinction must be made between benefit and competitive status seniority. **Benefit status seniority** is related to entitlement to organizationwide or bargaining unitwide benefits established in the contract. For example, if the contract specifies that vacation length depends on seniority, then the date of hire (as adjusted by any layoffs or leaves) establishes a benefit status. Most contracts base benefit entitlements on the total length of employment.

Competitive status seniority relates to entitlement to bid on promotions and transfers and to avoid layoffs. Benefit and competitive status seniority occasionally overlap, but competitive status seniority is usually accumulated within a job or department. Assume that an employee with five years' total service bids on an inspection job from a present job in assembly work. Competitive status seniority among the inspectors would begin as of the date of the job change. If a subsequent

---

[30] K. G. Abraham and H. S. Farber, "Returns to Seniority in Union and Nonunion Jobs: A New Look at the Evidence," *Industrial and Labor Relations Review* 42 (1988), pp. 3–19.

layoff occurred in which employees with four or fewer years of service on the job were furloughed, this inspector would be laid off. The inspector's benefit status seniority would be five years, but competitive status seniority would begin only from the date of obtaining the inspector job. Competitive status seniority is more likely to be companywide than departmentwide when the employer is small, capital intensive, in a single-employer bargaining unit, and when the production technology requires substantial training by the employer.[31]

Layoff Procedures

Layoffs are usually in inverse order of seniority, protecting the most senior worker for the longest period. Many contracts specify layoffs on the basis of departmental seniority; some permit **bumping,** whereby a senior employee is entitled to replace a junior employee in another department or job as long as the senior employee is qualified for it. In almost 60 percent of the contracts surveyed in a recent sample, seniority was the sole provision for determining layoff or job retention rights during cutbacks.[32] In another 30 percent of the contracts, seniority was the determining factor if the individual was qualified for the remaining jobs.

Promotions and Transfers

The CBNC survey found seniority is less frequently a criterion for promotions and transfers than for layoffs. In about half of contracts, seniority is the sole or determining factor for promotions if qualifications are essentially equal. For transfers, seniority is also a sole or determining factor in half of the contracts.[33]

Depending on the contract, seniority for someone promoted out of the bargaining unit (e.g., to first-line supervision) may continue to be accumulated, frozen, or lost after time. Employers usually desire clauses protecting accumulated seniority for supervisors because rank-and-file employees may be more willing to vie for promotions where risks of job loss are less if they fail or if employment is later reduced.

Time Away from Work

Contracts usually have provisions covering holidays, vacations, rest periods, and leaves. On average, unionized employees enjoy about one more paid holiday per year than the national average for all workers.

---

[31] J. F. Schnell, "An Ordered Choice Model of Promotion Rules," *Journal of Labor Research* 8 (1987), pp. 159–78.

[32] *Collective Bargaining Negotiation and Contracts* (Washington, DC: Bureau of National Affairs, updated as necessary), tab sect. 60.

[33] Ibid., tab sect. 68.

Also included are provisions related to paid breaks, lunches, changing and cleanup, and other periods in which no production work occurs but employees are compensated.

Most vacation clauses link entitlement to length of service, some contracts allow five weeks or more, usually after 20 or more years of service. Employers experience higher vacation costs for senior employees due to both the greater time away from work and the higher pay that senior employees are likely to be earning.

A variety of situations in which paid or unpaid leave will be granted are also included. Paid leaves often include time for funerals, sick leave, and jury duty. Unpaid leaves are available for civic responsibilities (such as elected office), union work (such as local president, etc.), and family leave (over and above that required by law).

No Discrimination

Virtually all contracts have a no-discrimination pledge. This is important because employees who allege discrimination can have their complaints heard quickly under the terms of the grievance clause without giving up their right to later pursue claims under civil rights law.

EFFECTS OF UNIONS ON NONWAGE OUTCOMES

Unions influence nonwage outcomes for both employers and the employees, predominantly in hiring, promotions, transfers, turnover, and retirement. Employee satisfaction is also related to union membership. This section explores research on the effects of unions on these types of nonwage outcomes.

Union Influences on Hiring

Lower-skilled workers prefer union jobs. Given this preference, unionized employers may be able to select more qualified job applicants. Applicants who do not initially obtain union employment find union jobs become less attractive as time passes because opportunities for promotion are at least partially related to seniority.[34] Among the unemployed, people with higher reservation wages (asking pay requirements), women, minorities, and former union members are more likely to wait for a union job opening. However, this tendency is inversely related to the level of unemployment and duration of individual unemployment.[35] Unionized employers use fewer recruiting sources and methods, probably because they get more applicants from chosen sources. They increase the number of selection

---

[34] J. M. Abowd and H. S. Farber, "Job Queues and the Union Status of Workers," *Industrial and Labor Relations Review* 36 (1983), pp. 354–67.

[35] J. S. Heywood, "Who Queues for a Union Job?" *Industrial Relations* 29 (1990), pp. 119–27.

hurdles, primarily because the likelihood of quitting or discharge for unsatisfactory workers is decreased. Figure 10–1 shows a model suggesting why these differences occur.[36]

Unionized employment positively influences wages for both black and white males. The effects are greater for blacks than whites and much greater for young blacks. However, greater proportions of unionized employment in an area depress employment opportunities for younger workers and wages for young black males.[37] But minorities are a higher proportion of new hires in unionized organizations compared with nonunion organizations.[38]

Employers who actively avoid unionization may attempt to screen out prounion applicants. This practice, while rare, violates the Taft-Hartley Act. Unfair labor practice charges are most likely to be upheld where the employer is involved in an organizing campaign or is openly hostile to the union, or the applicant is applying for a skilled position.[39]

Promotions, Transfers, and Turnover

Most contracts specify the methods for filling vacant positions requiring promotions or transfers. In nonunion organizations, unless policy or custom dictates otherwise, the employer may use any legal criterion for filling jobs.

Turnover in nonunion organizations is greater than in unionized employers with equivalent jobs. Chapter 6 suggested a relatively stable workforce is necessary for a successful organizing campaign. A plausible explanation for lower turnover following unionization would be the stable base preceding it. But employers with represented workforces are no more likely than other employers to hire innately stable applicants.[40] Lower turnover is probably related to wage premiums of about 3 to 8 percent for taking a unionized job, but wage losses from leaving one are about 7 to 11 percent.[41]

Contract provisions requiring that promotion and transfer decisions be based on seniority may explain union-nonunion differences in quit rates. The greater the weight given to seniority in job assignments, the lower the turnover rates.[42]

---

[36] M. J. Koch and G. Hundley, "The Effects of Unionism on Recruitment and Selection Methods," *Industrial Relations* 36 (1997), pp. 349–70.

[37] H. J. Holzer, "Unions and the Labor Market Status of White and Minority Youth," *Industrial and Labor Relations Review* 35 (1982), pp. 392–405.

[38] J. S. Leonard, "The Effect of Unions on the Employment of Blacks, Hispanics, and Women," *Industrial and Labor Relations Review* 39 (1985), pp. 115–32.

[39] T. L. Leap, W. H. Hendrix, R. S. Cantrell, and G. S. Taylor, "Discrimination against Prounion Job Applicants," *Industrial Relations* 29 (1990), pp. 469–78.

[40] R. B. Freeman, "The Effect of Unionism on Worker Attachment to Firms," *Journal of Labor Research* 1 (1980), pp. 29–61.

[41] J. D. Cunningham and E. Donovan, "Patterns of Union Membership and Relative Wages," *Journal of Labor Research* 7 (1986), pp. 127–44; and P. Kuhn and A. Sweetman, "Wage Loss Following Displacement: The Role of Union Coverage," *Industrial and Labor Relations Review* 51 (1998), pp. 384–400.

[42] R. N. Block, "The Impact of Seniority Provisions on the Manufacturing Quit Rate," *Industrial and Labor Relations Review* 31 (1978), pp. 474–88.

FIGURE 10–1

Union Effects on Hiring Practices

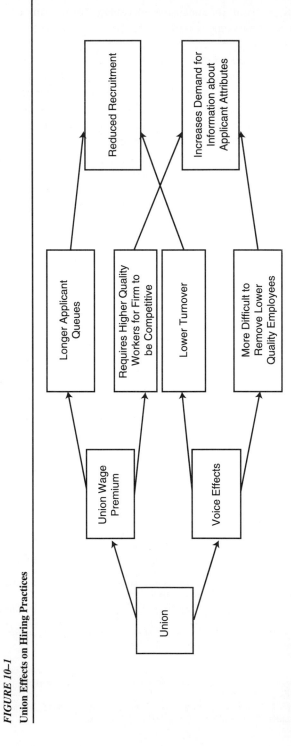

SOURCE: M. J. Koch and G. Hundley, "The Effects of Unionism on Recruitment and Selection Methods," *Industrial Relations*, 36 (1997), p. 352.

Collective bargaining also provides employees with a voice in how the organization is managed. Grievance procedures and contract negotiations provide a vehicle for changing the work environment. Without collective bargaining, employees must quit to escape unsatisfactory conditions.[43]

Unless nonunion employers have established grievance procedures, employees with grievances must accept the employer's unilateral action or leave, assuming the action was not unlawful. In unionized employers, employees are entitled to due process, and grievances might be allowed. Lags in the grievance process will extend tenure until a grievance is finally decided against the employee. Other inducements to stay in a unionized firm relate to expected progress in the next round of negotiations and perceptions about the likelihood of vacancies for which the individual can qualify through seniority.[44]

Unionization does not change the likelihood of layoffs and discharges, but laid-off unionized employees are much less likely to quit while awaiting recall than nonunion employees.[45] Compared with nonunion employees, they are more likely to be recalled from layoffs but are less likely to find a new job if permanently separated.[46] Unionized employees are 23 percent more likely to receive unemployment insurance benefits when laid off compared with similar nonunion workers.[47] In the absence of supplemental unemployment benefit packages, unionized employers should have a cost advantage—recall that costs are lower because of fewer vacancies and training of new employees. Management can store labor for future demand at relatively minimal costs.[48]

Seniority provisions may also result from management attention toward the interests of senior bargaining unit members (they are much more likely to be represented on negotiating committees than junior members) and away from the impact of the external labor market on the establishment of employment policy. Thus, where cost differences are not significant and the experience of senior employees is related to productivity, negotiated seniority clauses may benefit both the employer and longer-tenure employees. Bargaining unit members are probably more willing to ratify contracts with significant benefits for seniority, because many of them will likely have longer seniority if turnover in union situations is less; unionized employees may also anticipate achieving these benefits in later years.

If seniority clauses actually create opportunities for senior employees, over time unionized employees should have more internal job changes than nonunion

---

[43] R. B. Freeman, "Individual Mobility and Union Voice in the Labor Market," *American Economic Review* 67 (1976), pp. 361–68.

[44] Freeman, "Effect of Unionism," pp. 29–61.

[45] Ibid.

[46] T. L. Idson and R. G. Valletta, "Seniority, Sectoral Decline, and Employee Retention: An Analysis of Layoff Unemployment Spells," *Journal of Labor Economics* 14 (1996), pp. 654–76.

[47] J. W. Budd and B. P. McCall, "The Effect of Unions on the Receipt of Unemployment Insurance Benefits," *Industrial and Labor Relations Review* 50 (1997), pp. 478–92.

[48] J. L. Medoff, "Layoffs and Alternatives under Trade Unions in U.S. Manufacturing," *American Economic Review* 70 (1979), pp. 380–95.

employees. One study found quit rates for white union members were substantially below those of nonunion employees, and transfer and promotion rates were significantly higher. Almost all union members who had been with the same employer for more than 10 years had made at least one internal job change. Education was negatively related to a bargaining unit promotion but positively related to a promotion out of the bargaining unit. Promotions are more likely with more seniority in unionized situations, while they are less likely in nonunion employment. Unlike the nonunion situations in which women were less likely to receive promotions, gender made no differences in situations where employees were represented.[49] Interests in career flexibility within the employer were found to be higher among unionized employees.[50]

Retirement Programs

While retirement benefits are a wage issue, the age of retirement takes on a non-wage flavor for individuals (even though it has economic consequences for employers). In the past, 65 was the established retirement age across most employers within most occupations, but the age rules have changed. For example, the 1979 UAW agreement with the automakers provided that an individual could retire after accumulating 30 years of service (25 in foundries) regardless of age. Although past contracts have specified mandatory retirement at age 65, no new contracts may be negotiated requiring retirement at any specific age, given the amendments to the Age Discrimination in Employment Act becoming effective in 1987. Thus, employees in the auto industry could choose to retire as early as age 43 (with 25 years in foundry operations) and could not be forced to retire.

Early retirement decisions appear to be strongly influenced by the retiree's economic expectations and general health. The better the expectations and the worse the health, the more likely the individual is to retire early.[51] Married men plan to retire earlier when they expect larger pensions from both private and public sources, when their pensions have a known benefit level, when they are home owners, when they have earned relatively higher wages, when they are in poorer health, and when they work in jobs with a compulsory retirement age.[52] Union members have greater predictability in benefits because a larger share are covered by defined benefit pension plans.[53]

---

[49] C. A. Olson and C. J. Berger, "The Relationship between Seniority, Ability, and the Promotion of Union and Nonunion Workers," in D. B. Lipsky and J. M. Douglas, eds., *Advances in Industrial and Labor Relations* (Greenwich, CT: JAI Press, 1983), pp. 91–129.

[50] K. E. Boroff and K. W. Ketkar, "Investigating Career Flexibility among Union-Represented Employees," *Proceedings of the Industrial Relations Research Association* 46 (1994), pp. 268–78.

[51] R. Barfield and J. Morgan, *Early Retirement: The Decision and the Experience* (Ann Arbor: Survey Research Center, University of Michigan, 1969).

[52] A. Hall and T. R. Johnson, "The Determinants of Planned Retirement," *Industrial and Labor Relations Review* 33 (1980), pp. 241–54.

[53] J. Stewart, "The Retirement Behavior of Workers Covered by Union and Nonunion Pension Plans," *Journal of Labor Research* 18 (1997), pp. 121–36.

As benefit levels increase and as retirement decisions cover a range of time periods rather than a particular date, greater retirement planning by individuals and organizations is probable. Many contracts offer social security, private pension benefits, and tax advantages that, when combined, impose an actual cash penalty on one who continues to work after eligibility for social security begins.

Job Satisfaction

Union effects on job satisfaction are not clear-cut. Chapter 6 noted that dissatisfaction was a significant predictor of prounion voting in organizing campaigns.[54] Receiving the benefits a union might gain is expected to increase job satisfaction, but a large-scale cross-sectional study found that job satisfaction was lower for union members than for nonunion employees when other variables were held constant.[55]

Job satisfaction increases for union members whose jobs change as the result of a transfer or promotion but not from a turnover. The reverse was found for nonunion employees: Their satisfaction increased with turnover and did not change as the result of internal job movements.[56]

A national cross-sectional study found the overall job satisfaction of unionized employees was somewhat lower than that of nonunion employees, but results varied when facets of satisfaction were compared. Union members were more satisfied with their pay because they received more and because they valued pay outcomes more than nonunion employees did. Promotion satisfaction was also greater, largely because union members place lower value on promotions than other union achievements. This result can be partially accounted for by relatively lower pay differentials among jobs in unionized situations. Union members were less satisfied with supervisors and co-workers, largely through lower perceptions of supervisory behavior. They were also less satisfied with their jobs, largely as the result of lower job scope (or less varied tasks) than that of nonunion employees.[57] Unions could influence the satisfaction level of employees toward supervisors and the job if they point out those features as potential sources of problems that the union will help employees solve. An adversarial position might be necessary to create the need for continued representation. Within bargaining units, however, one study found no differences between union members and nonmembers on job satisfaction or intentions to quit.[58]

---

[54] J. G. Getman, S. B. Goldberg, and J. B. Herman, *Union Representation Elections: Law and Reality* (New York: Russell Sage Foundation, 1976), pp. 53–57.

[55] R. B. Freeman, "Job Satisfaction as an Economic Variable," *American Economic Review* 69 (1978), pp. 135–41.

[56] Olson and Berger, "Relationship between Seniority," pp. 91–129.

[57] C. J. Berger, C. A. Olson, and J. W. Boudreau, "Effects of Unions on Job Satisfaction: The Role of Work-Related Values and Perceived Rewards," *Organizational Behavior and Human Performance* 32 (1983), pp. 289–324; for additional confirmatory evidence, see S. Schwochau, "Union Effects on Job Attitudes," *Industrial and Labor Relations Review* 40 (1987), pp. 209–34.

[58] M. E. Gordon, and A. S. DeNisi, "A Re-examination of the Relationship between Union Membership and Job Satisfaction," *Industrial and Labor Relations Review* 48 (1995), pp. 222–36.

Finally, the strength of the union reduces fears that the employer might be able to increase work effort through threats.[59] At the same time, the degree of unionization appears positively related to job satisfaction, the willingness to cooperate, be productive, and reduce waste.[60]

SUMMARY

Nonwage issues in contracts are related primarily to hours of work, lengths of contracts, management rights, union security, and seniority provisions. All of these have economic consequences for the employer and represented employees.

Hours of work issues relate to establishing the length of the workday, entitlements to overtime, shift assignments, and the number of days worked during given periods. Evidence suggests that employers may prefer innovative schedules with fewer days and longer hours in some operations.

Management rights clauses spell out areas in which management exercises decision-making control. It also establishes rights to make and enforce reasonable rules. Grievance and arbitration clauses provide due process rules when bargaining unit members disagree with management's interpretation and operation of the contract.

Union security clauses provide requirements related to dues payment and membership in the union. Union shops require all bargaining unit members to belong to the union, while agency shop agreements require nonmembers to pay dues.

Seniority and job security can be broken into competitive and benefit status seniority. Competitive status seniority relates to entitlements to jobs while benefit status relates to compensation benefits.

Union jobs are preferred by lower-skilled workers, particularly among younger applicants because seniority is a factor in promotions in most union settings. Promotions and transfers occur more often in unionized settings and turnover is lower. Job satisfaction among union members is about equivalent to that of nonunion employees, but differences in the facets of satisfaction are found.

DISCUSSION QUESTIONS

1. Do the lower turnover rates that unionization seems to include offer an advantage to the organization?

---

[59] F. Green and S. McIntosh, "Union Power, Cost of Job Loss, and Workers' Effort," *Industrial and Labor Relations Review* 51 (1998), pp. 363–83.

[60] M. Kizilos and Y. Reshef, "The Effects of Workplace Unionization on Worker Responses to HRM Innovation," *Journal of Labor Research* 18 (1997), pp. 641–56.

2. Why would union officials be likely to oppose flexible work hours and other innovative work schedules?

3. What are the potential problems and benefits from early or flexible retirement programs?

4. Should either unions or managements be concerned with the apparently slight effect of higher economic outcomes on overall union member satisfaction?

KEY TERMS

Fair Labor Standards Act   *287*

Davis-Bacon Act   *288*

Walsh-Healy Government Contracts Act   *288*

Outsourcing   *292*

Management rights clauses   *292*

Grievance procedures   293

Wildcat strikes   *294*

Union security   *294*

Closed shop   *294*

Union shop   *294*

Modified union shop   *294*

Agency shop   *296*

Maintenance of membership   *296*

Checkoff   *296*

Benefit status seniority   *298*

Competitive status seniority   *298*

Bumping   *299*

CASE
GMFC ATTITUDE SURVEY

GFMC is a member of the Heritage Group, a consortium of employers with personnel research departments who participate in employment studies and share information. All members agreed this year to administer the same attitude surveys to their employees and relate the measures to variables such as turnover and productivity. To gain union cooperation in Central City, GMFC agreed to share the results of the survey and the broader study with Local 384. In return, Local 384 urged members to complete the surveys they received.

When comparative information became available, the results shown in the table were sent to Central City.

If you were a union or management representative, what would you make of the results? What impact might this have on the potential for negotiations in the next round of contract talks?

	Satisfaction	
	Central City	Total
Pay	53	50
Promotions	36	50
Work itself	62	50
Supervision	27	50
Co-workers	86	50
	Turnover	
Rate per hundred	18	50

(Results are in percentiles for all participating establishments.)

11

CONTRACT

NEGOTIATIONS

*T*he negotiation of a labor contract is critically important to both parties. The agreement governs the relationship between them for a definite contractual period. For the employer, the contract has cost impacts and constrains management decision making. For the union, it spells out union members' rights in their employment relationship.

Why does a contract emerge in the form that it does? How do the parties prepare for bargaining? What influences do the rank and file or the various functional areas within an organization have on the demands made in the negotiations? How does each group organize for bargaining? What constitutes success or failure in negotiations? What sequence of activities usually occurs during negotiations?

In this chapter, the activities preceding the negotiations are examined first, from both union and management perspectives. Then the theory and tactics of the negotiating process are covered. The steps necessary for agreement and ratification are detailed. Finally, management's assessment of bargaining is examined.

As you study this chapter, consider the following questions:

1. How do management and union prepare for negotiations?
2. How are negotiating teams constituted for bargaining?
3. What processes are involved in negotiations?
4. How are agreements reached, and what processes are necessary to obtain approval by the union rank and file for ratification?

Except for initial contracts and unusual financial conditions, when negotiations occur is largely determined by the expiration of a previous contract and the law. Under the Taft-Hartley Act, if either party desires modification at expiration, it must give at least 60 days' notice. In all negotiations, parties are required to meet at reasonable times to bargain. Under the Railway Labor Act, a party must indicate an interest in modifying the agreement; however, regardless of the expiration date the current contract remains in effect until a new one is agreed upon or an impasse period has been declared and completed.

Figure 11–1 portrays the general sequence of activities likely to be found in the bargaining process. The diagram lays out the basic prenegotiation activities, the proposals and responses in bargaining, and the possible outcomes of bargaining together with settlement procedures. Both parties have an idea how they would like a new contract to be shaped. They either have taken positions during an organizing campaign or have experience with an existing agreement.

MANAGEMENT PREPARATION

Because labor is a large share of total operating costs for most organizations, management must be well aware of the cost implications of contract proposals. The more heavily organized the firm, the more attention it pays to contract terms. Less-organized firms should also be aware of contract implications because benefits won at the bargaining table are frequently passed on to unorganized employees.

Department Involvement

In heavily organized firms, the chief executive officer (CEO) generally establishes the limits for possible concessions and targets needed changes for bargaining. The top human resource/industrial relations (HRIR) executive is responsible for coordinating preparations for bargaining and may be the lead management negotiator. Various functional departments contribute to preparations for bargaining and have interests in seeing certain issues pursued at the bargaining table. Production managers may be interested in work rules and costs. Marketing managers want a contract that will minimize shipping disruptions. Accounting personnel supply many of the cost figures used in bargaining.

Reviewing the Expiring Contract

The expiring contract is reviewed by top management, the labor relations staff, and first-line supervisors. This review centers on contract language that contributed to cost or operating difficulties during the contract, areas in which frequent grievances were encountered, the results of arbitration over unresolved grievances, current practices not covered in the contract, and other contract supplements that affect operations.

FIGURE 11–1

Bargaining Process Events

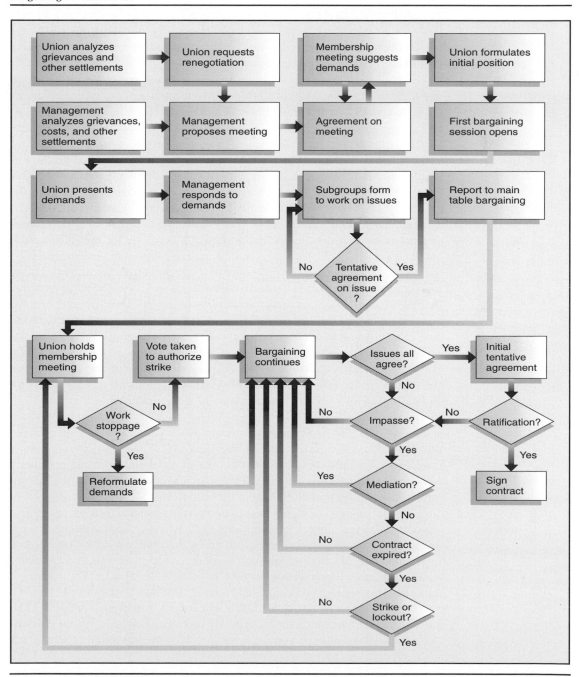

Preparing Data for Negotiations

Pay and benefit data are necessary and include relevant comparisons, such as rates paid within the industry, local labor market rates for occupations governed by the agreement, settlements gained by unions known as pattern setters, and changes in cost-of-living figures since the last negotiations.

Employee demographics such as seniority, age, sex, job classification, shift, and race are important. Because entitlement to many benefits is related to seniority, an increasingly senior workforce will incur higher benefit costs, even without an increase in benefit levels in a given negotiation. For example, if vacations increase from two to three weeks after five years' service, a workforce that had 200 employees with three years' seniority at the beginning of a three-year agreement would have 200 with six years at the end (assuming no turnover). This change would mean an increase of 200 weeks of vacation by the end of the agreement. Possible implications include paying for 200 unworked weeks and hiring four more employees to work the lost production time. Knowing the number of persons on each shift allows consideration of demands for shift differentials and their costs.

Internal economic data—such as the cost of benefits, participation in discretionary benefit plans (recreation, etc.), overall earnings levels, and the amount and cost of overtime—are important. Management prefers broadly used benefits because they improve employees' perceptions of the competitiveness of the compensation program. Information on competitive overall earning levels is important because some employee groups may feel underpaid when they actually are not. For example, skilled trades employees in industrial plants earn less per hour than their counterparts in contract construction, but they are laid off less frequently for weather or lack of work and thus may have higher gross earnings.[1]

Legal requirements are scrutinized. While minimum wage increases would seldom affect a unionized situation, an employer also tracks the implications of other employment law modifications. For example, Social Security tax increases raise costs without wage increases. Changes in equal employment opportunity laws and regulations may also suggest that employers negotiate changes in promotion and transfer procedures.

Knowledge of the union's negotiation and ratification procedures is also important. The bargaining team needs to know how the union signals concessions and drops demands during the process. If the union negotiator is new, information on his or her negotiating style and outcomes is important. The time necessary for ratification and whether the union usually works after contract expiration are important from a deadline standpoint.

The organization's current level of operations and anticipated future changes are important in assessing bargaining power on certain issues. For example, if little inventory is available and customer orders have increased recently but there

---

[1] T. A. Mahoney, "The Real Cost of a Wage Increase," *Personnel*, May–June 1967, pp. 22–32.

are several competitive sources available for similar products and services, then a strike might be disastrous.

Identification of Probable Union Demands

Using information from grievances under the expiring contract and feedback from first-line supervision, management may be able to assess the likelihood of certain demands and the likely tenacity of the union during bargaining. In large companies entering into national-level negotiations, attention to union bargaining conventions should inform management about the issues to which the union has committed itself. Other pattern settlements should offer clues to management.

Costing the Contract

As noted in Chapter 9, the wages and fringe benefits included in the ultimate settlement have a definite cost impact for the organization. To make rational choices among possible demands and to counteroffer with an acceptable package minimizing its costs, management must accurately cost contract demands.

A variety of costing methods, varying in their sophistication, can be used. An example of a relatively simple approach highlighting many of the issues is portrayed in Table 11–1. This example shows some of the important dynamics in long-term contracts. For example, Social Security tax rates and taxable bases may change during the term of the contract. Unemployment insurance rates may increase or decline, depending on the economy and a firm's individual layoff rate. It also shows that the rates of increase for benefits may change at different rates than wages.

The cost implications of certain contract terms are not straightforward and must be examined closely to capture real cost impacts.[2] First, the "roll-up," or amount by which overtime and wage-tied fringes are increased by changes in the base rate, must be tracked. Second, overtime premiums greater than required by law should cause the firm to consider the controllability of its overtime hours and whether labor cost increases can be passed on to customers. Third, vacation costs need to be critically examined. For example, vacations for maintenance employees may be essentially costless if some work can be postponed until vacations are over. On the other hand, production employees' vacations may require scheduling overtime, thereby increasing vacation costs by the premium rate, or hiring an equivalent number of full-time employees. Fourth, relief time may cost more if it is broken up into short periods. Some time may be necessary to begin the break and then return to work. This slippage will require adding more employees to sustain production volume.[3]

---

[2] M. H. Granof, *How to Cost Your Labor Contract* (Washington, DC: Bureau of National Affairs, 1973).

[3] Ibid, pp. 55–56.

TABLE 11–1

Costing Out Changes in Contract Terms

	Current	Demand	Year 1	Demand	Year 2	Demand	Year 3
Direct payroll—Annual cost per employee							
Average straight-time pay per hour	$10.00	$0.40	$10.40	$0.30	$10.70	$0.25	$10.95
Straight-time pay (2,080 hr. × avg. wage)	20,800		21,632		22,256		22,776
Shift differential	0.15	0.16	0.16	0.00	0.16	0.00	0.16
Shift differential (30% of employees × 2080)	94		100		100		100
Overtime (50% standard FLSA rate ×100 hr. per employee)	1,507		1,567		1,612		1,650
Overtime (100% holiday rate × 8 hr. per employee)	161		167		172		176
Total Payroll	22,561		23,466		24,140		24,702
Increase over current level			905		1,579		2,140
Percent increase over current level			4.01%		7.00%		9.49%
Statutorily required additions to payroll							
FICA and Medicare, 7.65%	1,726		1,795		1,847		1,890
FUTA, 2.5% × $7,000	175		175		175		175
Worker's compensation (2.8% × payroll)	564		587		604		618
Total statutory requirements	2,465		2,557		2,625		2,682
Increase over current level			92		160		217
Percent increase over current level			3.73%		6.50%		8.81%
Benefit costs							
Insurance—company portion (anticipated increases*)							
Health	3,114	480	3,594	216	3,810	216	4,026
Dental	185	5	190	20	210	6	216
Optical	0	200	200	10	210	10	220
Prescriptions	85	5	90	5	95	5	100
Life	50	1	51	1	52	1	53
Disability	40	1	41	1	42	1	43
Total	3,474		4,166		4,419		4,658
Cost per hour (2080 + 100 + 8 total hours)	1.59		1.90		2.02		2.13
Increase over current level			692		945		1,184
Percent Increase over current level			19.92%		27.20%		34.08%
Pension—5% straight-time match	1,040		1,082		1,113		1,139

	Current	Demand	Year 1	Demand	Year 2	Demand	Year 3
Pay for time not worked**							
Holidays	720	9	749	10	856	10	876
Vacation	1,200	15	1,248	15	1,284	16	1,402
Sick leave	400	5	416	5	428	5	438
Breaks	1,155	:30	1,201	:30	1,231	:30	1,254
Paid-time off for union activities	385	:10	400	:10	410	:10	418
Total	3,860		4,014		4,209		4,387
Cost per hour (2080 + 100 + 8 total hours)	1.76		1.83		1.92		2.01
Increase over current level			154		349		527
Percent increase over current level			4.00%		9.03%		13.66%
Total statutory and negotiated benefits	10,839		11,819		12,366		12,866
Increase over current level			980		1,527		2,027
Percent increase over current level			9.04%		14.09%		18.70%
Percent of total payroll	48.04%		50.37%		51.23%		52.09%
Total cost per employee	33,400		35,285		36,506		37,568
Increase over current level			1,885		3,106		4,168
Percent increase over current level			5.64%		9.30%		12.48%
Expected productivity improvement		2.50%		2.50%		2.50%	
Adjusted labor cost	33,400		34,424		35,615		36,652
Labor cost per unit increase			3.07%		6.63%		9.74%

* Benefit demand costs in italics include cost of demand plus anticipated premium increases, others reflect anticipated premium increases only.

** Assumes costs associated with hiring additional employees to work periods that employees take holidays, vacations, and sick leave.

Benefits costing also poses problems for organizations. Pension costs depend not only on a defined contribution requirement in some cases (e.g., 5 percent of base wages) but also on experience factors, vesting (personal ownership of benefits) requirements, and possible defined benefit levels at retirement. For example, if the contract provided for vesting of benefits after five years of service but only 20 percent of employees ever accrue five years, the cost of the pension would be far less than the 5 percent of base wages used in the example. Health insurance is generally negotiated to provide a certain level of benefits (e.g., all hospital and physician expenses up to $100,000 annually with $250 deductible). Unfortunately, organizations have little control over the premium charged for the benefits. Thus, future costs can only be estimated.[4]

Organizations may not closely evaluate salary increase costs during the term of the agreement. For example, given interest rates and the total amounts paid, agreeing to increases of 50 cents, 50 cents, and 75 cents, respectively, over a three-year agreement might cost the company less than 90 cents, 40 cents, and 30 cents. In the former case, the total increase is $1.75, while in the latter it is $1.60. But in the former case, an employee would earn 50 cents per hour more for three years ($1.50), 50 cents more for two years ($1.00), and 75 cents more for one year—a total of $3.25 more over the contract period. In the latter case, the employee would get 90 cents more for three years ($2.70), 40 cents for two years ($.80), and 30 cents for one year—a total of $3.80. But postponing increases to give a larger total increase during the agreement raises the base wage rate for subsequent negotiations.[5] Management should also consider the costs of wages and fringe benefits that will be granted to nonunion employees to preserve wage differentials and equity.

A detailed example of costing contract demands is given in the introduction to the negotiating exercise at the end of this chapter. Whatever method is used for costing should allow management to calculate the effects of various union proposals quickly and provide a true estimate of their financial ramifications.

Negotiation Objectives and the Bargaining Team

Contract objectives should support the goals of the organization. For example, to avoid production disruptions, clauses providing for arbitration of grievances that cannot be mutually resolved in return for no-strike agreements will serve this purpose. If cost certainty is important, avoiding fringe benefits and cost-of-living clauses and including **gainsharing,** profit sharing, and/or piece-rate pay plans provide a path to these ends.

Bargaining team members often represent particular interest areas (e.g., production) or have expertise in specific negotiated areas (e.g., employee benefits manager). The management team is frequently led by the organization's top HRIR

---

[4] Ibid., pp. 60–69.
[5] Ibid., pp. 83–126.

executive. The CEO may delegate responsibilities for negotiating the contract but retains authority to approve the ultimate agreement.

Bargaining Books

A **bargaining book** is a cross-referenced file enabling a negotiator to quickly determine what contract clauses would be affected by a demand. The book contains a general history of specific contract terms and a code to indicate the relative importance of the proposals to management. Many bargaining books are now automated and tied to spreadsheets so "what-if" questions can be answered, and the cost implications of demands and concessions can be rapidly calculated. Following is information likely to be contained for each clause:

1. The history and text of the particular clause as it was negotiated in successive agreements.
2. Comparisons of the company's experience with that of other companies in the industry, including comments on similarities and differences.
3. Company experience with the clause, both in operation and in grievances.
4. Legal issues pertaining to the clause, including both NLRB determinations and judicial decisions.
5. Points the company would like to have changed with regard to the clause, differentiated into minimum, maximum, and intermediate possibilities.
6. Changes the union may have previously demanded in the clause, the union's justification for these demands, and arguments management used to rebut them.
7. Data and exhibits with regard to the clause, including cost and supporting analysis.
8. Progress with regard to the clause in the current negotiation, together with drafts of various company proposals.[6]

Strike Preparation

As noted, anticipating vulnerability to a strike may substantially improve management's bargaining power. The organization also needs to plan how it will handle a potentially disruptive situation, particularly if it expects to continue operations.

The organization must determine the costs and benefits of operating during a strike. Labor relations will undoubtedly be troublesome after a contract is negotiated, particularly if replacements have been hired. Additional security may be required, and picket-line observation will be important. Suppliers, customers,

---

[6] M. S. Ryder, C. M. Rehmus, and S. Cohen, *Management Preparation for Bargaining* (Homewood, IL: Dow Jones-Irwin, 1966), pp. 65–66.

and government agencies will require notification if a strike occurs. For important customers, alternative methods of supply, including supply through competitors, may be necessary. A credible threat to replace strikers is seen by management to increase bargaining power, but it may not have a major effect on outcomes.[7]

Strategy and Logistics

Finally, the strategies to be used to move toward an agreement must be constructed. Questions about who has the power to make concessions and the final positions beyond which management will not go must be answered.

A place to hold bargaining meetings must be arranged. If meetings will be held away from the employer's premises, cost-sharing questions must be resolved before negotiations start. The union will probably prefer a neutral site, given evidence (explored later in this chapter) that the employer takes a tougher bargaining stance on its home ground. Table 11–2 on pp. 322–323 shows time frames and functions involved in preparations for negotiations.

UNION PREPARATION

To an extent, union preparations parallel those of management, with important distinctions. Traditionally, unions see contract negotiations as an event that should lead to improving their outcomes. Politically, leaders are expected to gain ground or face membership problems. The union may not be as well prepared for possible management demands as management is for union demands, especially if the national union is not involved in the negotiations.

National-Level Activities

National union research departments track settlements in contract negotiations. Research is also done to assess employers' abilities to improve pay and benefits. The ability of union members to take strikes is assessed. If the union has been involved recently in a long strike, it may not have the resources to provide subsistence strike benefits for a long strike in the present negotiations. The national must also consider the target company's ability to withstand a strike and its vulnerability to competition.

If the negotiations involve many units of a single company or are conducted on an industrywide basis, the national is usually responsible for negotiating economic issues. The bargaining team usually comprises national officers and officers of some key locals.

---

[7] J. W. Budd and W. E. Pritchett, "Does the Banning of Permanent Strike Replacements Affect Bargaining Power?" *Proceedings of the Industrial Relations Research Association* 46 (1994), pp. 370–78.

Before commencing negotiations, the national union may call a **bargaining convention** at which delegates from the locals hear the national's plans for bargaining and propose their own issues. The bargaining convention has two major purposes. First, members are heard, thus fulfilling grass-roots political requirements for involvement in specifying bargaining issues. Second, the union's leadership has a forum for publicly committing itself to certain bargaining positions. Commitment to issues strengthens the union's bargaining power, because conceding these committed issues later at the bargaining table will be more difficult. The union is also interested in homogenizing member attitudes around the salience of important issues and heightening adversarial attitudes.[8] A study of teacher union members found attitudes were less varied during negotiation years than "out" years. Attitudes toward pay and management declined while attitudes related to teaching were unchanged.[9]

If the local is to carry the major role in bargaining, the national often supplies a representative to assist and ensure the local's agreement is consistent with the national's interest. Exhibit 11–1 on page 324 is an example of how one national recently opened negotiations.

Local-Level Preparations

At the local level, the negotiating committee is usually elected with the other officers and has responsibility for negotiating contracts and processing grievances. The committee reaches some conclusions about portions of the contract (e.g., allocation of overtime) susceptible to more than one interpretation or viewed as inequitable by the membership.

Locals are also served by the national union's field representatives. As a result, members learn about settlements reached by other locals. They also learn which issues the national considers critically important to include in all contracts.

The employer's performance (in terms of profitability, sales, and so on) is known if the employer is publicly owned, and the union may use it to gauge the level of its economic demands. However, in companies that participate in several industries (e.g., General Electric is involved in building power plant equipment, home appliances, broadcasting, financial services, and other industries), the relative contributions of each division may be difficult to separate. The union also knows the perishability of the employer's products, its competition, and its ability to operate during a strike. The union may also be aware of industry trends to move plants to other geographic regions and the likelihood of the company to introduce labor-replacing equipment if high economic demands were won.

---

[8] R. A. Friedman, *Front Stage, Back Stage: The Dramatic Structure of Labor Negotiations* (Cambridge, MA: MIT Press, 1994), pp. 27–45.

[9] M. A.Griffin, P. E. Tesluk, and R. R. Jacobs, "Bargaining Cycles and Work-Related Attitudes: Evidence for Threat-Rigidity Effects," *Academy of Management Journal* 38 (1995), pp. 1709–25. See also J. W. Budd, "The Internal Union Political Imperative for UAW Pattern Bargaining," *Journal of Labor Research* 16 (1995), pp. 43–55.

TABLE 11–2
Management Planning for Contract Negotiations

	8 to 12 Months before Contract Expires	4 to 8 Months	1 to 4 Months before Commencement of Negotiations	During Negotiations	Postnegotiations
Local unit management	1. Assigns responsibilities for community surveys estimating union demands and employee attitude. 2. Assesses the total corporate community and union compensation/benefits plans. 3. Assesses union/employee motivation and goals for impending negotiations.	1. Division management, corporate E.R., and corporate insurance project alternate benefit proposals that are to be designed and costed. 2. Continues all steps in the planning process.	1. Secures division approval of strategy, negotiating plans, and cost estimates.	1. Continues negotiations, clears significant cost variances from plan and division management. 2. Integrates benefit negotiations with all other items. 3. Secures agreement in accord with plan. 4. Agrees with union on method and expense to inform employees of new contract terms.	1. Evaluates previous negotiations against plan within 30 days. 2. Assigns responsibilities for the planning process so as to integrate with the division's plans. 3. Identifies tentative objectives for next contract. 4. Completes wage/benefit adjustment form.
Division headquarters management	1. Assures local unit is preparing for negotiations. 2. Plans through annual financial plan projected impact of inventory buildup. Possible settlement costs, etc. 3. Identifies internal responsibilities and relationships (corporate, law, E.R., insurance, benefits, etc.). 4. Keeps corporate employee relations informed.	1. Coordinates the development of strategy and negotiating plan, consulting with corporate employee relations and benefits. 2. Develops with local management, corporate E.R., and insurance projected alternative benefit proposals that are to be designed and costed. 3. Makes broad judgment of impact on company and expected proposals in relation to division and corporate goals, strategy, and plans.	1. Approves negotiating plan strategy. 2. Clears benefit and corporate policy variances from plan with corporate employee relations. 3. Communicates progress to senior management and corporate employee relations. 4. Approves cost variances from plan. 5. Identifies strike issues.	1. Provides in addition to those points in "1 to 4 months" column, identification of "end" position and supports local negotiators in maintaining such position.	1. Evaluates all aspects of the previous negotiations within 45 days. 2. Identifies and communicates all long-range needs to executive management and corporate employee relations. 3. Integrates planning process in the division growth plan.

	4. Evaluates plans to control costs and deviations from plan/strategy.				
Corporate employee relations	1. Advises division and local management of union's national position on economics, benefits, and other issues. 2. Counsels on any anticipated conflict with corporate policy, other divisions, etc. 3. Provides available historical information pertinent to planning.	1. Consults with division on strategy and plans; available for on-the-scene assistance or to consult with international union officers; recommends corporate point of view on issues. 2. Approves all variances from corporate personnel policy and benefit plan proposals. 3. Assures that all issues are resolved at the required levels	1. Assists division, local management, and corporate insurance in projecting and preparing alternate benefit proposals that are to be designed and costed. 2. Keeps division and local unit informed of any external developments having impact on its planning.	1. Provides same as "1 to 4 months" column. 2. Identifies to division management potential problems having corporate impact; if necessary, advises corporate management of unresolved major issues.	1. Counsels with union and/or unit management on negotiating experiences and/or evaluation of new contract. 2. Informs other units of results 3. Initiates needed objectives for study, policy change, or corporate decision
Corporate law department	1. Counsels on request.	1. Counsels on request and reviews current contract as required. 2. Approves benefit plan drafts to assure legal compliance.	1. Counsels and drafts contract language on request. 2. Makes counsel available to review contract language before signing.	1. Provides same as "1 to 4 months" column.	1. Reviews new contracts for possible problems; advises division and corporate employee relations.

SOURCE: A. Freedman, *Managing Labor Relations* (New York: Conference Board, 1979), p. 24. Copyright © The Conference Board, 1979, used by permission.

EXHIBIT 11–1

UAW Delegates Direct Union to "Get Tough" in Talks with Big Three

DETROIT—Some 2,000 delegates attending the United Auto Workers bargaining convention approved broad resolutions on job security, outsourcing, health care, and other key issues that will guide upcoming talks with the Big Three automakers.

After some debate, delegates easily endorsed the 200-page resolution, directing top UAW officials to get tough with companies on subcontracting and workforce levels. It also rules out givebacks on health care and seeks to cut overtime in favor of additional new hires.

The union opens talks in June with General Motors, Ford, and Chrysler. The national contracts covering 400,000 workers expire September 14. . . . The convention is intended to set the general tone for national talks with the three automakers.

The convention's most vocal faction made it clear . . . that it wants to see cost-of-living increases on workers' pensions. . . . Automakers can retire after 30 years on the job. Many do not, partly because they are afraid that inflation will erode living standards.

The practice of sending work to outside suppliers, called outsourcing, is worrisome to the UAW because it moves large numbers of jobs out of its reach, the union says.

Three years ago, the automakers' practice of shipping work to outside, nonunion parts makers was a contentious issue. Thanks to GM's resolve, it's back again this year with added volume.

Health care will be another hot topic during this summer's talks. Customers pay an average $2,800 per new car to cover the automakers' health care tab for employees. In 1994, GM spent $1.7 billion on employee health care.

SOURCE: *Labor Relations Week,* April 3, 1996, p. 315.

Local unions hold membership meetings before the negotiations to inform members about important issues and to solicit more input. These meetings also help determine the commitment of local members to bargaining issues in case a strike is called.

After negotiations are under way, the union usually calls another membership meeting. The negotiating committee reports on progress and requests authorization to call a strike if necessary. Usually, overwhelming approval is given. A strike vote does not mean a strike will occur but that bargainers have the authority to call one after the contract expires.

Effects of Union Characteristics on Bargaining Outcomes

Bargaining outcomes could be influenced by such union characteristics as size, union democracy, complexity, propensity for striking, involvement in political activities, level of dues, recent success in organizing relative to the total size of its membership, and the diversity of the workers it represents. When a variety of other characteristics is controlled, wage rates in negotiated agreements appear influenced by national control of the *content* of bargaining, less control of the bargaining *process* by the national, smaller sizes of locals in the national union, local union autocracy, membership diversity, little recent organizing, and higher dues. Higher job security outcomes result from smaller national unions, more involvement of the national in the bargaining process, higher salary levels of union officers, political activity, lower complexity, and lower dues. Overall union democracy is related to higher job security and lower wages. Higher outcomes occur when the union has a relatively small number of large locals organized in several industries. Strikes may enhance outcomes, but present attention to organizing and political activity is related to lower outcomes.[10]

NEGOTIATION REQUESTS

Section 8(d) of the Taft-Hartley Act requires the party desiring a renegotiation of the contract (usually the union) to notify the other party of its intention and to offer to bargain a new agreement. Notice must come at least 60 days before the end of the contract if the requesting party intends to terminate the agreement at that time.

Employers usually propose a time—often not immediate—and place for negotiations to begin. Often this means that initial demands are not made until 30 days or less before the contract expires. After notice is served, both parties start final bargaining preparations.

WHAT IS BARGAINING?

Several academic disciplines have studied bargaining. Following is a description of bargaining or negotiating from an economic perspective:

1. Negotiation occurs if both parties will benefit by an agreement. In labor-management relations, the employer benefits by continued operations and the union benefits by better conditions for its members.

2. Concessions made during negotiations are voluntary. Concessions, in number and degree, may be influenced by the size of the demands and the opponent's beliefs about the demander's willingness to concede, but any movements made are still voluntary.[11]

3. Negotiations are seen as productive. They may disclose areas of agreement or alternatives not previously considered by either party.

4. Negotiations used in labor-management relations are characterized by verbal and/or written demands and concessions.

---

[10] J. Fiorito and W. E. Hendricks, "Union Characteristics and Bargaining Outcomes," *Industrial and Labor Relations Review* 40 (1987), pp. 569–84.

[11] F. Zeuthen, *Problems of Monopoly and Economic Warfare* (Boston: Routledge & Kegan Paul, 1930).

5. The bargaining process requires competition before the benefits available accrue to the parties involved in the bargaining.[12]

Bargaining, in its simplest format, is the communication by both parties of the terms they require for consummation of a transaction and the subsequent acceptance or rejection by both of the bargainers. Negotiation is the set of techniques used to translate bargaining power into the ultimate settlement.[13]

Bargaining requires that the parties have a conflict of interest on issues jointly affecting them. The parties' activities include dividing resources and other intangible issues in which they have joint interests. Negotiation requires the presentation of positions, their evaluation by the other party, and counterproposals. The process requires a sequential rather than simultaneous mode because each party must have time to evaluate the other's proposals before responding.[14]

A definition of collective bargaining from a behavioral perspective includes the following:

1. Collective bargaining includes some issues that generate conflict between the parties and others that require collaboration to accommodate the separate interests of both.

2. Attitudes and feelings play a part in the outcome of negotiations over and above what results from the bargainers' rationally defined attributes. Further, they come together not only for this negotiation, but must maintain an ongoing relationship. Thus, the results of the negotiations affect the long-run nature of the bargaining relationship.

3. The bargainers are often acting on behalf of others rather than for their own ends. They are representing constituents who evaluate their performance and may affect their tenure in negotiating positions.[15]

Thus, bargaining processes involve parties who have a mutual interest in reaching agreement on a variety of issues. Negotiators represent others who stand to have their positions altered as a result of bargaining. The personal characteristics of bargainers, as well as the power of the organizations they represent, are likely to influence the outcome. The union has strong interests in a continuing relationship while management has no intrinsic interest in its continuation.

Attributes of the Parties

Labor negotiations are seldom conducted in privacy. Although the general public and most management and union constituents are excluded, the negotiating teams

---

[12] J. G. Cross, *The Economics of Bargaining* (New York: Basic Books, 1969), pp. 4–6.

[13] C. M. Stevens, *Strategy and Collective Bargaining Negotiations* (New York: McGraw-Hill, 1963), pp. 2–4.

[14] J. Z. Rubin and B. R. Brown, *Social Psychology of Bargaining and Negotiation* (New York: Academic Press, 1975), pp. 2–18.

[15] R. E. Walton and R. B. McKersie, *A Behavioral Theory of Labor Negotiations* (New York: McGraw-Hill, 1965), pp. 3–4.

witness the bargainers' behavior. Audiences make it more difficult for bargainers to concede. The difficulty increases if the bargainer is highly loyal to the group or if the group has a strong commitment to the bargaining issue. If the other party views a concession as a sign of weakness, retaliation is likely in subsequent negotiations.[16] Bargainers might use two tactics to overcome these problems. First, to promote an opponent's willingness to concede, the bargainer should respond to an opponent's concession in another area important to the opponent or should indicate that a major concession will require hard bargaining. Second, the negotiator should realize that public commitment to an issue reduces the degree to which objective data can modify the position. But a skilled negotiator is aware that public commitment may be a tactic to justify support for an issue not really viewed as important.

It's important to remember that the union is the employees' bargaining *agent*. Members expect that their bargainer will have an expertise in negotiations which they lack. The lead negotiator may be an international representative, an experienced local negotiator, or an attorney hired by the local. Management is similarly represented by an experienced negotiator, an HRIR executive, attorney, or trade association representative. This lead negotiator also has the responsibility to structure interactions within the negotiating team and to coordinate communications between members. The lead must maintain a public hard line to maintain the commitment of constituents, but also be willing and able to make concessions to reach an agreement.[17]

Where several parties are involved in bargaining for each side, some bargainers act as brokers in negotiations with regard to information while others broker trust. As bargaining deadlines approach, the roles of these negotiators blur while the roles of gatekeeper and group representative become more distinct.[18]

Unless the initial demands of both parties are acceptable to their opponents, one or both must concede to achieve an agreement. A problem occurs in offering concessions, however, because the value of a particular concession may be reduced in the eyes of the recipient once it is made by the offerer. To avoid this problem, parties should know the priority of particular demands so the concession is perceived as having the highest value.[19] Alternatively, a concession costing a certain amount might be made and the opponent would be offered the choice of the area to which the concession will be applied.

The bargaining environment, perceptions of the bargainers, and complexity of the negotiations all influence outcomes. Conducting the negotiations in a neutral environment is important because there is less willingness to make concessions on one's home ground. Thus, unions should avoid bargaining at the plant. The

---

[16] J. Z. Rubin and B. R. Brown, *Social Psychology*, pp. 43–54.

[17] Friedman, *Front Stage, Back Stage,* pp. 47–112.

[18] R. A. Friedman and J. Polodny, "Differentiation of Boundary Spanning Roles: Labor Negotiations and Implications for Role Conflict," *Administrative Science Quarterly* 37 (1992), pp. 28–47.

[19] M. A. Neale and M. H. Bazerman, *Cognition and Reality in Negotiation* (New York: Free Press, 1991), pp. 75–77.

perceived characteristics of the opponent are also important. If the opponent is perceived as nondeferring, then concessions will not be sought as vigorously. As more issues are injected into the bargaining, **logrolling**—trading blocks of apparently dissimilar issues, such as union shop for a wage increase—occurs frequently. Also, a sequence of offers, counteroffers, and issue settlement will result from bargaining on numerous issues.[20] Where several bargaining issues exist, simultaneous consideration of the issues rather than following a sequential approach is more likely to produce an agreement.[21]

Perceived fairness of offers depends on the perspective of the recipient of the offer. Bargaining experiments have found situations in which both sides submit offers they believe are fair and would actually result in settlement, but do not because they aren't perceived as fair by the opponent.[22] Offers from parties who label them as "fair" but don't supply additional information are often lower.[23]

Aspiration levels of bargainers influence outcomes, and expectations of settlement improve chances of reaching an agreement. However, differences in expectancies may lead to impasses where settlements could actually have been reached.[24]

The interaction of interpersonal orientation, motivational orientation, and power affects the bargaining relationship. Interpersonal orientation reflects responsiveness to others—reacting to, interest in, and appreciation of variations in another's behavior.[25] Motivational orientation refers to whether one's bargaining interests are individual (seeking only one's own interest), competitive (seeking to better an opponent), or cooperative (seeking positive outcomes in the interests of both).[26] Power refers to the range of bargaining outcomes through which the other party may be moved.[27] Power is low if the negotiator has few alternatives when an agreement is not reached.[28]

Given these individual differences and contextual variables, bargaining effectiveness should be greatest when interpersonal orientation is high, motivational orientation is cooperative, and power is equal and low.[29] The interaction of these

---

[20] J. Z. Rubin and B. R. Brown, *Social Psychology*, pp. 130–56.

[21] L. R. Weingart, R. J. Bennett, and J. M. Brett, "The Impact of Consideration of Issues and Motivational Orientation on Group Negotiation Process and Outcomes," *Journal of Applied Psychology* 78 (1993), pp. 504–17.

[22] L. Babcock, G. Loewenstein, S. Issacharoff and C. Camerer, "Biased Judgments of Fairness in Bargaining," *American Economic Review* 85 (1995), pp. 1337–43; and L. Babcock and G. Loewenstein, "Explaining Bargaining Impasse: The Role of Self-Serving Biases," *Journal of Economic Perspectives* 11, no. 2 (1997), pp. 109–26.

[23] M. M. Pillutla and J. K. Murnighan, "Being Fair or Appearing Fair: Strategic Behavior in Ultimatum Bargaining," *Academy of Management Journal* 38 (1995), pp. 1408–26.

[24] S. B. White and M. A. Neale, "The Role of Negotiator Aspirations and Settlement Expectancies in Bargaining Outcomes," *Organizational Behavior and Human Decision Processes* 57 (1994), pp. 303–17.

[25] J. Z. Rubin and B. R. Brown, *Social Psychology*, p. 158.

[26] Ibid., p. 198.

[27] Ibid., p. 213.

[28] R. L. Pinkley, "Impact of Knowledge Regarding Alternatives to Settlement in Dyadic Negotiations: Whose Knowledge Counts?" *Journal of Applied Psychology* 80 (1995), pp. 403–17.

[29] Brown and Rubin, *Social Psychology*, pp. 256–57.

variables may have no effect on how the parties structure their negotiating teams. Much of the structuring must depend on the goals of the party (e.g., breaking ground on productivity issues requires cooperation) and on beliefs about the tactics an opponent may use (e.g., assigning low interpersonal orientation bargainers to a team). It should also be noted that the evidence regarding the interaction of individual differences and their effect on negotiation outcomes is mixed.[30]

The types and levels of concessions convey information about the party's true position. For example, several concessions on a given issue followed by no subsequent movement could signal that the party's resistance point has been reached. A retreat toward an original position may signal toughening of a stand. Concessions appearing to reward the requester's behavior may increase cooperation between the parties and strengthen the role of an attractive counterpart to the requester's constituency.[31]

Perceptions of Bargainers

Besides the personal attributes of the parties, the negotiators form perceptions about the bargaining situation. A variety of characteristics may influence the willingness to concede and, thus, the outcome of negotiations. Perceived strategic power is one characteristic. A bargainer would have high strategic power if (1) agreement is less advantageous for the bargainer than it is for the opponent, (2) more ways exist to satisfy the bargainer's needs than those of the opponent, (3) more credible threats can be made by the bargainer than by the opponent, (4) maintenance of the relationship is more important to the opponent, and (5) the opponent is under heavier time pressure.[32]

Within this framework, an example of condition 1 is an organization with a large backlog of orders. The company might be more motivated to settle because large profits would be lost. Relatively little pressure might exist for the union because it reasonably believes lost wages would be made up with overtime when the plant reopened. As an example of condition 2, an employer struck in one of many plants producing the same output as others would have a distinct bargaining advantage. Condition 3 could involve beliefs that threatened actions will be taken. It reinforces the idea that a strike may have value for future bargaining situations. In condition 4, unions are expected to be more responsive because the bargaining process is necessary to maintain the relationship. Finally, condition 5 involves employers dealing in perishable goods, such as food producers and transportation companies (e.g., holiday travel lost because of strikes). These are under greater pressure to settle on the union's terms.

---

[30] L. Thompson, "Negotiation Behavior and Outcomes: Empirical Evidence and Theoretical Issues," *Psychological Bulletin* 108 (1990), pp. 515–32.

[31] J. Z. Rubin and B. R. Brown, *Social Psychology*, pp. 276–78.

[32] J. M. Magenau and D. G. Pruitt, "The Social Psychology of Bargaining: A Theoretical Synthesis 1," in G. M. Stephenson and C. J. Brotherton, eds., *Industrial Relations: A Social Psychological Approach* (New York: John Wiley & Sons, 1979), pp. 197–99.

In the later stages of the bargaining process, lead negotiators may conduct private sidebar conferences in which they convey information about their willingness to concede, the relative importance of issues, and the like. The ability to use sidebars productively requires a climate of trust between the negotiators.[33]

THEORIES OF BARGAINING TACTICS

Bargaining occurs because either or both parties are unwilling to agree to the other's demands. The following rules govern bargaining.

Rule 1 states an impending contract expiration is necessary for the commencement of bargaining. During the course of the agreement, the parties have essentially agreed not to bargain, so the anticipated expiration allows the renewal of bargaining.

Rule 2 states the initial bargaining demand should be large. Even though both parties are fairly certain the initial positions are substantially different from what each is willing to settle for, the large initial demand creates room for bargaining and allows relatively large concessions when the time is right.

Rule 3 explains that the negotiating agenda is determined by the initial demands and counterproposals. In other words, the issues initially raised by the parties constitute the focus of the bargaining. Additions to the initial agenda are seldom made, and offers made in regard to these items can rarely be retracted.

Rule 4 precludes strikes or lockouts before a certain time and requires notice that a strike is possible after this point.

Rule 5 provides that negotiations terminate when an agreement is reached. Within this rule may be a requirement that unresolved issues be arbitrated or operations continued to preclude an emergency while an agreement is reached.

Rule 6 requires the parties to negotiate in good faith. To do this, the parties must respond to each other's demands and take no unilateral action to change the existing conditions before the end of negotiations.[34]

Bluffing

Bluffing has been studied extensively. In most negotiations, neither party expects to win its initial demands, and the other knows the demands are greater than the expected settlement.

Bluffing serves several valuable purposes. If one stated a final position first, concessions would be impossible. A failure to concede could destroy the relationship required in collective bargaining. Bluffing also allows a bargainer to test the firmness of an opponent's demands without a full commitment to a settlement. Thus, one learns more about the opponent's expectations through bluffing.[35]

---

[33] Friedman, *Front Stage, Back Stage*, pp. 94–97.
[34] Stevens, *Strategy*, pp. 27–56.
[35] Cross, *Economics of Bargaining*, pp. 169–80.

If bluffing is used to gain information for a final settlement, the union may reasonably make extreme demands on financial issues because it lacks information on management's ability to pay. When management has a good deal of information on a settlement point, its initial offer may be close to its expected settlement point. An examination of contract settlements between the Tennessee Valley Authority and its unions shows that, in most instances, final agreements on economic issues are closer to management than union proposals. However, if management is pressured by outside forces, settlements tend to be closer to the union's positions.[36] The union runs a risk in making very high demands, because these may increase management's cost expectations and lead to a strike over points the union may ultimately be willing to concede.[37]

BEHAVIORAL THEORIES OF LABOR NEGOTIATIONS

Distributive Bargaining

Four behavioral components are involved in bargaining. The first, **distributive bargaining,** occurs when the parties are in conflict on a particular issue and the outcome will involve a loss for one party and a gain for the other.[38] Suppose the union wants a 60-cent hourly wage increase, and the parties ultimately settle for 30 cents. The 30-cent increase is a gain to the union and a loss to the company, which is not to say the loss is greater than the company expected. The company may have believed a settlement for anything less than 35 cents would be better than it expected to win. Distributive bargaining simply means some resource is in fixed supply, and one's gain of that resource is the other's loss.

Because distributive bargaining involves the division of outcomes on a bargaining issue, much of the negotiation process involves providing the opponent information about the importance of a particular position, the likelihood of future movement on that position, and possible trade-offs that might be made for a concession. Through bargaining, both sides may pick up cues concerning where the other is willing to settle. An important part of this process is identifying the commitment a bargainer attaches to a position. One bargaining strategy would be to demand most of what would constitute an acceptable outcome and then threaten the other party that a strike will follow a rejection of this demand. Evidence from bargaining experiments suggests, however, that fairness in outcomes is incorporated into the bargainers' sequences of offers.[39] Table 11–3 portrays

[36] R. C. Bowlby and W. R. Schriver "Bluffing and the 'Split-the-Difference' Theory of Wage Bargaining," *Industrial and Labor Relations Review,* 32 (1979), pp. 161-71.

[37] H. S. Farber, "The Determinants of Union Wage Demands: Some Preliminary Empirical Evidence," *Proceedings of the Industrial Relations Research Association* 30 (1977), pp. 303–10.

[38] Walton and McKersie, *Behavioral Theory,* p. 4.

[39] J. Ochs and A. E. Roth, "An Experimental Study of Sequential Bargaining," *American Economic Review* 79 (1989), pp. 355–84.

TABLE 11–3

Interpretive Comments about the Degree of Firmness in Statements of Commitments

Statement of Commitment (1)	Degree of Finality of Commitment to a Position (2)	Degree of Specificity of That Position (3)	Consequences or Implications Associated with a Position (the Threat) (4)
From a negotiation involving a middle-sized manufacturing plant in 1953: "We have looked very seriously and must present this (10-cent package) as our final offer."	The statement "must present this as our final offer" is not as strong as "this is our final offer." The strength of the word *final* is somewhat hedged by the more tentative phrase "must present this as."	The reference to the "10-cent package" was fairly specific.	No reference to the consequences. What the other party is expected to associate with the company's position would depend on the company's reputation or other confirming tactics. It would seem to imply that company is ready to take a strike.
A union replied later, "The membership disagreed" with the company's economic proposal. "The present contract will not extend beyond 12:00 tonight."	Significantly, the membership was reported as only having "disagreed"; it did not "reject."	Reference to "economic proposal" is not specific. Hence the degree of disagreement is unclear.	By stating "the present contract will not extend," they do not state there would be a strike. And in the particular context it was not clear they would strike.
From the public statements regarding the 1955 negotiations between the UAW and the Ford Motor Company: Henry Ford II suggested alternative ways of achieving security "without piecemeal experimenting with dangerous mechanisms or guinea pig industries . . ." This was a statement of opposition to the union's GAW proposal.	The statement contained no hint about the finality of his commitment of opposition.	The phrase "piecemeal experimenting . . ." clearly avoided reference to just what was objected to.	There were no references to the consequences to be associated with ultimate failure to agree.
From the transcripts of a negotiation in the oil industry: Management stated, "If you say now or never or else (on a wage increase demanded by the union), I would say go ahead; we are prepared to take the consequences."	This was an explicit, binding commitment.	The company's position was also clear in this instance—it was not prepared to make any concession on the issue at hand.	Company was indicating its readiness for a work stoppage.

Later the union spokesman replied, "My advice to your employees will be not to become a party to any agreement which binds them to present wages."	Regarding what the union leader's advice will be, that is final. It says nothing about the finality of that position of the party, however.	The advice "not to become a party to any agreement which binds them to present wages" is hardly specific. Any increase would meet the test of this statement. In fact, even a reopening clause would avoid "binding the union to present wages."	Although at first glance this statement seems to commit the union to a wage increase "or else," it leaves them the option of continuing with no contract and with signing a contract that has a way of adjusting wages in the future. The context did nothing to clarify just what consequences were to be associated with the union's position.
"I don't believe that they (the rest of the union committee) can recommend acceptance" (of the company's offer).	"I don't believe" is more tentative than "I know they cannot."	"I don't believe that they can recommend acceptance" leaves unanswered whether the union committee would recommend that the membership not accept the offer or merely make no recommendation. Moreover, the reference is only to the company's *offer as it now stands.*	Not specified here, but the union had begun to refer to economic sanctions.

SOURCE: B. M. Selekman, S. K. Selekman, and S. H. Fuller, *Problems in Labor Relations*, 2nd ed. (New York: McGraw-Hill, 1958) pp. 221, 226, 233: Material from these pages used in formulating table by R. E. Walton and R. B. McKersie in *A Behavioral Theory of Labor Negotiations* (New York: McGraw-Hill, 1965), pp. 96, 97. Copyright © 1965 McGraw-Hill. Used with permission.

various management and union commitment statements and analyzes them for their finality, specificity, and consequences for ignoring them.

Integrative Bargaining

The second component is **integrative bargaining,** which occurs when parties face a common problem.[40] For example, a company may be experiencing high employee turnover. As a result, union membership is eroded, and union officials need to spend an inordinate amount of time recruiting new members. Both parties may seek a solution to their joint problem by attacking any causes of turnover existing in their contract.

Integrative bargaining occurs when employers and unions accommodate each other's needs without cost or through simultaneous gains. Integrative bargaining frequently involves the desire of employers to improve flexibility and the desire of unions for increased job security.[41] Much attention is currently being paid to so-called **mutual gains bargaining,** an example of integrative bargaining in which the parties approach the negotiations with the idea that when it's concluded, both sides will have benefited. Exhibit 11–2 details this approach.

Attitudinal Structuring

Attitudinal structuring refers to activities parties use to create atmospheres of cooperation, hostility, trust, and respect.[42] Changed attitudes are expected to change predispositions to act. Relationship patterns will have an effect on or be a result of one's action toward the other, beliefs about legitimacy, level of trust, and degree of friendliness.[43] The predominant patterns of these attitudinal dimensions (see Figure 11–2) fall within the categories of conflict, containment-aggression, accommodation, cooperation, and collusion.

Conflict occurs when both parties seek to destroy the other's base. Neither acknowledges the legitimacy of the other, and activities are pursued to interfere with the other's existence. *Containment-aggression* involves demonstrating a high degree of militancy while recognizing the other's right to exist. *Accommodation* occurs when each party accords the other a legitimate role and allows the other to represent its position as a legitimate interest. *Cooperation* occurs when the other's position is seen as legitimate and when common issues are of simultaneous concern to both parties. *Collusion* takes place when both parties join to subvert the goals of the parties they represent; for example, when

---

[40] Walton and McKersie, *Behavioral Theory,* p. 5.
[41] Ibid., p. 129ff.
[42] Ibid., p. 5.
[43] Ibid., pp. 184–280.

EXHIBIT 11–2

GCIU, Printing Industry Group Endorse Mutual Interest Bargaining

An alternative approach to collective bargaining, variously known as mutual interest bargaining, win-win bargaining, or [mutual gains bargaining] has been jointly endorsed by the Graphic Arts Employers of America, an industry group representing unionized printing firms and the Graphic Communications International Union.

According to William Solomon, GAE president, the printing industry group and the union are the only industrywide management and labor organizations to jointly support this type of innovative bargaining technique. "The days of adversarial bargaining are over," said Solomon. "We can't afford to keep beating the hell out of each other. We've been spending all our energy on this [adversarial approach] and not looking at our mutual survival."

GAE and the international union are promoting among their respective constituents a series of two-day workshops on mutual interest bargaining. The workshops were developed by the Cornell University School of Industrial and Labor Relations and the Human Incentive and Resource Education Institute, a non-profit group offering education and training in labor relations and human resources management for the printing industry.

Solomon said that the workshops, the first of which was held in Rochester, N.Y., . . . are intended to reshape the bargaining process in the printing industry . . . , substituting the new integrative approach for the old adversarial one. The objective . . . is to develop collective bargaining agreements that will enable unionized printing firms and their employees to better compete in the marketplace.

The joint support for mutual interest bargaining by the industry association and GCIU is a second step in a new atmosphere of cooperation between GAE and the union . . . Last year the governing bodies of both GAE and the union formally endorsed the concept of total quality management [TQM] as a means of increasing quality and productivity in printing firms through a positive labor-management environment. At the union's convention . . . delegates approv[ed] a resolution supporting TQM.

[James] Norton [president of the GCIU] said that union members are "buying in" on the TQM concept because they recognize that the education and training, which are key components of the program, will make them more proficient at their jobs. Union members accept that their employers must be able to produce quality products in order to compete in the marketplace.

SOURCE: *Daily Labor Report,* March 1, 1993, pp. A-12–A-13.

---

management covertly assists a union to organize in return for a nonmilitant stance on bargaining.[44]

Attitudes toward bargaining have polarized since the 1970s. Almost 20 percent of a sample of large U.S. manufacturing employers adopt strategies beyond containment-aggression with a goal of eliminating unions. Conversely, almost one-third have adopted a cooperative approach, emphasizing joint

---

[44] Ibid., 186–88.

FIGURE 11–2

Attitudinal Components of the Relationship Patterns

Attitudinal Dimensions	Pattern of Relationship				
	Conflict	Containment-Aggression	Accommodation	Cooperation	Collusion
Motivational orientation and action tendencies toward other	Competitive tendencies to destroy or weaken other		Individualistic policy of hands off	Cooperative tendencies to assist or preserve	
Beliefs about legitimacy of other	Denial of legitimacy	Grudging acknowledgment	Acceptance of status quo	Complete legitimacy	Not applicable
Level of trust in conducting affairs	Extreme distrust	Distrust	Limited trust	Extended trust	Trust based on mutual blackmail potential
Degree of friendliness	Hate	Antagonism	Neutralism—courteousness	Friendliness	Intimacy—"sweetheart relationship"

SOURCE: R. E. Walton and R. B. McKersie, *A Behavioral Theory of Labor Negotiations* (New York: McGraw-Hill, 1965), p. 189. Copyright © 1965 McGraw-Hill. Used with the permission of McGraw-Hill Book Company.

union-management programs, while another third mix containment-aggression and cooperation strategies. Union-busting tactics were linked with lower financial performance while cooperation was related to higher performance. In both cases, however, employers closed union facilities and opened new nonunion plants.[45] Tougher approaches by management to labor relations are linked to low sympathy for union goals, larger plant size, low capital intensity, low market share, and required education for the job.[46]

Intraorganizational Bargaining

Intraorganizational bargaining is the process for achieving agreement within one of the bargaining groups.[47] For example, a management bargainer's efforts might convince fellow management representatives that a 40-cent raise is necessary to avoid a strike although management had determined previously that the union would most likely settle for 35 cents. Intraorganizational bargaining also refers to the activities union negotiators engage in to sell an agreement to the membership.

The union negotiators must be able to sell an agreement to members once it has been reached. To do this, the team has to balance competing needs of subgroups within the union. One tactic is estimating some reasonable range of contract outcomes to members. Suggesting that excessive demands could damage the bargaining relations (see attitudinal structuring) can help moderate initial demands.

An analysis of the dramatic characteristics of labor negotiations suggests "front-stage" activities are directed at different audiences—the lead negotiator performing for the negotiating team, team members for each other and their constituencies. The show aims to demonstrate adherence and effort toward bargaining goals.[48] Figure 11–3 diagrams the acting and audiences.

One tactic, used particularly by management, limits participation by those who are likely to take militant stances or are unwilling to modify positions as bargaining continues. This gives the negotiator greater freedom to respond during the bargaining process.[49]

Negotiators are concerned with their reputations after the agreement is reached. A settlement may help or hinder a negotiator's career depending on the outcome and the degree to which he or she is associated with it. Negotiators who have particular information may control the direction of the negotiations and have greater effects on their outcome.[50]

---

[45] D. G. Meyer and W. N. Cooke, "U.S. Labour Relations in Transition: Emerging Strategies and Company Performance?" *British Journal of Industrial Relations* 31 (1992), pp. 531–52.

[46] J. Godard, "Whither Strategic Choice Do Managerial IR Ideologies Matter?" *Industrial Relations* 36 (1997), pp. 206–28.

[47] Walton and McKersie, *Behavior Theory*, p. 5.

[48] Friedman, *Front Stage, Back Stage*, pp. 85–99.

[49] Ibid., pp. 281–340.

[50] K. L. Valley, S. B. White, M. A. Neale, and M. H. Bazerman, "Agents as Information Brokers: The Effects of Information Disclosure on Negotiated Outcomes," *Organizational Behavior and Human Decision Processes* 51 (1992), pp. 220–36.

FIGURE 11–3

Audience Structure for Main-Table Negotiations

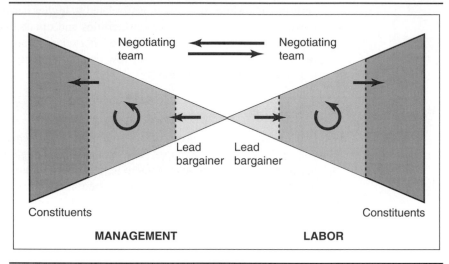

SOURCE: R. A. Friedman, *Front Stage, Back Stage: The Dramatic Structure of Labor Negotiations* (Cambridge, MA: MIT Press, 1994), p. 86.

Negotiations are seldom settled until close to a deadline.[51] Two reasons explain this: first, the more time available for negotiating, the more information that might be disclosed to lead to a better final solution; second, the constituents of the bargainers may believe that settlement before the deadline constitutes poor effort and their position could have been improved.[52] The presence of a deadline increases the rate of concessions.[53] The deadline effect may help to explain why negotiations under Taft-Hartley jurisdiction usually take substantially less time than negotiations under the Railway Labor Act.

Use of the Components in Bargaining

The four bargaining processes and their degree of use may result from certain preexisting conditions and the behaviors of the negotiators.[54] Figure 11–4 shows the predictors of the processes. Conditions such as high bargaining power are expected to be related to early commitment to a position. This in turn should lead to the use of distributive bargaining.

---

[51] A. E. Roth, J. K. Murnighan, and F. Schoumaker, "The Deadline Effect in Bargaining: Some Experimental Evidence," American Economic Review 78 (1988), pp. 806–23.

[52] B. P. McCall, "Interest Arbitration and the Incentive to Bargain: A Principal-Agent Approach," *Journal of Conflict Resolution* 34 (1990), pp. 151–67.

[53] S. G.-S. Lim and J. K. Murnighan, "Phases, Deadlines, and the Bargaining Process," *Organizational Behavior and Human Decision Processes* 58 (1994), pp. 153–71.

[54] R. B. Peterson and L. Tracy, "Testing a Behavioral Theory Model of Labor Negotiations," *Industrial Relations* 16 (1977), pp. 35–50.

FIGURE 11–4

Model of Conditions and Behaviors Related to Walton and McKersie's Four Goals of Bargaining

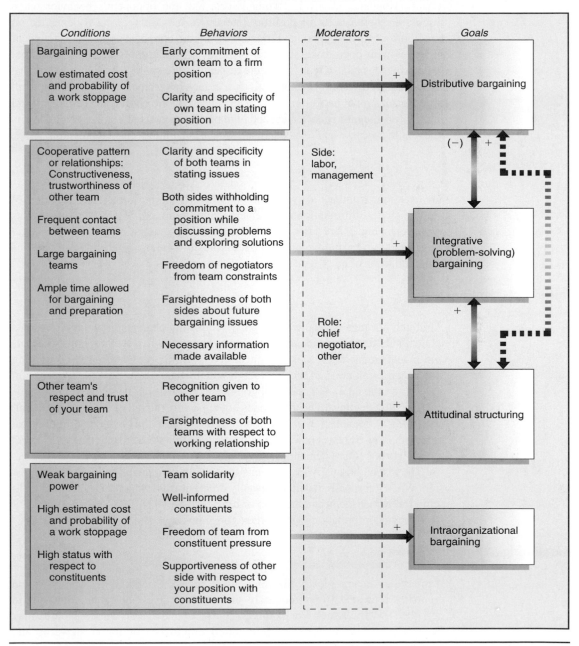

SOURCE: Richard B. Peterson and Lane Tracy, "Testing a Behavioral Theory Model of Labor Negotiations," *Industrial Relations*, February 1977, p. 17.

Responses of union and management negotiators to questionnaires indicate distributive bargaining success was influenced by bargaining power, low probability of a work stoppage, clarity in stating issues, and the opponent's behavior when discussing the basis for its position. Integrative bargaining success depended on conditions of trust, support, and friendliness by the opponent and a clear statement of issues with open discussion and plentiful information. Success in attitudinal structuring was related to management respect for the union, generally constructive relationships toward management, and a lack of criticism of the opponent. Intraorganizational bargaining success depended on the confidence bargainers had in their constituents' endorsement and high perceived costs of a stoppage. Behaviors relevant to success were related to team solidarity and low outside pressures.

NEGOTIATIONS

This section examines activities involved in bargaining a new contract. Issues include tactics, information requirements, and union and employer requirements for agreements. Labor laws require the parties to meet at reasonable times and places and to bargain in good faith over issues involving wages, hours, and terms and conditions of employment.

Initial Presentations

Although not legally required, the party requesting changes in its favor presents its demands first. Thus, the union presents demands when seeking improvements and management when seeking concessions. At this presentation, the initiating side specifies all areas of the contract in which changes are desired. This session also allows the union to present all grievances or positions developed through the membership meetings. The union does not expect to gain all of these changes, but, as a political organization, it has an obligation to state the positions of individual members. It also creates new bargaining positions that alert management to expect more vigorous future demands in these areas.

The responding party may not choose to reply to demands at the opening session. When it responds, its offer is usually different from what it would be willing to settle for. If management adheres to or refuses to move past its original position, it must provide information to support any positions based on an inability to pay.[55]

Bargaining on Specific Issues

If the issues are complex or the company is large, the negotiating committee and company representatives frequently divide themselves into subcommittees to negotiate specific issues. For example, contract language on work standards may be handled by a subgroup of production employees or union stewards and production supervisors.

---

[55] *NLRB* v. *Truitt Mfg. Co.*, 351 U.S. 149 (Sup. Ct., 1956).

Usually the subgroups do not have the authority to finalize issues they discuss, because these form part of a trade-off package, but they may bring tentative agreements or positions back to the main table for consideration.

At the main table, issues not forming part of a combined package or to be used as trade-offs may be initialed by the parties as finalized for the ultimate agreement. Thus, the final settlement is not necessarily a coalescence on all issues simultaneously but a completion of negotiations on final areas in which disagreement existed.

In most negotiations, nonwage issues—union security clauses, seniority provisions, work rules, and the like—are decided first. Wage and benefit issues are often settled as a package near the end of negotiations. As noted earlier in discussing the certainty of outcomes and the potential costs of package characteristics, wages and benefits are issues management must consider carefully.

TACTICS IN DISTRIBUTIVE BARGAINING

Each party enters the negotiations with certain positions it hopes to win. Management has an economic position it wants to protect. The union has specific wage and benefit demands it perceives as achievable. Bargaining is the process by which the parties influence the perceptions of the other to adopt their positions as a final outcome.

The following represents the types of tactics both parties use to influence the resistance points of their opponents through information transmission:

I do not think you really feel that strongly about the issues you have introduced.

I believe that a strike will cost you considerably more than you are willing to admit.

I believe a strike will cost me almost nothing in spite of your statements to the contrary.

I feel very strongly about this issue regardless of what you say.[56]

Certain tactics may be used during negotiations to assess the actual point at which an opponent would prefer to settle. Responses to questions addressed to various members of the negotiating team may gain an overall flavor of the most important issues. To highlight the importance of a particular issue, the party proposing it may provide detailed information to clearly establish its position. For example, a firm faced with a large wage demand may provide detailed data on the wage costs of its competition and its inability to pass increases through to its customers.

One tactic is to get the opponent to see that its demands will not result in as positive an outcome as it expects. For example, a demand for more paid time off may be seen by the union as a way to increase employment, but the company may show that increased costs will result in replacing existing workers with robots.

Another successful tactic changes the costs of a strike for an opponent. For example, a strike by the UAW is much more critical if close to a new model year

---

[56] Walton and McKersie, *Behavioral Theory*, p. 60.

when auto companies do not have inventories of vehicles ready for delivery (as they would in the spring). Employers may build up inventories before contract expirations by working at full capacity or by scheduling overtime to reduce the potential costs of a strike.

Committing to a Position

Commitment to a position can be a powerful bargaining tool. If the opposition perceives no more movement will be made on a specific issue, it may then concede to the offered point if it is within its settlement range. Three components of a position signal commitment: finality (communication indicating no further movement will be made), specificity (the clarity of the position), and the consequences (the contingent outcomes, such as a strike that will occur if the demand is not accepted as proposed).[57]

Several tactics may telegraph commitment to the opposition. Most relate to the issue of consequences. For example, a strike authorization vote signals union commitment. A company preparing to close operations or refusing to accept new orders signals it is prepared to call the union's bluff. Consider the 1981 Federal Aviation Administration–Professional Air Traffic Controllers Organization dispute in which President Reagan indicated the government would not bargain during a strike (finality) and that all strikers must return to work within 48 hours (specificity) or be permanently severed from federal employment (consequences).

Settlements and Ratifications

When the negotiators agree upon a new contract, the union team still has responsibilities to fulfill before the final agreement is signed. In most unions, two hurdles remain to be cleared before the tentative agreement becomes permanent. First, the international union must approve the agreement. This ensures that a local will not negotiate an agreement substantially inferior to other contracts in the international or other unions. Second, most unions require a referendum among the bargaining unit's membership to ratify the contract. To do this, the bargaining team conducts a membership meeting and explains the contract gains won in negotiations. The team then generally recommends settlement, and the members vote to accept or reject.

If the negotiating committee recommends acceptance, the membership nearly always votes to ratify. However, some exceptions occur. Reasons for contract rejections include an inability to alter positions through bargaining, final positions outside the opponent's settlement range, hostile relationships between the parties, poor coordination in bargaining, or a failure to estimate correctly the priorities of the membership.[58] A study of a specific contract ratification found votes for

---

[57] Ibid., p. 93.
[58] D. R. Burke and L. Rubin, "Is Contract Rejection a Major Collective Bargaining Problem?" *Industrial and Labor Relations Review* 26 (1973), pp. 820–33.

approval were more likely to come from union members who were satisfied with their pay, believed they had few alternative employment options, were positively disposed toward the quality of the union's representation, and had lower job satisfaction.[59] Contract rejection occurred in several major **concession bargaining** situations in the 1980s, even after the national union recommended the agreement. Exhibit 11–3 displays some major examples of recent rejections.

When the negotiating committee unqualifiedly recommends ratification but the contract is rejected, union negotiators are placed in a precarious position. Management may rightfully question whether the union actually speaks for its members. During the negotiations, management may have conceded on issues of seeming importance to the bargainers but of questionable relevance to its members. The negotiating committee also may have difficulty selling a subsequent settlement to the membership because its credibility was undermined by the earlier rejection.

Sometimes, management will question whether the bargaining committee is representing the true wishes of the membership. Management bargainers may suggest a package be submitted to the membership for ratification. The company may not insist on taking a proposal to the membership, however, because this is not a mandatory bargaining issue.[60] If the negotiating committee is reasonably certain a proposal will be rejected, it may encourage the membership to reject it in order to strengthen its bargaining position by putting management on notice that its position is unacceptable.

Nonagreement

Occasionally, the parties may fail to reach an agreement, either before or after the contract expires. A variety of activities may then occur, including mediation, strikes, lockouts, replacements, management's implementation of its last offer, and arbitration. Impasses lead to very complex issues, which will be detailed in the next chapter.

RECENT CHANGES IN BARGAINING OUTCOMES

During the 1980s when companies requested concessions, unions responded most frequently by asking for greater job security, limits on subcontracting, or some form of profit-sharing or gainsharing program. They were most successful in obtaining job security and gainsharing but very unsuccessful in limiting subcontracting.[61]

---

[59] J. E. Martin and R. D. Berthiaume, "Predicting the Outcome of a Contract Ratification Vote," *Academy of Management Journal* 38 (1995), pp. 916–28.

[60] *NLRB* v. *Wooster Division of Borg Warner Corp.*, 356 U.S. 342 (1958).

[61] A. Freedman, *The New Look in Wage Policy and Employee Relations* (New York: Conference Board, 1985), pp. 10–15.

EXHIBIT 11–3

Rank-and-File Rejections of Contract Negotiation Settlements

Union Employer	Dispute
1996	
Food & Commercial Workers (UFCW) Giant Foods Inc.	Local 27, with 7,000 members, rejected Giant's proposal which con tained a combination of general wage increases and lump-sum pay ments, along with substantial increases in pension benefits.
United Steelworkers of America Kaiser Permanente	Local 7600 representing 2,600 employees at Kaiser and related clinics overwhelmingly rejected the final offer from Kaiser Permanente.
1997	
Food & Commercial Workers (UFCW) Excel Corp.	Local 2, covering 2,400 hourly employees, voted to reject the settle ment offer. Excel Corp. is still putting the 4-year contract into place despite this rejection. The union leaders accepted this offer because the strike vote did not pass.
Allied Pilots Association (APA) American Airlines Inc.	The pilots union representing 9,000 employees rejected a tentative 4-year agreement to raise pay by 5%, provide stock options, and protect pilots from furlough.
1998	
Electronic Workers (IUE) Telescope Casual Furniture Inc.	Local 36 FW rejected their contract and thus Telescope Casual Furniture Inc. implemented a less favorable contract proposal. The NLRB ruled that this was not an illegal action in a 2–1 decision.
Airline Pilots Association (ALPA) Atlantic Southeast Airlines	The agreement that would have covered 450 pilots was rejected with 413 pilots voting against and 43 voting in favor of the agreement.
International Association of Machinists (IAM) Northwest Airlines	Mechanics, baggage handlers, ground support, and reservation and gate agents reject settlement recommended by negotiating team.

SOURCE: *Labor Relations Week*, 1996–1998.

Previous evidence has shown that companies vulnerable to strikes or that struck in the past are more likely to settle above their wage targets. This trend lends credence to the suggestion that striking may constitute an investment in bargaining power for the union. Companies emphasizing union containment goals as well as bargaining goals are more likely to achieve their targets.[62] However, one must not necessarily attribute a hard-line approach to success in bargaining because a heavily unionized firm cannot readily have a credible containment policy. Containment may be related to the unionization of relatively small proportions of employees, which in turn increases bargaining leverage. Conservative accounting practices, such as the use of LIFO (last-in-first-out) inventory

---

[62] Freedman, *Managing Labor Relations*, p. 48.

valuation and accelerated depreciation practices were related to more success in obtaining concessions from unions.[63]

The deregulation of the trucking industry and the resulting increased ease of entry of new freight haulers led to substantial reductions in Teamster coverage and bargaining power. Over the period from 1977 to 1990, wages decreased by 27 percent and unionized carriers saw returns on equity drop by 22 percent. The entry of a large number of nonunion carriers substantially reduced the ability to impose uniform high wage rates.[64]

An extensive study of smaller unionized firms in Michigan examined collective bargaining negotiations between 1987 and 1991. Only about one-third of the settlements were achieved through traditional bargaining. The rest were either highly contentious or cooperative. Fully one-sixth were not settled within a week after expiration of the previous agreement. Long delays were associated with unilateral imposition of a new contract by management. In contracts involving multiple rounds of concessions, wages were reduced first, benefits second, and few promised increased job security. Open warfare seemed to make a transition that led the parties to move from traditional to either highly contentious or cooperative bargaining relationships. Strikes tended to speed settlement but could only be used successfully when the union had reasonable levels of bargaining power.[65]

Firms with higher amounts of asset-specific investments had lower bargaining power. Unions captured a larger portion of profits through wage increases in these situations. In the longer run, high union density lowers investment and employment growth.[66]

SUMMARY

Managements prepare for bargaining by gathering internal and comparative data, including employee distributions by job, seniority, shift, and so forth. Other data relate to wage increases in other negotiations, local labor market rates, and so on. Many different functional departments obtain information and help in formulating a management negotiating position. Contract terms that may be renegotiated must be costed to assess their relative financial impacts on the employer. Bargaining books assist in negotiations.

Unions prepare for bargaining by determining what their members view as important issues. The political nature of unions requires attention to interests of major employee groups. National-level preparation involves collecting and

---

[63] R. D. Mautz, Jr., and F. M. Richardson, "Employer Financial Information and Wage Bargaining: Issues and Evidence," *Labor Studies Journal* 17, no. 3 (1992), pp. 35–52.

[64] M. H. Belzer, "Collective Bargaining after Deregulation: Do the Teamsters Still Count?" *Industrial and Labor Relations Review* 48 (1995), pp. 636–55.

[65] J. Cutcher-Gershenfeld, P. McHugh, and D. Power, "Collective Bargaining in Small Firms: Preliminary Evidence of Fundamental Change," *Industrial and Labor Relations Review* 49 (1995), pp. 195–212.

[66] J. K. Cavanaugh, "Asset-Specific Investment and Unionized Labor," *Industrial Relations* 37 (1998), pp. 35–50.

analyzing data, while local-level preparation formulates bargaining positions and involves members in forming a negotiating team.

Bargaining occurs in situations where both parties expect the act of bargaining to improve their positions. One side may expect an improvement in benefits, while the other gains certainty through the contracting process. Attributes of the bargaining situation and the personalities of the parties involved influence outcomes. Bluffing appears important because it allows the parties to explore the significance and reasons behind demands without initially stating positions from which they might later want to retreat.

Collective bargaining has four components: distributive bargaining (one's gain is the other's loss), integrative bargaining (a settlement improves both parties' positions), attitudinal structuring (attempts to create atmospheres most likely to obtain desired concessions), and intraorganizational bargaining (the parties try to convince constituents within their own organizations to change positions).

Bargaining usually begins with the party seeking a change presenting its positions. Changes are handled sequentially, although logrolling occurs on occasion. Following a tentative agreement, union members must ratify it. Failure to ratify appears related primarily to difficulties in attitudinal structuring and intraorganizational bargaining.

DISCUSSION QUESTIONS

1. To what extent should management allow the union to select the components of an economic package in a contract negotiation?
2. What balance should exist between local- and national-level influences in negotiations? Should this balance differ according to bargaining issue?
3. How could an opponent in bargaining overcome what appears to be a strong commitment to an issue by its opposite member?
4. What strategies should management use in bargaining when a settlement that was unanimously recommended by the union's bargaining team is rejected?
5. Why would it be harder for heavily unionized organizations than organizations with a small proportion of unionized employees to settle on their bargaining targets?
6. What attitudinal structuring and intraorganizational bargaining tactics would be different for integrative bargaining compared with distributive bargaining?

KEY TERMS

Gainsharing *318*
Bargaining book *319*
Bargaining convention *321*
Logrolling *328*
Distributive bargaining *331*
Integrative bargaining *334*
Mutual gains bargaining *334*
Attitudinal structuring *334*
Intraorganizational bargaining *337*
Concession bargaining *343*

MOCK NEGOTIATING EXERCISE

This negotiating exercise helps develop an appreciation of and insight into principles and problems of collective bargaining. Using information covered to this point in the text, you will act as a member of a union or management bargaining team in formulating strategies and tactics for negotiations. Following a more detailed approach to contract costing and instructions, the exercise presents a copy of the expiring contract between General Materials & Fabrication Company (GMFC) and Local 384 of the United Steelworkers of America.

A. Contract Costing

Contract costing is not straightforward. The cost changes often depend on changes in employee seniority, how increased vacations are handled, and similar issues not directly associated with the amount of an hourly wage increase. A costing example will be created so you can see the effects. Assume a bargaining unit containing 100 employees will renegotiate its contract. Five pay grades presently have pay rates, given length of service in the organization, as shown in Table MN–1.

The 100 employees are distributed by grade and seniority, shown in Table MN–2.

Table MN–3 shows the historic turnover rates—the proportion of employees who quit or retire in a given year—of bargaining unit employees by grade and seniority level.

The organization's retirement plan provides for full vesting of benefits at five years of service. Employees who quit before accruing five years of service lose their benefits. The plan is fully funded to provide for pensions for present employees, taking anticipated turnover into account. The retirement program provides that employees will have an equivalent of 5 percent of their gross pay (regular and overtime) contributed to their pension funds.

The health care program provides hospital and medical coverage paid by the employer. Twenty-five percent of the employees are single and without dependents. The other 75 percent have families, but of these, 5 percent are families in which both the husband and wife are employed by this company, so premiums need not be paid for both. Health care premiums are $150 per month for single employees and $350 per month for those with dependents. Premiums are expected to increase 7 percent next year for both single and family policies.

Under the contract, overtime is apportioned (within grade) on the basis of seniority, with each employee entitled to five hours of overtime before the next junior employee in that grade is entitled. If all employees within the grade have received the overtime, the cycle is repeated. During the last year, overtime was available in the following number of hours by grade: grade 1, 520 hours; 2, 840; 3, 1,640; 4, 1,020; and 5, 780. The overtime premium for all these hours was 50 percent. Table MN–4 shows the average number of hours of overtime per employee by seniority and grade level during the past year.

All employees receive nine paid holidays and three paid sick days. The average employee takes two sick days, independent of grade or seniority levels. Vacations are tied to length of service. Employees with less than one year's service do not accrue vacation time. Those with 1 to 2 years are entitled to one week; 3 to 5 years, two weeks; 6 to 10 years, three weeks; and more than 10 years, four weeks.

All employees are presently working on one shift, and all have two paid break periods of 10 minutes in the morning and afternoon.

TABLE MN–1
Pay Rates

	Seniority				
Grade	< 1 yr.	1–2 Yr.	3–5 Yr.	6–10 yr.	> 10 yr.
1	$ 8.50	$ 9.00	$ 9.50	$ 9.50	$ 9.50
2	9.50	10.00	10.50	11.00	11.00
3	10.50	11.00	11.50	12.00	12.50
4	11.50	12.00	12.50	13.00	13.50
5	12.50	13.00	13.50	14.00	14.50

TABLE MN–2
Employment Levels

	Seniority					
Grade	< 1 yr.	1–2 Yr.	3–5 Yr.	6–10 yr.	> 10 yr.	Total
1	8	2	–	–	–	10
2	2	4	14	–	–	20
3	–	5	15	20	5	45
4	–	–	3	6	6	15
5	–	–	–	2	8	10
Total	10	11	32	28	19	100

TABLE MN–3
Turnover Rates by Seniority and Grade

	Seniority				
Grade	< 1 yr.	1–2 Yr.	3–5 Yr.	6–10 yr.	> 10 yr.
1	0.25	0.10	0.10	0.10	0.10
2	0.10	0.05	0.05	0.00	0.00
3	0.05	0.05	0.05	0.00	0.02
4	0.00	0.00	0.00	0.00	0.03
5	0.00	0.00	0.00	0.00	0.10

TABLE MN–4
Hours of Overtime

	Seniority					
Grade	< 1 yr.	1–2 Yr.	3–5 Yr.	6–10 yr.	> 10 yr.	Total
1	51.25	55.00				520
2	40.00	40.00	42.86			840
3		35.00	35.00	37.00	40.00	1640
4			65.00	67.50	70.00	1020
5				75.00	78.75	780

Table MN–5 shows the average wage cost per employee by grade and seniority level under the expiring contract. It is calculated by multiplying the wage rate by 2,080 (the number of hours in a normal work year) plus the number of overtime hours from the appropriate cell in Table MN–4 times 1.5 (to account for the overtime premium rate).

Social Security and Medicare tax rates total 7.65 percent. Unemployment insurance is 4 percent on the first $10,000 of earnings, and worker's compensation insurance premiums are 2.2 percent of total payroll. With pensions vesting in five years, the pension contribution for people with less than six years' service must be multiplied by the likelihood that they will remain for that period to get the total contribution required. Table MN–6 is a matrix of probabilities of an employee remaining long enough to receive vested benefits.

Present pension costs by grade and seniority (number of employees times wage cost times retention factor) are shown in Table MN–7.

Present wage costs (straight time and overtime at time and a half) are obtained by multiplying the cells in Table MN–2 by corresponding cells in Table MN–5. The results are shown in Table MN–8.

The total labor costs in the last year of the expiring contract were:

Wages	$2,503,628
Pension contributions	118,855
Social security (.0765 × Wages)	191,528
Unemployment insurance (.04 × $10,000 × number of employees)	40,000
Worker's compensation (.022 × wages)	55,080
Health insurance (25 singles × $150 × 12 months)	45,000
Health insurance (75 families × $350 × 12 months)	315,000
(Less health insurance for five husband-wife duplications)	(21,000)
Total	$3,248,091

For the coming year, assume a set of contract demands as follows:

1. A 50¢ across-the-board wage increase.
2. 10¢ additional per grade from grade 2 on.
3. A 6 percent pension contribution.
4. One week additional vacation for all employees with more than five years' service.

Assume turnover rates are the same next year, all terminees and retirees are replaced at grade 1, and present employees are promoted to fill their vacancies. Five will be lost: grade 1, < 1 year, 2; grade 2, 3–5 years, 1; grade 3, 3–5 years, 1; and grade 5, >10 years, 1. Employees will also increase one year in seniority. Assume employees within seniority groups are relatively evenly distributed and those promoted are most often the most senior person applying, but in only two-thirds of cases is the most senior person eligible. The vacation demand will result in losing 56 weeks' work. Assume an additional employee must be hired at grade 1 to make up for 42 weeks of the loss and the other 14 weeks must be worked as overtime, evenly distributed among employees in grades 3 to 5 according to seniority rules. This results in 560 additional hours, with 200 hours apportioned to grade 5 and 180 each to grades 3 and 4. At the end of the contract year, the grade and seniority matrix (after turnover) could look as shown in Table MN–9.

Table MN–10 shows the seniority level and distribution of employees after promotions have been made and new hires added.

If the union wins its demands, the new wage rates would be as shown in Table MN–11.

Overtime for the coming year (assuming the same as last year except for additional hours necessary if the vacation demand is won) is shown in Table MN–12.

Table MN–13 shows the average wage cost per employee for straight time and overtime, given the proposed demands.

Multiplying Table MN–10 by Table MN–13 yields the total wage cost (less fringes) under the

TABLE MN–5

Average Wage Cost per Employee

Grade	< 1 yr.	1–2 Yr.	3–5 Yr.	6–10 yr.	> 10 yr.
			Seniority		
1	$18,333	$19,463	$19,760	$19,760	$19,760
2	20,330	21,400	22,515	22,880	22,880
3	21,840	23,458	24,524	25,626	26,750
4	23,920	24,960	27,219	28,356	29,498
5	26,000	27,040	28,080	30,695	31,873

TABLE MN–6

Pension Vesting Probabilities

Grade	< 1 yr.	1–2 Yr.	3–5 Yr.	6–10 yr.	> 10 yr.
			Seniority		
1	0.61	0.81	0.90	1.00	1.00
2	0.81	0.90	0.95	1.00	1.00
3	0.86	0.90	0.95	1.00	1.00
4	1.00	1.00	1.00	1.00	1.00
5	1.00	1.00	1.00	1.00	1.00

TABLE MN–7

Total Pension Costs·

Grade	< 1 yr.	1–2 Yr.	3–5 Yr.	6–10 yr.	> 10 yr.	Total
			Seniority			
1	$4,455	1,576	0	0	0	6,031
2	1,651	3,863	14,973	0	0	20,487
3	0	5,293	17,473	25,626	6,688	55,079
4	0	0	4,083	8,507	8,849	21,439
5	0	0	0	3,070	12,749	15,819
Total	$6,106	10,732	36,528	37,202	28,286	118,855

*All figures rounded to nearest dollar.

TABLE MN–8

Total Wage Costs

Grade	< 1 yr.	1–2 Yr.	3–5 Yr.	6–10 yr.	> 10 yr.	Total
			Seniority			
1	$146,668	$ 38,925	$ 0	$ 0	$ 0	$ 185,593
2	40,660	85,600	315,211	0	0	441,471
3	0	117,288	367,856	512,520	133,750	1,131,414
4	0	0	81,656	170,138	176,985	428,779
5	0	0	0	61,390	254,983	316,373
Total	$187,328	$241,813	$764,723	$744,048	$565,718	$2,503,628

TABLE MN–9

Remaining Employees

Grade	Seniority					Total
	< 1 yr.	1–2 Yr.	3–5 Yr.	6–10 yr.	> 10 yr.	
1	6	2	0	0	0	8
2	2	4	13	0	0	19
3	0	5	14	20	5	44
4	0	0	3	6	6	15
5	0	0	0	2	7	9
Total	8	11	30	28	18	95

TABLE MN–10

Seniority Levels with Promotions and New Hires

Grade	Seniority					Total
	< 1 yr.	1–2 Yr.	3–5 Yr.	6–10 yr.	> 10 yr.	
1	6	5	0	0	0	11
2	0	6	12	2	0	20
3	0	2	12	23	8	45
4	0	0	2	6	7	15
5	0	0	0	2	8	10
Total	6	13	26	33	23	101

TABLE MN–11

Postnegotiation Pay Rates

Grade	Seniority				
	< 1 yr.	1–2 Yr.	3–5 Yr.	6–10 yr.	> 10 yr.
1	$ 9.00	$ 9.50	$10.00	$10.00	$10.00
2	10.10	10.60	11.10	11.60	11.60
3	11.20	11.70	12.20	12.70	13.20
4	12.30	12.80	13.30	13.80	14.30
5	13.40	13.90	14.40	14.90	15.40

TABLE MN–12

Postnegotiation Overtime Distribution

Grade	Seniority					Total
	< 1 yr.	1–2 Yr.	3–5 Yr.	6–10 yr.	> 10 yr.	
1	45.00	50.00				520
2		40.00	42.50	45.00		840
3		40.00	40.00	40.00	42.50	1,820
4			80.00	80.00	80.00	1,200
5				95.00	98.75	980

new contract. The results are shown in Table MN–14.

Multiplying turnover probability (Table MN–6) by total wages in Table MN–14 gives the pension costs under the new contract. These are shown in Table MN–15.

Pension costs increase by $37,078 (or 31 percent more) because of increased seniority, which leads to a greater likelihood of staying, combined with the 20 percent increase in contribution rates. Following are the total costs in the first year of a new contract:

Wages	$2,706,283
Pension contributions	155,933
Social Security	207,031
Unemployment insurance (101 × 4% × 10,000)	40,400
Workers' compensation (2.2% of payroll)	59,538
Health insurance (26 singles @ $160.50 per month)	50,076
Health insurance (75 families @ 374.50 per month)	337,050
(Less health insurance for five husband-wife duplications)	(22,470)
Total	$3,587,841

Under the proposed new contract, total labor costs would increase by 10.5 percent even though average straight-time percentage wage increases would rise between 5.3 and 7.2 percent by grade and seniority level as shown in Table MN–16.

B. Approach

Assume the GMFC–Local 384 contract is due to expire soon and the union has made a timely notification to management that it desires renegotiations. It is your responsibility to negotiate a new contract. Following are the demands of both labor and management and supplemental information that will help in choosing contract demands.

TABLE MN–13

Postnegotiation Wage Cost per Employee

Grade	Seniority				
	< 1 yr.	1–2 Yr.	3–5 Yr.	6–10 yr.	> 10 yr.
1	$19,328	$20,473	$20,800	$20,800	$20,800
2	21,008	22,684	23,796	24,911	24,128
3	23,296	25,038	26,108	27,178	28,298
4	25,584	26,624	29,260	30,360	31,460
5	27,872	28,912	29,952	33,115	34,313

TABLE MN–14

Postnegotiation Total Wage Cost

Grade	Seniority					Total
	< 1 yr.	1–2 Yr.	3–5 Yr.	6–10 yr.	> 10 yr.	
1	$115,965	$102,363	0	0	0	$ 218,328
2	0	136,104	$285,548	$ 49,822	0	471,474
3	0	50,076	313,296	625,094	$226,380	1,214,846
4	0	0	58,520	182,160	220,220	460,900
5	0	0	0	66,231	274,505	340,736
Total	$115,965	$288,543	$657,364	$923,307	$721,105	$2,706,283

C. Demands

1. Union Demands

The union may formulate its demands from the following set, including all items from *a* through *d* and choosing any four from *e* through *k*:

a. A general wage increase of 60 cents per hour during each year of the contract, plus an additional 50 cents per hour at the effective date.

b. The company will neither subcontract work the bargaining unit is capable of performing nor close the plant or move any of the plant's operations during the life of the agreement.

c. A 50-cent per hour additional increase will be given to maintain wage differentials for employees outside the assembler classifications.

d. Reimplementation of a COLA based on 6 cents per hour for each one point increase in the consumer price index.

e. The company will create and operate a child-care center to be used by employees' children while they are on the job.

f. When employees achieve 25 years of service, if an employee retires, the company will provide an annual lifetime benefit equal to the difference between the annual return on the present value of retirement contributions and the present value of the retirement contributions of employees with 30 years of service.

g. Vacations will be increased one week for employees with 15 or more years of service.

h. The company's pension contribution will be increased from 5 percent of straight-time earnings to 6 percent of straight- and overtime earnings. Benefits will be 100 percent vested in three years.

i. A union shop clause will be implemented, with membership required after 60 days of employment.

TABLE MN–15

Postnegotiation Total Pension Costs

Grade	< 1 yr.	1–2 Yr.	3–5 Yr.	6–10 yr.	> 10 yr.	Total
		Seniority				
1	$4,227	$ 4,975	0	0	0	$ 9,202
2	0	7,370	$16,276	$ 2,989	0	26,636
3	0	2,712	17,858	37,506	$13,583	71,658
4	0	0	3,511	10,930	13,213	27,654
5	0	0	0	3,974	16,470	20,444
Total	$4,227	$15,056	$37,645	$55,398	$43,266	$155,593

TABLE MN–16

Postnegotiation Percentage Wage Increases

Grade	< 1 yr.	1–2 Yr.	3–5 Yr.	6–10 yr.	> 10 yr.
	Seniority				
1	5.9%	5.6%	5.3%	5.3%	5.3%
2	6.3	6.0	5.7	5.5	5.5
3	6.7	6.4	6.1	5.8	5.6
4	7.0	6.7	6.4	6.2	5.9
5	7.2	6.9	6.7	6.4	6.2

j. Double pay will be given for all overtime after nine hours in a day and for all Sunday or holiday work.

k. Mandatory overtime cannot exceed 10 hours in any given week.

2. Company Demands

The company's offers and demands will be formulated from the following list. All demands between *a* and *d* will be included in the offer, and any four demands between *e* and *k* may be included:

a. The length of the agreement will be three years.

b. Management shall have the right to subcontract or move any work to another plant without consulting the union.

c. Wage increases of 2.0 percent the first year, 2.5 percent the second year, and a 3.0 percent lump sum the third year will be given at the beginning of each year of the contract.

d. The supplementary unemployment benefit will be discontinued.

e. Due to the reduction in the size of the bargaining unit during the last several years, the number of union representatives from the plant serving on committees while being reimbursed by the company will be reduced from seven to five.

f. Persons promoted to supervisory positions will continue to accrue seniority within the bargaining unit after their promotion.

g. The annual increase in cost of the employee health care benefit will be limited to the percentage wage increase negotiated.

h. Employees may not refuse Saturday overtime and/or up to two additional hours per day, including Saturday.

i. Bargaining unit members who elect to join the union must maintain membership during the life of the agreement. With each contract expiration, individuals who had been members will be free to withdraw during the first week of the subsequent agreement.

j. The losing party in arbitration shall be responsible for all expenses of the arbitration procedure.

D. Organization for Negotiations

Each labor team will be headed by a chief negotiator. One member of labor's team should assume the role of international representative. Team sizes should be not less than three nor more than eight. Each management team will be headed by the plant labor relations director and may include managers from other functional areas—manufacturing, accounting, shipping, and so forth. Management team sizes should be about the same as labor's.

Before negotiations, each team should:

1. Construct its demand or offer package and identify the relative priority of the issues being included.

2. Identify issues it would be willing to trade off.

3. Develop bargaining books tying demands to provisions in the present contract. Identify for each demand a desired settlement position, an expected settlement position, and a maximum concession position before bargaining.

4. Cost the provisions of the contract that would be changed. (Both parties should do this.)

5. Identify and develop strategies and tactics to be used during the negotiations. Structure the roles of each member.

E. Negotiations

1. At the first bargaining session, labor and management shall first agree on an agenda and order of presentation. If a mutually satisfactory agenda cannot be achieved, the following may be used:

   a. Each demand or offer will be presented separately, with the other party responding. Normally, where both sides will make offers on the same issue, the union will present its demand first.

b. All demands will be presented and responded to before any concession is made.

2. As you begin to bargain, you should remember that once a concession is made, it is very difficult to retract. Thus, carefully consider changes in your positions before announcing them.

3. During the process, it is often beneficial to suspend face-to-face negotiations to hold a caucus of your bargaining group to consider a demand or concession.

4. As you negotiate, consider the impact the bargaining outcomes you attain will have on the bargaining relationship after the contract is signed. Is this a concession the other side can live with?

5. After the contract is agreed to, management must determine the final cost impact of the agreement, and the union must develop a strategy for gaining rank-and-file ratification.

F. Additional Information

1. The terms of the contract may have some cost impact outside the bargaining unit because improved fringe benefits are usually passed on to nonunion white-collar workers.

2. Over the last contract, the average amount of overtime per year has been distributed as shown in Table MN–17.

3. The plant has experienced several layoffs since 1981. The bargaining unit totaled 1,208 at the end of 1980, the largest ever achieved. In 1981, the production workforce was cut 20 percent in January and 20 percent in March. In April 1982, 10 percent was recalled, an additional 10 percent in October, and 10 percent in May 1983. In 1981, maintenance and craft employment was cut 10 percent in January, 10 percent in March, 10 percent in June, and 10 percent in September. Recalls of 10 percent were made in January and June 1982 and May 1983. Of those who were laid off, all were recalled except five employees with less than one year of service at the time of the layoffs. In January 1991, after adequate contractual notice, the plant was shut down for two weeks. In June 1991, 10 percent of the maintenance workforce was laid off. In July 1991, 20 percent of the production workforce was laid off. All were recalled in October. In November 1992, as part of a cost-cutting campaign during an economic slowdown, GMFC offered an early retirement program to all employees in which five years' contributions were added to retirees' accounts at rates corresponding to present salaries, under the assumption it was deposited five years ago. Between 1987 and 1991 (inclusive), the compound annual rate of return on the retirement plan's assets was 15 percent. Of the 95 employees with 25 or more years of service,

TABLE MN–17

Average Overtime Hours Worked per Employee under the Expiring Agreement

	Production			Nonproduction (Maintenance and Craft)		
	1996	1997	1998	1996	1997	1998
Saturdays (10-hour shift)	160	200	200	60	60	90
Weekdays	200	280	240	60	80	86
Holidays (8 hours)	0	0	0	0	0	16
Sundays (8 hours)	0	0	0	0	8	24
Totals	360	480	440	120	140	216

86 took advantage of the offer. The company did not hire any replacements until 1994, when 22 were hired. The present seniority list (as of January 1, 1999) is shown in Table MN–18. Turnover includes quits, retirements, and promotions and transfers out of the bargaining unit. All bargaining unit employees have retired when they reached 30 years of service.

4. The Central City plant was built 50 years ago and was expanded repeatedly during the early to middle 1970s. Presently, no expansion is planned. The company has similar U.S. and foreign operations. One relatively new plant in the Sunbelt is unorganized. Across the company, about 75 percent of production employees are represented, all by the Steelworkers.

5. Presently, 879 bargaining unit members belong to the union.

6. The average arbitration case cost the company and the union $6,500 each during the last contract. Arbitrators heard 14 cases and ruled for the company on 10.

7. Table MN–19 gives a distribution of employees by job and seniority.

8. Productivity changes over the past five years are as follows: 1994, up 6 percent; 1995, up 4 percent; 1996, down 3 percent; 1997, up 4 percent; 1998, up 2 percent. Over the past four years, product prices have increased by 1.5 percent in 1995, 1.8 percent in 1996, 2.0 percent in 1997, and down 4.0 percent in 1998. The equivalent number of units shipped in each of the past four years was up 8.2 percent in 1995, up 6.9 percent in 1996, 9.5 percent in 1997, and down 3.7 percent in 1998.

9. You should consider the costs of health fringes, Social Security and other wage-tied benefits, and changes in the consumer price index (if applicable) when costing contract terms.

10. For wage-comparison purposes, GMFC operations are in Standard Industrial Classification (SIC) codes 3441 (Fabricated Structural Metals), 3443 (Fabricated Plate Work), 3531 (Construction Machinery and Equipment), and 3537 (Industrial Trucks, Tractors, Trailers, and Stackers).

11. Recent selected financial information for this location is shown in Table MN–20.

TABLE MN–18

Seniority of Employees and Turnover Rates by Length of Service (seniority list as of January 1, 1999)

Years of Seniority	Number of Employees	Cumulative Number	Percent Turnover
30	13	13	100.0%
29	9	22	1.0
28	11	33	1.0
27	12	45	1.0
26	92	137	1.0
25	130	267	1.0
24	95	362	1.0
23	107	469	1.0
22	25	494	1.0
21	54	548	1.0
20	85	633	1.0
19	60	693	1.0
18	16	709	1.0
17	52	761	1.0
16	7	768	1.0
15	2	770	1.0
14	0	770	1.0
13	0	770	1.0
12	5	775	1.0
11	7	782	1.0
10	2	784	1.0
9	6	790	1.5
8	4	794	2.0
7	4	798	2.5
6	0	798	3.0
5	0	798	4.0
4	13	811	5.0
3	24	835	6.0
2	41	876	8.0
1	34	910	10.0
<1	17	927	30.0

TABLE MN–19

Seniority Level by Job Classification as of January 1, 1999

Job Title	Total	<1	1	2	3	4	5	6	7	8	9	10	11	12	13	14	15	16	17	18	19	20	21	22	23	24	25	26	27	28	29	30
												Years of Seniority																				
Assembler, level 1	180	14	32	40	23	11	0	0	3	3	5	2	7	5	0	0	2	6	24	1	2	0	0	0	0	0	0	0	0	0	0	0
Assembler, level 2	385	0	0	0	0	0	0	0	0	0	0	0	0	0	0	0	0	0	28	13	53	70	45	15	78	59	24	0	0	0	0	0
Assembler, level 3	230	0	0	0	0	0	0	0	0	0	0	0	0	0	0	0	0	0	0	0	0	0	0	3	8	21	85	79	10	9	8	7
Skilled production, level 1	23	0	0	0	0	0	0	0	0	0	0	0	0	0	0	0	0	0	0	0	0	4	3	1	5	4	3	0	0	0	0	3
Skilled production, level 2	23	0	0	0	0	0	0	0	0	0	0	0	0	0	0	0	0	0	0	2	2	2	1	1	3	3	4	4	0	0	0	1
Skilled production, level 3	23	0	0	0	0	0	0	0	0	0	0	0	0	0	0	0	0	0	0	0	0	2	2	2	2	4	6	4	0	0	0	1
Skilled maintenance, level 1	4	0	0	0	0	0	0	0	0	0	0	0	0	0	0	0	0	1	0	1	1	0	0	1	0	0	0	0	0	0	0	0
Skilled maintenance, level 2	8	0	0	0	0	0	0	0	0	0	0	0	0	0	0	0	0	0	0	0	1	0	0	0	2	2	3	0	0	0	0	0
Skilled maintenance, level 3	12	0	0	0	0	0	0	0	0	0	0	0	0	0	0	0	0	0	0	0	0	0	0	0	3	1	4	3	0	1	0	0
Material handling & prod. support	23	2	1	1	1	1	0	0	1	0	0	0	0	0	0	0	0	0	0	0	0	5	1	0	4	0	1	1	1	1	0	1
Maintenance	16	1	1	0	0	1	0	0	0	1	0	0	0	0	0	0	0	0	0	0	0	2	2	2	1	0	1	1	0	1	0
	927	17	34	41	24	13	0	0	4	4	6	2	7	5	0	0	2	7	52	16	60	85	54	25	107	95	130	92	12	11	9	13

TABLE MN–20

**Selected Financial Information for This Location
(Income Statement, Balance Sheet, and Employment)
(Financial Data in Thousands [$000])**

	1994	1995	1996	1997	1998
Net sales	$173,486	$190,528	$207,340	$231,578	$214,089
Materials	100,622	111,050	120,494	132,600	125,779
Depreciation	3,604	4,088	4,181	4,051	3,408
Compensation	45,349	50,131	59,348	63,627	61,902
Interest expense	2,028	1,851	1,667	1,529	1,340
Extraordinary charges	0	0	0	0	0
Income from operations	$ 21,883	$ 23,407	$ 21,650	$ 29,771	$ 21,661
Profit sharing	2,188	2,341	2,165	2,977	2,166
Net income from operations	19,694	21,066	19,485	26,794	19,495
Income from investments	9,696	9,367	9,357	9,399	9,748
Total income	$ 29,390	$ 30,433	$ 28,843	$ 36,193	$ 29,242
Provision for taxes	12,344	12,782	12,114	15,201	12,282
Net income	17,046	17,651	16,729	20,992	16,961
(less corporate asset return)	15,736	15,619	15,599	15,519	16,074
Plant surplus	1,310	2,032	1,130	5,473	887
Current assets	$ 6,086	$ 5,634	$ 5,109	$ 4,886	$ 8,891
Plant and equipment	79,086	85,108	89,662	93,191	94,027
(less accumulated depreciation)	61,065	64,669	68,757	72,938	76,989
Net plant and equipment	18,021	20,439	20,905	20,253	17,038
Investments	80,800	78,055	77,978	78,324	81,230
Total assets	$104,907	$104,128	$103,992	$103,463	$107,159
Current liabilities	2,879	2,992	3,026	3,569	3,994
Long-term debt	20,813	18,611	16,409	14,207	12,005
Retained earnings	81,215	82,525	84,557	85,687	91,160
Total liabilities and capital	$104,907	$104,128	$103,992	$103,463	$107,159
Average number of employees	1,002	1,041	1,103	1,099	1,052
Bargaining unit employees	895	921	963	966	927

AGREEMENT

between

GENERAL MANUFACTURING & FABRICATION COMPANY

CENTRAL CITY, INDIANA,

and

LOCAL 384, UNITED STEELWORKERS OF AMERICA

AFL-CIO/CLC

Effective March 1, 1996

CONTENTS

ARTICLE 1.   PURPOSE

1.01   It is the intent and purpose of the parties hereto that this Agreement will promote and improve industrial and economic relations between the employees and the COMPANY, and to set forth herein a basic agreement covering rates of pay, hours of work, and other conditions of employment to be observed by the parties and to ensure the peaceful settlement of disputes and to prevent stoppages of work.

ARTICLE 2.   RECOGNITION

2.01   The COMPANY recognizes Local Union No. 384, United Steelworkers of America, AFL–CIO/CLC, as the exclusive bargaining agent for all hourly paid employees designated in the bargaining unit by the National Labor Relations Board for the Central City plant and warehouses, which includes all production and maintenance employees including machine shop employees and receiving department and warehouse employees but excluding boiler room employees, clerical employees, watchpersons, guards, assistant supervisors, supervisors, and any other supervisory employees with authority to hire, promote, discharge, discipline, or otherwise effect changes in the status of employees or effectively recommend such action.

2.02   Any employee who is a member of the UNION on the effective date of this Agreement shall, as a condition of employment, maintain his/her membership in the UNION to the extent of paying membership dues.

2.03   Any employee who on the effective date of this Agreement is not a member of the UNION shall not be required to become a member of the UNION but shall be required to pay an amount equal to the UNION's regular monthly dues. Any such employee, however, who during the life of the Agreement joins the UNION must remain a member as provided in Section 2.02.

ARTICLE 3.   CHECKOFF OF UNION DUES

3.01   Upon individual authorization from members, monthly UNION DUES in an amount to be determined by the UNION shall be deducted by the COMPANY from each member's first pay in each month. Such sums shall be forwarded by the COMPANY to the financial secretary of the UNION before the 15th day of the month.

ARTICLE 4.   MANAGEMENT

4.01   The UNION and its members recognize that the successful and efficient operation of the business is the responsibility of management and that management of the plant and the direction of the working force is the responsibility of the COMPANY, provided, in carrying out these management functions, the COMPANY does not violate the terms of this Agreement.

4.02   The COMPANY retains the sole right to discipline and discharge employees for cause, provided that in the exercise of this right it will not act wrongfully or unjustly or in violation of the terms of this Agreement.

ARTICLE 5.   REPRESENTATION

5.01   The UNION shall designate a UNION COMMITTEE of no more than 10 members who shall represent the UNION in meetings with the COMPANY, with no more than 7 employees actively working in the plant as members of the committee.

5.02   The COMPANY agrees that during meetings held with management, members of the UNION required to attend shall be paid at their regular hourly base rate plus their departmental incentive for all time lost from their regularly assigned work schedule.

ARTICLE 6.   HOURS

6.01   *Work Day*   A day starts at the beginning of the first shift and ends at the close of the third shift. The first shift is any shift that starts after midnight. Normally the first shift starts at 7:00 A.M. or 8:00 A.M. Present shift schedules will continue unless changes are mutually agreed to by the COMPANY and the UNION.

6.02   *Payroll Week*   The payroll week starts at the beginning of the first shift on Monday and ends at the end of the third shift on Sunday.

6.03   *Daily Overtime*   Time and one-half shall be paid for all hours worked in excess of eight in any one day.

6.04   *Weekly Overtime*   Time and one-half shall be paid for all hours worked in excess of 40 in any one payroll week for which overtime has not been earned on any other basis.

6.05   *Saturday Work*   Time and one-half shall be paid for work performed on Saturday between the hours of 7:00 A.M. or 8:00 A.M. Saturday to 7:00 A.M. or 8:00 A.M. on Sunday.

6.06   *Sunday Work*   Double time shall be paid for work performed on Sunday between the hours of 7:00 A.M. or 8:00 A.M. Sunday to 7:00 A.M. or 8:00 A.M. Monday.

6.07   *Consecutive Hours over 8*   Time and one-half shall be paid for all hours worked over 8 but less than 12.

6.08   *Consecutive Hours over 12*   Double time shall be paid for all consecutive hours worked over 12.

6.09   ***Distribution of Overtime***   Overtime shall be distributed on an equitable basis within the department in a manner to be decided by the supervision and the UNION representatives in that department, giving consideration to seniority and ability to perform the work. Refused overtime hours shall be credited as overtime hours worked for purposes of distributing overtime.

6.10   ***Shift Premium***

A.   A shift premium of 30 cents per hour will be paid to all employees for all hours worked on a particular day if 50 percent or more of the hours worked on that day fall between the hours of 3:00 P.M. and 11:00 P.M.

B.   A shift premium of 40 cents per hour will be paid to all employees for all hours worked on a particular day if 50 percent or more of the hours worked on that day fall between the hours of 11:00 P.M. and 7:00 A.M.

C.   The incentive premium will not be applied to the shift premium.

6.11   ***Holidays***

A.   After completion of the probationary period, an hourly employee not working on the holiday will be granted holiday benefit consisting of eight hours' straight-time pay at his/her regular hourly base rate on the following holidays:

New Year's Day   Thanksgiving
Memorial Day   Christmas
Independence Day   December 24
Labor Day   December 31
Floating holiday

B.   Double time in addition to the holiday pay, as stated in Section 6.11a, will be paid for all hours worked on the above holidays.

C.   The floating holiday will be designated by the COMPANY. The UNION will be notified at least 90 days prior to the day set by the COMPANY.

D.   A holiday starts at the beginning of the first shift and ends at the close of the third shift. When one of these holidays falls on Sunday, the holiday shall be observed on Monday. When one of these holidays falls on Saturday, the holiday shall be observed on Friday.

E.   To be eligible, the employee must be at work on the day for which he/she is scheduled prior to the holiday and following the holiday unless absence is established for any of the following reasons:

1.   Unavoidable absence caused by sickness or injury.
2.   Emergencies in the immediate family.
3.   Regularly scheduled vacation. The holiday will not count against vacation.

4. Any other justifiable absence previously approved by his/her supervisor.

ARTICLE 7. WAGES

7.01   Effective March 1, 1996, a lump-sum bonus of $1,000 will be paid to all bargaining unit employees.

7.02   Effective March 1, 1982, 10 percent of profits (net income from operations before provision for income taxes) generated by the plant for the calendar year ending on December 31, 1982, and continuing thereafter on December 31 of each calendar year will be divided among members of the bargaining unit. Each employee will receive an amount equal to his/her hours worked divided by the total number of hours worked by the bargaining unit during the calendar year times the profit proportion (if any). Profit-sharing payments will be made not later than March 31 of the following year for distributions earned for the preceding calendar year.

7.03   ***Skill-Based Pay Plan***   Effective March 1, 1997, a skill-based pay plan will be implemented. Pay will be based on employees' demonstrated skills. Skill blocks associated with ability to perform work in five job categories will be defined jointly by the COMPANY and the UNION. The five categories are assembler, skilled production, skilled maintenance, material handling and production support, and maintenance. Three levels in each of the assembler, skilled production, and skilled maintenance categories require significantly increasing skill levels. There is a single level in the material handling and production support and maintenance categories.

A.   ***Assembly Category***   The skills associated with the former Assembler grades 1, 2, and 3 will constitute those required to perform as an Assembler, level 1. All employees currently assigned to these grades will be initially qualified as Assembler, level 1. The skills associated with the former Assembler grades 4, 5, and 6 will constitute those required to perform as an Assembler, level 2. All employees currently assigned to these grades will be initially qualified as Assembler, level 2. The skills associated with the former Assembler grades 7, 8, 9 and 10 will constitute those required to perform as an Assembler, level 3. All employees currently assigned to these grades will be initially qualified as Assembler, level 3.

B.   ***Skilled Production Category***   The skills associated with the following jobs will be associated with skilled production, level 3: tool and model maker, tool and die maker, jig grinder operator, machinist, welder, and precision grinder. The skills associated with the following jobs will be associated with skilled production, level 2: layout and setup worker, painter, profile mill operator, machinist trainee, capital assembly worker, and weldment finisher. The skills associated with the following jobs will be associated with skilled production, level 1: metal fabricator, grinder operator, milling machine operator, lathe operator, head assembly worker, developmental assembler, experimental assembler, and assembler.

C.   ***Skilled Maintenance Category***   The skills associated with the following jobs will be associated with skilled maintenance, level 3: systems control technician, measurement and control technician, instrument maintenance technician, electrician, refrigeration and air-conditioning mechanic, steamfitter, development electronics technician, millwright mechanic, maintenance mechanic, and millwright. The skills associated with the following jobs will be associated with skilled maintenance, level 2: none. The skills associated with the following jobs will be associated with skilled maintenance, level 1: cabinetmaker, locksmith, specialist, oiler, and trades helper.

D.   ***Material Handling and Production Support***   The skills associated with the following jobs are associated with the material handling and production support skill set: steelroom handler, head stockroom clerk, yardworker, stock service worker, truck driver, tool crib attendant, stockroom clerk, waste hauler, and yard laborer.

E.   ***Maintenance***   The skills associated with the following jobs are associated with the maintenance skill set: air conditioning cleaner and janitor.

7.04   ***Skill Level Rates***   Skill level rates effective March 1, 1997, are as shown in the appendix. Effective March 1, 1998, all rates will be increased 3 percent.

7.05   ***Certification of Qualifications***   All employees will be given skill tests each March 1 to determine their current skill levels. If employees pass the next higher level skill test, they will be promoted to that level (not more than one level per year). If employees fail a test at their current level, level 1 employees have one year to requalify or be terminated. Level 2 or above retain their current pay rates for one year and then will be demoted if they don't qualify on the next test. There are no fixed number of openings at any level. When employees qualify, they will be advanced at the rate of one level per year or less. Certification tests will be developed jointly by the COMPANY and the UNION and will be administered jointly annually on March 1 by the COMPANY and UNION. For its part, the COMPANY will offer no less than 30 hours of skill training annually to employees who request it.

7.06   ***Promotional Increases***   When an employee is promoted to a higher level, he/she will receive the classified rate for the job the first Monday on or after his/her promotion.

7.07   ***Temporary Transfers between Departments***   When in the interest of effective and economical operation or as a means of deferring layoffs it is desirable to transfer employees temporarily from one department to another, such temporary transfers may be made for a maximum period of four weeks, if mutually agreeable to both the COMPANY and the UNION. Wherever possible, departmental seniority will be given due consideration in determining employees to be transferred. The UNION agrees to cooperate with the COMPANY in arranging such temporary interdepartment transfers. The COMPANY agrees not to request temporary interdepartment transfers except in the interests of efficient and economical operation or as a means of deferring layoff.

7.08   ***Employee Reporting and No Work Available***   Employees reporting for work according to their regularly assigned work schedules without being notified in advance not to report and work is not available shall be allowed a minimum of four hours' pay at the employees' regular straight-time hourly base rate except in cases beyond the control of the COMPANY.

7.09   ***Call-in Pay***   Employees who have been recalled to work after they have completed their regularly scheduled shift and have left the plant shall be given a minimum of four hours' work if they so desire. If four hours' work is not available, the employee shall be paid the hours worked according to the wage and premium pay policy, and the remainder of the four hours not worked shall be paid at the employee's regular straight-time hourly rate.

7.10   ***Jury Duty***   The COMPANY agrees to pay the difference between jury duty pay and the employee's straight-time hourly base rate earnings when called for jury duty. When called, the employee will be scheduled to work on the first shift whenever possible. The employee shall be required to report for work whenever he/she is able to work four consecutive hours or more of the first shift.

ARTICLE 8.   SENIORITY

8.01   ***Plant Seniority***   Plant seniority shall be determined from the employee's earliest date of continuous employment with the COMPANY and shall apply to divisional and plant layoffs and plant recalls after layoff.

8.02   ***Departmental Seniority***   Departmental seniority shall be determined from the employee's earliest date of continuous employment in the department and shall apply to promotions, demotions, and reductions in force within the department.

8.03   ***Termination of Seniority***   Seniority shall terminate for the following reasons:

A.   Voluntary resignation.
B.   Discharge for proper cause.

C. Absence for three successive working days without notice, unless satisfactory reason is given.

D. Failure to report to work after layoff within five working days after being notified by registered letter (return receipt requested) at the employee's last available address, unless satisfactory reason is given. A copy of the written offer shall be sent to the UNION.

8.04   *Employees on Layoff*

A. Employees who are or shall be laid off due to lack of work and later reemployed shall retain their seniority as of the time of the layoff but will not accumulate seniority during the layoff period. If an employee after the first six months of layoff declines to return to work when contacted by the production personnel office regarding an opening, his/her seniority rights shall be terminated.

B. Employees shall be given three working days' notice of impending layoff from the plant or three days' pay in lieu thereof.

8.05   *Probationary Employees*

A. A new employee shall be on probation without seniority for 40 days actually worked after date of employment by the COMPANY, during which period the COMPANY shall determine the employee's ability to perform satisfactorily the duties and requirements of the work. Layoff or discharge of an employee during such probationary period shall not be subject to the grievance procedure.

B. Upon satisfactorily completing the probationary period, the employee will be placed on the department's seniority list, and his/her departmental seniority shall date from the beginning of the probationary period. If an employee is transferred to another department during his/her probationary period, his/her departmental seniority shall date back to the date of transfer to the new department upon completion of the probationary period.

8.06   *Transfers*

A. When an employee leaves his/her department to accept a job in another department, his/her seniority rights in the department that he/she left shall not be forfeited for a period of 90 days. If the employee chooses to return to his/her home department (home department is where he/she has recall and return rights) within 90 days from the date of such transfer, he/she shall be returned to his/her former job not later than the third Monday following his/her request. If he/she requests transfer to another department within 12 months of his/her return to his/her home department, he/she shall, upon being transferred, forfeit all departmental seniority rights.

B. If an employee signs a plant posting and during the 90-day period in that job signs another plant posting, he/she has the original 90 days to return to his/her home department but has no right of return to the second department he/she left.

8.07   *Layoffs*

A. *Departmental*   When the number of employees in a department is reduced, layoffs shall be made on the basis of departmental seniority, providing those remaining are qualified to perform the work.

B. *Divisional*   The employee ultimately laid off from a department shall be entitled to bump into the department of the least senior employee in the plant on the basis of plant seniority, provided he/she has the necessary qualifications to perform the job to which he/she is assigned. In multiple reductions involving the displacement of employees in the department in which reduction is taking place, the employees with the most departmental seniority of those on the original reduction schedule will be retained in the department, providing employees in the reducing department do not have sufficient plant seniority to allow them to remain in the plant. Others reduced from the department will be assigned to one or two shifts according to plant seniority. Upon notification to the production personnel department, special shift requests will be given consideration.

C. *Plant*   The employee laid off from his/her division shall be entitled to bump into the department of the least senior employee in the plant, providing the claiming employee has the necessary qualifications to perform the job to which he/she is assigned and has more than six months of plant seniority to his/her credit. In case any of the jobs vacated by the least senior employees in the plant are on a one- or two-shift basis as opposed to the ordinary three-shift basis, the employees being laid off from a division who have the most plant seniority shall automatically be given these one- or two-shift jobs. Upon notification to the production personnel department, special shift requests will be given consideration.

D. The employee so transferred shall accept, according to his/her seniority, the position vacated to make room for him/her. The supervisor shall have the right to place the crew as he/she sees fit on jobs carrying the same classified rate in all cases of emergencies and vacancies, taking into account the most efficient utilization of his/her working force.

E. When a classification is eliminated, the employee(s) occupying that classification may exercise his/her seniority to claim any classification within the department to which his/her seniority entitles him/her. The employee(s) then affected will follow the normal layoff procedure.

8.08   *Recall after Layoff*

A. When it is necessary to employ additional employees, employees laid off due to lack of work will be recalled in order of their plant seniority, providing they are qualified to handle the jobs, before new employees are hired.

B.   When an employee is recalled after layoff for a job in another department and accepts, he/she will retain his/her home departmental seniority until such time as he/she declines an opportunity to return to his/her home department, subject to Section 8.06. If a laid-off employee declines, he/she shall remain on recall to his/her home department for a period not to exceed six months after layoff date. If, during the six months' period, the employee wishes to be considered for an opening in another department, he/she may do so by notifying the production personnel office. Thereafter, he/she must return to work when offered employment by the COMPANY or his/her seniority will be terminated.

8.09   *Leaves of Absence*

A.   Members of the UNION, not to exceed three in number at any one time, shall be granted leaves of absence for the duration of this Agreement to work directly for the local UNION. It is further agreed that four additional leaves shall be granted to any employees of the COMPANY covered by this Agreement who have been or who may in the future be elected to or appointed to a full-time office in the international union or the state federation of labor, AFL–CIO, providing that such leaves do not exceed the duration of this Agreement. Upon being relieved of their official positions, they will be entitled to full seniority rights as though they had been employed by the COMPANY continuously.

B.   Employees, not to exceed 1 percent of the UNION's membership, who are members of the UNION when delegated or elected to attend a UNION convention or conference shall be granted such leaves of absence as may be necessary, providing reasonable notice is given the COMPANY.

C.   Any employee elected to or appointed to any federal, state, or city public office shall be granted a leave of absence during the period he/she is actively engaged in such service.

D.   Maternity leave.

1.   An employee who becomes pregnant will be granted a leave of absence upon request at any time during pregnancy and extending for three months after the birth of the child. Where leave of absence is taken, such employee shall not lose seniority that was acquired before the beginning of such leave of absence.

2.   All employees placed on maternity leave of absence shall have their seniority dates adjusted upon their return by an amount of time equal to the number of days absent prior to and after the birth of the child.

8.10   *Supervisory and Other Salaried Positions*

A.   It is recognized that all supervisory employees are representatives of management and the assignment of their duties, promotions, demotions, and transfers is the responsibility of the COMPANY and cannot be determined on the basis of seniority.

B.   Any supervisory employees, including quality supervisors, promoted from any hourly job shall maintain seniority as follows:

1.   Hourly employees promoted to supervisory positions prior to January 1, 1980, shall continue to accumulate seniority while holding a supervisory position.

2.   Hourly employees promoted to a supervisory position after January 1, 1980, shall accumulate seniority until such a time that he/she holds a supervisory position continuously for six months. After six continuous months, his/her seniority in the bargaining unit shall be frozen as of the date of promotion. If later reduced to an hourly job, he/she shall be assigned to the skill class to which his/her accumulated or frozen seniority entitles him/her in the department that he/she left to become a supervisor. Supervisors who are reduced to hourly jobs will be required to certify at a given skill level within their classifications not later than 18 months following reduction. No supervisor as herein defined shall have posting privileges until 30 days following his/her reassignment to an hourly production job. In return for protecting an employee's seniority while he/she is in a supervisory position as well as allowing him/her the right to claim a job in the bargaining unit if reduced from his/her supervisory position, supervisors who are reduced to hourly jobs shall become members of the UNION within 30 days.

C.   Supervisory and other salaried employees will not perform the work of hourly production employees except in cases of emergency.

ARTICLE 9.   GRIEVANCE PROCEDURE AND NO-STRIKE AGREEMENT

9.01   *Departmental Representatives*   The UNION may designate representatives for each section on each shift and in each department for the purpose of handling grievances that may arise in that department. The UNION will inform the production personnel office in writing as to the names of the authorized representatives. Should differences arise as to the intent and application of the provisions of this Agreement, there shall be no strike, lockout, slowdown, or work stoppage of any kind, and the controversy shall be settled in accordance with the following grievance procedures:

9.02   *Grievances*

Step 1.   The employee and the departmental steward, if the employee desires, shall take the matter up with his/her supervisor. If no settlement is reached in Step 1 within two working days, the grievance shall be reduced to writing on the form provided for that purpose.

Step 2.   The written grievance shall be presented to the supervisor or the general supervisor and a copy sent to the production personnel office. Within two working days after receipt of the grievance, the general supervisor shall hold a meeting, unless mutually agreed otherwise, with the supervisor, the employee, and the departmental steward and the chief steward.

Step 3.   If no settlement is reached in Step 2, the written grievance shall be presented to the departmental superintendent, who shall hold a meeting within five working days of the original receipt of the grievance in Step 2 unless mutually agreed otherwise. Those in attendance shall normally be the departmental superintendent, the general supervisor, the supervisor, the employee, the chief steward, departmental steward, a member of the production personnel department, the president of the UNION or his/her representative, and the divisional committee person.

Step 4.   If no settlement is reached in Step 3, the UNION COMMITTEE and a national representative of the UNION shall meet with the MANAGEMENT COMMITTEE for the purpose of settling the matter.

Step 5.   If no settlement is reached in Step 4, the matter shall be referred to an arbitrator. A representative of the UNION shall meet within five working days with a representative of the COMPANY for the purpose of selecting an arbitrator. If an arbitrator cannot be agreed upon within five working days after Step 4, a request for a list of arbitrators shall be sent to the Federal Mediation and Conciliation Service. Upon obtaining the list, an arbitrator shall be selected within five working days. Prior to arbitration, a representative of the UNION shall meet with a representative of the COMPANY to reduce to writing wherever possible the actual issue to be arbitrated. The decision of the arbitrator shall be final and binding on all parties. The salary, if any, of the arbitrator and any necessary expense incident to the arbitration shall be paid jointly by the COMPANY and the UNION.

9.03   In order to assure the prompt settlement of grievances as close to their source as possible, it is mutually agreed that the above steps will be followed strictly in the order listed and no step shall be used until all previous steps have been exhausted. A settlement reached between the COMPANY and the UNION in any step of this procedure shall terminate the grievance and shall be final and binding on both parties.

9.04	The arbitrator shall not have authority to modify, change, or amend any of the terms or provisions of the Agreement or to add to or delete from the Agreement.
9.05	The UNION will not cause or permit its members to cause or take part in any sit-down, stay-in, or slowdown in any plant of the COMPANY or any curtailment of work or restriction of production or interference with the operations of the COMPANY.
9.06	The UNION will not cause or permit its members to cause or take part in any strike of any of the COMPANY's operations, except where the strike has been fully authorized as provided in the constitution of the international union.

ARTICLE 10. VACATIONS

10.01	The vacation year shall be from April 1 to and including March 31. Wherever possible, however, vacations shall be taken before December 31 of any one year. Vacations for any two years shall not be taken consecutively. Unused vacations may be accumulated across years; however, the time accrued will be discounted each year by the average percent increase of the bargaining unit hour wage. For example, if 20 days are accumulated and unused and there is a 5 percent increase, the accumulated days will be reduced to 19.
10.02	***One Week's Vacation*** One week's vacation with pay (see Section 10.07) will be granted to an employee who has accumulated 12 months or more of service credit prior to September 30 of the vacation year, provided he/she has accumulated a minimum of 6 months' service credit during the 12-month period immediately preceding April 1 of the vacation year and is actively working on or after April 1 of the vacation year.
10.03	***Two Weeks' Vacation*** Two weeks' vacation with pay (see Section 10.07) will be granted to an employee who has accumulated 36 months or more of service credit by December 31 of the vacation year, provided he/she has accumulated a minimum of 6 months' service credit during the 12-month period immediately preceding April 1 of the vacation year and is actively working on or after April 1 of the vacation year.
10.04	***Three Weeks' Vacation*** Three weeks' vacation with pay (see Section 10.07) will be granted to an employee who will complete 120 months or more of service credit by December 31 of the vacation year, provided he/she has accumulated a minimum of 6 months' service credit during the 12-month period immediately preceding April 1 of the vacation year and is actively working on or after April 1 of the vacation year.
10.05	***Four Weeks' Vacation*** Four weeks' vacation with pay (see Section 10.07) will be granted to an employee who will complete 180 months or more of service credit by December 31 of the vacation year, provided

he/she has accumulated a minimum of 6 months' service credit during the 12-month period immediately preceding April 1 of the vacation year and is actively working on or after April 1 of the vacation year.

10.06   ***Five Weeks' Vacation***   Five weeks' vacation with pay (see Section 10.07) will be granted to an employee who will complete 300 months or more of service credit by December 31 of the vacation year, provided he/she has accumulated a minimum of 6 months' service credit during the 12-month period immediately preceding April 1 of the vacation year and is actively working on or after April 1 of the vacation year.

10.07   One week of vacation pay shall consist of 40 hours' pay at the employee's regular straight-time hourly base rate plus the average incentive percentage of the eight weeks prior to April 1 of the department in which he/she is working at the time the vacation is taken.

10.08   If a holiday recognized within this Agreement falls within an employee's vacation period, he/she shall be granted an extra day of vacation, provided the employee is eligible for holiday pay on that holiday.

10.09   Any employee who is discharged for proper cause forfeits his/her accrued unused vacation earned during the current vacation year.

10.10   Vacations shall be granted at such times of the year as the COMPANY finds most suitable, considering both the wishes of the employee according to plant seniority and the requirements of plant operations.

10.11   Employees who are laid off will be granted the vacation to which they are otherwise ineligible if they have worked a minimum of 1,600 straight-time hours since the previous April 1.

ARTICLE 11. SICK LEAVE

11.01   ***Employees with One- to Five-Year Service Credit***   Employees who have accumulated 12 months but less than 60 months of service credit shall be entitled to a maximum of four working days' sick leave (32 hours straight-time pay at the employee's regular hourly base rate) in any one year calculated from April 1 to March 31, inclusive. Such benefits, not to exceed eight hours in any day, will apply only to time lost from scheduled work for reasons of personal illness or injury except that no benefits will be paid for the first two scheduled working days of any period of such absence.

11.02   ***Employees with Five or More Years of Service Credit***

A.   ***Eligibility***   A five-year employee who has accumulated 60 months of service credit will receive the difference between sickness and accident insurance or workers' compensation benefits for which he/she is eligible and his/her regular hourly base rate for time lost due to unavoidable absence as defined in Section 11.02E, which occurs during the first 40 hours he/she is scheduled to work in any week, not to exceed 8 hours in any one day, and subject to Section 11.02D.

B. ***Amount of Benefits***   The benefits made available each year shall be 80 hours. The year starts April 1. Combined benefits on any day of qualified absence shall total the amount equal to the number of qualified hours multiplied by the employee's base rate. In no instance shall this payment total more than base rate earnings of 8 hours per scheduled workday nor more than base rate earnings of 40 hours per scheduled workweek. In other words, the COMPANY shall supplement with sick leave payments any compensation or insurance payments from a company-financed private or government plan with an amount of money sufficient to make the combined total payment equal to 8 hours of base rate pay per day of qualified absence or 40 hours per week of qualified absence.

1. If the employee qualifies for compensation from a company-financed private or governmental plan, his/her available sick leave benefits will be charged 19.9 hours per 40-hour week or 49.8 percent of the eligible working hours absent for part weeks. If the employee does not qualify for compensation from a company-financed private or governmental plan, his/her available sick leave benefits will be charged with 100 percent of the eligible working hours absent.

C. ***Accumulation***   Sick leave benefits unused in any year of the plan may be accumulated for possible use in the next two years. When fourth-year benefits become available, the unused benefits from the first year automatically cancel and so on for each succeeding year. Order of sick leave usage is, first, the current year's benefits and, second, the oldest year's benefits. Employees out sick before April 1 whose absence due to that illness extends through April 1 will first use those benefits that were available at the commencement of the absence.

D. ***Waiting Period***   There shall be no waiting period for the first five days (40 hours) of sick leave usage in a benefit year. However, no benefits shall be payable for the first normally scheduled working day in any period of absence commencing thereafter.

E. Unavoidable absence is defined as follows:
1. Unavoidable absence caused by sickness or injury.
2. Emergencies in the immediate family.

F. Immediate family shall consist of the following with no exceptions:

Spouse	Son	Sister
Mother	Daughter	Mother-in-law
Father	Brother	Father-in-law

In addition, the death of the employee's grandfather or grandmother will be recognized as an emergency in the immediate family to the extent of allowing one day's benefit, provided it is necessary that he/she be absent.

11.03   A.   A 15-year hourly employee will receive straight-time pay at his/her regular hourly base rate for time lost due to hospitalization in a recognized hospital or convalescence thereafter that occurs during the first 40 hours he/she is scheduled to work in any week not to exceed 8 hours in any day. The total amount of such allowance will not exceed 80 hours in any one year, calculated from year to year. Benefits provided in this paragraph will not apply to days of unavoidable absence for which benefits are paid under the provisions of Section 11.02

             B.   A 25-year hourly employee will receive straight-time pay at his/her regular hourly base rate for time lost due to hospitalization in a recognized hospital or convalescence thereafter that occurs during the first 40 hours he/she is scheduled to work in any week not to exceed 8 hours in any day. The total amount of such allowance will not exceed 160 hours (an additional 80 hours to [A] above) in any one year, calculated from year to year. Benefits provided in this paragraph will not apply to days of unavoidable absence for which benefits are paid under the provisions of Section 11.02 above.

11.04   In order to obtain these benefits, the employee shall, if required, furnish his/her supervisor satisfactory reason for absence.

11.05   The COMPANY and the UNION agree to cooperate in preventing and correcting abuses of these benefits.

ARTICLE 12.   GENERAL

12.01   *Bulletin Boards*   The COMPANY shall provide bulletin boards that may be used by the UNION for posting notices approved by the industrial relations manager or someone designated by him/her and restricted to:

             A.   Notices of UNION recreational and social affairs.
             B.   Notices of UNION elections.
             C.   Notices of UNION appointments and results of UNION elections.
             D.   Notices of UNION meetings.
             E.   And other notices mutually agreed to.

12.02   *Relief Periods*

             A.   Relief periods of 25 minutes for every eight-hour work period will be on COMPANY time at such times in each department as will be most beneficial to the employees and the COMPANY. A lunch period on COMPANY time and premises may be substituted for relief period, provided the total time allowed for lunch and relief period in an eight-hour work period does not exceed 25 minutes.

             B.   Employees leaving the COMPANY premises for lunch during their shifts must clock out during the time they are away.

             C.   The relief and lunch periods in each department will be determined by the department supervisors and the UNION stewards, considering both the wishes of the employees and the requirements of efficient departmental operations.

12.03   All benefits now in effect and not specifically mentioned in this Agreement affecting all hourly paid employees of the COMPANY shall not be terminated for the duration of this Agreement.

12.04   ***Sickness and Accident***   The COMPANY agrees to maintain its current sickness and accident insurance plans, as amended, effective December 1, 1985. Benefits begin one month after the sickness and accident initially occurred and continue for six months. Benefits will be equal to 60 percent of the employee's straight-time wage at the time of the sickness or accident.

12.05   ***Long-Term Disability Plan***   Subject to the provisions and qualifications of the long-term disability (LTD) plan, there will be available monthly income benefits commencing after 26 weeks of continuous disability and continuing until recovery or death but not beyond the normal retirement date. The monthly amount will be $25 per $1,000 on the first $10,000 of group life insurance.

12.06   ***Group Life Insurance***

    A.   The COMPANY will pay for the first $1,000 of group life insurance available to employees. Employees will have the option of purchasing an additional amount of insurance in accordance with their earnings class schedule.

    B.   The present permanent and total disability benefit is replaced by a disability waiver-of-premium provision under which coverage will be continued during periods of total disability while LTD payments are being made, but reduced each month by the amount of the LTD benefit. Reductions will cease when the amount of insurance in force is equal to the greater of (a) 25 percent of the original amount or (b) the employee's postretirement life amount calculated as of the date of commencement of LTD payments. Coverage will be reduced to the latter amount at the earlier of (a) normal retirement age or (b) commencement of any employee retirement income.

12.07   ***Retirement Income Plan***

    A.   The COMPANY will contribute an amount equal to 5 percent of each employee's straight-time earnings to the retirement trust fund administered by Commonwealth National Bank, Central City, Indiana.

    B.   The COMPANY will provide for 100 percent vesting in pension benefits after five (5) years' service.

    C.   Contributions and any investment income earned on them that are forfeited by employees who terminate prior to the vesting of pension benefits will be returned to the COMPANY.

12.08   For the first $2,500 in medical costs incurred by an employee and his/her family each calendar year, the COMPANY will pay 80 percent of the cost when provided by a Preferred Provider Organization (PPO) approved by the employer. If the employee chooses care from another provider, the employer will pay 80 percent of the cost of the treatment as determined by the PPO fee schedule. For coverage beyond the first $2,500, the COMPANY will contract with Indiana Blue Cross–Blue Shield to provide hospitalization and medical insurance for all employees and their family members residing at home (except children over 21). The COMPANY will pay all premiums necessary to provide full coverage of necessary and approved surgical, medical, and hospital care under Blue Cross–Blue Shield fee schedules when performed by a participating doctor in a participating hospital according to procedures approved by Indiana Blue Cross–Blue Shield.

12.09   Departmental agreements between COMPANY and UNION representatives shall not supersede provisions contained in this Agreement should controversies arise. In no case, however, shall any retroactive adjustment be made if and when such a departmental agreement is canceled. Wherever possible, the UNION shall receive a copy of the agreement.

12.10   ***Optical Care Insurance***   The company will self-insure optical care for bargaining unit members. The company will provide for one eye exam per year for each employee and his/her dependents as provided by the company's PPO. Examinations conducted by other providers will be reimbursed up to $15 per employee and/or dependent per year. The company will pay for one pair of standard prescription glasses every other year for employees and/or their dependents whose vision prescriptions are measured by the employer's PPO, and eyeware is dispensed by the employer's PPO. If eyeware is not dispensed by the PPO, the employer will reimburse up to $100 per employee and/or dependent every two years. In odd-numbered years of this agreement, employees with birth years ending in odd numbers will be eligible for new prescription eyeware, in even-numbered years, employees with even-numbered birth years will be eligible. Employees must submit claims not later than three months after expenses are incurred to Employee Benefits Coordinators, Inc., the COMPANY'S payment coordinator. Forms for requesting payment are available in the production personnel office.

12.11   ***Safety***

A.   The COMPANY will make reasonable provisions for the safety and health of the employees of the plant during the hours of their employment. Such protective devices and other safety equipment as the COMPANY may deem necessary to protect properly employees from injury shall be provided by the COMPANY without cost to the employees. The supervisor in each department will arrange for this equipment.

B.   Gloves and uniforms required on such jobs and in such departments as the COMPANY may deem necessary shall be furnished and maintained by the COMPANY.

C. The UNION agrees in order to protect the employees from injury and to protect the facilities of the plant that it will cooperate to the fullest extent in seeing that the rules and regulations are followed and that it will lend its wholehearted support to the safety program of the COMPANY.

D. Rotating UNION departmental representatives chosen by the UNION will participate in periodic safety inspections conducted by departmental supervision and safety staff.

E. The COMPANY agrees that it will give full consideration to all suggestions from its employees or their representatives in matters pertaining to safety and health, including proper heating and ventilation, and if these suggestions are determined to be sound, steps will be taken to put them into effect.

F. It shall be considered a regular part of each employee's regular work to attend such safety meetings as may be scheduled by the COMPANY. Hours spent at safety meetings will be compensated for as hours worked.

G. It is understood that the COMPANY shall not be required to provide work for employees suffering from compensable or other injuries; the COMPANY, however, will offer regular work that may be available to such employees, provided that they can perform all duties of the job.

12.12   Other than the recall provisions of the Agreement and the privileges accorded an employee under the COMPANY group insurance plans, employees on layoff shall not be entitled to the benefits of this Agreement.

12.13   *Supplementary Unemployment Benefit Plan*

A. *Objective*   To provide a greater measure of income protection during periods of unemployment for all eligible employees by supplementing state unemployment benefit payments.

B. *Principles*

1. To provide income protection for permanent full-time employees as mentioned in (A) above.

2. To preserve the necessary differential between amount received while unemployed and straight-time weekly earnings while working so as to provide an incentive for the unemployed to become employed. This differential is defined to be 65 percent of straight-time weekly earning less any normal deductions that are not of the savings variety.

3. The COMPANY will pay the difference between 65 percent of straight-time weekly earnings less normal deductions and the state unemployment benefit for which the employee qualifies. In the event the state benefit check is reduced because of ineligibility, the SUB payment will be reduced in the same proportion. The straight-time weekly earnings will be based on the week of layoff. The number of weeks an employee qualifies for would depend on length of service.

    C.   ***Eligibility***
1. Permanent, full-time employees covered under this Agreement.
2. Five years or more of service.
3. On layoff from the COMPANY per seniority provisions in the UNION-MANAGEMENT Agreement and with the following conditions present:
   - *a.* Be able and available for work.
   - *b.* Maintain an active and continuing search for work.
   - *c.* Register and maintain constant contact with the State Employment Office.
   - *d.* Accept referral by the COMPANY to other employers in the area and accept resulting employment offers if deemed suitable under terms of the existing state system.
   - *e.* Layoff not due to a strike, slowdown, work stoppage, or concerted action.
   - *f.* Layoff not due to a labor dispute with the COMPANY or labor picketing conducted on the COMPANY premises which interferes with the COMPANY's operations.
   - *g.* Layoff not due to voluntary quit.
   - *h.* Layoff not due to disciplinary suspensions or discharges.
   - *i.* Layoff not due to leaves of absence.
4. Weeks of eligibility.
   0–5 years' service credit—0 weeks of SUB.
   5–26 years' service credit—1 week of SUB for each full year of service credit.
   26 or more years' service credit—26 weeks of SUB.

    D.   ***Reinstatement***   When an employee has received any benefits for which he/she is eligible under this plan per the schedule, he/she will have his/her full benefits reinstated after six months of continuous service.

    E.   ***To Obtain Benefits***   To obtain benefits, the employee must initiate the claim by preparing the necessary forms and presenting his/her state unemployment check weekly to the personnel office for verification and processing of claim.

12.14   The COMPANY will contract with Delta Dental Plan to provide full coverage for preventive dental care and basic restorations up to a limit of $200 annually. The plan will also provide for a lifetime orthodontic benefit of $2,000 for each employee and/or his/her spouse and children when a Delta Dental Plan dentist determines that orthodontia is necessary to prevent higher costs of future dental treatments if left uncorrected.

12.15   In the event any section or any article of this Agreement shall be found to be illegal or inoperable by any government authority of competent jurisdiction, the balance of the Agreement shall remain in full force and effect.

12.16   *Nondiscrimination Agreement*

A. The COMPANY and the UNION agree that the provisions of this agreement shall apply to all employees covered by the Agreement without discrimination, and, in carrying out their respective obligations, it will not discriminate against any employee on account of race, color, national origin, age, sex, or religion.

B. In an effort to make the grievance procedure a more effective instrument for the handling of any claims of discrimination, special effort shall be made by the representatives of each party to raise such claims where they exist and at as early a stage in the grievance procedure as possible. If not earlier, a claim of discrimination shall be stated at least in the third-step proceedings. The grievance and arbitration procedure shall be the exclusive contractual procedure for remedying discrimination claims.

ARTICLE 13. RENEWAL

13.01   This Agreement shall become effective as of March 1, 1996, and shall continue in full force and effect until 11:59 P.M., February 28, 1999, and thereafter from year to year unless written notice to modify, amend, or terminate this Agreement is served by either party 60 days prior to the expiration of this Agreement, stating in full all changes desired.

13.02   After receipt of such notice by either party, both parties shall meet for the purpose of negotiating a new agreement within 30 days from the date of service of said notice, unless the time is extended by mutual agreement.

APPENDIX   CLASSIFIED BASE RATES

Job Title	Wage Rate	Job Title	Wage Rate
Assembler, level 1	11.00	Skilled maintenance, level 1	11.50
Assembler, level 2	12.50	Skilled maintenance, level 2	13.00
Assembler, level 3	14.00	Skilled maintenance, level 3	14.50
Skilled production, level 1	12.00	Material handling & prod. supp.	11.50
Skilled production, level 2	13.50	Maintenance	9.50
Skilled production, level 3	15.00		

12

IMPASSES AND

THEIR RESOLUTION

*N*egotiations don't always yield an agreement. If you're buying a car and the dealer won't accept your highest offer, there is no sale. The same happens in collective bargaining when employers and unions can't agree on terms of new contracts. The failure to reach agreement is called an impasse. Unlike a car purchase, unions aren't free to find new employers to deal with, and employers must still be willing to negotiate with their employees' representatives.

Most negotiations do not result in an impasse. The parties usually find a common ground for settlement without strikes or third-party interventions. Data from 1997 find only about 0.01 percent of time available for work was lost to strikes.[1]

This chapter examines the causes of impasses, tactics used to resolve them, and interventions of third parties. The focus in this chapter is on the private sector. Public-sector impasse resolution procedures, which are generally more complex and often applicable only to certain occupational classifications, are covered in Chapter 16.

As you study this chapter, consider the following issues:

1. What actions can labor and management legally take after an impasse is reached?
2. What is involved in third-party interventions?
3. What tactics do employers and unions use when they reach an impasse?
4. What are the effects of strikes on employers?

---

[1] http://146.142.4.24/cgi-bin/dsrv, Bureau of Labor Statistics, U.S. Department of Labor.

IMPASSE DEFINITION

A bargaining **impasse** occurs when the parties are unable to move further toward settlement. The impasse may result from nonoverlapping settlement ranges—the least the union is willing to take is more than the most the employer is willing to offer—or from the inability or unwillingness of the parties to communicate enough information about possible settlements for an agreement to be reached. The first type is more difficult to overcome because it requires at least one party to adjust its settlement range to reach a solution. The second type may be helped by mediators who facilitate communication and keep the parties working toward a settlement.

THIRD-PARTY INVOLVEMENT

Major types of third-party interventions include mediation, fact-finding, and arbitration. Each becomes progressively more constraining on the freedom of the parties, but in most private-sector negotiations not covered by the Railway Labor Act (except for health care organizations under federal legislation), the parties must agree voluntarily before any third-party involvement can occur. The only major exception involves national emergency disputes under the Taft-Hartley Act, in which outside fact-finding is required. However, Taft-Hartley procedures have not been imposed for more than a decade.

Because employees in most public-sector jobs are legally precluded from striking, third parties are used more frequently there. General types of third-party interventions used across both public and private sectors are covered here, and their application in public jurisdictions is explained in greater detail in Chapter 16.

MEDIATION

In **mediation,** a neutral third party tries to assist principals to reach an agreement. Procedures are tailored to the situation and aimed at opening communications and identifying settlement cues the parties may have missed.

While some parties use mediation before an impasse, the mediator most often deals with parties who are unable to agree on their own, are at impasse, and have broken off negotiations. The mediator may have trouble not only in getting a settlement but also in resuming bargaining. To show strength, both sides may refuse to propose a bargaining session; if one appeared willing to reopen bargaining, the other might interpret it as weakness.

The mediator must ultimately get the parties face-to-face to reach a settlement, but the mediator and a party may meet several times just to assess possibilities of movement. Changing the location of a meeting to the mediator's office may increase the mediator's strength in the process. Mediation requires parties to continue to communicate and negotiate, but not at an intensity leading to hardening positions.[2]

Bargainers are rewarded by their constituencies for getting the best possible deal. To an extent, reaching an impasse indicates they have represented their positions vigorously. Mediators are rewarded for gaining agreements. Their concern is not what either party achieves; thus, they are unlikely to influence the direction of the outcome.[3]

The mediator has to keep communications open and also move the parties toward settlement, if possible. Mediators apparently use one of two approaches. In the public sector, with less experienced bargainers, mediators may try to create an acceptable package by obtaining the facts in dispute and the parties' priorities in a settlement. With this information, they attempt to "make a deal" both parties can accept. In private-sector mediation involving federal mediators, settlements are "orchestrated" through information exchanges enabling the parties to build a settlement they consider acceptable. Mediators let parties establish their own priorities and help them prepare negotiating proposals.[4]

To assess settlement possibilities, the mediator may try out hypothetical settlements to see the parties' reactions. The relative rigidity of a party's position must be determined so the mediator knows whether the party is willing to compromise on given issues. As a strike deadline approaches, the mediator communicates assessments of the likelihood of a strike, possible settlement packages available, and the costs of striking compared with settling on the current proposal.

Mediator Behavior and Outcomes

Mediators operate in a crisis atmosphere requiring a special mix of experience, talents, and behaviors. Mediators may be either "deal makers" or "orchestrators." The former approach is used more when mediators believe their clients are inexperienced in negotiations. Deal makers are more likely than orchestrators to run into problems in consummating their deals and getting agreements.[5]

Mediation involves establishing a working relationship between the parties, improving the negotiating climate by facilitating communications and using single-party caucuses, addressing issues, and applying pressure for settlement.[6] Mediation facilitates settlement by (1) reducing hostility by focusing on

---

[2] W. E. Simkin, *Mediation and the Dynamics of Collective Bargaining* (Washington, DC: Bureau of National Affairs, 1971).

[3] M. H. Bazerman, M. A. Neale, K. L. Valley, E. J. Zajac, and Y. M. Kim, "The Effect of Agents and Mediators on Negotiation Outcomes," *Organizational Behavior and Human Decision Processes* 53 (1992), pp. 55–73.

[4] D. M. Kolb, "Strategy and the Tactics of Mediation," *Human Relations* 36 (1983), pp. 247–68.

[5] D. M. Kolb, "Roles Mediators Play: Contrasts and Comparisons in State and Federal Mediation Practice," *Industrial Relations* 20 (1981), pp. 1–17.

[6] K. Kressel and D. G. Pruitt, "Conclusion: A Research Perspective on the Mediation of Social Conflict," in K. Kressel, D. G. Pruitt, and associates, eds., *Mediation Research* (San Francisco: Jossey-Bass, 1989), pp. 394–435.

bargaining objectives, (2) enhancing understanding of the opponent's position, (3) adjusting negotiating formats through chairing, subcommittee creation, and so forth, (4) assuming the risk in exploring new solutions, (5) affecting perceptions regarding the costs of conflict, and (6) contributing to face-saving facilitating concessions.[7] Table 12–1 shows a set of mediator behaviors and how they can be grouped into clusters.

Other variables influencing mediator behavior and bargaining outcomes involve dispute intensity and mediator activities. Intense disputes reduce the likelihood of mediated settlements, particularly for impasses where the employer is unable to pay the increase demanded. Mediators achieve settlements more frequently if they act aggressively when negotiations have broken down.[8] Impasses characterized by conditions such as a new bargaining relationship, dislike between key negotiators, conflict within management or union teams, union strength, pattern bargaining, and an inability to pay are more often resolved by intensive mediation. Intense mediation includes a willingness to get true feelings before the parties and discuss real costs of the proposed packages. Low-intensity mediation is more successful when an impasse also is low intensity.[9]

A study examining reactions of managements and unions to mediated settlements found management believed mediator expertise and impartiality increased the likelihood of settlements, while the union attributed settlements to mediator neutrality and persistence. Mediation strategies most often cited by management as facilitating settlement included discussions of costs of disagreement, suggestions of face-saving proposals, and gains in the parties' trust. Unions said changing expectations and devising an improved negotiating framework hastened settlement.[10]

Although mediation is an art, behaviors of mediators and levels or types of disputes can be classified; thus, an appropriate style of mediation can be selected to match the intensity of the dispute to exert the greatest likelihood of a settlement. Alternatively, mediators whose styles best fit the impasse could be assigned to the case.[11]

Mediator Backgrounds and Training

The Federal Mediation and Conciliation Service (FMCS) uses no specific criteria for selecting mediator trainees. This does not mean they are not carefully selected

---

[7] A. Karim and R. Pegnetter, "Mediator Strategies and Qualities and Mediation Effectiveness," *Industrial Relations* 22 (1983), pp. 105–14.

[8] T. A. Kochan and T. Jick, "A Theory of the Public Sector Mediation Process," *Journal of Conflict Resolution* 22 (1978), pp. 209–41.

[9] P. F. Gerhart and J. E. Drotning, "Dispute Settlement and the Intensity of Mediation," *Industrial Relations,* 19 (1980), pp. 352–59.

[10] Ibid.

[11] See J. Webb, "Behavioral Studies of Third-Party Intervention," in G. M. Stephenson and C. J. Brotherton, eds., *Industrial Relations: A Social Psychological Approach* (New York: John Wiley & Sons, 1979), pp. 309–31; and J. A. Wall, Jr., "Mediation: A Categorical Analysis and a Proposed Framework for Future Research," *Academy of Management Proceedings* 40 (1980), pp. 298–302.

TABLE 12–1

Mediator Tactics and Behaviors

Reflexive	Try to gain their trust/confidence
	Develop rapport with them
	Attempt to speak their language
	Avoid taking sides in important issues
	Express pleasure at their progress
	Use humor to lighten the atmosphere
	Let them blow off steam in front of me
	Control their expression of hostility
Facilitating	*Face Saving*
	Suggest proposals to help avoid appearance of defeat
	Help save face
	Take responsibility for their concessions
	Constituency
	Suggest review of needs with constituency
	Help them deal with problems with constituents
	Bridging
	Clarify the needs of the other party
	Argue their case to the other party
	Assure them that the other party is being honest
Maneuvering	*Make Suggestions*
	Suggest a particular settlement
	Make substantive suggestions for compromise
	Suggest trade-offs among the issues
	Discuss other settlements
	Pressing
	Express displeasure at their progress
	Press them hard to make compromise
	Point out costs of disagreement
	Tell them the next impasse step is no better
	Try to change their expectations
	Tell them their position is unrealistic
	Agenda Implementation
	Keep negotiations focused on the issues
	Control the timing or pace of negotiations
	Keep the parties at the table and negotiating
	Use late hours, long mediation
	Call for frequent caucuses
Contextual	*Agenda Structuring*
	Attempt to simplify agenda
	Have them prioritize the issues
	Attempt to settle simple issues first
	Teach them impasse procedures

SOURCES: P. J. D. Carnevale and R. Pegnetter, "The Selection of Mediator Tactics in Public Sector Disputes: A Contingency Analysis," *Journal of Social Issues* 41, no. 2 (1985), p. 73; and M. E. McLaughlin, P. Carnevale, and R. G. Lim, "Professional Mediators' Judgments of Mediation Tactics: Multidimensional Scaling and Cluster Analysis," *Journal of Applied Psychology* 76 (1991), p. 471.

EXHIBIT 12–1

Cyrus Ching and the 1949 Steel Negotiations

In 1949, when the United Steelworkers and the large steel producers were approaching the showdown over employer-subsidized pensions, Ching felt the only way to avert a strike was through appointment of a presidential fact-finding board. Truman, whose early experiences with labor in the White House made him reluctant ever to get back into the middle of a major industrial confrontation, was cool to the idea . . . Philip Murray assured Ching that his union would keep its members at work if the companies agreed to appear before the fact-finders. Ching anticipated no difficulty on that score, because any recommendations made by the panel would not be binding.

The board of directors of U.S. Steel proved wary, however, and the rest of the industry held off, awaiting "Big Steel's" response. The first word from the board was a telegram to Truman raising questions about the function of the fact-finders. Ching regarded all of these inquiries as legitimate, and he had a telegram designed to overcome U.S. Steel's apprehensions sent over the president's signature. The company directors came back with a second telegram to Truman, raising further questions, and Ching was called to the White House for a decision on what the government's next step should be. Ching advised Truman not to answer the wire, but instead to empower the FMCS chief to call Benjamin Fairless, the company's chairman, and tell him he was speaking in the president's name. Given a green light by Truman to proceed, Ching was blunt in his conversation with Fairless the next day.

"My conversation is going to be very short this morning," Ching said. "Number one, I want to tell you that you can't bargain with the president of the United States and, number two, will you send an answer, yes or no, this morning. Either you will or you won't, no more exchanging of telegrams." Fairless gasped. "You're quite plainspoken this morning," he said. "Yes, I intended to be. And that is the message I'm giving you from the president in answer to your telegram." That conversation ended the holdout, and the fact-finding panel began its vain effort to head off a strike.

SOURCE: A. H. Raskin, "Cyrus S. Ching: Pioneer in Industrial Peacemaking," *Monthly Labor Review* 112, no. 8 (1989), pp. 33–34.

---

or are untrained. Persons with experience in negotiating contracts are preferred, regardless of whether they bargained for managements or unions. This mixture of backgrounds and the independence of the FMCS was ensured by its first director, Cyrus Ching.[12] Exhibit 12–1 displays the toughness and impartiality he established for the FMCS.

Almost all FMCS mediators have significant experience as management or union negotiators, or as neutrals in labor relations disputes. FMCS mediators are most often over 45 years of age and many have long experience in the service.[13] A newly appointed mediator generally begins with a two-week training program in

---

[12] A. H. Raskin, "Cyrus S. Ching: Pioneer in Industrial Peacemaking," *Monthly Labor Review* 112, no. 8 (1989), pp. 22–35.

[13] Simkin, *Mediation,* pp. 57–69. More recent work suggests the pattern hasn't changed. See Kolb, "Roles Mediators Play."

Washington and then is sent to a regional office to learn procedures and to work with experienced mediators. By the end of the first year, a first case has probably been assigned. Summaries and specialized training supplement experience as the mediator is assigned to increasingly complex cases.

Mediator Activity

Under Taft-Hartley, parties are required to notify the FMCS 30 days before the expiration of a contract when negotiations are under way and an agreement has not been reached. Table 12–2 shows notification and caseloads for the FMCS during fiscal years 1993–97. The figures indicate the FMCS is involved in just over 33 percent of cases in which 30-day notifications had been received.

Most cases do not require the intervention of mediators. Data from the FMCS Annual Report series show mediation is used more often when first contracts are being negotiated and the term of the contract is three years. Thus, negotiator inexperience and/or the permanency of the agreement appear to inhibit agreement without outside assistance.

Mediation is one third-party intervention method. It is an active process of keeping the parties together using a neutral approach. Mediation allows the parties to settle on their own terms when they have been unable to do so on their own.

FACT-FINDING

Fact-finding has a long history in U.S. labor relations. Fact-finding doesn't involve facts, only values associated with the possible positions taken on outcomes in the dispute. In the 19th century, it was used to fix blame on one party rather than to find the underlying causes of the dispute.[14] In present-day fact-finding, a neutral party studies the issues in dispute and renders a public recommendation for settlement.[15]

Fact-finding uses neutrals who act on behalf of the public.[16] If the fact-finders' published findings are not adopted in a settlement, private-sector parties are free to return to bargaining as they see fit.

In the United States, fact-finding has been used primarily to meet Taft-Hartley emergency dispute requirements (in which it has been relatively ineffectual) and in railroad and airline disputes where presidential emergency boards have been created under the Railway Labor Act.[17] While Congress continues to legislate

---

[14] T. J. McDermott, "Fact-Finding Boards in Labor Disputes," *Labor Law Journal* 11 (1960), pp. 285–304.

[15] C. M. Rehmus, "The Fact-Finder's Role," *The Proceedings of the Inaugural Convention of the Society of Professionals in Dispute Resolution* (1973), pp. 34–44.

[16] J. T. McKelvey, "Fact-Finding in Public Employment Disputes: Promise or Illusion?" *Industrial and Labor Relations Review* 22 (1969), p. 529.

[17] Rehmus, "Fact-Finder's Role," pp. 35–36.

TABLE 12–2

Analysis of Dispute Notifications (Number of Dispute Notifications Received by FMCS for Years 1993 through 1997)

Receipt of Notifications	1993	1994	1995	1996	1997
30-day notices required by the LMRA	66,137	64,806	55,035	57,989	58,585
Union and employer requests	1,784	1,656	1,649	1,702	2,122
NLRB and FLRA certifications	1,489	1,507	1,566	1,402	1,530
Public Sector Board Requests	329	308	218	257	273
Total notifications and requests	69,741	68,278	58,470	61,350	62,510
Cases requiring mediation	24,536	22,184	20,199	19,535	20,844
Percent of cases requiring mediation	35.2	32.5	34.5	31.8	33.3

SOURCE: http://www.fmcs.gov/annuals/97/dm.dtm

some railroad settlements, national emergency boards are less frequent and Taft-Hartley fact-finding has almost ceased occurring.[18]

Fact-Finding and the Issues

Private-sector fact-finders are not very successful on distributive bargaining issues. They make recommendations but do not personally facilitate bargaining. Neither party may accord legitimacy to an outside group in determining or recommending what either is entitled to.

On the other hand, presidential emergency board fact-finders appear to have had some success in integrative bargaining areas. In the rail industry, new technology raised job security issues for the union and survival issues for management. The parties can implement solutions proposed by neutrals without as much resistance from constituents. Thus, fact-finding boards facilitate integrative bargaining through the proposal of solutions and encourage intraorganizational bargaining by legitimizing positions the principal negotiators may be willing to raise but see as unacceptable to the memberships.

INTEREST ARBITRATION

Interest arbitration is an impasse resolution method that has seen considerable use in a variety of forms in the public sector. Arbitration differs substantially from mediation and fact-finding. While mediation assists the parties to reach their own settlement, arbitration hears the positions of both and decides on binding settlement terms. While fact-finding recommends a settlement, arbitration dictates it.

---

[18] C. M. Rehmus, "Emergency Strikes Revisited," *Industrial and Labor Relations Review* 43 (1990), pp. 175–90.

Two classes of arbitration are central to labor relations—rights and interest. **Interest arbitration** occurs where no agreement exists or a change is sought and where the parties have an interest in the outcome because the contract will specify future rights. **Rights arbitration** involves the interpretation of an existing agreement to determine which party is entitled to a certain outcome or to take a certain action.[19]

In the United States, interest arbitration was used by the National War Labor Board during World War II and has been imposed on railroads by Congress on a number of occasions since the 1960s. If interest arbitration is mandated, it eliminates the parties' need to settle on their own. Some believe the availability and use of interest arbitration has a "narcotic" effect. This controversy will be explored in greater detail in Chapter 16.

The government also may get involved in an informal manner without resorting to statutory processes. For example, in the Northwest Airlines–Air Line Pilots Association strike of 1998, Bruce Lindsey, counsel to the president, and Rodney Slater, secretary of transportation, joined Maggie Jacobson, chairwoman of the National Mediation Board, to arm-twist the parties into reaching an agreement (see Exhibit 12–2).

REVIEW OF THIRD-PARTY INVOLVEMENTS

Of the three methods of third-party involvements, only one—arbitration—guarantees an impasse resolution. However, interest arbitration has not been embraced by the private sector. Fact-finding also has a relatively checkered past. When used, it has been imposed on the parties, who are free to ignore its recommendations. Mediation is neutral in that it requires the parties to bargain their own terms. It has been relatively successful in keeping parties at the table, given the FMCS caseload and success rate reported earlier.

Sometimes parties at an impasse are not involved with mediation, fact-finding, or arbitration. Mediation and fact-finding don't always break impasses. Then strikes, lockouts, or other pressuring activities occur. Strikes pressure employers to settle on union terms. Lockouts or hiring replacements are attempts to get unions to settle on employer terms. Their use, effectiveness, and legality are examined next.

STRIKES

The four major types of strikes have one thing in common: a withholding of effort by employees. An **economic strike** occurs after a failure to agree on contract terms. It is called to pressure the employer to settle on the union's terms. The union believes the cost of the strike (both economic and political) will be less to it

---

[19] *Elgin, Joliet, & Eastern Railway Co. v. Burley,* 325 U.S. 71 (1945).

EXHIBIT 12–2

Clinton Administration Arm-Twisting

When the Northwest Airlines pilots strike ended Saturday and the gags were lifted on union officials, they spoke in respectful tones about the role White House deputy counsel Bruce Lindsey and other government officials played in ending the biggest walkout of pilots in aviation history.

"It helps when you've got the president's pager number," said Mark Innerbichler, one of 17 voting members on the Master Executive Council of the Northwest Air Line Pilots Association (ALPA).

Innerbichler and other union leaders were briefed Saturday on the government's "arm-twisting" campaign before they ratified the proposed four-year agreement, ending the 15-day strike by 6,200 Northwest pilots.

In coaxing the settlement, Lindsey overtly threatened ALPA and Northwest negotiators with White House intervention if they didn't each soften their positions and craft an agreement of their own, Innerbichler said.

At that point in the talks, neither side wanted a Presidential Emergency Board, which would have ordered the pilots back to work.

The company feared that the board would be stacked with arbitrators sympathetic to labor, and the union clung to its original worry that White House interference would set a dangerous precedent for labor groups throughout the airline industry.

"[Lindsey] looked at the clock, and he said, 'In one hour I'm going to pick up the phone. The executive order is already written because I wrote it myself before I left Washington,'" Innerbichler said.

He said Lindsey, working in tandem with National Mediation Board Chairwoman Maggie Jacobsen and federal mediator Jack Kane, backed up his words Thursday morning by packing his suitcases and threatening to leave. By about 1 p.m., ALPA and Northwest negotiators agreed on a proposed pact that would end the strike. Only then did Lindsey return to Washington. He never commented publicly about his role in the settlement and he avoided the press during his visit to the Twin Cities.

SOURCE: T. Kennedy, "Clinton Aide Lindsey Was Pivotal in Ending Strike, Both Sides Say," *Minneapolis Star Tribune,* September 14, 1998.

than to the employer, and benefits of the expected solution are greater than the strike's costs. Even though it is called an economic strike, the disputed issues do not always involve wages. An economic strike can occur over any mandatory bargaining issue. But if a union insists on going to impasse and strikes over a permissive issue, it commits an unfair labor practice (ULP).[20] An economic strike involves unique rules, which are explained later.

An **unfair labor practice strike** protests employer labor law violations. If an employer commits illegal acts, the employees' right to strike in protest and be reinstated at its end is absolutely protected by NLRB and court interpretations of the labor acts. A **wildcat strike** is an unauthorized work stoppage during the

---

[20] *Detroit Resilient Floor Decorators Union,* 136 NLRB 756 (1962).

contract. Employees may face disciplinary action if the strike breaches a no-strike clause. A **sympathy strike** occurs when one union strikes to support another union's strike. These occur where more than one union represents employees in a single establishment, or several plants have separate contracts. The union's right to support another union is guaranteed by the Norris-LaGuardia Act, even if its contract contains a no-strike clause and provides for arbitration of unresolved grievances,[21] unless it's clear that the no-strike clause is intended as well to prohibit sympathy strikes.[22]

If the company bargained in good faith to an impasse, an economic strike ensued, and both parties refused to move further, the gulf would be permanent. If employees continue the strike, new employees would have to be hired for the employer to remain in business. Employers can legally replace economic strikers and resume operations.[23] However, new employees become bargaining unit members and are represented by the striking union. Decertification is necessary to remove the bargaining representative.

Strike Votes and Going Out

Unions usually take strike votes during negotiations to strengthen their bargaining positions. This doesn't mean a strike will occur, only that the union may go on strike at the contract's expiration. A local union usually needs its parent national's approval to strike. If it strikes without approval, the local and its officers may be disciplined, the international may place the local under trusteeship, or strike benefits may not be paid.

If an impasse is encountered and a strike has been authorized, the negotiators must decide whether to actually go on strike or to continue to work under terms of the expired contract. Holdouts probably occur in more conditions than strikes. Evidence indicates strikes are more likely to occur if unemployment rates have decreased recently and/or employees in the bargaining unit have suffered a drop in their real wages.[24]

Unions usually require members to participate in strike activities, such as picketing, to receive strike benefits and may discipline members who refuse to strike. A strike may increase cohesiveness and solidarity of the union. UAW members involved in contract negotiations in 1976 and 1977 were surveyed four times. During the talks, Ford was struck, but GM and Chrysler were not. While on strike, Ford employees' attitudes toward their international union and its leaders were

---

[21] *Buffalo Forge Co.* v. *United Steelworkers of America, AFL–CIO,* 92 LRRM 3032 (Sup. Ct., 1976).

[22] *John Morrell & Co.* v. *UFCW, Local 304A,* U.S. Court of Appeals, 8th Circuit, 1990, 135 LRRM 2233.

[23] *NLRB* v. *MacKay Radio & Telegraph,* 304 U.S. 333 (1938).

[24] P. C. Cramton and J. S. Tracy, "Strikes and Holdouts in Wage Bargaining: Theory and Data," *American Economic Review* 82 (1992), pp. 100–21.

more positive than before the strike and more positive than those of fellow union members at GM and Chrysler.[25]

Strikes are often seen as resulting from a failure to obtain enough information to clearly know what the opponent's likely settlement range will be. It may also be argued, however, that strikes reflect the use of collective voice in demonstrating to the employer that workers need not continually comply. Evidence from Canadian strikes indicates that behavioral variables such as the rigidity of management practices and internal union politics influence the willingness to strike and its subsequent length.[26] A study of Temple University faculty members whose union voted to reject a contract offer and three days later voted not to comply with an injunction to end the strike identified determinants of voting behavior and militant union activity. Votes against the contract offer were predicted by low job satisfaction, low commitment to the employer, perceived instrumentality of the strike, being a woman, and not being in an engineering or hard science department. Votes to defy the injunction were related to low pay satisfaction, commitment to the union, strike support within the member's department, and perceived instrumentality of the strike. Predictors of militant activity included commitment to the union, strike support within the member's department, perceived instrumentality of the strike, comfort with demonstrative or confrontational forms of militancy, and being in upper professorial ranks (i.e., not assistant professors or instructors, so probably tenured).[27]

Picketing

Picketing is one of the most noticeable strike activities. In picketing, the union informs the public about the dispute and may appeal to others to stop doing business with their employer during the dispute. Before Norris-LaGuardia, state and federal courts often enjoined picketing. Since then, federal courts have been forbidden to enjoin strikes unless a clear and present danger to life or property is shown. States may not restrict peaceful picketing because it is protected by the First Amendment.[28] Some restrictions, however, are imposed on **recognitional picketing** under Landrum-Griffin.

To be protected from employer reprisals, employees must publicize that they are involved in a labor dispute when they picket or inform the public about the employer or its products and services.[29] The site and manner of the picketing are also of concern, because the union can be accused of illegal secondary activity in

---

[25] R. Stagner and B. Eflal, "Internal Union Dynamics During a Strike: A Quasi-Experimental Study," *Journal of Applied Psychology* 67 (1982), pp. 37–44.

[26] J. Godard, "Strikes as Collective Voice: A Behavioral Analysis of Strike Activity," *Industrial and Labor Relations Review* 46 (1992), pp. 161–75.

[27] J. A. McClendon and B. Klaas, "Determinants of Strike-Related Militancy: An Analysis of a University Faculty Strike," *Industrial and Labor Relations Review* 46 (1993), pp. 560–73.

[28] *Thornhill* v. *Alabama*, 310 U.S. 88 (1940).

[29] *NLRB* v. *Local Union, 1229, International Brotherhood of Electrical Workers,* 346 U.S. 464 (1953).

certain instances. The next sections examine various types of picketing. Legal picketing is not necessarily associated with strikes; it may also involve informational and recognitional activities.

Picket lines inform members of other unions about the dispute and ask that they not cross. They also aim at deterring their members from working. However, differences exist among members concerning their potential willingness to honor picket lines. Those with less positive attitudes toward the union and who are earning lower wages than average are less willing to strike as long and more willing to cross picket lines.[30] Where represented employees cross picket lines, the union's bargaining power is decreased because it increases the employer's ability to operate. In one situation, crossing behavior after a strike authorization vote was taken was related to a vote against the authorization, satisfaction with management, perceived hardship, and negatively with union commitment and co-worker social support. Crossing after a contract rejection was associated with a vote to accept, and negatively with union commitment and co-worker social support.[31]

Strikes are a powerful weapon with strong social overtones. There are mixed reactions to strikes largely dependent on social status, irrespective of union membership. People with a higher social status generally disapprove of strikes and coercive picketing, while persons in lower social status groups are more likely to approve militant action.[32]

Common Situs Picketing

The place where picketing occurs may affect secondary employers. This issue is important in construction, where a prime contractor and subcontractors work simultaneously on a common site. Each utilizes different trades, may or may not be unionized, and may have different wages, terms, and expiration dates in contracts. If unions strike in sympathy with a primary dispute, even if a dispute involves only one contractor, a whole site may be shut down.

A primary employer is one involved in a dispute, and a neutral employer is one affected by the picketing activity of the primary's employees. The rules governing **common situs picketing** in construction were established in the *Denver Building Trades Council* cases.[33] Picketing began when it was learned the prime contractor on the site had employed a nonunion subcontractor. The picketing was aimed at forcing the general contractor to drop the subcontractor. When picketing began, all other union workers refused to cross the picket line. The prime contractor maintained the dispute was with the subcontractor and that general picketing of the site was an illegal secondary boycott designed to force neutral employers to cease dealing with the subcontractor. The court agreed, and since

[30] M. H. LeRoy, "Multivariate Analysis of Unionized Employees' Propensity to Cross Their Union's Picket Lines," *Journal of Labor Research* 13 (1992), pp. 285–92.

[31] B. S. Klaas and J. A. McClendon, "Crossing the Line: The Determinants of Picket Line Crossing During a Faculty Strike," *Journal of Labor Research* 16 (1995), pp. 331–46.

[32] G. M. Saltzman, "The Impact of Social Class on Attitudes Towards Strikes: A Four Country Study," *Labor Studies Journal* 22, no. 3 (1997), pp. 28–56.

[33] *NLRB* v. *Denver Building Trades Council,* 341 U.S. 675 (1951).

then construction unions have been forbidden to picket sites to force a primary employer to cease doing business with a nonunion subcontractor. The usual practice at construction sites is to establish reserved gates for each employer. Primary dispute pickets may then patrol only the gate of their employer.

Ambulatory Site

Sometimes the objects of a strike move from place to place, such as a ship being struck by a seafarers union. In one case, when the ship was moved to dry dock for repairs, the union sought to picket beside the ship. Dry-dock managers refused to allow this, and a picket line was set up at the entrance to the dock. Such picketing was ruled legal if (1) the object is currently on the secondary employer's site, (2) the primary employer continues to engage in its normal business, (3) the picketing is reasonably close to the strike object, and (4) the picketing discloses that the dispute is with the struck employer and not the site owner.[34]

Multiple-Use Sites

An employer's site is usually easily identified, but recent changes in retailing, for example, have blurred this identity. Enclosed shopping centers make it difficult to picket a primary employer without disrupting secondary businesses. The employer has usually leased the site from another company that owns the shopping mall. The Supreme Court has held that unions do not interfere with a neutral owner and other stores by peacefully informing the public about a labor dispute with one of the stores within the mall.[35]

Slowdowns

The incidence of strikes has recently declined markedly. Employers have occasionally replaced economic strikers and have become more automated and thus better able to operate for extended periods with only supervisory employees. In response, unions are increasingly using slowdowns to pressure employers to settle contracts. A slowdown most often involves **working to rules.** Employees refuse to perform activities outside their job descriptions, follow procedures to the letter, and refuse overtime and other voluntary employment duties. Because they are complying with the contract and company work rules, they can seldom be disciplined.[36] The most visible example of slowdown or work-to-rule activities was the reaction of UAW member workers at Caterpillar following the company's unilateral imposition of new economic terms following a long impasse. Exhibit 12–3 contains details of worker responses.

---

[34] *Sailors' Union of the Pacific (Moore Dry Dock Co.),* 92 NLRB 547 (1950).

[35] *Edward J. DeBartolo Corp.* v. *Florida Gulf Coast Building and Construction Trades Council and NLRB,* Sup. Ct., No. 86-1461, 1988.

[36] "Labor's Shift: Finding Strikes Harder to Win, More Unions Turn to Slowdowns," *The Wall Street Journal,* May 22, 1987, pp. 1, 6; see also a publication for union members, *The Inside Game: Winning with Workplace Strategies,* Industrial Union Department, AFL–CIO, 1987.

EXHIBIT 12–3

Caterpillar UAW Members "Work-to-Rules"

. . . The 2½-year-old labor dispute between the [UAW and Caterpillar] began in October 1991. It was capped by a 5½-month UAW strike and company lockout that ended in April 1992 after the company issued an ultimatum for the workers to return to work or risk losing their jobs.

Once the workers returned the union began its "Work to Rule" in-plant strategy whereby its members do only what is required based on their job description and nothing else.

"If the in-plant strategy works the way it should, there should never be the chance of going out again," [UAW Secretary-Treasurer Bill] Casstevens said.

And Caterpillar seems to be concerned about this, Casstevens said. He held up Caterpillar's 1993 earning report—where the company recorded its first profitable year since 1990—and pointed to a statement about the uncertainties of continued success with the unresolved labor dispute.

. . . stronger business conditions for Caterpillar products also give the union more leverage to affect production by either a strike or continuing the in-plant strategy.

It's like they (Caterpillar) are sitting in California waiting for the next earthquake. They know they've had some strikes here and there . . . but they know the big one's out there and it could come at any time and come when it could really interrupt the opportunity to make some real big profits," said Bill Stewart, UAW Region 4 director.

SOURCE: B. Bouyea, "Casstevens: Strike Still in Picture," *Peoria Journal Star,* January 26, 1994, p. 1.

Corporate Campaigns

In a **corporate campaign,** the union exerts pressure on points where the employer might be vulnerable to support a collective bargaining effort. A corporate campaign successfully forced the J. P. Stevens Company to negotiate a first contract with the Clothing and Textile Workers, which had won representation rights several years earlier.

The first phase of a corporate campaign explores the corporation's business activity to uncover any possible regulatory violations recorded by government agencies, such as the Environmental Protection Agency or Occupational Safety and Health Administration. The campaign also finds which other corporations are closely linked as suppliers, customers, financial backers, and the like. Corporate investigations will also include detailed analyses of the firm's publicly reported financial data.

The second phase involves publicizing items detrimental to the employer's interests that support the union's demands. The campaign tries to get outsiders to pressure the employer to settle with the union on terms beneficial to the employees. Some of the activities may be held to motivate consumer boycotts.[37]

---

[37] H. Datz, L. Geffner, J. M. McLaughlin, and S. Kellock, "Economic Warfare in the 1980s: Strikes, Lockouts, Boycotts, and Corporate Campaigns, " *Industrial Relations Law Journal* 9 (1987), pp. 82–115.

Shutdowns

A variety of responses are available to the employer when struck, generally falling into three categories: (1) shut down the affected area, (2) continue operating, or (3) contract out work for the duration. Each has its own consequences and can cause retaliatory action.

Shutdowns are designed to have the least consequences in terms of union activity. But a shutdown has consequences the employer would like to avoid. First, production revenues are lost. Second, competitors may gear up to take over the lost production, thus permanently reducing the struck company's market share. Third, if a firm is a sole supplier, its customers may encourage others to enter the market as alternative sources, thus reducing the possibilities of temporary shortages. And fourth, during periods of scarcity, the firm may lose its suppliers as they fill orders from more reliable customers.

Continued Operations

Continued operations may be accomplished by two strategies. Neither is relished by the union, but the second will almost certainly lead to militant action. The first strategy is to continue operations using supervisors and other nonproduction workers, which is feasible if the firm is not labor intensive and if maintenance demands are not high. Automated and continuous-flow operations, such as those found in the chemical industry, fall into this category. If this strategy is used, supervisory-employee relations may be strained after the strike because the supervisors' work may have enabled the company to prolong the strike.

The second strategy is to hire strike replacements. Because this places strikers' jobs in direct jeopardy, violence often ensues. During the 1980s, employers were much more likely to hire replacements, given their availability when unemployment was high. Exhibit 12–4 describes the responses of some employers to work stoppages. A company's ability to attract replacements substantially reduces union bargaining power. Strike replacements face a difficult situation. They are reviled as "scabs" by strikers (see Exhibit 12–5 for a definition almost invariably used when strike replacements are hired) and, due to low seniority, may be vulnerable to layoff after a new contract is signed. On the other hand, if the employer can operate for a year without settling the strike, new employees may succeed in decertifying the union. Major strikes involving violence occur when employers attempt to continue operations with supervisors or replacement workers. Recent examples include the *New York Daily News* and *Detroit Free Press–Detroit News* strikes.

Strike Replacements and Public Policy
Since the *Mackay Radio* decision, employers have been free to hire strike replacements. However, the practice increased during the 1980s. With the increased threat or use of replacements, unions have proposed to legislatively prohibit replacing

EXHIBIT 12–4

More Firms Get Tough and Keep Operating Despite Walkouts

To an increasing number of companies, *strike* is no longer a frightening word. These companies are prepared to continue operating right through a labor walkout.

The latest example is Continental Airlines, which decided to keep flying on a curtailed schedule despite strikes by its pilots, flight attendants, and ground personnel. When the Machinists union struck Continental last summer, the carrier immediately hired replacements. And when the company recently filed a bankruptcy petition to bail itself out of its labor and financial problems, it rehired about 35 percent of its former work force at drastically reduced pay and then resumed flights.

Operating during strikes is nothing new for many companies . . . But now many labor-intensive concerns are adopting the strategy as a continuation of the hard-nosed concession bargaining pressed during the recession. Companies that have chosen to operate despite strikes recently have included, in addition to Continental, Phelps Dodge Corp., Magic Chef, Inc., and Whirlpool Corp.

Labor experts say the time is ripe for such aggressive management tactics . . . "We have a president who says let's confront them, fire them, and keep on rolling. That makes it legitimate to operate during strikes, and private employers have followed the lead," says John Zalusky, an economist in the AFL–CIO's research department.

SOURCE: R. S. Greenberger, "More Firms Get Tough and Keep Operating in Spite of Walkouts." Reprinted from *The Wall Street Journal,* October 11, 1983, p. 1. © 1983 Dow Jones & Company. All Rights Reserved Worldwide.

EXHIBIT 12–5

What Is a Scab?

After God had finished the rattlesnake, the toad, and the vampire, he had some awful substance left with which He made a scab. A scab is a two-legged animal with a corkscrew soul, a water-logged brain, and a combination backbone made of jelly and glue. Where others have hearts, he carries a tumor of rotten principles.

When a scab comes down the street, men turn their backs, and angels weep in heaven, and the devil shuts the gates of hell to keep him out. No man has a right to scab as long as there is a pool of water deep enough to drown his body in, or a rope long enough to hang his carcass with. Judas Iscariot was a gentleman compared with a scab. For betraying his Master, he had character enough to hang himself. A scab hasn't!

Esau sold his birthright for a mess of pottage. Judas Iscariot sold his Savior for 30 pieces of silver. Benedict Arnold sold his country for a promise of a commission in the British Army. The modern strikebreaker sells his birthright, his country, his wife, his children, and his fellow men for an unfulfilled promise from his employer, trust, or corporation.

Esau was traitor to himself. Judas Iscariot was a traitor to his God. Benedict Arnold was a traitor to his country.

A strikebreaker is a traitor to his God, his country, his family, and his class!

SOURCE: P. S. Foner, *Jack London, American Rebel* (New York: Citadel Press, 1947), pp. 57–58.

economic strikers. Most Canadian provinces prohibit strike replacements. Employers argue that eliminating the use of replacements as a potential labor relations tactic would substantially reduce their bargaining power. However, a study of the effects of these laws in Canada, where they vary across provinces, indicates little effect on the economic outcomes in bargaining.[38]

Replacing strikers has severe negative consequences for union survival. A replacement tactic also lengthens strike duration. Evidence indicates that employers in most industries are able to continue operating without using permanent replacements.[39]

The use of strike replacements has varied widely over time, with higher numbers after the *Mackay Radio* decision in the late 1930s, and increasing again in the 1980s after President Reagan replaced striking air traffic controllers.[40] Table 12–3 shows details of these longitudinal changes.

Employers run some legal and operating risks using replacements. The NLRB finds unfair labor practices present in most strikes where replacements are used.[41] If the ULPs involve a refusal to bargain, the employer may face potentially large back-pay liabilities. Where employers continue operations using nonproduction workers or hiring replacements, higher injury rates follow, accompanied by the likelihood of higher workers' compensation insurance rates.[42]

Rights of Economic Strikers

If replacements are hired, strikers may still get their jobs back. First, if they offer unilaterally to return and if their jobs or others they qualify for are unfilled, refusing to rehire them is an ULP since strikes are protected by Section 7 of the National Labor Relations Act. Second, if employees ask for reinstatement at the strike's end, they are entitled to their jobs, if open, or to preference in hiring when positions become open.[43] Nevertheless, employers may give job preferences to replacements or employees who crossed the picket line before the end of the strike.[44] They are not required to reinstate employees who break rules during the strike, such as sabotage and picket line violence. But discharges must be for cause, and the grievance procedure would be open for hearing disputes over these discharges.

---

[38] J. W. Budd, "Canadian Strike Replacement Legislation and Collective Bargaining: Lessons for the United States," *Industrial Relations* 35 (1996), pp. 245–60.

[39] C. L. Gramm, "Empirical Evidence on Political Arguments Relating to Replacement Worker Legislation," *Labor Law Journal* 42 (1991), pp. 491–96.

[40] M. H. LeRoy, "Regulating Employer Use of Permanent Striker Replacements: Empirical Analysis of NLRA and RLA Strikes 1935–1991," *Berkeley Journal of Employment and Labor Law* 16 (1995), pp. 169–208.

[41] M. H. LeRoy, "The Changing Character of Strikes Involvement Permanent Striker Replacements," *Journal of Labor Research* 16 (1995), pp. 423–38.

[42] W. D. Allen, "How Strikes Influence Work-Injury Duration: Evidence from the State of New York," *Proceedings of the Industrial Relations Research Association* 46 (1994), pp. 306–14.

[43] *NLRB* v. *Fleetwood Trailer Co., Inc.,* 389 U.S. 375 (1967).

[44] *TWA* v. *Independent Federation of Flight Attendants,* Sup. Ct., 1989, 130 LRRM 2657.

TABLE 12–3

Historical Incidence of Strikes Where Replacements Were Used

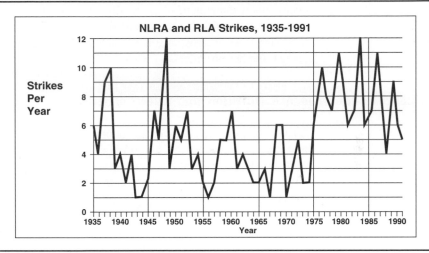

SOURCE: M. H. LeRoy, "Regulating Employer Use of Permanent Striker Replacements: Empirical Analysis of NLRA and RLA Strikes 1935–1991," *Berkeley Journal of Employment and Labor Law* 16 (1995), p. 208.

Contracting Out

Strikes have serious consequences for employers with major customers whose businesses require output on a fixed schedule, particularly if competitors offer the same services. One strategy is to arrange for a competitor to temporarily handle the work.

On its face, this seems foolproof: no problems with strikebreakers and the union, and customers get their work done on time. It's not, however. If the subcontractor is unionized, its employees legally can refuse to perform the work when a struck employer has initiated the order. Such refusals are allowed under the so-called **ally doctrine.**

For example, a printing firm responsible for providing Sunday supplements to newspapers was struck by its employees. To maintain its ability to meet the weekly schedule, it subcontracted the work to another firm. When the second firm's employees learned why they were doing the work, they refused to perform it. The first employer charged this was a secondary boycott, but the NLRB reasoned the dispute became primary through the handling of the struck work for the primary employer.[45]

An exception to the ally doctrine is granted to health care providers. Sick patients can't wait for care until a strike is over. Hospitals accepting struck work (patient care) cannot risk the extension of the strike to them. Congress modified

---

[45] *Blackhawk Engraving Co.,* 219 NLRB 169 (1975).

Section 8(b)(4) of the Taft-Hartley Act to allow a limited exemption to the ally doctrine for health care providers. If a hospital is struck and another supplies an occasional technician to assist, an ally relationship is not established. But if shifts of nurses were provided by a group of hospitals, they would become allies. Thus, the magnitude of assistance is the determining factor in whether a strike could spread to other providers.

Evidence on the Incidence, Duration, and Effects of Strikes

Strikes are popularly viewed as counterproductive. Those not directly involved might be inconvenienced, and often a winner is not apparent. Companies lose profits on lost sales, and workers lose wages that take years to make up even if the strike secured higher wages than companies offered before the walkout. But striking or taking a threatened strike may be a long-term investment. If a union never supports its demands with militant action, the employer may doubt the credibility of its threats. Short strikes may be a relatively low-cost investment in gaining large future demands. From an employer standpoint, taking a strike may be necessary for gaining permission to introduce new work methods or for lowering expectations.[46]

The number of strikes and the amount of time lost to strikes has diminished precipitously since the end of the 1970s. Compared to the early 1950s, there are fewer than 8 percent as many strikes in large employers, and about 8 percent as many days lost due to strikes. Compared to the late 1970s, strikes occur only 12 percent as often, and fewer than 20 percent as many days are lost. Table 12–4 displays historical strike data.

Incidence of Strikes

Several studies identify variables linked to the incidence of economic strikes. Strikes are more frequent when the costs of disagreeing or the parties' relative risks have substantially changed from earlier negotiations. For example, declining real wages or failing to win settlements comparable to other contracts increase the likelihood of strikes.[47] Strike incidence is procyclical; that is, strikes increase as

---

[46] For arguments supporting this position, see C. R. Greer, Stanley A. Martin, and Ted E. Reusser, "The Effect of Strikes on Shareholder Returns," *Journal of Labor Research* 1 (1980), pp. 217–29; and M. J. Mauro, "Strikes as a Result of Imperfect Information," *Industrial and Labor Relations Review* 35 (1982), pp. 522–38.

[47] See O. Ashenfelter and G. E. Johnson, "Bargaining Theory, Trade Unions, and Industrial Strike Activity," *American Economic Review* 59 (1969), pp. 35–49; D. J. B. Mitchell, "A Note on Strike Propensities and Wage Developments," *Industrial Relations* 20 (1981), pp. 123–27; M. I. Naples, "An Analysis of Defensive Strikes," *Industrial Relations* 26 (1987), pp. 96–105; and C. L. Gramm, "The Determinants of Strike Incidence and Severity: A Micro-Level Study," *Industrial and Labor Relations Review* 39 (1986), pp. 361–76.

TABLE 12–4

Work Stoppages Involving 1,000 or More Workers (1947–1997)

Year	Number of Strikes	Workers Involved (000)	Person- Days Idle (000)
1947	270	1,629	25,720
1952	470	2,746	48,820
1957	279	887	10,430
1962	211	793	11,760
1967	381	2,192	31,320
1972	250	975	16,764
1977	298	1,212	21,258
1982	96	656	9,061
1987	46	174	4,481
1988	40	122	4,381
1989	52	454	16,996
1990	50	200	5,926
1991	45	412	4,584
1992	41	383	3,989
1993	36	184	3,981
1994	45	322	5,021
1995	34	207	5,771
1996	38	275	4,889
1997	34	351	4,497

SOURCE: http://www.146.142.4.24/cgi-bin/dsrv: U.S. Bureau of Labor Statistics.

unemployment falls and inflation rises.[48] Employer and union stability[49] and stability in the employer's supplier market is associated with lower rates of strike incidence.[50] Strikes are longer when companies are not performing well relative to competitors or other industries.[51] Economic strikes in the auto industry were more prevalent when productivity was low, while intracontract strikes are more frequent

[48] See J. Kennan, "Pareto Optimality and the Economics of Strike Duration," *Journal of Labor Research* 1 (1980), pp. 77–94; B. E. Kaufman, "The Determinants of Strikes over Time and across Industries," *Journal of Labor Research* 4 (1983), pp. 159–75; C. L. Gramm, W. E. Hendricks, and L. M. Kahn, "Inflation Uncertainty and Strike Activity," *Industrial Relations* 27 (1988), pp. 114–29; S. B. Vroman, "A Longitudinal Analysis of Strike Activity in U.S. Manufacturing: 1957–1984," *American Economic Review* 79 (1989), pp. 816–26; and S. McConnell, "Cyclical Fluctuations in Strike Activity," *Industrial and Labor Relations Review* 44 (1990), pp. 130–43.

[49] B. E. Kaufman, "The Determinants of Strikes in the United States: 1900–1977," *Industrial and Labor Relations Review* 35 (1982), pp. 473–90.

[50] J. M. Cousineau and R. Lacroix, "Imperfect Information and Strikes: An Analysis of Canadian Experience, 1967–82," *Industrial and Labor Relations Review* 39 (1986), pp. 539–49.

[51] McConnell, "Cyclical Fluctuations."

when productivity was increasing.[52] Strikes of 14 days or less during the last negotiation increase the odds of strikes in the present round.[53] Higher proportions of unionized employees in an industry are related to higher strike and wage levels, reflecting successful use of union bargaining power.[54]

Several demographic and industry variables are related to strike incidence. Urban, southern, and female-dominated bargaining units strike less often.[55] Unions in high-injury industries strike more frequently, perhaps reflecting risk-taking behavior in taking these types of jobs.[56] Foreign owned firms in Canada have lower strike rates, possibly due to more care in sharing information with unions to increase the company's credibility.[57]

Rank-and-file involvement increases the propensity to strike, since strikes increased after the Landrum-Griffin Act guaranteed union democracy.[58] Younger members appear more militant, while personal hardship decreases militancy.[59]

Public policy has a mixed effect on strikes. Availability of Aid to Families with Dependent Children or welfare payments is unassociated with strikes.[60] Right-to-work laws, on the other hand, are related to higher strike rates.[61] Canadian legal mandates for conciliation and strike votes reduce incidence rates.[62] Where public policy reduces risks to strikers, such as where they are entitled to unemployment compensation[63] or, as in Canada, where employers cannot legally replace them, the incidence rate is higher.[64]

---

[52] S. Flaherty, "Strike Activity, Worker Militancy, and Productivity Change in Manufacturing, 1961–1981," *Industrial and Labor Relations Review* 40 (1987), pp. 585–600; and S. Flaherty, "Strike Activity and Productivity Change: The U.S. Auto Industry," *Industrial Relations* 26 (1987), pp. 174–85.

[53] D. Card, "Longitudinal Analysis of Strike Activity," *Journal of Labor Economics* 6 (1988), pp. 147–76.

[54] J. M. Abowd and J. S. Tracy, "Market Structure, Strike Activity, and Union Wage Settlements," *Industrial Relations* 28 (1989), pp. 227–50.

[55] Kaufman, "The Determinants of Strikes over Time."

[56] J. P. Leigh, "Risk Preferences and the Interindustry Propensity to Strike," *Industrial and Labor Relations Review* 36 (1983), pp. 271–85.

[57] J-M. Cousineau, R. Lacroix, and D. Vachon, "Foreign Ownership and Strike Activity in Canada," *Relations Industrielles* 46 (1991), pp. 616–29.

[58] Ashenfelter and Johnson, "Bargaining Theory."

[59] J. E. Martin, "Predictors of Individual Propensity to Strike," *Industrial and Labor Relations Review* 39 (1986), pp. 214–27; see also A. W. Black, "Some Factors Influencing Attitudes toward Militancy, Solidarity, and Sanctions in a Teachers' Union," *Human Relations* 36 (1983), pp. 973–85.

[60] R. Hutchens, D. Lipsky, and R. Stern, *Strikes and Subsidies: The Influence of Government Transfer Programs on Strike Activity* (Kalamazoo, MI: Upjohn Institute for Employment Research, 1989).

[61] Gramm, "Determinants of Strike Incidence and Severity,"

[62] M. Gunderson and A. Melino," The Effects of Public Policy on Strike Duration," *Journal of Labor Economics* 8 (1990), pp. 295–316.

[63] Hutchens et al., *Strikes and Subsidies.*

[64] Gunderson and Melino, "Effects of Public Policy".

Duration of Strikes

Strike duration is related to a number of variables, increasing during low-performing economic periods.[65] Employer costs do not necessarily increase at a constant rate with duration because costs for a short strike may be small if shipments can be made from inventory or if customers have stocked up in anticipation. As strikes lengthen, revenue losses from forgone orders increase rapidly, and long-run profits are reduced as market share is lost to more reliable competitors. Duration is longer in booming industries, suggesting strong earnings by both companies and union members may allow longer holdouts.[66] Employers who are diversified across industries can usually take a longer strike.[67] For strikers, direct marginal costs rise rapidly as savings are exhausted and the disparity between strike benefits and wages becomes apparent. Strikes last longer where union members have relatively low debt-to-income ratios.[68] Striker job security is important; durations are longer in Canada where they cannot be replaced.[69] In the United States, however, either announcing an intent to replace or actually replacing strikers increased strike durations by an average of 30 percent.[70]

Issues are related to duration. Renegotiation strikes are almost always over economics (85 percent of cases), while intracontract strikes almost always involve working conditions or job security (90 percent of cases). The median duration of renegotiation strikes in one sample was 15 days, while the median for intracontract strikes was just 3 days.[71] Wildcat strikes most frequently involve plant administration issues and generally last three days or less. They are predicted by high unionization rates within the industry, unsafe working conditions, low inventories, liberal political environment, and moderate degree of bargaining experience. Wildcat strikes are inhibited by the employer's likelihood of filing an ULP, high unemployment rates, high real wages in the industry, a higher percentage of women in the bargaining unit, location in the South, and a long-term bargaining relationship.[72]

Ironically, the shorter the strike, the more easily it appears to be settled. Almost 13 percent of strikes are settled in the first day. At 10 days, the rate drops

---

[65] Kennan, "Pareto Optimality"; Kaufman, "Determinants of Strikes over Time and Across Industries"; Vroman, "Longitudinal Analysis of Strike Activity"; and A. Harrison and M. Stewart, "Cyclical Fluctuations in Strike Duration," *American Economic Review* 79 (1989), pp. 827–41.

[66] McConnell, "Cyclical Fluctuations."

[67] D. Rose, "Firm Diversification and Strike Duration: Is There a Connection?" *Industrial Relations* 33 (1994), pp. 482–91.

[68] Gramm, "Determinants of Strike Incidence and Severity."

[69] Gunderson and Melino, "Effects of Public Policy."

[70] J. F. Schnell and C. L. Gramm, "The Empirical Relations between Employers' Strike Replacement Strategies and Strike Duration," *Industrial and Labor Relations Review* 47 (1994), pp. 189–206.

[71] S. Flaherty, "Contract Status and the Economic Determinants of Strike Activity," *Industrial Relations* 22 (1983), pp. 20–33.

[72] D. M. Byrne and R. H. King, "Wildcat Strikes in the U.S. Manufacturing, 1960–1977," *Journal of Labor Research* 7 (1986), pp. 387–401.

to 4.8 percent; at 30 days, to 3.2 percent; and at 50 days, only 2.4 percent of the remaining strikes are settled. Once a strike exceeds this length, the probability of settling does not change, indicating that the parties' relative costs of continuing the strike do not change.[73]

Effects of Strikes

Some argue strikes are strictly random events not known before they occur. If this were true, outsiders who could be hurt by strikes could not take action to insulate themselves. During the 1960s and early 1970s, steel customers learned to stock up before contract expirations in the expectation of strikes. Studies of shareholder behavior suggest that investors anticipate strikes; rates of return on shares of struck companies decline in value before a strike occurs. Investors discount stocks as the duration increases over relatively short runs.[74] However, only about one third of the total decline in share price is discounted before the strike is announced.[75] The costs of strikes spread to supplier industries as well. Auto strikes were associated with declines in stock prices for steel companies roughly equal to those found in autos.[76] On the other hand, there are few intraindustry strike effects on share prices. This may relate to defensive strategies such as building inventories, expectations of concessions, or pattern bargaining expectations for other nonstruck firms.[77] Very long strikes appear related to situations in which firms have done better than average before the strike (ability to pay), and investors bid up these stocks after the strike, perhaps anticipating that management gained major concessions.[78] This appears rational because data indicate wages negotiated after a strike are about 3 percent lower than when no strike occurs.[79] From the standpoint of an individual employer in the lumber industry, work stoppages do not appear to appreciably affect supplies of products or prices.[80]

Short-run profitability and productivity decreases occur in struck employers. However, effects are even stronger in suppliers or customers of struck firms. Two reasons may explain these findings. First, it may be more difficult for suppliers or customers to predict strikes than the target employer. Second, relative to struck firms, suppliers and customers are less likely to lay off employees.[81]

---

[73] Kennan, "Pareto Optimality."

[74] G. R. Neumann, "The Predictability of Strikes: Evidence from the Stock Market," *Industrial and Labor Relations Review* 33 (1980), pp. 525–35.

[75] B. E. Becker and C. A. Olson, "The Impact of Strikes on Shareholder Equity," *Industrial and Labor Relations Review* 39 (1986), pp. 425–38.

[76] O. S. Persons, "The Effects of Automobile Strikes on the Stock Value of Steel Suppliers," *Industrial and Labor Relations Review* 49 (1995), pp. 78–87.

[77] J. K. Kramer and G. M. Vasconcellos, "The Economic Effect of Strikes on the Shareholders of Nonstruck Competitors," *Industrial and Labor Relations Review* 49 (1995), pp. 213–22.

[78] Greer, et al., "Effect of Strikes."

[79] S. McConnell, "Strikes, Wages, and Private Information," *American Economic Review* 79 (1989), pp. 810–15.

[80] H. J. Paarsch, "Work Stoppages and the Theory of the Offset Factor: Evidence from the British Columbian Lumber Industry," *Journal of Labor Economics* 8 (1990), pp. 387–411.

[81] R. McHugh, "Productivity Effects of Strikes in Struck and Nonstruck Industries," *Industrial and Labor Relations Review* 44 (1991), pp. 722–32.

Negotiators may make subjective estimates of the effects of striking in deciding on bargaining tactics. In a study of the perceived results of striking, chief negotiators believed management appeared to gain more from strikes than unions. The ability to remain in operation and/or to have a large proportion of a plant's employees involved in the strike increased management's perceived advantage.[82] Unions may also use strikes to influence internal politics. For example, locals voting not to ratify the 1981 United Mine Workers–Bituminous Coal Operators Association agreement were very likely to vote to replace the international's leadership during the next election. Dissidents campaigned actively against the contract.[83]

Overview

Depending on which data are examined, it could be argued that involvement in strikes is higher than suggested. This chapter's introduction noted that time lost due to strikes was not large in comparison to total time worked. The relatively low number of days lost and the declining percentage of days lost may be due to short strike durations and the decreasing proportion of unionized workers.

BOYCOTTS

Boycotts are used infrequently with mixed results. As noted in Chapter 2, the *Danbury Hatters'* and *Buck's Stove* boycotts were declared violations of the Sherman Antitrust Act, exposing unions to treble damages until the Clayton Act exempted them from antitrust provisions.

Boycotts are used infrequently for a number of reasons: (1) They require a great deal of publicity to alert customers, (2) customers may not respond unless a clear-cut social issue is involved, (3) keeping a boycott from becoming a secondary boycott is sometimes difficult, and (4) boycott effects are not turned off as easily as strike effects because after a settlement the public may continue identifying the producer with poor labor relations. Boycotts are generally seen as having little economic effect; stock prices of boycotted companies fall for only about 15 days before returning to preboycott levels.[84]

One boycott technique informs the public of a labor dispute at a location where the struck business's products are sold. However, this activity risks being declared a secondary boycott. Consider the following: A major television and radio receiver manufacturer is struck by its production employees. To pressure the

---

[82] A. Shirom, "Strike Characteristics as Determinants of Strike Settlements: A Chief Negotiator's Viewpoint," *Journal of Applied Psychology* 67 (1982), pp. 45–52.

[83] T. Ghilarducci, "The Impact of Internal Union Politics on the 1981 UMWA Strike," *Industrial Relations* 27 (1988), pp. 114–29.

[84] S. W. Pruitt, K. C. J. Wei, and R. E. White, "The Impact of Union-Sponsored Boycotts on the Stock Prices of Target Firms," *Journal of Labor Research* 9 (1988), pp. 285–90.

employer to settle, the union pickets retail stores selling the TV sets. The signs read, "Don't shop here. This store sells XYZ TV sets produced under unfair conditions. ABC union on strike for justice against XYZ." Suppose the union uses a different message on its signs: "ABC on strike against XYZ Co. Don't buy an XYZ TV while shopping here today. ABC has no dispute with this store." Only the second strategy is legal. In the second instance, the picket calls attention to the labor dispute and the struck product but does not ask people to boycott the neutral store. If the union follows the second strategy and does not impede customers or deliveries, the action is considered primary and legal.[85]

During the 1980s, boycotts were used against Adolph Coors Company (to force recognition) and J. P. Stevens & Company (to force recognition and bargaining on initial contracts). The Coors boycott had some effect on the ultimate willingness of the firm to recognize the union, but the J. P. Stevens action was much more difficult because many of its products were sold under labels that were hard to identify with the employer.

An unanswered concern in boycotts is what responsibility unions have to secondary employers. If boycotted products are sold in a large department store, the impact may be minimal. But if the secondary employer was a franchisee of the primary employer and the boycott was successful, the impact could be great.

Degree of impact was dismissed as an improper test of a boycott's legality in the *Tree Fruits* case, but it was raised later in a boycott having a much greater impact on a secondary employer. Steelworkers Local 14055 struck the Bay Refining division of Dow Chemical Company at Bay City, Michigan. Gasoline from the struck refinery was marketed through Bay stations in Michigan. To pressure Dow, pickets informed customers in heavily unionized areas that Dow supplied Bay gasoline and asked consumers not to buy it when patronizing Bay stations. Over 80 percent of station revenues came from gasoline sales, so the impact on the secondary employer was great where the boycott was effective. Because gasoline refining was only a small part of Dow's business, the effect of the boycott on its sales was minimal. Furthermore, gasoline was easily marketed through other firms. The appeals court dismissed ULP complaints against the Steelworkers under the *Tree Fruits* impact doctrine. The Supreme Court overruled and remanded the issue to the NLRB. The board did not reconsider the impact issue because Local 14055 had been disestablished, leaving the issue undecided.[86]

Unions cannot use boycotts to make political statements. The International Longshoremen's Association refusal to handle Soviet goods in response to the invasion of Afghanistan was an illegal secondary boycott because no primary dispute existed with the dockworkers' employer.[87]

---

[85] *NLRB* v. *Fruit & Vegetable Packers, Local 760,* 377 U.S. 58 (1964).

[86] Bureau of National Affairs, *Daily Labor Report,* May 5, 1977, p. A-4.

[87] *International Longshoremen's Association, AFL–CIO* v. *Allied International, Inc.,* No. 80-1663, Sup. Ct., 1982; for a critique of this decision, see J. Rubin, "The Primary-Secondary Distinction: The New Secondary Boycott Law of *Allied International, Inc.* v. *International Longshoremen's Association,*" *Industrial Relations Law Journal* 6 (1984), pp. 94–124.

LOCKOUTS

Lockouts are the flip side of the strike coin. Employers use them most frequently when faced with strikes involving (1) perishable goods and (2) multiemployer bargaining units.

Perishable Goods

An employer dealing with perishable goods is frequently at the mercy of the union. For example, California vegetable canners were struck in 1976 just before harvest. Because their revenues depended on packing the produce when it was mature, a strike during the pack would have caused the produce to rot. Thus, the employers were under great pressure to settle quickly.

Similar situations occur when goods and services are perishable, but the employer has control over their perishability. For a packer, the timing of the crop's maturity is not within its control. But a brewer can decide when to start a new batch of beer, and a contractor can elect when to begin a tract of houses. For the brewer, if the beer is started, it must be bottled on a certain date or the batch will spoil. For the contractor, customers may become dissatisfied waiting for an unfinished house and spread their displeasure to other home buyers. Lockouts are legitimate employer tactics to decrease union power in situations when it is done to avoid economic loss[88] or to preserve customer goodwill.[89]

Multiemployer Lockouts

As discussed in Chapter 8, several small employers engaged in the same business whose employees are represented by the same union often form a multiemployer bargaining unit. But if the union strikes only one employer and attempts to break the solidarity of the group by using a **whipsaw** strategy, can the remainder lock out their employees? When one member of a multiemployer unit is struck and the remaining members lock out their employees, the lockout is defensive in nature; without its use the continued integrity of the bargaining unit could not be assured.[90] Multiemployer groups can also lock out employees when one is struck and temporarily replace them for the duration of the lockout to continue operations.[91]

---

[88] *Duluth Bottling Association,* 48 NLRB 1335 (1943).
[89] *Betts Cadillac-Olds, Inc.,* 96 NLRB 268 (1951).
[90] *NLRB* v. *Truck Drivers' Local 449,* 353 U.S. 87 (1957).
[91] *NLRB* v. *Brown,* 380 U.S. 278 (1965).

Single-Employer Lockouts

In a single-employer negotiation, there is no need to defend against a whipsaw. Thus, the question of whether a lockout interferes with employee rights to engage in concerted activities must be scrutinized more closely for single employers. Unless an impasse occurs, a lockout cannot be implemented.[92]

When an impasse has been reached and the contract has expired, employers are permitted to lock out employees[93] although refusing to bargain simply to gain an impasse allowing the use of a lockout would be unlawful. In addition, single employers may hire temporary replacements to pressure the union after a lockout is imposed.[94]

BANKRUPTCIES

While bankruptcies are not impasses, some firms have used them to gain concessions or to escape existing contracts without negotiating. Bankruptcy law allows companies to abrogate contracts with suppliers and renegotiate on more favorable terms. Under Chapter 11 of the bankruptcy code, the firm continues operations and gains protection from its creditors while trying to reorganize. Bankruptcy courts oversee the changes made to contracts to safeguard the interests of both the creditors and the debtor-in-possession.

When companies attempted to abrogate labor agreements, unions filed refusal-to-bargain charges with the NLRB. Early in 1984, however, the Supreme Court ruled bankruptcy courts may allow rejection of collective bargaining agreements if the debtor-in-possession shows their continuance burdens the business.[95] Congress responded by amending the bankruptcy code to require negotiations with unions over changes thought to be necessary. The bankruptcy court can allow contract repudiation only if the union rejected modifications without good cause.

Some argue that relatively liberal provisions of Chapter 11, which don't require insolvency, will lead to "going concerns" electing to file bankruptcy to escape contract terms unavoidable through collective bargaining. Conflicts between labor legislation and bankruptcy law lead to controversy whenever bankruptcy is declared.[96]

---

[92] *Quaker State Oil Refining Corp.,* 121 NLRB 334 (1958).

[93] *American Ship Building Co.* v. *NLRB,* 380 U.S. 300 (1965).

[94] *Harter Equipment, Inc.,* 122 LRRM 1219 (1986).

[95] *NLRB* v. *Bildisco & Bildisco,* 115 LRRM 2805, Sup. Ct., 1984.

[96] For further details, see T. R. Haggard and M. S. Pulliam, *Conflicts between Labor Legislation and Bankruptcy Law,* Labor Relations and Public Policy Series, No. 30 (Philadelphia: Industrial Relations Unit, The Wharton School, University of Pennsylvania, 1987).

SUMMARY

Impasses occur when the parties fail to reach an agreement during negotiations. Several methods are used to break impasses. The parties may strike or lock out, agree to mediation, or invoke interest arbitration.

Mediation brings the parties together through a third party who helps to reopen communications, clarify issues, and introduce a realistic approach to bargaining issues that continue to separate the parties. Interest arbitration turns the dispute over to a neutral party to decide the terms of a final settlement.

Typical tactics used by unions in impasses include strikes, picketing, boycotts, and corporate campaigns. Employers respond by hiring replacements, locking out employees, or declaring bankruptcy.

Strikes usually occur as the result of a disagreement upon the terms of a new contract. These strikes are called economic strikes. Other strikes occur over ULPs, sympathy with other unions, and violations of no-strike clauses. The strikers' rights to employment in each category have been clearly defined by the courts.

Lockouts involve a refusal to provide work. Although strikes can occur anytime after the termination of the contract, lockouts seldom occur because the employer loses revenues when not in operation. Most lockouts involve multiemployer bargaining units whose members seek to preserve the bargaining relationship by countering the strike of a single member.

Strikes occur more often when unions have failed to keep up with relevant comparison settlements. Good economic conditions are also associated with more strikes. Strikes are longer if economic issues are the major concern.

Bankruptcies allow employers to abrogate labor agreements. Present interpretations of bankruptcy laws permit employers who undergo reorganization to unilaterally dissolve labor agreements just as they do other contracts.

DISCUSSION QUESTIONS

1. Why don't more firms use lockouts to break impasses?
2. What conditions are necessary for mediation to assist in settling an impasse?
3. Do you believe the present rights given to strikers by the NLRB are appropriate? Should they be increased or decreased?
4. What are the potential consequences for labor relations of the present interpretation of the bankruptcy statutes?

KEY TERMS

CASE
GMFC IMPASSE

Assume you are director of industrial relations for GMFC. The company and the union have failed to agree on a new contract, and the old contract expired last week. Two issues remain unresolved, and no movement has been made on these for more than 10 days. The union is demanding 10 cents an hour more than the company is willing to offer, and management continues to demand some co-payment by employees for medical care. This is the first negotiation in 15 years in which a new contract has not been ratified before the old one expired.

Local 384 voted a strike authorization about a month ago, but the leaders have not yet indicated whether they intend to strike. In your organization, production managers are lobbying for a lockout to avoid material losses if the heated steel treating process must be shut down rapidly. Marketing managers want production maintained to meet orders scheduled for shipment. They argue that the union doesn't intend to strike because it hasn't already done so.

In the executive council meeting this morning, financial officers briefed the top executives of GMFC and indicated the company could accept a wage settlement of 5 cents an hour more, but only if this were a firm figure and not subject to increases over the term of the contract. Unfortunately, the union appeared adamant that it will not agree to any health care co-payment.

It is now your turn to recommend strategy to the company in this impasse. Considering the evidence, what action should the company take? Outline the action, including processes used and timetables. Consider the possibility that your strategy may trigger a strike or other union activity.

13

UNION-MANAGEMENT

COOPERATION

*M*any labor relations practices are adversarial—organizing, bargaining over wages, disputing contract interpretations, and the like. But it is increasingly argued that unions and managements both can achieve improved outcomes through cooperation. As noted earlier, the bargaining unit depends on employment for its existence. If the employer's viability is threatened and the union perceives the threat is credible, both are likely to cooperate to devise a survival strategy. Economic concessions by unions in many of the nation's primary industries during the 1980s were rooted in a recognition that members' jobs were on the line.

This chapter explores the mechanisms and programs involved in union-management cooperation, including regional labor-management cooperation projects, joint union-management productivity programs, employee involvement programs, work and organization redesign, gainsharing, and innovative methods for improving negotiations.

As you study this chapter, consider the following questions:

1. How are cooperative problem-solving methods different from traditional bargaining?
2. Can a cooperation program violate labor laws?
3. What are some results of cooperative programs? Are they equally likely to lead to successes for both unions and managements?
4. What types of cooperation programs are in current use by employers and unions?

LABOR AND MANAGEMENT ROLES AND THE CHANGING ENVIRONMENT

Chapter 2 examined the history of labor relations in the United States. A number of economic cycles influenced the outcomes for labor and management. Labor supply and union power have been altered by several waves of immigration. The Railway Labor, Norris-LaGuardia, and Wagner acts strengthened labor's ability to organize. Taft-Hartley and Landrum-Griffin increased management's powers. At various points, new production technologies substantially reduced the need for low-skill union members.

A major difference between present and previous eras is increasing global competition and its effect on profitability and employment stability. During the past 25 years, industries that virtually monopolized domestic markets have encountered heavy foreign competition: steel, motor vehicles, consumer electric and electronic products, textiles, shoes, and others. Foreign competitors benefited from investment and technology transfer that boosted their productivity while costs of domestic producers increased faster than productivity. Some of this was due to the ability of unions to increase wages and some to failures by employers to invest in technology. Jointly, there was a lack of attention to the way in which work and production were organized as foreign producers implemented the latest in U.S. and international production methods.[1] Some companies failed and local unions were decimated, while others survived and prospered. This chapter examines mechanisms used to meet the challenge and adapt, recognizing the different roles and objectives of management and labor.

Organizing and the Evolving Bargaining Relationship

Unionization has traditionally been fought by U.S. employers. Even in heavily unionized industries, beginning in the 1970s, employers implemented active union avoidance programs by fighting new organizing, shifting production from unionized plants to new **greenfield operations,** and reducing investment in unionized plants.[2]

Adversarial relationships carry over from organizing to bargaining and implementing contracts. The union needs to gain in bargaining for its officers to be reelected and to avoid decertification. Its exclusive representation right and agency responsibility require it to be responsive to all bargaining unit members. The legal specification of mandatory bargaining issues increases the union's emphasis on immediate economic issues and away from employer and union survival issues. As noted earlier, managers have generally been judged on their ability to avoid unionization or to limit its impact. In their dealings with the union, managers tend to view cooperative relationships as those in which the union has

---

[1] J. Hoerr, *And the Wolf Finally Came* (Pittsburgh: University of Pittsburgh Press, 1989).

[2] T. A. Kochan, H. C. Katz, and R. B. McKersie, *The Transformation of American Industrial Relations* (New York: Free Press, 1986).

an insignificant role in decision making.[3] Thus, neither party's leaders are initially motivated to seek cooperation.

Evidence also suggests that unions win initial certification as the result of employees' interests in exercising "voice" in the employment relationship. Creating opportunities for this to occur through cooperation may seem to management as a legitimation of union efforts.

Preferences of Management and Labor

Management seeks the highest profit level it can achieve through investing its capital. It makes investment decisions that shift resources from product lines with lower returns to those with higher profits. To do this, it needs to be able to adapt. From an unconstrained standpoint, it would prefer to open, close, and retool plants as needed; hire labor on a flexible basis; and adjust wage rates to meet changing product market conditions and respond to shifts in the labor market.

Employees are generally assumed to be risk averse, while employers are assumed to be risk neutral. This means employers are looking for the highest rate of return, consistent with the risks they expect to encounter, while employees are assumed to accept lower pay if they can simultaneously reduce unemployment and other risks. Employees are risk averse not because they have an inherent dislike of risk, but because their skills are often occupationally specific, and perhaps specifically tailored to their present employer's requirements. Thus, their human capital is not diversifiable. They depend on continued employment, often with their present employers and in their present occupations, to be able to earn a satisfactory return. Employees are also interested in improving their economic outcomes, particularly when it can be demonstrated that the employer is able to do so. This means employers would prefer great flexibility in employment, while employees would prefer employment security and wages that are not contingent on employer performance.

Levels of Cooperation and Control

Given the way mandatory bargaining issues are defined in the labor acts and the antipathy of employers toward organized labor, managers have sought to retain as much control of the workplace as possible. Labor has generally been reluctant to seek shared responsibility for decision making given its adversarial role and the economic concessions it might have to make to gain a greater say in decision making. Both employers and unions began to consider cooperation during the 1980s in situations where companies or facilities were in extremis.

In return for economic concessions, unions have sometimes won greater claims on the rights to control processes and share in profits. Provisions have been

---

[3] M. M. Perline and E. A. Sexton, "Managerial Perceptions of Labor-Management Cooperation," *Industrial Relations* 33 (1994), pp. 377–85.

negotiated to increase the proportion of employees' pay at risk, usually to help ensure employer survival and increase employment security. The effect of labor–management participation in gaining rights can flow along two dimensions: control and return rights. Control rights involve the degree to which labor participates in organizational decision making. Unionization in itself introduces a degree of control rights because the employer can no longer unilaterally determine mandatory bargaining issues. At the extreme, control rights would include works council arrangements (as in Germany—covered in Chapter 17) and representation on corporate boards of directors. Return rights begin with wage payments, and progress through incentive plans, profit-sharing and gainsharing programs, and ultimately to employee stock ownership of the enterprise.[4]

Conflicts over participation rights, the historical antipathy of employers, and adversarial relationships in bargaining have made the creation of joint problem solving difficult. This chapter explores initiatives in union-management cooperation to jointly accomplish their separate goals. Part of this is done through integrative bargaining during contract negotiations and part through the development of ongoing cooperative relationships. Many cooperation experiments are initiated through side letters in the contract or through agreements to suspend contract provisions to experiment with new methods.

INTEGRATIVE BARGAINING

Integrative bargaining is a set of activities leading to the simultaneous accomplishment of nonconflicting objectives that solve a common problem for both parties.[5] Conflict occurs when parties have different goals and either the need to share resources or task interdependencies block one party's goal attainment if the other party pursues a certain course.[6] For example, shared resources may be available hours of work, and different goals may be overtime premium earnings for the union and high profits for management. One's accomplishment will interfere with the other's. Integrative bargaining occurs when one party's goal will not block the other's. The parties may not immediately know the integrative issues that might emerge from a failure of distributive bargaining to achieve the goals they desire.

Two major types of integrative solutions are suggested. The first is a situation in which both parties experience an absolute gain over their previous positions. As an example, autoworkers at Ford in the 1980s achieved permanent job security in return for new work rules to reduce costs. Second, integrative bargaining may involve both parties sacrificing simultaneously (in distributive bargaining, one's

---

[4] A. Ben-Ner and D. C. Jones, "Employee Participation, Ownership and Productivity: A Theoretical Framework," *Industrial Relations*, 34, (1995), pp. 532–54.

[5] R. E. Walton and R. B. McKersie, *A Behavioral Theory of Labor Negotiations* (New York: McGraw-Hill, 1965), p. 5.

[6] S. M. Schmidt and T. A. Kochan, "Conflict: Toward Conceptual Clarity," *Administrative Science Quarterly* 17 (1972), pp. 359–70.

gain is the other's loss).[7] Steel industry wage concessions in the early 1980s reduced labor costs enough in several situations to keep certain mills open that had been considered for closure because of their technological inefficiency, thus increasing the likelihood of job security for many steelworkers.

Change processes within union-management situations require certain conditions to exist. Increasing internal or external pressures should lead to the consideration of new joint ventures. Multiple constituencies within the union and/or management would stimulate efforts to arrive at innovative procedures for dealing with joint problems. Where the normal collective bargaining process and its attention to crisis situations is used exclusively, innovation is less likely. Joint commitments are more likely when a program is seen as accomplishing important ends for both parties and when both are willing to compromise on goals they desire. Programs should enable early measurable progress toward goals for both to maintain support from their constituents. Many of each group's members must experience benefits, and these benefits should not detract from accomplishing other important goals. Programs should be insulated from the formal bargaining process, and usual methods for distributive bargaining would continue.[8]

While management may propose integrative bargaining in situations where the effects of economic change need to be addressed, distributive effects often underlie the overture. If a change can't be negotiated, management may indicate its intent to close a facility. Capital is far more mobile than labor. A plant can be closed and resources redeployed, but the financial burdens workers face in moving, particularly if the firm is the dominant employer in the area, are often onerous.[9]

A three-step integrative bargaining model requires that (1) the problem as perceived by each party is identified and each conveys information germane to the problem, (2) parties discover how they will reach their individually important goals simultaneously, and (3) parties compare and evaluate the alternatives for reaching simultaneous goals to determine the actions having the greatest benefits to both.[10]

Several conditions are necessary for facilitating problem solving. First, parties must be jointly motivated to reach a solution. Second, communications between parties must reveal as much information addressing the problem as possible. Third, parties must have created a climate in which they can trust each other to deliberate over the issues without taking advantage of disclosed information.[11]

---

[7] Walton and McKersie, *Behavioral Theory*, pp. 128–29.

[8] T. A. Kochan and L. Dyer, "A Model of Organizational Change in the Context of Union-Management Relations," *Journal of Applied Behavioral Science* 12 (1976), pp. 59–78.

[9] E. A. Mannix, C. H. Tinsley, and M. Bazerman, "Negotiating over Time: Impediments to Integrative Solutions," *Organizational Behavior and Human Decision Processes* 62 (1995), pp. 241–51.

[10] Walton and McKersie, *Behavioral Theory*, pp. 137–39.

[11] Ibid., pp. 139–43.

Integrative bargaining is appropriate for both immediate and long-run problems. For example, an integrative solution may be appropriate when a contract issue causes grievances during the agreement. Rather than waiting until the next negotiation, addressing the problem immediately may lead to positive outcomes for both parties. On the other hand, anticipated consequences of technology changes may be long run and require an open-ended relationship extending beyond the contract period.

Mutual Gains Bargaining

As noted in Chapter 11, distributive bargaining essentially "slices up the pie." In addition to reflecting the relative bargaining power of the parties, the bargain establishes certainty in the employment relationship, including costs the employer will encounter. On the other hand, the contract usually assumes that current conditions will continue for the time horizon covered by the agreement. By the time a situation reaches the point that both parties will suffer if the contract is not changed, each may have lost a substantial amount (e.g., employer profits and union members' job security).

A climate in which both the employer and the union would be continually concerned with problem solving and mutual improvement in their situations calls for a living agreement.[12] This requires the parties to determine, a priori, what types of events would trigger problem solving. Contracts that typically include the possibility of reopeners based on the passage of time would require that certain employer and employee outcomes trigger joint problem solving to deal with them.

Unions and managements have been involved in adversarial relationships from organizing onward. As noted in Chapter 11, the parties engage in a number of tactics associated with attitudinal structuring. These are aimed at conveying information to the other party about the strength of commitment to certain bargaining positions. Intraorganizational bargaining also occurs to convince negotiators within the parties to adopt certain positions or to accept certain offers from their opponents.

One problem with certain attitudinal structuring techniques, such as withholding information or threatening opponents, is the breakdown of trust. It's difficult to define and address problems straightforwardly unless parties trust the information each provides. **Principled negotiations** require that bargaining be on the merits of the issue, providing information that would enable both to arrive at a mutually agreeable solution.[13] The process requires that parties trust each other, but trust does not occur spontaneously. Evidence indicates it follows from attitudes toward trust itself, and experience the parties have with the perceived

---

[12] C. Hecksher and L. Hall, "Improving Negotiations: Two Levels of Mutual-Gains Interventions," *Proceedings of the Industrial Relations Research Association* 44 (1992), pp. 160–68.

[13] R. Fisher and W. Ury, *Getting to Yes: Negotiating Agreement without Giving In* (Boston: Houghton Mifflin, 1981).

trustworthiness of their opponents.[14] Where a trusting relationship doesn't exist, the parties will need training and an opportunity to build trust in simulated relationships before beginning to experiment with it in situations in which the parties are at risk.

Creating and sustaining a trusting relationship can be difficult, particularly because much bargaining involves simultaneously both distributive and integrative issues. So-called **"relations by objectives"** programs have been used to train negotiators to take a more problem-solving approach to negotiations and contract administration. Evidence about the effectiveness of these programs is mixed, with some short-term effects on reducing the amount of time necessary to negotiate agreements. However, adverse economic environments erase the effects of change, especially if the negotiators for either side change.[15]

CREATING AND SUSTAINING COOPERATION

U.S. employers basically oppose unions, particularly their involvement in decision making.[16] For more than 60 years, efforts have been made to implement union-management cooperation in a variety of situations, but most have not been sustained.[17] Since the early 1980s, however, an increased number of cooperative initiatives outside contracts and integrative bargains within contracts have enhanced firm performance and improved job security. Efforts are going forward in about half of all unionized firms in the private sector.[18] Given management's long-standing antipathy toward unions, it's reasonable to expect it to collaborate only where improved performance is expected. Where cooperation has been successful, communications between the parties are open, management accepts the representational role of the union, and the union is concerned about the success of the enterprise.[19]

Figure 13–1 depicts a model of the proposed impact of collaboration on performance. It suggests that the intensity of cooperation is influenced by the

---

[14] S. C. Currall, "Labor-Management Trust: Its Dimensions and Correlates," *Proceedings of the Industrial Relations Research Association* 44 (1992), pp. 465–74.

[15] R. Hebdon and M. Mazerolle, "Mending Fences, Building Bridges: The Effect of Relationship by Objectives on Conflict," *Relations Industrielles* 50 (1995), pp. 164–85.

[16] D. Lewin, "Industrial Relations as a Strategic Variable," in M. M. Kleiner, R. N. Block, M. Roomkin, and S. W. Salsburg, eds., *Human Resources and the Performance of the Firm* (Madison, WI: Industrial Relations Research Association, 1987), pp. 1–41.

[17] W. N. Cooke, *Labor-Management Cooperation* (Kalamazoo, MI: W. E. Upjohn Institute for Employment Research, 1990), pp. 4–5.

[18] Kochan et al., *Transformation*; J. T. Delaney, C. Ichniowski, and D. Lewin, "Employee Involvement Programs and Firm Performance," *Proceedings of the Industrial Relations Research Association* 41 (1988), pp. 148–58; and P. B. Voos, "Managerial Perceptions of the Impact of Labor Relations Programs," *Industrial and Labor Relations Review* 40 (1987), pp. 556–68.

[19] R. W. Miller, R. W. Humphreys, and F. A. Zeller, "Structural Characteristics of Successful Cases of Cooperative Union-Management Relations," *Labor Studies Journal* 22, no. 2 (1997), pp. 44–65.

FIGURE 13–1

Model of the Effect of Cooperation on Performance and Labor Relations Outcomes

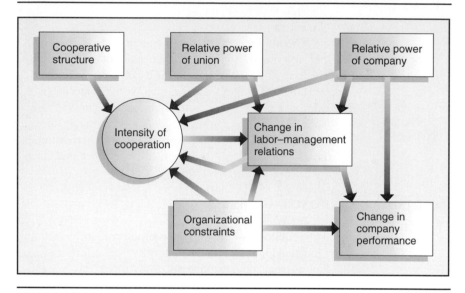

SOURCE: W. N. Cooke, *Labor–Management Cooperation* (Kalamazoo, MI: W. E. Upjohn Institute for Employment Research, 1990), p. 94.

cooperative structure and the relative power of the company and union, as modified by organizational constraints. Over time, the climate of labor-management relations also influences intensity, while changing labor-management relations, the relative power of the company, and organizational constraints lead to changes in company performance. The availability of power to the union and company implies they will use it to influence cooperation. The application of relatively equal power should enhance cooperative efforts where both parties prefer it as a mode for achieving important ends.[20]

Methods of Cooperation

The next section examines methods of cooperation, covering assumptions about types of cooperation, mechanisms used to achieve it, union and management personnel involved, and results of cooperative efforts. Several generic approaches to labor-management cooperation are examined, including areawide labor-management committees, improvement of the atmosphere for contract negotiation, productivity improvement and employee involvement plans, gainsharing, and employee stock ownership plans. Within bargaining relationships, several of these may be combined to enhance joint outcomes. This will be followed by

---

[20] Cooke, *Labor-Management Cooperation*, pp. 93–95.

examining the changing roles of managers and union officials, political changes that occur, and the processes involved in the diffusion and institutionalization of innovation in workplace design.

AREAWIDE LABOR-MANAGEMENT COMMITTEES

Areawide labor-management committees (AWLMCs) are jointly sponsored organizations in given geographic areas. They neither engage in collective bargaining nor form multiemployer or multiunion bargaining units. Instead, they advise their constituents concerning how to deal with jointly experienced employment issues.

AWLMCs are most often a response to significant regional employment problems. They have been concentrated in the Northeast and Midwest, which have experienced industrial and employment declines. There is often a history of plant closings with parent companies expanding elsewhere. High wages and/or union-management relations may have led to some of the employment problems.

A health care labor-management council in Minneapolis-St. Paul enhanced communications between labor and management in an industry undergoing major structural changes in what had become an increasingly adversarial union-management situation. With support from the Minnesota Bureau of Mediation Services, the group aimed at building trust to improve labor-management relations.[21]

The primary assumption behind the creation of AWLMCs is that labor and management's peer members may pressure each to identify sources of problems and use cooperative methods to reduce or avoid conflict. The identification of joint issues, such as reduced profits and declining job security, may lead to joint efforts to resolve them.

AWLMCs are typically managed by an executive director hired by a coalition of top-level business and union leaders. AWLMCs engage in four major types of activities: (1) sponsoring social events to improve labor-management communications, (2) establishing labor-management committees in local plants, (3) providing assistance in negotiations, and (4) fostering local economic development.[22] These activities are aimed at creating an environment in which problems can be solved and an outward appearance of labor and management cooperation for the betterment of both.

The effectiveness of AWLMCs is difficult to assess because they do not encompass all employers and all are not facing similar problems. In Buffalo, New York, in-plant committees were established to facilitate negotiations in a utility company undergoing a 17-week strike and in four cargo-handling firms faced

---

[21] "Nearly 30 Twin Cities Area Hospitals, Unions Form Labor-Management Council," *Labor Relations Week*, July 18, 1990, p. 681.

[22] R. D. Leone, *The Operation of Area Labor-Management Committees* (Washington, DC: U.S. Department of Labor, Labor-Management Services Administration, 1982).

with declining shipping volumes. The negotiating and cargo volume objectives have been partially achieved.

In Jamestown, New York, several committees were begun in small- to medium-size plants. The community had little success in involving the two largest local employers. In-plant committees succeeded in improving productivity and reducing overhead, but because inadequate attention was paid to implementation and gaining agreement on the effects of changes, many of the efforts foundered.

Generally, evidence suggests AWLMCs need the backing of major employers who have visibility in the community and a competent executive director who is willing and able to stay in the post for an extended period to accomplish the goals.[23]

JOINT LABOR-MANAGEMENT COMMITTEES

An examination of the retail food industry **joint labor-management committee** (JLMC) indicates that this forum involving top union and management leaders helps managers understand the national-local union relationship in a decentralized industry. Successful projects involved research in occupational safety and health issues, the introduction of new technology, health care cost-containment, and competitiveness issues.[24] AT&T and the Communications Workers of America (CWA) developed a corporate-national union method for helping local unions and managements cope with cutbacks and job changes resulting from divesting telephone operating companies and introducing new technology. Many of the projects involved retraining for new jobs in AT&T or with local employers.[25] JLMCs are most often implemented in industries with many employers and a dominant union with locals in many employers and locations.

Joint labor-management committees have been used in most situations to deal with particular problems rather than to address the entire scope of the bargaining and employment relationship. Some joint efforts, triggered by particular problems, have led to continuing and expanded cooperation efforts. Notable among these have been the relationships between Xerox Corporation and the Amalgamated Clothing and Textile Workers (ACTWU) begun as a result of rapidly growing competitive pressures faced by Xerox in the early 1980s and the effects this was having on job security,[26] and the Employee Involvement (EI)

---

[23] Ibid.; and R. W. Ahern, "Discussion of Labor-Management Cooperation," *Proceedings of the Industrial Relations Research Association* 35 (1982), pp. 201–6.

[24] Kochan et al., *Transformation*, pp. 182–89.

[25] C. Alexander, "The Alliance for Employee Growth and Development," *Labor-Management Cooperation Brief*, No. 17, U.S. Department of Labor, Bureau of Labor-Management Relations and Cooperative Programs (1989); and more recently D. K. Allen, "BellSouth-CWA Partnership: Teaming Up to Meet the Challenges of a Changing Industry," *Employee Relations Today* 21 (1994), pp. 163–72.

[26] P. Lazes, "Unions and the Choice of Employee Involvement Activities," *Workplace Topics* 2, no. 2 (1991), pp. 1–12.

program developed by Ford Motor Company and the United Auto Workers to respond to higher levels of quality and value in imported vehicles and decreasing profits and job security in an industry under siege. Another example is the introduction of joint building trades–union contractor committees in the construction industry. Here one study found improvements in safety, training, and absenteeism; a reduction in jurisdictional disputes between unions; and a decline in jobs going to nonunion contractors.[27]

WORKPLACE INTERVENTIONS

Workplace interventions are projects initiated at the plant or office level. They may reside in a single location within an employer and involve a single union, or they may be part of a larger joint union-management program. Typically, changes are sought by employers to improve product quality, productivity, and profitability. Unions seek enhanced employment security, an opportunity for economic gains, and continued operation of local facilities.

Workplace interventions often lead to new designs for work and organization through increased use of team-based methods, lean production, cell manufacturing, self-directed work teams, and the like. Jobs are made broader and their classifications consolidated, increasing the employer's flexibility in assigning work as demands change and reducing the likelihood of layoff that might be associated with the decrease in demand for jobs in which narrow skills are represented. Pay programs are often changed so employees share in productivity or profitability gains while reducing employers' risks during periods of economic difficulty. Employees find pay more frequently tied to their skill level rather than to their current job or seniority level.

The prevalence of joint programs varies widely across manufacturers. Table 13–1 shows a sample of over 200 company and union situations. Of these, quality and productivity are most frequently addressed by programs based on work teams, while productivity and labor-management climate are more frequently handled by structures based on committees. Programs were generally initiated by the company without outside assistance. U.S. government agency support was the most frequently used outside help.[28]

A variety of workplace interventions has been implemented. Table 13–2 summarizes key program dimensions for seven major types. They can be divided roughly into gainsharing and nongainsharing plans. Gainsharing plans increase pay when labor becomes more productive following an intervention than during a base period. Nongainsharing approaches may include a changed reward structure

---

[27] J. Remington and B. Londrigan, "Construction Industry Labor-Management Cooperation Committees: Defining Essential Elements," *Labor Studies Journal* 19, no. 2 (1994), pp. 67–80.

[28] W. N. Cooke, "Labor-Management Collaboration: New Partnerships or Going in Circles" (Ann Arbor: University of Michigan, 1988).

TABLE 13–1

Type and Extent of Joint Programs across Manufacturing

Type of Program	Percent of Plants with Program*
Quality circles	31
Quality-of-work-life/employee involvement	19
Work teams	18
Productivity committees	17
Labor–management committees	15
Scanlon or other gainsharing (with employee involvement)	7
Employee stock ownership (with employee involvement)	6
Profit sharing (with employee involvement)	6
Other than above	12

*Based on 194 company responses and 40 unique responses.
SOURCE: W. N. Cooke, "Improving Productivity and Quality: Juxtaposing Relative and Collaborative Power" (Ann Arbor: Graduate School of Business Administration and Joint Labor-Management Relations Center, University of Michigan, 1988), p. 4.

(primarily nonmonetary) in the intervention, but no contingency between productivity and pay is established. The table summarizes each intervention method's guiding philosophy, primary change goal, degree of worker participation, role of supervisors and management, any bonus formulas, role of the union, and other method characteristics.

Scanlon, Rucker, and Impro-Share plans are designed to improve productivity. Scanlon and Rucker plans depend on employee suggestions. The **Scanlon plan** allows employee groups to screen and implement suggestions, while management controls the suggestion system in the **Rucker plan.** The **Impro-Share plan** shares savings resulting from performance improvements over an engineered standard and allows employers to make "buyouts" of productivity improvements if new technologies are introduced. If gainsharing plans are implemented at the same time that base pay levels are reduced, greater proportions of an employee's pay would be at risk.

Quality circles, originally developed in Japan, enable employees to solve production problems and implement solutions. No bonus is explicitly tied to improvements. Under Japanese systems, however, all employees share in bonuses resulting from the organization's performance at six-month or yearly intervals. Labor-management committees are formed to deal with pervasive employment problems within the organization. **Quality-of-work-life programs** aim at improving the workplace environment and increasing the satisfaction of employees, with productivity changes as a welcomed by-product if they are positive. Team-based approaches are aimed at increasing flexibility, utilizing employees, eliminating management layers, and enabling employees to control the process within their work units. They have become increasingly utilized with the implementation of total quality management (TQM) programs.

TABLE 13-2
Comparative Analyses of Workplace Interventions

Program Dimension	Gainsharing			Nongainsharing			
	Scanlon	Rucker	Impro-Share	Quality Circles	Labor-Management Committees	Quality-of-work-life Projects	Self-Managed Work Teams
Philosophy/theory	Share improvements; people willing to make suggestions, want to make ideas work	Primarily economic incentive; some reliance on employee participation	Economic incentives; increased performance	People capable/willing to offer ideas/make suggestions	Improve attitudes; trust	Improve environment (physical, human, systems aspects)	Reduce layers of management; increase employees' control over work environment
Primary goal	Productivity improvement	Productivity improvement	Productivity improvement	Cost reduction, quality	Improve labor-management relations, communications	Improve psychological well-being at work; increase job satisfaction	Productivity improvement; reduce levels of supervision
Subsidiary goals	Attitudes, communication, work behaviors, quality, cost reduction	Attitudes, communication, work behaviors, quality, cost reduction	Attitudes, work behaviors	Attitudes, work behaviors, quality, productivity	Work behaviors, quality, productivity, cost reductions	Attitudes, communication, work behaviors, quality, productivity, cost reduction	Worker autonomy, quality, cost reduction, flexibility
Worker participation	Two levels of committees: screening (1), production (many)	Screening committee, production committee (sometimes)	Bonus committee	Screening (1); circles (many)	Visitor subcommittees (many)	Steering committees; ad hoc to work on problem; informal	Control over work assignments, production methods
Suggestion making	Formal system	Formal system	None	Context of committee	None, informal	Possibly informal, depending on project	Determined within team

TABLE 13–2
(Concluded)

Program Dimension	Gainsharing			Nongainsharing			
	Scanlon	Rucker	Impro-Share	Quality Circles	Labor-Management Committees	Quality-of-work-life Projects	Self-Managed Work Teams
Role of supervisor	Chair, production committee	None	None	Circle leaders	None	No direct role	No supervisor
Role of managers	Direct participation in bonus committee assignments	Ideas coordinator evaluates suggestions, committee assignments	None	Facilitator evaluates proposed solutions	Committee members	Steering committee membership	Communicates with work team on production targets; problem-solving
Bonus formula	Sales/payroll	Bargaining unit payroll/Production value (sales-materials, supplies, services)	Engineered std. × BPF/Total hours worked	All savings/improvements retained by company	All savings/improvements retained by company	All savings/improvements retained by company	All savings/improvements retained by company
Frequency of payout	Monthly	Monthly	Weekly	Not applicable	Not applicable	Not applicable	Not applicable
Role of union	Negotiated provisions, screening committee membership	Negotiated provisions, screening committee membership	Negotiated provisions	Tacit approval	Active membership	Negotiated provisions, screening committee membership	Job design negotiated into collective bargaining agreement
Impact on management style	Substantial	Slight	None	Some	Some	Substantial	Substantial

SOURCE: Expanded from M. Schuster, *Union-Management Cooperation: Structure, Process, and Impact* (Kalamazoo, MI: W. E. Upjohn Institute for Employment Research, 1984), p. 73.

The Scanlon Plan

The Scanlon plan was born in the late 1930s in a struggling steel mill. With no profits and employees demanding higher wages and better working conditions, their union leader, Joseph Scanlon, saw that gaining the demands would force the company's closure. To meet the company's profit goals and the union's wage and working condition demands, he proposed the parties work together to increase productivity to which a wage bonus would be linked. Two underlying foundations of the Scanlon Plan are participation by all production employees in a unit and equity in reward distribution.[29]

The participation system is based on the recognition that abilities are widely distributed in the organization and that change in the organization's environment is inevitable. Because change occurs and employees at all levels may have solutions to problems or suggestions to improve productivity, the system includes an open suggestion procedure. Suggestions are evaluated and acted on by joint worker-management committees who make recommendations up the line. Figure 13–2 details a typical committee structure and their actions.

A suggestion is evaluated by a work unit's **production committee.** If a suggestion has merit and can be implemented in the unit, the production committee can implement it. If the suggestion is questionable or has wide impact, it is sent to a **screening committee** (comprised of executives and employee representatives) for evaluation and possible implementation.

The screening committee is also responsible for determining the bonus to be paid each month or quarter. The bonus is calculated by comparing the usual share of product costs attributed to labor with the most recent actual costs. For example, if each $1 of sales has traditionally required 30 cents worth of labor, then any improvement, to 29 or 25 cents, for example, would represent a productivity improvement. Table 13–3 represents a simple formula in which labor costs are 30 percent of the total production value.

Companywide and individual bonuses are calculated after the screening committee receives operating results for the previous period. Table 13–4 gives an example of a company bonus report.

The Scanlon plan's major purposes are to increase rewards to both parties for productivity gains, encourage and reward participation, and link pay to employer performance. The plan focuses on reducing labor costs for a given level of output—a factor more directly within workers' control. Thus, the behavior-outcome relationship is higher than it is for profit sharing. Productivity gains are shared across work groups, encouraging solutions that mutually benefit several departments.

Over a nine-year period, one Scanlon plan failed to pay a bonus only 13 times. While productivity was not significantly better, its direction was up. Employment

---

[29] C. F. Frost, J. H. Wakeley, and R. A. Ruh, *The Scanlon Plan for Organization Development: Identity, Participation, and Equity* (East Lansing: Michigan State University Press, 1974), pp. 5–26.

FIGURE 13–2

Scanlon Plan Production Committee

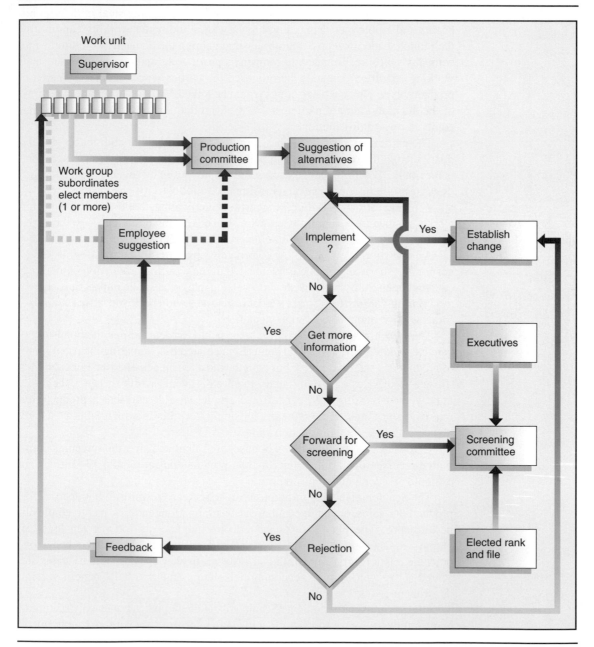

TABLE 13–3

Simple Labor Formula

Sales	$ 98,000
Returned goods	3,000
Net sales	95,000
Inventory +	5,000
Production value	$100,000
Labor bill	
Wages	$ 16,000
Salaries	8,000
Vacations and holidays	1,800
Insurance	1,700
Pensions	500
Unemployment	500
F.I.C.A.	1,500
Total labor bill	$ 30,000
Ratio	.30

SOURCE: C. F. Frost, J. H. Wakeley, and R. A. Ruh, *The Scanlon Plan for Organization Development: Identity, Participation, and Equity* (East Lansing: Michigan State University Press, 1974), p. 103.

TABLE 13–4

Bonus Report

a. Scanlon ratio	0.40/1.00
b. Value of production	$100,000
c. Expected costs (*a* × *b*)	40,000
d. Actual costs	30,000
e. Bonus pool (*c* − *d*)	10,000
f. Share to company—20% (*e* × 0.20)	2,000
g. Share to employees—80% (adjusted pool) (*e* × 0.80)	8,000
h. Share for future deficits—25% of adjusted pool (*g* × 0.25)	2,000
i. Pool for immediate distribution (*g* − *h*)	6,000
j. Bonus for each employee* as a percentage of pay for the production period (*i* ÷ *d*)	20%

The June pay record might look like this for a typical employee:

Name	Monthly Pay for June	Bonus Percent	Bonus	Total Pay
Mary Smith	$900	20%	$180	$1,080

* This example assumes all employees are participating in the plan at the time this bonus is paid; for example, there has been no turnover and no employees are in their initial 30-, 60-, or 90-day trial periods.

SOURCE: Modified from C. F. Frost, J. H. Wakeley, and R. A. Ruh, *The Scanlon Plan for Organization Development: Identity, Participation, and Equity* (East Lansing: Michigan State University Press, 1974), p. 15.

decreased over time but not as rapidly as in the industry as a whole.[30] Another more recently implemented plan often fails to pay bonuses because of declining prices, but employee suggestions for savings have continued to increase.[31] In another organization, the focus of productivity suggestions has shifted from material and in-house work improvements to improving work processes and product design.[32]

Although comparing the results of Scanlon plans has limitations, evidence suggests that (1) perceived participation is necessary for successful implementation, (2) company or plant size is not a factor, (3) managerial attitudes toward the plan predict its success, (4) successful implementation takes considerable time, (5) plans are more successful where expectations are high but realistic, (6) a high-level executive must lead implementation for it to be successful, and (7) the type of production technology is not related to success or failure.[33]

Rucker Plans

Rucker plans (named after the industrial engineer who developed them) have some participative elements of Scanlon plans, but management names an idea coordinator to handle suggestions. Bonuses are calculated by determining the historical value added by direct labor. Any improvement in value added will earn a bonus. Employees may receive bonuses based on output increases, lower scrap rates, and other material or subcontracting savings. If their costs increased, even in the face of improved productivity, it could result in an inability to pay bonuses. Rucker plans might be suggested for an employer not ready to participate to the degree a Scanlon plan requires, but they may be difficult to obtain in a collective bargaining agreement.[34] Table 13–5 shows how Rucker plan bonus pools are calculated.

Impro-Share

Impro-Share ties pay to improved productivity. While consultative management is suggested, participation is minimal except a bonus committee is responsible for determining some aspects of the bonus formula. The bonus formula is somewhat

---

[30] C. S. Miller and M. Schuster, "A Decade's Experience with the Scanlon Plan: A Case Study," *Journal of Occupational Behavior* 8 (1987), pp. 167–74.

[31] G. Pearlstein, "Preston Trucking Drives for Productivity," *Labor-Management Cooperation Brief*, No. 13., U.S. Department of Labor, Bureau of Labor-Management Relations and Cooperative Programs, 1988.

[32] J. B. Arthur and L. Aiman-Smith, "Gainsharing as Organizational Learning: An Analysis of Employee Suggestions over Time," *Proceedings of the Industrial Relations Research Association* 48 (1996), pp. 270–77.

[33] J. K. White, "The Scanlon Plan: Causes and Correlates of Success," *Academy of Management Journal* 23 (1979), pp. 292–312.

[34] M. Schuster, *Union-Management Cooperation: Structure, Process, and Impact* (Kalamazoo, MI: W. E. Upjohn Institute for Employment Research, 1984).

TABLE 13–5
Rucker Plan Bonus Calculation

Historic labor input percentage	45%
Employees' share	50%
Value of production	$1,000,000
Materials and supplies	$550,000
Outside purchases, nonlabor costs	$125,000
Value added (VA)	$325,000
Allowed labor costs (VA times .45)	$146,250
Actual labor costs	$134,500
Bonus pool	$11,750
Employee share	$5,875
Participating payroll	$117,500
Bonus percentage	5%

complex, but the result subtracts the actual hours employees work from the "base value earned hours" of their output. If the result is positive, the employees' share (say, 50 percent) is divided by the actual number of hours worked to obtain a bonus percentage. For example, if an employee worked 1,000 hours during a period, and base value earned hours were 1,100 with a 50 percent share, the bonus would be 5 percent. Table 13–6 shows how the Impro-Share bonus is determined.

Impro-Share allows employers to direct incentives toward specific jobs or groups and decreases competitors' abilities to determine wage costs based on bonus formulas. However, employees have difficulty calculating what they will receive.[35] A study of Impro-Share plans in both union and nonunion environments found that productivity increased an average of 8 percent the first year after its introduction. By the third year, productivity was up an average of 17.5 percent. Much of the gains can be attributed to reductions in defects and downtime. Larger workplaces had lower rates of improvement, suggesting free riding is less of a problem in smaller plants.[36]

Quality Circles

Quality circles (QCs) are teams of employees supported by management who meet periodically to focus attention on product and service quality or other issues. In both union and nonunion settings, the leaders or facilitators in the QCs are not usually the supervisors of the work group, particularly where the circle cuts across functional areas (e.g., production and quality assurance).

---

[35] Ibid.

[36] R. T. Kaufman, "The Effects of Improshare on Productivity," *Industrial and Labor Relations Review* 45 (1992), pp. 311–22.

TABLE 13–6

Calculation of Impro-Share Bonus

Base Productivity Factor Calculation

$$\frac{\text{Direct labor hours} + \text{Indirect labor hours}}{\text{Direct labor hours}}$$

Example:
   40 Direct labor employees
   20 Indirect labor employees
   40 Hours per week

$$\frac{40(40) + 20(40)}{40(40)} = 1.5$$

Work Hour Standard

$$\frac{\text{Total production work hours}}{\text{Units produced}}$$

Example:

Direct employees	20
Hours per employee	40
Pieces produced	1,000
Total hours	800
Hours per piece	.8

Bonus Calculation

Units produced	1,100
Allowed hours	.8
Base productivity factor	1.5
Impro-Share base	1,320
(Units times allowed hours × BPF)	
Base hours	1,320
Actual hours	1,200
Gained hours	120
Pay per hour	$10.00
Employee share	.50

Bonus

$$\frac{\text{Pay per hour} \times \text{Gained hours} \times \text{Employee Share}}{\text{Actual hours}}$$

$$\frac{10 \times 120 \times .5}{1,200} = \$.50$$

One study found that the opportunity for participation in quality circles was most attractive to employees who were younger, believed the union should be involved, were less likely to be involved in union activities, were more often involved in on-the-job activities such as suggestion programs, desired more participation, and had more information on quality circles. The results suggested that unions shouldn't be concerned about employee involvement programs as a means of weakening union control. Rather, employees will identify increasingly with the company if the union doesn't support opportunities for interested employees to be involved.[37]

Labor-Management Committees

Labor-management committees focus on organizational problems if labor-management relations have been deteriorating and may lead to one of the more formal plans previously described. Representatives and methods are determined on an ad hoc basis. The success of the committees depends on the ability of the parties to focus on problems threatening their mutual interests.

At Xerox, study-action teams are groups of employees removed from their regular jobs to deal with a particular problem. Product development and liaison teams are involved with designing and implementing programs to accommodate the manufacture and sale of new products.[38] Cooperative efforts are motivated by a need to reduce costs to compete effectively in a maturing product line. At Xerox, a team was developed to study this problem, propose and implement solutions, working six months away from their regular jobs. Implementation was the least rewarding phase for the group.[39]

Quality-of-Work-Life and Employee Involvement Programs

From an overall standpoint, quality-of-work-life (QWL) programs include three components: (1) improving workplace climate, (2) generating commitment, and (3) implementing change. However, three alternative developmental patterns involving these three components exist. In planned programs, climate and commitment lead to change; in evolved programs, climate leads to change, which leads in turn to commitment; and in induced programs, change leads to appropriate climate and commitment.[40] Union willingness to become involved in QWL programs appears related to the progressiveness of the company and increased foreign competition. Increased involvement in traditional workplace decisions is related to deregulation, changing demographics, and support (but not pressure) by a parent national union. Cooperation in strategic decision making is related positively to foreign competition and negatively to domestic competition—probably because the same national union often represents employees in other companies in the industry.[41]

---

[37] A. Verma and R. B. McKersie, "Employee Involvement: The Implications of Noninvolvement by Unions," *Industrial and Labor Relations Review* 40 (1987), pp. 556–68.

[38] P. Lazes, "Unions and the Choice of Employee Involvement Activities," *Workplace Topics* 2, no. 2 (1991), pp. 1–12.

[39] P. Lazes, L. Rumpeltes, A. Hoffner, L. Pace, and A. Costanza, "Xerox and the ACTWU: Using Labor-Management Teams to Remain Competitive," *National Productivity Review* 10 (1991), pp. 339–50.

[40] R. W. Keidel, "QWL Development: Three Trajectories," *Human Relations* (1982), pp. 743–61.

[41] I. Goll, "Environment, Corporate Ideology, and Employee Involvement Programs," *Industrial Relations* 29 (1990), pp. 501–12.

A study examining industrial relations performance, quality, productive efficiency, and QWL components in GM–UAW plants found that grievances, discipline, absenteeism, number of local contract demands, and negotiating time were
significantly related. Grievances and absenteeism also tended to rise during periods of strong demand for automobiles. Product quality and productivity-efficiency
measures were negatively related to industrial relations problems. Managerial attitudes were positively related to both labor relations and productivity-efficiency
measures. Evidence also suggests QWL programs were associated with higher
product quality and reduced grievance rates. Absenteeism, ironically, was associated with higher quality, possibly because less-careful workers were absent more
often. QWL program ratings were not associated with productivity-efficiency
changes.[42]

Other studies indicate QWL programs are associated with reductions in
absences, accidents, grievances, and quits even when unemployment rates are
held constant.[43] Participation in programs leads to greater loyalty to the union
rather than undermining commitment. However, perceived effectiveness of the
grievance procedure is a stronger predictor of attitudes toward the union than participation in QWL programs.[44]

Employee involvement program (EI) participation was associated with
improved job satisfaction and enhanced communication skills. Union empowerment is a possible outcome.[45] EI programs were found to increase the organizational citizenship behavior of participants, both through participation and
changing job characteristics that require more task sharing. Other employment
practices had little effect.[46] Finally, union antagonism toward EI doesn't appear to
influence employee attitudes, but it does reduce participation.[47]

Team-Based Approaches

The restructuring of organizations that began in the 1980s has increasingly
involved team-based approaches. Work teams are constructed of employees who
are responsible for a particular function or who operate in a given work area. They

[42] H. C. Katz, T. A. Kochan, and K. R. Gobeille, "Industrial Relations Performance, Economic
Performance, and QWL Programs: An Interplant Analysis," *Industrial and Labor Relations Review* 37
(1983), pp. 3–17.

[43] S. J. Havlovic, "Quality of Work Life and Human Resource Outcomes," *Industrial Relations*
30 (1991), pp. 469–79.

[44] A. E. Eaton, M. E. Gordon, and J. H. Keefe, "The Impact of Quality of Work Life Programs
and Grievance System Effectiveness on Union Commitment," *Industrial and Labor Relations Review*
45 (1992), pp. 591–604.

[45] T. Juravich, "Empirical Research on Employee Involvement: A Critical Review for Labor,"
Labor Studies Journal 21, no. 2 (1996), pp. 51–69.

[46] P. Cappelli and N. Rogovsky, "Employee Involvement and Organizational Citizenship:
Implications for Labor Law Reform and 'Lean Production'," *Industrial and Labor Relations Review*
51 (1998), pp. 633–53.

[47] R. E. Allen and K. L. Van Norman, "Employee Involvement Programs: The Noninvolvement
of Unions Revisited," *Journal of Labor Research* 17 (1996), pp. 479–95.

are given responsibility for the output from the area, including how tasks are to be assigned to employees, and how their assigned outputs are to be produced given the equipment they have.

Each member of the team is expected to be able to perform any of the tasks necessary to produce the output for which the team is responsible. The greater the number of skills employees possess, the greater the variety of tasks they can perform. As such, many team-based programs are supported by skill-based pay (SBP) plans. SBP plans tie employees' pay levels to the number of specific skills they can demonstrate they have acquired.[48] Within a team, an employee who has acquired the entire set of applicable skills can perform any of the jobs. Further, broader skills mean the organization can readily accommodate changes in demands for products because employees can assume new responsibilities quickly. Less equipment downtime occurs because one of the skill sets includes equipment maintenance. Multiskilling also improves an individual's job security.[49]

Creating teams and training them to take responsibility for work assignments and output allows the elimination of supervisors, creating a leaner organization. Teams at Saturn Corporation are led by a management and a union representative. There is no increase in costs, however, because many more employees are associated with these facilitators than reported to two or more supervisors in a traditional setting.[50] The Saturn teams are involved in decision making in areas outside of the mandatory bargaining issues, including choosing suppliers, product design, and vehicle types to be produced. Figures 13–3 and 13–4 demonstrate aspects of the team process at Saturn. At Chrysler's Jefferson North plant, a **"modern operating agreement"** was implemented as the company's quid pro quo for rebuilding the plant in Detroit. Team leaders are elected in this operation as well, but rotation is infrequent. The team structure encourages equal effort and reduced absenteeism. This plant was staffed primarily by senior employees who would have been laid off if a new plant had not been built.[51]

Team members team are expected to learn all skills required by jobs performed by the team. The team decides how work will be accomplished. Supervisors act as facilitators rather than directing work. In organizations where **team concepts** have been implemented, relatively small numbers of distinct jobs exist. Employee-supervisor relations improve more when there is substantial participation by union leaders and teams are very active. They do best where employment

---

[48] For additional details on skill-based pay plans, see G. T. Milkovich and J. Newman, *Compensation,* 6th ed. (Burr Ridge, IL: Irwin-McGraw-Hill, 1999).

[49] C. Ichniowski, "Human Resource Practices and Productive Labor-Management Relations," in D. Lewin, O. S. Mitchell, and P. D. Sherer, eds., *Research Frontiers in Industrial Relations and Human Resources* (Madison, WI: Industrial Relations Research Association, 1992), pp. 239–72.

[50] S. Rubinstein, M. Bennett, and T. Kochan, "The Saturn Partnership: Co-Management and the Reinvention of the Local Union," in B. E. Kaufman and M. M. Kleiner, eds., *Employee Representation: Alternatives and Future Directions* (Madison, WI: Industrial Relations Research Association, 1993), pp. 339–70.

[51] H. Shaiken, S. Lopez, and I. Mankita, "Two Routes to Team Production: Saturn and Chrysler Compared," *Industrial Relations* 36 (1997), pp. 17–45.

FIGURE 13–3

Saturn's Organizing Principles

- Treat people as a fixed asset. Provide opportunities for them to maximize their contributions and value to the organization. Provide extensive training and skill development to all employees.
- The Saturn organization will be based on groups which will attempt to identify and work collaboratively toward common goals.
- Saturn will openly share all information including financial data.
- Decision making will be based on consensus through a series of formal joint labor-management committees, or Decision Rings. As a stakeholder in the operation of Saturn, the UAW will participate in business decisions as a full partner, including site selection and construction, process and product design, choice of technologies, supplier selection, make-buy decisions, retail dealer selection, pricing, business planning, training, business systems development, budgeting, quality systems, productivity improvement, job design, new product development, recruitment and hiring, maintenance, and engineering.
- Self-managed teams or Work Units will be the basic building blocks of the organization.
- Decision-making authority will be located at the level of the organization where the necessary knowledge resides, and where implementation takes place. Emphasis will be placed on the Work Unit.
- There will be a minimum of job classifications.
- Saturn will have a jointly developed and administered recruitment and selection process, and Work Units will hire their own team members. Seniority will not be the basis for selection, and the primary recruiting pool will consist of active and laid off GM/UAW employees.
- The technical and social work organization will be integrated.
- There will be fewer full-time elected UAW officials and fewer labor relations personnel responsible for contract administration.
- Saturn's reward system will be designed to encourage everyone's efforts toward the common goals of quality, cost, timing and value to the customer.

SOURCE: S. Rubinstein, M. Bennett, and T. Kochan, "The Saturn Partnership: Co-Management and the Reinvention of the Local Union," in B. E. Kaufman and M. M. Kleiner, eds., *Employee Representation: Alternatives and Future Directions* (1993), pp. 343, table; 345, figure.

has not changed appreciably, where workers are experienced and management does not subcontract.[52]

While team approaches to job designs have been broadly implemented, they have been controversial in the auto industry, particularly at General Motors. GM's initial foray into cooperation involved QWL programs begun before major economic downturns hit the industry. Since then, the introduction of teams has been primarily aimed at improving productivity with more positive worker outcomes a potential by-product.

Team approaches have been quite successful in New United Motors Manufacturing, Inc. (NUMMI), the GM–Toyota joint venture in Fremont,

[52] W. N. Cooke, "Factors Influencing the Effect of Joint Union-Management Programs on Employee-Supervisor Relations," *Industrial and Labor Relations Review* 43 (1990), pp. 587–603.

FIGURE 13–4

Saturn Partnership Structure

Work units are organized into teams of 6 to 15 members, electing their own leaders who remain working members of the unit. They are self-directed and empowered with the authority, responsibility, and resources necessary to meet their day-to-day assignments and goals including producing to budget, quality, housekeeping, safety, and health, maintenance, material and inventory control, training, job assignments, repairs, scrap control, vacation approvals, absenteeism, supplies, recordkeeping, personnel selection and hiring, work planning, and work scheduling.

Saturn has no supervisors in the traditional sense. Teams interrelated by geography, product, or technology are organized into modules. Modules have common Advisors.

Modules are integrated into three Business Units: Body Systems (stamping, body fabrication, injection molding, and paint); Powertrain (lost foam casting, machining and assembly of engines and transmissions); and Vehicle Systems (vehicle interior, chassis, hardware, trim, exterior panels and assembly).

Joint labor-management Decision Rings meet weekly:

- At the corporate level the Strategic Action Council (SAC) concerns itself with company-wide long-range planning, and relations with dealers, suppliers, stockholders, and the community. Participating in the SAC for the union is the local president and, on occasion, a UAW national representative.

- The Manufacturing Action Council (MAC) covers the Spring Hill manufacturing and assembly complex. On the MAC representing the local is the union president and the four vice presidents who also serve as the UAW bargaining committee.

- Each Business Unit has a joint labor-management Decision Ring at the plant level. The local president appoints an elected executive board member who is joined by UAW Module Advisors and Crew Coordinators in representing the union.

- Decision Rings are also organized at the module level. Module Advisors and the elected Work Unit Counselors (team leaders) participate in the module Decision Rings.

SOURCE: S. Rubinstein, M. Bennett, and T. Kochan, "The Saturn Partnership: Co-Management and the Reinvention of the Local Union," in B. E. Kaufman and M. M. Kleiner, eds., *Employee Representation: Alternatives and Future Directions* (1993), pp. 343, table; 345, figure.

California, which is managed by Toyota. Before the joint venture, this GM assembly plant had the worst absentee and quality records in the corporation. When NUMMI started, the UAW remained as the employees' representative, and most of the newly hired employees had previously been with the plant. The team concept was agreed to before hiring and start-up, and extensive training in statistical process control and teamwork approaches was undertaken. Ultimately, the pace is faster than when GM ran the plant, but there is also a no-layoff policy. Absentee rates are very low.[53] The employee involvement program helped improve ergonomics for the introduction of the 1993 models.[54]

---

[53] C. Brown and M. Reich, "When Does Union-Management Cooperation Work? A Look at NUMMI and GM-Van Nuys," *California Management Review* 31, no. 4 (1989), pp. 26–37; P. D. Staudohar, "Labor-Management Cooperation at NUMMI," *Labor Law Journal* 42 (1991), pp. 57–63.

[54] P. S. Adler, B. Goldoftas, and D. I. Levine, "Ergonomics, Employee Involvement, and the Toyota Production System: A Case Study of NUMMI's 1993 Model Introduction," *Industrial and Labor Relations Review* 50 (1997), pp. 416–37.

At GM-Van Nuys, California, however, a bare majority voted for the team concept in return for keeping the assembly plant open. Some members saw the vote as pitting workers in different plants against each other to save their plants. Opponents saw the team concept as eroding local and national union power and reducing returns to seniority through the virtual elimination of promotion opportunities.[55] At Van Nuys, implementation involved training in interpersonal skills but, unlike NUMMI, no employment security was promised.[56] Since then, the critics' arguments appear to be justified since the plant has been closed.

Teams seem to be most productive where workers have the requisite skills, particularly in statistical process control, and where management has designed a great deal of autonomy for the teams.[57] Teams have more trouble when working with problems that occur outside the organization, such as supplier quality, shipping schedules, and inventory management. Product-line changes can disrupt teams as employment levels change.[58] Because teams were implemented about the same time wage concessions were granted, they are very controversial in many plants. Dissidents claim concessions haven't saved jobs and that teamwork is harder than the assembly-line approach. They also claim their locals discourage grievances and create a layer of union bureaucrats who are not in elected office, and thus not accountable.[59]

Alternative Governance Forms

Union-management cooperation changes both the production process and workplace governance. Employee involvement in decision making shifts the focus of collective bargaining from structural rules to processes. Traditional collective bargaining offers less participation than other forms of governance.[60] Table 13–7 shows the relationship between employee relations practice and various employee involvement areas influencing governance of the organization.

Union Political Processes and the Diffusion of Change

Collaboration is foreign to an adversarial environment. Major political changes are necessary to implement cooperation at national and local union levels. This is

[55] E. Mann, *Taking on General Motors* (Los Angeles: Center for Labor Research and Education, Institute of Industrial Relations, University of California, 1987).

[56] Brown and Reich, "Union-Management Cooperation."

[57] J. Hoerr, "The Cultural Revolution at A. O. Smith," *Business Week*, May 29, 1989, pp. 66–68.

[58] W. Zellner, "GM's New 'Teams' Aren't Hitting Any Homers," *Business Week*, August 8, 1988, pp. 46–47.

[59] W. Zellner, "The UAW Rebels Teaming up against Teamwork," *Business Week*, March 27, 1989, pp. 110–14.

[60] A. Verma and J. Cutcher-Gershenfeld, "Joint Governance in the Workplace: Beyond Union-Management Cooperation and Worker Participation," in B. E. Kaufman and M. M. Kleiner, eds., *Employee Representation: Alternatives and Future Directions* (Madison, WI: Industrial Relations Research Association, 1993), pp. 197–234.

TABLE 13–7
Joint Governance and Other Governance Forms

Dimensions	High-Involvement Nonunion Systems	Traditional Collective Bargaining	Traditional Labor-Management Committees	Labor Representatives on the Board	German-style Works Councils	Mutually-agreed-to Joint Governance
Conflict vs. Cooperation	Heavy emphasis on cooperation; only interpersonal avenues for conflict resolution	Formal conflict resolution procedures with limited emphasis on cooperation	Cooperative forum with no decision-making role and no formal conflict resolution procedure	More of a cooperative forum; some room for expressing conflict	Potential for cooperation; conflicts can be taken to labor courts	Potential for cooperation and room for surfacing and resolving conflicts
Procedural vs. Substantive Work Rules	Few formal work rules; heavy emphasis on informal resolution	Heavy reliance on substantive rules enforced by the grievance procedure	Procedural rule-making	Procedural decision-making	Heavy emphasis on procedural decision-making	Heavy emphasis on procedural decision-making
Direct vs. Indirect Participation	Heavy emphasis on direct participation	Mostly indirect; little emphasis on direct participation	Mostly indirect; little emphasis on direct participation	Indirect	Indirect; informal direct participation	Indirect; creates pressures to introduce direct participation
Administrative vs. Political Skills	Administrative skills taught to employees at all levels	Management concentrates on administrative skills; union on political skills	Some overlap but lack of decision-making role prevents further diffusion	Labor representatives develop administrative skills but only marginal diffusion of political skills among management	Labor develops administrative skills; plant management develops political skills	Labor develops administrative skills; management develops political skills
Joint and Equal Decision-making Power	No	Yes, but in bargainable issues and at bargaining time only	May contain equal number of labor and management reps, but equality is less significant because the role is mostly advisory	No, with the exception of the German law of 1951 covering the iron, steel, and coal industries	Yes	Yes

SOURCE: A. Verma and J. Cutcher-Gershenfeld, "Joint Governance in the Workplace: Beyond Union-Management Cooperation and Worker Participation," in *Employer Alternatives and Future Directions*, ed. B. E. Kaufman and M. M. Kleiner (Madison, WI: Industrial Relations Research Association, 1993), pp. 204–205.

one reason a stable plant environment and progressive management are necessary to ensure the safety net union leaders need to advocate change. Unions adopt one of five different approaches to innovative workplace changes: "just say no," let management lead and see what results, become involved to protect itself politically, cooperate or collaborate, or use to assert union interests.[61] Local union defensiveness is not irrational because managers interpret cooperation as a willingness to make economic concessions and increase productivity even as management efforts to undermine the union continue.[62] When unions see themselves in an unequal power relationship with management, cooperation is hard to introduce. At Western Airlines, participation became effective only when unions gained power to constrain management rights and jointly formed a vision for survival.[63] Union leaders can take advantage of communication about economic problems to further worker interests. Cooperative programs offer an opportunity to negotiate permanence for participation in contracts.[64]

Program development is enhanced by international union education efforts and the willingness of locals to be involved.[65] Participation programs can benefit unions since active participants are more satisfied with their unions and involved in union activities. Union support is not undermined by member involvement.[66] Proactive behavior of leaders toward participation increases member commitment to the union, but members who are negative toward the company and union before participation programs are not changed regardless of the success of the programs.[67]

Management Strategy

Labor-management cooperation efforts are frequently carried out at the plant level although there have been some corporatewide strategies such as the Ford–UAW Employee Involvement program. Management may also frequently encounter situations in which its employees, across plants, are represented by several different international unions, each with its own approach toward union-management cooperation.

---

[61] A. E. Eaton and P. B. Voos, "The Ability of Unions to Adapt to Innovative Workplace Arrangements," *American Economic Review* 79, no. 2 (1989), pp. 172–76.

[62] P. B. Voos and T-Y Cheng, "What Do Managers Mean by Cooperative Labor Relations?" *Labor Studies Journal* 14 (1989), pp. 3–18.

[63] K. R. Wever, "Toward a Structural Account of Union Participation in Management: The Case of Western Airlines," *Industrial and Labor Relations Review* 42 (1989), pp. 600–609.

[64] J. Cutcher-Gershenfeld, R. B. McKersie, and K. R. Wever, *The Changing Role of Union Leaders* (Washington, DC: Bureau of Labor-Management Relations, U.S. Department of Labor, 1988).

[65] A. E. Eaton, "The Extent and Determinants of Local Union Control of Participative Programs," *Industrial and Labor Relations Review* 43 (1990), pp. 604–20.

[66] A. Verma, "Joint Participation Programs: Self-Help or Suicide for Labor?" *Industrial Relations* 28 (1989), pp. 401–10.

[67] M. W. Fields and J. W. Thacker, "The Effects of Quality of Work Life on Commitment to Company and Union: An Examination of Pre-Post Changes," *Proceedings of the Industrial Relations Research Association* 41 (1988), pp. 201–9.

Initial research results on management strategies toward collective bargaining, cooperation, union avoidance, and firm performance suggested that firms improve profitability through extensive collaboration between management and labor. Performance is also improved by closing existing unionized facilities and opening or acquiring new nonunion plants. Deunionizing activity in any existing plant has a negative effect on performance.[68]

Evidence from steel minimills indicates they follow either a cost-reduction or product-differentiation strategy. Cost-reduction strategies are associated with conflict and the use of formal grievance procedures while product differentiation requires flexible manufacturing and is associated with employee commitment, collective bargaining, and the informal solution of problems. Wages in minimills following a product-differentiation strategy are higher and employees add more value to the products.[69]

Research on the Effects of Cooperation across Organizations

A study of several hundred organizations has yielded important information on the effects of contextual and cooperative structures on productivity and quality. The more active team-based programs are, the greater their effect. Top union leader participation is important as well. Larger plants have more difficulty improving productivity through cooperative efforts. Technology changes improve productivity at a rate faster than any negative effects from unilateral management implementation. Higher union security predicts more positive results. Subcontracting apparently reduces gains, as do more frequent layoffs. Interestingly, the larger the proportion of women in the workforce, the greater the productivity gains.[70]

Gains in product quality were greater in unionized firms under joint labor-management programs. Adversarial programs produced better results than programs run by management only, which were equal to results from companies with no program. Joint programs in unionized facilities were as effective as participation programs in nonunion firms. If the firm coupled cooperation with significant capital investments, quality was improved substantially. Factors reducing the effectiveness of joint programs included subcontracting, earlier concessions, downsizing, and larger unit size.[71] Table 13–8 details the effects of various union-management cooperation plans, demographic characteristics, and program performance on measures of quality, productivity, cost reduction, production processes, and bonus payouts.

---

[68] D. G. Meyer and W. N. Cooke, "Labor Relations in Transition: Strategic Activities and Financial Performance," *British Journal of Industrial Relations* 31 (1993), pp. 531–52.

[69] J. B. Arthur, "The Link between Business Strategy and Industrial Relations Systems in American Steel Minimills," *Industrial and Labor Relations Review* 45 (1992), pp. 488–506.

[70] Cooke, "Improving Productivity and Quality."

[71] W. N. Cooke, "Product Quality Improvement through Employee Participation: The Effects of Unionization and Joint Union-Management Administration," *Industrial and Labor Relations Review* 46 (1992), pp. 119–34.

TABLE 13–8

Perceived Effectiveness of Involvement and Gainsharing Programs on Performance Measures

Program or Characteristic	Improved Quality	Improved Labor Productivity	Cost Reduction	Improved Production Process	Bonus Payout Level
Employee involvement	**			**	
Frequent bonus			*(-)		**
Employee bonus share				***	—
Employee bonus share squared				***(-)	—
Bonus payouts	**	***	***	***	—
Bonus payouts-squared		***(-)	**(-)		—
Small bonus group	*				**
Scanlon plan	***			***	
Modified Scanlon plan				**	**(-)
Rucker plan				*	
Customized plan	**			**	
Consultant involvement	*				
Employee vote	***		***	*	**(-)
Labor intensity		*	**		
Market growth				**	**
Financial situation					**
Average education	*(-)				
Average seniority	**	***	***		*
Union	***(-)	***(-)	**(-)	***(-)	
Program age		*(-)	**(-)	*	***
MU(1)	***	***	***	***	***
Union support (if union present)	**		*	*	***

* Likelihood that effect of program or characteristic is zero is less than 10 percent.
** Likelihood that effect of program or characteristic is zero is less than 5 percent.
*** Likelihood that effect of program or characteristic is zero is less than 1 percent.
(-) Direction of effect is negative.
— Effect is not measured in this specification.
SOURCE: Adapted from D. O. Kim, "Factors Influencing Organizational Performance in Gainsharing Programs," *Industrial Relations* 35 (1996), pp. 232–233.

An examination of performance across 24 units in the same company found adversarial labor-management relations associated with higher costs, more scrap, lower productivity, and lower returns to direct labor hours than areas with increased cooperation and improved grievance handling.[72] Another study across firms found that employee involvement programs were just as likely in union as

---

[72] J. Cutcher-Gershenfeld, "The Impact of Economic Performance of a Transformation in Workplace Relations," *Industrial and Labor Relations Review* 44 (1991), pp. 241–60.

in nonunion settings, but unionized firms allowed employees less authority. The programs, in themselves, were not related to measures of returns on assets.[73]

Participation programs appeared to have more influence on firm performance in unionized firms while profit-sharing and gainsharing programs were more effective in nonunion firms when value-added per employee was the influenced measure. In general, unionized firms had higher value-added, lower labor costs, and more experienced and skilled workforces.[74]

Another study of outcomes across a set of employers found that union officer-management relations were positively related to forming general committees but not to decisions involving profit sharing or **employee stock ownership plans** (ESOPs). Grievances were reduced where committees or gainsharing plans were implemented. General labor-management committees kept grievance handling more informal and resolved problems more quickly. Flexibility and reduced absenteeism and turnover were related to all types of participation as catalogued in workplace interventions (above).[75] Table 13–9 summarizes the results of this study.

Managers perceive greater employee support from employees who are covered by profit-sharing and participation plans. Employee input on issues and authority to implement suggestions are related to managerial perceptions that employees support change.[76]

Research on the Long-Run Effects of Cooperation

Several studies have been made on the long-run effects of union-management cooperation. However, one study found large differences in the philosophies underlying cooperation initiatives. Scanlon and quality circle programs have the greatest participation, while Rucker and Impro-Share programs are mostly associated with economic incentives. The plans cannot substitute for good management, but where that does not exist, labor-management committees can be a springboard for progress. In the absence of management commitment to participation, Scanlon and other high-participation programs will fail.[77] Critical factors for the ongoing success of the programs are the training and commitment of supervisors and the construction and understanding of the bonus formulas.

Companies and unions generally begin programs to improve labor relations, increase the level of pay available, and so on. The motives of the parties will influence the type of plan chosen. Gainsharing affects productivity more than

---

[73] J. T. Delaney, C. Ichniowski, and D. Lewin, "Employee Involvement Programs and Firm Performance," *Proceedings of the Industrial Relations Research Association* 41 (1988), pp. 148–58.

[74] W. N. Cooke, "Employee Participation Programs, Group-Based Incentives, and Company Performance: A Union-Nonunion Comparison," *Industrial and Labor Relations Review* 47 (1994), pp. 594–609.

[75] P. B. Voos, "The Influence of Cooperative Programs on Union-Management Relations, Flexibility, and Other Labor Relations Outcomes," *Journal of Labor Research* 10 (1989), pp. 103–17.

[76] S. Schwochau, J. Delaney, P. Jarley, and J. Fiorito, "Employee Participation and Assessments of Organizational Policy Changes," *Journal of Labor Research* 18 (1997), pp. 379–401.

[77] Schuster, *Union-Management Cooperation.*

TABLE 13–9

Managers' Mean Evaluations of the Impact of Selected Committees and Programs on Six Labor Relations Outcomes

	Union Officer-Management Relations	Grievance Rate	Ability to Resolve Grievances Informally	Flexibility in Utilizing Labor	Absenteeism	Turnover
General plant committees	1.23* (.08)	1.03* (.08)	1.24* (.08)	.54* (.08)	.41* (.07)	.31* (.06)
Specialized plant committees	.77* (.07)	.71* (.06)	.66* (.05)	.25* (.05)	.32* (.05)	.25* (.04)
Local area cooperation committees	.82* (.25)	.18 (.12)	.36* (.14)	.00 (.00)	.00 (.00)	.00 (.00)
Employee participation programs	.47* (.10)	.53* (.08)	.55* (.07)	.47* (.06)	.30* (.06)	.27* (.05)
Gainsharing plans	.57* (.17)	.76* (.20)	.76* (.19)	.57* (.18)	.57* (.16)	.47* (.16)
Profit-sharing plans	.36* (.12)	.17 (.09)	.28* (.09)	.20* (.10)	.25* (.10)	.46* (.12)
Employee stock-ownership plans	.38* (.13)	.12 (.08)	.12 (.08)	.12 (.08)	.12 (.08)	.23* (.11)

* Significant at the .05 level on a 2-tailed test.

All mean evaluations have been based on the following scaling of responses: Large positive effect = 2, small positive effect = 1, no effect = 0, small negative effect = −1, and large negative effect = −2.

SOURCE: P. B. Voos, "The Influence of Cooperative Programs on Union-Management Relations, Flexibility, and Other Labor Relations Outcomes," *Journal of Labor Research* 10 (1989), p. 109.

labor-management committees or QWL programs. And no matter which method is chosen, it will not be necessary if traditional collective bargaining methods are successful. Companies and unions both appear to bargain rather than to use cooperative alternatives unless difficulties arise in accomplishing their goals.

A study of cooperation at 23 sites found productivity improvements in 12 and no change in 10 others. In 16 sites, subsequent experience enabled employees to earn bonuses supplementing what they would have earned solely as a result of collective bargaining. Bonus levels are directly influenced by the rate of suggestions generated by the employees.[78] Employment levels are relatively unaffected by cooperative programs, and labor relations are seen as improved.[79]

Finally, evidence suggests that productivity improvements usually involve a one-shot increase rather than a long, steady improvement. And the workplace intervention most likely to produce the productivity improvement appears to be the Scanlon plan.

---

[78] M. Schuster, "The Scanlon Plan: A Longitudinal Analysis," *Journal of Applied Behavioral Science* 20 (1984), pp. 23–38.

[79] M. Schuster, "The Impact of Union-Management Cooperation on Productivity and Employment," *Industrial and Labor Relations Review* 37 (1983), pp. 415–30.

THE LEGALITY OF COOPERATION PLANS

Among unionized employers, cooperation plans meet the requirements of the labor acts because they are jointly agreed to by unions and managements. Many employers in nonunion companies have established joint management-employee committees to deal with a variety of production and employment issues. However, it's possible these committees violate labor law. Section 8(a)(2) of the Taft-Hartley Act forbids employers from creating and operating employer-dominated labor organizations.[80] Discussion of employment issues or proposals by committees for taking action on areas related to wages, hours, and terms and conditions of employment intrude into the mandatory bargaining issues specified in the act.[81]

The NLRB was faced with ruling on the legality of an employer-sponsored committee in the *Electromation* case.[82] In its deliberation, the NLRB asked: "When does an employee committee lose its protection as a communication device and become a labor organization?" and "What employer conduct constitutes interference or domination of such committees?"

The company had set up five volunteer committees to look at absenteeism, pay, bonuses, and so forth. The company initiated the committees, drafted their goals, and had management representatives there to facilitate discussions. The NLRB ruled this constituted an employer-dominated labor organization and thus violated Section 8(a)(2).

At this point, it would be difficult to determine what would be a legal employee involvement program in a nonunion environment because pay will undoubtedly be an issue if productivity is discussed.[83] At the same time, it should be noted that the NLRB has accepted and pursued very few cases alleging 8(a)(2) violations where employers have established teams and committees.

EMPLOYEE STOCK OWNERSHIP PLANS

Employee stock ownership plans (ESOPs) were first permitted by the Employee Retirement Income Security Act (ERISA) of 1974. Under ERISA, employees may receive their employer's stock through profit sharing, productivity gains, or subtractions from wages. Since the early 1980s, several companies (e.g., Chrysler) have agreed to give employees stock in exchange for labor concessions. In some companies, such as Weirton Steel, the employees became majority owners.

---

[80] A. B. Cochran, III, "We Participate, They Decide: The Real Stakes in Revising Section 8(a)(2) of the National Labor Relations Act," *Berkeley Journal of Employment and Labor Law* 16 (1995), pp. 458–519.

[81] R. Hanson, R. I. Porterfield, and K. Ames, "Employee Empowerment at Risk: Effects of Recent NLRB Rulings," *Academy of Management Executive* 9, no. 2 (1995), pp. 45–56.

[82] *Electromation, Inc.*, 309 NLRB No. 163 (1992).

[83] A. E. Perl, "Employee Involvement Groups: The Outcry over the NLRB's *Electromation* Decision, *Labor Law Journal* 44 (1993), pp. 195–207.

Recently, the airline industry has implemented ESOPs and partial ownership plans. Employees at Northwest Airlines agreed to take stock and have their representatives join the board of directors in return for wage concessions. Unionized employees at United Air Lines have purchased a majority of the company from shareholders.

ESOPs will not, in themselves, improve productivity. Employee-owned firms in Israel don't function much differently than privately owned firms. Pay, productivity, and job security are somewhat higher.[84] Workers are generally productive regardless of the source of ownership.[85] Ownership affects attitudes through greater perceived influence and control and the financial value of ownership.[86] Workers may not automatically favor ESOPs either; the firm governance role involved in ESOPs may induce fear and anxiety as well as expanded commitment. Where performance of the firm is linked to retirement security, workers may wish to avoid ESOPs because their investments lose substantial diversification.[87]

THE DIFFUSION AND INSTITUTIONALIZATION OF CHANGE

An important issue for labor and management is how successful changes get diffused throughout the organization and become institutionalized. Participation needs a stable environment to grow. The parties need to avoid or isolate collective bargaining shocks and strategic shocks. Layoffs create problems for teams because workers use competitive seniority rights to bump in and out. Changes are aided by implementing them in new facilities with new workers. Diffusion of successful changes can then move toward established settings. Unions can markedly assist change when they have a role in strategic decision making such as plant locations. They may also provide needed concessions and work rule changes to make retrofitting of existing facilities economically feasible. Training in the introduction of new technology and increasing employment security are important to employees and can help to make change permanent. Gainsharing will probably follow as a logical consequence of innovative participation.[88]

The ability to institutionalize change depends on high levels of trust and commitment by union leaders and members, supervisors, plant managers, and corporate executives. Evidence shows there are substantially different perceptions in

---

[84] A. Ben-Ner and S. Estrin, "What Happens When Unions Run Firms? Unions as Employee Representatives and as Employers," *Journal of Comparative Economics* 15 (1991), pp. 65–87.

[85] J. R. Blasi, "The Productivity Ramifications of Union Buyouts," *National Productivity Review* 9 (1990), pp. 17–34.

[86] A. A. Buchko, "Effects of Ownership on Employee Attitudes: A Test of Three Theoretical Perspectives," *Work and Occupations* 19 (1992), pp. 59–78.

[87] J. L. Pierce, S. A. Rubenfeld, and S. Morgan, "Employee Ownership: A Conceptual Model of Process and Effects," *Academy of Management Review* 16 (1991), pp. 121–44.

[88] T. A. Kochan and J. Cutcher-Gershenfeld, *Institutionalizing and Diffusing Innovations in Industrial Relations* (Washington, DC: U.S. Department of Labor, Bureau of Labor-Management Relations and Cooperative Programs, 1988).

many situations held by labor and management regarding the degree of commitment, feelings of manipulation and co-optation, and delivery on promises that the efforts undertaken have not always followed their planned course. Establishing and continuing trust is an underlying critical factor to the success of cooperation programs.[89]

SUMMARY

The employment environment has changed substantially during the last 20 years, spurred by global competition. Most union-management activity has been adversarial, but the needs of both parties have increasingly led toward cooperative approaches in a variety of situations. Employers would like to earn as large a return as possible on their investment while labor would like continuous economic improvements and an avoidance of employment security risks. Given the requirements for negotiations on mandatory issues and the inability of unions to demand negotiations on permissive issues, room for cooperation in traditional bargaining environments is sparse.

Integrative bargaining is the set of activities leading to simultaneous accomplishment of unconflicting objectives in solving a common problem. Mutual gains bargaining has been increasingly practiced. To implement integrative solutions, both parties must have as much available information as possible on the problem they are attempting to solve.

A variety of methods are used by employers and unions to create and sustain cooperation. These include areawide labor-management committees dealing with regional employment problems in unionized environments, joint labor-management committees operating at the industry or firm level, gainsharing plans (the Scanlon plan, Rucker plan, and Impro-Share) and nongainsharing interventions (labor-management committees, quality circles, quality-of-work-life programs, and team-based approaches).

Increasing numbers of companies are implementing (with unions) team-based action groups to improve productivity and quality. Perceived productivity seems to increase most where the union is secure, top union officials are involved in the process, and significant numbers of union members are in team-based activities. The introduction of new technology continues to lead the way in improving productivity. Unions are learning how to participate in and benefit from cooperation while retaining their distributive bargaining roles. Innovation is institutionalized through success and stability in organizations where experiments are tried.

Employee stock ownership plans aim at increasing employee commitment to the company through the long-run improvement of the value of ownership gained through higher productivity.

---

[89] Cooke, *Labor-Management Cooperation*, pp. 121–36.

DISCUSSION QUESTIONS

1. Why would the inclusion of such programs as QWL in the collective agreement be difficult?

2. Under what conditions would a Scanlon plan be likely to be effective over relatively long periods?

3. What are the potential long-run problems for unions in agreeing to labor-management cooperation programs?

4. Should unions be guaranteed a seat on an organization's board of directors?

5. Should the *Electromation* decision be overturned?

KEY TERMS

Greenfield operations   *418*

Principled negotiations   *422*

"Relations by objectives"   *423*

Areawide labor-management committees   *425*

Joint labor-management committees *426*

Scanlon plan   *428*

Rucker plan   *428*

Impro-Share plan   *428*

Quality circles   *428*

Quality-of-work-life programs   *428*

Production committee   *431*

Screening committee   *431*

Labor-management committees   *437*

Employee involvement program   *438*

"Modern operating agreement"   *439*

Team concepts   *439*

Employee stock ownership plans   *447*

CASE

CONTINUING OR ABANDONING THE SPECIAL-ORDER FABRICATION BUSINESS

It is about three months since the effective date of the GMFC–Local 384 contract. In GMFC's executive council meeting this morning, financial officers reported on an in-depth study on the profitability of the special-order fabrication operations. They recommended GMFC take no more orders for this area and close the operation when present commitments were shipped. Their data showed the operations lost money two out of the last three years, and they argued the Speedy-Lift assembly lines could be expanded into that area for meeting the increasing demand for GMFC forklift trucks.

Top-level management in the special-order fabrication operations conceded that profits, when earned, were low but pointed out that, from a return-on-investment standpoint, they had been among the best in the company during the 1968–73 period. Besides, they argued, many of the special orders were from some of the largest customers in the standard product lines, and GMFC could not afford to lose that business if it had to depend on occasional custom orders as well.

The finance people reiterated their recommendations to terminate the operation, pointing out that labor costs had risen over the past several contracts and, because of the custom nature of the work, productivity gains had been small because new technologies could not be introduced.

After both sides presented their final summations, the chief executive officer announced the firm should prepare to terminate operations. After the announcement, the industrial relations director pointed out that GMFC would have to negotiate the termination with Local 384. The union might demand severance pay, job transfers, and so forth. The point was also raised that this decision offered the union and the company the opportunity to devise a method for reducing and controlling labor costs.

The CEO designated the vice president of finance, the general manager of special-order fabrications, and the industrial relations director as the bargaining team to present the company's decision and bargain a resolution. The CEO made it clear that the company intended to abandon these operations but could reverse its position with the right kind of labor cost reductions.

Although this meeting was not publicized, Local 384's leadership had been concerned about the special-order fabrications area for some time. Management had frequently grumbled about low productivity, and stewards were frequently harassed about alleged slowdowns. Union members in the shop often grieved about work rule changes. The stack of grievances, coupled with management's inaction on them, led the leadership to request a meeting with the industrial relations director to solve the problems.

Directions

1. Rejoin your original labor or management bargaining team.

2. Reach an agreement for continuation or termination of the special-order fabrication operations.

   a. Company negotiators must reduce labor costs by 10 percent and stabilize them for project bids if operations are to continue (labor costs are 30 percent of the total costs, and return on investment (ROI) would be 7 percent if costs were cut by 10 percent).

b. Union members are unwilling to have their pay rates cut.

c. All of the employees in this area are level 2 or 3 assemblers, and most have more than 20 years' experience.

3. Use the agreement you previously reached or the contract in Chapter 11 to specify current terms for these workers.

CONTRACT

ADMINISTRATION

After a contract is negotiated and ratified, the parties are bound by its terms. But contract clauses may be interpreted differently, so mechanisms are needed to resolve disputes. Almost all contracts contain a grievance procedure to resolve intracontractual disputes. This chapter identifies types and causes of disputes and the contractual means used for resolving them.

As you study this chapter, consider the following questions:

1. What areas of disagreement emerge while the contract is in effect?
2. What actions by the parties violate the labor acts?
3. Are disagreements solved by bargaining or by evaluating the merits of a given issue?
4. What does the union owe individual members in grievance processing?

THE DUTY TO BARGAIN

Parties do not end their obligation to bargain by concluding an agreement. The National Labor Relations Board (NLRB) and courts have interpreted the duty to bargain to cover the entire labor relationship from recognition onward. Any disputes regarding wages, hours, or terms and conditions must be mutually resolved through the contractual grievance procedure.

Although the parties have rendered a written agreement, it is possible that differences in its interpretation could occur. There may also be differences about the creation and implementation of rules that are enabled by the contract but not actually within it.

Management generally takes the initiative in **contract administration**. It determines how it will operate facilities and discipline employees. The union reacts if it senses a result is inconsistent with its interpretation of the contract and work rules.

When a grievance procedure exists and management changes its operations, employees are expected to conform to the change. If the change is considered unjust, employees must file a grievance rather than refuse to follow orders. If the latter occurred, employees can be discharged for insubordination even if the management practice was later found to be in violation of the contract, unless the violation was flagrant.

ISSUES IN CONTRACT ADMINISTRATION

Disputes during the contract may focus on several issues. Disputes result from initiatives taken by the employer. The employer usually does not file a grievance when the union or a worker allegedly violates the contract; it simply acts and waits for a union response. For example, if a worker swears at a supervisor, the company may suspend the worker for five days. The company does not contact the union and ask it to discipline its members. If the union believes the discipline is unjust, it protests the action through a grievance. Some of the major contract areas leading to grievances will be examined next.

Discipline

Discipline imposed by the employer for infractions of rules is one of the most frequently disputed issues. Discipline often involves demotion, suspension, or discharge, and it is meted out for insubordination, dishonesty, absenteeism, rule violations, or poor productivity. Rule violations include issues such as substance abuse and sexual harassment. A discharge is the industrial equivalent of capital punishment and often results in a grievance, regardless of its ultimate merit, because political solidarity often requires the union to extend itself in trying to save a member's job.

Discipline is imposed for violations of employer rules. Employees must be aware of the rules in order to conform to them. Employers use discipline to deter employees from behavior that damages the employers' performance. Before discipline can be imposed, unsatisfactory behaviors must be observed by or reported to an authority who can act. The authority must decide whether violations are sufficiently important for action to be taken. If behaviors exceed the threshold of punishment, discipline is imposed.[1] Unions are particularly interested that employers, when imposing discipline, have reliably observed the unsatisfactory behaviors and have consistently applied similar penalties in similar situations and that the magnitude of the penalties is commensurate with the violations.

When an employee has repeatedly breached rules and been disciplined and no improvement in performance has been observed, employers and unions may implement a **"last chance agreement"** in an attempt to save the employee's job. In return for not discharging the employee for the most recent offense, the employer, union, and employee conclude a written agreement stipulating that if another violation of the same rule occurs within a specified time period, the employee will be discharged automatically and the union will not grieve.

Incentives

A contract may have an incentive scheme in which employees are paid by the piece or receive bonuses for productive efficiency. Frequently, these contracts will establish groups of jobs that work on incentive rates and identify others that don't. If an employee is moved from an incentive to a nonincentive job, wages will probably decrease. If the job seems highly similar to the incentive job, grievances may result. A grievance might also result if the assignment is considered arbitrary or punitive.

Problems also may arise if a new production process is introduced and management seeks to establish higher base rates or time standards before incentive earnings begin. New standards must be bargained collectively.

Work Assignments

Disputes may occur over which classification is entitled to perform certain work. For example, assume an electrical generating plant using coal-fired boilers for steam generation shuts down a boiler for rebricking. To do this, a wall has to be knocked down with some care to avoid damage to other boiler parts. Who should do the work? General laborers might do the work under a supervisor's direction. But the work requires some care and is preparatory to rebricking, so the job might be assigned to skilled masonry workers. The company may assign the job to

---

[1] R. D. Arvey and A. P. Jones, "The Use of Discipline in Organizational Settings: A Framework for Future Research," in L. L. Cummings and B. M. Staw, eds., *Research in Organizational Behavior*, vol. 7 (Greenwich, CT: JAI Press, 1985), pp. 367–408.

helpers because the cost is less and skill requirements are believed to be low. But masons may believe the task is an integral part of their job and thus grieve.

Individual Personnel Assignments

These grievances most often concern promotions, layoffs, transfers, and shift assignments. Most contracts specify that seniority, seniority and merit, or experience on a particular job will govern personnel assignments. Disputes often relate to layoffs and shift preference. People who are laid off may believe they are entitled to the jobs of junior workers in other departments who have been retained. While contracts normally specify that employees must be qualified for a job if they are bumping junior employees, opinions may differ whether claimed qualifications are actually possessed.

Hours of Work

Hours grievances involve overtime requirements and work schedules. For example, if the firm has maintained an 8 A.M. to 4 P.M. shift to mail customer orders and finds that its freight company has moved its shipping schedule from 4 P.M. to 3 P.M., then a 7 A.M. to 3 P.M. shift better meets its needs. This change will affect employees, and grievances may result.

Supervisors Doing Production Work

Most contracts forbid supervisors from performing production work except when demonstrating the job to a new employee or handling an emergency. Absence of an employee is usually not considered an emergency. This is basically a job security issue.

Production Standards

Employers and unions often agree on output rates in assembly line technologies or standards for incentives in piece-rate output. If management speeds up the line or reengineers the standards, more effort is required for the same amount of pay, and grievances often result.

Working Conditions

These issues relate to health and safety concerns. For example, if workers believe excessive fumes are present or an existing convenience (e.g., heating) fails, grievances may result.

Subcontracting

Unless the contract allows complete discretion to the company in subcontracting, work performed by bargaining unit members may not be subcontracted before bargaining with the union.[2] Subcontracting can affect job security, so if grievances result, management would be involved in a refusal to bargain if it did not discuss the subcontracting issue.

Past Practice

Many employment practices are not written into contracts, but unions consider them to be obligations. For example, an employer may provide below-cost cafeteria food services to workers. If the cafeteria is closed, the union may grieve even though there is no contract language on food services, and management must respond.[3] If stopping work 15 minutes before the end of a shift to wash up is usual practice, then extending working time to the shift's end changes past practice.

Rules

Employers occasionally institute rules to improve efficiency or to govern the workforce. Many contracts establish the employer's right to do so under the management rights clause. Employees may grieve the establishment of rules as altering a term or condition of employment.

Work rules relating to smoking, drug testing, and sexual harassment have the potential to create divisions within the bargaining unit, depending on employee attitudes and how the rules are implemented. While a large majority of union members questioned in one survey approved of limited drug testing, those who were subject to testing were more negative about probable cause testing, random testing, and terminating those who tested positive.[4]

---

[2] The Supreme Court decision in *Fibreboard Paper Products* v. *NLRB*, 379 U.S. 203 (1964), requires bargaining by management if the union requests when subcontracting is being considered, unless the union has expressly waived its right in this area; however, this rule has been relaxed somewhat by *First National Maintenance* v. *NLRB*, 107 LRRM 2705 (Sup. Ct., 1981), and later by the NLRB when it held that removal of union work to another facility of the company would be permissible if bargaining had reached an impasse (*Milwaukee Spring Div. of Illinois Coil Spring Co.*, 115 LRRM 1065 [1984], enforced by the U.S. Court of Appeals, District of Columbia Circuit, 119 LRRM 2801 [1985]), or for a legitimate business reason if there were no antiunion animus (*Otis Elevator Co.*, 115 LRRM 1281 [1984]).

[3] *Ford Motor Co.* v. *NLRB*, No. 77-1806, Sup. Ct., 1979.

[4] M. H. LeRoy, "The Presence of Drug Testing in the Workplace and Union Member Attitudes," *Labor Studies Journal* 16, no. 3 (1991), pp. 33–42.

Prevalence of Issues

Grievances occur across a number of areas, as noted above. There are some differences in the extent to which they relate to different issues. A study of four organizations in different industries found the seven largest grievance categories were distributed as follows: pay (17 percent), working conditions (16 percent), performance and permanent job assignments (16 percent), discipline (14 percent), benefits (14 percent), management rights (7 percent), and discrimination (6 percent).[5]

GRIEVANCE PROCEDURES

Most contracts specify procedures for resolving interpretive disagreements. While contracts vary, most procedures contain four or five steps. In the absence of a grievance procedure, the employee is still entitled to press grievances individually under guarantees contained in Section 9 of the Taft-Hartley Act. Individual employees may also file grievances if the contract has such a procedure, but they generally do not, leaving the union the right to participate in the process.

Steps in the Grievance Procedure

The usual steps in the grievance procedure are as follows:

Step 1
This step varies considerably across companies. In some companies, an employee who believes the company has violated the contract complains to the union steward, who may accept or assist in writing up a grievance. The steward then presents the grievance to the grievant's supervisor, who has the opportunity to answer or adjust it.

In some companies, few grievances are settled at Step 1. The company won't delegate power to supervisors because their decisions can establish precedents for future grievance settlements. Thus, supervisors often simply "deny" grievances at Step 1. In other companies, an oral grievance is presented directly to the supervisor, and settlements can be negotiated immediately. (Figure 14–1 is an example of a fairly complex grievance at its first step.)

Supervisory style affects grievance rates and their disposition. In a large manufacturing plant, autocratic supervisors had lower grievance rates and fewer overtime, supervisor-related, and discipline grievances than democratic supervisors. Management was less likely to reverse grievance decisions for autocratic

---

[5] D. Lewin and R. B. Peterson, *The Modern Grievance Procedure in the United States* (Westport, CT: Quorum, 1988).

FIGURE 14–1

Example of a Written Grievance

I have just been given a job review, as a result of which I am now on the second highest eligibility list. I now want clear and accurate answers with supporting information to the following questions:

1. Why was this job review given five months after its effective date and on the day before my vacation?

2. Why change my rating for "manner and interest" from excellent to good? It was admitted that I am excellent in this category, but only to those whom I think will buy, and that the reviewer did not know of any mistakes in judgment I had made.

3. Why change "alertness to service" from excellent to good? Since I was told by the reviewer that I was too "selective" in both this and the previous category, I think that *(a)* one or the other should be eliminated, or *(b)* perhaps they should be combined, or *(c)* both reviewer and employees should be made aware of whatever difference there may be.

4. Why change "cooperation" from excellent to good? Since I was told that my cooperation with the other eight people in the department was excellent, I would like to know exactly what incidents took place and who was involved, resulting in this change.

It also seems that there is a clear, consistent pattern of downgrading everyone in the department from their previous ratings and that job reviews will be given to employees just prior to their going on vacation. It is my distinct impression that the present reviewers are not only ignorant of previous reviews but also feel that they do the job much better than the previous reviewers. If they can't come up with some better reasons for the changes than those I have heard, then I think they are doing a remarkably poor job.

SOURCE: M. S. Trotta, *Handling Grievances: A Guide for Labor and Management* (Washington, DC: Bureau of National Affairs, 1976), pp. 141–42.

supervisors.[6] Stewards may have more knowledge of the contract if they are experienced and have contract administration as their full-time job. But supervisors and stewards usually do not understand the contract well. About 7 of 10 grievances examined in one study were screened by stewards, and about half used their authority to adjust grievances. Steward training is likely to be provided equally by the employer or the union.[7]

Present grievances in an informal, oral manner may allow supervisors and stewards greater latitude in reaching a quick solution before a written record is established. One study found that moving toward oral from written grievances was favored by supervisors, stewards, union leaders, and top management, but oral grievances ultimately failed because of opposition from plant managers who believed they undermined their authority.[8]

---

[6] R. L. Walker and J. W. Robinson, "The First-Line Supervisor's Role in the Grievance Procedure," *Arbitration Journal* 32 (1977), pp. 279–92.

[7] S. Briggs, "The Steward, the Supervisor, and the Grievance Process," *Proceedings of the Industrial Relations Research Association* 34 (1981), pp. 313–19.

[8] V. G. Devinatz, "A Program for Building Cooperative Shop Floor Labor Relations: The UAW, The International Harvester Corporation and the 'New Look' Procedure," *Labor Studies Journal* 20, no. 3 (1995), pp. 5–18.

Several levels of activity may lead to filing grievances. Stewards may hear complaints from members and act on them. A large-scale study of Canadian bargaining units found that stewards reported more complaints from members if the supervisor had low knowledge of the contract and if the work unit was relatively large. Informal grievance resolution was related to the supervisor's knowledge of the contract and the steward's commitment to the employer, education, and training. The likelihood of a steward initiating a grievance where the member declined to do so or where the steward observed a contract violation and filed on behalf of the group was increased by a supervisor's considerate supervisory style and lack of contract knowledge, and this likelihood was positively related to union commitment and a contested vote in the unit for the steward's position, and negatively related to employer commitment. Grievance rates were related to many of these same factors, but were reduced by informal settlements and increased by steward initiation. Behaviors of stewards and supervisors were more important predictors of initiation and settlement than were workplace characteristics.[9]

Stewards are generally more satisfied in their grievance-processing roles if the procedure permits oral grievances and some grievance committee screening takes place. Dissatisfaction is related to high grievance rates and large work groups. Satisfaction is higher if a larger proportion of grievances are resolved—and resolved successfully for the grievant.[10]

Step 2

Many grievances are settled at Step 1. If denied there, the steward presents the grievance to a plant industrial relations (IR) representative. Both are very familiar with the contract, and both are aware of how previous grievances have been settled. In routine cases, the company allows the IR representative to apply and create precedents.

Step 3

Most grievances have been settled by Step 2. However, if a grievance has major precedent-setting implications or involves potentially major costs but may have merit, the IR representative may deny it and send it to Step 3. If the case involves discharge of an employee, the union is likely to send it to Step 3. The Step 3 participants vary depending on the contract. The grievance may be settled locally, with the union represented by its local negotiating committee and management by its top IR manager or plant manager. In more complex situations or in larger firms, the parties may be an international union representative with or without the local negotiating committee and a corporate-level IR director. Most unresolved grievances are settled here.

---

[9] B. Bemmels, Y. Reshef, and K. Stratton-Devine, "The Roles of Supervisors, Employees, and Stewards in Grievance Initiation," *Industrial and Labor Relations Review* 45 (1991), pp. 15–30.

[10] B. Bemmels, "Shop Stewards' Satisfaction with Grievance Procedures," *Industrial Relations* 34 (1995), pp. 578–92.

Step 4

When a grievance is unresolved at the third step, the parties submit the dispute to an arbitrator who hears evidence from both sides and renders an award. A number of methods for choosing an arbitrator are available. First, the parties may name a permanent arbitrator, or **umpire,** in their contract. Second, they may ask a private agency, such as the American Arbitration Association, to provide an arbitration panel. A panel consists of an odd number of members (usually five) from which each party rejects arbitrators in turn until one remains. He or she becomes the arbitrator unless one party objects, in which case a new panel is submitted. Third, the same process may be followed by petitioning the Federal Mediation and Conciliation Service, which also supplies panels of arbitrators listed by the agency. A hearing date is set, and the arbitrator renders an award some time after the evidence is presented. Chapter 15 examines arbitration as a separate topic. Figure 14–2 is an example of a contract clause dealing with grievance handling.

Grievance rates among unionized employers probably run about 10 per 100 employees per year. Of each 100 grievances, between 0.5 and 2.5 require arbitration for resolution.[11] About half of all written grievances are settled at Step 1, 60 percent of open grievances at Step 2, and 80 percent of the rest at Step 3.[12] Settlements at higher levels are associated with required written grievances, rigid procedural rules, larger bargaining units, adversarial bargaining relationships, low costs, and low supervisor and steward knowledge of the contract.[13] One study of several employers found that settlement at Step 1 is higher with written grievances and authorization by management, the union, or both to allow supervisors and/or stewards to settle the grievance. Settlement before arbitration is higher in larger units and where more grievances are filed.[14]

Grievances may be granted, denied, partially granted, or withdrawn at any step in the process. A study of grievances in a Canadian firm found 46 percent were denied, 36 percent partially or fully granted, and 18 percent withdrawn at the first step. Of those proceeding to Step 2 (which could include some of those partially granted at Step 1), 62 percent were denied, 24 percent partially or fully granted, and 14 percent withdrawn. At Step 3, 4 percent were partially or fully granted, 80 percent denied, and 16 percent withdrawn. Prior decisions for a particular type of grievance reduced their submission for a period of time.[15]

---

[11] Lewin and Peterson, *Modern Grievance Procedure*, p. 89.

[12] Ibid., p. 170.

[13] Ibid., pp. 98–100.

[14] J. A. Davy, G. Stewart, and J. Anderson "Formalization of Grievance Procedures: A Multi-Firm and Industry Study," *Journal of Labor Research* 13 (1992), pp. 307–16.

[15] R. P. Chaykowski, G. A. Slotsve, and J. S. Butler, "A Simultaneous Analysis of Grievance Activity and Outcome Decisions," *Industrial and Labor Relations Review* 45 (1992), pp. 724–37.

FIGURE 14–2
Grievance Procedure Clause

9.02 *Grievances*

Step 1   The employee and the departmental steward, if the employee desires, shall take the matter up with his or her supervisor. If no settlement is reached in Step 1 within two working days, the grievance shall be reduced to writing on the form provided for that purpose.

Step 2   The written grievance shall be presented to the supervisor or the general supervisor and a copy sent to the production personnel office. Within two working days after receipt of the grievance, the general supervisor shall hold a meeting, unless mutually agreed otherwise, with the supervisor, the employee, the departmental steward, and the chief steward.

Step 3   If no settlement is reached in Step 2, the written grievance shall be presented to the departmental superintendent, who shall hold a meeting within five working days of the original receipt of the grievance in Step 2 unless mutually agreed otherwise. Those in attendance shall normally be the departmental superintendent, the general supervisor, the supervisor, the employee, the chief steward, departmental steward, a member of the production personnel department, the president of the UNION or his representative, and the divisional committeeman.

Step 4   If no settlement is reached in Step 3, the UNION COMMITTEE and an international representative of the UNION shall meet with the MANAGEMENT COMMITTEE for the purpose of settling the matter.

Step 5   If no settlement is reached in Step 4, the matter shall be referred to an arbitrator. A representative of the UNION shall meet within five working days with a representative of the COMPANY for the purpose of selecting an arbitrator. If an arbitrator cannot be agreed upon within five working days after Step 4, a request for a list of arbitrators shall be sent to the Federal Mediation and Conciliation Service. Upon obtaining the list, an arbitrator shall be selected within five working days. Prior to arbitration, a representative of the UNION shall meet with a representative of the COMPANY to reduce to writing wherever possible the actual issue to be arbitrated. The decision of the arbitrator shall be final and binding on all parties. The salary, if any, of the arbitrator and any necessary expense incident to the arbitration shall be paid jointly by the COMPANY and the UNION.

Time Involved

Generally, speedy resolution of grievances is preferred. Typical contracts allow 2 to 5 days for resolution at the first two steps and 3 to 10 days at Step 3. If management denies the grievance at Step 3, the union has 10 to 30 days to demand arbitration. If it doesn't, the dispute may no longer be arbitrable because it was not referred to arbitration in time. After arbitration is demanded, the time frame is less rigid because a panel must be requested and received, an arbitrator selected, hearing dates arranged and the hearing held, and a final award written and rendered. While an arbitrated dispute could conceivably be resolved in two months or less, the time lapse is usually considerably longer. (See Chapter 15 for information on the length of the entire process when a grievance goes to arbitration.) One study found the average grievance was settled in 10 to 14 days.[16] Settlements take longer where bargaining units are large, the union requires written grievances, both parties follow procedures closely, an adversarial bargaining relationship exists, and the contractual knowledge of supervisors is low.[17]

Most contracts rely on a four step procedure, settlement rates are higher in steps 2 and 3, where contractual procedures and time schedules are closely followed, and few differences exist in filing periods when disciplinary and other contractual grievances are compared.[18] Figure 14–3 presents the flow of decisions in a typical grievance process.

METHODS OF DISPUTE RESOLUTION

Disputes not resolved by negotiations are handled in two major ways: arbitration and strikes. Arbitration is used far more often, but strikes are traditionally used by some unions or in some types of disputes.

Striking over Grievances

Disputes where time is of the essence are most likely to lead to strikes. Arbitration usually involves a considerable time lag, so certain unions (e.g., building trades) seldom use it because of the short periods their members work for a given employer. By the time a grievance is arbitrated, the job would be completed, with the employer dictating the working conditions.

The same holds for grievances over safety and working conditions in industrial situations where a stable employment relationship exists. When these conditions occur, a strike may be used by the union to force the company to interpret

---

[16] Lewin and Peterson, *Modern Grievance Procedure,* p. 89.
[17] Ibid., pp. 98–100.
[18] J. A. Davy and G. W. Bohlander, "Recent Findings and Practices in Grievance-Arbitration Procedures," *Labor Law Journal* 43 (1992), pp. 184–90.

FIGURE 14–3
Grievance Procedure Steps

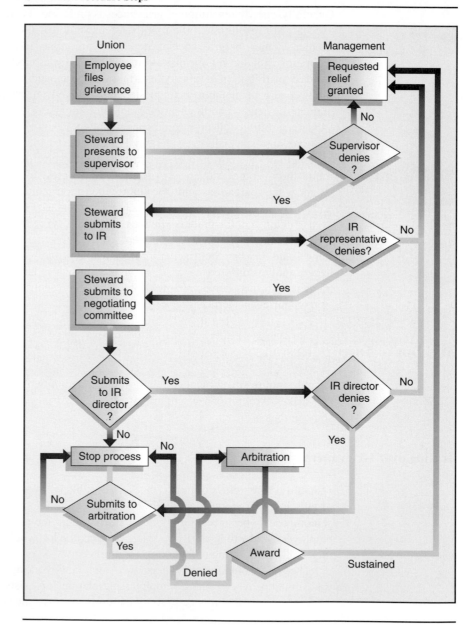

the contract as it demands. With a contract in effect, these strikes may or may not be breaches of the agreement and may or may not be enjoinable by the courts.

Project Labor Agreements

Recently, building trades unions and contractors have often concluded **project labor agreements** (PLAs) prior to bidding on major projects. PLAs include provisions about pay rates, hiring procedures, work rules, and the like that will apply to the project at hand during its duration. A PLA also includes dispute resolution procedures and union agreement to forgo strikes during its term.[19]

Wildcat Strikes

If a no-strike clause has been negotiated, a strike during the agreement period is called a wildcat strike because it contradicts the contract and is unauthorized by the parent national union. Wildcat strikes are particularly prevalent in the coal mining industry.[20]

Research on the characteristics of wildcat strikes in coal mining found high-strike mines were larger than low-strike mines, perhaps reflecting the increased formality of grievance handling in large mines. Working conditions were not related to wildcat strikes, but supervisory friction was. Strikes were higher where miners perceived supervisors as being unable to handle grievances and in mines where disputes could not be dealt with locally. Confidence in the grievance procedure did not relate to strike incidence. Miners at both high- and low-strike mines believed strikes resolved disputes in favor of the miners, but the high incidence rates of strikes appeared related to perceptions that a strike was the best method to get management to listen.[21]

When companies agree to submit unresolved grievances to arbitration, they are giving up some of their initiative in changing conditions. As a quid pro quo, they usually demand and win a no-strike clause. Under that provision, the union agrees not to strike during the term of the contract, because it has an arbitral forum available. But what if the union strikes? Does the company have a legal recourse? The Norris-LaGuardia Act prohibits injunctions against lawful union activities, which includes strikes. However, the Supreme Court ruled that where a bona fide no-strike clause exists, with a grievance procedure available and where the union has not sought to arbitrate its dispute, federal courts could enjoin a wildcat strike in violation of the contract.[22] The Court will not apply this doctrine when the employer is unwilling to include an arbitration agreement along with the no-strike clause.

---

[19] See *Journal of Labor Research* 19, no. 1 (1998), pp. 1–24, for additional details.

[20] J. M. Brett and S. B. Goldberg, "Wildcat Strikes in Bituminous Coal Mining," *Industrial and Labor Relations Review* 32 (1979), pp. 465–83.

[21] Ibid.

[22] *Boys Markets, Inc.*, v. *Retail Clerks Union Local 770,* 398 U.S. 235 (1970).

Discipline for Wildcat Strikes

What tools do employers have to counteract a wildcat strike? First, if the strike concerned an unfair labor practice and the union correctly judged that the action was illegal, the strike would be protected under the law, and the employer could not legally retaliate. But if the strike were in violation of a no-strike clause, several factors would come into play.

Both the national and local union participate in ratifying an agreement. Both also share in the joint responsibility for enforcing it. Unfortunately for management, little in damages can be gained unless a union's leaders clearly fomented a wildcat strike.[23] However, if a union demands that its members return to work and they fail to obey, they are subject to union discipline as well as to employer retaliation. Employers cannot sue individual union members for breach of contract for violating a no-strike clause,[24] but where a union defies an injunction to return to work, it may be found in contempt of court and fined.[25]

Grievance Mediation

As noted earlier, wildcat strikes have been a troublesome feature of labor relations in coal mining. An experiment in the mediation of grievances found costs and time to settlement were reduced by using a mediationlike process to deal with contract disputes. A large share of the grievances headed for arbitration were settled with the help of mediation. The union, in particular, was highly satisfied with mediation, especially as it related to the union's belief regarding the mediator's understanding of the grievance. Mediation may allow the parties to uncover and deal with the real reason for the conflict rather than require framing the reason as a specific contract violation. Mediation did not increase the likelihood of settlements at lower levels and was used neither for discharge grievances nor for those involving financial claims of more than $5,000.[26] In a utility setting where suspension and discharge grievances were included in grievance mediation, managements were equally satisfied with mediation and arbitration except with the settlements. About two-thirds of all final step grievances were settled by mediation; thus, the number going to arbitration was cut to one-third. The overall level of grievances did not decline as a result of mediation.[27]

---

[23] *Carbon Fuel Co.* v. *United Mine Workers*, 444 U.S. 212 (1979).

[24] *Complete Auto Transit* v. *Reis*, 107 LRRM 2145, Sup. Ct., 1981.

[25] *United Mine Workers* v. *Bagwell*, 114 S. Ct. 2552 (1994).

[26] S. B. Goldberg and J. M. Brett, "An Experiment in the Mediation of Grievances," *Monthly Labor Review* 106, no. 3 (1983), pp. 23–30.

[27] M. T. Roberts, R. S. Wolters, W. H. Holley Jr., and H. S. Feild, "Management Perceptions of Grievance Mediation," *Arbitration Journal* 45, no. 3 (1990), pp. 15–23.

Grievance mediation tends to shift the focus from a "rights" (who wins) orientation towards a problem-solving mode. Evidence from one plant indicates that mediation is unrelated to "win" rates of management or the union.[28]

EMPLOYEE AND UNION RIGHTS IN GRIEVANCE PROCESSING

One important grievance issue concerns an employee's right to union representation in disciplinary proceedings. For example, if a supervisor suspects an employee of quitting work early, which normally merits a suspension, can the supervisor confront and interrogate the employee without allowing union representation? The Supreme Court ruled that employees who are suspected of offenses that could result in discipline are entitled to union representation if they request it.[29] The employer cannot proceed with the interrogation unless a union steward is present to advise its member.

To What Is the Employee Entitled?

Not every grievance constitutes a bona fide contract violation, and not every legitimate grievance is worth pursuing to arbitration. For example, suppose a supervisor performed bargaining unit work during a rush—but not an emergency—period. The union may have a legitimate grievance, and the workers are entitled, as a group, to receive pay for the period the supervisor worked. If it is an isolated incident, bringing it to management's attention should reduce the likelihood of its recurrence, even if management denies the relief requested.

The merits of individual cases vary. For example, a discharge case is more serious than a case where the grievant claims entitlement to two hours' pay for overtime given to another. How far can an individual union member pursue a grievance or force a union to process it through arbitration if necessary? This subject is not entirely resolved, but opinions of legal experts and court discussions provide some direction. The issue is referred to by terms such as individual rights and **fair representation.** In the discussion, the latter term applies to the vigor and equality of the union's advocacy, not necessarily to its competence (the competence issue is covered in Chapter 15).

Occasionally, an employer disciplines a union activist more harshly than other offenders for a rule violation. If the individual charges the company with violating his or her rights to engage in union activity, the NLRB will apply the following test. First, the general counsel for the board must make a prima facie case that the discipline was motivated by the employee's union activity. Then, the employer

---

[28] R. N. Block and A. R. Olson, "Low Profile/High Potential," *Dispute Resolution Journal* 51, no. 4 (1996), pp. 54–61.

[29] *NLRB* v. *J. Weingarten, Inc.*, 420 U.S. 251 (1975).

could rebut an unfair labor practice charge if it can show the same punishment would have occurred in the absence of union activity.[30]

Fair Representation

The question of fair representation is a complex issue in which the rights and duties of those involved are not completely spelled out.[31] Generally, however, representation rights of nonunion employees are substantially less, unless employers grant them by policy.[32] All employees, represented or not, are able to seek legal redress for employer actions violating civil rights, wage and hour, or health and safety laws. In other areas, however, unrepresented employees have no legal right to review an arbitrary decision.

Individual Rights under the Contract

Several decisions clarify individual rights under collective bargaining agreements. Major decisions before passage of the Taft-Hartley Act helped to specify minority rights in grievance processing. In *Elgin, Joliet, and Eastern Railway* v. *Burley*, the Supreme Court held that a concession of a grievance by the union does not necessarily insulate the employer from being sued.[33] The employees must have authorized the union to act for them, and some vigorous defense must be shown. Because the union is the exclusive bargaining agent for all employees, the courts will watch to ensure that all classes and subgroups are entitled to and receive equal protection and advocacy from their representatives.

Taft-Hartley enables represented employees to grieve directly to employers. However, employers cannot process grievances without union observation, if demanded by the union, or adjust the grievance in a manner inconsistent with the contract. For example, if the contract entitles senior employees to promotions, a junior employee cannot personally insist on receiving a promotion to which a senior employee is entitled.

An individual's rights under the contract are not clearly established. Three possible positions might be suggested: (1) individuals have a vested right to use the grievance procedure through arbitration if they choose; (2) individuals should be entitled to grievance processing for discharge, seniority, and compensation cases; and (3) the union as a collective body should have freedom to

---

[30] *Wright Line*, 251 NLRB No. 150 (1980).

[31] For a detailed review of fair representation issues, see E. C. Stephens, "The Union's Duty of Fair Representation: Current Examination and Interpretation of Standards," *Labor Law Journal* 44 (1993), pp. 685–96.

[32] J. Stieber, "The Case for Protection of Unorganized Employees against Unjust Discharge," *Proceedings of the Industrial Relations Research Association* 32 (1979), pp. 155–63.

[33] 325 U.S. 711 (1945).

decide what constitutes a meritorious grievance and how far the grievance should be pursued.[34]

The NLRB and courts seldom assert jurisdiction over the merits of grievances. But a few rulings help explain union member entitlements and employer and union responsibilities. In *Miranda Fuel Company,* an employee was permitted to start vacation before the date in the contract.[35] After the employee returned late because of illness, other bargaining unit members demanded the union require his discharge. The NLRB ruled this was an unfair labor practice because the union acquiesced to a majority demand even though the discharged employee had seniority.

The second case involved a merger.[36] Here the same union represented employees of both acquired and surviving companies. After the merger, the union credited the seniority of the workers from the acquired company instead of starting seniority at the acquisition date. Several employees from the surviving company claimed they were unfairly represented because their union granted seniority to employees coming from the other firm. The Supreme Court held that the employees must use Taft-Hartley remedies rather than the state courts to redress unfair representation.

In *Vaca* v. *Sipes*, an employee returning from sick leave was discharged because the employer believed he was no longer capable of holding a job.[37] He filed a grievance and the union pressed his case, obtaining medical evidence and requesting that he be given a less physically demanding job. The doctors' reports were in conflict on whether the employee could safely continue working. Although the union vigorously pursued the grievance through the final step before arbitration, it did not demand arbitration when the company refused to reinstate the grievant.

The grievant sued his union for unfair representation and his employer for breach of contract. The court held that an employee may not go to court on a grievance unless contractual remedies have been exhausted, except where the employer and/or the union have refused to use these remedies. If the grievant contends the union has unfairly represented him or her, he or she must prove this. The court found individual bargaining unit members have no inherent right to invoke arbitration. In representing all bargaining unit members, the union is both an advocate and an agent which must judge whether claims are frivolous or inconsistent with past practice or contract interpretation. If the union weighs the grievance's merit and treats the grievant in the same manner as others in the same situation, that is not unfair representation.

---

[34] B. Aaron, "The Individual's Legal Rights as an Employee," *Monthly Labor Review* 86 (1963), pp. 671–72.

[35] 140 NLRB 181 (1962).

[36] *Humphrey* v. *Moore*, 375 U.S. 335 (1964).

[37] 386 U.S. 171 (1967).

An appeals court decision can place the union "between a rock and a hard place."[38] In this case, the contract provided that promotions would be based on seniority and merit. When the company promoted junior employees, the union processed grievances of senior employees to arbitration. The arbitrator awarded the jobs to senior employees. The displaced junior employees sued their union for failing to represent their positions in the arbitration. The court held that the union owed equal obligations to both groups. Although the union certainly favored seniority as the basis for promotion, it must advocate management's position as well because the contract provides benefits to two potential groups with opposite interests.

Another case extends union liability for damages. If an employee can prove the employer violated the contract to the employee's detriment and the union dealt with the grievance in an arbitrary and capricious manner, the employee can collect damages from both. The employee collects damages from the employer up to the point at which the union fails to process a meritorious claim and from the union until relief is granted.[39]

A review of Supreme Court decisions on fair representation has extracted the following six principles: (1) employees have the right to have contract terms enforced to their benefit, (2) an employee has no right to insist on his or her personal interpretation of a contract term, (3) no individual can require a union to process a grievance to arbitration, but each should have equal access to grievance procedures, (4) settlement on the basis of personal motives by union officials constitutes bad faith, (5) the individual should have a grievance decided on its own merits, not traded for other grievance settlements, and (6) while the union is entitled to judge the relative merit of grievances, it must exercise diligence in investigating the situation that led to the grievance.[40]

GRIEVANCES AND BARGAINING

As noted in the chapters on union structure, organizing, and negotiation, the processes involved can be specified, but the actual behavior does not always duplicate the model. The grievance procedure, as described, provides a method for resolving disputes over the contract's meaning. The process consigns the union to the role of responding to management's actions and management to the role of initiating some action leading to the dispute. Grievance resolution has been dealt with as a serial process, from both the steps involved (which duplicate reality rather closely) and the presentation order (first in, first out—which is an unlikely duplication). This section looks at grievances from a political standpoint and as a bargaining tool.

---

[38] *Smith* v. *Hussman Refrigerator Co. & Local 13889, United Steelworkers of America* (U.S. Court of Appeals, 8th Circuit, 1979); certiorari denied by Sup. Ct., 105 LRRM 2657 (1980).

[39] *Bowen* v. *U.S. Postal Service*, 112 LRRM 2281, Sup. Ct., 1983.

[40] C. W. Summers, "The Individual Employee's Rights under the Collective Agreement: What Constitutes Fair Representation?" in J. T. McKelvey, ed., *Duty of Fair Representation* (Ithaca: New York State School of Industrial and Labor Relations, Cornell University, 1977), pp. 60–83.

Union Responses to Management Action

In many cases, grievances have a number of ramifications for the union. A novel grievance may establish a precedent for or against the union if it is arbitrated. In the past, the situation may have been informally handled on a case-by-case basis usually favorable to the union, but now the risks of losing may be too great. Other grievances may lead to internal disputes, such as entitlements to work or overtime. Politically powerful minorities within the union may also need accommodation. Upcoming union election activity may also influence grievance activity and its resolution. Candidates may take militant positions, and management may grant fewer grievances or take more time, particularly in areas where it sees strength in certain campaigning candidates who it expects will be difficult to deal with in the future.

Besides the responses of union officials to grievances, rank-and-file members may engage in tactics affecting the grievance process. If a large number of grievances build up or if settlement is slow (particularly for those alleging a continuing violation), then pressure tactics such as slowdowns, quickie strikes, and working to rules may be used to pressure management to settle or grant the grievances.[41] Grievants might not wait passively for an ultimate response but rather use tactics to speed up a favorable settlement.

Evidence indicates the union gains bargaining power by shaping employee complaints so they fit a clear grievance category. At the same time, the union is more successful in winning its grievance if the category is different from one particularly important to the employer.[42]

Fractional Bargaining

Because most grievances concern an individual employee or a single work group and relate only to one or a few contract terms, tactics aimed at modifying the practice of contract administration are called **fractional bargaining.**[43] Fractional bargaining affects work groups in the same way an employer with multiple bargaining units suffers a reduction in bargaining power. An organization consists of interdependent parts; when one part is embroiled in disputes that lessen its productivity, the remainder will be affected.

Fractional bargaining occasionally poses problems for the union because one critical group may win grievances others fail to achieve. If a negotiating committee stops grievances of a powerful small group, internal political pressures will increase. A steward of a powerful small group may successfully pressure for settlement at lower levels to avoid local officer involvement. The company may accede to lessen chances of production disruptions.

---

[41] J. W. Kuhn, *Bargaining in Grievance Settlement* (New York: Columbia University Press, 1961).

[42] P. Suschnigg, "Measuring Bargaining Power through Grievance Outcomes: Results from an Ontario Steel Mill," *Relations Industrielles* 48 (1993), pp. 480–500.

[43] Kuhn, *Bargaining in Grievance Settlement,* p. 79.

Management may also take the initiative by assigning work to political opponents of the existing union leadership and by handling some disciplinary cases by the book and being lenient with others. These practices may increase internal political pressures and cause more of its energies to be devoted to healing these rifts rather than to additional grievance activity. Thus, as in contract negotiations, each side pressures the other, but some mutual accommodation enabling the survival of both is usually reached.

Union Initiatives in Grievances

The union may take the initiative with grievances. Stewards may solicit grievances, looking for potential contract violations.[44] A violation need not actually occur for a grievance to be filed, only the belief that one did occur and the linking of that belief to some contract clause. If the union believes it has problems with one area or supervisor, it may simply flood management with grievances. These create work for management, because they must be answered in a certain time under the contract. If higher management has to spend more time on grievances, it may simply tell supervisors to "clean up their act," usually resulting in a more lenient approach to demonstrate to management that supervision has "cured" the grievance problem.

Union stewards may stockpile grievances as threats or trade-offs for larger issues. If an issue of importance to the steward comes up, the supervisor may be told informally that unless a change is made, a variety of grievances will be filed with higher-ups later in the day.

In large plants, the steward has an advantage over the supervisor. Many contracts specify the steward is a full-time union representative, although paid by the company. As such, a steward's full-time work involves contract administration, while the supervisor is responsible for personnel, equipment, production, and other matters. The two are usually no match in interpreting the contract because the contract is a much more integral part of the steward's job and the steward has studied it in greater detail.

The steward's personality may also play a role. One study found that stewards who informally settled grievances with supervisors were likely to have higher needs for autonomy, affiliation, and dominance than those who used formal processes. The study also found that stewards who had higher needs for achievement and dominance were involved in greater numbers of grievances.[45] Higher commitment to the union predicted higher grievance activity levels, while higher company commitment and job satisfaction were related to lower grievance activism.[46]

---

[44] Ibid., p. 14.

[45] D. R. Dalton and W. D. Todor, "Manifest Needs of Stewards: Propensity to File a Grievance," *Journal of Applied Psychology* 64 (1979), pp. 654–59.

[46] D. R. Dalton and W. D. Todor, "Antecedents of Grievance-Filing Behavior: Attitude/Behavioral Consistency and the Union Steward," *Academy of Management Journal* 25 (1982), pp. 158–69.

Higher grievance rates are related to inexperienced stewards, union policies that influence grievance filing, and periods close to negotiations or political choice within the union.[47] A longitudinal study of an auto plant with a single UAW local found that grievances with high factual clarity were decided for the union more often during periods of high production importance such as model changeovers and heavy schedules, when few grievants were involved, when the steward was politically entrenched, and in nonassembly plants. In cases where grievances had low factual clarity, political issues had a greater effect, such as the shorter the time until the next union election, the lower the settlement rate; the more grievances, the lower the union win rate; the more likely the grievance claimed a right given to another bargaining unit member, the lower the union win rate; and the more entrenched the steward, the lower the win rate. Other factors involved with low clarity outcomes for the union included high production pressure situations and skilled trades occupations.[48] All these indicate management's response could be seen as pressuring the union politically and facilitating the production process.

Management practices may also have an influence on grievance rates. A study of grievances and productivity in an aircraft manufacturing plant found that the highest productivity occurred at a grievance rate significantly above zero. Very low grievance rates might indicate a lack of management monitoring and enforcement, while high levels consume extra effort in their settlement.[49]

Stewards are often elected. Grievance handling influences the election process. Stewards who file more grievances, who resolve them at lower levels, and who take more time with them are more frequently reelected and with higher margins. As the relationship between supervisors and stewards matures, the process becomes more efficient and effective.[50]

Individual Union Members and Grievances

Chapter 1 noted that people may unionize to exercise a voice in governing the workplace.[51] Negotiating a contract and obtaining ratification by the bargaining unit create an employment equilibrium. This equilibrium represents the exercise of bargaining power by both parties and their preferences for the structure of the agreement. In grieving, an individual member exercises voice and expresses dissatisfaction or takes advantage of an opportunity for gain that a specific situation such as increased production rates might allow. Workers in high-paying jobs or those facing few alternative job opportunities are more likely to use the grievance process and

---

[47] C. E. Labig, Jr., and C. R. Greer, "Grievance Initiation: A Literature Survey and Suggestions for Future Research," *Journal of Labor Research* 9 (1988), pp. 1–27.

[48] D. Meyer and W. Cooke, "Economic and Political Factors in Formal Grievance Resolution," *Industrial Relations* 27 (1988), pp. 318–35.

[49] M. M. Kleiner, G. Nickelsburg, and A. Pilarski, "Monitoring, Grievances, and Plant Performance," *Industrial Relations* 34 (1995), pp. 169–89.

[50] D. Meyer, "The Political Effects of Grievance Handling by Stewards in a Local Union," *Journal of Labor Research* 15 (1994), pp. 33–51.

[51] R. B. Freeman and J. L. Medoff, *What Do Unions Do?* (New York: Basic Books, 1984).

less likely to engage in absenteeism or turnover, availing themselves of their voice opportunities.[52] The strength of the grievance procedure influences the beliefs that employees have about their ability to influence outcomes within their employers because quit rates, as one study discovered, were negatively related to the strength of the grievance procedure.[53] Figure 14–4 portrays a model of the grievant's choices and potential outcomes. Some grievance opportunities occur because of workplace changes or actions taken against the grievant. The model suggests negative outcomes will occur to the employee and employer unless the process leading to the ultimate outcome is perceived to be procedurally just.[54]

Differences exist among employees in grievance behavior and characteristics. Demographic and job-related aspects are generally poor predictors of grievance activity,[55] although evidence found that younger,[56] male,[57] minority,[58] and better-educated employees[59] have higher rates. An attitudinal study examining employees across many employers found grievants more likely to have lower job satisfaction, higher satisfaction with the union, and be an active participant in union affairs.[60] Another study using the same sample found employees who filed more grievances had declining job satisfaction during the four years between the waves of the study, were in larger plants, perceived themselves as expending lower effort, and anticipated working for the same employer in five years. Factors relating to perceived union effectiveness, poor or changing working conditions, or the openness of the supervisor did not influence grievance-filing behavior.[61] An experimental study using a hypothetical situation found union members more likely to indicate they would file grievances when the situation evoked strong reactions and when management's action was perceived to be intentional.[62]

[52] P. Cappelli and K. Chauvin, "A Test of an Efficiency Model of Grievance Activity," *Industrial and Labor Relations Review* 45 (1991), pp. 3–14.

[53] D. I. Rees, "Grievance Procedure Strength and Teacher Quits," *Industrial and Labor Relations Review* 45 (1991), pp. 31–43.

[54] B. S. Klaas, "Determinants of Grievance Activity and the Grievance System's Impact on Employee Behavior: An Integrative Perspective," *Academy of Management Review* 14 (1989), pp. 445–58.

[55] Labig and Greer, "Grievance Initiation."

[56] P. Ash, "The Parties to the Grievance," *Personnel Psychology* 23 (1970), pp. 13–38; J. Price, J. Dewire, J. Nowack, K. Schenkel, and W. Ronan, "Three Studies of Grievances," *Personnel Journal* 55, no. 1 (1976), pp. 32–37; Lewin and Peterson, *Modern Grievance Procedures*, p. 174; and M. E. Gordon and R. C. Bowlby, "Reactance and Intentionality Attributions as Determinants of the Intent to File a Grievance," *Personnel Psychology* 42 (1989), pp. 309–29.

[57] Lewin and Peterson, *Modern Grievance Procedures*, p. 174.

[58] Ibid.; and Ash, "Parties to the Grievance."

[59] Ash, "Parties to the Grievance"; Lewin and Peterson, *Modern Grievance Procedures*, p. 174; and Price et al., "Three Studies."

[60] R. E. Allen and T. J. Keaveny, "Factors Differentiating Grievants and Nongrievants," *Human Relations* 38 (1985), pp. 519–34.

[61] B. Klaas and G. G. Dell'Omo, "The Determinants of Grievance Filing Behavior: A Psychological Perspective," paper presented at the Academy of Management Meetings, Anaheim, CA, 1988.

[62] Gordon and Bowlby, "Reactance and Intentionality."

FIGURE 14–4

An Integrative Model of Individual Grieving Behavior

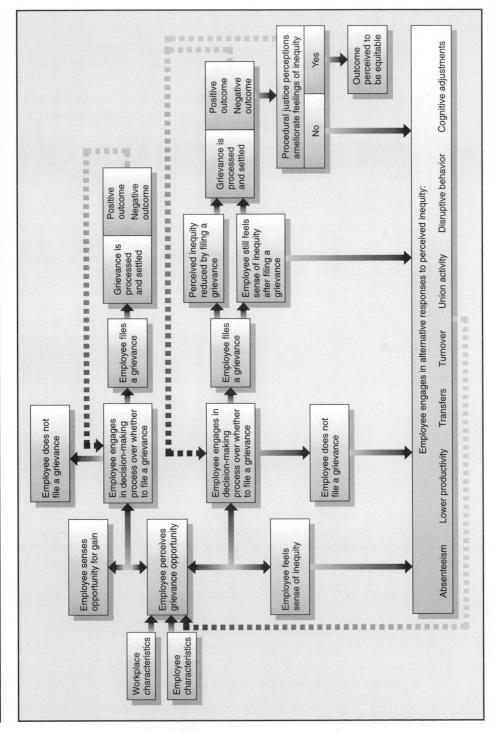

SOURCE: B. S. Klaas, "Determinants of Grievance Activity and the Grievance System's Impact on Employee Behavior: An Integrative Perspective," *Academy of Management Review* 14 (1989), p. 449.

EFFECTS OF GRIEVANCES ON EMPLOYERS AND EMPLOYEES

Both employers and employees may be influenced by the filing, processing, and outcome of grievances. A study of grievances in a government agency found that employees filing two grievances within one rating period received lower performance ratings. Winning or losing the grievance was not associated with the rating. Employees who grieved were no more likely to transfer; however, employees who filed a second grievance were more likely to receive a disciplinary sanction, and a second negative adjustment to a grievance was associated with an increased probability of quitting. From the employer's standpoint, grievance filing was associated with higher absenteeism and fewer production hours.[63] Absenteeism appears to increase in association with policy grievances and is reduced by disciplinary grievances. Absenteeism falls following negative outcomes from disciplinary grievances, possibly because of escalating consequences for further discipline problems.[64] In a study of a steel mill, grievants were usually better employees during the year in which they grieved and, if their grievance was settled at a low level and/or they lost the grievance, they were more likely to be rated higher, have better attendance, lower turnover, and more likely to be promoted in the subsequent year.[65] Managers and supervisors of units in which grievance rates were higher were somewhat more likely to be rated lower in the next period.[66]

From the perspective of the ongoing bargaining relationship, evidence across 118 bargaining units in 1976–77 followed up by a study of 18 units in 1979–80 found that high grievance rates were associated with conflictual rather than cooperative labor relations.[67]

A study of public-sector management and union representatives found explicit performance and disciplinary standards were associated with higher grievance rates. Rivalry between unions within the same employer increased grievances. Positive management attitudes and willingness to compromise were related to lower rates, but consultation with the union about items of mutual interest did not reduce grievances.[68]

Grievance resolution provides information to assist in resolving subsequent cases at lower levels. The evidence suggests that only management used prior decisions to guide initial decisions on a grievance. The higher the level of settlement of a grievance, the more likely the parties were to use formal settlements of

---

[63] B. S. Klaas, H. G. Heneman III, and C. A. Olson, "Grievance Activity and Its Consequences: A Study of the Grievance System and Its Impact on Employee Behavior" (Columbia: University of South Carolina, 1988).

[64] B. S. Klaas, H. G. Heneman III, and C. A. Olson, "Effects of Grievance Activity on Absenteeism," *Journal of Applied Psychology* 76 (1991), pp. 818–24.

[65] Lewin and Peterson, *Modern Grievance Procedures*, pp. 185–87.

[66] Ibid., p. 189.

[67] J. Gandz and J. D. Whitehead, "The Relationship between Industrial Relations Climate and Grievance Initiation and Resolution," *Proceedings of the Industrial Relations Research Association* 33 (1981), pp. 320–28.

[68] C. E. Labig, Jr., and I. B. Helburn, "Union and Management Policy Influences on Grievance Initiation," *Journal of Labor Research* 7 (1986), pp. 269–84.

previous grievances as precedents. Earlier decisions are used most frequently as precedents in discipline and work assignment cases.[69] In a Canadian public-sector union, grievances were more likely to be settled favorably in the early steps, for more highly paid employees, and for working condition rather than work assignment issues.[70] (Management may settle grievances to the grievant and union's benefit "without precedent" for subsequent similar cases.)

Employees who frequently grieve do not necessarily have better work outcomes. But what effect do grievances have for employers? Each grievance requires involvement of stewards, the grievant, and supervisors at the first step; industrial relations representatives, national union representatives, and the union negotiating committee at subsequent steps; and attorneys or representatives, witnesses, and an arbitrator at arbitration. A study of 10 paper mills (9 union and 1 nonunion) found higher grievances associated with lower plant productivity. The presence of a grievance procedure (only in the union mills) was associated, however, with higher productivity, perhaps because employees had an outlet for complaints that would operate while production occurred.[71]

SUMMARY

Contract administration is the joint activity in which labor and management spend the most time. Not only do the parties respond voluntarily to differences in interpretation, but they also must, by law, bargain on practices related to mandatory items over the life of the contract.

Both sides deal with a variety of issues, with job security, seniority, and discipline among the most important. Methods for handling disputes involve the presentation and resolution of grievances in a stepwise manner, culminating in arbitration if necessary.

Unions must represent employees in a consistent manner in grievance proceedings, and employees who can show they were not accorded fair treatment may hold the union and the employer in breach of contract.

All grievances are not equally meritorious, and political factions within unions may obtain power to gain more favorable outcomes. Grievances also may accompany periodic union political elections. Management may influence these by the way in which it responds to the source of grievances during campaigning.

Grievants have been found less satisfied with their jobs, more satisfied with their unions, and more involved in union activities. They are also more likely to grieve if they see fewer alternatives (such as quitting) available to them.

---

[69] T. R. Knight, "Feedback and Grievance Resolution," *Industrial and Labor Relations Review* 39 (1986), pp. 585–98.

[70] I. Ng and A. Dastmalchian, "Determinants of Grievance Outcomes: A Case Study," *Industrial and Labor Relations Review* 42 (1989), pp. 393–403.

[71] C. Ichniowski, "The Effects of Grievance Activity on Productivity," *Industrial and Labor Relations Review* 40 (1986), pp. 75–89.

Grievances, in general, do not lead to stronger positive outcomes for employees. Employers with high grievance rates appear to have slightly lower productivity.

DISCUSSION QUESTIONS

1. Should management be required to consult with the union about discipline before it is imposed rather than simply providing for grievance processing after its imposition?
2. Should unions be allowed to drop an employee's grievance if the employee desires arbitration?
3. How does the grievance procedure make subtle changes in the meaning of the contract possible over time?
4. What are the advantages and disadvantages of a program to reduce the number of written grievances?

KEY TERMS

Contract administration   *458*

"Last chance agreement"   *459*

Umpire   *465*

Project labor agreements   *469*

Fair representation   *471*

Fractional bargaining   *475*

CASE

Carolyn Foster had just returned to her office from the weekly plant IR representatives' meeting. Her secretary had left a note to call George Lowrey, the superintendent of the forklift assembly operation. She called back and immediately recognized from the seriousness of George's tone that a major problem must be brewing in his area. They both agreed she would come right over.

After George had welcomed her into his office, he leaned forward and, putting his chin in his hands, said, "Carolyn, I feel like I'm sitting on a powder keg here. Last year we put in the new Simplex Process assembly line for our forklifts. It had a rated capacity of 35 units an hour. When we installed it, we started up at 28 units, which is the same as the old line, to shake it down and get the bugs out. The new line automates more of the assembly, so each worker has less of a physical demand than before. Well, last week we figured we had everything ironed out on the bugs, so we raised the speed to 35. We figure each worker has to put out about the same amount of effort as under the old system.

"This morning, Steve Bonneville, the shop steward, and three of my general supervisors came in, all arguing. Bonneville had a fistful of grievances and was yelling about a 'speedup.' Anyway, the upshot is that he wants the employees to be advanced one skill level to compensate for the additional effort and more difficult working conditions under Section 7.03 of the contract.

"Carolyn, we can't give them a penny more and remain competitive. Besides, if they get a raise, the whole plant will paper us with classification grievances. Bonneville is running for union president because Matt Duff is retiring, and if he's successful with this grievance, he's a shoo-in. All we need for a long strike over some penny-ante issue is a bunch of hotheads like him running the show. What can you do to help me?"

Carolyn had been busy taking notes about the problem. She asked, "Do you have the grievances?" George nodded and handed them to her. Then she said, "I'll study the grievances, the contract, and the union situation and get back to you in time for us to plan a Step 3 response. I'll be back to you this afternoon."

Directions

1. Draft a strategy for the company to follow. Consider the immediate problem and the possibilities of precedents being set by your action. List the advantages and disadvantages of your chosen strategy.

2. Prepare a scenario in which your response is presented to Steve Bonneville. How is he likely to react? What steps do you expect he will take as a result of your response?

3. What conditions do you consider necessary for these grievances to be resolved at Step 3?

GRIEVANCE

ARBITRATION

*T*his chapter is about the final step in most grievance procedures—arbitration. Arbitration is not solely a labor relations process, and within labor relations it does not deal solely with grievances. The chapter covers the definition of arbitration, its legal place in labor relations, the process itself, difficulties associated with its practice, and results associated with arbitration of employee discharge and discipline cases.

As you study this chapter, consider the following questions:

1. How have Supreme Court decisions influenced arbitration?
2. How is arbitration aided or interfered with by the National Labor Relations Board?
3. What procedures are used during arbitration?
4. What problems do critics of arbitration point out?

WHAT IS ARBITRATION?

Arbitration is a quasi-judicial process in which parties agree to submit unresolved disputes to a neutral third party for binding settlement. Both parties submit their positions, and the arbitrator decides what each party is entitled to. This chapter is concerned with labor arbitration, but the method is also applied to disputes between buyers and sellers, contractors and real estate developers, stockbrokers and customers, and doctors and patients.

Two major types of labor arbitration are "interest" and "rights." This chapter is primarily concerned with rights arbitration. Chapter 16 covers interest arbitration which is primarily applied in the public sector. The Supreme Court distinguishes between interest and rights arbitration this way:

> The first relates to disputes over the formation of collective agreements or efforts to secure them. They arise where there is no such agreement or where it is sought to change the terms of one, and therefore the issue is not whether an existing agreement controls the controversy. They look to the acquisition of rights for the future, not to assertion of rights claimed to have vested in the past.
>
> The second class, however, contemplates the existence of a collective agreement already concluded or, at any rate, a situation in which no effort is made to bring about a formal change in terms or to create a new one. The dispute relates either to the meaning or proper application of a particular provision with reference to a specific situation or to an omitted case. In the latter event the claim is founded upon some incident of the employment relation, or asserted one, independent of those covered by the collective agreement. In either case the claim is to rights accrued, not merely to have new ones created for the future.[1]

Thus, rights arbitration applies to interpreting and applying terms of an existing contract, and interest arbitration decides unresolved future issues.

DEVELOPMENT OF ARBITRATION

The Knights of Labor preferred arbitration for resolving interest differences but was never able to use it. No federal law requires arbitration of private-sector labor disputes. During World War II, however, the National War Labor Board required labor agreements to provide for arbitration of intracontract disputes.[2] Beginning in 1957, the Supreme Court and the NLRB defined the role and scope of arbitration in their decisions.

---

[1] *Elgin, Joliet & Eastern Railway Co.* v. *Burley,* 325 U.S. 711 (1945).

[2] F. Elkouri and E. A. Elkouri, *How Arbitration Works*, 3rd ed. (Washington, DC: Bureau of National Affairs, 1973), p. 15.

Lincoln Mills

The *Lincoln Mills* case first established arbitration as the final forum for contract disputes.[3] In *Lincoln Mills*, the Supreme Court held that Section 301 of the Taft-Hartley Act required federal courts to enforce collective bargaining agreements, including those with provisions for arbitrating future grievances. If the contract called for arbitration and if the federal court agreed with the arbitrator, the award would be enforced by the court if either party failed to comply with it.

Steelworkers' Trilogy

The legitimacy and finality of rights arbitration was decided by the Supreme Court in 1960.[4] The question facing the Court was whether arbitrators' decisions were subject to judicial review. In a set of decisions, the court essentially said no, laying down three basic protections for arbitration. First, arbitration clauses require parties to arbitrate unresolved grievances. Second, the substance of grievances and their **arbitrability** are to be determined by arbitrators, not courts. And third, if an arbitration clause exists, the courts will order arbitration unless a dispute is clearly outside the scope of the contract. The decisions state that arbitrators are presumed to have special competence in labor relations and are thus better able than courts to resolve labor disputes.

In the *Warrior and Gulf* case, the Supreme Court held, that where a broad arbitration clause is included in the contract, even a dispute not covered in other sections is arbitrable. In this case, the employer subcontracted work while the firm's employees were in a partial layoff status. While lower courts held subcontracting to be a potential management right, the Supreme Court held that the broad arbitration agreement coupled with the no-strike provision brought the dispute within the arbitral arena.

The *American Manufacturing* case involved an employee who became disabled and accepted worker's compensation. His doctor later certified his ability to return to work, but the company refused to reinstate him. He grieved, but the company refused to process the grievance, claiming it was frivolous. The Supreme Court ordered arbitration.

Enterprise Wheel involved several employees who had been fired for walking out to protest the firing of another employee. After the company refused to arbitrate the discharge grievances, the federal district court ordered it. The arbitrator reinstated the employees with back pay for all but 10 days of lost time. The award

---

[3] *Textile Workers Union v. Lincoln Mills*, 355 U.S. 448 (1957).

[4] *United Steelworkers of America v. Warrior & Gulf Navigation Co.*, 363 U.S. 574; *United Steelworkers of America v. Enterprise Wheel and Car Corp.*, 363 U.S. 593; and *United Steelworkers of America v. American Manufacturing Co.*, 363 U.S. 564 (1960).

was rendered five days after the contract expired, but the Supreme Court ordered compliance.

Four propositions follow from the decisions in the **Steelworkers' trilogy.**

1. The existence of a valid agreement to arbitrate and the arbitrability of a specific grievance sought to be arbitrated under such an agreement are questions for the courts ultimately to decide (if such an issue is presented for judicial determination) unless the parties have expressly given an arbitrator the authority to make a binding determination of such matters.

2. A court should hold a grievance nonarbitrable under a valid agreement to use arbitration as the terminal point in the grievance procedure only if the parties have clearly indicated their intention to exclude the subject matter of the grievance from the arbitration process, either by expressly so stating in the arbitration clause or by otherwise clearly and unambiguously indicating such intention.

3. Evidence of intention to exclude a claim from the arbitration process should not be found in a determination that the labor agreement could not be interpreted properly in such manner as to sustain the grievance on its merits, for this is a task assigned by the parties to the arbitrator, not the courts.

4. An award should not be set aside as beyond the authority conferred upon the arbitrator, either because of claimed error in interpretation of the agreement or because of alleged lack of authority to provide a particular remedy, where the arbitral decision was or, if silent, might have been the result of the arbitrator's interpretation of the agreement; if, however, it was based not on the contract but on an obligation found to have been imposed by law, the award should be set aside unless the parties expressly authorized the arbitrator to dispose of this as well as any contract issue.[5]

The trilogy decisions enable arbitrators to decide whether disputes are arbitrable, and if arbitrable, to decide—free from federal court intervention—what awards should be.[6] Where companies or unions have gone to court over arbitration procedures or awards, courts have most often compelled arbitration if a party has tried to avoid it or enforced awards if one has failed to implement them. Less than 1 percent of arbitration cases involve court proceedings. About 25 percent of postarbitration appeals succeed.[7]

The Steelworkers' trilogy protects a union's right to insist on arbitration and to have arbitral awards enforced without court review. But could management also expect similar treatment if it agreed to arbitrate, received a favorable award, and was struck to prevent enforcement (given that the Norris-LaGuardia Act

---

[5] R. A. Smith and D. L. Jones, "The Supreme Court and Labor Dispute Arbitration," *Michigan Law Review* 63 (1965), pp. 759–60.

[6] Ibid., p. 761.

[7] P. Feuille and M. LeRoy, "Grievance Arbitration Appeals in the Federal Courts: Facts and Figures," *Arbitration Journal* 45, no. 1 (1990), pp. 35–47; M. H. LeRoy and P. Feuille, "The Steelworkers Trilogy and Grievance Arbitration Appeals: How the Federal Courts Respond," *Industrial Relations Law Journal* 13 (1991), pp. 78–120.

prevents federal courts from enjoining most union activities, including strikes for any purpose as long as they do not threaten life or property)?

The 1962 Trilogy

The 1962 trilogy involves the requirement to arbitrate damages for violating a no-strike clause rather than taking the disputes directly to the federal courts.[8] The *Drake* decision held that management should request arbitration when a no-strike clause exists to determine whether the contract has been violated. In the *Sinclair* cases, the court held that federal courts could not enjoin a strike in violation of a no-strike clause because the Norris-LaGuardia Act prevented injunctions against labor activities.

The decision in *Sinclair* v. *Atkinson* questioned the utility of no-strike clauses for employers. Without court enforcement of no-strike clauses, a strike over an arbitrator's adverse award or striking rather than using the grievance procedure could not be enjoined. In a later reversal, the Supreme Court held that a strike in violation of a no-strike clause before arbitration is enjoinable if the company is willing to arbitrate the dispute.[9]

Recent Supreme Court Decisions on Arbitration

Three cases involving arbitration procedures and awards modified and reaffirmed the basics of the Steelworkers' trilogy. In the first case, the company and the union couldn't agree whether the disputed situation involved the contract. The union argued that a decision on coverage should be made by the arbitrator after appointment, while the company maintained that arbitrability should be up to the courts. The Supreme Court agreed with the company and declared the courts are ultimately responsible for deciding the arbitrability of contract disputes. This doesn't mean an arbitrator can't rule on arbitrability, but a decision is subject to court review, and, if a dispute existed, a party could petition the courts to decide arbitrability before the case was heard.[10]

The second case involved a situation in which an arbitrator had reinstated an employee who had been fired for smoking marijuana. The company appealed the decision, which was later overturned by the courts as inconsistent with public policy on drug use. The Supreme Court, however, reversed the lower courts' decisions, holding that in the absence of fraud or dishonesty, courts may not review a decision on its merits, for errors of fact, or possible contract misinterpretations. Further, to overturn an award on the basis of public policy, a court must show that

---

[8] *Sinclair Refining Co.* v. *Atkinson*, 370 U.S. 195 (1962); *Atkinson* v. *Sinclair Refining Co.*, 370 U.S. 238 (1962); and *Drake Bakeries* v. *Local 50*, 370 U.S. 254 (1962).

[9] *Boys Markets, Inc.* v. *Retail Clerks Union Local 770*, 398 U.S. 235 (1970).

[10] *AT&T Technologies, Inc.*, v. *Communications Workers of America*, 106 Sup. Ct., 1415 (1986).

the policy is well defined, dominates the interests of the employee or employer, and has a history of laws and legal precedents to support it.[11]

The third case held that where a contract has expired and the employer takes a unilateral action (in this case a layoff) that was not begun under the expired contract, the employer cannot be compelled to arbitrate a grievance where a new contract has not been agreed upon.[12]

NLRB Deferral to Arbitration

Occasionally, a dispute involves both a grievance and a charge of an unfair labor practice. For example, bargaining unit members claim certain work may have been given to nonunion employees outside the bargaining unit. The grievance would allege a violation of the contract on work assignments, and the union might charge the employer with discrimination based on union membership. To prevent "forum shopping" and to reduce its caseload, the NLRB has adopted rules for deferring to arbitration when a contract violation and an unfair labor practice are alleged simultaneously.

In developing its policy, the NLRB first held that where a grievance also alleged an unfair labor practice and the arbitration award had been adverse to, say, the union, the union could not then pursue the unfair labor practice.[13] The board decreed it would defer to arbitral awards if the parties had agreed in the contract to be bound by the decisions, the proceedings were fair and regular, and the results were consistent with the provisions of the labor acts.

In 1971 in *Collyer,* the NLRB went further by deferring hearings on pending charges of unfair labor practices until arbitration had been completed, as long as the process was consistent with *Spielberg.*[14] In 1977, the NLRB retreated somewhat from the **Collyer doctrine,** which deferred the disposition of unfair labor practices to pending arbitration, by limiting deferral only to cases where the alleged unfair labor practice was not in violation of an employee's Section 7 rights.[15] Ironically, a study of several awards in cases where the board deferred to arbitration in 1977 and 1978 in the Detroit region found that the decisions on unfair labor practices involving violation of Section 7 rights were seldom incompatible with board decisions, while refusal to bargain unfair labor practices decisions were frequently incompatible. Unions frequently received more favorable treatment from arbitrators than they would have from the NLRB.[16] In 1984, the board extended deferral to arbitration awards unless the decision was "palpably

---

[11] *United Paperworkers International Union, AFL-CIO* v. *Misco, Inc.,* 108 Sup. Ct., 364 (1987).

[12] *Litton Financial Printing Division* v. *NLRB,* 501 US 190 (1991)

[13] *Spielberg Manufacturing Co.,* 112 NLRB 1080 (1955).

[14] *Collyer Insulated Wire Co.,* 192 NLRB 150 (1971).

[15] *Roy Robinson Chevrolet,* 228 NLRB 103 (1977); *General American Transportation Corporation,* 228 NLRB 102 (1977).

[16] B. W. Wolkinson, "The Impact of the *Collyer* Policy of Deferral: An Empirical Study," *Industrial and Labor Relations Review* 38 (1985), pp. 377–91.

wrong."[17] The NLRB declared it would defer to arbitration if the arbitrator had adequately considered the alleged unfair labor practice and contractual and unfair labor practice issues were essentially parallel. Even before the *Olin* case, regional directors of the NLRB deferred about 90 percent of cases alleging unfair labor practices. Following *Olin*, this rate increased even though appeals courts have not enforced cases similar to *Olin*.[18]

Exceptions to Deferral

Although the Supreme Court led the way in endorsing the finality of arbitration in contract disputes, and the NLRB allowed arbitrators to decide cases simultaneously alleging violations of federal labor relations law and the contract, there are limits on deferral.[19] Individual rights granted under other statutory employment laws cannot be decided in a collectively bargained arbitral procedure if a party objects to the outcome. Thus, if a grievant is dissatisfied with an arbitrator's ruling, the case could be started again by complaining to the appropriate federal compliance agency.

In *Alexander*, an African-American maintenance employee bid on a skilled job. After his promotion, he was warned that his performance was substandard. After completing the probationary period (and the expiration of his right to revert to his former position), Alexander was terminated. He charged his termination was racially motivated. However, the arbitrator ruled it had been performance motivated and upheld the decision.

Alexander complained to the Equal Employment Opportunity Commission (EEOC). Early in the process, the company refused conciliation because the arbitrator had ruled in its favor. The district court dismissed the suit because the contract had an EEO clause and an arbitrator had ruled. Ultimately appealed to the Supreme Court, the case was remanded when the Court ruled the law would not permit deferral to an arbitral award. On remand, the district court determined that Alexander had been discharged for performance reasons.

Employers and unions could still arbitrate discrimination cases if a grievance alleged a violation of both contract and law. Appropriate procedure would require a single grievant to allege discrimination and not argue the contract is discriminatory. Individuals would be entitled to their own lawyers and a transcript would be kept. Arbitrators would be required to render written awards. Thus, courts might be willing to defer on a case-by-case basis because the procedure would meet the suggested requirements in *Alexander*.[20]

---

[17] *Olin Corporation*, 268 NLRB 573 (1984).

[18] P. A. Greenfield, "The NLRB's Deferral to Arbitration before and after *Olin*: An Empirical Analysis," *Industrial and Labor Relations Review* 42 (1988), pp. 34–49.

[19] *Alexander* v. *Gardner-Denver Co.*, 415 U.S. 36 (1974); and *Barrentine* v. *Arkansas-Best Freight System*, 2 WH Cases 1284, Sup. Ct., 1981.

[20] H. T. Edwards, "Arbitration as an Alternative in Equal Employment Disputes," *Arbitration Journal* 33, no. 12 (1978), pp. 23–27.

Few EEO grievances are relitigated and, where they are, arbitrators' awards are almost always upheld. A survey of management and union advocates suggests they prefer more attention to arbitration than the extension of Title VII law to the adjudication of the grievance.[21]

In some public-sector situations, employees are subject to both the labor agreement and the rules of administrative agencies. The Supreme Court requires arbitrators to apply the same standards as administrative bodies in deciding employee performance cases.[22] This prevents the grievant from shopping for the most hospitable forum.

ARBITRATION PROCEDURES

This section examines the prearbitration processes, arbitrator selection, conduct of the arbitration hearing, preparing and rendering an award, and the magnitude of arbitration in the United States.

Prearbitration Matters

The contract specifies how a dispute goes to arbitration. Normally, cases have proceeded through the preceding steps of the contractual arbitration process. At the last step, if management denies a grievance or fails to modify its position sufficiently for the union to agree, the union can demand arbitration.

If the parties have agreed to concessions before arbitration, these may not be communicated to the arbitrator. In most cases, the parties can return to their own initial positions without establishing precedents. Also, in cases settled before arbitration, the company may explicitly state that it will not consider the granting of that specific grievance as precedent setting.

The union's request for arbitration must be timely. The contract specifies time limits for the various steps of the grievance process. If management denies the grievance at the last step, the union has a certain time to demand arbitration. If it does not exercise its rights within this period, management's decision becomes final.

Selection of an Arbitrator

Procedures for selecting an arbitrator are in the contract. The usual forms for arbitration are either to (1) use one impartial arbitrator who hears the evidence and renders an award or (2) have a tripartite board consisting of company and union

---

[21] M. M. Hoyman and L. E. Stallworth, "Arbitrating Discrimination Grievances in the Wake of *Gardner-Denver*," *Monthly Labor Review* 106, no. 10 (1983), pp. 3–10.

[22] *Cornelius v. Nutt*, 472 U.S. 648 (1985).

representatives and an impartial chairperson. In large organizations or where a long-term bargaining relationship exists, the contract may specify an individual or group from whom arbitrators are selected. When a specific individual is named, the position is called a **permanent umpire.** Permanence, however, is relative, because arbitrators continue to serve only as long as both parties rate performance satisfactory. Permanent umpires may be more vulnerable when a militant union presents less meritorious cases than with a union that saves arbitration for very important issues. The arbitrator would be likely, in dealing with a militant union, to rule much more frequently for management; as a result, the union might rate performance unsatisfactory quite soon.[23]

A common type of selection is the **ad hoc arbitrator,** appointed to hear only one case or set of cases. The appointment expires when the award is rendered, and the company and the union may coincidentally appoint other ad hoc arbitrators to hear unrelated cases at or near the same time.

Both methods of arbitrator selection have advantages and disadvantages. Less may be known about an ad hoc arbitrator, although information about potential arbitrators is usually available through résumés, previously published decisions, fields of expertise, and so on. But the appointment constitutes no continuing obligation by the parties. The permanent umpire has a better grasp of the problems the parties encounter because of continuing experience with both. Because the relationship is continuous, however, whether the umpire will engage in award splitting may always be open to question.

In a study of arbitrator acceptability based on caseload volume, the visibility of the arbitrator rather than personal background or practice characteristics was the factor most highly related to caseload. Also particularly important was a listing with referral agencies, publication of awards, membership in professional organizations, and background as a permanent umpire.[24] Another study suggests managements and unions should not pay too much attention to the personal background characteristics of arbitrators in making choices for a particular case because they account for little variance in arbitrators' rulings for the union or the company.[25] One study of decisions in suspension cases found male arbitrators were more lenient with female than male grievants, while female arbitrators dealt similarly with both men and women.[26] However, another study found that rulings in the public sector were more often favorable to men.[27] Exhibit 15–1 reports a conversation between two experienced arbitrators on gaining acceptability.

---

[23] R. W. Fleming, *The Labor Arbitration Process* (Urbana: University of Illinois Press, 1965), pp. 219–20.

[24] S. S. Briggs and J. C. Anderson, "An Empirical Investigation of Arbitrator Acceptability," *Industrial Relations* 19 (1980), pp. 163–74.

[25] H. G. Heneman III and M. H. Sandver, "Arbitrators' Backgrounds and Behavior," *Proceedings of the Industrial Relations Research Association* 35 (1982), pp. 216–23.

[26] B. Bemmels, "Gender Effects in Grievance Arbitration," *Industrial Relations* 30 (1991), pp. 150–62.

[27] D. J. Mesch, "Arbitration and Gender: An Analysis of Cases Taken to Arbitration in the Public Sector," *Journal of Collective Negotiations in the Public Sector* 24 (1995), pp. 207–18.

EXHIBIT 15–1

Gaining Acceptability as an Arbitrator

"Paul, you've been an active arbitrator for over 25 years. For several of those years arbitration was your principal means of livelihood. You're an old-timer. How did you get started?"

"Like many if not most of the old-timers, I started with the War Labor Board. I was a graduate of the Wharton School at the University of Pennsylvania and studied under Prof. George W. Taylor. When Dr. Taylor was appointed in 1942 to be vice chairman of the War Labor Board, he recruited a number of his students to the W.B., including me."

"Did most of the W.B. staff continue as arbitrators after the war?"

"No, only a small fraction survived the rough-and-tumble of voluntary arbitration in the postwar years. Throughout this book, Pete, we've frequently referred to the 350 members of the National Academy of Arbitrators who do most of the arbitrating. 'Mainline' arbitrators, they're often called, to distinguish them from 'fringe' arbitrators trying to get into the main current."

"At what point did you personally cease to be a fringe arbitrator and consider yourself a mainliner?"

"Not on any one single case, I can assure you. A fringe arbitrator can be broken by a bad opinion in just one arbitration, but becoming a mainliner is a process rather than the result of a single spectacular case."

"Is there any condition or status you can describe which clearly defines a mainline arbitrator?"

"When you put it that way, Pete, I can make the line of demarcation between a fringe arbitrator and a mainliner quite distinct. When I was a fringe arbitrator, the losing party would scrutinize my opinion to find out where *I* was wrong. I knew I had arrived at the mainline stage when in many cases the loser would study my opinion to find out where *he* was wrong."

SOURCE: P. Prasow and E. Peters, *Arbitration and Collective Bargaining: Conflict Resolution in Labor Relations* (New York: McGraw-Hill, 1970), pp. 284–85.

Sources and Qualifications of Arbitrators

There are no absolute qualifications to be an arbitrator. Anyone could simply declare him- or herself to be an arbitrator and seek appointments. However, to arbitrate one must be selected by the parties to a grievance. Where do arbitrators come from? Arbitrators are those who have arbitrated. Parties involved in ad hoc arbitration want someone with experience and expertise because some of the participants have done little arbitrating and need an experienced arbitrator to assist them in procedural matters. They also look for someone with a background in handling the disputed area. For parties with much arbitration experience, a permanent umpire may be named, and this individual is likely to have an outstanding reputation in arbitration.

Arbitrators are generally from two groups: increasingly, attorneys who are full-time arbitrators, and academics who teach labor law, industrial relations, and economics. Another source of arbitrators is new entrants. However, many offer their services but are never chosen. Since 1975, the average mainline arbitrator has become older and more experienced; many have more than 30 years of experience and are over 65 years old.[28] One method for getting started is to serve an informal apprenticeship under an experienced arbitrator, gaining practice in writing decisions and learning hearing techniques. This exposure with a highly regarded neutral may lead to later appointments. Another method is to attend training courses for arbitrators; however, few of these are available. A few training programs have been successful, particularly for minority arbitrators.[29] Evidence suggests that the arbitrator acceptability of those who complete training is quite high.

Three major sources refer arbitrators. Each serves a slightly different function, but all have interests in providing arbitrator services in labor disputes.

National Academy of Arbitrators

The National Academy of Arbitrators consists of highly regarded active arbitrators who are invited to join. The academy holds meetings and issues proceedings, commenting on difficult problems in arbitration and offering alternative solutions. For example, it offered a variety of approaches in handling arbitration of discrimination cases, given the *Alexander* v. *Gardner-Denver* decision.[30] The group is comprised largely of full-time arbitrators, law school professors, and professors of industrial relations in major universities.

The academy does not offer panels to disputants, but its directory provides a source of recognized, highly qualified arbitrators the parties can contact directly.

American Arbitration Association

Many contracts specify that the parties use American Arbitration Association (AAA) services for its unresolved grievances. The AAA does not employ arbitrators but acts more as a clearinghouse to administer matters between the parties and the arbitrators.

If a contract specified AAA to assist in choosing an arbitrator, the following occurs: First, AAA is notified that a dispute exists. AAA responds with a list of arbitrators—usually five and almost always an odd number. The arbitrators may have particular expertise in the disputed area (e.g., job evaluation) or may practice in a particular geographic area. Second, names are rejected alternately until only one remains. This person will be the nominee unless either party objects. In that case, AAA sends out another panel. Generally, referral agencies usually refuse to

---

[28] D. F. Jennings and A. D. Allen, Jr., "A Longitudinal Analysis of Content Issues in Labor Arbitration: View from Arbitrators Themselves," *Labor Studies Journal* 16, no. 2 (1991), pp. 35–49.

[29] W. A. Nowlin, "Arbitrator Development: Career Paths, a Model Program, and Challenges," *Arbitration Journal* 43, no. 1 (1988), pp. 3–13.

[30] H. T. Edwards, "Arbitration of Employment Discrimination Cases: A Proposal for Employer and Union Representatives," *Labor Law Journal* 27 (1976), pp. 265–77.

send more than three panels for any dispute. Third, after a name has been agreed upon, AAA contacts the appointee to offer the dispute, and the appointee accepts or declines. If accepted, arrangements are made directly with the parties for a hearing date. Fourth, AAA will provide hearing facilities and court reporters if the parties request. Finally, AAA follows up to see what decisions were rendered.

Federal Mediation and Conciliation Service

The FMCS maintains a roster of arbitrators from which it can select panels. The arbitrators are not FMCS employees but private practitioners. If FMCS assistance is specified in a contract, it would provide panels as AAA does but would not have reporting or facilities assistance available.

FMCS screens persons who seek listing as arbitrators. People with obvious conflicts of interest (e.g., union organizers, employer labor consultants) are not included, and listees who fail to be selected are purged from subsequent lists.[31] Figure 15–1 contains some of the requirements for being listed.

FMCS follows up on referral by requiring arbitrators to render awards within 60 days of the hearing's close and the receipt of posthearing briefs.

Once the arbitrator has been selected, processes related to the scheduled hearing begin. The phases of this process include prehearing, hearing, and posthearing activities.

Prehearing

Elkouri and Elkouri detailed a number of steps both parties should go through before an arbitration hearing:

a. Review the history of the case as developed at the prearbitral steps of the grievance procedure.

b. Study the entire collective agreement to ascertain all clauses bearing directly or indirectly on the dispute. Also, compare current provisions with those in prior agreements to reveal possible changes significant to the case.

c. To determine the general authority of the arbitrator and the scope of the arbitration, examine the instruments used to initiate the arbitration.

d. Talk to all persons (even those the other party might use as witnesses) who might be able to aid development of a full picture of the case, including different viewpoints. You will thus better understand not only your own case but also your opponent's; if you can anticipate your opponent's case, you can better prepare to rebut it.

e. Interview each of your own witnesses (a) to determine what they know about the case; (b) to make certain they understand the relation of their testimony to the

---

[31] *Code of Federal Regulations,* Title 29, Chap. 12, Part 1404.

FIGURE 15–1

Requirements for Listing as an Arbitrator with the FMCS

Section 1404.5   Listing on the Roster; Criteria for Listing and Retention

Persons seeking to be listed on the Roster must complete and submit an application form which may be obtained from the Office of Arbitration Services. Upon receipt of an executed form, OAS will review the application, assure that it is complete, make such inquiries as are necessary, and submit the application to the Arbitrator Review Board. The Board will review the completed applications under the criteria set forth in paragraphs (a), (b), and (c) of this section, and will forward to the Director its recommendation on each applicant. The Director makes all final decisions as to whether an applicant may be listed. Each applicant shall be notified in writing of the Director's decision and the reasons therefore.

(a) General Criteria. Applicants for the Roster will be listed on the Roster upon a determination that they:
   (1) Are experienced, competent, and acceptable in decision-making roles in the resolution of labor relations disputes; or
   (2) Have extensive experience in relevant positions in collective bargaining; and
   (3) Are capable of conducting an orderly hearing, can analyze testimony and exhibits, and can prepare clear and concise findings and awards within reasonable time limits.

(b) Proof of Qualification. The qualifications listed in paragraph (a) of this section are preferably demonstrated by the submission of actual arbitration awards prepared by the applicant while serving as an impartial arbitrator chosen by the parties to disputes. Equivalent experience acquired in training, internship or other development programs, or experience such as that acquired as a hearing officer or judge in labor relations controversies may also be considered by the Board.

(c) Advocacy
   (1) Definition. An advocate is a person who represents employers, labor organizations, or individuals as an employee, attorney, or consultant, in matters of labor relations, including but not limited to the subjects of union representation and recognition matters, collective bargaining, arbitration, unfair labor practices, equal employment opportunity, and other areas generally recognized as constituting labor relations. The definition includes representatives of employers or employees in individual cases or controversies involving worker's compensation, occupational health or safety, minimum wage, or other labor standards matters. The definition of advocate also includes a person who is directly associated with an advocate in a business or professional relationship as, for example, partners or employees of a law firm.
   (2) Eligibility. Except in the case of persons listed on the Roster before November 17, 1976, no person who is an advocate, as defined above, may be listed. No person who was listed on the Roster at any time who was not an advocate when listed or who did not divulge advocacy at the time of listing may continue to be listed after becoming an advocate or after the fact of advocacy is revealed.

(d) Duration of Listing, Retention. Initial listing may be for a period not to exceed three years, and may be renewed thereafter for periods not to exceed two years, provided upon review that the listing is not canceled by the Director as set forth below. Notice of cancellation may be given to the member whenever the member:
   (1) No longer meets the criteria for admission;
   (2) Has been repeatedly and flagrantly delinquent in submitting awards;
   (3) Has refused to make reasonable and periodic reports to FMCS, as required in Subpart C of this part, concerning activities pertaining to arbitration;
   (4) Has been the subject of complaints by parties who use FMCS facilities and the Director, after appropriate inquiry, concludes that just cause for cancellation has been shown.
   (5) Is determined by the Director to be unacceptable to the parties who use FMCS arbitration facilities; the Director may base a determination of unacceptability on FMCS records showing the number of times the arbitrator's name has been proposed to the parties and the number of times it has been selected.

No listing may be canceled without at least 60 days' notice of the reasons for the proposed removal, unless the Director determines that the FMCS or the parties will be harmed by continued listing. In such cases an arbitrator's listing may be suspended without notice or delay pending final determination in accordance with these procedures. The member shall in either case have an opportunity to submit a written response showing why the listing should not be canceled. The Director may, at his discretion, appoint a hearing officer to conduct an inquiry into the facts of any proposed cancellation and to make recommendations to the Director.

whole case; (c) to cross-examine them to check their testimony and to acquaint them with the process of cross-examination. Make a written summary of the expected testimony of each witness; this can be reviewed when the witness testifies to ensure that no important points are overlooked. Some parties outline in advance the questions to ask each witness.

f.   Examine all records and documents that might be relevant to the case. Organize those you expect to use and make copies for use by the arbitrator and the other party at the hearing. If needed documents are in the exclusive possession of the other party, ask that they be made available before or at the hearing.

g.   Visit the physical premises involved in the dispute to visualize better what occurred and what the dispute is about. Also, consider the advisability of asking at the hearing that the arbitrator (accompanied by both parties) also visit the site of the dispute.

h.   Consider the utility of pictorial or statistical exhibits. One exhibit can be more effective than many words, if the matter is suited to the exhibit form of portrayal. However, exhibits which do not "fit" the case and those which are inaccurate or misleading are almost certain to be ineffective or to be damaging to their proponent.

i.   Consider what the parties' past practices have been in comparable situations.

j.   Attempt to determine whether there is some "key" point on which the case might turn. If so, it may be to your advantage to concentrate on that point.

k.   In "interpretation" cases, prepare a written argument to support your view as to the proper interpretation of the disputed language.

l.   In "interests" or "contract-writing" cases, collect and prepare economic and statistical data to aid in evaluating the dispute.

m.   Research the parties' prior arbitration awards and the published awards of other parties on the subject of the dispute for an indication of how similar issues have been approached.

n.   Prepare an outline of your case and discuss it with other persons in your group. This ensures better understanding of the case and will strengthen it by uncovering matters that need further attention. Then, too, it will tend to underscore policy and strategy considerations that may be very important in the ultimate handling of the case. Use of the outline at the hearing will facilitate an organized and systematic presentation of the case.[32]

   In addition, the parties may continue to seek a settlement or reduce the time necessary to settle a case. Anytime during the prehearing phase, the arbitration request may be withdrawn by joint consent. Contracts will often specify whether withdrawal is "with prejudice" (nonresubmittable) and whether a withdrawal is precedent setting. The parties may also stipulate certain facts in a case, agree on applicable contract terms, and prepare joint exhibits. Settlement after arbitration is

---

[32] Elkouri and Elkouri, *How Arbitration Works*, pp. 198–99.

requested but before the hearing occurs, settlement is more frequent when the parties' representatives are not attorneys.[33]

Hearing Processes

The actual hearing may take many forms. Most simply, a case may be completely stipulated, with the arbitrator ruling on an interpretation of the contract based on the written documents submitted. This option is not entirely up to the parties, however, because the arbitrator may insist on calling witnesses and examining evidence on site.

Representatives of the Parties

The parties' positions may be advocated by anyone they choose, which means the representatives may be attorneys, company or union officials, the grievant, and so on. In most cases involving smaller companies, a national union field representative or local union officer and an industrial relations director or personnel officer are the advocates. A party appears to have an advantage when represented by an attorney and the other side is not. When only one side retains an attorney, it is more frequently management that does so.[34]

Presentation of the Case

Because the union generally initiates grievances, it is responsible for presenting its case first, except in cases of discipline and discharge. A union presents joint exhibits relevant to its case and calls witnesses. Management may object to exhibits and cross-examine witnesses. When the union has completed its case, management offers its evidence in a similar manner. Rules of evidence in arbitration are more liberal than in courts of law. At the end of the hearing, both sides may present closing arguments. The arbitrator may question witnesses but is not required to do so.

Posthearing

Following the hearing, the parties may submit briefs supporting their positions. The arbitrator studies the evidence, takes briefs into account, and perhaps examines similar cases.

---

[33] C. R. Deitsch and D. A. Dilts, "Factors Affecting Pre-Arbitral Settlement of Rights Disputes: Predicting the Methods of Rights Dispute Resolution," *Journal of Labor Research* 7 (1986), pp. 69–78.

[34] R. N. Block and J. Stieber, "The Impact of Attorneys and Arbitrators on Arbitration Awards," *Industrial and Labor Relations Review* 40 (1987), pp. 543–55.

The arbitrator then prepares an award and sends it to the parties. In some cases, the arbitrator maintains jurisdiction until the award has been implemented in case additional proceedings are necessary to iron out differences in its application.

Evidentiary Rules

Where AAA rules apply, Rule 28 states: "The arbitrator shall be the judge of the relevancy and the materiality of the evidence offered, and conformity to legal rules of evidence shall not be necessary."[35] However, arbitrators must weigh the relevance or credibility of evidence when considering a grievance.

Two basic types of evidence are direct and circumstantial. Direct evidence is information specifically tying a person to a situation. The search for the "smoking gun" is an attempt to find direct evidence. Circumstantial evidence suggests a connection between events and an individual. For example, if shortages in a cash register occur only when one particular employee is scheduled, that circumstance, when connected with others, may establish guilt.

Evidence is relevant if it addresses the issue at hand. For example, if an arbitrator hears a case involving drinking on the job, evidence related to the subject's work assignment is not highly relevant. The evidence must also be material. For example, testimony that the subject bought a six-pack of beer the week before the alleged offense has little impact on establishing a connection with the offense.

In arbitration hearings, the union must prove management violated the contract, except in discipline cases. The level of proof required in discipline cases varies among arbitrators, but it is usually greater if the potential consequences are more severe.

Generally, employees are expected to know that published rules apply and prior written warnings they received were correctly given unless challenged. Past discipline may be used to corroborate that an employee committed this type of offense, but the longer the time since the discipline, the less weight it is usually given.

If another arbitrator has ruled on the same issue in this company and no contract changes have occurred in the area, the present arbitrator will probably rule that the issue has already been decided. In discipline cases where criminal proceedings have also occurred, the arbitrator is not bound by the same rules for evaluating evidence to prove the offense beyond a reasonable doubt.

Arbitrators must also assess the credibility of witnesses. Persons who have little inherent interest in the case might be considered more credible, and one's reputation for honesty may also be considered.[36]

---

[35] 30 *Labor Arbitration* 1086, 1089.

[36] M. Hill, Jr., and A. V. Sinicropi, *Evidence in Arbitration* (Washington, DC: Bureau of National Affairs, 1980), pp. 1–108.

Occasionally, one party has information that would aid the other in the preparation of a case. Four rules have been suggested for the production of material held by one party:

1. If the arbitrator requests it.
2. If refused, the arbitrator may weigh the refusal as he or she sees fit in the award.
3. The document or information could be used to attack the credibility of a witness.
4. The arbitrator may admit only the parts relevant to the hearing.[37]

For cross-examination and confrontation, the following have been recommended:

1. Depositions and previous testimony be admitted if a witness is unavailable.
2. Hearsay be accepted when a direct witness declines to testify against a fellow employee.
3. Investigation should generally not be attempted by the arbitrator.
4. Where exposing the identity of a witness would damage legitimate interests of either party, the witness should be questioned by counsel in the sole presence of the arbitrator.[38]

Self-incrimination is prohibited in criminal trials and may also be an issue in arbitral proceedings. Arbitrators probably will not grant absolute immunity against self-incrimination but will weigh refusals to testify as if they were evidence. However, arbitrators should not consider refusals to testify as sufficient to sustain a case.[39]

Arbitral Remedies

When a case is submitted to an arbitrator, the issues usually are specified and the grievant has indicated what relief is desired. The relief requested tends to vary given the type of case, but generally arbitrators will grant relief when it is found that the aggrieved party has been wronged, up to but not exceeding the relief desired.

In discipline and discharge cases, requested relief is usually for back pay for periods out of work, restoration of employment, recission of a demotion or transfer, elimination of reprimands from personnel files, and the like. If reinstatement and/or back pay is to be granted, the arbitrator must determine the amount through the likely job history of the grievant, less pay earned on other jobs, and so forth.

---

[37] Fleming, *Labor Arbitration Process*, p. 175.
[38] Ibid., p. 181.
[39] Ibid., p. 186.

Arbitrators might also reduce discipline if it exceeds what the offense merits, given similar situations in the employer or other workplaces with similar settings.

More difficult cases to remedy involve subcontracting, plant closures, entitlements to overtime, assignment of work, and other economic issues. Usual remedies may require the restoration of work to the bargaining unit and payment of wages forgone by employees who would have been entitled to the work.[40]

Preparation of the Award

The award conveys the arbitrator's decision in the case, including (in most cases) a summary of the evidence presented, the reasoning behind the decision, and what action must be taken to satisfy the decision.

To prepare the award, the arbitrator must determine whether the dispute was arbitrable. Did the grievance allege an actual violation of the contract? Were the steps in the grievance procedure followed in a prescribed manner so the grievance and union follow-up were timely? If these criteria are met, the arbitrator examines the merits.

While the arbitrator has no statutory obligation to do so, it is important that the reason for a particular award be included to guide the parties in the future. Even though the grievance may appear trivial, the decision will guide employer and union conduct during the contract, so it is important for them to know why the issue was decided as it was.

The arbitrator must be careful to ensure that the award draws from the essence of the contract. Most contracts prohibit arbitrators from adding to, subtracting from, or modifying the agreement. The arbitrator must show how the interpretation is within the four corners of the contract.

Occasionally, an arbitrator will find a conflict between contract language and federal labor or civil rights laws or interpretations. No clear-cut guidance for this situation exists. Some argue that the arbitrator is to give primacy to a contractual interpretation,[41] while others suggest that federal employment laws must supersede contract terms and influence the shape of an award where they would govern.[42]

PROCEDURAL DIFFICULTIES AND THEIR RESOLUTIONS

Time delays are a major problem in arbitration. It is not unusual for some cases to take up to two years to resolve. Table 15–1 provides time data from almost 600

---

[40] M. Hill, Jr., and A. Sinicropi, *Remedies in Arbitration* (Washington, DC: Bureau of National Affairs, 1981).

[41] B. Meltzer, "Ruminations about Ideology, Law, and Labor Arbitration," in *The Arbitrator, the NLRB, and the Courts: Proceedings of the National Academy of Arbitrators* (Washington, DC: Bureau of National Affairs, 1967), p. 1.

[42] R. Howlett, "The Arbitrator, the NLRB, and the Courts," in *The Arbitrator, the NLRB, and the Courts: Proceedings of the National Academy of Arbitrators* (Washington, DC: Bureau of National Affairs, 1967), p. 67.

TABLE 15–1

Time Involved in Arbitrated Grievances

	Mean	Median	Minimum	Maximum
Pre-arbitration grievance steps (days)	54.7	41.5	0	334
Arbitrator selection (days)	77.7	50.0	0	428
Scheduling (days)	128.3	112.0	9	623
Decision preparation (days)	65.2	55.9	0	347
Total procedure (days)	333.6	161.2	14	936
Length of award (pages)	15.1	13	1	105

SOURCE: A. Ponak, W. Zerbe, S. Rose, and C. Olson, "Using Event History Analysis to Model Delay in Grievance Arbitration," *Industrial and Labor Relations Review* 50, p. 112.

arbitrated cases in the province of Alberta between 1985–1988.[43] The total time is very similar to U.S. data.

The arbitral process can take more time, but the data show an average of 184 days from appointment to award. The 65 days from the termination of the hearing to the award date is greater than the 60-day limit previously established by the FMCS, but it may include time during which briefs are submitted.[44] The median of 50 days is within the period. One arbitrator noted that the time between the close of the hearings and rendering a decision in about 150 cases varied from zero to 94 days with a mean of 30 days or less in every industry except railroads. For these cases, the time lapse between the grievance and the hearing was zero to 1,426 days, with a mean of over 100 days in all industries and a mean of over one year in steel, railroads, and the federal government.[45]

Time delays occur at various points. From the original grievance to referral to arbitration, the complexity of the dispute and nondischarge grievances increase the time required. Delay in arbitrator selection is related to the use of attorneys and the size of the arbitration board. Delays in scheduling relate to the use of outside attorneys; hours, wages, and benefits; and job entitlement issues. Delay in decisions was related to complexity; discipline, hours, wages, benefits, and other issues; board size; legal counsel; and the arbitrator's workload. Public-sector arbitrations took longer than those in the private sector.[46]

Problems still exist with the length of time. The quote "justice delayed is justice denied" is not an empty platitude. It is important to individuals who have been disciplined to have their cases decided so they can make a new employment life or return to work made whole. For firms, a grievance involving many employees can lead to heavy back-pay liabilities if long-delayed findings are adverse.

---

[43] A. Ponak, W. Zerbe, S. Rose, and C. Olson, "Using Event History Analysis to Model Delay in Grievance Arbitration," *Industrial and Labor Relations Review* 50 (1996), pp. 105–21.

[44] Ibid.

[45] G. Mangum, "Delay in Arbitration Decisions," *Arbitration Journal*, 42, no. 1 (1987), p. 58.

[46] Ponak et al, *Using Event History Analysis*, pp. 105–21.

Arbitration costs also cause problems, particularly for unions. Because unions and managements usually share arbitration costs, a poorly financed union may be reluctant to use arbitration as much as it would like. Table 15–2 estimates the costs for a typical, relatively uncomplicated arbitration case, using 1990 per diem figures for arbitrators and doubling most other costs from those determined when the table was first constructed in 1976.[47]

Expedited Arbitration

Since the early 1970s, some larger companies and unions have used **expedited arbitration** to reduce time delays and costs. Instead of hearing a single case in a day, arbitrators hear several cases and submit very short written awards. Most expedited arbitration cases involve individual discipline and discharge or emergencies. Expedited arbitration also will provide for the entry of new arbitrators because relatively simple and straightforward cases are generally handled by this process. Table 15–3 contains examples of expedited arbitration procedures.

Inadequate Representation

Chapter 14 noted that employees in certain situations successfully argued they were not fairly represented by their unions in the grievance procedure. In arbitration, inadequate representation can arise. It could be malicious or occur through ineptitude. Because arbitration determinations are viewed as final by courts, the quality of the advocacy a grievant receives is of substantial concern.

The Supreme Court reversed an arbitration award discharging an over-the-road trucker accused of padding expenses.[48] An adequate prehearing investigation would have disclosed that the apparent dishonesty was the result of a motel clerk charging more than the published rate and pocketing the difference. The trucker was actually blameless.

During hearings, arbitrators may become aware of differences in the quality of representation. Although arbitrators may question witnesses and probe into other matters, their impartiality in an adversarial hearing could be questioned as a result. Is it ethical for an arbitrator to "make a case" for an advocate who has inadequately prepared a case? This issue has not been settled. However, if it is clear to the arbitrator that the grievant's rights are not adequately represented, a later appeal could reverse the award.[49]

---

[47] D. F. Jennings and A. D. Allen, "Labor Arbitration Costs and Case Loads: A Longitudinal Analysis," *Labor Law Journal* 41 (1990), pp. 80–88.

[48] *Hines* v. *Anchor Motor Freight, Inc.*, Sup. Ct., 74-1025, 1976.

[49] See J. T. McKelvey, "The Duty of Fair Representation: Has the Arbitrator a Responsibility?" *Arbitration Journal* 41, no. 2 (1986), pp. 51–58, for one arbitrator's opinion.

TABLE 15–2

The Union's Cost of Traditional Arbitration for a One-Day Hearing

Prehearing	
Lost time: Grievant and witnesses @ $15/32 hours	$ 480
Lawyer:	
Library research @ $100/4 hours	400
Interviewing witnesses @ $200/4 hours	800
Filing fee: AAA (shared equally) $200	100
Total prehearing costs	$1,780
Hearing expense	
Arbitrator:	
Fee (shared equally) 1 hearing day @ $600	$ 300
Expenses for meals, transportation, etc. (shared equally)	200
Travel time one-half day (shared equally)	150
Transcript: $10 per page with two copies and 10-day delivery of 200 pages	
(shared equally)	1,000
Lawyer: Presentation of case @ $200 per hour	1,200
Lost time: Grievant and witnesses @ $15/32 hours	480
Hearing room: Shared equally	100
Total hearing	$3,430
Posthearing expense	
Arbitrator: 1¾ days study time (shared equally)	$ 525
Lawyer: Preparation of posthearing brief @ $200/8 hours	1,600
Total posthearing	$2,125
Total cost to union	$7,335

ARBITRATION OF DISCIPLINE CASES

Many arbitration cases are employee appeals to reconsider evidence related to employer discipline or to reassess the severity of a punishment. Any punishment that includes discharge is very likely to go to arbitration. What principles do arbitrators apply to evaluating evidence and establishing fair punishment in industrial discipline cases?

Role of Discipline

Employees and employers have certain contractual rights and obligations. Employees have rights to their jobs as the contract reads, and employers are entitled to performance from their workers. An employer expects employees to carry out orders, regardless of the employees' interpretation of the rightness of the orders, unless they are unsafe, unhealthful, or illegal.[50] If employees believe

[50] D. L. Jones, *Arbitration and Industrial Discipline* (Ann Arbor: Bureau of Industrial Relations, University of Michigan, 1961), pp. 17–18.

TABLE 15-3
Examples of Expedited Methods

	Steelworkers—Basic Steel Industry	American Arbitration Association Service	AIW Local 562 Rusco, Inc.	American Postal Workers—U.S. Postal Service	Miniarbitration Columbus, Ohio
Source of arbitrators	Recent law school graduates and other sources	Special panel from AAA roster	FMCS roster	AAA, FMCS rosters	Its own "Joint Selection and Orientation Committee" from FMCS roster
Method of selecting	Preselected regional panels; administrator notifies in rotation	Appointed by AAA regional administrators	Preselected panel by rotating FMCS contracts	Appointed by AAA regional administrators	FMCS regional representative by rotation
Lawyers	No limitation, but understanding that lawyers will not be used	No limitation	No lawyers	No limitation but normally not used	No limitation
Transcript	No	No	No	No	May be used
Briefs	No	Permitted	No	No	May be used
Written description of issue	Last step grievance report	Joint submission permitted	No	Position paper	Grievance record expected
Time from request to hearing date	10 days	Approximately 3 days depending on arbitrator availability	10 days	Approximately 7 days depending on arbitrator availability	Not specified
Time of hearing to award	Bench decision or 48 hours	5 days	48 hours	Bench decision; written award, 48 hours	48 hours
Fees (plus expenses)	$100/½ day $150/day	$100 filing fee Arbitrator's normal fee	$100/½ day $150/day	$100 filing fee $100 per case	$100/½ day, 1 or 2 cases; $150/full day, 1 or 2 cases; $200/day, 3 or 4 cases

SOURCE: John Zalusky, "Arbitration: Updating a Vital Process," *American Federationist* 83, no. 11 (November 1976), p. 4.

orders violate the union contract, they are entitled to file grievances and seek relief. But if employees take matters into their own hands, they are guilty of insubordination and may be punished. Punishment can serve two basic purposes: (1) to motivate employees to avoid similar conduct in the future and (2) by example, to deter others.

Evidence

Because discipline cases are extremely important to the grievant, arbitrators require the company to present evidence showing the grievant actually committed the offense and the punishment is consistent with the breach of the rules. Arbitrators tend to make decisions in discipline cases based on their assessment of what caused the discipline problem to occur.[51] Arbitrators who overturn discipline decisions generally cite a lack of supporting evidence; mitigating circumstances; arbitrary, capricious, or disparate treatment; inappropriate administration or rules; or procedural errors.[52]

Given this evidence, arbitrators may uphold or deny punishment or modify it downward (but not upward) to follow the disciplinary breach more closely. Arbitrators also require the discipline to be given for just cause and not on some capricious basis.

Uses of Punishment

Punishment can be thought of in two contexts as it relates to discipline. The first sees punishment as a legitimate exercise of authority resulting from a breach of rules. The second sees punishment as a corrective effort to direct the employees' attention to the consequences but also to change their attitudes toward the punished behaviors.[53] Arbitrators may be concerned with these approaches, but they are perhaps more concerned with the procedural regularity of the discipline in the case at hand, in the evenness of its application across persons within the same firm, and in its fundamental fairness given societal norms.[54]

A study of arbitral decisions found that applications of authoritarian or corrective discipline were equally divided, with a small additional proportion using humanitarian discipline (using rules only as guidance and taking into account individual intentions). Table 15–4 shows the results. Corrective discipline is used more often for absenteeism and incompetence, while authoritarian approaches are

---

[51] B. Bemmels, "Attribution Theory and Discipline Arbitration," *Industrial and Labor Relations Review* 44 (1991), pp. 548–62.

[52] G. W. Bohlander and D. Blancero, "A Study of Reversal Determinants in Discipline and Discharge Arbitration Awards: The Impact of Just Cause Standards," *Labor Studies Journal* 21, no. 3 (1996), pp. 3–18.

[53] Jones, *Arbitration and Industrial Discipline,* pp. 2–4.

[54] Ibid., pp. 16–20.

TABLE 15–4

Analysis of Arbitration Decisions Relating to Discharge and Discipline by Theory of Discipline and Type of Offense, as Reported in *Labor Arbitration Reports,* **May 1970 through March 1974**

	Humanitarian	Corrective	Authoritarian	Total
Absenteeism, tardiness, leaving early	2	20	8	30
Dishonesty, theft, falsification of records	2	13	28	43
Incompetence, negligence, poor workmanship, violation of safety rules	1	27	9	37
Illegal strikes, strike violence, deliberate restriction of production	0	12	19	31
Intoxication, bringing intoxicants into plant	1	10	7	18
Fighting, assault, horseplay, troublemaking	3	16	15	34
Insubordination, refusal of job assignment, refusal to work overtime, also fight or altercation with supervisor	2	42	54	98
Miscellaneous rule violations	2	20	26	48
Totals	13	160	166	339
Percent	4%	47%	49%	

SOURCE: Hoyt N. Wheeler, "Punishment Theory and Industrial Discipline," *Industrial Relations,* May 1976, p. 239.

used more often for dishonesty and illegal strike activity.[55] In the increasingly important area of substance abuse, arbitrators appear to use corrective discipline for cases of alcohol abuse and punishment for drug abuse when solid evidence exists that the offense occurred in the workplace.[56]

Given that corrective discipline is applied about half the time, is it effective? One intensive study concluded that in no case did an unsatisfactory employee receiving corrective discipline later perform satisfactorily. A number of reasons are suggested for this finding. First, the individual is often restored to the original work group, where behavior that resulted in the punishment is reinforced. Second, the grievant may be unclear which behavior the punishment was related to. And third, in some cases, placing an employee in a probationary status rather than punishing him or her may be reasonable, so the contingency is on future rather than past behavior.[57]

An employee's previous work record is apparently predictive of job performance after reinstatement. Poor performance after reinstatement among a large sample of employees was predicted by the number of warnings and other disciplinary action before being discharged and by discharges for absenteeism or

---

[55] H. N. Wheeler, "Punishment Theory and Industrial Discipline," *Industrial Relations* 15 (1976), pp. 235–43.

[56] K. W. Thornicroft, "Arbitrators and Substance Abuse Discharge Grievances: An Empirical Assessment," *Labor Studies Journal* 14 (1989), pp. 40–65.

[57] Jones, *Arbitration and Industrial Discipline,* pp. 71–74.

dishonesty.[58] Among another group of reinstated employees, the evidence suggested most discharges had been for attendance problems, and the performance of reinstated employees was about average.[59]

Substance Abuse Cases

Since 1970, increasing numbers of contracts and/or work rules recognize alcoholism and addiction to narcotics as diseases. Employers and unions have agreed generally to facilitate treatment for employees who make their conditions known and to avoid discipline for the substance abuse itself.[60] Some substance abuse problems become known to employers through drug testing. Since testing is a condition of employment, it is a mandatory bargaining issue. In general, where probable cause exists (rather than random testing), failure to submit to a drug test will usually lead an arbitrator to uphold a discharge.[61]

Arbitrators in alcohol and drug cases have upheld company discipline depending on the company's ability to prove misconduct, the reasonableness of its action, and appropriateness of the penalty. Other factors weighing in the decision include proper notice to employees of the consequences of drug and alcohol offenses, equal treatment, and proper investigation.[62]

Where last chance agreements are violated, courts have held that they supersede the contract and discharges under them are not arbitrable if the facts are incontrovertible.[63]

Sexual Harassment Violations

Sexual harassment is a violation of Title VII of the Civil Rights Act of 1964. Employers are liable for damages if an employee is sexually harassed and the employer has taken no affirmative action to prevent its occurrence. Thus, most employers have promulgated policies forbidding supervisors from soliciting sexual favors in return for positive employment treatment and forbidding employees

---

[58] C. E. Labig, Jr., I. B. Helburn, and R. C. Rodgers, "Discipline History, Seniority, and Reason for Discharge as Predictors of Post-Reinstatement Job Performance," *Arbitration Journal* 40, no. 3 (1985), pp. 44–52.

[59] W. E. Simkin, "Some Results of Reinstatement by Arbitration," *Arbitration Journal* 41, no. 3 (1986), pp. 53–58.

[60] T. Schneider-Denenberg and R. V. Denenberg, "Arbitration of Employee Substance Abuse Rehabilitation Issues," *Arbitration Journal* 46, no. 1 (1991), pp. 17–33.

[61] C. L. Reder and A. Abbey, "The Arbitration of Drug Use and Testing in the Workplace," *Arbitration Journal* 48, no. 1 (1993), pp. 80–85.

[62] S. M. Crow, E. C. Stephens, and W. H. Sharp, "A New Approach to Decision-Making Research in Labor Arbitration Using Alcohol and Drug Disciplinary Cases," *Labor Studies Journal* 17, no. 3 (1992), pp. 3–18.

[63] D. S. McPherson and B. R. Metzger, "'Last Chance' Discharges at Arbitration: Emergent Standards of Judicial Review," *Proceedings of the Industrial Relations Research Association* 46 (1994), pp. 315–23.

from creating and maintaining a sexually hostile environment. Courts have generally interpreted harassment from the standpoint of the potential target (e.g., if the target is a woman, what would a "reasonable woman" consider harassment). Many companies have "zero tolerance" for harassment (i.e., employees who harass will be terminated).

An analysis of arbitration awards involving charges of sexual harassment found that 72 percent involved co-workers, 5 percent supervisors, and 4 percent nonemployees, with 92 percent involving complaints of unwanted sexual advances or hostile work environments.[64] Arbitrators face a difficult issue in dealing with harassment discipline grievances. If they find a violation but don't view it as serious enough to merit discharge, there is the potential problem of restoring the employee to the same work area as the person who was harassed, thereby continuing a threatening or hostile workplace.[65]

ARBITRATION OF PAST PRACTICE DISPUTES

Certain work practices or benefits may not be mentioned explicitly in the contract but may have been applied so consistently that there is an understanding they will continue to be applied in a similar manner. Unions may frequently negotiate clauses stating that both parties agree existing conditions will not be lowered during the present agreement.

In a variety of situations, arbitrators have ruled certain practices not mentioned in the contract are protected to the initiator: union or management. If management confers a benefit but announces special circumstances each time it confers it, the employer does not establish a continuing practice. On the other hand, if management mentions a benefit as a reason for not conceding in some area during negotiations, the benefit tends to assume binding characteristics. If conditions change and management decides to drop a practice, it must do so within a reasonably short time after the change to defend itself against **past practice** grievances.[66]

One arbitrator suggested that eight criteria should be examined in ruling on past practice grievances.

1. Does the practice concern a major condition of employment?
2. Was it established unilaterally?
3. Was it administered unilaterally?
4. Did either party seek to incorporate it into the body of the written agreement?
5. What is the frequency of repetition of the practice?

---

[64] V. E. Hauck and T. G. Pearce, "Sexual Harassment and Arbitration," *Labor Law Journal* 43 (1992), pp. 31–39.

[65] T. J. Piskorski, "Reinstatement of the Sexual Harasser: The Conflict between Federal Labor Law and Title VII," *Employee Relations Law Journal* 18 (1993), pp. 617–23.

[66] P. Prasow and E. Peters, *Arbitration and Collective Bargaining: Conflict Resolution in Labor Relations* (New York: McGraw-Hill, 1970), pp. 96–121.

6. Is the practice of long standing?

7. Is it specific and detailed?

8. Do the employees rely on it?[67]

If the answers to these questions are yes or frequent, the condition will likely take on the same legitimacy as a negotiated benefit.

ARBITRAL DECISIONS AND THE ROLE OF ARBITRATION

For arbitration to be accepted by both parties, neither expects to fare worse in the results. In a survey of published decisions, win rates for union and managements were divided evenly. The party with the burden of proof (management in discipline cases, the union in others) wins in 43 percent of cases.[68]

The parties negotiate the agreement and provide for arbitration in their grievance procedure. Most contracts indicate arbitrators cannot add to the agreement or decide a case using criteria outside the agreement. Yet the parties encounter situations in which they cannot agree on the interpretation of the contract. One commentator suggested that the role of the arbitrator is to add to the agreement by setting terms to cover one of a number of infinite work situations the parties could not contemplate when the agreement was negotiated.[69] The method continues to be the choice of parties to resolve intracontractual differences that cannot be negotiated or mediated.

The FMCS gathers data on the number of cases going to arbitration and the issues involved for panels it supplies. Table 15–5 shows the progression from 1973 through 1997.

SUMMARY

Arbitration is a process for resolving disputes through the invitation of a neutral third party. The use of arbitration is encouraged by the courts, and the outcome of arbitral awards is generally considered nonreviewable. Supreme Court decisions in the Steelworkers' trilogy laid the groundwork for the present status of arbitration.

Arbitral hearings are quasi-judicial in nature and resolve alleged contract violations. Arbitrators hear evidence from both parties and rule on the issue in dispute.

---

[67] *Jacob Ruppert* v. *Office Employees International Union Local 153*, October 19, 1960, 35 LA 505; Arbitrator, Burton B. Turkus.

[68] D. A. Dilts and C. R. Deitsch, "Arbitration Win/Loss Rates as a Measure of Arbitrator Neutrality," *Arbitration Journal* 44, no. 3 (1989), pp. 42–47.

[69] D. Feller, "The Remedy Power in Grievance Arbitration," *Industrial Relations Law Journal* 5 (1982), pp. 128–37.

TABLE 15–5

Number and Percent Change in Issues Reported to Applicable FMCS Closed Arbitration Award Cases for Fiscal Years 1973, 1981, 1985, 1990 and 1997; Percent Change from 1981

Specific Issues	1973	1981	1985	1990	1997	Percent Change from 1981
Total	4,255	8,126	5,380	5,916	3,787	−53.4
General issues	1,130	1,962	1,378	1,419	779	−60.3
Overtime other than pay						
Distribution of overtime	187	202	112	143	63	−68.8
Compulsory overtime	17	23	17	21	12	−47.8
Other	—	49	25	50	20	−59.2
Seniority						
Promotion and upgrading	203	215	156	214	108	−49.8
Layoff, bumping, and recall	264	361	267	198	129	−64.3
Transfer	96	92	61	66	44	−52.2
Other	90	93	73	74	65	−30.1
Union officials	27	41	27	19	15	−63.4
Strike and lockout	19	13	1	6	4	−69.2
Working conditions	48	57	33	64	21	−63.2
Discrimination	—	63	51	47	22	−65.1
Management rights	—	199	139	156	81	−59.3
Scheduling of work	179	150	105	88	82	−45.3
Work assignments	—	404	311	273	140	−65.3
Pay issues	581	930	546	671	409	−56.0
Wage issues	—	107	54	98	69	−35.5
Rate of pay	—	176	105	133	91	−48.3
Severance pay	—	18	19	13	13	−27.8
Reporting, call-in, and call-back pay	86	72	47	48	13	−81.9
Holidays and holiday pay	119	129	76	87	40	−69.0
Vacations and vacation pay	113	142	92	91	74	−47.9

A large number of arbitration proceedings are associated with individual discipline and discharge cases. Arbitration cases appear to be split about evenly in applying authoritarian or corrective standards in the use of punishment.

Arbitration has been criticized for its time delays and costs and because some decisions appear to go outside the scope of the contract or dispute. But opponents and proponents are relatively satisfied with the system.

Specific Issues	1973	1981	1985	1990	1997	Percent Change from 1981
Pay issues—*Cont.*						
Incentive rates or standards	82	74	41	38	15	−79.3
Overtime pay	181	212	112	163	94	−55.7
Fringe benefit issues	161	228	156	251	110	−51.8
Health and welfare	51	86	58	124	40	−53.5
Pensions	24	23	20	27	18	−21.7
Other	86	119	78	100	52	−56.3
Discharge and disciplinary issues	1,302	3,231	2,050	2,546	1,941	−40.0
Technical issues	400	380	296	299	163	−57.1
Job posting and bidding	—	108	99	98	58	−47.3
Job evaluation	400	75	65	75	30	−60.0
Job classification	—	197	132	126	75	−61.9
Scope of agreement	186	231	136	191	120	−48.1
Subcontracting	95	127	98	131	79	−37.8
Jurisdictional disputes	40	49	14	30	25	−49.0
Supervision, etc.	42	47	23	24	13	−72.3
Mergers, consolidations, accretion of other plants	9	8	1	6	4	−50.0
Arbitrability of grievances	223	734	584	275	99	−86.5
Procedural	143	434	301	168	29	−93.3
Substantive	70	218	146	77	59	−72.9
Procedural and substantive	10	82	67	30	11	−86.6
Other	—	—	70	0	0	NM
Not elsewhere classified	243	320	234	264	188	−41.2

NM = not meaningful

SOURCE: U.S. Federal Mediation and Conciliation Service, *Thirty-Eighth Annual Report, Fiscal Year 1986* (Washington, D.C.: U.S. Government Printing Office, 1986), pp. 38–39; U.S. Federal Mediation and Conciliation Service, *Forty-Third Annual Report, Fiscal Year 1990* (Washington, D.C.: U.S. Government Printing Office, 1990), p. 44; http://www.fmcs.gov/annuals/97/arb.htm.

DISCUSSION QUESTIONS

1. Given the rulings of the Supreme Court and NLRB, what is the scope and finality associated with rights arbitration proceedings in the private sector?

2. What possible drawbacks do you see associated with the expansion of expedited arbitration?

3. What duty, if any, does an arbitrator owe to the parties to see that both are competently represented?
4. Give arguments for and against the greater involvement of attorneys—as both advocates and umpires—in arbitration.
5. Forecast what you see as the future of labor arbitration in terms of the expansion or contraction of issues within its jurisdiction and the finality of its decisions.

KEY TERMS

Arbitrability   *487*

Steelworkers' trilogy   *488*

Collyer doctrine   *490*

Permanent umpire   *493*

Ad hoc arbitrator   *493*

Expedited arbitration   *504*

Past practice   *510*

CASES

About six months after the new GMFC–Local 384 contract was ratified, four grievances were sent to arbitration by the union. The company and the union agreed that all four grievances would be heard on separate dates by the same arbitrator. Your name was on the panel the FMCS sent to the parties, and they selected you to arbitrate the grievances. You agreed and have heard all four over the past three days. Now you have to prepare your awards.

Case 1

George Jones was a level 1 assembler in the heavy-components assembly department. He worked with six other assemblers of the same grade, constructing cabs for power shovels. The supervisor, Ralph Barnes, was in charge of three of these heavy-assembly crews. Jones had been with GMFC for about four years. Over the past six months, he had spent all of his time with his present work crew. His work record had been unremarkable. He had two unexcused absences but no problems with supervision.

On May 6, Jones struck a co-worker, Elliot Johnson, with his fist, rendering him unconscious. As soon as Barnes arrived on the scene and gave first aid, he asked the work crew what had happened. They had only seen Jones strike Johnson. After Johnson regained consciousness, Barnes asked him what happened. Johnson stated he and Jones had been talking when Jones suddenly turned and swung at him. Barnes then asked Jones what happened. Jones, who is the only African-American employee in his work group, said Johnson had been directing racial slurs toward him ever since he joined the crew, and this morning he had been pushed over the brink when Johnson said, "If it weren't for affirmative action, welfare would be the only thing that would keep a shirt on your back."

From his supervisor training course, Barnes knew it was company policy to discharge anyone who struck another employee or started a fight. Thus, he called security to take Jones to the HR department for termination. When Jones arrived there, he demanded to see Ralph Murphy, the union steward in his area. After conferring, Murphy filed a grievance on Jones's behalf, alleging the company had violated Section 4.02 of the contract by discharging him without cause. His grievance stated that the attack on Johnson was justified given his past harassment, and punching him seemed to be the "only way to get him off my back."

When Murphy gave the grievance to Barnes, it was immediately denied. Barnes said, "The rule is ironclad, as far as I'm concerned. Management said we supervisors didn't have any latitude on this issue."

Murphy then presented copies of the grievance to the shift IR representative, Carolyn Foster, and Neal Young, the general supervisor. In her examination of the grievance, Foster called Johnson and Cronholm, Jensen, and Albers (three other employees in the work group) to her office separately. When questioned, Johnson repeated his allegation that Jones's attack was unprovoked and adamantly denied ever making racial slurs toward him. Information from Jensen and Albers supported Johnson's denial of racial slurs, but Cronholm said he had repeatedly heard Johnson make disparaging remarks to Jones and Jones had asked him to stop. After weighing this information and considering company policy on fighting, she upheld Barnes's action.

The union continued to demand Jones's reinstatement with full back pay, and management adamantly refused.

When the case was heard, the union's grievance alleged that not only had Jones been discharged without cause (Section 4.02) but that the discharge had also been racially motivated, violating the EEO section (12.16a). In its opening argument, the company asked you to find the grievance nonarbitrable because Jones could file a charge with the EEOC under Title VII if your award upheld the discharge. The company also said the discrimination issue was not arbitrable because it had not been raised in Step 3 as provided in 12.16b. You noted the arguments but reserved your ruling on arbitrability for the decision you would prepare.

Both sides presented their evidence. All of it was in substantial agreement with what Barnes and Foster had found in their investigation. Jones and Johnson held to their stories, as did Jensen, Albers, and Cronholm. The company introduced evidence to show that without exception employees had been terminated for fighting. It also provided statistics showing 12 percent of the eight employees discharged for fighting over the past three years were African Americans and 14 percent of the production labor force was African-American.

In this case, your award should contain:

1. Your ruling on the arbitrability of the grievance.
2. Your rationale in finding on the merits of the case (if arbitrable).
3. If arbitrable, the degree to which you would grant the relief Jones is asking or uphold management.

Case 2

Until the present grievance was filed, GMFC had always used its own janitors for cleaning and maintenance. Because of operational requirements, most of this work was performed on the third shift. About 16 janitors were required to maintain the Central City facilities. GMFC had always had problems with absences among its janitors, but since the last contract was signed, the absence rate

had increased from about 2 percent per day to 10 percent. Because of this increase, housekeeping lagged, and GMFC officials started to worry about fire code violations resulting from the superficial cleaning. Management considered discharging those who were chronically absent but found on investigation that absences seemed to rotate systematically among members of the crew, as if they were planned.

As a result of management's investigation, Carolyn Foster contacted Matt Duff, Local 384's president, and asked him to enforce the contract and get the janitors' absence rate down. She told Duff the company considered the employees' action the equivalent of a slowdown, and strong action would be taken if absence rates were not reduced. Duff protested, saying there was no concerted activity behind the absences.

When the high rate and rotating pattern persisted, the company discharged the janitors and subcontracted their work to Dependa-Kleen, a full-time janitorial service. To the company's pleasure, Dependa-Kleen was able to take over the entire operation at a cost lower than that incurred by the in-house operation before the problem of absenteeism.

On behalf of the janitors, Duff filed a grievance arguing that the discharges violated Section 4.02. He also filed an unfair labor practice charge with the NLRB, claiming the company violated Section 8(a)(5) of the Taft-Hartley Act through its unilateral action in subcontracting the work without consulting or bargaining with the union.

The company argued that it was justified in replacing the janitors because their systematic absences were a violation of the contract's no-strike or slowdown clause (Section 9.05). The company argued it was entitled to replace the participants consistent with the management rights clause, Section 4.02.

Assume the testimony at the hearing does not seriously challenge the evidence management has gathered on the increase in absences among the janitors. In this case, decide the following:

1. Would you find the grievance arbitrable given the unfair labor practice charge filed by the union?

2. Assuming you find the grievance arbitrable, frame an award and justify it.

Case 3

The maintenance electricians in the unit are assigned to repair jobs around the Central City facilities shortly after they report to work at their central shop at the beginning of a shift. Before ratification of the most recent contract, electricians traditionally returned to the shop for their afternoon coffee breaks. All of the electricians left their work so they would arrive at the shop at the beginning of the break and all left the shop at the end of the break to return to work.

The electrical shop supervisor, Ken Bates, issued a new policy after the new contract was approved, stating the break would commence once work stopped at the assigned location and end when work was restarted. This policy change meant some electricians would have insufficient time to return to the shop for their breaks.

The union filed a grievance alleging that the company had revoked a prevailing practice that had the effect of a contract term. It also argued it had not been consulted as Article 12.03 required. The company denied the grievance, citing the language in Section 12.02.

1. Should the grievance be sustained?

2. If the grievance is sustained, what is your reasoning and what should the award be? If denied, what is the basis for the denial?

Case 4

Two months ago, GMFC decided to change its health care preferred provider organization (PPO) from the Central Indiana Medical Group (CIMG) to UniCare of Indiana, a local affiliate of UniCare of America. This shift meant that GMFC employees must change from their present family doctors in CIMG to employee doctors of UniCare if they are to receive PPO coverage. If they remain with their present doctors, they will have to pay the difference in treatment costs between the UniCare and CIMG schedules which are, on average, about 20 percent higher. In addition, UniCare does not cover some of the treatments offered by CIMG, such as chiropractic treatments when referred by a medical doctor.

The union grieved this change, arguing that the chosen provider would be expected to remain in place over the term of the agreement. It argued that a significant negotiated benefit issue was unilaterally changed by the employer. Employees' compensation suffered as a result. The union also filed a refusal to bargain an unfair labor practice charge with the NLRB.

The company argued that Section 12.08 of the negotiated agreement permitted it to choose the PPO. It further argued that none of the provisions of Section 12.08 had been changed. The company still stands ready to pay 80 percent of the first $2,500 in treatment provided by the PPO. It has simply made a business decision to change suppliers to maximize performance.

1. Should the grievance be sustained or denied?

2. If sustained, what should the award be?

3. Has an unfair labor practice been committed? If so, what action can the NLRB take? Given the evidence on NLRB actions in cases where unfair labor practices are charged, how would it be likely to act in this one?

PUBLIC-SECTOR

LABOR RELATIONS

*T*his chapter covers collective bargaining practices in the public sector and highlights the differences between public and private sectors and within public-sector levels. The public sector consists of the myriad of levels and jurisdictions of governmental units (federal, state, municipal, and so on). The "customer" group affected by outcomes in public-sector labor relations is generally much larger (e.g., homeowners and apartment dwellers in a garbage collection strike) and settlement costs are much more likely to be directly passed on to customers in the short run than in the private sector. Little collective bargaining occurred before the early 1960s in the public sector, compared with the middle to late 1930s in the private sector.

This chapter covers the evolution of federal and state labor law, differences in coverage among jurisdictions and across occupations, union structure and organizational issues, bargaining methods and outcomes, and impasse procedures and their effectiveness.

As you study this chapter, consider the following questions:

1. How do the public- and private-sector bargaining relationships differ, particularly concerning impasse procedures?
2. How do laws regulating labor relations in the public sector differ across both states and occupations?
3. How successful has the application of fact-finding been in the public sector?
4. How do the conduct of collective bargaining and the determinants of bargaining power differ in the public and private sectors?
5. What variables seem to have the greatest effect on bargaining outcomes?

PUBLIC-SECTOR LABOR LAW

As Chapter 3 noted, federal labor-management relations are governed by a separate law, and state and local employees are governed by state laws, if legislation has been passed to permit collective bargaining.

Federal Labor Relations Law

Federal employees have been involved in union activities since the 1830s. The federal government did not oppose employee union activities until the 1880s, when postal employees began to organize. Before the Lloyd-LaFollette Act (1912), federal employees were forbidden to communicate with Congress about employment conditions. Union activities increased during the 1930s, but President Franklin D. Roosevelt asserted normal collective bargaining could not occur at the federal level.

After President John F. Kennedy was elected, the federal government promulgated the first in a series of executive orders governing federal employment labor relations. A bill to allow collective bargaining for federal employees was pending in Congress when the president preempted the legislation with Executive Order 10988. The order enabled unions representing a majority of federal employees within a unit to negotiate exclusive written agreements with an agency. However, these agreements could cover only noneconomic and nonstaffing issues. Other labor organizations representing less than a majority but more than 10 percent of employees in a unit were entitled to consultation with the employer but could not negotiate agreements. Arbitration of grievances was allowed, but it was advisory to agency heads, not binding. Most employees were entitled to organize, with the exception of managers and nonroutine personnel workers.

Civil Service Reform Act, Title VII

In January 1979, the executive orders of Presidents Kennedy, Nixon, and Ford were supplanted by the Federal Service Labor-Management Relations statute, Title VII of the Civil Service Reform Act of 1978. The act applied to federal agencies except the Postal Service (covered under Taft-Hartley), the FBI, the General Accounting Office, the National Security Agency, the CIA, and agencies dealing with federal employee labor relations. Employees of the legislative and judicial branches were also excluded. A **Federal Labor Relations Authority** (FLRA) was created with responsibilities similar to those of the NLRB. The FMCS assists the agencies involved in bargaining impasses, and unresolved impasses are referred to the Federal Services Impasses Panel (FSIP). The FSIP deals with approximately 200 to 300 cases a year, all involving noneconomic issues.[1]

---

[1] G. W. Bohlander, "The Federal Services Impasses Panel: A Ten-Year Review and Analysis," *Journal of Collective Negotiations in the Public Sector* 24 (1995), pp. 193–206.

Bargaining rights remain limited under the statute. Federal employees cannot bargain on wages and benefits, participation in political activities, classification of positions, missions or budgets of agencies, hiring or promotion, or subcontracting. They are, however, allowed consultation rights in these areas and may negotiate on these issues if the agency allows. Federal labor organizations may not advocate the use of strikes, and unauthorized strikes may lead to decertification and discipline of individual members. Picketing is also unlawful if it disrupts an agency's activities.

Grievance procedures must be negotiated and must provide for binding arbitration of unresolved issues. The FLRA may review appealed arbitration awards and set them aside if they conflict with laws, rules, or regulations.

The law enumerates a number of unfair labor practices similar to those in the private sector, except employers and unions must not refuse the use of impasse procedures if necessary. Unions may not call strikes, work stoppages, or slowdowns. If violations occur, the FLRA may issue cease-and-desist orders, require the renegotiation of agreements, reinstate employees with back pay, or initiate other actions necessary to redress unfair practices.[2]

State Labor Laws

Public-sector labor relations differ widely among the 50 states. Several have no public-sector bargaining laws, a few prohibit at least some occupations from bargaining, and most prohibit strikes. Where state labor laws have been passed, they generally follow Taft-Hartley procedures except for the strike prohibitions.[3] Labor laws are generally more comprehensive and were passed earlier in states in which private-sector unionization is heaviest. Unlike the private sector, some states permit collective bargaining for public-sector supervisors and managers. Many states have established public employment labor relations boards to act in the same role as the NLRB in recognition of unfair labor practice situations. Union security provisions in state labor laws increase the likelihood that employees will be represented, while right-to-work laws do not reduce coverage below that of states with no union security provisions. The degree of union coverage of public employees in a state is associated with pay levels.[4] The requirement for compulsory arbitration for negotiation impasses for some employee groups probably reduces dispute costs but results in higher wage costs.[5] Reductions of dispute costs may be

[2] H. B. Frazier III, "Federal Employment," in M. K. Gibbons, R. B. Hersby, J. Lefkowitz, and B. Z. Tener, eds., *Portrait of a Process—Collective Negotiations in Public Employment* (Fort Washington, PA: Labor Relations Press, 1979), pp. 421–34.

[3] D. A. Dilts, W. J. Walsh, and C. Hagmann, "State Labor-Management Relations Legislation: Adaptive Modeling," *Journal of Collective Negotiations in the Public Sector* 22 (1993), pp. 79–86.

[4] G. Hundley, "Collective Bargaining Coverage of Union Members and Nonmembers in the Public Sector," *Industrial Relations* 32 (1993), pp. 72–93.

[5] J. Currie and S. McConnell, "Collective Bargaining in the Public Sector: The Effect of Legal Structure on Dispute Costs and Wages," *American Economic Review* 81 (1991), pp. 693–718.

beneficial to the citizenry, however, even at the cost of higher wages given disruption of services such as sanitation and education.

A study of the development of state labor laws found that private-sector unionization levels within a state predict public sector bargaining statutes. The passage of public-sector bargaining legislation is related to low relative public-sector wages, larger proportions of nonwhite employees, a favorable political climate, and the spread of laws from neighboring states. Prospects for prolabor legislation is reduced by management opposition and single-party dominance of the legislature.[6]

Unlike employees in the private sector, public-sector employers are simultaneously bargainers and legislators. Thus, they pass the laws under which they bargain. Legislators are elected by voters who are also essentially the customers for the services the state provides. The outcomes of prior contract negotiations might be expected to influence legislative changes. Research found that states make favorable policy changes in public-sector bargaining laws and procedures for management or labor depending on recent difficulties each might have had in negotiations.[7]

Jurisdictions and Employees
While exemptions from federal labor law coverage are relatively few in the private sector, many differences exist in the public sector. In the private sector, only agricultural workers, domestic workers, and supervisors and managers are exempt from coverage. In the public sector, differences in coverage exist by types of employees and political jurisdictions.

Sources of Employment
Some states distinguish between employees within and outside a statutory civil service system. Persons who are politically appointed are usually unprotected, although the ability of public officials to use political party membership as a criterion for maintaining a public position is limited.[8] In some states, civil service employees are not permitted to bargain collectively.

Levels of Government
Large differences also exist in the jurisdictions of bargaining units involved. Within states, a variety of lesser jurisdictions and semiautonomous agencies exist. For example, a statewide university system may be largely autonomous of a legislature in terms of its governance. Counties, cities, school boards, sewer districts, transportation authorities, and the like are all publicly governed, but each is

---

[6] M. S. Waters, R. C. Hill, W. J. Moore, and R. J. Newman, "A Simultaneous-Equations Model of the Relationship between Public Sector Bargaining Legislation and Unionization," *Journal of Labor Research* 15 (1994), pp. 355–72.

[7] S. Schwochau, "Effects of Employment Outcomes on Changes to Policy Covering Police," *Industrial Relations* 35 (1996), pp. 544–65.

[8] *Elrod* v. *Burns*, Sup. Ct., No. 74-1520 (1976).

responsible to a different constituency and perhaps dependent on a different source of funding.

Types of Employee Groups

Frequently, state labor laws have different provisions for employees by occupation and jurisdiction, such as teachers, police, firefighters, state employees, and local employees. Large differences exist between states and across employee groups in terms of collective bargaining rights and restrictions.

Teachers   Teacher bargaining laws apply primarily to elementary and secondary public school teachers. Most states with laws permitting bargaining for teachers also confer exclusive recognition on a majority union; impose a mutual duty on both the employer and the union to bargain; have defined impasse procedures, normally including mediation and fact-finding; and prohibit strikes. Some states allow strikes when the school district refuses to arbitrate at a bargaining impasse. A study of teacher bargaining laws found that, other things being equal, the right to strike is associated with a 11.5 percent wage premium and 37 minutes less time in the workday. States that do not grant—but do not prohibit—the right of teachers to strike, have a 5.7 percent premium and 49 minutes less time in the workday, while states where mandatory arbitration is required at impasse have a 3.6 percent premium and 70 minutes less time. Fact-finding and voluntary arbitration states have no premiums or less time in the workday than states prohibiting strikes and offering no other impasse procedures.[9]

Police   Most police statutes cover uniformed officers employed by cities or counties. Most states permit collective bargaining by the police and grant exclusive recognition to a majority union. Where bargaining is allowed, most statutes impose a mutual duty on both union and employer, but some only allow the union to meet and confer. Most laws require mediation or fact-finding at impasse, and many require arbitration if agreement is not reached. Only Hawaii allows police a limited right to strike. Evidence shows that unionized police are slightly less productive with regard to minor crimes.[10]

Firefighters   The International Association of Fire Fighters (IAFF) is one of the oldest public-sector unions and has been very successful in obtaining bargaining rights. Most states grant exclusive recognition to a majority union and require a mutual duty to bargain. Impasse procedures are generally similar to those for police and, except in Idaho, all firefighters are forbidden to strike.

---

[9] M. A. Zigarelli, "The Linkages between Teacher Unions and Student Achievement," *Journal of Collective Negotiations in the Public Sector* 23 (1994), pp. 299–320.

[10] D. Byrne, H. Dezhbakhsh, and R. King, "Unions and Police Productivity: An Economic Investigation," *Industrial Relations* 35 (1996), pp. 566–84.

State Employees Fewer states permit bargaining for general state employees than for special occupational groups. Where permitted, bargaining is generally a mutual duty. There are fewer formal procedures for breaking impasses than for specific occupational groups. Some states allow strikes if an impasse has been reached.

Local Employees Provisions for local employees in other occupational classifications are largely similar to those of state employees. More states permit strikes for local employees than for other classifications.

While many states forbid strikes, enforcing the prohibition is often difficult. A long history of public employee strikes shows that legally permissible steps to end strikes are not often taken, and statutorily mandated reprisals, such as discharges, have seldom been invoked. Table 16–1 is a compilation of provisions in state labor laws across the 50 states.

PUBLIC EMPLOYEE UNIONS

The four major classifications of nonfederal public-sector labor organizations are:

1. All-public-sector employee unions.
2. Mixed public- and private-sector unions.
3. State and local employee associations.
4. Unions and associations representing uniformed protective services.[11]

Major mixed unions include the Service Employees International Union (SEIU), which is increasingly involved in health care, and the Teamsters. In the uniformed services, the International Association of Fire Fighters (IAFF) and the Fraternal Order of Police (FOP) are among the largest.

Several unions represent public-sector employees exclusively or predominantly. The American Federation of State, County, and Municipal Employees, AFL–CIO (AFSCME), represents state and local unit employees (see Chapter 4 for a description of its structure). The American Federation of Government Employees, AFL–CIO (AFGE), represents federal employees. Postal service employees are represented by several national unions, such as the National Association of Letter Carriers (NALC).

Some public-sector bargaining representatives began as professional associations and were involved primarily in establishing standards and occupational licensing requirements and lobbying for improved funding and facilities. Others began as civil service employee associations before collective bargaining rights were available; they were involved primarily in meeting and conferring with management and lobbying with legislatures. Some, like the California State Employees Association, were large enough to exercise political influence through

---

[11] J. Stieber, *Public Sector Unionism* (Washington, DC: Brookings Institution, 1973).

large blocs of voters in districts where state employment was high. Associations are most prevalent where laws forbid bargaining but where legislative lobbying representing numerical strength is important. Professional associations are usually organized on occupational bases and have begun to bargain more recently than unions, often as a response to organizing by unions that demanded to bargain collectively rather than to meet and confer with employers.

Most national unions bargaining at state and local levels are organized along a federal model, such as the National Education Association (NEA). Because education laws and funding methods vary by state and most bargaining occurs at the local school board level, state-level services are largely devoted to lobbying and negotiation assistance. Public-sector local unions seldom need approval from the national for contract ratifications and strikes.

Membership in public-sector unions has increased during the 1990s, while private-sector unionization has declined. About 37 percent of public-sector employees are union members. Organizing has become more intense in the public

TABLE 16–1

Provisions of State Labor Laws by Occupational Group

	Duty to Bargain			
State	Police & Fire	State Employees	P/S Teachers	Municipal
Alabama	Meet and confer	No	No	Meet and confer
Alaska	Mutual duty	Mutual duty	Mutual duty	Mutual duty
Arizona	No	No	No	No
Arkansas	No	No	No	No
California	Meet and confer	Meet and confer	Mutual duty	Meet and confer
Colorado	No	No	No	No
Connecticut	Mutual duty	Mutual duty	Mutual duty	Mutual duty
Delaware	Mutual duty	Mutual duty	Mutual duty	Mutual duty
District of Col.	Mutual duty	(No employees)	Mutual duty	Mutual duty
Florida	Mutual duty	Mutual duty	Mutual duty	Mutual duty
Georgia	Mutual duty (fire fighters)	No	No	No
Hawaii	Mutual duty	Mutual duty	Mutual duty	Mutual duty
Idaho	Mutual duty (fire fighters)	No	Mutual duty	No
Illinois	Mutual duty	Mutual duty	Mutual duty	Mutual duty
Indiana	No	No	Mutual duty (wages only)	No
Iowa	Mutual duty	Mutual duty	Mutual duty	Mutual duty
Kansas	Meet and confer (Mutual duty by local option)	Meet and confer	Mutual duty	Meet and confer

TABLE 16–1

(Continued)

	Duty to Bargain			
State	Police & Fire	State Employees	P/S Teachers	Municipal
Kentucky	Mutual duty (fire fighters)	No	No	No
Louisiana	No	No	No	No
Maine	Mutual duty	Mutual duty	Mutual duty	Mutual duty
Maryland	Voluntary for fire fighters	No	Mutual duty	Mutual duty (Baltimore only)
Massachusetts	Mutual duty	Mutual duty	Mutual duty	Mutual duty
Michigan	Mutual duty	Mutual duty	Mutual duty	Mutual duty
Minnesota	Mutual duty	Mutual duty	Mutual duty	Mutual duty
Mississippi	No	No	No	No
Missouri	No	Meet and confer	No	Meet and confer
Montana	Mutual duty	Mutual duty	Mutual duty	Mutual duty
Nebraska	Mutual duty	Mutual duty	Mutual duty	Mutual duty
Nevada	Mutual duty	No	Mutual duty	Mutual duty
New Hampshire	Mutual duty	Mutual duty	Mutual duty	Mutual duty
New Jersey	Mutual duty	Mutual duty	Mutual duty	Mutual duty
New Mexico	Mutual duty	Mutual duty	Mutual duty	Mutual duty
New York	Mutual duty	Mutual duty	Mutual duty	Mutual duty
North Carolina	No	No	No	No
North Dakota	No	No	Mutual duty	No
Ohio	Mutual duty	Mutual duty	Mutual duty	Mutual duty
Oklahoma	Mutual duty	No	Mutual duty	No
Oregon	Mutual duty	Mutual duty	Mutual duty	Mutual duty
Pennsylvania	Mutual duty	Mutual duty	Mutual duty	Mutual duty
Rhode Island	Mutual duty	Mutual duty	Mutual duty	Mutual duty
South Carolina	No	No	No	No
South Dakota	Mutual duty	No	Mutual duty	Mutual duty
Tennessee	No	No	Mutual duty	No
Texas	Mutual duty (by local option)	No	No	No
Utah	No	No	Mutual duty	No (except Salt Lake City)
Vermont	Mutual duty	Mutual duty	Mutual duty	Mutual duty
Virginia	No	No	No	No
Washington	Mutual duty	No	Mutual duty	Mutual duty
West Virginia	No	No	No	No
Wisconsin	Mutual duty	Mutual duty	Mutual duty	Mutual duty
Wyoming	Mutual duty (fire fighters only)	No	No	No

TABLE 16–1

(Continued)

Permissibility of Strikes and Impasse Resolution Procedures

State	Police & Fire	State Employees	P/S Teachers	Municipal
Alabama	No bargaining	No bargaining	No bargaining	No bargaining
Alaska	Prohibited with fines, arbitration of economic issues	Prohibited, other impasse procedures	Prohibited, other impasse procedures	Prohibited, other impasse procedures
Arizona	No bargaining	No bargaining	No bargaining	No bargaining
Arkansas	No bargaining	No bargaining	No bargaining	No bargaining
California	No provision	Strikes allowed, mediation	Strikes allowed, voluntary fact-finding	Strikes allowed, mediation
Colorado	Strikes allowed, no provision	Strikes allowed, no provision	Strikes allowed, no provision	Strikes allowed, no provision
Connecticut	Strikes allowed, fact-finding	Strikes allowed, fact-finding, arbitration	Strikes prohibited, final-offer arbitration on total package	Strikes allowed, fact-finding, arbitration
Delaware	Strikes prohibited, fact-finding	Strikes prohibited, fact-finding	Strikes prohibited, fact-finding	Strikes prohibited, fact finding
District of Columbia	Strikes prohibited, final offer arbitration whole package on economics, issue-by-issue on others	No state employees	Strikes prohibited, final offer arbitration whole package on economics, issue-by-issue on others	Strikes prohibited, final offer arbitration whole package on economics, issue-by-issue on others
Florida	Strikes prohibited, union can be decertified, fact-finding, final resolution by legislative body	Strikes prohibited, union can be decertified, fact-finding, final resolution by legislative body	Strikes prohibited, union can be decertified, fact-finding, final resolution by legislative body	Strikes prohibited, union can be decertified, fact-finding, final resolution by legislative body
Georgia	Strikes prohibited, fact-finding	Strikes prohibited, employees disciplined	No bargaining	No bargaining

TABLE 16–1
(Continued)

Permissibility of Strikes and Impasse Resolution Procedures

State	Police & Fire	State Employees	P/S Teachers	Municipal
Hawaii	Strikes prohibited, arbitration	Strikes allowed with proper notice, fact-finding, voluntary arbitration	Strikes allowed with proper notice, fact-finding, voluntary arbitration	Strikes allowed with proper notice, fact-finding, voluntary arbitration
Idaho	Strikes allowed, mandatory fact-finding	No bargaining	Strikes prohibited, voluntary fact-finding	No bargaining
Illinois	Strikes prohibited, final-offer arbitration by issue	Strikes allowed with notice, voluntary fact-finding	Strikes allowed with sufficient notice, voluntary fact-finding and/or arbitration	Strikes allowed with notice, voluntary fact-finding
Indiana	No bargaining	Strikes prohibited, union decertified	Union loses dues checkoff if illegal strike, mandatory fact-finding	No bargaining
Iowa	Strikes prohibited, union can be decertified, fact-finding, final-offer arbitration issue-by-issue	Strikes prohibited, union can be decertified, fact-finding, final-offer arbitration issue-by-issue	Strikes prohibited, union can be decertified, final-offer arbitration issue-by-issue	Strikes prohibited, union can be decertified, fact-finding, final-offer arbitration issue-by-issue
Kansas	Strikes prohibited, mandatory fact-finding, final resolution by legislative body	Strikes prohibited, mandatory fact-finding, final resolution by legislative body	Strikes prohibited, mandatory fact-finding, final resolution by legislative body	Strikes prohibited, mandatory fact-finding, final resolution by legislative body
Kentucky	Strikes prohibited, voluntary fact-finding	No bargaining	No bargaining	No bargaining
Louisiana	Strikes prohibited	Strikes allowed	Strikes allowed	Strikes allowed
Maine	Strikes may be ULP, voluntary fact-finding and/or advisory arbitration	Strikes may be ULP, voluntary fact-finding and/or advisory arbitration	Strikes may be ULP, voluntary fact-finding and/or advisory arbitration	Strikes may be ULP, voluntary fact-finding and/or advisory arbitration
Maryland	No provision	No bargaining	Union decertified if strike, voluntary fact-finding	Union decertified if strike, mandatory fact-finding

State	Police & Fire	State Employees	P/S Teachers	Municipal
Massachusetts	Strikes prohibited, arbitration	Strikes prohibited, mandatory fact-finding, voluntary arbitration	Strikes prohibited, mandatory fact-finding, voluntary arbitration	Strikes prohibited, mandatory fact-finding, voluntary arbitration
Michigan	Strikes prohibited, final offer arbitration issue-by-issue	Strikes prohibited, mediation	Strikes prohibited, mediation	Strikes prohibited, mediation
Minnesota	Strikes are possible ULP, arbitration	Strikes allowed with proper notice, arbitration	Strikes allowed with proper notice, arbitration	Strikes allowed with proper notice, arbitration
Mississippi	No bargaining	No bargaining	No bargaining	No bargaining
Missouri	No bargaining	Strikes prohibited	No bargaining	Strikes prohibited
Montana	Strikes not prohibited, arbitration	Strikes not prohibited, mandatory fact-finding, voluntary arbitration	Strikes not prohibited, mandatory fact-finding, voluntary arbitration	Strikes not prohibited, mandatory fact-finding, voluntary arbitration
Nebraska	Strikes prohibited, mediation, voluntary fact-finding	Strikes prohibited, mediation	Strikes prohibited, mediation, voluntary fact-finding	Strikes prohibited, mediation, voluntary fact-finding
Nevada	Strikes prohibited with discipline, arbitration	No bargaining	Strikes prohibited with discipline, arbitration	Strikes prohibited with discipline, mandatory fact-finding
New Hampshire	Strikes are possible ULP, fact-finding with legislative review	Strikes are possible ULP, fact-finding with legislative review	Strikes are possible ULP, fact-finding with legislative review	Strikes are possible ULP, fact-finding with legislative review
New Jersey	Strikes not prohibited, arbitration or other method devised by parties	Strikes permitted, mandatory fact-finding	Strikes permitted, mandatory fact-finding	Strikes permitted, mandatory fact-finding
New Mexico	Strikes prohibited, union decertified, mandatory fact-finding	Strikes prohibited, union decertified, fact-finding with legislative review	Strikes prohibited, union decertified, fact-finding with legislative review	Strikes prohibited, union decertified, fact-finding with legislative review

TABLE 16–1
(Concluded)

Permissibility of Strikes and Impasse Resolution Procedures

State	Police & Fire	State Employees	P/S Teachers	Municipal
New York	Strikes prohibited with discipline, arbitration	Strikes prohibited with discipline, fact-finding with legislative review	Strikes prohibited with discipline, fact-finding with legislative review	Strikes prohibited with discipline, fact-finding with legislative review
North Carolina	No bargaining	No bargaining	No bargaining	No bargaining
North Dakota	No bargaining	No bargaining	Strikes prohibited with discipline, mandatory fact-finding	No bargaining
Ohio	Strikes prohibited, final-offer arbitration issue-by-issue	Strikes allowed with notice, mandatory fact-finding, other procedure determined by parties	Strikes allowed with notice, mandatory fact-finding, other procedure determined by parties	Strikes allowed with notice, mandatory fact-finding, other procedure determined by parties
Oklahoma	Strikes prohibited with discipline, final offer arbitration on total package	No bargaining	Strikes prohibited with discipline, mandatory fact-finding	No bargaining
Oregon	Strikes prohibited, arbitration	Strikes allowed with notice, mandatory fact-finding, voluntary arbitration	Strikes allowed with notice, mandatory fact-finding, voluntary arbitration	Strikes allowed with notice, mandatory fact-finding, voluntary arbitration
Pennsylvania	Strikes not prohibited, arbitration	Strikes allowed, mandatory fact-finding, voluntary arbitration	Strikes allowed, arbitration or other procedure determined by parties	Strikes allowed, mandatory fact-finding, voluntary arbitration
Rhode Island	Strikes prohibited, arbitration	Strikes prohibited, arbitration	Strikes prohibited, arbitration	Strikes prohibited, arbitration
South Carolina	No bargaining	No bargaining	No bargaining	No bargaining
South Dakota	Strikes prohibited with discipline, mediation	Strikes prohibited with discipline, mediation	Strikes prohibited with discipline, mediation, final resolution by legislative body	Strikes prohibited with discipline, mediation
Tennessee	No bargaining	No bargaining	Strikes prohibited and may be ULP, mandatory fact-finding	No bargaining
Texas	Strikes prohibited with discipline, arbitration	No bargaining	No bargaining	No bargaining
Utah	No bargaining	No bargaining	Strikes not prohibited, mandatory fact-finding	No bargaining

Vermont	Strikes allowed but may be ULP, mandatory fact-finding, voluntary arbitration	Strikes are possible ULP, final-offer arbitration on total package	Strikes allowed, fact-finding with review by legislative body	Strikes allowed but may be ULP, mandatory fact-finding, voluntary arbitration
Virginia	No bargaining	No bargaining	No bargaining	No bargaining
Washington	Strikes prohibited with discipline, arbitration	Strikes prohibited, fact-finding with review by legislative body	Strikes not prohibited, mandatory fact-finding, voluntary arbitration	Strikes prohibited, fact-finding with review by legislative body
West Virginia	No bargaining	No bargaining	No bargaining	No bargaining
Wisconsin	Strikes may be allowed or may result in discipline, arbitration	Strikes prohibited with discipline and may be ULP, mandatory fact-finding	Strikes prohibited with discipline, final-offer arbitration on total package	Strikes prohibited with discipline, final-offer arbitration on total package
Wyoming	Strikes not prohibited, arbitration	No bargaining	No bargaining	No bargaining

SOURCE: Adapted from J. Lund & C. L. Maranto (1996) "Public Sector Law: An Update," in D. Belman, M. Gunderson, & D. Hyatt (eds.), *Public Sector Employment in a Time of Transition*, Madison, WI: Industrial Relations Research Association, 52–56. For more details on specific provisions for each state, consult this reference.

sector, while management resistance to unions has lowered.[12] Prospects for future growth depend on the level of demand for public services, a decline in the trend toward privatization of services, and the increasing adoption of state laws permitting expanded bargaining rights.[13] Duty-to-bargain laws substantially increase unionization beyond other public policy measures favorable to public-sector unions.[14]

Union organization also depends on the structure of bargaining units permitted under governing legislation. The next section explores more issues in organizing in the public sector.

BARGAINING RIGHTS AND ORGANIZING

Because of the variety of representatives involved and differences in dates when organizing occurred, employers often bargain with several unions. Public-sector bargaining units are generally not as inclusive as in industry but more akin to the building trades in construction. In a given geographical area, public employee unions bargain with a variety of statutory agencies. For example, a large city may have a local government, school board, transit authority, sewer district, public utility, and so forth, all with autonomous powers to bargain, levy taxes, and provide specific services. Separate bargaining units may exist within each. For example, a school board may bargain with an AFT local representing teachers, a SEIU local representing custodians, an AFSCME local representing clericals, and a Teamsters local representing bus drivers. This situation makes it possible to whipsaw an unsophisticated management, but the costs ultimately result in higher taxes, which bring either legislative or taxpayer referendums into play.

Bargaining unit composition depends on what state laws allow and the interests of the organizing union. From the employer's standpoint, the scope of the bargaining unit is usually limited by the extent of the taxing authority. For example, a statewide clerical bargaining unit would be appropriate for state employees but not for local government clericals, because the city may not have the revenue-producing capabilities necessary to finance wages negotiated at a state level.

PUBLIC-SECTOR BARGAINING PROCESSES

This section examines the differences between public- and private-sector bargaining and evolving bargaining structures found in nonfederal negotiations. Management

[12] J. F. Burton, Jr., and T. Thomason, "The Extent of Collective Bargaining in the Public Sector," in B. Aaron, J. M. Najita, and J. L. Stern, eds., *Public Sector Bargaining*, 2nd ed. (Washington, DC: Bureau of National Affairs, 1988), pp. 1–51.

[13] L. N. Edwards, "The Future of Public Sector Unions: Stagnation or Growth," *American Economic Review* 79, no. 2 (1989), pp. 161–65.

[14] J. S. Zax and C. Ichniowski, "Bargaining Laws and Unionization in the Local Public Sector," *Industrial and Labor Relations Review* 43 (1990), pp. 447–62.

in most public-sector bargaining consists of two levels: appointed civil service officials (e.g., city managers and school superintendents) and elected officials (e.g., mayors, city councils, and school boards). Although appointed managers may be directly responsible for negotiations, elected officials can pressure them to modify positions toward the union. Intraorganizational bargaining may need to be intense among management parties in public-sector negotiations.

Bargaining Structures

Bargaining is much more fragmented in the public than in the private sector, partly because of legislation imposing different recognition, bargaining, impasse, and strike rules on various jurisdictions and occupations. Another reason relates to the relatively narrow governmental jurisdictions involved. For example, although teachers are a relatively homogeneous occupational group, a rather small geographic area may have several municipalities with separate school boards and separate negotiations.

In Illinois, coordinated teacher bargaining on the local level in 45 southern counties led to higher salary levels. Efforts have also gone forward in the East San Francisco Bay and Portland, Oregon, areas. In Michigan, local teacher union successes in enforcing regional patterns led to legislation outlawing higher-level union approval of negotiated contracts.

Management Organization for Bargaining

Unlike the private sector, the public sector has an ambiguous management structure. The top leadership is politically elected, while the ongoing management is frequently in the hands of career civil servants. In addition, managers may belong to their own bargaining units. Bargaining structures become increasingly centralized over time to gain budgetary control and coordinate bargaining within an office with an expert bargainer who will have long-term responsibility for the collective bargaining agreement.[15]

Multilateral Bargaining

A major distinction exists between public- and private-sector contract negotiations. In the public sector, employees may strongly influence management because they also vote, and organizations to which they belong may be part of a political power bloc. Also, relatively large numbers of people in a defined jurisdiction utilize services provided or see their taxes affected by the outcome of an agreement. Elected officials who have been endorsed by unions representing their

---

[15] M. Derber, "Management Organization for Collective Bargaining in the Public Sector," in B. Aaron, J. M. Najita, and J. L. Stern, *Public Sector Bargaining*, 2nd ed. (Washington, DC: Bureau of National Affairs, 1988), pp. 90–123.

employees may influence negotiations. Thus, public-sector collective bargaining is probably multilateral, with public officials being approached to influence the negotiating positions of management members who are ultimately responsible to these elected officials.

Multilateral bargaining occurs when more than two groups with interests in the outcome are engaged simultaneously. It more likely occurs where there is internal conflict between management bargainers, the union is politically active and involved, and the union attempts to use a variety of impasse procedures. Multilateral bargaining activities involve (1) public officials influencing negotiations outside the process, (2) union representatives discussing contract terms with managers who are not on the bargaining team, (3) community interest groups, (4) city officials failing to implement the agreement, and (5) elected officials attempting to mediate. With data collected from 228 firefighter negotiations in cities nationwide, multilateral bargaining was most strongly related, in order of importance, to (1) general conflict among city officials, (2) union political pressure tactics, (3) union impasse pressure tactics, and (4) management commitment to collective bargaining. The incidence of multilateral bargaining increased with the age of the bargaining relationship, but comprehensiveness of state laws and experience of management negotiators had little impact.[16]

In Texas, cities are allowed to hold referenda on whether police and firefighters should be permitted to bargain collectively. Cities with high union membership, unions endorsing police and firefighter positions, and police and firefighter cooperation were more likely to permit bargaining. Denials were associated with active business opposition, active opposition by current elected city officials or an ad hoc group, and a concurrent city council election.[17] Both bargaining outcomes and the ability to bargain may be influenced multilaterally.

A study of the effectiveness of multilateral bargaining tactics by firefighters found several factors significantly related to positive union outcomes: (1) fact-finding or compulsory arbitration at impasse, (2) comprehensiveness of the state's bargaining law, (3) the decision-making power of management's negotiator, (4) city council–negotiator goal incompatibility, and (5) elected official intervention at impasse. The first two factors reflect the legal environment, the next two reflect management characteristics, and the last is a multilateral bargaining component. Union pressure tactics were not significantly related to outcomes.[18]

The scope of public-sector bargaining laws reflects the relative wealth of a state.[19] The coincidence of comprehensive laws and greater ability to pay influences bargaining outcomes toward the union. A comprehensive law legitimizes unions, reduces management's costs of recognition, and may legally

[16] T. A. Kochan, "A Theory of Multilateral Collective Bargaining in City Government," *Industrial and Labor Relations Review* 28 (1974), pp. 525–42.

[17] D. T. Barnum and I. B. Helburn, "Influencing the Electorate: Experience with Referenda on Public Employee Bargaining," *Industrial and Labor Relations Review* 35 (1982), pp. 330–42.

[18] T. A. Kochan and H. N. Wheeler, "Municipal Collective Bargaining: A Model and Analysis of Bargaining Outcomes," *Industrial and Labor Relations Review* 29 (1975), pp. 46–66.

[19] T. A. Kochan, "Correlates of State Public Employee Bargaining Laws," *Industrial Relations* 12 (1973), pp. 322–37.

decrease management's use of contract rejection, refusals to bargain, and similar tactics.[20] Environmental characteristics affect not only the makeup of bargaining teams and their interrelationships but also the power and tactics available to parties during negotiations.

Bargaining outcomes are related to institutional and public opinion characteristics. Bargaining outcomes for unions in medium-sized municipalities were better (1) where only certain trades were involved, rather than a large general unit; (2) where no statutory penalty for striking existed; (3) where the union was affiliated with a public-sector national; (4) where strike activity in the state was above average; and (5) where public opinion had led to or favored a bargaining law.[21]

Political activity can have an indirect effect on union outcomes for particular occupations. For example, police and firefighter union support for better police and fire protection is associated with higher departmental budgets which lead to the employment of larger forces.[22]

Bargaining Outcomes

Bargaining outcomes may have immediate effects for the employment relationship or long-run effects on the occupation as a whole. This section examines several studies of public-sector bargaining outcomes.

Public employees who bargain are often part of a monopoly. Their service is provided only by the government (e.g., police protection); thus, obtaining better contracts should be easier because the government can more easily pass on the costs to the consumer (at least in the short run). In a study of cities with either public or private waste management systems, the effect of unions on wages in privately managed systems was not significant, but in publicly managed systems, the effects were between 10 and 17 percent. In privately managed systems, several competing waste haulers were usually involved in the market.[23] These results indicate monopoly power available to public employers can be used to increase wages.

Research on the effects of collective bargaining on wages, employment, and productivity of unionized compared with nonunion government employees found that union wages and benefits were eight to 12 percent higher, less than in the private sector.[24] Wage differences increased as employees gained recognition and bargaining rights. Spillovers to unorganized areas also occurred.[25] Evidence on

[20] P. F. Gerhart, "Determinants of Bargaining in Local Government Labor Negotiations," *Industrial and Labor Relations Review* 29 (1976), pp. 331–32.

[21] Ibid., p. 349.

[22] R. Gely and T. D. Chandler, "Protective Service Unions' Political Activities and Departmental Expenditures," *Journal of Labor Research* 16 (1995), pp. 171–85; and K. M. O'Brien, "The Effect of Political Activity by Police Unions on Nonwage Bargaining Outcomes," *Journal of Collective Negotiations in the Public Sector* 25 (1996), pp. 99–116.

[23] L. N. Edwards and F. R. Edwards, "Wellington-Winter Revisited: The Case of Municipal Sanitation Collection," *Industrial and Labor Relations Review* 36 (1982), pp. 307–18.

[24] H. G. Lewis, "Union/Nonunion Wage Gaps in the Public Sector," *Journal of Labor Economics* 8 (1990), pp. S260–S328.

[25] J. S. Zax, "Wages, Nonwage Compensation, and Municipal Unions," *Industrial Relations* 27 (1988), pp. 301–17.

specific occupations found that state bargaining laws and mandatory impasse procedures increased police wages. Nonunion police received almost as much due to the threat of organizing.[26] Firefighter unionization influenced total compensation, entry, and maximum salary levels. The greatest impact was on fringe benefits, similar to findings in the private sector.[27] For teachers, greater union activity was related to lower male/female and elementary/secondary pay differences. Unionization also increased pay for advanced education, years of experience, and years of experience in the district. Measurable, job-related aspects assumed a greater value for pay outcomes in situations where more union activity was present.[28] A 10 percent increase in union density was associated with a 2.6 percent increase for teacher's wages at the top end of the structure but only 0.2 percent at the bottom.[29] This finding probably reflects the presence of larger proportions of the bargaining unit closer to the top end of the structure in most teacher situations. In higher education, unionized faculty received about 2 percent higher pay, with greater returns to length of service and less to publications than in nonunion colleges and universities.[30] Employment in represented units increased 3 percent faster than in nonunion units around 1980. While employment usually falls as wages increase, lobbying and other activities to influence the electorate led to net expansions.[31] In general, local unit wages were related to union density, enabling legislation, mandatory arbitration, household income in the local area, and private sector union density. At the state level, wages were positively related to public-sector union density and household incomes, but negatively related to the right to strike, voluntary arbitration at impasse, and private union density.[32]

Productivity results are not clear; but in the private sector, only unionized blue-collar occupations were more productive. Research on public school teachers indicates that high school SAT scores were 4.7 percent higher in unionized schools (other things being equal)[33] and 13 percent higher for African-American

[26] P. Feuille and J. T. Delaney, "Collective Bargaining, Interest Arbitration, and Police Salaries," *Industrial and Labor Relations Review* 39 (1986), pp. 228–40; and C. Ichniowski, R. B. Freeman, and H. Lauer, "Collective Bargaining Laws, Threat Effects, and the Determination of Police Compensation," *Journal of Labor Economics* 7 (1989), pp. 191–209.

[27] C. Ichniowski, "Economic Effects of the Firefighters' Union," *Industrial and Labor Relations Review* 33 (1980), pp. 198–211.

[28] A. B. Holmes, "Union Activity and Teacher Salary Structure," *Industrial Relations* 18 (1979), pp. 79–85.

[29] H. L. Zwerling and T. Thomason, "Collective Bargaining and the Determinants of Teachers' Salaries," *Journal of Labor Research* 16 (1995), pp. 467–84.

[30] D. A. Barbezat, "The Effect of Collective Bargaining on Salaries in Higher Education," *Industrial and Labor Relations Review* 42 (1989), pp. 443–55.

[31] L. M. Spizman, "Public Sector Unions: A Study of Economic Power," *Journal of Labor Research* 1 (1980), pp. 265–74; and J. S. Zax, "Employment and Local Public Sector Unions," *Industrial Relations* 28 (1989), pp. 21–31.

[32] D. Belman, J. S. Heywood, and J. Lund, "Public Sector Earnings and the Extent of Unionization," *Industrial and Labor Relations Review* 50 (1997), pp. 610–28.

[33] C. A. Register and P. W. Grimes, "Collective Bargaining, Teachers, and Student Achievement," *Journal of Labor Research* 12 (1991), pp. 99–109.

FIGURE 16–1

Union Impact on Supervisory Policy Usage

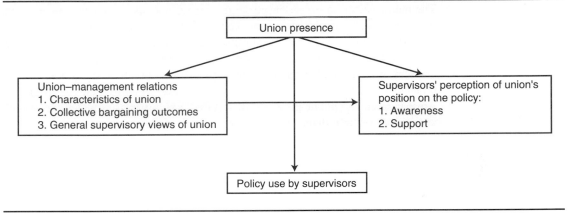

SOURCE: Janice M. Beyer, Harrison M. Trice, and Richard E. Hunt, "The Impact of Federal-Sector Unions on Supervisors' Use of Personnel Policies," *Industrial and Labor Relations Review* 34 (1980), p. 214.

students.[34] During the 1980s, concessions were much larger in the private sector, but the union wage advantage was also greater there previously.[35] Collective bargaining increased expenditures in municipal departments that were covered, but it did not appear to influence property taxes, total revenues, or total expenditures.[36]

The advent of federal collective bargaining has affected supervisors' uses of personnel policies. Agencies may have personnel policies that are not part of the contract, but which lead to grievances, depending on the way supervisors implement them. Figure 16–1 suggests that supervisors are influenced by the union's presence and their perceptions about the union's position on specific policies. One study found that supervisors in situations where a union was well entrenched and had negotiated certain policies into contracts were more aware of union positions and used them more often.[37]

[34] P. W. Grimes and C. A. Register, "Teacher Unions and Black Students' Scores on College Entrance Exams," *Industrial Relations* 30 (1991), pp. 492–500.

[35] D. J. B. Mitchell, "Collective Bargaining and Compensation in the Public Sector," in B. Aaron, J. M. Najita, and J. L. Stern, eds., *Public Sector Bargaining*, 2nd ed. (Washington, DC: Bureau of National Affairs, 1988), pp. 124–59.

[36] R. G. Valletta, "The Impact of Unionism on Municipal Expenditures and Revenues," *Industrial and Labor Relations Review* 42 (1989), pp. 430–42.

[37] J. M. Beyer, H. M. Trice, and R. E. Hunt, "The Impact of Federal Sector Unions on Supervisors' Use of Personnel Policies," *Industrial and Labor Relations Review* 34 (1980), pp. 212–31.

Union-Management Cooperation

The public sector has experienced some of the same environmental changes that have occurred in the private sector. The electorate has shown greater interest in increasing efficiency in providing public services and offering more choice for users, particularly in public education. In some municipalities, publicly provided services such as sanitation have been privatized. In other situations, union-management cooperation programs have been developed to increase efficiency while maintaining public provision of services. Exhibit 16–1 provides excerpts of such initiatives in Indianapolis.

IMPASSE PROCEDURES

Because public-sector employees are often prohibited from going on strike, the following may occur when an impasse is reached: work continues under terms of the expired contract, mediation, legal or illegal strikes or "sickouts", fact-finding, interest arbitration, or a mandated agreement by a legislative body.

What leads to impasses in public-sector negotiations? A study of New York state police and firefighter negotiations proposed the model shown in Figure 16–2. Environmental factors related to impasses included previous impasse experience, percentage of the local electorate voting Democratic in 1972 (for police), and prior starting salary (for police). Structural variables associated with impasses included union pressure tactics, adherence to pattern settlements (police), lack of authority for management negotiators, internal management conflict, and pressure on union leaders (police). Interpersonal/personal factors included hostility, lack of management negotiator skills (firefighters), lack of union or management in-house negotiators, and management negotiator experience.

Negotiations requiring formal procedures at or beyond fact-finding were more likely to take place with higher starting salaries, with previous impasse experience, in large cities (police), when union pressure tactics were used, and when management negotiators had little authority. Hostility and negotiator experience were also related, while negotiator skill (for firefighters) was negatively related.[38]

Fact-Finding

Fact-finding began in the private sector through the establishment of fact-finding boards under the Taft-Hartley Act and emergency board procedures in the Railway Labor Act. Today, however, fact-finding is far more prevalent in the public sector.

---

[38] T. A. Kochan, M. Mironi, R. G. Ehrenberg, J. Baderschneider, and T. Jick, *Dispute Resolution under Fact-Finding and Arbitration* (New York: American Arbitration Association, 1979), pp. 32–3.3

EXHIBIT 16–1

Union-Management Cooperation in the Public Sector

When Stephen Goldsmith ran for mayor of Indianapolis, he vowed to engage in widescale privatization; in other words, transferring delivery of services to private contractors. Convinced that Indianapolis was in a struggle with its neighbors for both business and residents, raising taxes to pay for improved city services did not seem a viable option. Goldsmith believed that market forces and competition would ultimately serve citizens better than what he and his staff call the government "monopoly."

Once in office, however, he says he quickly came to realize that the real answer to improving service delivery was not privatization because "monopolies, public or private, are inefficient." Instead, Indianapolis launched a comprehensive effort that features labor-management cooperation and, in some areas, fosters competitions between city departments and private contractors. In these instances, it treats city departments as businesses and gives workers a voice in ways to cut costs. If the department can put in a winning bid against private competitors, the city workers continue to provide that particular service.

In addition, city workers also bid for new work and work that was previously contracted out—returning those services to the public sector when it can be done there in a competitive fashion. For example, both the sign shop and fleet maintenance services are now performing work purchased by community organizations, by other governments and by local utilities.

Although Indianapolis receives much attention for its competitive initiatives, the Task Force found in its site visit that the structured, cooperative relationship pervading city operations is the unsung hero of the service and cost improvements.

In fact, where the union has bid, city and union officials estimate that public employees have won the bulk of the contracts put up for competition by examining methods, systems and cost structures in conjunction with management.

"I was increasingly impressed with the inherent ability of our own employees to perform better when the system allowed them to; I underestimated what they could do if we unloaded the bureaucracy off the top of their heads," Goldsmith said.*

His goal then became providing the best service at the lowest cost for citizens—a goal embraced by the city's workers, largely represented by the American Federation of State, County and Municipal Employees (AFSCME). AFSCME leadership viewed the competitions as a way to help eliminate the myth that the private sector always is more efficient than the public sector, as well as to take back work that had been contracted out years ago.

"Using the private sector as a yardstick with which to measure ourselves, we're fine with that institutionally," said Steve Fantauzzo, executive director of Indiana's State Council 62, AFSCME. "But to simply say that the private sector is always a better answer, that's simply not true." Fantauzzo points out that under public management, for example, refuse collection routes have been redesigned and worker productivity has doubled, producing annual savings close to $15 million.†

*Rob Gurwitt, "Indianapolis and the Republican Future," *Governing,* February 1994, 24–28

†"Indianapolis Wins Big on Savings, Safety, Effluent Quality Under Contract O&M," *Public Works Financing,* March 1995, 14–16

SOURCE: *Working Together for Public Service,* Report of the U.S. Secretary of Labor's Task Force on Excellence in State and Local Government through Labor-Management Cooperation, May 1996, p. 35.

In a private-sector impasse, the fact-finder's role is to establish a reasonable position for settlement by studying the context and issues and preparing a report based on the setting. A primary end result sought by this process is the publication of the disputed issues and a recommended settlement. In this way, public opinion may be galvanized to pressure a settlement on a factual conclusion. Fact-finding may also lead to economizing a legislature's time when it expects to impose a solution.[39]

The role of providing facts for a legislature is not very appropriate in the public sector because it is frequently a party in the dispute (school boards, city councils, etc.). Here the fact-finder's role is to educate the public about the costs of a reasonable settlement. Fact-finding may be sought by parties fearing adverse public opinion if they bargain a settlement. They might expect a fact-finder to recommend something similar to a negotiated settlement, but "facts" from a neutral party may seem more reasonable.[40]

Statutory Role of the Fact-Finder

Wisconsin was one of the first states to pass a comprehensive fact-finding statute. While the law was in effect, fact-finding could be initiated by either party at impasse or if the other refused to bargain. The Wisconsin Employee Relations Board (WERB) investigated the request and attempted to mediate. If mediation failed, a fact-finder was appointed to examine the evidence and recommend a settlement. The recommendation was sent to the parties and publicized by the WERB. Although parties may have asked for fact-finding, they were under no obligation to accept the report's recommendations.[41] If dispute resolution is the criterion, fact-finding is less successful than other methods once an impasse has been reached.

Criteria for Fact-Finding Recommendations

In early experiences with fact-finding in Wisconsin, wage comparisons were most often used for economic recommendations. Ability to pay was also frequently considered. Some fact-finders decided what the wage settlement would have been

---

[39] J. T. McKelvey, "Fact-Finding in Public Employment Disputes: Promise or Illusion," *Industrial and Labor Relations Review* 23 (1969), pp. 528–30.

[40] Ibid., pp. 530–31.

[41] J. L. Stern, "The Wisconsin Public Employee Fact-Finding Procedure," *Industrial and Labor Relations Review* 20 (1966), pp. 4–5.

FIGURE 16–2

Determinants of Impasses

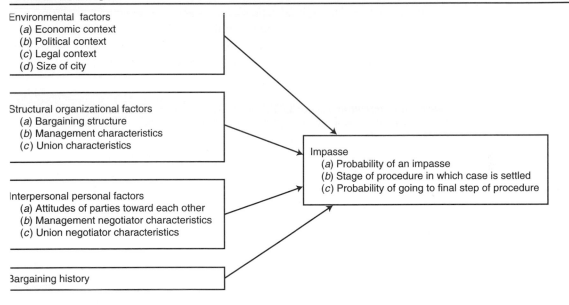

SOURCE: T. A. Kochan, M. Mironi, R. G. Ehrenberg, J. Baderschneider, and T. Jick, *Dispute Resolution under Fact-Finding and Arbitration: An Empirical Evaluation* (New York: American Arbitration Association, 1979), p. 32.

if the union were permitted to strike. Productivity and cost-of-living issues were seldom mentioned, although management and labor raised them in their presentations.[42]

Arbitration

Some laws require arbitration at impasse. They apply more often to uniformed services and are considered to be a quid pro quo for not granting the right to strike. With arbitration at impasse, the union does not face the prospect of management unilaterally continuing past terms without recourse to some other bargaining weapon. Other laws allow unions and managements to agree voluntarily to interest arbitration as a means for settling negotiating impasses.

---

[42] Ibid., pp. 15–17.

Arbitrators who handle public-sector interest cases are normally selected in the same way as arbitrators in private-sector ad hoc rights cases. The hearing procedure is also similar. Both sides present evidence supporting their positions, and the arbitrator determines the contract on the basis of the evidence and whatever criteria are to be used for the award. The less information the parties have about the arbitrator's decision-making tendencies, the more likely they are to avoid an impasse and settle on their own.[43]

Interest Arbitration Variants

Several methods are used in public-sector interest arbitrations. In a typical situation, an arbitrator hears the case and determines an appropriate settlement. However, it has been argued this has a **chilling effect** on bargaining because the parties might believe an arbitrator will split differences between them. For example, if a union wants 90 cents an hour and management is willing to give 30 cents, they may believe an arbitrator will settle on 60 cents—halfway between. It is also argued that arbitration becomes habit forming. Parties supposedly skip negotiations and go directly to impasse, thereby availing themselves of an effortless and less risky remedy: arbitration. This is the so-called **narcotic effect.** Beliefs regarding the presence of a narcotic effect have led to implementation of several variants of interest arbitration. Early evidence suggests a narcotic effect existed because negotiations in states that provided for arbitration went to impasse more frequently.[44]

Final-Offer Arbitration

To reduce its use, final-offer arbitration has been implemented in some states. **Final-offer arbitration** was proposed as a "medicine" to cure parties from using arbitration. In final-offer arbitration, each party presents its positions and the arbitrator is required to choose one position without modification. Supposedly, this results in an extreme contract the loser would do anything to avoid in the future.[45]

Some jurisdictions opt for entire-package approaches (Massachusetts and Wisconsin); others use issue-by-issue methods (Michigan). Entire-package selections increase the need to make a reasonable final-offer submission because one unreasonable position in an otherwise reasonable package may tip the arbitrator's preferences toward the other party. Where final-offer selection is available on an issue-by-issue basis, more unresolved issues reach the arbitrator.[46] Arbitrators appear to give equal weight to wage and nonwage issues in fashioning awards.[47]

---

[43] L. C. Babcock and L. J. Taylor, "The Role of Arbitrator Uncertainty in Negotiation Impasses," *Industrial Relations* 35 (1996), pp. 604–10.

[44] H. N. Wheeler, "Compulsory Arbitration: A 'Narcotic Effect'?" *Industrial Relations* 14 (1975), pp. 117–20.

[45] C. M. Stevens, "Is Compulsory Arbitration Compatible with Bargaining?" *Industrial Relations* 5 (1966), pp. 38–50.

[46] P. Feuille, *Final-Offer Arbitration* (Chicago: International Personnel Management Association, 1975), pp. 35–48.

[47] C. A. Olson, "Arbitrator Decision Making in Multi-Issue Disputes," *Proceedings of the Industrial Relations Research Association* 44 (1992), pp. 392–401.

One way interest and rights arbitration differ is that many contracts and statutes permit parties to alter their final offers and to settle after the process begins. Since public-sector interest arbitration is often conducted before a tripartite board (one labor, one management, and one neutral member), partisans may sense which direction the neutral appears to be leaning and concede an issue rather than lose entirely.[48]

Results of Final-Offer Laws

Final-offer procedures can be evaluated by examining whether parties accept and comply with awards and whether the process chills or encourages future bargaining.[49] Several studies have examined the issues.

Michigan. Michigan uses issue-by-issue offers for economic aspects and a conventional approach for others. The process has had no appreciable effect on arbitration frequency in the uniformed services. There has been a slight tendency for deputy sheriff negotiations to use the procedure more often than police or firefighters, but this was partially attributed to a relatively newer collective bargaining relationship.[50] Police arbitrations occur more frequently in larger cities where there are more police officers per capita and where property values are lower, indicating some decreased ability to pay.[51]

Wisconsin. Wisconsin uses a package-type, final-offer procedure. The Wisconsin experience does not support the idea that arbitration use declines in a package-selection environment over time,[52] but evidence does indicate its use decreases when management wins.[53] The relative use of arbitration in Wisconsin is less than in Michigan, an issue-by-issue state.

Negotiators in Wisconsin public teacher negotiations appear to engage in strategic behavior because in about half of all cases referred to arbitrators, the parties either negotiated an agreement after the arbitrator had been appointed or accepted a consent settlement. In 86 percent of cases, the settlement ranges of the parties overlapped.[54] In fashioning their awards, arbitrators in Wisconsin appear to

---

[48] Feuille, *Final Offer Arbitration*. 35–48

[49] Ibid., pp. 15–16.

[50] J. L. Stern, C. M. Rehmus, J. J. Loewenberg, H. Kasper, and B. D. Dennis, *Final-Offer Arbitration,* (Lexington, MA: Lexington Books, 1975), pp. 37–75.

[51] B. R. Johnson, G. Warchol, and K. A. Bailey, "Police-Compulsory Arbitration in Michigan: A Logistic Model Analysis of Environmental Factors," *Journal of Collective Negotiations in the Public Sector* 26 (1997), pp. 27–42.

[52] Stern et al., *Final-Offer Arbitration,* pp. 77–115.

[53] C. A. Olson, "Final-Offer Arbitration in Wisconsin after Five Years," *Proceedings of the Industrial Relations Research Association* 31 (1978), pp. 111–19.

[54] L. C. Babcock and C. A. Olson, "The Causes of Impasses in Labor Disputes," *Industrial Relations* 31 (1992), pp. 348–60; and L. C. Babcock, "Strategic Behavior in Negotiations and the Use of Arbitration," *Proceedings of the Industrial Relations Research Association* 44 (1992), pp. 375–84.

have compared settlements from other schools in the same athletic conference from earlier rounds of teacher negotiations.[55]

Parties that used arbitration in the previous round and lost, made better offers to their opponents in the next contract round. Variance in settlements was down and the negotiated wage structure was closer to what the arbitrator imposed in the last settlement.[56]

Massachusetts.   Massachusetts has a package final-offer procedure. After its passage, arbitrations increased almost 70 percent. Almost 40 percent of negotiations went to impasse, but only 7 percent were ultimately arbitrated. The awards of arbitrators closely paralleled the reports of fact-finders issued earlier during the impasse.[57]

New Jersey.   Bargainers can elect to use conventional arbitration, final-offer arbitration on a single package, final-offer on an issue-by-issue basis, final-offer on the economic package and issue-by-issue on others, or two forms of fact-finding. Parties choose which type of arbitration they want to use. Results indicate relatively fewer negotiations have arbitrated settlements, and arbitrators are acting more frequently in mediating roles.[58]

The evidence suggests that states with issue rather than package approaches have more arbitrations and more issues going before arbitrators.

What Is a "Final Offer"?

One problem frequently encountered in final-offer arbitration is what is a final offer? In Wisconsin, parties must state their positions to the WERB when an impasse is declared. But it has been the practice there and in Michigan (where mediation by the arbitrator appears to be encouraged) to allow negotiations to narrow differences after a request for arbitration. Some see this as an advantage because the parties settle the issues, but others see it as a no-win situation because, if they adhere to a well-thought-out final position and only their opponent expresses a willingness to move, the arbitrator may award the point to the opponent based on the apparent intransigence of the adamant party. Thus, a party may provoke an impasse to achieve what it believed it could not get from true bargaining. Evidence indicates that unions gained 1 to 5 percent more in economic settlements as a result of arbitration than they would have gained in bargaining a settlement.[59]

---

[55] C. A. Olson and P. Jarley, "Arbitrator Decisions in Wisconsin Teacher Wage Disputes," *Industrial & Labor Relations Review* 44 (1991), pp. 536–47.

[56] C. A. Olson and B. L. Rau, "Learning from Interest Arbitration: The Next Round," *Industrial and Labor Relations Review* 50 (1997), pp. 237–51.

[57] D. B. Lipsky and T. A. Barocci, "Final-Offer Arbitration and Public-Safety Employees: The Massachusetts Experience," *Proceedings of the Industrial Relations Research Association* 30 (1977), pp. 65–76.

[58] R. A. Lester, "Analysis of Experience under New Jersey's Flexible Arbitration System," *Arbitration Journal* 44, no. 2 (1989), pp. 14–21.

[59] Stern et al., *Final-Offer Arbitration*, pp. 77–115.

Evidence on the Narcotic Effect

A study of New York police and firefighter impasses found that after the impasse law was changed to allow arbitration rather than legislative action as the final step, negotiations increasingly went to impasse and were likely to proceed to the final step. However, there was no evidence that the parties were less likely to move before impasse and little evidence that the awards were different from outcomes in similar situations where bargaining was completed.[60] The availability of arbitration seemed to chill the ability to reach a bargained settlement but not the ability to bargain.

A longitudinal study of the New York law's effect found that a positive narcotic effect during early negotiation rounds later became negative.[61] Following changes in Minnesota's public-sector law in 1979, there was an "epidemic effect" with units using arbitration largely because other units in the same bargaining round used it. In subsequent rounds, parties appeared to avoid arbitration.[62]

Evidence on the narcotic effect is mixed. Arbitration is used more widely when it becomes available but less often when it has been experienced. Once the novelty has dissipated, there are neither negative nor positive effects in its use level.[63] Use of arbitration in the previous negotiation increases its likelihood in the next round, but aggregate use across negotiations reduces aggregate use in the next round.[64] The availability of arbitration is not associated with perfunctory negotiations. Parties going to arbitration, held more negotiating sessions than those who settled without it.[65]

Arbitration and Maturing Labor Relations

Strikes have almost always been prohibited in the public sector. Because the private-sector model included them and little experience existed with other mechanisms, a great deal of experimentation has occurred. Fact-finding has decreased, both statutorily and at the individual impasse level. Surveys suggest that the use of arbitration is low and decreasing.[66] The effectiveness of arbitration may also

[60] Kochan et al., *Dispute Resolution*, pp. 158–59.

[61] R. J. Butler and R. G. Ehrenberg, "Estimating the Narcotic Effect of Public Sector Impasse Procedures," *Industrial and Labor Relations Review* 34 (1981), pp. 3–20.

[62] F. C. Champlin and M. F. Bognanno, "Chilling under Arbitration and Mixed Strike-Arbitration Regimes," *Journal of Labor Research* 6 (1985), pp. 375–87; and F. C. Champlin, M. F. Bognanno, and P. L. Schumann, "Is Arbitration Habit Forming? The Narcotic Effect of Arbitration Use," *Labour* 11 (1997), pp. 23–52.

[63] J. R. Chelius and M. M. Extejt, "The Narcotic Effect of Impasse Resolution Procedures," *Industrial and Labor Relations Review* 38 (1985), pp. 629–38.

[64] J. Currie, "Who Uses Interest Arbitration? The Case of British Columbia's Teachers, 1947–1981," *Industrial and Labor Relations Review* 42 (1989), pp. 363–79.

[65] J. J. Loewenberg, "Bargaining Intensity and Interest Arbitration," *Proceedings of the Industrial Relations Research Association* 44 (1992), pp. 385–91.

[66] C. A. Olson, "Dispute Resolution in the Public Sector," in B. Aaron, J. M. Najita, and J. L. Stern, eds., *Public-Sector Bargaining*, 2nd ed. (Washington, DC: Bureau of National Affairs, 1988), pp. 160–88.

depend on prehearing processes. Where experienced negotiators are bargaining, mediation may be much more helpful in fashioning an acceptable settlement.[67]

It is difficult for parties to determine an appropriate settlement point where third-party interventions exist. Neither party knows for certain what an arbitrator would view as a correct solution. They also may doubt the workability of an imposed solution. The choices may also vary substantially given what constitutes a last offer.

Arbitral Criteria

Arbitrators apply certain criteria in deciding awards in both grievance and interest cases. Some criteria are specified by law, others by arbitrators. The criteria can cause problems for both arbitrators and disputants.

One factor often considered is ability to pay. Nevada statutes require its assessment in arriving at an award.[68] The ability-to-pay issue may retard gains when revenues do not support wage demands. However, arbitrators are less concerned than elected officials about the actual ability to pay.[69] (This is hardly surprising since officials are generally closer to their managements than to their rank and file, who are coincidentally constituents.) A study of Wisconsin arbitrators found economic awards were most frequently shaped by internal and external comparability of pay packages, less so by cost of living, and least by ability to pay.[70] Comparability was stressed by police impasse arbitrators, and offers by the city had greater influence than the union.[71]

Managements and unions have some common and dissimilar preferences in their choice of an arbitrator. A study of New Jersey arbitrations found management and union preferences were moderately similar and stressed the arbitrators' experience levels. Unions preferred lawyer arbitrators while managements preferred economists. Both sides were influenced by the direction of the arbitrator's previous awards.[72]

The Utility of Arbitration for Unions

Public safety unions are strong advocates of binding arbitration to resolve impasses. While it is obvious that arbitration provides a method for resolving interest differences when strikes are prohibited, less information is available on the impact of the process on bargaining outcomes. Two studies found relatively

---

[67] P. F. Gerhart and J. F. Drotning, "The Effectiveness of Public-Sector Impasse Procedures," in D. B. Lipsky and J. Douglas, eds., *Advances in Industrial and Labor Relations*, vol. 2 (Greenwich, CT: JAI Press, 1985), pp. 143–95.

[68] J. R. Grodin, "Arbitration of Public-Sector Labor Disputes," *Industrial and Labor Relations Review* 27 (1974), pp. 89–102.

[69] R. D. Horton, "Arbitration, Arbitrators, and the Public Interest," *Industrial and Labor Relations Review* 27 (1975), pp. 497–507.

[70] G. G. Dell'Omo, "Wage Disputes in Interest Arbitration: Arbitrators Weigh the Criteria, *Arbitration Journal* 44, no. 2 (1989), pp. 4–13.

[71] S. Schwochau and P. Feuille, "Interest Arbitrators and Their Decision Behavior," *Industrial Relations* 27 (1988), pp. 37–55.

[72] D. E. Bloom and C. L. Cavanagh, "An Analysis of the Selection of Arbitrators," *American Economic Review* 76 (1986), pp. 408–22.

minimal wage effects (0 to 5 percent) associated with arbitration.[73] However, arbitration should serve to raise management offers, particularly in final-offer selection states. Management might be expected to concede toward an anticipated award, rather than risk the choice of a union's extreme position. For the union's part, it might be likely to take a harder line where it has a final resolution available that does not entail the risk of an illegal strike. A study of firefighter arbitration laws found arbitration was associated with higher salaries and shorter working hours the longer the law was in effect. Wage increases averaged about 11 to 22 percent higher in arbitration states.[74]

The expected utility of arbitration to settle a dispute depends on the perceived threat presented by arbitration to both sides. The lower the expected utility from arbitration, the less favorable a settlement a party would be willing to accept.[75] Part of utility is related to direct costs. The higher the costs, the more likely parties are to negotiate their own settlement. Where this occurs, the less risk averse party achieves higher outcomes.[76] In some situations, a union bargainer chooses arbitration where a satisfactory settlement might be negotiated to signal to members that it isn't shirking negotiations and settling for less than it could have gotten.[77]

Strikes

Most states prohibit public employee strikes and have injunction and penalty provisions if they occur. The right to strike is granted to certain occupations in Alaska, Hawaii, Idaho, Minnesota, Montana, Oregon, Pennsylvania, Vermont, and Wisconsin under specific circumstances. Although most states forbid strikes, enforcing the prohibition is difficult. The long history of public employee strikes shows that legally permissible steps to end them are not often taken, and statutorily mandated reprisals, such as discharges, are not often invoked. In any case, the incidence of strikes in the public sector is quite low. About 42 percent of all union members work in the public sector, but only 20 percent of strikes occur there with only 12 percent of days lost.[78] Table 16–2 shows the relative incidence of public sector strike activity across occupations and jurisdictions.

---

[73] Stern et al., *Final-Offer Arbitration*, pp. 77–115; and Kochan et al., *Dispute Resolution*, pp. 158–59.

[74] C. A. Olson, "The Impact of Arbitration on the Wages of Firefighters," *Industrial Relations* 19 (1980), pp. 325–39.

[75] F. C. Champlin and M. F. Bognanno, "A Model for Arbitration and the Incentive to Bargain," in D. Lipsky and J. Douglas, eds., *Advances in Industrial and Labor Relations* (Greenwich, CT: JAI Press, 1986), pp. 153–90.

[76] H. S. Farber, M. A. Neale, and M. H. Bazerman, "The Role of Arbitration Costs and Risk Aversion in Dispute Outcomes," *Industrial Relations* 29 (1990), pp. 361–84.

[77] B. P. McCall, "Interest Arbitration and the Incentive to Bargain: A Principal-Agent Approach," *Journal of Conflict Resolution* 34 (1990), pp. 151–67.

[78] R. Hebdon, "Public Sector Dispute Resolution in Transition," in D. Belman, M. Gunderson, and D. Hyatt, eds., *Public Sector Employment in a Time of Transition* (Madison, WI: Industrial Relations Research Association, 1996), p. 88.

TABLE 16–2

Major (over 1000) Public Sector Strikes by Employer and Occupation, 1983–94

	Number	Percent
All Employers	78	100.0
Board of Education	52	66.7
University	7	9.0
Utility	6	7.7
County	4	5.1
State	4	5.1
City	3	3.8
Transit	1	1.3
Welfare	1	1.3
All Occupations	78	100.0
Teacher	55	70.5
Blue collar	14	17.9
State/comprehensive	3	3.8
Hospital/comprehensive	2	2.6
Nurse	1	1.3
Police and fire	1	1.3
Social work	1	1.3
Unknown	1	1.3

SOURCE: R. Hebdon, "Public Sector Dispute Resolution in Transition," in. D. Belman, M. Gunderson, and D. Hyatt, eds., *Public Sector Employment in a Time of Transition* (Madison, WI: Industrial Relations Research Association, 1996), p. 90.

The table shows that most strikes occurred at the local level, with school employees involved in strikes more often than any other group. More days are lost from strikes by school employees, and the duration of strikes is longest for school disputes. One reason for the level and duration of school strikes is that they are often essentially costless to both employers and employees. Legislatures establish school years of certain lengths, so if a strike disrupts the first three weeks of school, the school year is simply extended three weeks. The only cost to the school or the teachers is the delay in school aid receipts and wages. The incidence and duration of school strikes are associated with state laws governing the length of the school year and the local district's willingness to tax itself for greater educational costs.[79] The subsequent incidence of strikes was decreased by not rescheduling lost school days. Duration was predicted by the salaries of neighboring teachers, variation in comparison salaries (uncertainty about an appropriate settlement point), and the unemployment rate (reduced bargaining power and willingness to be taxed). Duration was decreased by average income of residents

---

[79] C. A. Olson, "The Impact of Rescheduled School Days on Teacher Strikes," *Industrial and Labor Relations Review* 38 (1984), pp. 515–28.

(ability to pay), percent of teachers with master's degrees, and school days not rescheduled (forgone income).[80]

There is mixed evidence regarding the incidence of strikes. The evidence suggests that police strikes occur less often when there is a provision for collective bargaining and arbitration to settle impasses.[81] On the other hand, strikes appear to be used when they are legal or not prevented as vehicles for increasing public employee bargaining power. Well-enforced penalties or threats of firing reduce public-sector strikes, while poorly enforced laws have no effect, and permissive laws increase their frequency.[82] Strike incidence declines with both the length of experience of the bargainers and the relative equality of their experience level.[83] Where strikes are banned, grievance rates are higher, particularly on economic issues.[84]

Generally, strikes in the public sector are positively influenced by the rate of wage increase for private-sector employees, increases in the cost of living, and fiscal belt-tightening. Unemployment in the private sector and recessions are related to reduced public-sector strike activity.[85]

Recent studies of teacher strikes suggest they are not used as an offensive weapon to improve outcomes more than other comparison groups but are used as defensive weapons to maintain a relative position or to reverse erosion. Among Illinois and Iowa teachers, strikes are worth only about $285 annually. Evidence suggests that the availability of impasse resolution procedures influences wages by about 10 percent.[86]

SUMMARY

The legal environment is a critical factor in public employee unionization because management ultimately determines the scope of bargaining rights. Public opinion predicts changes in these laws in some states, but generally rights are more restrictive than in the private sector. Legislation is most conducive to bargaining in the

---

[80] X. Wang and L. Babcock, "Salary Comparisons and Public School Teachers Strikes," *Proceedings of the Industrial Relations Research Association* 48 (1996), pp. 224–30.

[81] C. Ichniowski, "Arbitrators and Police Bargaining: Prescriptions for the Blue Flu," *Industrial Relations* 21 (1982), pp. 149–66; and R. N. Horn, W. J. McGuire, and J. Tomkiewicz, "Work Stoppages by Teachers: An Empirical Analysis," *Journal of Labor Research* 3 (1982), pp. 487–95.

[82] C. A. Olson, "Strikes, Strike Penalties, and Arbitration in Six States," *Industrial and Labor Relations Review* 39 (1986), pp. 539–51; and D. M. Partridge, "Teacher Strikes and Public Policy: Does the Law Matter?" *Journal of Collective Negotiations in the Public Sector* 25 (1996), pp. 3–22.

[83] E. Montgomery and M. E. Benedict, "The Impact of Bargainer Experience on Teacher Strikes," *Industrial and Labor Relations Review* 42 (1989), pp. 380–92.

[84] R. P. Hebdon and R. N. Stern, "Tradeoffs among Expressions of Industrial Conflict: Public Sector Strike Bans and Grievance Arbitration," *Industrial and Labor Relations Review* 51 (1998), pp. 204–21.

[85] W. B. Nelson, G. W. Stone, Jr., and J. M. Swint, "An Economic Analysis of Public Sector Collective Bargaining and Strike Activity," *Journal of Labor Research* 2 (1981), pp. 77–98.

[86] J. T. Delaney, "Strikes, Arbitration, and Teacher Salaries: A Behavioral Analysis," *Industrial and Labor Relations Review* 37 (1983), pp. 431–46.

industrialized North and East and is least in rural or southern areas. Right-to-work laws for the private sector predict statutes prohibiting union activity in the public sector.

Where bargaining is permitted, issues are much the same as in the private sector. Unionization varies, with AFSCME organized along an industrial-union approach and the uniformed services generally organized on a craft basis.

Impasse resolution varies widely by jurisdiction and occupation. In the federal government, the Federal Services Impasses Panel resolves disputes. In states providing for impasse resolution by statute, arbitrators usually handle uniformed services disputes. In other areas, fact-finding, mediation, and other methods are prescribed. Strikes are forbidden in most jurisdictions.

Evidence suggests that unions benefit from mandatory interest arbitration and strikes. Final-offer selection may reduce reliance on arbitration, but more recent evidence suggests that any experience with arbitration lessens its future usage.

DISCUSSION QUESTIONS

1. If government employees were to be given a limited right to strike, which occupations should be prohibited from striking, and under what conditions should the prohibition be enforced?
2. Since arbitrators are not responsible to the electorate, should they be allowed to make binding rulings on economic issues?
3. Civil service rules provide many public employees with a large measure of protection from arbitrary action, so why should public employees be allowed to organize?
4. Because fact-finding publicizes the major areas in dispute and a proposed settlement, why has it not been more successful given the public's stake in the outcome?

KEY TERMS

Federal Labor Relations Authority *520*

Chilling effect *542*

Narcotic effect *542*

Final-offer arbitration *542*

CASE

The annual contract negotiations between the Pleasant Ridge Board of Education and the Pleasant Ridge Classroom Teachers Association (PRCTA) are due to begin July 1, one week from now. Under state law, the new contract has to be signed by September 1 or an impasse will be declared. Following an impasse, state law requires simultaneous mediation and fact-finding. The fact-finder's report must be published no later than September 20. Under the law, the parties could arbitrate unresolved contract issues using a total-package, final-offer selection approach if both agree to binding arbitration. The state law prohibits teachers from striking, but about 10 short strikes occurred in the state last year at the time school opened.

The contract at Pleasant Ridge was not signed until November 10 last year, even though mediation and fact-finding occurred. The PRCTA had repeatedly requested arbitration of the contract dispute, but the school board refused. Although no strike occurred, two "sickouts" took place in October when teacher absence rates exceeded 90 percent and schools had to be closed. For the upcoming contract, apparently considerable sentiment exists for "hitting the bricks" if negotiations are unsatisfactory.

About 5,000 students are enrolled at Pleasant Ridge from kindergarten through 12th grade. There are 250 teachers, of whom 240 are PRCTA members. Like many established school systems, enrollment at Pleasant Ridge had declined for several years because of the baby bust. The impact had been greatest in the secondary grades (dropping about 6 percent annually). Now with the baby boomlet, enrollments are increasing in the elementary grades by about 10 percent annually.

The school system's operating budget is funded from two sources: state school aid based on student enrollments and local property taxes. The legislature has passed a 5 percent increase in per student funding for the upcoming school year. Local property taxes presently provide the other 60 percent, based on a 22 mill levy against assessed market value. Fifteen mills are permanently required by state law. The other seven are supplemental and are periodically reconsidered by local voters. Five of the seven mills expire this November and will be subject to reapproval by the voters in the general election. Property values are presently appreciating by 4 percent annually.

School costs are divided approximately equally between salaries and plant, equipment, supplies, and reduction of bonded indebtedness. Of the 50 percent allocated to salaries, 80 percent is paid to the instructional staff represented by the PRCTA. Nonwage costs are increasing at an annual rate of 3 percent.

The PRCTA bargaining committee has just completed its contract demands. Major areas in which it demands changes include a 6 percent salary increase, a reduction in maximum class size from 30 to 25 students in the elementary grades (K–6), and the granting of tenure after the second year of teaching, instead of the fourth. Because about 2,500 students are in the K–6 program, a reduction in class sizes would boost teacher employment. The tenure change would affect 25 second-year and 25 third-year teachers now uncovered. In case of staff reduction, tenured employees who are terminated are entitled to one year's pay under the contract. As part of its preparations for negotiations, the PRCTA surveyed comparable schools and found that the pay of its members is about 5 percent below the market rate, tenure is normally granted after three years, and the median elementary class size (by contract) is 27.

As the school's governing body, the Pleasant Ridge Board of Education must ultimately approve the contract if arbitration is not used. The district's superintendent, personnel director, high school principal, and two elementary principals form the management bargaining team. The school board consists of five persons. Two of these are union members, and three (including these two) were endorsed by the Pleasant Ridge Central Labor Union (PRCLU) at the last election. Two others endorsed by the PRCLU lost to the other present members. At that last election, two mills of the supplementary tax were approved, but the margin in favor was only 500 out of 10,000 votes cast.

Questions

1. What should be the initial bargaining position of the school board? What data justify this position?

2. What should the PRCTA consider a reasonable settlement?

3. If fact-finding occurs, what should the fact-finder use as criteria in recommending a settlement? What should the recommendation be?

4. Should the board go to arbitration if an agreement cannot be negotiated?

5. What strategies should the management and union negotiators use to win their demands?

6. If the negotiations go to arbitration as a final-offer package, what should each party's offer be for the arbitrator?

17

A SURVEY OF LABOR

RELATIONS IN

MARKET ECONOMIES

This chapter provides an overview of labor relations in modern industrial market economies around the world. Labor organizations vary substantially in their involvement in political activity, collective bargaining, and decision making within societies, industries, and enterprises. Their organizational structures differ as well. The previous chapters dealt with a variety of development, structure, and process issues that influence and describe labor relations in the United States. This chapter is an overview of differences in the development of labor movements and structures and the manner in which processes are implemented in market economies. The chapter emphasizes the basics of labor relations among European Union (EU) members, Australia, Japan, and the developing economies of East Asia and Eastern Europe.

An entire text could be written on any of these countries; thus, by its brief nature, the chapter provides a sketchy overview that should acquaint and direct the reader to more detailed and analytical treatments.

As you study this chapter, consider the following issues:

1. What are the major differences in the prevalence and operation of labor unions in North America and Western Europe?
2. How are the plant-level needs of workers addressed in countries where bargaining occurs at the industry and employer association level?
3. How does the role of the government in labor-management relations differ across developed market-based economies?
4. What are the advantages and disadvantages to workers, unions, and employers of the various structures of labor-management relations examined in this chapter?

THE DEVELOPMENT OF LABOR MOVEMENTS

In comparing industrial relations systems across countries and economies, an examination of where and when they developed helps explain current approaches. In the United States, uplift, revolutionary, business, and predatory unions were identified as representing a typology of unions. Another basis for classification identifies unions as utilitarian (rational or instrumental values), idealistic (commitment or identification values), affective (emotional values), or traditional (values based on the results of previous outcomes such as utilitarian or idealistic approaches). Cultural values, ideologies, and political policies strongly influence the approach chosen by a union.[1] Table 17–1 explains this typology in greater detail.

The development of European labor unions roughly paralleled developments in the United States, with some variation across countries depending on political activities. German unions began to form with the 1848 revolution but did not gain momentum until after the repeal of the antisocialist laws promulgated under Otto von Bismarck.[2] Swedish unions gained adherents in the late 19th and early 20th centuries. British unions began to organize about the same time and in the same manner as the Knights of Labor in the United States. As this chapter will note, only British collective bargaining resembles U.S. labor relations, with initial recognition obtained primarily at the plant level and generally adversarial bargaining at the establishment or corporate level.

As in the United States, several types of unions emerged during the formative period. In the United States, the National Labor Union and the Knights of Labor espoused uplift unionism; while later the Industrial Workers of the World (IWW), anarchists, and syndicalists advocated revolutionary unionism. Germany and Great Britain were early spawning grounds of revolutionary approaches to government and employment. Karl Marx advocated the takeover of the state by the proletariat (rank and file) together with state ownership of the means of production to end the exploitation of workers. Under the Marxian approach, the goals of unions and the state are synonymous. Anarchists and syndicalists advocated abolishing the state and/or capitalistic ownership of the means of production. The Fabians in Great Britain and other socialists favored state ownership and planned economies to better allocate wealth among a population and to choose desired outputs.

In the late 1890s, Swedish labor organized into a variety of federations forming the Swedish Confederation of Trade Unions (LO). This was followed around 1900 by employers forming the Swedish Employers' Confederation (SAF). In 1906, the SAF recognized the LO's right to unionize and the LO recognized managerial prerogatives. Industrywide agreements were negotiated during 1900–10

---

[1] M. Poole, *Industrial Relations: Origins and Patterns of National Diversity* (London: Routledge and Kegan Paul, 1986).

[2] "Germany: Industrial Relations Background," *European Industrial Relations Review* 216 (1992), pp. 21–27.

TABLE 17–1

Strategies and Categories of Social Action

General Categories of Social Action (orientations)	Strategies
1. *Instrumental-rational* (Zweckrational)—that is, determined by expectations as to the behavior of objects in the environment and of other human beings; these expectations are used as 'conditions' or 'means' for the attainment of the actor's own rationally pursued and calculated ends	Utilitarian, based on material interests and a 'will to power'
2. *Value-rational* (Wertrational)—that is, determined by conscious belief in the value for its own sake of some ethical, aesthetic, religious, political, or other form of behavior, independently of its prospects of success	Idealistic, based on identification and commitment
3. *Affectual* (especially emotional)—that is, determined by the actor's specific affects and feeling states	Not strategic but sentiments and emotions can enhance value-rational commitments
4. *Traditional*—that is, determined by ingrained habituation	The institutionalization of previous strategic decisions of an utilitarian or idealistic character

SOURCE: M. Poole, *Industrial Relations: Origins and Patterns of National Diversity* (London: Routledge and Kegan Paul, 1986), p. 14.

after major strikes.[3] Substantial conflict continued between labor and management until the 1930s when the government moved into the hands of the Social Democrats, whose agenda meshed closely with labor, separating the political and economic power of employers for the first time. After some adjustments, an era of consultation and cooperation was begun that continues to some extent today.

Japanese unions emerged in the 1890s after that country's industrial revolution. They were active before World War II and were encouraged by the United States during the period of U.S. military rule after the war. Following the war, unions exhibited Marxist tendencies when real wages were low, but became more enterprise oriented as productivity and wages increased. As in most industrialized countries, unions in Japan affiliated with federations.[4]

While many unions have supported socialist agendas and been affiliated with labor parties in Europe, the trend has been increasingly toward accommodation of capitalism and free market economies. In Germany, unions have moved from

---

[3] W. Korpi, "Industrial Relations and Industrial Conflict: The Case of Sweden," in B. Martin and E. M. Kassalow, eds., *Labor Relations in Advanced Industrial Societies: Issues and Problems* (Washington: Carnegie Endowment for International Peace, 1980), pp. 89–108.

[4] K. Koike, *Understanding Industrial Relations in Modern Japan* (New York: St. Martin's Press, 1988).

having Marxist perspectives toward acting as intermediaries who represent worker interests and try to ameliorate the effects of change in supporting a dynamic economy within democratic capitalism.[5] At the same time, where the economic system of the country implies less shareholder interest in the organization, managers appear to be more pluralistically oriented.[6]

Unions in socialist economies are expected to assist in meeting production goals and maintaining discipline since everyone is expected to conform to statist objectives. The community of interests of the state and its citizens precludes legitimate goal conflict. Pay inequality in most socialist economies was smaller than in capitalist societies except in the old Soviet Union. In transformed economies, unionization remained high in the state-owned sector, but not in the private sector. Private wages are generally higher. When state-owned companies are sold off to private investors in Hungary, new owners must establish works councils. In Poland, one-third of the board of director's seats are given to workers' representatives.[7]

Major changes in unionization in Eastern Europe followed the fall of communism. In Poland, the Solidarity movement was largely responsible for catalyzing the breakdown of the communist system. Its leader, Lech Walesa, led the government following the collapse of martial law. In Bulgaria, new labor organizations emerged in an economy beset by inflation and falling real output. Tripartite structures (unions, employers, and the government) are trying to deal with the problems there.[8] In the former East Germany, rapid privatization undermined union influence, but extension of the West German codetermination law and centralized bargaining offset the decline.[9]

Changes in union philosophies in Poland toward supporting a market economy occurred gradually as state intervention was seen as a decreasingly viable alternative for catalyzing change.[10] Compared to Western countries, former Communists were more egalitarian, expressed low job satisfaction, and were more supportive of strong trade unions. As actual wage differentials increased in Eastern Europe following the collapse of communism, support for egalitarianism decreased.[11]

---

[5] O. Jacobi, "World Economic Changes and Industrial Relations in the Federal Republic of Germany," in H. Juris, M. Thompson, and W. Daniels, eds., *Industrial Relations in a Decade of Economic Change* (Madison, WI: Industrial Relations Research Association, 1985), pp. 211–46.

[6] Poole, *Industrial Relations.*

[7] R. J. Flanagan, "Institutional Reformation in Eastern Europe," *Industrial Relations* 37 (1998), pp. 337–57.

[8] D. C. Jones, "The Changing Face of Labor Markets and Industrial Relations in Bulgaria," *Proceedings of the Industrial Relations Research Association* 44 (1992), pp. 578–85.

[9] U. Jurgens, L. Klinzing, and L. Turner, "The Transformation of Industrial Relations in Eastern Germany," *Industrial and Labor Relations Review* 46 (1992), pp. 229–44.

[10] M. Sewerynski, "Changes in Polish Labour Law and Industrial Relations during the Period of Post-Communist Transformation," *Bulletin of Comparative Labour Relations* 31 (1996), pp. 85–108.

[11] D. G. Blanchflower and R. B. Freeman, "The Attitudinal Legacy of Communist Labor Relations," *Industrial and Labor Relations Review* 50 (1997), pp. 438–59.

THE STRUCTURE OF LABOR MOVEMENTS

In the United States, primary authority in the labor movement is vested in the national unions, organized on a craft or industrial basis. This model does not hold for most free-market industrialized world economies. The unions in many other industrialized countries concentrate their control in labor federations or at the local level.

Swedish unions concentrate power in the LO which deals with the employers' SAF. In Germany, a small number of national unions do most of the bargaining. British unions organize into nationals, but locals retain a good deal of authority. Local unions in many countries have primarily geographic (somewhat similar to the early U.S. Knights of Labor), rather than corporate relationships.[12] Italy, France, and the Netherlands have politically or religiously based national federations. Dutch employers also organize along religious lines.[13] National unions are increasingly merging in the EU, similar to the United States.[14] Union leaders in Europe are more entrenched than in the United States, particularly at the local level, because there are fewer union elections in Europe.[15] In Japan, although most bargaining is conducted at the local or enterprise level, most locals affiliate with a national.[16] Enterprise unions usually include both blue- and white-collar workers.[17]

In the United States, a variety of characteristics are related to interest and participation in union activities. Japanese union member activity is predicted somewhat similarly. For example, length of membership in the union, pay levels, dissatisfaction with pay and working conditions, interaction with others in the work group, and perceptions of union effectiveness and democracy predict participation in Japan. Contrary to United States unions, age and educational attainment of Japanese members were negatively related and job status was unrelated.[18]

Because union members in many European countries have little involvement in contract negotiations at the plant or enterprise level, there is little rank-and-file participation in union activities. In Germany, most establishments are required to have **works councils.** These councils advise management on employment matters and may also be consulted on the overall strategy of the organization. There may be an operational conflict between unions and works councils. Evidence suggests that works councils may be more interested in preserving plant interests than those

---

[12] J. P. Windmuller, "Comparative Study of Methods and Practices," In J. P. Windmuller, ed., *Collective Bargaining in Industrialized Market Economies: A Reappraisal* (Geneva: International Labour Office, 1987), pp. 3–158.

[13] T. Kennedy, *European Labor Relations* (Lexington, MA: Lexington Books, 1980).

[14] Windmuller, "Comparative Study."

[15] Poole, *Industrial Relations.*

[16] Koike, *Understanding Industrial Relations.*

[17] Ibid.

[18] S. Kuruvilla, D. G. Gallagher, J. Fiorito, and M. Wakabayashi, "Union Participation in Japan: Do Western Theories Apply?" *Industrial and Labor Relations Review* 43 (1990), pp. 374–89.

TABLE 17–2

Important Participation Rights of the Works Council

Kind of Right	Social Concerns	Personnel Issues	Economic Matters
Codetermination rights (can be enforced)	Beginning and end of daily working time; planning of holidays; design of payment system; piecework and premium rates; humane organization of work in accordance with established scientific knowledge	Staff file; selection criteria; in-firm training	Social plan
Veto rights		Recruitment; redeployment; assignment to wage group; dismissal	
Consultation and information rights	Labor protection; accident prevention	Personnel planning; right to be heard before dismissal	Information about major business plans or changes in the firm; consultation about: building or extending plant and changing/ introducing equipment; changes in work processes or places; economic committee.

SOURCE: C. Lane, *Management and Labour in Europe* (Hampshire, England: Edward Elgar, 1989), p. 230.

of the union with which many of its employees are associated.[19] Table 17–2 shows the types of issues and level of authority works councils have in Germany. In Germany, a corporatist approach is taken with labor and management operating as "social partners." German unions also have extensive technical expertise through their employment of an extensive professional administration. German unions are highly consolidated; only 17 major nationals currently exist.[20]

Since the early 1980s, economic globalization has accelerated. Various regions of the world have experienced rapid economic development, usually involving extensive investment in manufacturing either by state-directed activities or through infusions of foreign capital. In Asia, development has been most rapid in China, Indonesia, Korea, Malaysia, Singapore, Taiwan, and Thailand, although all have been deeply affected by the recession that began in late 1997. Eastern Europe has shifted from communism toward market economies at varying rates,

---

[19] K. R. Wever, "Industrial Relations Developments in France, West Germany, the U. K., and Sweden: An American Assessment," *Proceedings of the Industrial Relations Research Association* 41 (1988), pp. 361–64.

[20] C. Lane, *Management and Labour in Europe* (Hampshire, England: Edward Elgar, 1989).

with stronger economies seen in the Czech Republic, Hungary, and Poland. Mexico and Latin America have also been strongly influenced by globalization and foreign investment.

During this same period, treaties have been enacted to create economic regions in various areas of the world. The most prominent include the European Union, North American Free Trade Agreement (NAFTA), and Mercosur (the southern common market of Argentina, Brazil, Paraguay, and Uruguay). The regionalization and globalization of the economy has put increasing pressure on trade unions and reduced the ability to gain wage increases given the increasingly competitive nature of the product market. Trade unions have tried to influence the "social dimension" of the EU and NAFTA, but have had only limited success.[21] One of the major difficulties that national unions face in regionalization and globalization is that they have little ability to coordinate pressure across political boundaries. In Mexico, divisions in the labor movement, labor's political isolation, undemocratic union structures, and a lack of innovative strategies and tactics disabled efforts to influence extension of some protective labor regulations during the development of NAFTA.[22] Militant responses were more likely to come from autonomous and democratic unions who were not part of Mexico's state-corporatist labor confederation.[23]

Transnational organizations and neoconservative political control of developed economies have contributed to market integration and the decline in union bargaining power and interest in the welfare state.[24]

Developing economies may adopt one of two basic approaches (or a mix of them) to industrialize: import-substitution industrialization (ISI) or export-oriented industrialization (EOI). ISI strategies have limited growth implications because there is probably some limit on the potential level of internal consumption, particularly given income levels. EOI strategies require that output be either substantially cheaper or of better quality than the domestic products with which they will compete.[25] Figure 17–1 presents a model of industrialization strategies, national industrial relations policy goals, and their likely consequences.

Figure 17–1 indicates that countries in the first stage of EOI are competing primarily through their abilities to contain costs. Some of this may result from repressive measures such as relaxing labor standards and banning labor organizations. Movement to a second stage, which requires high quality, higher

---

[21] R. Hyman, "Trade Unions and European Integration," *Work and Occupations* 24 (1997), pp. 309–31.

[22] W. Vanderbush, "Mexican Labor in the Era of Economic Restructuring and NAFTA: Working to Create a Favorable Investment Climate," *Labor Studies Journal* 20, no. 4 (1996), pp. 58–86.

[23] J. P. Tuman, "Unions and Restructuring in the Mexican Automobile Industry: A Comparative Assessment," *Industrial Relations Journal* 27 (1996), pp. 317–30.

[24] T. Boswell and D. Stevis, "Globalization and International Labor Organizing," *Work and Occupations* 24 (1997), pp. 288–308.

[25] S. C. Kuruvilla, "Economic Development Strategies, Industrial Relations Policies and Workplace IR/HR Practices in Southeast Asia," in K. S. Wever and L. Turner, eds., *The Comparative Political Economy of Industrial Relations* (Madison, WI: Industrial Relations Research Association, 1995), pp. 115–50.

FIGURE 17–1

Economic Development Strategies, Industrial Relations Policies and Workplace IR/HR Practices

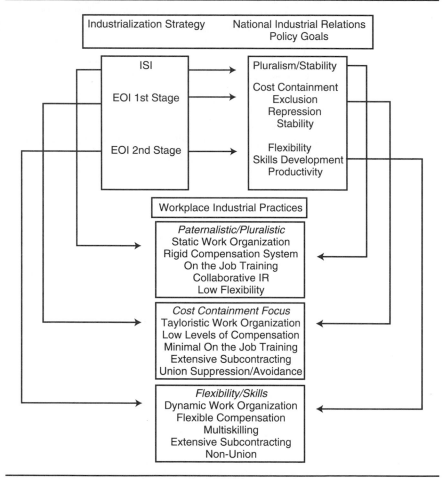

SOURCE: S. C. Kuruvilla, "Economic Development Strategies, Industrial Relations Policies and Workplace IR/HR Practices in Southeast Asia," in K. S. Wever and L. Turner, eds., *The Comparative Political Economy of Industrial Relations* (Madison, WI: Industrial Relations Research Association, 1995), p. 120.

value-added output, requires increases in worker skills and productivity. Repression ceases to be an effective strategy as a developing middle class gains the opportunity to exercise political power. Strikes, even if outlawed, are more likely to lead to change.

Competition leads employers and the state to look for ways to attract investment. One way to do this is to enhance labor's effectiveness to the benefit of capital. In the short run, holding down real wages while boosting productivity will accomplish this. The willingness of the state employers in this process is related to exposure to foreign investors, but is also related to the nation's culture and politics.[26]

It is argued that political regimes, especially in countries without a democratic tradition, make a choice about whether to adopt a repressive or benign policy toward labor unions. Where unions are likely to create an opposition political force, repressive approaches may be more likely. Repressive forces may also be used when the state has a strong need (possibly for corrupt reasons) for tapping the results of economic growth. Figure 17–2 depicts systematic relationships between state and labor components under repressive and benign strategies.[27] Arrows show the direction of effects, ellipses relate to state policy variables (labor and wage), and broken lines represent long-term effects. Growth permits wage increases, but rapid wage growth would reduce economic growth. Dictatorships would be likely to repress unionization and directly influence labor discontent which, in the absence of unionization, would have no expression except to reduce growth. In the benign strategy, wage growth could reduce labor discontent, which would reduce unionization. On the other hand, democracy would also lead to greater opportunities to unionize which would have a likelihood of raising wages.[28]

Given recent economic experience, repressive regimes have encountered labor force problems (e.g., Indonesia) while, given global competition, unions have had less success in gaining wage increases in nonrepressive regimes.

ORGANIZING AND REPRESENTATION

Organizing and representation in the industrialized economies outside North America is quite unlike what occurs in the United States. With the exception of Great Britain, members of the EU have no mechanism for workers to vote on representation. Rather, unions are recognized at the national or federation level by their employer counterparts and bargaining over a basic contract occurs at that level.

Exclusive representation is uncommon outside of the United States. In several European countries, employers may deal with many unions in the workplace, each with slightly different representational agendas. This type of situation is particularly prevalent in countries with unions having religious ties. As will be noted below, this multiplicity in representation and the lack of exclusive jurisdiction do not appear to be problems.

Union security differs substantially across Europe. Closed shops can be negotiated in Great Britain, but in most other countries, union security is not an issue

---

[26] S. J. Frenkel and D. Peetz, "Globalization and Industrial Relations in East Asia: A Three-Country Comparison," *Industrial Relations* 37 (1998), pp. 282–310.

[27] R. B. Freeman, "Repressive Labor Relations and New Unionism in East Asia," *Proceedings of the Industrial Relations Research Association* 46 (1994), pp. 231–38.

[28] Ibid.

FIGURE 17–2

State Policy—Unionization Relationships

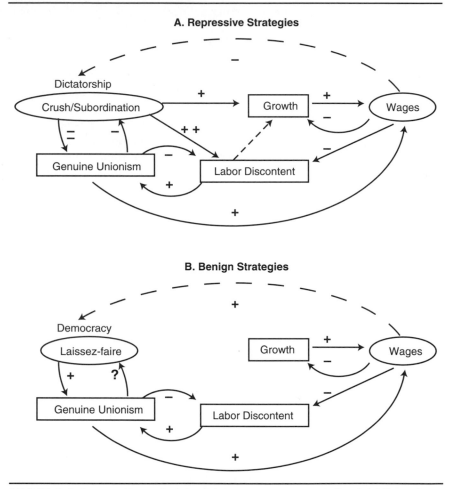

SOURCE: R. B. Freeman, "Repressive Labor Relations and New Unionism in East Asia," *Proceedings of the Industrial Relations Research Association* 46 (1994), p. 235.

because several unions may represent employees in what would be considered a bargaining unit in the United States.[29] In Great Britain, representation is possible only when employers give voluntary recognition. While compulsory union membership declined in Great Britain between 1979 and 1991, there

---

[29] T. Kennedy, *European Labor Relations*.

was no increase in the rate at which employers decline to recognize worker representatives.[30]

Japanese unions have difficulty organizing in new firms. This is partly due to an enterprise orientation which makes it difficult to take wages out of competition. Thus, their direct effect on pay and benefits is rather small. The lack of wage premiums make them unattractive to unorganized workers since "voice" issues are not generally problems with Japanese employers.[31]

Union density varies widely among industrialized nations. Table 17–3 notes a membership rate of over 96 percent in Sweden to about 17 percent in France. The Nordic countries have the highest rate, with only Belgium, Ireland, and New Zealand also exceeding 50 percent. Density is lower in countries with adversarial relations.[32]

Union density is quite low in the United States and has declined more than in other countries, reflecting, among other things, the more adversarial relationship found in this country. Union wage premiums are generally higher in the United States. Additionally, the variation in earnings is lowered more by unionization in the United States than in all other developed countries except Switzerland.[33] Trade union density in Great Britain has declined recently; like the United States, substantial proportions of the decline are unrelated to an adversarial relationship per se. Demographic, legal, and occupational changes account for about 30 percent of the British decline.[34] Similar declines are beginning to occur in other more heavily unionized industrial countries.

Strong local unions and the official institution of work participation mechanisms are associated with higher union density among nations of the European Union. The local level is the point at which most workers assess whether unionization is to their benefit. France has unimportant locals with little voice in participation (France also has the lowest unionization rate), although legislation passed in the early 1980s encouraging participation has led to more bargaining and employee involvement.[35] Great Britain and Italy (with unionization rates at about 40 percent) have strong locals, but no participation mechanisms are assured.

---

[30] M. Wright, "The Collapse of Compulsory Unionism? Collective Organization in Highly Unionized British Companies, 1979–1991," *British Journal of Industrial Relations* 34 (1996), pp. 497–514.

[31] T. Tsuru and J. B. Rebitzer, "The Limits of Enterprise Unionism: Prospects for Continuing Union Decline in Japan," *British Journal of Industrial Relations* 33 (1995), pp. 459ff.

[32] "International: Unions 'Forward March' Reversed?", *European Industrial Relations Review* 212 (1991), pp. 16–17.

[33] D. G. Blanchflower and R. B. Freeman, "Unionism in the United States and Other Advanced OECD Countries," *Industrial Relations* 31 (1992), pp. 56–79.

[34] F. Green, "Recent Trends in British Trade Union Density," *British Journal of Industrial Relations* 30 (1992), pp. 445–58.

[35] "France: A Decade of the 'Auroux' Laws," *European Industrial Relations Review* 233 (1993), pp. 30–32.

TABLE 17–3

Union Membership of Nonagricultural Workers as a Percentage of Nonagricultural Wage and Salary Employees, 1970–86/87 (percentages)

Country	1970	1979	1986–87	1970–79	1979–86	1970–87
With sharp rises in density						
Denmark	66	86	95	+20	+9	29
Finland	56	84	85	+28	+1	29
Sweden	79	89	96	+10	+7	17
With 1970s rises in density stable in 1980s						
Belgium	66	77	76	11	−1	10
Ireland	44	49	51	5	2	7
West Germany	37	42	43	5	1	6
Australia	52	58	56	6	−1	5
Canada	32	36	36	4	0	4
Switzerland	31	34	33	3	−1	2
Norway	59	60	61	1	1	2
With 1970s rises in density decline in 1980s						
Italy	39	51	45	12	−6	6
United Kingdom	51	58	50	7	−8	−1
New Zealand	43	46	41	3	−5	−2
With declining density						
Austria	64	59	61	−5	2	−3
Netherlands	39	43	35	4	−8	−4
France	22	20	17	−2	−3	−5
Japan	35	32	28	−3	−4	−7
United States	31	25	17	−6	−8	−14
Unweighted average (exclusive of U.S.)	48	54	53	6	−1	6
Deviation of U.S. from unweighted average	−16	−28	−34	−12	−7	−20

SOURCE: D. G. Blanchflower and R. B. Freeman, "Unionism in the United States and Other Advanced OECD Countries," *Industrial Relations* 31, (1992) p. 59.

Germany, Sweden, and Belgium (with rates between 33 and 85 percent) have strong locals with participation assured.[36]

BARGAINING ISSUES

Bargaining issues in countries outside the United States are both broader and narrower. Because most countries do not have a statute that enables collective

---

[36] B. Hancke, "Trade Union Membership in Europe, 1960–90: Rediscovering Local Unions, *British Journal of Industrial Relations* 31 (1993), pp. 593–614.

bargaining, bargaining issues or methods are unspecified. Thus, no definition of or distinction among mandatory, permissive, or prohibited issues exists. The bargaining issues and outcomes also differ from country to country, depending on the economic policies of the government and the degree to which central planning or income policies exist.[37] Further, except in Sweden and France, there is no legal duty to bargain, although it is implied in employer recognition of unions.[38] Work rules and seniority issues are seldom found in contracts and may evolve from tradition, particularly in Great Britain. These clauses are less necessary in most EU countries because there is substantial social legislation to deal with **redundancy** (dismissal from a job, especially by layoff) because of economic reverses and technological change.[39] More recent negotiations in Great Britain have introduced changes in traditional work practices, including them in contracts. Where work rules were negotiated, wage settlements were generally higher. Large productivity gains have resulted.[40]

From an economic standpoint, the bargaining power of employers is reduced in Australia because arbitration courts have indexed wages, although their influence is beginning to weaken in the face of global competition problems. A form of multilateral bargaining also occurs because Australian states can legislate directly on wages and working conditions.[41]

In France, contracts are usually negotiated annually, but the length of agreements may be indeterminate in some countries.[42] This is very contrary to U.S. approaches where contracts have tended toward longer periods and the only intra-contractual issues open to change are wages, and then only annually.

In Japan, unions have little say on promotion procedures but do exert control on transfers between workshops or employee groups. The group's supervisor has great influence in promotion decisions and is usually a union member. Regular and contract workers are from noncompeting groups. Because there is no distinction between classes of bargaining issues in Japan, unions have more influence in managerial decision making than in the United States. Issues requiring consultation or consent at the enterprise level involve improvement in production methods, conditions of labor, shop-floor environment and safety, and fringe benefits. Occasionally, consultation occurs regarding investments, product development, financial situations, recruiting, mergers, and training policies.[43] In contrast to the

---

[37] Poole, *Industrial Relations*.

[38] Windmuller, "Comparative Study."

[39] A. Sturmthal, *Comparative Labor Movements* (Belmont, CA: Wadsworth, 1972).

[40] P. N. Ingram, "Changes in Working Practices in British Manufacturing Industry in the 1980s: A Study of Employee Concessions Made During Wage Negotiations," *British Journal of Industrial Relations* 29 (1991), pp. 1–14.

[41] B. Dabscheck and J. Niland, "Australian Industrial Relations and the Shift to Centralism," in H. Juris, M. Thompson, and W. Daniels, eds., *Industrial Relations in a Decade of Economic Change* (Madison, WI: Industrial Relations Research Association, 1985), pp. 41–72.

[42] S. Dayal, "Collective Bargaining and Contemporary Management-Labor Relations: Analysis and Prospects," in S. B. Prasad, ed., *Advances in International Comparative Management* (Greenwich, CT: JAI Press, 1989), pp. 45–59.

[43] Koike, Understanding Industrial Relations.

United States, information sharing in Japanese union-management negotiations is associated with lower union wage demands and shorter negotiations.[44]

BARGAINING STRUCTURES

With the exception of Great Britain, bargaining in most EU countries occurs at the industry level where it involves national unions or federations and employer associations. In Italy, unions may bargain with the government on social issues, at the employer association and industry levels on economics, and at plant levels on working conditions.[45]

Industry-level bargaining, coupled with works councils, enhances the introduction of technological change because contracts address issues of redundancy. Unions may take a broader look at employment security, and employers may be able to take the costs of retraining out of competition since all organizations in the industry would be vulnerable at the same levels. Great Britain's tendency to negotiate at the enterprise level has been cited as one reason British firms may be less able to incorporate technological change than other EU members.[46] The fact that several unions frequently represent employees and obtain contracts in British firms also leads to employer and employee resistance to workplace concessions involving technological issues.

While most union-management relationships occur within national boundaries, the increasing importance of multinational employers may lead to changes. Changes in local economic climates increasing global competition make information availability increasingly critical for both labor and management in the future. In turn, this should increase multinational consultation. But owing to their interests in maintaining national and geographical pay differentials, employers will resist multinational negotiations.[47] In multinational companies, union officials frequently have difficulty getting access to executives who make overall industrial relations policy for their companies.[48]

Ironically, as product markets have globalized, the tendency for labor negotiations has been to move from the industry to the local level to cope with

---

[44] M. Morishima, "Information Sharing and Collective Bargaining in Japan: Effects on Wage Negotiation," *Industrial and Labor Relations Review* 44 (1991), pp. 469–85.

[45] Kennedy, *European Labor Relations.*

[46] W. Brown, "The Effect of Recent Changes in the World Economy on British Industrial Relations," in H. Juris, M. Thompson, and W. Daniels, eds., *Industrial Relations in a Decade of Economic Change* (Madison WI: Industrial Relations Research Association, 1985), pp. 151–75.

[47] H. R. Northrup, D. C. Campbell, and B. J. Slowinski, "Multinational Union-Management Consultation in Europe: Resurgence in the 1980s?" *International Labour Review* 127 (1988), pp. 525–43.

[48] D. Kujawa, "Labor Relations of U.S. Multinationals Abroad," in B. Martin and E. M. Kassalow, eds., *Labor Relations in Advanced Industrial Societies: Issues and Problems* (Washington, DC: Carnegie Endowment for International Peace, 1980), pp. 14–42.

increasingly diverse production practices and local job security issues linked with potential plant closings.[49]

There is a generally corporatist approach to industrial relations in northern and central Europe, although some decentralization is developing in response to global competition and some proliferation of occupation-based confederations is taking place in the Scandinavian countries.[50] In Sweden and Germany, bargaining has taken place at the employer association–national union level. However, increasing competition leading to pressures to reduce labor costs is shifting negotiations toward the enterprise level.[51] Centralized bargaining in Sweden began to break down in the mid-1980s following several rounds of pay increases higher than in other countries belonging to the Organization for Economic Cooperation and Development (OECD). In the 1993 metalworking agreement negotiated at the industry level, a 3.3 percent overall pay increase was provided, but the actual distribution of the increase was left to plant-level decision making.[52] In Germany, IG Metall (one of the largest unions) and Gesantmetall (an employer organization) bargained with the help of the Bundesbank (German central bank). IG Metall has a policy of maintaining or increasing employment of its members. New contracts contain incentives for skill development and keep wages in line with productivity and inflation increases.[53] German and Swedish employers act as cartels to take wages out of competition and sanction whipsaw strikes. Contractual wage terms are often extended to nonrepresented workers, thus decreasing the incentive to avoid unionization.[54] While enterprise unions have had little bargaining power in Japan, unions have occasionally combined to implement a "Shunto" approach in which the state pressures employers to improve wages in line with productivity and inflation increases.[55]

Developing labor relations in rapidly developing Asian nations have been highly varied. Korean unions developed strongly during the 1980s, but employers are large and involved in several industries simultaneously, reducing bargaining power of unions within any given industry sector. In Taiwan, labor is dominated

[49] R. Locke, T. Kochan, and M. Piore, "Reconceptualizing Comparative Industrial Relations: Lessons from International Research," *International Labour Review* 134 (1995), pp. 139–64.

[50] M. Wallerstein, M. Golden, and P. Lange, "Unions, Employer Associations, and Wage-Setting Institutions in Northern and Central Europe, 1950–1992," *Industrial and Labor Relations Review* 50 (1997), pp. 379–401.

[51] W. Streeck, "More Uncertainties: German Unions Facing 1992," *Industrial Relations* 30 (1991), pp. 317–49.

[52] "Sweden: Collective Bargaining in Transition," *European Industrial Relations Review* 234 (1993), pp. 15–16.

[53] D. Soskice, "The German Wage Bargaining System," *Proceedings of the Industrial Relations Research Association* 46 (1994), pp. 349–58.

[54] M. Reder and L. Ulman, "Unionism and Unification," in L. Ulman, B. Eichengreen, and W. T. Dickens, eds., *Labor and Integrated Europe* (Washington, DC: Brookings Institution, 1993), pp. 13–44.

[55] L. Ulman and Y. Nakata, "Enterprise Bargaining and Social Contract in Japan," *Proceedings of the Industrial Relations Research Association* 46 (1994), pp. 339–48.

by employers and the ruling political party. Only consultation and constrained collective bargaining are available.[56]

IMPASSES

The incidence and duration of strikes vary substantially across industrialized nations. Incidence is high in Australia and New Zealand. Australia, Italy, Finland, Spain, Israel, Portugal, and New Zealand are high in involvement levels per 1,000 workers. Strikes are longest in the United States, Ireland, and Canada, while days lost to strikes per 1,000 workdays scheduled are highest in Italy, Spain, Canada, Ireland, and Australia.[57] Italy frequently has intracontract strikes.[58] Within Great Britain, strike incidence is higher in plants where employees are represented by several unions. Unlike the United States, incidence of strikes was countercyclical. Incidence rates have declined markedly in the last few years in Great Britain, less so in France, and slightly in Spain. Strike frequency is negatively related to duration and intensity. In general, rates in southern Europe are considerably higher than in northern Europe.[59] Reduced incidence since the early 1980s is attributed to changes in British industrial relations laws.[60]

Australia offers conciliation and arbitration to settle disputes.[61] Arbitration courts establish wage rates for occupations across a broad class of employers. Ironically, frequent but short strikes may follow arbitration awards to hasten their implementation. France requires conciliation when agreements can't be reached.

UNION-MANAGEMENT COOPERATION

Different mechanisms have been developed to enhance union-management or worker-manager cooperation. These mechanisms can be involved with three primary levels of decision making: shop floor (work methods and production processes), core (wages, hours, and terms and conditions of employment), and strategic (production levels, product lines, designs, pricing, and so on). Levels of involvement might be split roughly into three categories: advisory (providing suggestions to management that may be undertaken), collective bargaining (ability to negotiate and contract on issues), and codetermination (mutual consensus on

---

[56] A. Kleingartner and H.-Y. Peng, "Taiwan: An Exploration of Labour Relations in Transition," *British Journal of Industrial Relations* 29 (1991), pp. 427–46.

[57] Poole, *Industrial Relations*.

[58] Kennedy, *European Labor Relations*.

[59] M. Aligisakis, "Labour Disputes in Western Europe: Typology and Tendencies," *International Labour Review* 136 (1997), pp. 73–94.

[60] P. Ingram, D. Metcalf, and J. Wadsworth, "Strike Incidence in British Manufacturing in the 1980s," *Industrial and Labor Relations Review* 46 (1993), pp. 704–717.

[61] B. Dabscheck and J. Niland, "Recent Trends in Collective Bargaining in Australia," in J. P. Windmuller, ed., *Collective Bargaining in Industrialized Market Economies: A Reappraisal* (Geneva: International Labour Office, 1987), pp. 161–76.

TABLE 17–4

Cooperation Types and Involvement Dimensions

Country	Involvement Dimension	Advisory	Collective Bargaining	Codetermination
United States	Strategic	No	No	No
	Core	No	Yes	No
	Shop floor	Yes	Yes	No
Japan	Strategic	Yes	No	No
	Core	Yes	Yes	No
	Shop floor	Yes	No	No
Germany	Strategic	Yes	No	Yes
	Core	Yes	Yes	No
	Shop floor	Yes	No	Yes

SOURCE: Table developed from J. Bellace, "Managing Employee Participation in Decision-Making: An Assessment of National Models," *Bulletin of Comparative Labour Relations* 27 (1993), pp. 5–15.

goals and/or processes).[62] Table 17–4 diagrams the current relationships between cooperation types and involvement dimensions in the United States, Japan, and Germany.

There is a great variation in Europe regarding the degree to which employees are entitled to information, consultation, and participation, even though the development of the European Union has been aimed at reducing national differences in a host of business and legal areas. Among the EU countries, only Germany allows unionists on boards of directors. Works councils are legislated in most countries, but union involvement in them varies. With regard to collective bargaining, employers *must* disclose information necessary to unions to assist in preparing their positions.[63]

In Germany, members of works councils are equally appointed by management and elected by employees. Work council members need not be employees and frequently are union officials elected by union members in the various plants. Works councils must be involved in all decision making having an effect on employment. This means that many strategic decisions are included in their menu of subjects. Evidence about their effect on organizational performance is mixed. One study found that works councils have no significant effect on profitability, but some positive effect on wages and some negative effect on investment.[64]

---

[62] J. Bellace, "Managing Employee Participation in Decision-Making: An Assessment of National Models," *Bulletin of Comparative Labour Relations*, no. 27 (1993), pp. 5–15.

[63] R. Blainpain, "Management Initiatives and Rights to Information, Consultation, and Workers' Participation in the EC Countries," *Bulletin of Comparative Labour Relations* no. 27 (1993), pp. 25–42.

[64] J. T. Addison, K. Kraft, and J. Wagner, "German Works Councils and Firm Performance," in B. E. Kaufman and M. M. Kleiner, eds., *Employee Representation: Alternatives and Future Directions* (Madison, WI: Industrial Relations Research Association, 1993), pp. 305–38.

Turnover and dismissal rates are lower in firms where there is works council representation.[65]

In Japan, enterprise-level labor councils often exist in the steel and auto industries. Managements and unions have negotiated profit sharing to make pay more flexible and enhance worker job security. Many plants may periodically have large-scale job shifts to introduce variety and broaden employee skills.[66] However, participation has not led to greater workplace democracy. Strategic decisions continue to be made at higher levels. Suggestions from the work floor are forwarded to supervisors for possible implementation.[67] Employee stock option plans (ESOPs) are popular in Japan; 91 percent of companies listed on Japanese stock exchanges have implemented them. Firms adopting ESOPs were likely to be more labor intensive, to experience high employment growth, and to have below average business performance. Implementation of an ESOP increased productivity.[68]

In Europe, worker cooperatives are more common than in the United States. In a worker cooperative, employees own the firm, hire its managers, and direct its strategy. A study of cooperatives in northern Italy found they have higher productivity, more labor-intensive production functions, low differentials between pay of rank-and-file workers and managers, and more tranquil labor relations than privately held firms.[69]

Industrial democracy has developed to a much higher degree in most industrialized countries than in the United States. There is also a greater incidence of worker-owned cooperatives, input into managerial selection, and other consultations of unions. Table 17–5 shows the types of industrial democracy in industrialized nations.

CONTRACT ADMINISTRATION

Large differences exist in contract administration because there are such great differences in bargaining structure and because the contract is simply a basic agreement in many countries and individual plants and employees may add to it.

In Canada, labor law forbids intracontract strikes and requires binding arbitration of unresolved grievances even if the parties have not negotiated it into an

[65] B. Frick, "Co-determination and Personnel Turnover: The German Experience," *Labour* 10 (1996), pp. 407–30.

[66] K. Kawahito, "Labor Relations in the Japanese Automobile and Steel Industries, *Journal of Labor Research* 11 (1990), pp. 231–38.

[67] R. M. Marsh, "The Difference between Participation and Power in Japanese Factories," *Industrial and Labor Relations Review* 45 (1992), pp. 250–57.

[68] D. C. Jones and T. Kato, "The Scope, Nature, and Effects of Employee Stock Ownership Plans in Japan," *Industrial and Labor Relations Review* 46 (1992), pp. 352–67.

[69] W. Bartlett, J. Cable, S. Estrin, D. C. Jones, and S. C. Smith, "Labor-Managed Cooperatives and Private Firms in North Central Italy: An Empirical Comparison," *Industrial and Labor Relations Review* 46 (1992), pp. 103–18.

TABLE 17-5

A Comparative Analysis of the Main Types of Industrial Democracy

Type	Defining Characteristics	Structural Properties	Range of Incidence	Key Examples
1. Workers' self-management	Occurs in decentralized socialist economies; a substantial degree of workers' participation on the main decision-making bodies and the overall right of the work force to use but not to own the assets of the enterprise	Typical organs of administration include workers' assemblies, workers' councils, and representation on management committees	Algeria, Peru, Poland, Yugoslavia, and various Third World and Eastern European societies	Yugoslavia
2. Producer cooperatives	Occur in a variety of political economies; workers' ownership with market mechanisms	Many workers own stock, ownership is widely distributed, workers participate in enterprise management and control and share in the distribution of the surplus (profits)	Very wide ranging, including many Third World countries, France, Italy, Spain, United States, and United Kingdom	Mondragon (Basque provinces of Spain)
3. Codetermination	Rights of workers' representatives to joint decision making on actual enterprise boards in predominantly private enterprise economies	Single- or two-tier boards (supervisory and man-agement), varying rights to veto and proportion of workers' representatives on main board(s)	Widely practiced in Western Europe (e.g., Italy, Norway, Sweden, German), Africa (e.g., Egypt), and South America (e.g., Argentina)	Germany
4. Works councils and similar institutions	Varying political economies, bodies that regularly meet with management on enterprise issues	Representatives of work force elected, varying degree of legalism or voluntarism and extent to which committees are constituted solely by employees and are joint bodies	Broad ranging, including Finland, Indonesia, Netherlands, Spain, Sri Lanka, Germany, and Zambia	Netherlands Germany

TABLE 17-5
(Concluded)

Type	Defining Characteristics	Structural Properties	Range of Incidence	Key Examples
5. Trade union action a. Disjunctive via collective bargaining	Pluralist societies, acknowledgment of conflicting interests accommodated through trade union-management negotiations	Trade union channel of representation on workers' side, varying degrees of legalism and voluntarism and levels at which bargaining is conducted	The most common form of participation in pluralist societies. Examples include Australia, Canada, United States, and United Kingdom	United States United Kingdom
b. Integrative	State socialism or corporatism; trade union rights to determine various issues within a framework of harmoniously conceived interests of management, trade union, and the state	Trade unions have responsibility for areas such as holiday arrangements and influence decisions over dismissals, safety, welfare, and working conditions but are integrated into both management and the state	The typical role for trade unions in a planned economy whether under state socialism or corporatism	Former USSR
6. Shop-floor programs	Workers' initiatives and new concepts of work organization; participation by employees in the organization of work in various political economies (e.g., autonomous work groups and quality-of-work-life programs)	Influence of workers varies depending on program, though usually task based	Very wide-ranging worker practices and accommodative management techniques in First, Second, and Third Worlds	Scandinavia USA

SOURCE: Adapted from M. Poole, *Industrial Relations: Origins and Patterns of National Diversity* (London: Routledge and Kegan Paul, 1986), pp. 154–56.

agreement.[70] Where unresolved grievances remain in France, conciliation is required; while in Italy, they are referred to the courts.[71]

In Germany, disputes arise occasionally within works councils with worker and management representatives at odds. Strikes are not permitted to pressure a settlement. By law, disputes over works council discussions must be settled by arbitration.[72]

PUBLIC-SECTOR UNIONIZATION

Collective bargaining in the public sector internationally is somewhat akin to the differences found among states in the United States. Its level and practice depends largely on the relative development of private-sector unionism and the friendliness of the ruling political party. For example, public-sector unions were defensive during most of Margaret Thatcher's term as prime minister in the United Kingdom. As in the United States, a variety of impasse procedures are used and significant differences exist about what are considered permissible bargaining issues.[73]

COMPARATIVE EFFECTS OF UNIONIZATION

A variety of general changes in industrial relations have followed from increased globalization. Common patterns of transformation include a stronger focus at the enterprise level, increased flexibility in production and job assignments, skill development, and declining unionization. Some of the decline can be attributed to changes in skill mix.[74]

Direct investment abroad by U.S. firms is negatively related to union density, centralized collective bargaining, layoff restrictions, and contract extension policies, but positively related to education levels and works councils. This suggests that investors wish to avoid situations in which bargaining power is reduced and prefer situations with skilled workforces and institutionalized methods for continuous conflict resolution and problem solving.[75]

Among European countries, the United Kingdom has the most adversarial system with very decentralized bargaining. Many decisions are made at the firm

---

[70] R. J. Adams, B. Adell, and H. N. Wheeler, "Discipline and Discharge in Canada and the United States," *Labor Law Journal* 41 (1990), pp. 596–600.

[71] Kennedy, *European Labor Relations.*

[72] International Labour Office, *World Labour Report*, vol. 2 (Geneva: International Labour Office, 1985), pp. 5–52.

[73] International Labour Office, *World Labour Report, 1989* (Geneva: International Labour Office, 1989), pp. 105–25.

[74] R. Locke, "The Transformation of Industrial Relations? A Cross-National Review," in Wever and Turner, eds., *Comparative Political Economy,* pp. 9–32.

[75] W. N. Cooke, "The Influence of Industrial Relations Factors on U.S. Foreign Direct Investment Abroad," *Industrial and Labor Relations Review* 51 (1997), pp. 3–17.

or plant level. Effects of unions in the United Kingdom might be close to those in the United States. Investment rates of firms that recognized manual unions were 23 percent below nonunion firms. Taking the higher wages of their unionized employees into account, the decrease due primarily to unionization was between 4 and 13 percent.[76] Dual allegiance among British workers is quite low; less than 10 percent of unionized electronics workers are committed to both their union and their employer. Most workers had low commitment to both.[77]

In Germany, even though unions see themselves as cooperative rather than confrontational, unionization is related to slightly lower productivity.[78] However, unionization does not reduce the proportional expenditures of firms on research and development (R&D) or employment in R&D activities.[79]

In the Far East, enterprise unionization in Japan has not influenced worker satisfaction but has reduced company commitment. The negative relationship between job satisfaction and unionization in the United States appears to be related to lower job complexity, less worker autonomy in shop-floor decision making, lower promotional opportunities, and less quality circle membership.[80] Unionized firms in Singapore have become more capital intensive and add technology to improve product quality. More attention is paid to communications and work design, tighter control systems, and dominance of the workplace.[81]

In Korea, unionization increases wages and reduces turnover, while works councils are associated with increases in employee satisfaction and productivity (but less so).[82] Interest in works councils in Korea was increased by demands for increased democracy in the late 1980s. Some firms have instituted a bonus policy. Labor productivity is positively influenced by the bonus policy, however unionization reduces the productivity effect. Under poorer labor relations since 1987, the effect is negative. It increasingly appears that worker participation is necessary for the bonus to have a positive productivity effect.[83]

---

[76] K. Denny and S. Nickell, "Unions and Investment in British Manufacturing Industry," *British Journal of Industrial Relations* 29 (1991), pp. 113–22.

[77] D. E. Guest and P. Dewe, "Company or Trade Union: Which Wins Workers' Allegiance? A Study of Commitment in the UK Electronics Industry," *British Journal of Industrial Relations* 29 (1991), pp. 75–96.

[78] C. Schnabel, "Trade Unions and Productivity: The German Evidence," *British Journal of Industrial Relations* 29 (1991), pp. 15–24.

[79] C. Schnabel and J. Wagner, "Unions and Innovative Activity in Germany," *Journal of Labor Research* 13 (1992), pp. 391–406.

[80] J. R. Lincoln and J. N. Boothe, "Unions and Work Attitudes in the United States and Japan," *Industrial Relations* 32 (1993), pp. 159–87.

[81] C.-T. Foo, "Union Presence and Corporate Productivity Practices: Evidence from Singapore," *British Journal of Industrial Relations* 29 (1991), pp. 123–28.

[82] M. M. Kleiner and Y.-M. Lee, "Works Councils and Unionization: Lessons from South Korea," *Industrial Relations* 36 (1997), pp. 1–16.

[83] M. B. Lee and Y. Rhee, "Bonuses, Unions, and Labor Productivity in South Korea," *Journal of Labor Research* 17 (1996), pp. 219–38.

SUMMARY

Labor relations in other industrialized countries is conducted in a variety of modes. Generally, union power tends to reside in labor federations on the European continent and at the enterprise level in Great Britain and Japan. Works councils are most prominent in Germany and Sweden. Employees may be represented by more than one union in a workplace, and recognition is gained through the bargaining process. Trade unions are continuing to undergo transformations in the former Warsaw Pact nations. In some nations of East Asia, unions are either outlawed, highly restricted, or controlled by the government and employers.

Bargaining issues are much more broadly defined in European Union countries than in the United States because there is no legislation in most EU countries differentiating between so-called mandatory and permissive issues. Bargaining structures are more centralized, employer associations represent a large number of employers within an industry, and federations or national unions bargain with them. By contrast, most decisions in Japan are made on the enterprise level.

Most European countries have strikes of shorter duration than in the United States, but strike incidence rates are higher in Australia and New Zealand, Italy, and Finland. Conciliation is mandated in some countries, and arbitration precedes contracting for wages in Australia.

Union-management cooperation is higher in the European Union, although there are wide variations. A common mechanism for cooperation is the works council which is involved in any decisions affecting employment.

The effects of unions on firm performance tend to be similar in Europe and the United States. Wage differences due to unionization are less in Europe than the United States, and the degree of wage differentiation is associated negatively with the level of investment.

DISCUSSION QUESTIONS

1. Given the degree of democracy found in U.S. political jurisdictions, why isn't there more democracy in the workplace?
2. Why are there such large differences in Germany and Japan in the structure of unions and managements for negotiation, yet such similar levels of consultation in the workplace?
3. Could religious or politically affiliated unions have an effective role in labor relations in the United States?
4. Are the concepts of exclusive representation and mandatory bargaining issues anachronisms in a modern industrial society?

KEY TERMS

works councils   *559*   redundancy   *567*

GLOSSARY

Ability to pay The economic ability of the employer to grant a wage increase.

Accretion The adding of a group of employees to an existing bargaining unit.

Across-the-board increase An equal cents-per-hour increase for all jobs in a bargaining unit.

Ad hoc arbitrator An arbitrator appointed to hear a particular case or set of cases.

Administrative law judge A judge charged with interpreting the application of federal labor law in unfair labor practice cases that are not settled between the parties.

Agency fee The portion of union dues that non-members must pay when employed under a contract with an agency shop clause.

Agency shop A union security clause that requires employees who are not union members to pay a service fee to the bargaining agent.

Ally doctrine The employees of a secondary employer do not commit an unfair labor practice by refusing to perform struck work.

American Federation of Government Employees (AFGE) An industrial-type union asserting jurisdiction over employees of the federal government.

American Federation of Labor The first permanent national labor organization. It brought together a set of craft unions in 1883 and evolved a business unionism approach toward influencing employers and public policy.

American Federation of Labor–Congress of Industrial Organizations (AFL–CIO) The primary labor federation for international union affili-

ation in the United States. It coordinates national public policy initiatives for the labor movement.

American Federation of State, County, and Municipal Employees (AFSCME) The dominant industrial-type union organizing nonfederal publicsector employees.

American plan A strategy used by employers in the 1920s that aimed at casting organized labor in an outsider role to employees. It fostered company unions and opposed nonemployees from being able to act as bargaining representatives.

Appropriate bargaining unit A group of employees the National Labor Relations Board determines to be a reasonable unit in which a representation election will be held.

Arbitrability A grievance is arbitrable if it alleges a violation under the contract and if the contract terms allow it to be settled through arbitration.

Arbitration A dispute resolution procedure in which a neutral third party hears the positions of the parties and renders a decision binding on both. The arbitrator draws his or her power from the agreement of the parties to abide by the decision and/or the creation of the position in a contract to handle any disputes arising under the contract.

Area-wide labor management committee (AWLMC) An organization of industrial and trade union leaders in a given geographical region whose goal is to deal with employment problems of common concern. Usually these are aimed at promoting labor-management cooperation to enhance job security and competitiveness, especially in an area experiencing economic decline.

Associate member A proposed status for union membership in which an individual who is not in a bargaining unit can receive group benefits through union membership.

Attitudinal structuring The techniques and processes aimed at changing a party's position toward bargaining issues in negotiations.

Authorization card A card signed by an employee to authorize the union to act as his or her bargaining representative. It is necessary for establishing a sufficient interest to request an election from the NLRB.

Bad faith bargaining A practice by an employer or union that constitutes a refusal to bargain, a refusal to discuss mandatory issues, or to insist until impasse on a permissive issue.

Bargaining book A collection of contract clauses and their history, the desired position of the party on an issue in negotiation, and acceptable levels for settlement.

Bargaining convention A meeting of union delegates to determine the union's position on mandatory bargaining issues in an upcoming negotiation.

Bargaining order An order from the NLRB requiring an employer to bargain with a union where a representation election failed, but the employer's egregious conduct eroded the union's majority.

Bargaining power The ability of one side in a dispute to inflict heavier loss on the other than it will suffer.

Bargaining structure The organizational nature of the relationship between union(s) and employer(s) in contract negotiations including a specification of the employees and facilities covered.

Bargaining unit A collection of employees with similar interests who are represented by a single union representative. For organizing purposes, bargaining units would be within the same employer. For bargaining purposes, they might involve several employers.

Benefit status seniority The seniority in a bargaining unit entitling an employee to a certain level of benefits, usually dating from date of hire (adjusted by layoffs or leaves).

Board-directed (or petition) election A representation election in which the NLRB determines the bargaining unit in which the election will be conducted.

Boycott A refusal by individuals not directly involved in a labor dispute to deal with the employer directly involved. For example, if a clerks' union struck a store, a boycott would occur when some segment of the general public (usually union members) refused to patronize the store until the dispute was settled.

Bumping The assertion of a competitive status seniority right of an employee who is going to be laid off to claim a different job held by another employee who has lower competitive status seniority.

Business agent A permanent union employee who administers the contract and provides services to union members in a local union representing employees across several employers, particularly in the construction industry.

Business unionism An approach in which collective bargaining is the union's primary objective, leading to the betterment of the workers they represent.

"C" (charge) cases The NLRB cases involving allegations of unfair labor practices against an employer or union.

Capital-labor accords A period during the 1950s and 1960s in which employers conceded the legitimacy of unions and negotiated wage increases closely tracked to productivity growth.

Cease and desist orders The orders by the NLRB to stop conduct that violates labor law.

Central bodies The collections of local unions at the city or state level for the purposes of political activity. Their support is directly from the AFL-CIO.

Certification This occurs when the NLRB determines the results of a representation election.

Certification bars an election in the same unit for one year.

Certification election　An election under the auspices of the National Labor Relations Board to determine whether a group of employees desires initially to be represented by a union for collective bargaining purposes.

Checkoff　A collective bargaining agreement provision in which the employer agrees to deduct union dues from employees' pay.

"Chilling" effect　The assumption that the availability of interest arbitration decreases the willingness of the parties to negotiate an agreement.

Civil service system　A public-sector employment system defining rules for hiring and promotion. It insulates employees from political patronage by preserving certain jobs as not vulnerable to loss when political parties change.

Closed shop　A collective bargaining clause requiring that a prospective employee be a union member before employment. It is unlawful under federal labor law.

Coalition bargaining　A bargaining structure in which a group of unions simultaneously bargains with a single employer.

Collective bargaining　The collective aspect of collective bargaining is the exclusive representation by the union of the collection of people in a bargaining unit. Bargaining represents the negotiation of labor agreements and their administration during the period in which they are in effect.

Collyer doctrine　The NLRB's policy of deferring the disposition of unfair labor practice charges to pending arbitration.

Committee for Industrial Organization (later Congress of Industrial Organizations)　A group of trade unionists interested in the early 1930s in organizing unskilled workers by industry. Later, as they were successful, the unions that were created formed the Congress of Industrial Organizations.

Committee on Political Education　A department within the AFL–CIO that endorses candidates friendly to labor, provides information on political positions to members, and mobilizes voters.

Common situs picketing　The picketing of a facility used by several employers. An action aimed at a single employer may cause unionized employees of other employers to refuse to cross the picket line.

Community action　A union tactic seeking to link the interests of a local union with those of the larger community in order to gain public support for its positions.

Community of interests　The degree to which the employees in a proposed unit have common interests in bargaining outcomes. It is one of the most frequent criteria the NLRB uses to determine the scope of a bargaining unit in petition elections.

Company union　An employer-established labor organization established for a single firm's employees. It is unlawful under federal labor law.

Competitive status seniority　The seniority levels of employees that entitle them to certain jobs, bid on certain jobs, bump, or avoid layoffs. It is usually calculated from the date of promotion into a given job or job group.

Concession bargaining　A negotiating situation in which the union is asked to give back previously won economic levels.

Consent elections　A representation election in which there is no dispute between the employer and union about which employees would be represented if the union won.

Conspiracy doctrine　The legal approach holding that any union activity among a collection of individuals was ultimately aimed to restrain trade through the fixing of wages.

Constitutional conventions　Periodic national meetings required by the constitutions of labor unions to elect officers, adopt positions, and amend their constitutions (as necessary).

Contract administration　The process a union and management pursue in complying with the contract during its term.

Coordinated bargaining The cooperation between two or more unions in bargaining with a single employer. This method may involve observation of bargaining by other unions or coordinating bargaining demands.

Corporate campaign An activity by unions in difficult organizing or bargaining situations to pressure companies whose officers are members of the board of directors of the target company with public relations campaigns. It is frequently used against banks and aimed at informing the public of the connection between the target company and potential supporting companies.

Corporatist A labor-management-public policy approach in which employers, unions, and the government work together to create and maintain a stable labor-relations climate involving essentially equal roles for management and labor with government overseeing the relationship.

Cost-of-living adjustments The contract terms that adjust pay in response to changes in the level of the consumer price index. These terms are aimed at keeping the real value of pay constant over the term of the agreement.

Craft A skilled occupation or trade.

Craft severance An action by the NLRB to remove craft employees from a bargaining unit because their community of interests is dissimilar.

Craft union A national union representing predominantly employees in one occupation, such as the Carpenters Union.

Davis-Bacon Act A federal law requiring that employers involved in contract construction work for the federal government pay prevailing area wages for the crafts that they employ.

Decertification election An election to determine whether a majority of bargaining unit employees still favors union representation.

Defined benefit pension plan A pension plan guaranteeing a certain payment level at retirement. It is usually based on the average of the final two or three years' pay and length of service.

Defined contribution pension plan A pension plan with a specific formula for calculating employer contributions toward retirement. The ultimate level of benefits depends on the amount of contributions and the investment experience of the plan.

Distributive bargaining The bargaining over issues in which one party's gain is the other party's loss.

Doctrinaire organization An employer adopting an employee relations approach aimed at closely duplicating conditions likely under collective bargaining in order not to be a target of unionization.

Drive system A production system in which supervisors have a great deal of power in rewarding and punishing subordinates.

Dual commitment The notion that an individual can be simultaneously committed to his or her employer and union.

Dual governance The notion that individuals have opportunities for the governance of their workplace through electing officers of their bargaining unit representatives and voting on contract ratification.

Duty to bargain The duty by both parties under federal labor law, following recognition or certification of a union, to bargain over wages, hours, and terms and conditions of employment.

Economic strike A strike following the expiration of a contract over an impasse on any mandatory bargaining issue. Strikers may be replaced.

Election bar The certification of an election prohibits another election in the same unit for a year.

Employee Any person who is not an employer or supervisor and who is involved in a labor dispute, according to Taft-Hartley.

Employee involvement A name for a variety of plans in which employers provide more employee voice in the operation of the work setting. It is usually included with problem-solving activity.

Employee stock ownership plan A plan in which employees acquire part or all of the shares of stock in a private-sector organization.

Employee relations   The set of activities engaged in by employers to systematically address employment problems in the workplace.

Employer   An organization or manager acting for an organization within the jurisdiction of the labor acts.

Excelsior list   A list of employees and their addresses that employers must turn over to the union when the NLRB authorizes a representation election.

Exclusive representation   All individuals within a bargaining unit are represented by the union for purposes of collective bargaining regardless of whether they voted for representation or whether they are union members.

Executive committee   The elected executive officers of a local union.

Executive order 10988   An order issued by President Kennedy allowing federal employee bargaining units where a majority of employees vote for representation. Bargaining was limited to terms and conditions of employment.

Expedited arbitration   An arbitration method that speeds the process and reduces the formality of the proceedings.

Fact-finding   A third-party method used to develop information about the issues in dispute and recommend a potential settlement.

Fair Labor Standards Act   A federal law requiring that employers pay overtime premiums when 40 hours are exceeded in a week for covered employees, and that at least a minimum wage be paid.

Fair representation   The requirement that the union treat all bargaining unit members equally in processing grievances.

Federal Labor Relations Authority   The federal employment equivalent of the National Labor Relations Board. It oversees representation elections and rules on unfair labor practice allegations.

Federal Mediation and Conciliation Service   A federal agency created by the Taft-Hartley Act to assist employers and unions in bargaining through mediation, particularly in situations where they have reached impasses.

Federal service labor-management relations statute   Title VII of the Civil Service Reform Act of 1978 codifying the right of federal employees to organize. Bargaining rights do not extend to economic or staffing issues. It created the Federal Labor Relations Authority.

Field representatives   The full-time international union employees who provide organizing services and services to local unions in negotiations and grievance processing.

Final-offer arbitration   A variant of interest arbitration in which the arbitrator must choose one of the offers of the parties. Variants of final-offer arbitration may require an arbitrator to select the entire package or to select one or the other party's offers on each issue.

Fractional bargaining   A tactic a union might use in contract administration to pressure the employer to make concessions on issues that could not be won in bargaining.

Fraternal Order of Police   A major collective bargaining representative for police. It began as a benevolent organization and turned to collective bargaining when legislation enabled it and unions to begin to organize police.

Free-riding   A condition in which a bargaining unit member does not pay dues; possible under an open shop or in a right-to-work law state.

Functional democracy   The availability of union member checks on their environment through voting for local union members and ratification of contracts in their establishments.

Gainsharing   A flexible compensation system in which employees receive bonuses based on labor and/or material savings as compared to a base period.

Good faith bargaining   The willingness of the parties to meet at reasonable times and places to discuss mandatory bargaining issues.

Greenfield operation   A newly opened plant in a location in which the employer has never had operations previously. It is usually part of an employer strategy to avoid unions or reduce the proportion of employees represented.

Grievance   Any complaint any employee has against an employer. In collective bargaining, an allegation that the employer has violated the collective bargaining agreement.

Grievance procedures   The negotiated provisions in the contract that specify how alleged contract violations will be resolved.

Hiring hall   The union office, in the building trades, at which tradespeople congregate to take available jobs for which employers have asked the unions to provide workers.

Hot cargo   The goods made by nonunion labor that unionized employees refuse to transport or install.

Human resource manager   A person responsible for developing and implementing employment policies and practices and advising line managers on employment issues.

Impasse   An inability to agree on a contract which follows an unwillingness by both parties to concede further.

Implied contract   A pattern of practices and expectations that lead employees to assume employers will continue to treat them in an established manner.

Impro-share   A gainsharing plan in which groups of employees receive bonuses as a result of producing products in fewer hours than standards require.

Industrial relations manager   In a unionized employer, a person responsible for developing and implementing policies and practices consistent with the collective bargaining agreement, and for negotiating and administering contracts.

Industrial union   A national union representing predominantly employees employed in a single industry, such as United Auto Workers.

Industrial Workers of the World   A revolutionary union founded in the late 1800s that urged the end of the capitalistic system and worker control of the means of production. It was strongly opposed by employers, and its leaders were jailed during World War I for opposing the war.

Industrywide bargaining   A bargaining structure in which all (or many) employers in an industry bargain simultaneously with a single union.

Injunctions   The court orders requiring that certain actions be stopped.

Integrative bargaining   Bargaining over issues in which both parties may achieve a better position than the one held previously.

Interest arbitration   Arbitration over the contents of the contract.

Internal labor market   The pattern of rules and practices governing promotions and transfers within an organization among the set of jobs for which employees are not hired externally.

International Association of Fire Fighters (IAFF)   The dominant craft-type union organizing fire fighters. The IAFF has been highly successful in influencing public-sector legislation enabling bargaining for municipal employees.

International unions   The organizations chartering local unions representing certain crafts, industries, or as general unions. International unions are the level at which control ultimately resides in the labor movement.

Intraorganizational bargaining   The activities that occur within a bargaining team that lead to agreements on positions and concessions in negotiations.

Job evaluation   A procedure used to measure the relative value of jobs to an organization. It usually examines factors such as skill, effort, responsibility, and working conditions.

Job posting   A procedure for publicizing to employees the availability of open positions and eligibility rules for being considered for them.

Job security   The retaining of employment with a given employer until the employee voluntarily retires or quits once a probationary period is completed.

Joint labor-management committee   An organization of employers and a labor union designed to deal with common industrywide problems in an integrative manner.

Journeyman   The job level in a skilled trade one attains following successful completion of an apprentice program.

Jurisdictional dispute   A dispute between two unions over the representation of a specific group of employees.

Knights of Labor   A post-Civil War national union movement in which employees joined city central unions. Leaders advocated arbitration to settle disputes. The knights declined rapidly after the formation of the American Federation of Labor in 1883.

Labor-management committee   A form of consultation in which representatives of a local bargaining unit and management confer on employment and production problems that are not included within the contract.

Labor relations   The activities of unions and management in negotiating and implementing collective bargaining agreements.

Laboratory conditions   The environment the NLRB has desired to surround union representation elections to allow the employee to make a free and uncoerced choice regarding representation.

Landrum-Griffin Act   A law passed in 1959 aimed at increasing democracy in unions and ensuring individual rights. It also modified Taft-Hartley.

"Last change agreement "   In lieu of possible termination for a disciplinary infraction, when an employee, union, and management agree that another instance of a similar violation will result in immediate termination without access to the grievance procedure.

Line manager   A manager who has responsibility for some part of the actual process of producing or delivering an organization's products or services.

Local union   The union body closest to the members. It is usually established in a particular geographic location to represent employees in either one employer or one industry. Officers are elected and frequently remain employed fulltime.

Logrolling   A practice in bargaining in which sets of dissimilar issues are traded.

Maintenance of membership clause   A union security clause in which employees who become union members during the agreement are required to remain members.

Make-whole orders   The orders by the NLRB to restore employment and back pay to employees who are victims of unfair labor practices.

Management rights clause   A contract clause specifying certain areas in which management reserves the right to make and implement decisions.

Mandatory bargaining issue   An issue that is statutorily required to be disclosed if one of the parties in bargaining raises it.

Marginal revenue product   The value of the additional production resulting from a one unit addition of a productive input (usually the value of production produced by adding an additional worker—all else equal).

Marginal supply curve   The functional representation of the additional costs associated with hiring each additional unit of labor.

Median voter   The middle person, from an opinion perspective, in a bargaining unit. For any two alternate decisions, assuming that voter opinions lie along a continuum, the median voter must vote for the winning alternative.

Mediation   A process involving a neutral party who maintains communications between bargainers in an attempt to gain agreement.

Mediators   The neutral people who attempt to help parties to settle disputes. Mediators have no power to impose solutions but rather focus on keeping lines of communication open and exploring alternative settlements with disputing parties.

"Modern operating agreement" The agreement between Chrysler Corporation and the United Auto Workers in which the amount of supervision was reduced, and team concepts and broader jobs were introduced in return for rebuilding a plant in Detroit.

Modified union shop A union security clause in which employees who are hired after a specified date are required to become union members.

Mohawk Valley formula An employer approach toward organizing campaigns in the 1930s in which organizers were branded as outsiders and communists, and local public interests were stirred against organizing.

Monopoly power The ability of a union to increase wages as a result of controlling the labor supply to the firm.

Multiemployer bargaining A consensual relationship between employers and a union in which bargaining on a contract involves all employers in the unit and the terms and conditions of the ultimate agreement apply equally to all employers.

Multilateral bargaining The tendency of elected officials to become involved in public-sector labor negotiations, thus creating a tripartite bargaining situation in which the employer, the union, and elected officials are the parties.

Mutual gains bargaining An approach to bargaining in which labor and management enter negotiatings with the objective of simultaneously improving the outcomes of both.

Narcotic effect The assumption that parties who have experienced interest arbitration will be more likely to use it in the future than those who have not.

National departments The offices within unions created to bargain and administer contracts with major national employers.

National Education Association (NEA) A professional association of elementary and secondary public school teachers with chapters in all states that is now involved in organizing and collective bargaining where permitted and has expanded its jurisdiction to higher education.

National Labor Relations Board The federal agency created by the Wagner Act that has responsibility for investigating and ruling on unfair labor practice charges and holding and certifying the results of representation elections.

National Labor Union A post-Civil War uplift union.

National Mediation Board The agency that mediates contract disputes between employees and unions covered by the Railway Labor Act. It holds representation elections.

National Railroad Board of Adjustment The group originally designed to handle unresolved grievances under the Railway Labor Act. Since there were equal numbers of management and union representatives, an independent arbitrator renders the decision.

National union *See* international union.

Negotiation committee The local union committee responsible for contract negotiations and decisions on grievance handling above the entry-level steps.

Norris-LaGuardia Act An act passed in 1932 prohibiting federal courts from enjoining lawful union activities and forbidding enforcement of yellow-dog contracts.

Ombudsman An individual designated to expedite the settlement of disputes within an organization. The person usually has investigative powers and powers to impose settlements.

"Open door" policy A policy in which employees have access to higher-level management to complain about problems in their work unit. These programs are usually accompanied by investigative units and formal feedback to the employee about the disposition of the problem raised.

Open shop   An employment arrangement in which an employee would never be required to join a union as a condition of continued employment.

Organizing campaign   The set of activities involved in attempting to gain recognition for a union and representation for employees to collectively bargain with their employer.

Outsourcing   Purchasing components or services that have been produced by an organization's employees from an outside organization.

Past practice   A traditional work practice or rule on which the employees rely even though not a part of the collective agreement.

Pattern bargaining   A bargaining tactic in which employers or unions seek agreements that imitate those previously concluded in other bargaining rounds in the industry.

Pay form   The manner in which pay is provided, such as cash, deferred compensation, insurance, paid time off, etc.

Pay level   A comparison between the average pay rates of a given employer and the market averages for comparison jobs.

Pay structure   The rates and ranges of pay assigned to different jobs in the organization.

Pay system   The set of rules used by an organization or included in a contract to determine how an individual employee's pay will change.

Permanent umpire   An arbitrator named in a contract who hears all cases within his or her area that may come up under the agreement.

Permissive bargaining issue   An issue that does not statutorily require bargaining and one that cannot be used to go to impasse.

Philosophy-laden   Employee relations programs that consistently follow a particular value system that simultaneously renders unionization superfluous to employees.

Picketing   The act of parading at an employer's site to inform the public about the existence of a labor dispute and asking other union members and the public not to cross.

Political action committee (PAC)   An employer or union organization to raise and disburse funds to support political candidates.

Predatory unionism   A situation in which the primary goal of the union is to gain the dues of the employees and extract side payments from employers in return for beneficial contracts.

Principled negotiations   A negotiating process in which parties reveal all information necessary to reach an agreement early in the process and whenever asked by an opponent.

Production committee   A work unit-level committee consisting of rank-and-file employees and the unit's supervisor that acts on employee suggestions in the Scanlon plan.

Professional association   An organization formed to pursue the interests of professional employees without functioning as a collective bargaining representative.

Professional employee   An employee, under the Wagner Act, with substantial education and working without close supervision in a professional job. The employee cannot be included in a nonprofessional bargaining unit without majority vote of the professionals.

Profit sharing   A flexible compensation system in which employees receive bonuses based on the profitability of a unit or firm.

Prohibited bargaining issue   An issue the parties are statutorily forbidden to include in their contract.

Project labor agreements   In construction, an agreement that covers the period during which a project will be undertaken. Usually unions agree not to strike and employers agree to hire only union labor.

Quality circles   A group of employees who meet to apply statistical process control methods to improve the quality of production.

Quality-of-work-life   The programs aimed at improving the work environment to enhance employee safety and satisfaction. They usually involve joint labor-management committees.

"Quickie" strikes   Short strikes an employer can't anticipate designed to disrupt production and force an employer to bargain with or recognize a union.

"R" (representation) cases   Petitions for certification elections.

"Raid" elections   An election to determine whether a new union should succeed the present bargaining agent.

Railway Labor Act   The labor act passed in 1926 that applies to the rail and airline industries. It establishes craft-oriented bargaining units and requires bargaining with majority representatives who have exclusive rights to bargain for employees in unit. The act established by the National Mediation Board and the National Railroad Board of Adjustment.

Recognitional picketing   The act of picketing to inform the public that the employer is not represented and requesting recognition. It is prohibited after 30 days if the employer requests and wins an election.

Redundancy   In Europe, a situation in which technological or economic conditions leads to surplus workers who will be permanently terminated.

Regional director   The top NLRB official in each of its regions, having broad power to deal with representation election certifications and unfair labor practice charges and investigations.

Relations by objectives   A program initiated by the FMCS to train parties who have strained bargaining relationships to improve communications and focus more closely on desired bargaining outcomes.

Representation   The union's role as the employees' agent in employment matters.

Representation election   An election to determine whether unrepresented employees desire to be represented by a union for the purposes of collective bargaining.

Revolutionary unionism   An approach in which the union movement mobilizes to change the ownership of the means of production, commonly toward a socialist approach.

Right-to-work law   A state law, permitted under section 14b of the Taft-Hartley Act, prohibiting the negotiation of union or agency shop clauses, thereby forbidding the requirement of union membership as a condition of continued employment.

Rights arbitration   The arbitration over interpretation of the meaning of contract terms or entitlements to outcomes.

Roll up   The amount by which overtime payments and fringe benefits increase as the base wage rate is increased.

Rucker plan   A gainsharing program in which employees, as a group, receive bonuses for improvements in labor productivity and reductions in material costs.

Scanlon plan   A gainsharing program in which employees, as a group, receive bonuses for improvements in labor productivity.

Screening committee   A committee of employee and management representatives under the Scanlon plan that handles suggestions referred to it from lower-level production committees.

Secondary boycott   An action asking the public not to patronize an uninvolved party doing business with an employer who is involved in a labor dispute. It is unlawful under federal labor law.

Seniority   The period of time between an individual being hired or moved into a current job and the present.

Sherman Antitrust Act   A federal law prohibiting organizations from fixing prices or for a single organization to become and act as a monopolist.

"Sick-out"   A concerted action to withhold labor in situations where strikes are not permitted.

Sit-down strike   An illegal strike in which employees cease work in place and refuse to leave. This type of strike also denies the employer the use of the facility.

Skill-based pay   A pay plan basing pay rates on the acquired skills of employees specific to the work environment. Pay is based on skills or knowledge rather than the job the person happens to be assigned to.

Spillover   The adoption of an outcome from collective bargaining to nonrepresented employees.

Spillover effect   The tendency for economic gains won in collective bargaining to influence pay practices for nonunion employees and employers.

Standard of living   The absolute level of goods and services an individual can purchase with his or her pay.

Steelworkers' trilogy   A set of three Supreme Court decisions essentially establishing arbitration as the *final* decision-making step in the grievance procedure when the parties have agreed to include it in a contract.

Stewards   The elected or appointed shop floor union representatives responsible for interpreting the contract for union members and processing grievances.

Subcontracting   Contracting with another employer to perform work that bargaining unit employees could perform.

Superseniority   The state of having greater seniority than any other individual in the bargaining unit. It is usually conferred on stewards to protect union governance in case of layoffs.

Supervisor   An employee who is an agent of management and who has the power to effectively hire, fire, and make compensation decisions for subordinates.

Supplementary unemployment benefits   An employer-provided benefit added to unemployment benefits to bring an employee's payments during unemployment closer to pay for work.

Sympathy strike   A strike by a union not involved in negotiations in support of a union that is.

Taft-Hartley Act   The act amending and extending the Wagner Act to include union unfair labor practices. It also established the FMCS, provided for dealing with national emergency strikes, and regulated suits by union members against their unions.

Team concept   A work design in which groups of employees are assigned to produce a given product, assembly, or service. All employees in the group are expected to be able to perform all tasks. Worker autonomy is increased because the group is responsible for supervising its own activities.

Totality of conduct   The sum total of conduct of employers or unions, rather than each individual act, in organizing campaigns or bargaining may be determinative of unfair labor practices.

Trusteeship   A situation in which a national union takes over operation of a local union as a result of its violation of the union constitution.

Twenty-four-hour-rule   The NLRB rule forbidding union and management campaigning in certification elections in the last full day before the election.

Two-tier pay plan   A pay structure variant in which groups of employees are paid different rates for performing the same job. It is usually included as a concessionary clause with newly hired employees being paid at lower rates. Some plans merge employees after a period of time, while others create permanent differences.

Umpire   An arbitrator designated by name in a collective bargaining agreement to hear and rule on disputes between the parties during the life of the agreement.

Unfair labor practice strike   A strike by employees to pressure an employer to stop an unfair labor practice. Employees are entitled to reinstatement if they are fired or replaced.

Unfair labor practices   The activities by a management or union that violate Section 8 of the Taft-Hartley Act.

Union   An organization established to represent the interests of employees. Under U.S. statutes, to be considered as a union, an organization must seek to represent groups of nonsupervisory employees, and after being designated as a representative, collectively bargain for the employees it represents.

Union security   The level of permanency in representation negotiated into a labor agreement, such as a union shop.

Union shop   A contract clause requiring that all employees who are members of the bargaining unit must become union members following completion of a probationary period as new employees.

Uplift unionism   An approach in which the labor movement's primary goal is to better society as a whole.

Voice power   The ability that unionization provides to empower employees in having their complaints heard and acted upon by management.

Wagner Act   The law that provided for collective bargaining for handling labor disputes, recognized the right to representations, established the National Labor Relations Board, initiated exclusive representation within bargaining units, defined employer unfair labor practices, and specified rights and duties of employers and unions in bargaining.

Walsh-Healey Government Contracts Act   A federal law requiring employers who are producing goods for the federal government to pay industry prevailing wage rates and to comply with overtime pay requirements.

Whipsawing   A bargaining tactic in which a union settles contracts sequentially, demanding a higher settlement in each subsequent negotiation.

Wildcat strike   An intracontract strike in violation of a no-strike clause.

Working to rules   The act of meticulously following the contract and work rules to degrade productivity and pressure an employer to settle on the union's terms.

Works council   A bipartite board in Germany involving employee and management representatives in consultation over issues involving staffing, strategy, health and safety, technological change, and other issues of concern to workers in the organization.

Yellow-dog contract   An agreement between an employee and an employer in which the employee indicates that he or she is not a member of a labor union and that joining a labor union in the future will be sufficient grounds for dismissal.

NAME INDEX

SUBJECT INDEX